THE
ENGLISH
ROMANTIC
POETS

Ernest Bernbaum,
Samuel C. Chew, Frank Jordan,
James V. Logan, Jr., Ernest J. Lovell, Jr.,
David Perkins, Thomas M. Raysor,
Donald H. Reiman, Max F. Schulz,
Ford T. Swetnam, Jr.,
Clarence D. Thorpe, Bennett Weaver,
and René Wellek

1972
THE MODERN LANGUAGE ASSOCIATION OF AMERICA
NEW YORK

THE
ENGLISH
ROMANTIC
POETS

A Review of Research and Criticism

THIRD REVISED EDITION

Edited by Frank Jordan

cop. 1

Published by The Modern Language Association of America
62 Fifth Avenue
New York, New York 10011

Designed by The Etheredges

PREFACE

THIRD EDITION

Each chapter of the third edition of *The English Romantic Poets: A Review of Research and Criticism* has been substantially revised except for the chapter on Coleridge's philosophy and criticism, which Mr. Wellek has chosen to reprint with some slight changes and to supplement with a new account of the scholarship since 1956. The other authors have endeavored to preserve as much of the original chapters as possible, but the considerable differences in these chapters, as well as in the men revising them, have resulted in varying degrees of rewriting and varying proportions of new material. Ford T. Swetnam, Jr., has revised the chapter on Wordsworth; Max F. Schulz, the chapter on Coleridge's poetry; Ernest J. Lovell, Jr., the chapter on Byron; Donald H. Reiman, the chapter on Shelley; David Perkins, the chapter on Keats; and the editor, the chapter on Romanticism. In matters of procedure the authors have tried to be consistent, but where the materials dictated diverse practices, as in the citing of reprints, they have proceeded accordingly. Each chapter has been read by two or more of the contributors, who thus assisted the editor with his job; each author remains, however, the final authority on his work and assumes the final responsibility for it. The cut-off date for books and articles discussed is generally 1970, although a few items from early 1971 have been included.

F. J.

CONTENTS

ABBREVIATIONS IN REFERENCES

BB	Bulletin of Bibliography
BC	Book Collector
BJA	British Journal of Aesthetics
BNYPL	Bulletin of the New York Public Library
BR	Baltic Review
CBEL	Cambridge Bibliography of English Literature
CE	College English
CentR	The Centennial Review
CJ	Classical Journal
CL	Comparative Literature
CLAJ	College Language Association Journal
CLS	Comparative Literature Studies
CLSB	Charles Lamb Society Bulletin
CollG	Colloquia Germanica, Internationale Zeitschrift für Germanische Sprach- und Literaturwissenschaft
CW	Catholic World
DM	Dublin Magazine
DR	Dalhousie Review
E&S	Essays and Studies by Members of the English Association
EC	Etudes Celtique

ECS	Eighteenth-Century Studies
EDH	Essays by Divers Hands
EIC	Essays in Criticism
EIE	English Institute Essays
EJ	English Journal
ELH	Journal of English Literary History
ELN	English Language Notes
EM	English Miscellany
ES	English Studies
ESA	English Studies in Africa
EXP	Explicator
HJ	Hibbert Journal
HLB	Harvard Library Bulletin
HLQ	Huntington Library Quarterly
HTR	Harvard Theological Review
HudR	Hudson Review
HUS	Harvard University Studies
IJP	International Journal of Psychoanalysis
JAAC	Journal of Aesthetics and Art Criticism
JEGP	Journal of English and Germanic Philology
JHI	Journal of the History of Ideas
JWCI	Journal of the Warburg and Courtauld Institute
KR	Kenyon Review
KSJ	Keats-Shelley Journal
KSMB	Keats-Shelley Memorial Bulletin
L&P	Literature and Psychology
MinnR	Minnesota Review
MLN	Modern Language Notes
MLQ	Modern Language Quarterly
MLR	Modern Language Review
MP	Modern Philology
N&Q	Notes and Queries
NCBEL	New Cambridge Bibliography of English Literature
NM	Neuphilologische Mitteilungen

PBSA	Papers of the Bibliographical Society of America
PLL	Papers on Language and Literature
PMLA	Publications of the Modern Language Association of America
PQ	Philological Quarterly
PTRSC	Proceedings and Transactions of the Royal Society of Canada
QQ	Queen's Quarterly
QR	Quarterly Review
RBPH	Revue Belge de Philologie et d'Histoire
REL	Review of English Literature
RES	Review of English Studies
RLC	Revue de Littérature Comparée
RSSCW	Research Studies State College of Washington
RSWSU	Research Studies Washington State University
SAQ	South Atlantic Quarterly
SB	Studies in Bibliography
SEL	Studies in English Literature
SHR	Southern Humanities Review
SIR	Studies in Romanticism
SN	Studia Neophilologica
SP	Studies in Philology
SR	Sewanee Review
SSL	Studies in Scottish Literature
TexSE	Texas Studies in English
TLS	Times Literary Supplement
TSE	Tulane Studies in English
TSL	Tennessee Studies in Literature
TSLL	Texas Studies in Language and Literature
TWC	The Wordsworth Circle
UKCR	University of Kansas City Review
UTQ	University of Toronto Quarterly
VQR	Virginia Quarterly Review
WR	Western Review
YFS	Yale French Studies
YR	Yale Review

I
THE ROMANTIC MOVEMENT

Ernest Bernbaum
Frank Jordan

I. BIBLIOGRAPHIES

George Watson's edition of *The New Cambridge Bibliography of English Literature,* Volume III (1969), which combines volume three of the 1940 edition with the relevant section of the 1957 supplement and extends the whole through 1967, is doubtless the greatest single source of books and articles concerning the Romantic Movement.[1] By consulting the preliminary divisions one could compile an impressive but almost interminable li..t. Consequently efforts to discriminate from among these books and articles those items of lasting merit, resulting in much shorter but less formidable lists, continue to have real value for students of the subject. Two of the older lists—Hoxie N. Fairchild's thirteen books, in "Romanticism: A Symposium" (*PMLA,* 1940), and Ernest Bernbaum's approximately 325 items, in *Guide through the Romantic Movement* (1930; rev. ed., 1949)—are inevitably dated and must give way to more recent surveys, but they remain important landmarks in the history of the subject. Among the best of the more recent short surveys are Richard Harter Fogle's "The Romantic Movement," in *Contemporary Literary Scholarship: A Critical*

[1] In order to discuss the scholarship on the Romantic Movement since 1950 I have had to condense Professor Bernbaum's chapter, though I have tried always to retain the substance of his commentary and to identify his more pronounced judgments, especially where they might be confused with my own. I have kept his topical arrangement for treating the Pre-Romantic Movement, but I have simplified his elaborate scheme for treating the Romantic Movement so that I might have more space for the matter itself. Every effort has been made to consider the more important and accessible books and articles published in the last twenty years, but the essay is finally highly selective: those items omitted number many times those included in the following pages. For a title which recurs in the essay, the date of publication is given only once, usually in the first reference. Long titles when repeated are shortened; the names of editors for *Festschriften* and other such collections are dropped after the first citation. (F. J.)

Review, ed. Lewis Leary (1958), and René Wellek's "Romanticism Re-examined," in *Concepts of Criticism,* ed. Stephen G. Nichols (1963), and in *Romanticism Reconsidered,* ed. Northrop Frye (1963). At once sound, succinct, and lucid Fogle's essay begins by canvassing attitudes toward Romanticism in the twentieth century and discussing some of the more outstanding studies of the subject; it proceeds by recounting the fortunes of the major poets, including Blake, during the same period; and concludes by summarizing the fates of the minor poets and the prose writers. Wellek's essay, which seeks to demonstrate a growing area of agreement among scholars both American and European as to the nature of Romanticism, especially in the period from 1949 to 1963, is more than a bibliographical survey; the books and articles cited are the evidence for his thesis. But their special function aside, they constitute a useful list of the more important recent studies, particularly those of the 1950's. In 1967 Fogle returned to the subject at greater length, with *Romantic Poets and Prose Writers,* a compilation for the Goldentree Bibliographies series. Initial sections provide advanced undergraduate and graduate students with the basic resources for studying Romanticism in its historical, intellectual, and social backgrounds and its literary and aesthetic foregrounds and, through the special journals and reviews, in its ongoing interest.

Three British contributions to the subject are of widely varying merit. Boris Ford's edition of *The Pelican Guide to English Literature: Vol. V: From Blake to Byron* (1957) includes a full and reliable bibliography as a supplement to three essays that discuss Romanticism in its social and literary dimensions. Hugh Sykes Davies' *The Poets and Their Critics: Vol. II: Blake to Browning* (1962) omits Coleridge altogether and neglects the more modern criticism of the other poets, for reasons that are at best unsatisfactory. F. W. A. Bateson's *A Guide to English Literature* (1965; rev. ed., 1968) offers a reading list for the literature from 1800 to 1960, which, though highly selective and just as highly opinionated, is worth consulting for the works it highlights.

The annual bibliographies which allow one to ascertain quickly the most recent contributions to the study of Romanticism date back to 1919, when the English Association of London began to publish *The Year's Work in English Studies.* Increasingly, this annual has paid more attention to the criticism of outstanding new studies than to the extensive listing of new titles. Much fuller lists are found in the *Annual Bibliography of English Language and Literature,* compiled since 1920 by the Modern

Humanities Research Association. This annual contains no criticism, but does notice reviews of new studies that have appeared in the learned journals and literary periodicals. In 1922 the Modern Language Association of America began to publish its *Annual Bibliography* in *PMLA*. Originally restricted to the contributions of American scholars, in 1957 it became an international project and subsequently many times enlarged. Today it is easily the largest of the annual bibliographies. Solely devoted to Romanticism in English and European literature is *The Romantic Movement: A Selective and Critical Bibliography,* on the whole the most important of the annuals, which has appeared variously in *ELH,* 1937–49; in *PQ,* 1950–64; and in *ELN,* 1965–. It provides full reviews of major studies and brief notices of consequential ones; it describes or summarizes important articles; and it indicates reviews, sometimes with a hint as to their tone. Another specialized annual is the *Current Bibliography* of studies in Keats, Shelley, Byron, Hunt, and their circles, published since 1952 in *KSJ.* (In 1964 D. B. Green and E. G. Wilson collected the first ten years and extended backward to cover 1950–51.) One should note, too, "Recent Studies in Nineteenth-Century English Literature," which has appeared in the Autumn issue of *SEL* since 1961, with a different reviewer for each year. With no attempt, even where books are concerned, to be comprehensive, this last has achieved a reputation for severe remarks that *Blackwood's* itself might have envied. The latest journal in the field, *The Wordsworth Circle* (1970–   ), does not presently offer a formal review or bibliography, but under such headings as "Book News" and "Some Recent Articles" provides for word of late scholarship in this area.

Several review articles of the last decade attend to some of the more important scholarship of the late 1950's and the 1960's. Taken in order of appearance, they are: Edward E. Bostetter's "The New Romantic Criticism" (*SR,* 1961), which discusses eight books; Patrick Cruttwell's "Romantics and Victorians" (*HudR,* 1961–62), which includes four books on individual Romantic writers; Anne Kostelanetz's "Romantic Poets and Pontificators" (*MinnR,* 1964), which treats both general studies and specific ones; Herbert Lindenberger's "On Commentary, Romanticism, and Critical Method: Reflections on Three Recent Books" (*MLQ,* 1966); and J. R. MacGillivray's two-part "New Editors and Critics of the English Romantics" (*UTQ,* 1968, 1970). Although these articles are no substitute for the more systematic bibliographies and guides, they often single out from the crowd the more noteworthy of recent studies and put them into a context that can be valuable for the student of Romanticism who is overwhelmed by the deluge of contemporary scholarly writing.

II. THE PRE-ROMANTIC MOVEMENT

The modern study of Romanticism began at a time when literary study was increasingly devoted to the historical method, to a search for origins and influences, and to the belief that the essential and most valuable qualities of the masterpieces of the Romantics were "anticipated," "influenced by," "caused," or "determined" by Pre-Romantic predecessors. More attention was therefore likely to be paid to a great poet's supposed precursors than to himself, or to the movement's alleged antecedents than to its own nature. Such scholarly activity led to the idea of a coherent movement that prepared for the Romantic Movement and resulted in widespread use of the phrase which heads this section. When the roots were of more interest than the flower, the identification and classification of the flower were usually hasty, partial, and superficial, while the delving after the roots became a laborious pursuit in underground darkness with less and less certainty that the true roots were being traced. No sooner were some of the obvious larger roots followed down, than one by one, others and still others, slimmer and slimmer, in the entangled subterranean system appeared to require attention. The result was that the historical method, pursued too blindly and without help from other critical methods, often petered out in confusion and triviality. As was to be expected, reaction set in, stimulated in part by the New Criticism, with its emphasis on the literature itself. And to judge from the paucity of writing on the subject in the last twenty years, the concept of a Pre-Romantic Movement is still very much in disrepute. One seldom comes across the phrase these days, let alone books or articles that subscribe to the idea behind it. Symptomatic of this change is the latest major teaching text, David Perkins' *English Romantic Writers* (1967), which unlike its predecessors in the field ignores the Pre-Romantic writers altogether.

Reaction ranged from simple and silent neglect to vehement denouncement (see, for example, Morse Peckham's "A Survey of Romantic Period Textbooks," *CE,* 1958) but fortunately included considered rejection, as in R. D. Havens' "Discontinuity in Literary Development: The

Case of English Romanticism" (*SP*, 1950), which argues temperately and effectively against a direct development of Romantic poetry out of mid- and late-eighteenth-century literature; in Bertrand Bronson's "The Pre-Romantic or Post-Augustan Mode" (*ELH*, 1953; rpt. in *Facets of the Enlightenment*, 1968), which finds the label Pre-Romantic or Post-Augustan unsuitable for poets who are defined by their very uncommittedness to both the old (Augustan) and the new (Romantic); and in Northrop Frye's "Towards Defining an Age of Sensibility" (*ELH*, 1956; rpt. in *Fables of Identity: Studies in Poetic Mythology*, 1963), which maintains that, as a term for the age of sensibility, " 'pre-romantic' . . . has the peculiar demerit of committing us to an anachronism before we start, and imposing a false teleology on everything we study." Frye proceeds to show that the literature of sensibility follows an aesthetic neither Augustan nor Romantic. For all such cogent statements, it is only fair to note, however, that some of our best scholars, while recognizing the special merits and peculiar qualities of both the eighteenth century and the Romantic Period, continue to insist, particularly where aesthetics and psychology are concerned, on a real and significant continuity from the one to the other. One thinks of Walter Jackson Bate, who in his latest study, *The Burden of the Past and the English Poet* (1970), persists in seeing the Romantics as nothing less than the very children of the eighteenth-century writers, the Augustans as well as the sentimentalists. Where the one period is used not to denigrate but to elucidate the other, as in the case of Bate's essay, this perspective seems immanently sane, not to say rewarding.

Nevertheless, the statement that Ernest Bernbaum made early in the original form of this section remains true: there exists no recent monograph on the Pre-Romantic Movement as a whole. For many years scholars in the field have not attempted a general synthesis; if interested in pursuing the subject at all, they have concentrated their labors upon individual Pre-Romantics or upon special topics. Hence William Lyon Phelps's *The Beginnings of the English Romantic Movement: A Study in Eighteenth Century Literature*, though it appeared in 1893 and is amateurish and inaccurate, may perhaps still serve as an introductory outline, its tone and preoccupations being literary and its substance not being weighed down by pedantic antiquarianism. In the same elementary helpful category is the section in Emile Legouis's and Louis Cazamian's *Histoire de la littérature anglaise* (1924; tr. 1926–27; last rev. ed., 1967) entitled "The Pre-Romantic Period"; useful also are the chapters, even more up-to-date and dependable, in A. D. McKillop's handbook *English Literature from Dryden to Burns* (1948), entitled "Romanticism and Changing Taste," "Sentimentalism," "Primitivism," and "The Medieval Revival."

More sophisticated in approach are the several collections of essays and the *Festschriften* devoted to literature of the eighteenth and nineteenth centuries. These volumes, because their authors or contributors are usually not committed to tracing influences or assigning labels, often throw considerable light, though sometimes indirectly, on the relationship of the later eighteenth century to the Romantic Period. One such collection is Geoffrey Tillotson's *Augustan Studies* (1961), with its several essays on poetic diction and its single piece on "The Manner of Proceeding in Certain Eighteenth- and Early Nineteenth-Century Poems." Another is Earl Wasserman's *The Subtler Language: Critical Readings of Neoclassic and Romantic Poems* (1959), which by treating poems of Dryden, Denham, Pope, and Shelley traces the change from a mimetic to a creative conception of poetry. *Aspects of the Eighteenth Century* (1965), edited by Wasserman, is limited to neither literature nor England; rather it is a rich assortment of writings on eighteenth-century European culture, several of which have subsequently been developed into books. *Festschriften* such as *The Age of Johnson,* ed. Frederick W. Hilles (1949), and *From Sensibility to Romanticism,* ed. Frederick W. Hilles and Harold Bloom (1965), contain valuable essays (discussed elsewhere in this volume) by leading scholars on both Pre-Romantic and Romantic writers and, in some instances, essays which connect the two—for example, W. K. Wimsatt's "The Structure of Romantic Nature Imagery," in the Hilles volume, and A. D. McKillop's "Local Attachment and Cosmopolitanism—The Eighteenth-Century Pattern," in the Hilles and Bloom volume. (The latest of these is *The Augustan Milieu,* ed. Henry Knight Miller, Eric Rothstein, and G. S. Rousseau, 1970. For a fuller list of relevant *Festschriften,* see the Bibliographical Supplement to the third volume of *A Literary History of England,* ed. A. C. Baugh, 2nd ed., 1967.) Needless to say, the studies in these volumes are not all new, nor are they all equal in value, but some of them are major contributions to the literature.

Inasmuch as a conspicuous feature in many poems of Wordsworth and other Romantics is a faith in the instinctive goodness of human beings, combined with faith in the relatively high moral value of sympathy or benevolence, it is not strange that the appearance of such beliefs and inclinations in eighteenth-century literature was one of the first of the topics pursued by scholars in the Pre-Romantic field. Ernest Bernbaum's

The Drama of Sensibility: A Sketch of the History of English Sentimental Comedy and Domestic Tragedy, 1696–1780 (1915) belongs in that group of studies. Fifty years later, its approach and method, as Bernbaum himself pointed out, seem rather inept: it discusses playwrights as if they were, or should have been, systematic moralists; and it exaggerates the sharpness of the opposition between two schools of drama—one with conservative (classical?) ideas about man as an inseparable mixture of good and evil traits, the other inspired by Shaftesbury's enthusiasm for nature and confidence in the sensibilities and goodness of man (sentimental, and ultimately to become Romantic). This was followed by other studies in sentimentalism—C. A. Moore's "Shaftesbury and the Ethical Poets in England" (*PMLA*, 1916), his "Whig Panegyric Verse, 1700–1760: A Phase of Sentimentalism" (*PMLA*, 1926); Edith Birkhead's "Sentiment and Sensibility in the Eighteenth-Century Novel" (*E&S*, 1925); Johannes H. Harder's *Observations on Some Tendencies of Sentiment and Ethics, Chiefly in Minor Poetry and the Essay* . . . (1933); R. S. Crane's "Suggestions Toward a Genealogy of 'The Man of Feeling' " (*ELH*, 1934); and James H. Warner's " 'Education of the Heart': Observations on the Eighteenth-Century Sentimental Movement" (*Michigan Acad. of Science, Arts, and Letters*, 1943).

Arthur Sherbo's *English Sentimental Drama* (1957) takes advantage of all these studies but develops chiefly, as they do, out of Bernbaum's pioneering book. The author has no very high regard for the plays he treats; indeed his method of defining sentimental drama and testing plays against his definition is calculated to expose the inferior literary quality of the genre, which, according to Sherbo, is by definition without "artistic distinction and integrity." An earlier study, Joseph Wood Krutch's *Comedy and Conscience after the Restoration* (1949), and a later one, Norman Holland's *The First Modern Comedies* (1959), of necessity consider sentimentalism, but Paul Parnell's "The Sentimental Mask" (*PMLA*, 1963) is the only important theoretical essay in recent years. It suggests that the assumption of moral perfection—the belief that one's own nature is perfectible, if not already perfect—is the hallmark of the sentimental hero or heroine, for whom sentimentalism is thus a mask to hide any evidence to the contrary, for instance, self-seeking and hypocrisy. Arthur Friedman's "Aspects of Sentimentalism in Eighteenth-Century Literature," in the *Festschrift The Augustan Milieu*, is a late contribution to the subject.

Northrop Frye's "Towards Defining an Age of Sensibility," mentioned above, characterizes the literature of sensibility and hence the period in which it flourished as one of process; in this respect, Frye argues, it is distinct from both Augustan and Romantic literature, which is one of finished product. Frye's essay, written to suggest that later eighteenth-century literature is not "merely traditional" but "justifies and calls for a distinct kind of esthetic analysis," is convincing so long as one remembers the "not 'merely.' " That there is some agreement among scholars as to the wisdom of Frye's label for the age he interprets may be inferred from the title of the *Festschrift From Sensibility to Romanticism*. No one essay in this collection focuses generally on sensibility, but the Pre-Romantic poets, as well as certain motifs characteristic of their work, figure prominently. Gray's "Elegy," for example, is the central subject of three essays. Patricia Meyer Spacks, in writing about the later eighteenth-century, would seem to agree with Frye that the literature of sensibility must be judged according to its own aesthetics and valued for its own sake (see her *The Insistence of Horror: Aspects of the Supernatural in Eighteenth-Century Poetry*, 1962, and *The Poetry of Vision: Five Eighteenth-Century Poets*, 1967). Even so, her work inevitably adds to our understanding of the Romantics by exploring the context from which they derive. Louis I. Bredvold's series of lectures, *The Natural History of Sensibility* (1962), after establishing the ethics of feeling, examines the consequences of these ethics, which are seen to be something less than desirable.

The second topic which received early consideration is indicated by the title of Myra Reynolds' work *The Treatment of Nature in Poetry between Pope and Wordsworth* (1896; rev. ed., 1909). She detected Pre-Romanticism in poems which showed direct personal observation expressed in a somewhat realistic and concrete style that avoided general abstract terms. The specimens of the kind of poetry which she cites may be supplemented by those given in R. A. Aubin's *Topographical Poetry in XVIII-Century England* (1936). The interest in accurate concrete description as a sign of Pre-Romanticism was succeeded by a greater interest in the appearance of such sentimental, mystical, or philosophical implications in the nature-poetry as might be detected. This trend is seen in C. A. Moore's "The Return to Nature in English Poetry of the Eighteenth Century" (*SP*, 1917) and G. G. Williams' "The Beginnings of Nature Poetry in the Eighteenth Century" (*SP*, 1930). Moore emphasized the influence of Shaftesbury's philosophy of nature; but Herbert Drennon, "James Thomson and Newtonianism" (Univ. of Chicago, *Abstracts of Theses*, 1929), deemed Newton more important (see his articles in *PMLA*, 1934, and *SP*, 1934). The ramifications of this problem are pursued far and wide, among critics as well as poets, in Marjorie H. Nicolson's *Newton Demands the Muse: Newton's Opticks and the Eighteenth Century Poets* (1946; see A. D. McKillop's valuable review, *JEGP,* 1947). The distant background of the eighteenth-century ideas of nature is set forth in A. O. Lovejoy's *The Great Chain of Being* (1936). Beginning with Plato, it expounds the history of concepts about nature—its unity, plenitude, and diversity—lamenting what seem to Lovejoy the tragic and muddleheaded contradictions which they led to. He maintains, first, that the original Platonic theory of an absolute unity was logically irreconcilable with the need of diversity; and, second, that the Romantics discarded the idea of unity and promoted that of diversity. It seemed to Ernest Bernbaum in 1950—and to many others then and now—that both these contentions are erroneous: it can, he believed, be successfully maintained that Romanticism is not an admission of the irreconcilable inconsistencies of Platonic idealism, but on the contrary an enriched and corrected form of Platonism. Somewhat closer than Lovejoy to Pre-Romantic literature itself is Basil Willey's *The Eighteenth-Century Background: Studies on the Idea of Nature in the Thought of the Period* (1940), which deals with the philosophies of nature of Newton, Hartley, Priestley, and others, the aim being "to indicate some stages in that divinization of 'Nature' which culminates in Wordsworth." Closer still but much less ambitious is Bonamy Dobrée's "Nature Poetry in the Early Eighteenth Century" (*E&S,* 1965), which assesses Pre-Romantic nature poetry according to its own aesthetic and finds it appealing and successful. With R. W. Harris' *Reason and Nature in the Eighteenth Century, 1714–1780* (1968) we return to "nature" in the broadest sense of the term. Like his similar volume on the Romantics (see below), this one is essentially a social and intellectual overview of the period specified, with rather more attention to literature and art as evidence of attitudes and atmosphere than is customary with such studies.

A third topic arises out of the encouragement which the School of Sensibility, and especially its subdivision the Graveyard School, gave to the cultivation of sympathy and of its profuse emotional expression. The elegiac interest in bereavement, in mourning, in the melancholy induced by the mutability of man's estate, is studied in the following monographs: Amy Louise Reed, *The Background of Gray's Elegy: A Study in the Taste for Melancholy Poetry: 1700–1751* (1924); J. W. Draper, *The Funeral Elegy and the Rise of English Romanticism* (1929; see R. S. Crane's review, *PQ,* 1930); and Eleanor M. Sickels, *The Gloomy Egoist: Moods and Themes of Melancholy from Gray to Keats* (1932). Leo Shapiro, "Lucretian 'Domestic Melancholy' and the Tradition of Vergilian 'Frustration' " (*PMLA*, 1938), shows that some of the sorrowful strains in Thomson, Gray, and Collins may be echoes from Lucretius. The only later monograph devoted to the subject is John F. Sena's Princeton dissertation "The English Malady: The Idea of Melancholy from 1700 to 1760" (1968). His published essay "Smollett's Persona and the Melancholic Traveler: An Hypothesis" (*ECS*, 1968), which elaborates one part of the longer study, attends to the medical background of melancholy that is Sena's especial concern.

Pre-Romantic interest in social conditions of humanitarian reforms provides a fourth topic. One aspect of the social situation, slighted by students of English Pre-Romanticism, is dealt with by Paul Van Tieghem, "La Sensibilité et la passion dans le roman européen au XVIIIe siècle" (*RLC*, 1926), namely, the revolt of genuine love against conventional worldly standards and *mariages de convenance*. Edward A. Whitney gives a general survey, "Humanitarianism and Romanticism" (*HLQ*, 1939). Wylie Sypher's *Guinea's Captive Kings: British Anti-Slavery Literature of the XVIIIth Century* (1942) is a detailed study, and includes glimpses of pro-slavery writings. It should be supplemented with Earl L. Griggs's *Thomas Clarkson, the Friend of Slaves* (1936), Bernard Martin's *John Newton* (1950; rev. as *An Ancient Mariner*, 1960), and Martin and Mark Spurrell's edition of Newton's *Journal of a Slave Trader* (*John Newton*), *1750–1754* (1962). Ford K. Brown's *Fathers of the Victorians: The Age of Wilberforce* (1961) and James Pope-Hennessy's *Sins of the Fathers: A Study of the Atlantic Slave Traders, 1441–1807* (1967), while not primarily concerned with literature or literary figures, are important interpretations of the social and moral history of slavery and anti-slavery. Brown, for example, in his last chapter draws a parallel between the evangelicals and Mary Shelley's gothic hero Frankenstein; Pope-Hennessy writes about slavery with a view to long-term effects, including current racial problems. The interest in prison reform that is reflected in writing of the early Romantics, Godwin and Wordsworth, for example, is pinpointed in two studies of John Howard which appeared in the same year (1958): Derek L. Howard's *John Howard: Prison Reformer* and John Southwood's *John Howard, Prison Reformer: An Account of His Life and Travels*. Under the topic of humanitarian reform belongs, too, Dix Harwood's *Love for Animals and How It Developed in Great Britain* (1928).

The next topic, religion, is, as might be expected, one of the most involved and controversial. There is little if any agreement as to whether the religious revival was a cause of Pre-Romanticism, or a consequence; or whether it was even relevant and important thereto. Materials that might help one decide such questions may be found here and there in the following writings, though some of them are not chiefly concerned with literature: W. J. Warner, *The Wesleyan Movement in the Industrial Revolution* (1930); Umphrey Lee, *The Historical Background of Early Methodist Enthusiasm* (1931); A. W. Harrison, "Romanticism in Religious Revivals" (*HJ*, 1933); John M. Creed and John S. B. Smith, eds., *Religious Thought in the Eighteenth Century: Illustrated from Writers of the Period,* an anthology (1934); Frederick C. Gill, *The Romantic Movement and Methodism: A Study of English Romanticism and the Evangelical Revival* (1937; rpt. 1954); T. B. Shepherd, *Methodism and the Literature of the Eighteenth Century* (1940); and R. W. Wearmouth, *Methodism and the Common People of the Eighteenth Century* (1945). In the years since World War II, sectarian presses, in particular the Abingdon Press in this country and the Epworth Press in Britain, have turned out enough books and tracts on historical Methodism alone to stock a small library. When one adds to them the accounts of Shakers and other minor sects, the records of the Oxford evangelicals and other smaller groups within the larger movements, and the several biographies of George Whitefield and other important leaders, the library becomes many times too large to be described here. It is well catalogued, however, in the bibliography of English literature for the years 1660–1800, the third section, published annually in *Philological Quarterly.* The authors of these and of the earlier studies mentioned by title are by and large sympathetic to their material. But such is not always the case. Sidelights, brilliant, but from an unfriendly, agnostic point of view, are cast upon the subject in Leslie Stephen's *History of English Thought in the Eighteenth Century* (2 vols., 1876), where the prosaic and unaspiring tone of ordinary religion in that period is exposed. One would expect Hoxie N. Fairchild's *Religious Trends in English Poetry* (Vol. I, 1700–40: 1939; Vol. II, 1740–80: 1942), judging by its title, to be of special interest to the student of literature, but it may disappoint him. The author, a sincere and devoted Anglo-Catholic, looks upon all the varieties of Protestantism as unorthodox, and regards eighteenth-century Pre-Romanticism as "simply Protestant Christianity in a more or less delightfully phosphorescent state of decay." From that point of view he diligently surveys a vast body of eighteenth-century verse, much of it of slight poetic value, judges it systematically by the strict theological dogmas of Anglo-Catholicism, and of course condemns most of it, especially if it tends towards Romanticism, as deplorably heretical. His third volume (1780–1830: 1949), then, is predictable in its negative judgments of the Romantic poets, who like their immediate predecessors, but even more so, depart from the true faith as Fairchild sees it.

The sixth topic is the interest of the Pre-Romantics in the French Revolution, which brought to a burning focus their sympathies with various causes, such as democracy, the rights of man, political and economic freedom, and the improvement of labor conditions and of the status of women. The discussion of this exciting subject was brilliantly begun by Edward Dowden in his *The French Revolution and English Literature* (1897), which is rich in vivid character-sketches and biographical incidents. Among the best of the later studies are: A. E. Hancock, *The French Revolution and the English Poets: A Study in Historical Criticism* (1899); Charles Cestre, *La Révolution française et les poètes anglais (1789–1809)* (1906); Allene Gregory, *The French Revolution and the English Novel* (1915), sympathetic towards radicalism; B. Sprague Allen, "Minor Disciples of Radicalism in the Revolutionary Era" (*MP,* 1923); Crane Brinton, "The Membership of the Jacobin Clubs" (*Amer. Hist. Rev.,* 1929); and M. Ray Adams, *Studies in the Literary Backgrounds of English Radicalism, with Special Reference to the French Revolution* (1947). J. M. Thompson edited a collection, *English Witnesses of the French Revolution* (1938), containing quotations from the narratives of fifty witnesses, including Mary Wollstonecraft, Tom Paine, Samuel Rogers, and Wordsworth. More recent studies include the first two volumes of Simon Maccoby's six-volume history of *English Radicalism, 1762–1961* (1955–61), which cover the movement from its origins in Wilkes's era to its triumph in Cobbett's heyday; Carl B. Cone's *The English Jacobins: Reformers in Late Eighteenth-Century England* (1968); and Alfred Cobban's numerous studies of the French Revolution (or Revolutions, as he prefers) from its many different aspects. These items vary considerably in their attention to the connection between the Pre-Romantics and the French Revolution, but W. R. Freyer, in "Romantic Literature and the European Age of Revolution" (*Renaissance and Modern Studies,* 1964), has taken this connection as his theme, arguing persuasively that the link is neither tenuous nor fortuitous but precisely the contrary. Basic to Freyer's argument, with regard to both Pre-Romantics and Romantics, is his belief that the former were allies of the writers of the Enlightenment and the latter their inheritors.

Turning away from the relation of the Pre-Romantics to their own century, we come to the seventh topic, their so-called primitivism. First of the learned works in this group is Chauncey B. Tinker's *Nature's Simple Plan: A Phase of Radical Thought in the Mid-Eighteenth Century* (1922), which delightfully recounts their fancies about a golden age when men lived in a state of nature, free, virtuous, and happy, and enjoyed the highest kind of poetry, that of the primitive bards. This theme is elaborated in Hoxie N. Fairchild, *The Noble Savage: A Study in Romantic Naturalism* (1928); Lois Whitney, *Primitivism and the Idea of Progress in English Popular Literature of the Eighteenth Century* (1934); R. S. Crane, "Anglican Apologetics and the Idea of Progress, 1699–1745" (*MP,* 1934); R. T. Clark, Jr., "Herder, Percy, and the Song of Songs" (*PMLA,* 1946); and Rayner Unwin, *The Rural Muse: Studies in the Peasant Poetry of England* (1954). Unwin's account of the uneducated poet in England, though centered on the century that gave him birth, traces his tradition into the twentieth century and claims for it a small but enriching influence on English literature. Somewhat related to the subject is Donald M. Foerster, *Homer in English Criticism: The Historical Approach in the Eighteenth Century* (1947), and likewise Samuel Kliger, "The Gothic Revival and the German *Translatio*" (*MP,* 1947), which shows that some Pre-Romantics admired the (anti-classical) Goths as pioneers of a higher kind of insight and of religious reformation, a theme that Kliger has treated at greater length in *The Goths in England: A Study in Seventeenth and Eighteenth Century Thought* (1952). It should be remarked that in recent years little attention has been given to Pre-Romantic or Romantic primitivism, in part because of the over-emphasis it received in the first half of the century. The better Romantics scholars had recognized all along that to define Romanticism primarily as primitivism was more than risky. Put on the defensive by the attacks of the New Humanists and the New Critics, they saw that to do so was to play directly into the hands of the enemy. With not a little embarrassment they attempted to divert him to other less vulnerable fronts, with some success. Latter-day Romantics scholars are no longer embarrassed by Romantic primitivism; rather they simply refuse to accept so simple and inadequate an explanation for the movement, just as they dismiss its boon companions, orientalism and gothicism, the next topics in this section, and for much the same reason.

Henry A. Beers's *A History of English Romanticism in the Eighteenth Century* (1898) is an admirable work within its limitations; but its author regarded Romanticism as almost entirely confined to the revival of the medieval, and it is instructive to note that when he wrote the sequel, *A History of English Romanticism in the Nineteenth Century* (1901), he had little to say of Wordsworth, Byron, and Shelley.

Another feature of Pre-Romanticism, furnishing the eighth topic, is the translating and imitating of such fascinatingly strange literature as the Oriental, the Scandinavian, and the Celtic. The Oriental is less thoroughly but more variously treated than the other two. In addition to Martha B. Conant's *The Oriental Tale in England in the Eighteenth Century* (1908), we now have Arthur J. Weitzman's "The Oriental Tale in the Eighteenth Century: A Reconsideration" (*Studies on Voltaire and the Eighteenth Century,* 1967), which takes issue with Conant's explanation of the fashion. William W. Appleton has limited his scope to the Chinese, in *A Cycle of Cathay: The Chinese Vogue in England During the Seventeenth and Eighteenth Centuries* (1951); John D. Yohannan has concentrated on the Persian, in "The Persian Poetry Fad in England, 1770–1825" (*CL,* 1952); and Kenneth R. Stunkel has investigated the Indian, in "English Orientalism and India, 1784–1830" (*Ohio Univ. Review,* 1969), looking specifically at the English discovery and elucidation of India's Sanskrit-based civilization in these years. Previous to these more specialized items are R. W. Frantz, *The English Traveller and the Movement of Ideas, 1660–1732* (Univ. of Nebraska Studies, 1932–33), and Wallace C. Brown, "The Popularity of English Travel Books about the Near East, 1775–1825" (*PQ,* 1936). And basic to them all, broad or narrow, is Raymond Schwab, *La Renaissance orientale* (1951), a major study of the oriental movement in Europe in the nineteenth century. On the Scandinavian there are two thorough and systematic studies, Frank E. Farley, *Scandinavian Influences in the English Romantic Movement* (1903), and Sigurd B. Hustvedt, *Ballad Criticism in Scandinavia and Great Britain During the Eighteenth Century* (1916). On the Celtic we have Edward D. Snyder, *The Celtic Revival in English Literature: 1760–1800* (1923). It is profitable to study the treatises of Farley and Snyder side by side.

The ninth topic, the Gothic Novel, has been the occasion, whatever the reason, for much writing. Early studies in this century, some of them now little more than curiosities, include: A. M. Killen, *Le Roman terrifiant: ou Roman noir de Walpole à Anne Radcliffe et son influence sur la littérature française jusqu'en 1840* (1915); Dorothy Scarborough, *The Supernatural in Modern English Fiction* (1917); Edith Birkhead, *The Tale of Terror: A Study of the Gothic Romance* (1921); Eino Railo, *The Haunted Castle: A Study of the Elements of English Romanticism* (1927);

Michael Sadleir, "The Northanger Novels" (*Edinburgh Review,* 1927); and Jakob Brauchli, *Der englische Schauer-Roman um 1800 . . .* (1928). On the whole these studies, which depend heavily on the accumulation of illustrative detail or on lists and catalogues of "elements," present no very creditable picture of Romanticism, if one is defensive about the subject. The more standard works on the genre date from the 1930's and 1940's. Walter F. Wright's *Sensibility in English Prose Fiction, 1760–1814: A Reinterpretation* (1937) is perhaps the best account of its origins and development. Montague Summers' double bill *The Gothic Quest: A History of the Gothic Novel* (1938) and *A Gothic Bibliography* (1941) have made him the chief name in the field. But the *History of the Pre-Romantic Novel in England* (1949) by James R. Foster offers the most trustworthy because most scholarly treatment of the subject. Useful, too, are Paul Yvon, *Le Gothique et la renaissance gothique en Angleterre (1750–1880)* (1931); Mary M. Tarr, *Catholicism in Gothic Fiction* (1946); and Auguste Viatte, *Les Sources occultes de romantisme: Illuminisme-théosophie, 1170–1820,* 2 vols. (1928). From these last, it would appear that, if interest in the Gothic Novel be a sign of "low" taste, it is a descent peculiar to neither England nor America.

In the last two decades interest in the Gothic Novel has, if anything, waxed. Reputable publishers have come out with new editions of major and minor classics of the genre. The Oxford English Novels Series, for example, numbers several "Gothics"; the seven "Northanger Novels," edited by Devendra P. Varma, who is also the author of *The Gothic Flame* (1956), have been published by Folio Society (1968). One notices, too, that fiction decidedly in the Gothic vein now occasionally rivals in quality and popularity the better fiction being written. Signs of scholarly interest in the subject are such essays as Lowry Nelson's "Night Thoughts on the Gothic Novel" (*YR,* 1963); Francis Hart's "The Experience of Character in the English Gothic Novel," in *Experience in the Novel,* ed. Roy Harvey Pearce (1968); and Robert Hume's "Gothic Versus Romantic: A Revaluation of the Gothic Novel" (*PMLA,* 1969). (See the March 1971 issue of *PMLA* for Robert L. Platzner's rejoinder to Hume and the ensuing debate.) These essays have their different points to make, but they share the theme that the Gothic Novel must not be viewed as a bastard child in the family of Romanticism but rather as a legitimate offspring. Besides discriminating the good from the inferior novels, they also suggest that the development of English fiction will not be clearly in perspective until we recognize the contribution of the Gothic Novel. Indeed, a book such as

Masao Miyoshi's *The Divided Self: A Perspective on the Literature of the Victorians* (1969) implies that, unless we know the nature and history of the Gothic Novel, we are not likely to understand the modern literary sensibility, which (at least in the romance tradition) is divided against itself. The archetype of this divided mind, according to Miyoshi, is the Gothic villain. Paul Frankl's *The Gothic: Literary Sources and Interpretations through Eight Centuries* (1960) has chapters on the Romantic Period in Europe but very little on England or English writers at this time.

The next group of studies, the tenth, consists mostly of contributions to the history of Pre-Romantic poetry. Some decades ago such studies— e.g., the introduction to Ernest Bernbaum's *English Poets of the Eighteenth Century* (1918)—overstressed the contrasts between the Neo-Classical and the Pre-Romantic. Oswald Doughty's subdivisions in his otherwise admirable *English Lyric in the Age of Reason* (1922) illustrate the liking for sharp distinctions. But several early essays by R. D. Havens warned against too rigid classification of authors as either Classical or Romantic—"Romantic Aspects of the Age of Pope" (*PMLA*, 1912), "Thomas Warton and the Eighteenth-Century Dilemma" (*SP*, 1928), and "Changing Taste in the Eighteenth Century: A Study of Dryden's and Dodsley's Miscellanies" (*PMLA*, 1929). In the 1950's Havens returned to the subject, with the articles "Solitude and the Neoclassicists" (*ELH*, 1954) and "Simplicity, a Changing Concept" (*JHI*, 1953). The former demonstrated the popularity of solitude as a literary theme in the eighteenth century, while showing that before the Romantics took it up solitude was more a pastime than a passion. The latter discussed the motif of simplicity to the end of proving that by the time of Wordsworth simplicity was a value long accepted and widely believed in. A. M. Kinghorn was concerned with the gradual evolution of simplicity as aesthetic principle, in "Literary Aesthetics and the Sympathetic Emotion—a Main Trend in Eighteenth Century Scottish Criticism" (*SSL*, 1963). Paul S. Wood, "The Opposition to Neo-Classicism in England Between 1660 and 1700" (*PMLA*, 1928), held that not *all* such opposition should be termed Romantic. F. W. Bateson, *English Poetry and the English Language: An Experiment in Literary History* (1934), urged the use of "baroque" to denote the Pre-Romantic love of orderly disorder; but René Wellek demurred, "Literature and the Arts" (*EIE: 1941, 1942*). Geoffrey Tillotson's "Eighteenth-Century Poetic Diction" (*E&S*, 1939) was a strong defense; but see Wellek's criticism (*MP*, 1944). Tillotson later expanded and reprinted this essay, last published as *Augustan Poetic Diction*, 1964. Josephine Miles, *The Primary*

Language of Poetry in the 1740's and 1840's (1950), demonstrated that the primary language of poetry in 1840 was not at all the primary language of poetry in 1740, thereby establishing a basis in diction for distinguishing Romantic poetry from Augustan poetry. Donald Davie, *Purity of Diction in English Verse* (1952), has defended the diction of later eighteenth-century poetry against the charge of metaphorical poverty by reference to the principles of pure diction to which the poets subscribed. Davie calls attention to the same principles resulting in the same diction in "the movement" poetry of the 1950's. The rather special topic of *Personification in Eighteenth-Century English Poetry* (1955) is the contribution of Chester F. Chapin. The style and composition of Pre-Romantic poetry as it contrasts with that of Romantic poetry is the subject of P. W. K. Stone, who in *The Art of Poetry, 1750–1820* (1967) argues that the former is primarily indebted to a theory of rhetoric, the latter to a theory of imagination.

Other noteworthy contributions largely concerned with poetry are: Arthur Johnston, *Enchanted Ground: The Study of Medieval Romance in the Eighteenth Century* (1964); J. W. Draper, "The Metrical Tale in XVIII-Century England" (*PMLA,* 1937); Earl R. Wasserman, "The Return of the Enjambed Couplet" (*ELH,* 1940), on predecessors of Leigh Hunt, and *Elizabethan Poetry in the Eighteenth Century* (1947), a broad survey; David Nichol Smith, *Shakespeare in the Eighteenth Century* (1928); R. W. Babcock, *The Genesis of Shakespeare Idolatry, 1766–1799: A Study of English Criticism of the Late Eighteenth Century* (1931); Augustus Ralli, *A History of Shakespearian Criticism,* Vol. II (1932); Paul S. Conklin, *A History of Hamlet Criticism, 1601–1821* (1947); G. W. Stone, Jr., "Shakespeare in the Periodicals, 1700–1740: A Study of the Growth of a Knowledge of the Dramatist in the Eighteenth Century" (*Shakespeare Quarterly,* 1952); George C. Barnam, *Eighteenth-Century Adaptations of Shakespeare* (1956); and David Lovett, "Shakespeare as a Poet of Realism in the Eighteenth Century" (*ELH,* 1935). Still other forms and techniques are treated by the following scholars: Norman Mclean, "From Action to Image: Theories of the Lyric in the Eighteenth Century," *Critics and Criticism Ancient and Modern,* ed. R. S. Crane (1952); Earl Miner, "From Narrative to 'Description' and 'Sense' in Eighteenth-Century Poetry" (*SEL,* 1969); J. E. Congleton, *Theories of Pastoral Poetry in England, 1684–1798* (1952); William Bowman Piper, *The Heroic Couplet* (1969); and Wallace C. Brown, *The Triumph of Form: A Study of the Later Masters of the Heroic Couplet* (1948).

Bernard H. Stern, *The Rise of Romantic Hellenism in English Literature, 1732–86* (1940), treats a motif peculiar to no one form or technique, as does Martin Price, *To the Palace of Wisdom: Studies in Order and Energy from Dryden to Blake* (1964).

The eleventh topic is the literary theories and judgments of eighteenth-century philosophers and critics, a subject involving the meaning and value of such concepts as Genius, Beauty, Imagination, and Taste. John G. Robertson, *Studies in the Genesis of Romantic Theory in the Eighteenth Century* (1923), tried, not wholly successfully, to trace Romantic aesthetics back to critics of the Italian Renaissance; and A. E. Longueil studied "The Word 'Gothic' in Eighteenth Century Criticism" (*MLN*, 1923). The way in which the word "romantic" came to acquire its more familiar connotations was followed by Raymond Immerwahr in "The Ascending Romantic View in the Eighteenth Century" (*Pubs. of the Eng. Goethe Soc.*, 1966); Immerwahr walked much the same ground traveled earlier by Logan Pearsall Smith in "Four Words," discussed below. Hence the best new study of the term is François Jost's, in *Essai de littérature comparée*, Vol. II (1968). Significant changes in the meaning of "genius" were studied by Paul Kaufman, "Heralds of Original Genius" in *Essays in Memory of Barrett Wendell* (1926), and by Hans Thüme, *Beiträge zur Geschichte des Geniebegriffs in England* (1927); see also Ruth O. Rose, "Poetic Hero-Worship in the Late Eighteenth Century" (*PMLA*, 1933). In " 'Beauty': Some Stages in the History of an Idea" (*JHI*, 1961) Jerome Stolnitz traced the decline of beauty in modern aesthetics to its origins in the eighteenth century, where it first began to lose ground because of its intimate connection with the concept of genres. Imagination, ultimately the most important concept, was discussed in C. D. Thorpe, "Addison and Hutcheson on the Imagination" (*ELH*, 1935); D. F. Bond, "The Neo-Classical Psychology of the Imagination" (*ELH*, 1937); and John Bullitt and W. J. Bate, "Distinctions Between Fancy and Imagination in Eighteenth-Century English Criticism" (*MLN*, 1945). M. A. Goldberg, in "Wit and Imagination in Eighteenth-Century Aesthetics" (*JAAC*, 1958), attempted to show the changing relationships of wit, imagination, and judgment in the interval between Addison and Hazlitt, whose views on the three concepts are almost diametrically opposed. With essays on specific writers and works, *Eighteenth-Century Studies* devoted a special issue (Fall 1969), edited by Ronald Paulson, to *The Eighteenth-Century Imagination*. An article "On the Origins of 'Aesthetic Disinterestedness' " (*JAAC*, 1961) by Jerome Stolnitz prompted supplementary notes in the same journal on "critical disinterestedness" and "religious disinterestedness" and finally a second article, by Jerome Schiller, proposing "An Alternative to 'Aesthetic Disinterestedness' " (1964). The aesthetic of "organic unity" as it developed in the eighteenth century was the subject of James Benziger's "Organic Unity: Leibniz to Coleridge" (*PMLA*, 1951). R. Cohen, in "Association of Ideas and Poetic Unity" (*PQ*, 1957), demonstrated the connection between the new psychology and the new theory of poetry. In "Romantic Poetry and the Genius Loci" (*The Disciplines of Criticism* . . . , ed. Peter Demetz et al., 1968) Geoffrey Hartman characterized the later eighteenth-century poets as attempting to marry the visionary and prophetic temperament, or the ancient genius loci, with the rational temperament, or English poetic genius—in short, as attempting to anglicize the spirit of place. Gray and Wordsworth formed the outer boundaries for his investigations. E. N. Hooker's "The Discussion of Taste, from 1750–70, and the New Trends in Literary Criticism" (*PMLA*, 1934) was followed by S. A. Larrabee's "Il Poco Più and the School of Taste" (*ELH*, 1941), on the nameless grace, the *je ne sais quoi;* and R. L. Brett's "The Aesthetic Sense and Taste in the Literary Criticism of the Early Eighteenth Century" (*RES*, 1944).

Other noteworthy studies are: A. D. McKillop, "A Critic of 1741 on Early Poetry" (*SP*, 1933); L. I. Bredvold, "The Tendency toward Platonism in Neo-Classical Esthetics" (*ELH*, 1934); Kathleen Raine, "Thomas Taylor, Plato and the English Romantic Movement" (*BJA*, 1968; *SR*, 1968); René Wellek, *The Rise of English Literary History* (1941) and *A History of Modern Criticism*, Vol. 1 (1955); Samuel H. Monk, *The Sublime: A Study of Critical Theories in XVIII-Century England, 1674–1800* (1935; rpt. with new preface, 1960), wherein the admiration for the sublime is shown as hostile to Neo-Classicism, and as stimulating interest in the vastness and irregularities of nature; W. J. Hipple, Jr., *The Beautiful, the Sublime, and the Picturesque in Eighteenth-Century British Poetic Theory* (1957), which seeks to differentiate these three aesthetic types; and Martin Price, "The Picturesque Moment," in *From Sensibility to Romanticism,* which moment Price defines as "that phase of speculation . . . where the aesthetic categories are self-sufficient," i.e., requiring the support of neither morality nor metaphysics. In this group of works on literary theories there is an exceptionally high degree of erudition and astuteness. Perhaps the best introduction to the topic which they variously explore, however, is yet another study, W. J. Bate's *From Classic to Romantic: Premises of Taste in Eighteenth-Century England* (1946), which with remarkable precision and with much attention to the Imagination traces the steps that led from Neo-Classic intellectualism toward a theoretical preference for the intuitional assimilation of experience and the Romantic expression thereof. One should consult, along with Bate's book, A. S. P. Woodhouse's "Romanticism and the History of Ideas" (*English Studies Today*, 1951) for a different point of view on the development of the Romantic Imagination. Of great value for this topic, too, is Earl Wasserman's *The Subtler Language* with its account of the change in epistemology and its effect for poetry which took place between Dryden and Shelley. Stanley Hyman analyzes the change in literary taste from Augustan to Romantic by concentrating on two key poems, "The Rape of the Lock" and "Resolution and Independence," in *Poetry and Criticism: Four Revolutions in Literary Taste* (1961).

The relations of English Pre-Romanticism to foreign literatures, the twelfth topic, which receive occasional attention in some of the studies previously mentioned, are the main consideration in the following ones: Joseph Texte's brilliant *Jean-Jacques Rousseau et les origines du cosmopolitanisme littéraire* . . . (1895; tr., 1899), described the congruences between the English and French schools of sensibility; Henri Roddier's *J.-J. Rousseau en Angleterre en XVIIIe siècle: l'œuvre et l'homme* (1950) demonstrated how it happened that Rousseau was able to exert a forceful influence on English Romanticism. Paul Van Tieghem, *Le Pré-Romantisme: Etudes d'histoire littéraire européenne*, 3 vols. (1924–47), based on knowledge of many European literatures, amassed the evidences of widespread interest in such Pre-Romantic themes as Ossianism. Two studies which linked English Pre-Romanticism with two of France's most celebrated blue-stockings were Robert Escarpit, *L'Angleterre dans l'œuvre de Madame de Staël* (1954), and Magdi Wahba, "Madame de Genlis in England" (*CL*, 1961). On the whole, the relations to German literature are better explored. V. Stockley contributed *German Literature as Known in England, 1750–1830* (1929), a systematic account of the translations, with no discussion of what influence was exerted by them, a subject which was attacked, rather unsatisfactorily, in F. W. Stokoe's *German Influence in the English Romantic Period, 1788–1818* . . . (1926). A weighty philosophical contribution was Friedrich Meinecke's "Die englische Präromantik des 18. Jahrhunderts als Vorstufe des Historismus" (*Historische Zeitschrift*, 1935; rpt. and expanded in *Werke*, Vol. III, 1965). Subsequent studies include B. Q. Morgan and A. R. Hohlfeld, eds., *German Literature in British Magazines, 1750–1860* (1949); R. Pick, comp., *Schiller in England, 1787–1960: A Bibliography* (1961); and Theodore Grieder,

"The German Drama in England, 1790–1800" (*Restoration and 18th Century Theatre Research*, 1964). The current from England to Germany is the subject of several books by Lawrence Marsden Price, but particularly of *English Literature in Germany* (1953).

Finally, the thirteenth topic—the interrelations between literature and the arts—is treated in the following works, some of them illustrated. Kenneth Clark, *The Gothic Revival, an Essay in the History of Taste* (1928); Elizabeth Manwaring, *Italian Landscape in Eighteenth-Century England* (1926); Edward Malins, *English Landscaping and Literature* (1966); Christopher Hussey, *The Picturesque: Studies in a Point of View* (1927); Shan y Chan, "Chinese Gardening" (Univ. of Chicago *Abstracts of Theses*, 1932); A. O. Lovejoy, "The First Gothic Revival and the Return to Nature" (*MLN*, 1932) and "The Chinese Origin of a Romanticism" (*JEGP*, 1933; rpt. in *Essays in the History of Ideas*, 1948); Paul Zucker, "Ruins—An Aesthetic Hybrid" (*JAAC*, 1961); and Herbert M. Schueller, "Literature and Music as Sister Arts: An Aspect of Aesthetic Theory in 18th Century Britain" (*PQ*, 1947), "The Use and Decorum of Music as Described in British Literature, 1700 to 1780" (*JHI*, 1952), and "Correspondences Between Music and the Sister Arts, According to 18th Century Aesthetic Theory" (*JAAC*, 1953). An admirable, illustrated general survey is B. Sprague Allen, *Tides in English Taste (1619–1800): A Background for the Study of Literature*, 2 vols. (1937), which describes the new movement in art, decoration, gardening, etc. A very recent book, also of a general nature, is Lawrence Lipking, *The Ordering of the Arts in Eighteenth-Century England* (1970); it treats of the efforts in the second half of the century by such writers as Walpole, Reynolds, Warton, and Johnson to order the arts of painting, music, and poetry by establishing their histories and by guiding the tastes of their audiences. Not the least informative part of Lipking's impressive book is the Bibliographical Sketch with which it concludes.

III. THE ROMANTIC MOVEMENT

Although we are far from knowing all the facts of the Romantic Movement today, and far from understanding all their interrelations and significances, we know and understand them incomparably better than they were known and understood seventy years ago. Then the movement was represented as if it amounted to little more than a change in the fashion of poetic diction and verse-forms, the rise of a new kind of historical novel, and the expression of a greater love for nature and for the common man. In addition to superficiality of knowledge there was often some kind of strong prejudice. H. A. Taine, the positivist, in his popular *Histoire de la littérature anglaise* (1863; tr. 1871) appreciated only Byron. Georg Brandes, the political radical, in his Danish *Main Currents in Nineteenth Century Literature* (1871; tr. 1901–05) likewise slighted Wordsworth and Coleridge, and appreciated Shelley only because he was a social rebel. W. J. Courthope, whose taste was narrowly classical, in his *History of English Poetry*, Vols. v and vi (1903–05), described the movement as frustrate and deleterious. Today we apprehend better what the intent of the Romantics was, and how their movement, "the one spirit's plastic stress," affected every type of literature from ode to essay, and every form of intellectual and imaginative life from theology and philosophy to historiography and criticism. The following pages represent an effort to recognize the stepping stones whereby we have arrived at this better apprehension. Perhaps they will suggest as well those areas of our knowledge and understanding where the footing is still poor or in need of repair.

III A. HISTORIES, BACKGROUNDS, INTRODUCTIONS, AND GENERAL STUDIES

C. H. Herford's *The Age of Wordsworth* (1897; 3rd rev. ed., 1899) has some advantages over later surveys; it includes brief sketches of many of the minor authors, and of the economists, historians, theologians, and other persons of importance in fields outside literature. The chief sources of the movement are seen in Rousseau's revolutionary naturalism combined with German transcendentalism—a point of view recently reiterated by John Jones in "Postscript on Romantic Feeling," the conclusion to his *John Keats's Dream of Truth* (1969). George Saintsbury's chapters on the Romantics in his *A History of Nineteenth-Century Literature* (*1780–1895*) (1896) interpret the movement as the outcome of many not necessarily related forces—medieval and foreign literatures, the French Revolution, the usual ebb and flow of the world spirit, and pure accident—the result being a delightfully new kind of literature which explored the universe and the life of man, past and present, in innumerable different ways and directions. Legouis's and Cazamian's *History of English Literature* describes it as a renaissance of the emotions culminating in a renaissance of the imagination. Ernest Bernbaum's *Guide Through the Romantic Movement* concentrates upon the sixteen major Romantics from Blake to the young Carlyle, and tries to synthesize the best scholarly researches in the field. Samuel C. Chew's *The Nineteenth Century and After* (*1789–1939*), Volume IV of *A Literary History of England,* ed. A. C. Baugh (1948), has been the American graduate student's bible almost from its first appearance and no doubt continues to introduce him to the scholarly study of modern British literature. The uneven quality of Chew's work, however, limited its usefulness from the outset. The second edition (1967), for which Richard D. Altick replaced Chew, is no improvement on the first. The text and notes are largely unchanged, and the bibliographical supplement, if the section on Romanticism is any indication, offers little guidance through the maze of scholarly writing since 1948 except that implicit in omission. Present-day students of the Romantic Movement are better served by David Daiches' *A Critical History of English Literature* (1960) and by Ian Jack's *English Literature, 1815–1832,* Volume X of *The Oxford History of English Literature* (1963). This last in particular is accurate, current, and always critically responsible, sometimes critically provocative. Unfortunately, the preceding volume in the series and the intended companion to Jack's, W. L. Renwick's *English Literature, 1789–1815* (1963), is of less value.

Specific background studies will be taken up later; here it is sufficient to mention two collections of essays designed especially for the modern student: Leonard M. Trawick's *Backgrounds of Romanticism: English Philosophical Prose of the Eighteenth Century* (1967) and Karl Kroeber's *Backgrounds to British Romantic Literature* (1968). Trawick's volume includes eight excerpts from the writing of such intellectuals as Hartley, Duff, and Godwin. Kroeber's volume, which is not restricted to philosophical background, includes pieces by thirteen prominent social, intellectual, and art historians of the twentieth century. Both collections are provided with informative introductions and responsible reading lists.

No student of the Romantics these days, graduate or undergraduate, is complete without one or two "introductions" to the subject, usually paperback compilations of essays or parts of essays taken from scholarly journals and books and edited by a distinguished scholar in the field. Fortunately most of these introductions are respectable and some are much better than that. It is impossible to do more here than to describe briefly the more useful ones; some of the essays they contain are, however, identified and discussed elsewhere in this and subsequent chapters. Two volumes rather similar in purpose and format are M. H. Abrams' *English Romantic Poets: Modern Essays in Criticism* (1960) and Shiv Kumar's *British Romantic Poets: Recent Revaluations* (1966). On the whole, the former has more to offer. Two other volumes conceived as companions to the second edition of the present undertaking and to its counterpart on the minor Romantic writers—*The Major English Romantic Poets: A Symposium in Reappraisal,* ed. C. D. Thorpe, Carlos Baker, and Bennett Weaver (1957), and *Some British Romantics: A Collection of Essays,* ed. James V. Logan, John E. Jordan, and Northrop Frye (1966)—bear witness to the continuing reappraisal of the Romantic poets and assert or imply their continuing significance. The essays of a general character which these collections include are all mentioned later on in this chapter. The most distinguished effort of reappraisal, however, is *Romanticism Reconsidered,* four papers selected from those read at the English Institute in 1962 and edited by Northrop Frye (1963). Discussed elsewhere in this chapter, the papers are by Frye, Abrams, Trilling, and Wellek. *Romanticism: Points of View* (1962), by Robert F. Gleckner and Gerald E. Enscoe, rehearses the chief debates among scholars from Pater to Earl Wasserman. Anthony Thorlby's *The Romantic Movement* (1966), in the series Problems and Perspectives in History, is a more serious version of the Gleckner and Enscoe volume; the author has not left the problems and perspectives to identify themselves. Two additional items of some use perhaps are John B. Halsted's *Romanticism: Problems of Definition, Explanation, and Evaluation* (1965), an assortment of essays taken from the more or less standard studies, and *Romanticism* (1969), a group of documents arranged according to such topics as aesthetics, religion, and politics. Finally there is *The Romantic Reader,* ed. Howard E. Hugo (1957), a fat anthology of excerpts from Romantic poetry and prose ordered so as to picture the age of Romanticism in all its variety of subject and mood.

Oliver Elton's *Survey of English Literature, 1780–1830* (1912), although a history, pays more attention to individual authors than to historical causes. An old book, it remains valuable, especially for revealing the impact of Romanticism on the traditional literary forms. Graham Hough's *The Romantic Poets* (1953) is a relatively modest effort to discuss Romantic poetry according to the best lights of modern scholarship and criticism. Hough has no particular thesis to advance nor any particular critical approach to demonstrate; rather he offers simply an intelligent survey of Romantic poetry based upon analyses of selected key works. Another general study, Edward E. Bostetter's *The Romantic Ventriloquists: Wordsworth, Coleridge, Keats, Shelley, Byron* (1963), is altogether a different case. Taking issue with Earl Wasserman, who argued in *The Subtler Language* that the Romantics created a new cosmic syntax, Bostetter claims that they inherited one ready-made from the eighteenth century but, because it was only half a dialectic and thus unable to withstand the scrutiny of reason or experience, one that ultimately failed them. Bostetter builds his case for failure on the major unfinished poems of the five poets. The book can be and has been in part refuted, but it cannot be ignored by any serious student of the period. A third general introduction to the Romantics is Harold Bloom's *The Visionary Company: A Reading of English Romantic Poetry* (1961). Bloom's hallmark is not so much a theme as a method—he is one of the best "myth critics" of the present day. And though one can object to his "reading" as tending to make Blake the type of the Romantic poet and thus as tending to distort the others, still the book is full of valuable insights into single writers and of striking connections among the lot of them. It is worth noting that Bloom gives a chapter to Beddoes, Clare, Darley, and other writers traditionally labeled "minor." The myth approach of Bloom brings to mind an older but still important work, D. G. James's *The Romantic Comedy* (1948). Though James's objective is to trace the development of the Romantic spirit as it changed and matured over a period of thirty-odd years, he finds certain constants, among the most prominent the interest of the Romantic poets in mythology and their need to employ it. The great study of mythology and Romanticism is, however, Douglas Bush's *Mythology and the Romantic Tradition in English Poetry* (1937), a work which rises above its topic to become one of the three or four best general studies of the Romantic Movement. Bush shows how the myths of classical antiquity, which had become meaningless, were recreated by Wordsworth, Keats, Shelley, and others, and given new life and potency as well as high poetical values. Perhaps the only legitimate complaint one can make against Bush is that he has no very high regard for Blake, who consequently figures only incidentally in the book. A second book which transcends its topic to become a general study of the period is Joseph W. Beach's *The Concept of Nature in Nineteenth-Century English Poetry* (1936), which looks upon the development of that concept as a sad mistake. (For a counter opinion, see Ernest Bernbaum's "Is Wordsworth's Nature-Poetry Antiquated?" *ELH,* 1940.) While on the subject, I might mention Alfred North Whitehead's *Science and the*

Modern World (1925), the fifth chapter of which is a widely influential defense of the Romantics' use of nature in their revolt against scientific materialism. (Some years later, however, Charles G. Hoffmann, "Whitehead's Philosophy of Nature and Romantic Poetry" [*JAAC*, 1952], took the position that the Romantics rebelled not against eighteenth-century science and philosophy but against neoclassical poetic conventions and techniques.) More recent contributions to the subject than either Beach's or Whitehead's are F. E. L. Priestley's "Newton and the Romantic Concept of Nature" (*UTQ*, 1948) and Peter L. Thorslev's "Freedom and Destiny: Romantic Contraries" (*Bucknell Review*, 1966).

Several other general studies of Romanticism view the movement as a quest. James's book, discussed above, describes the quest as one for an adequate literary form. Hoxie N. Fairchild's *The Romantic Quest* (1931) locates the objectives in naturalism, medievalism, and transcendentalism and judges them as issuing in an "illusioned [false] view of the universe and of human life." The "devil's advocate" of Romanticism (see his essay in *The Major English Romantic Poets*), Fairchild has over the years consistently sounded this same note in his writing about the Romantics. As such, he has been useful in protecting sympathetic Romantics scholars from their own excessive enthusiasms. Magnus Irvine's *The Unceasing Quest* (1940) dwells on the Romantics' search for perfection.

Two additional studies of a general nature should be mentioned here: Margaret Sherwood's *Undercurrents of Influence in English Romantic Poetry* (1934), a rather desultory book which stresses "the organic idea" of the universe as a living and developing whole; and S. B. Liljegren's *Essence and Attitude in English Romanticism* (1945), a book which overemphasizes the importance in the movement of affectation in manners and attire.

III B. RELATIONS WITH THE CONTINENT

The relationship of the English Romantic writers to the continental Romantics or even to their American counterparts is still far from clear. Increasingly the efforts to define Romanticism (see below) take into account the European aspect of the movement, but the findings are not yet conclusive. Indeed, at present scholars continue to disagree on the basic issue of whether there was one international Romantic movement or several national ones. Students of comparative literature, though they have augmented our knowledge of the subject, have not succeeded to everyone's satisfaction in isolating a common denominator for Romanticism wherever it appeared. The more popular candidates, such as imagination, organicism, and revolution, have less competition than formerly, thanks to the diligence with which Romantics scholars have pursued the problem in this century. Superficial or merely glamorous candidates, particularly, seem to have been disposed of once and for all. But the very historical approach to literature which, in the Romantic Period, gave countenance to the concept of the *Zeitgeist* and gave rise to the comparative method of dealing with it is the favorite retreat of those who either cannot subscribe to the notion of a common origin or cannot live in the confusion and frustration that accompany the search for one. For the student who is not satisfied to view Romanticism as an historical period carefully circumscribed by comprehensive dates, seemingly coherent only in its continuum, there is every reason to regret the present state of affairs but every opportunity as well to remedy it. A few have pointed the way.

Two symposiums of some thirty years ago are convenient points of departure for a hasty look at the subject. "Romanticism: A Symposium" (*PMLA,* 1940) and "Symposium of Romanticism" (*JHI,* 1941) both indicate, though from somewhat different perspectives, the thinking then current about Romanticism in its European dimensions. The bibliographies or notes that figure prominently in these discussions are reliable guides to what is most valuable in the scholarship that antedates the Second World War. More extensive lists may be found in Richard Benz, *Die deutsche Romantik: Geschichte einer geistigen Bewegung* (1937); Jean Giraud, *L'Ecole romantique française: Les Doctrines et les hommes* (1927); Arturo Farinelli, *Il Romanticismo nel mondo latino* (1927); and E. Allison Peers, *History of the Romantic Movement in Spain* (1935). It seems unfair, however, at least not to mention Mario Praz's *The Romantic Agony* (1931; tr. 1933), still one of the best-known books in the field. Whatever the distortions of Romanticism that result from its specialized subject (the exotic, erotic, satanic, pathological elements of European Romanticism), Praz's study remains the authority for much that it treats. In 1948 Paul Van Tieghem published his *L'Ere romantique: Le Romantisme dans la littérature européenne,* the most ambitious general treatise up to that date and even today a common reference. But Van Tieghem's book, which overwhelms with its catalogues of works and themes, ultimately offers the reader little more; for all the author's great erudition, he fails to provide the overview that would give meaning to the pages and pages of descriptive material. A timely book from the same period is Paul Roubiczek's *The Misinterpretation of Man: Studies in European Thought in the Nineteenth Century* (1947), an account of the perversions of Romantic idealism in the nineteenth and earlier twentieth centuries, with their tragic results for modern man, and an appeal for a revival of Romantic idealism in its true form.

The most accessible and the most positive account of scholarly progress since World War II in the understanding of international Romanticism is René Wellek's essay "Romanticism Re-examined," discussed above. Wellek relates the newer studies to the older traditions of German and French scholarship, but he concentrates on the writing from 1949 to 1963. The author's optimism about recent scholarship when taken in toto has made the essay a rallying point for those of like mind, a focus of dissent for those who see little or no consensus as yet among Romantics scholars. American contributions to the study of continental Romanticism are identified in the two-volume Princeton series, *Humanistic Studies in America.* Volume I (1966), written by Henri Peyre, treats the literature of France; Volume II (1968), written by several authors, treats that of Italy, Spain, Germany, Russia, and the Orient. Peyre suggests that little of consequence has been written on French Romanticism. The only theoretical works he finds significant are Morse Peckham's *Beyond the Tragic Vision* (see below) and Wylie Sypher's *Loss of the Self in the Modern World* (see below). Those writing about the other national literatures are not quite so negative in their appraisals, but readers will be surprised to discover how few major studies, to judge from these surveys, Americans have in fact contributed. Rudolf Majut's "Englische Arbeiten 1950–1960 zur deutschen Literaturgeschichte bis zum Ausgang der Romantik" (*Germanische-romanische Monatsschrift,* N.S., 1961) devotes some six pages to the German Romantics as interpreted by Anglo-American scholars. And Joachim Müller's series of reviews for *Deutschunterricht* (XV, 1963; XVII, 1965; XX, 1968) of Romantics scholarship in the 1960's surveys comparative and general works before taking up studies of individual German writers. Unfortunately there is no room in this chapter to designate and describe the articles and books surveyed by Wellek, Peyre, Majut, Müller, and others, except where they are directly concerned with the English Romantics. The reader can only be advised here to consult first the essays of these men for such authors and titles as they supply and then to consult the appropriate bibliographies and reference works for additional materials.

Scholars like Morse Peckham, Wylie Sypher, and René Wellek, who characteristically range over European art and thought when writing about Romanticism, usually have a strong, if not controversial, thesis to argue. H. G. Schenk, in *The Mind of the European Romantics: An Essay in Cultural History* (1969), is content to offer a familiar concept of the Romantic mind—contradictory, dissonant, inner conflicting—in order that he might concentrate on integrating literature, philosophy, religion, painting, and music into a full cultural history of European Romanticism. For the most part, Schenk's method is to take up a traditional topic and present it through a "pen-portrait" of the Romantic who best illustrates it. Given his idea of the Romantic mind, Schenk's method is well chosen, but the pen-portrait inevitably suggests comparisons, some with master artists, with results that are not always favorable to Schenk. Still, his book is conspicuous for its lack of company and important for the same reason.

Of the foreign influences on English Romanticism there is no comprehensive study. Most attention has been given to the German, beginning with A. C. Bradley, *English Poetry and German Philosophy in the Age of Wordsworth* (1909; rpt. in *A Miscellany*, 1929). F. W. Stokoe, *German Influence in the English Romantic Period, 1788–1818,* believes the influence has been exaggerated; but see V. Stockley, *German Literature as Known in England, 1750–1830.* Of central importance is René Wellek, *Immanuel Kant in England, 1793–1838* (1931), a pioneering study that must now be considered in the light of more recent Coleridge studies, including Wellek's own. E. D. Hirsch's *Wordsworth and Schelling: A Typological Study of Romanticism* (1960) examines the literary relationships between England and Germany in the Romantic Period, not in terms of influences as traditionally conceived but in terms of an underlying *Weltanschauung* or common consciousness simultaneously and independently developed in the two countries, as demonstrated by the striking similarities in the outlook of Wordsworth and Schelling, writers who could not possibly have influenced each other in their formative years. The *Weltanschauung* that explains the similarities between English Romantic poetry and German Romantic philosophy is thus the phenomenon that explains the unitary and international movement we call Romanticism. But Hirsch is concerned to show that such a Romantic consciousness, which is the familiar one that intuits the organic unity of all things and strives to affirm that vision in imaginative or discursive discourse, may also be invoked to shed light on some of the cruxes in Romantic literature that do not become clear when approached from other angles.

Three other studies which compare English and German Romantics are Horst Oppel's "Englische und deutsche Romantik" (*Die neueren Sprachen*, 1956; incorporated into his *The Sacred River* [1959] and rpt. with slight changes in *Versdichtung der englischen Romantik: Interpretationen*, ed. Teut A. Riese and Dieter Riesner, 1968); Eudo C. Mason's *Deutsche und englische Romantik* (1959); and René Wellek's "German and English Romanticism: A Confrontation" (*SIR*, 1964; rpt. in *Confrontations*, 1965). Of the three, the first is the only one to give more or less equal attention to likenesses and differences; the last two emphasize strongly the peculiar characteristics of the two groups. Geoffrey Hartman's "Romanticism and 'Antiself-Consciousness' " (*CentR*, 1962; rpt. in *Romanticism and Consciousness*, ed. Harold Bloom, 1970), discussed below, also comments on similarities, though such is not the main purpose of the essay. Werner W. Beyer's *The Enchanted Forest* (1963), primarily about the influence of Wieland's *Oberon* on Coleridge, pays some attention to other Romantic poets.

On the French influence in general there is only Marcel Moraud, *Le Romantisme français en Angleterre de 1814 à 1848* . . . (1933), which maintains that the French Romantics were usually reinterpreted so as to make them more acceptable to English prejudices. Jacques Voisine, *J.-J. Rousseau en Angleterre à l'époque romantique: Les Ecrits autobiographiques et la légende* (1956) raises the question of whether or not Rousseau was not better understood in England than in France and implies an affirmative answer. Paul de Man, using a method similar to Hirsch's, associates Rousseau, Wordsworth, and Hölderlin in "Structure intentionelle de l'image romantique" (*Revue Internationale de Philosophie*, 1960; tr. for *Romanticism and Consciousness*). He concludes that, because the Romantics put into question the ontological priority of the sensory object, the status of the poetic image was crucially threatened and remains so to this day. Margaret Gilman, "Revival and Revolution in English and French Romantic Poetry" (*YFS*, 1950), explores the conventional explanation for the inferiority of French Romantic poetry to English—the failure of the French poets to achieve a real poetic revolution—and finds it correct but inadequate. Unlike the English poets, she maintains, the French were cut off from their own roots, with the result that they had nothing positive to put in place of what they sought to destroy—no Renaissance tradition to revive and refashion.

English-Italian literary relationships in the Romantic Period are increasingly well explored. The chief works are: Margaret C. W. Wicks, *The Italian Exiles in London: 1816–1848* (1937); Harry W. Rudman, *Italian Nationalism and English Letters: Figures of the Risorgimento and Victorian Men of Letters* (1940); C. P. Brand, *Italy and the English Romantics: The Italianate Fashion in Early Nineteenth-Century England* (1957); and Herbert Barrows, "Convention and Novelty in the Romantic Generation's Experience in Italy" (*BNYPL,* 1963). For the Romantics' knowledge and use of Dante, Boccaccio, and Tasso there are the studies of W. P. Friederich, "Dante and English Romanticism," in *Dante's Fame Abroad, 1350–1850* (1950); Oswald Doughty, "Dante and the English Romantic Poets" (*EM,* 1951); H. G. Wright, *Boccaccio in England from Chaucer to Tennyson* (1957); C. P. Brand, *Torquato Tasso: A Study of the Poet and of His Contribution to English Literature* (1964). The most distinguished contribution of recent years, however, is Karl Kroeber's *The Artifice of Reality: Poetic Style in Wordsworth, Foscolo, Keats, and Leopardi* (1964). Kroeber's book, which is concerned with the advent of a new style in poetry that he calls "Mediterranean," provides first-rate evidence for the fact of an international Romanticism while at the same time observing its fundamental diversity. Greco-Anglo literary relationships are best approached through Harry Levin's *The Broken Column: A Study in Romantic Hellenism* (1931), which maintains that the true spirit of ancient Greece was given a too sentimental interpretation in English Romantic literature, and through Terence Spencer's *Fair Greece, Sad Relic* (1954), the definitive study of philhellenism in English literature to date. This last is relevant, however, largely because of Byron. The same is true of James M. Osborn's "Travel Literature and the Rise of Neo-Hellenism in England" (*BYNPL,* 1963). Unlike Levin and Spencer, Osborn neglects belles-lettres and concentrates on pure travel literature.

George B. Parks, "The Turn to the Romantic in the Travel Literature of the Eighteenth Century" (*MLQ,* 1964), accounts for this phenomenon and dates it 1736–67. For Bernard Blackstone, Georg Roppen, and Richard Sommer, Romantic poetry is by and large travel literature because it is a poetry of movement, the Romantic poets "mental travellers." Blackstone, *The Lost Travelers: A Romantic Theme with Variations* (1962), works this theme through the six major poets, but Blake is his point of departure. Roppen and Sommer, *Strangers and Pilgrims: An Essay on the Metaphor of Journey* (1964), trace their metaphor from antiquity to Wordsworth before looking at the English Romantics, for whom the journey has become "The Individual Quest." Blackstone's study is interesting and informative if not especially revealing; the volume by Roppen and Sommer is too clumsy to be of much value.

III C. RELATIONS WITH THE OTHER ARTS

Contemporaneous developments in the arts is a subject that can take us far afield of the Romantic Movement in English poetry, but increasingly literary scholars themselves have turned to such developments in their efforts to understand more fully the Romantic literature that is their principal concern, with the result that we now have any number of studies which range freely among the arts as they seek to demonstrate this theory or that one about Romanticism. Morse Peckham and Wylie Sypher, for example, characteristically consider music and painting in their theoretical studies of modern art. H. G. Schenk in *The Mind of the European Romantics* (see above) and Eric Newton in *The Romantic Rebellion* (1962) follow suit. This last is, in fact, primarily about the arts. Both Frederick B. Artz, *From the Renaissance to Romanticism: Trends in Style in Art, Literature, and Music, 1300–1800* (1962), and Ulrich Weisstein, "Romanticism: Transcendentalist Games or 'Wechselseitige Erhellung der Künste'" (*CollG,* 1968), seek to find a distinctive style in Romantic art whatever the form. Artz's idea that Neoclassicism and Romanticism are parallel movements will strike some people as peculiar; Weisstein's failure, in a rambling article, to find a period style unless styles be defined as *Weltanschauung* may annoy readers who expect his quest to be more successful. An earlier essay by Edmund Blunden discusses "Romantic Poetry and the Fine Arts" (*Proceedings of the British Academy,* 1942). For the connections between poetry and painting, one should see Chauncey B. Tinker, *Painter and Poet: Studies in the Literary Relations of English Painting* (1938), which deals with Blake, Wilson, Turner, Constable, and others. Erich Heller's *The Artist's Journey into the Interior, And Other Essays* (1959), which is concerned throughout with the problem of defining "Romantic," takes its departure from the Tate Gallery's 1959 exhibit, "The Romantic Movement." (See the exhibition catalogue published in 1960 by the Arts Council of Great Britain and Alexandra Wedgwood's *Le Mouvement romantique,* 1969, a related project.) Heller found Friedrich's "The Wanderer" the most Romantic painting of the exhibit (see the essay "The

Romantic Expectation") and hence a Romantic touchstone, but he continually examines paintings and sculptures by other Romantics as he pursues a definition of them all. Friedrich, along with Runge, is also important to Gunnar Berefelt, who in "On Symbol and Allegory" (*JAAC*, 1969) draws upon the two painters for examples in support of his argument that distinguishing the two terms is the central problem of Romantic aesthetics. Roy Park's " 'Ut Pictura Poesis': The Nineteenth-Century Aftermath" (*JAAC*, 1969) recalls that most special inheritance of the Romantic poets from their eighteenth-century predecessors; Park is concerned with the ambivalence of Coleridge and Hazlitt toward this legacy. Two efforts of the more popular sort, Harold Nicolson's "The Romantic Revolt" (*Horizon*, 1961) and Peter Quennell's *Romantic England* (1970), are impressive testimony to the imaginative excitement of Romantic painting in particular, the general interest in which has been greatly stimulated by the Turner revival of the 1960's and the Blake revival of the last two decades. For most of the individual Romantic poets (see the subsequent chapters), there are now essays and books that treat of their response to painting, if not to the plastic arts in general.

Stephen A. Larrabee, *English Bards and Grecian Marbles: The Relationship between Sculpture and Poetry, Especially in the Romantic Period* (1943), remains the standard work on this subject, though it should be read in connection with Harry Levin's study, mentioned above. Larrabee shows the gradual development away from mere description of statues toward interpretation of their inner meaning. Romanticism in architecture is the subject in whole or in part of Warren H. Smith, *Architecture in English Fiction* (1934); Agnes Addison, *Romanticism and the Gothic Revival* (1938); Ronald Bradbury, *The Romantic Theories of Architecture of the Nineteenth Century, in Germany, England and France* (1934); Sacheverell Sitwell, *British Architects and Craftsmen: A Survey of Taste, Design, and Style During Three Centuries, 1600 to 1830* (1945). More recently Richard P. Adams has traced the course of Romantic architectural theory into the twentieth century, in "Architecture and the Romantic Tradition: Coleridge to Wright" (*Architects' Quarterly*, 1957). The relation between the terms "baroque," "rococo," and "romantic" was eagerly debated in letters to *TLS* in 1946. In the same year René Wellek, who earlier had warned against superficial "analogizing between the arts" ("The Parallelism Between Literature and the Arts," *EIE:1941*, 1942), discussed "The Concept of Baroque in Literary Scholarship" (*JACC*; rpt. in *Concepts of Criticism*, 1963). Wellek's warning is perhaps most to be heeded where music is concerned and hence the lack of studies comparable to those which link the poets with the painters and sculptors. Yet M. H. Abrams has reminded us in *The Mirror and the Lamp* (see below) that the Romantics themselves pointed to music rather than painting as the sister art to poetry—one need only remember their favorite analogy of the Aeolian harp. George Graham's "Toward a Definition of Romanticism in Music" (*QQ*, 1965), part of a symposium on Romanticism in the arts, is by implication at least aware of this affinity. But this article is primarily exploratory of traditional definitions to the end of showing their weaknesses. The aesthetics of Romantic art in general are best approached through Katherine E. Gilbert's and Helmut Kuhn's *A History of Aesthetics* (1939; rev. ed. 1953) and, somewhat more narrowly, through *The Mirror and the Lamp*.

III D. SPECIAL TOPICS

Earlier studies of religion or the supernatural in the Romantic Movement include Dean W. R. Inge, *The Platonic Tradition in English Religious Thought* (1926) and "Romanticism," in *Lay Thoughts of a Dean* (1926); Denis Saurat, *Literature and Occult Tradition: Studies in Philosophical Poetry* (1930); Sukumar Dutt, *The Supernatural in English Romantic Poetry, 1780–1830* (1938); J. Bronowski, *The Poet's Defense* (1939); and E. B. Hungerford, *Shores of Darkness* (1941), which examines myth in the poetry of Blake, Shelley, Keats, and Goethe as the vehicle of religious utterance. Hungerford's book traces the debts of these poets to the speculative mythologists of the later eighteenth and earlier nineteenth centuries, and should be supplemented by the more recent work of Albert J. Kuhn, "English Deism and the Development of Mythological Syncretism" (*PMLA*, 1956), a study of the syncretic mythology which flourished from 1775 to 1835 and promised, according to its deist practitioners, a key to the universe by removing barriers between Christianity and myth, and of Alex Zwerdling, "The Mythographers and the Romantic Revival of Greek Myth" (*PMLA*, 1964), a discussion of the mythographers responsible for bringing myth back into repute by showing its alliance with religion. A chapter on the Romantic Revival in Douglas Bush's *Pagan Myth and Christian Tradition in English Poetry* (1968) rehearses each major poet's use of Greek myth but contends that this use is always classical and secular;

the active relationship between pagan myth and Christian tradition that characterizes earlier English poetry has vanished. Vilhelm Gronbeck's *Religious Currents in the Nineteenth Century* (1964) includes chapters on Blake, Wordsworth, Coleridge, and the German Romantics. Murray Roston's *Prophet and Poet: The Bible and the Growth of Romanticism* (1965) treats a neglected subject, the debt of Romantic poetry to the Old Testament, with some interest and skill. Much concerned with Pre-Romanticism, Roston traces the discovery of the Old Testament as poetry and the subsequent recovery of the prophetic mode to English poetry. John Herman Randall's "Romantic Reinterpretations of Religion" (*SIR*, 1963), predicated on the belief that Romanticism was a religious world-view, sketches the efforts of the Romantics, particularly the religious liberals among them, to defend religion by reinterpreting or reconstructing it along the intellectual, aesthetic, and ethical lines suggested by the German pioneers in religious liberalism. Perhaps the most important item in this area is James G. Benziger's *Images of Eternity: Studies in the Poetry of Religious Vision, from Wordsworth to T. S. Eliot* (1962). Like Randall, Benziger is able to see Romanticism as broadly religious at heart, and he studies Romantic poetry for the images and intuitions of eternity, as apprehended by the transcendentalizing imagination, which characterize it. Benziger's work is especially a corrective to the narrow perspective of Hoxie N. Fairchild (see II above) but also an effort to overcome certain problems inherent in American criticism when it approaches the subject of Romantic poetry and traditional religious faith. Benziger has the grace to indicate clearly his own position on the subject, making it possible to separate the author from the poets he writes about. Finally, the student who wants a short but authoritative account, one which avoids the bias that is so likely to plague studies in this field, can hardly do better than the chapter on the Romantics in A. S. P. Woodhouse's *The Poet and His Faith: Religion and Poetry in England from Spenser to Eliot and Auden* (1965).

The discussions of the political attitudes and ideals of the Romantics began with S. F. Richardson, "A Neglected Aspect of the English Romantic Revolt" (Univ. of California Pubs. in Mod. Philol., 1915). There followed B. H. Lehman, "The Doctrine of Leadership in the Greater Romantic Poets" (*PMLA*, 1922); Crane C. Brinton, *The Political Ideas of the English Romanticists* (1926); Alfred Cobban's notably good *Edmund Burke and the Revolt against the Eighteenth Century* . . . (1929); and Eva B. Dykes, *The Negro in English Romantic Thought, or, A Study of Sympathy for the Oppressed* (1942). The best-known and liveliest book in this group is Jacques Barzun, *Romanticism and the Modern Ego* (1943), revised as *Classic, Romantic and Modern* (1961). The original book interpreted the Romantic Movement as fundamentally a social and political phenomenon, its art and philosophy as responses to the political desire for personal freedom within collective action. Because he saw the cultural history of the nineteenth and twentieth centuries as Romantic in nature, Barzun took seriously the connections he believed to exist between Romanticism and such modern political phenomena as Fascism and Nazism, just as he took seriously the connections he saw between Romanticism and such later aesthetic movements as Realism, Naturalism, Symbolism, and Cubism. His aim was to show that Romanticism, despite the efforts to kill it or to assert its demise in the 1920's and 1930's, was anything but dead and gone. The revised book simply provides an epilogue to the earlier one, bringing Barzun's story up to date. As in *The Energies of Art* (1956) and in "Romanticism Today" (*Encounter*, 1961), he argues that Romanticism by the Romantic act of abolition or annihilation, which has been the aesthetic of art since World War II, is at long last about to come to an end. Romanticism was a great symphony, its last three movements represented by Realism, Naturalism, and Symbolism; Modernism is the coda that proclaims the end of the music, which is to say, the death of art.

In recent years Barzun's essays have had considerable company, some of it first-rate work. There is Allan Rodway's *The Romantic Conflict* (1963), for example, a sociological study of Romanticism, which, because it accounts for the growth and development of the Romantic Movement by the circumstances of the age, especially the conflicts and ensuing mutations, allows for both casualties and victories—the failure of Romantic metaphysics and the triumph of Romantic human or psychological insights in a poetry which "does not give a creed for Life, but *is* a verbalised mode of living . . . at its rare best, a mode wherein destructive energies are converted to illumination, conflicts to alliances." A newer study is R. W. Harris' *Romanticism and the Social Order 1780–1830* (1969), a series of essays intended to convey the cross-currents of thought in the Romantic Period; all the major Romantics and many minor ones receive a chapter. Several studies of nineteenth-century society, politics, or culture include essays on the Romantics: Russell Kirk's *The Conservative Mind: From Burke to Santayana* (1953) and Judith Shklar's *After Utopia: The Decline of Political Faith* (1957) both analyze the Romantic mind as it responded to intellectual movements and currents. Raymond Williams' *Culture and Society: 1780–1950* (1959) pays particular attention to the way in which the Romantics responded to the Industrial Revolution. According to Williams, the Romantic artist saw his role in society, especially as time went on, as interlocking with the roles of others, not as antithetical to them. Hence he accepted the changes wrought by the Industrial Revolution and in doing so precipitated changes in the image of the artist—in himself. Jeremy Warburg, in "Poetry and Industrialism: Some Refractory Material in Nineteenth-Century and Later English Verse" (*MLR,* 1958), proposes that we can measure the impact industrialism made on poetry by noting, for example, when the train, originally appearing as simile, began to appear as metaphor.

The most influential essay of recent years is M. H. Abrams' "English Romanticism: The Spirit of the Age," in *Romanticism Reconsidered.* Following in the footsteps of Hazlitt and suggesting that more Romantic scholars should do likewise, Abrams insists that the climate of the Romantic Period was fundamentally revolutionary and that Romantic literature cannot be understood either in substance or form apart from this obsession with change. Carl Woodring's *Politics and English Romantic Poetry* (1970), the culmination of some years of work in this area, is the latest substantial contribution to the subject. Drawing heavily upon Wordsworth, Byron, and Shelley for proof of the interconnections of personal experience, political event, and poetic act, Woodring argues the thesis that politics was more of a generative force for Romantic poetry than is usually recognized. In passing it is worth noting that many of the above discussions implicitly or explicitly depend on the concept of the *Zeitgeist,* which though by no means universally accepted by Romantics scholars would seem to have considerable, even renewed currency in our time. Ernst Fischer's *Zeitgeist und Literatur: Gebundenheit und Freiheit der Kunst* (1964) addresses itself to this very subject.

Of the works on special topics of a more strictly literary nature, those concerned with the critical reception of Romantic poetry are properly considered first. Henri Peyre, in *Writers and Their Critics* (1944), inquired why contemporaries failed to understand the Romantics. A year later William S. Ward discussed "Some Aspects of the Conservative Attitude Toward Poetry: 1798–1820" (*PMLA,* 1945). The more balanced perspective that characterizes recent scholarship (and that results from it) is indicated by J. J. Welker's "The Position of the Quarterlies on Some Classical Dogmas" (*SP,* 1940), which shows that the journals were not as hostile to Romanticism as had been assumed, and by such book-length studies as John Clive's *Scotch Reviewers: The Edinburgh Review,*

1802–1815 (1957) and John O. Hayden's *The Romantic Reviewers 1802–1824* (1969). These and similar items, along with the new histories of leading reviews and biographies of their reviewers so popular as dissertation topics, have done much to dispel the long popular notion that Keats and other Romantic poets were killed by the journals. In addition, first John Wain and then Patricia Hodgart and Theodore Redpath have made accessible to anyone interested fair samples of the reviewers' work. In *Contemporary Reviews of Romantic Poetry* (1953) Wain uses extracts from the three leading critical quarterlies to assess the reception of the five Romantic poets plus Tennyson. His introductory essay not only surveys the reviews and magazines but also compares journalistic criticism then and now. The Hodgart and Redpath volume, *Romantic Perspectives . . .* (1964), is limited to the early Romantics, including Crabbe and Blake. The perspectives presented are taken from all sorts of contemporary prose, not just reviews.

Studies of language and form abound. First among the former are the essays and books of Josephine Miles, whose capacity to transform statistical surveys into sensitive analyses rarely fails her. Many of the essays are caught up in the two books *The Vocabulary of Poetry* (1946) and *The Primary Language of Poetry in the 1740's and 1840's* (1950). Changes in the diction of poetry with which Miss Miles is concerned in these volumes become important evidence for changes in the mode of poetry with which she is concerned in "The Romantic Mode of Poetry" (*ELH,* 1953), subsequently one of four chapters on the Romantics in *Eras & Modes in English Poetry* (1957). In general the book argues for the validity of the period concept of English literature; in particular, the chapters on the Romantics demonstrate the advent of a new or Romantic mode of poetry, the lyrical narrative of dramatic confrontation, or the new ballad. This new structure, which serves a new substance, a new attitude, justifies, in Miss Miles's opinion, our grouping of the five major poets (but not Blake) as Romantics. Three other books on the language of poetry are worthy of mention: Donald Davie's *Purity of Diction in English Verse*; Bernard Groom's *The Diction of Poetry from Spenser to Bridges* (1956); and R. A. Foakes's *The Romantic Assertion: A Study in the Language of Nineteenth-Century Poetry* (1958). Of these, Foakes's book, which distinguishes the poetry of the nineteenth century from that of the twentieth as poetry of assertion, not of conflict—as poetry committed to "images of impression," not to metaphor, is probably the most rewarding. Davie's book, as a 1966 Postscript makes clear, is ultimately a manifesto of "the movement." Essays on the language of Romantic poetry range from the largely descriptive—Irene P. McKeehan's "Some Observations on the Vocabulary of Landscape Description among the Early Romanticists" (Univ. of Colorado Studies, 1945)—to the largely theoretical—Elizabeth M. Wilkinson's "The Inexpressible and the Un-Speakable: Some Romantic Attitudes to Art and Language" (*German Life and Letters,* 1963).

Foakes's book focuses on two structural images in Romantic poetry, the journey of life and the vision of love. W. H. Auden, in *The Enchaféd Flood, or the Romantic Iconography of the Sea* (1951), published the previous year with a different subtitle, also attempts to understand the nature of Romanticism by exploring in detail an isolated image, the sea. He takes as his text Wordsworth's dream of the fleeing Bedouin in *The Prelude,* but before he is done *Moby Dick* has become as important to his thesis as Wordsworth's poem. Frank Kermode's often mentioned *Romantic Image* (1957) similarly does not stay within the confines of English Romanticism as historically defined, giving most attention to Yeats, but it argues brilliantly for the actual continuity of Romantic and twentieth-century poetry, using as its touchstone the Romantic doctrine of isolation and suffering as the source of joy, of pain and fear as the wellspring of art, most triumphantly realized for Kermode in Yeats's symbol of the dancer and the dance. David Perkins' *The Quest for Permanence: The Symbolism of Wordsworth, Shelley, and Keats* (1959) is appropriately discussed in the chapters that follow, but deserves mention here, for like Kermode's study it looks beyond the Romantics to the twentieth century and like it, too, discovers the key both to individual poets and to Romantic poetry in its symbols—in this case, symbols of permanence in a world "Where youth grows pale, and spectre-thin, and dies." Articles which discuss Romantic symbols are legion; many of them are named elsewhere in this volume, in connection with the poems from which they derive. But one of them must be cited here—M. H. Abrams' "The Correspondent Breeze: A Romantic Metaphor" (*KR,* 1957), revised for *English Romantic Poets: Modern Essays in Criticism*—because it deals with an image that is not only pervasive in Romantic poetry but also basic to an understanding of what Romantic poetry is.

The fragment, which is so common to Romantic poetry and which is the subject of Ilse Gugler's *Das Problem der fragmentarischen Dichtung in der englischen Romantik* (1944), continues to fascinate scholars. D. F. Rauber, in "The Fragment as Romantic Form" (*MLQ,* 1969), contends that the fragment is the perfect formal solution to the Romantic's problem of reflecting the infinite and indeterminate world of his vision. And Alethea Hayter, in *Opium and the Romantic Imagination* (1968), points up the causal connection between opium and the fragment: "It is the great plans that are destroyed."

The most valuable essays on form and structure in general are those by W. K. Wimsatt, "The Structure of Romantic Nature Imagery," in *The Verbal Icon: Studies in the Meaning of Poetry* (1954); by Elizabeth Nitchie, "Form in Romantic Poetry," in *The Major English Romantic Poets*; and by M. H. Abrams, "Structure and Style in the Greater Romantic Lyric," in *From Sensibility to Romanticism.* All three essays are concerned with characteristic Romantic poems as they resemble or differ structurally from their predecessors and successors; all three have much to say about Coleridge, organic form, and the poem as symbolic structure; and all three make convincing cases for the impressive artistry of the poems they study. So, too, does Albert Gérard's *English Romantic Poetry* (1968), discussed elsewhere in this chapter and in this volume. Two more restricted articles— Robert Daniel's "Odes to Dejection" (*KR*, 1953) and Irene H. Chayes's "Rhetoric as Drama: An Approach to the Romantic Ode" (*PMLA*, 1964)—attempt to come at the special quality of certain Romantic poems. Both help us to understand better the patterns of these poems, but neither is completely successful in describing the Romantic ode, which rather gloriously eludes those who would classify and categorize it too narrowly. Kurt Schlüter's *Die englische Ode: Studien zu ihrer Entwicklung unter dem Einfluss der antiken Hymne* (1964), which examines the English ode from the point of view specified in the title, devotes a chapter to the Romantic ode in general and a chapter to the political ode in particular.

Ballads and narrative poems in the Romantic period are the subjects of Albert B. Friedman's *The Ballad Revival: Studies in the Influence of Popular on Sophisticated Poetry* (1961) and of Karl Kroeber's *Romantic Narrative Art* (1960). The latter in particular is valuable for charting a course through a large and—in the instances of the minor poets especially—little-known territory, but at the same time it bears witness to the need for still more attention to the subject. Lionel Stevenson has responded to that need, in "The Mystique of Romantic Narrative Poetry" (*Romantic and Victorian: Studies in Memory of William H. Marshall,* ed. W. Paul Elledge and Richard L. Hoffman, 1971), where he eliminates from "the category of essentially Romantic art" those narrative poems, Romantic and Victorian, whose method is not calculated to induce spontaneous imaginative participation by the reader in the narrating or creating of the story.

Two books on epic poetry make a contribution to Romantics studies: D. M. Foerster's *The Fortunes of Epic Poetry: A Study in English and American Criticism, 1750–1950* (1962), which incorporates three articles published previously; and Brian Wilkie's *Romantic Poets and Epic Tradition* (1965). Though Foerster and Wilkie make the same apology for their work (the absence of any study of the epic after 1800 except for Tillyard's), Foerster is preoccupied with the fate of epic as genre in the nineteenth and twentieth centuries, Wilkie with some Romantic poems that evidence a strong epic intention. The titles of the two books are thus accurate (if in the case of Wilkie, modest) designations. Other Romantic forms which have been singled out for attention are the pastoral, in John Stevenson's "Arcadia Re-Settled: Pastoral Poetry and Romantic Theory" (*SEL,* 1967), and the epitaph, in Ernest Bernhardt-Kabisch's "The Epitaph and the Romantic Poets: A Survey" (*HLQ,* 1967). Finally, there is Robert Langbaum's study of the dramatic monologue, *The Poetry of Experience* (1957), one of the more influential books on modern poetry in recent years. The Victorians loom larger in Langbaum's work than the Romantics, as one would expect, but they, along with their successors the twentieth-century symbolists, are shown to be in the Romantic tradition of poetry, which is the poetry of experience. The distinctive form which this poetry takes is the dramatic monologue of Tennyson and Browning, but Langbaum traces the roots of the form to the dramatic lyrics of the Romantics and detects its influence in the symbolist poems of Eliot and Pound.

Prose forms in the Romantic Period seldom come in for general study. Stage drama, for example, even when poetic, is usually treated only in such surveys as Allardyce Nicoll's *A History of Early Nineteenth Century Drama* (1930; rev. ed., 1955). But there are some few exceptions. Newman Ivey White examined "The English Romantic Writers as Dramatists" (*SR,* 1922). A second, though specialized study, was Bertrand Evans' *Gothic Drama from Walpole to Shelley* (1947). Much more recently Richard M. Fletcher has devoted a book to the general subject: *English Romantic Drama, 1795–1843: A Critical History* (1966). Wordsworth and Coleridge are given a separate chapter. In addition, there is John Ehrstine's article "The Drama and Romantic Theory: The Cloudy Symbols of High Romance" (*Research Studies of Washington State Univ.,* 1966). Ehrstine suggests that Romantic drama failed, at least in the form of the play, because its theory—that drama is mental, interior, imaginative—was incompatible with the conventions of traditional drama. Most recent is Joseph Donohue's *Dramatic Character in the English Romantic Age*

(1970), which reiterates Ehrstine's view of Romantic dramatic theory but, in addition, shows how it developed from Jacobean drama and how it reflected the contemporary cultural milieu. One should note here, as well, the chapter in Patricia Ball's *The Central Self: A Sudy in Romantic and Victorian Imagination* (1968) on Romantic plays, which she claims are "central efforts of the Romantic imagination, not peripheral mistakes." Even so, at this point in the scholarly discussion of the subject it would seem that Shelley's *Cenci* is the only stage drama likely to prove an exception to the judgment of failure, and even this is dubious. The leap from play to film is easily made these days. In "The Visionary Cinema of Romantic Poetry" (*William Blake: Essays for S. Foster Damon,* ed. Alvin Rosenfeld, 1969) Harold Bloom compares what he calls the cinema of Romantic poetry to the film, with the plaudits going to the poetry, whose cinema, because it is visionary and not visual, takes us far deeper imaginatively than the film does. The novel in the Romantic Period is similarly neglected, though single novelists, Scott in particular, are increasingly coming in for serious attention. The same qualification should be made for a single type, the Gothic Novel, which is likewise a subject now of some interest (see II above). Students of the novel are still dependent on the comprehensive histories of Ernest Baker, Lionel Stevenson, Walter Allen, and others, and on the studies—considerable in number and quality—given over to the novel in the eighteenth century and the Victorian period, not to mention the twentieth century, for whatever light they may shed on the hiatus. Still, there are a few essays of note: Ernest Bernbaum, "The Views of the Great Critics on the Historical Novel" (*PMLA,* 1926); W. H. Rogers, "The Reaction Against Melodramatic Sentimentality in the English Novel, 1796–1830" (*PMLA,* 1934); and John T. Taylor, *Early Opposition to the English Novel: 1760–1830* (1943). The standard work on the familiar essay remains Marie H. Law's *The English Familiar Essay in the Early Nineteenth Century* (1934), which may be supplemented by M. R. Watson's "The 'Spectator' Tradition and the Development of the Familiar Essay" (*ELH,* 1946) and his *Magazine Serials and the Essay Tradition, 1746–1820* (1956).

For the aesthetics of the Romantics, Annie E. Powell's (Mrs. A. E. Dodds's) *The Romantic Theory of Poetry: An Examination in the Light of Croce's Aesthetic* (1926) may still be recommended. She compares the theories of Blake, Coleridge, Wordsworth, Shelley, Keats, and De Quincey with the newer aesthetic doctrine of Benedetto Croce, which she finds useful for pointing up the inadequacies of Romantic poetics, though in the process she also finds weaknesses in Croce. A much more recent study is Herbert Mainusch's *Romantische Ästhetik: Untersuchungen zur englischen Kunstlehre des späten 18. und frühen 19. Jahrhunderts* (1969). The finest work on the subject, however, is M. H. Abrams' *The Mirror and the Lamp: Romantic Theory and the Critical Tradition* (1953), without doubt the most distinguished piece of American literary scholarship in the Romantics field in some years. Abrams' book is far too rich and far too important to distort by summary. Suffice it to say that he sees the Western critical tradition as encompassing four theories of art—the mimetic, the pragmatic, the expressive, and the objective—and that in the book he treats the expressive or Romantic theory (symbolized by the lamp) as it differs from the others but especially from the mimetic theory (symbolized by the mirror) which dominated Western art from the beginnings to the eighteenth century. The break with tradition that characterizes the Romantic Movement at seemingly every point is no less evident, to judge from Abrams, in its aesthetics than in its politics or religion. Other treatises on Romantic aesthetics include P. W. K. Stone's *The Art of Poetry, 1750–1820* (see II above) and M. A. Goldberg's *The Poetics of Romanticism: Toward a Reading of John Keats* (1969). The former is concerned to show that Romantic poetics is a new birth, not a higher species of neo-classic poetics; the latter goes beyond its subtitle to make precisely the opposite point, namely, that Romanticism is another version of Classicism, perhaps an up-dating of it.

Some individual elements of Romantic aesthetics have been singled out for concentrated study. Marjorie Hope Nicolson, in *Mountain Gloom and Mountain Glory: The Development of the Aesthetics of the Infinite* (1959), traces a change in taste fundamental to the advent of Romanticism. John Press, in *The Chequer'd Shade: Reflections on Obscurity in Poetry* (1958), discusses both the charge of obscurity against the poets and their response to it. Stuart M. Tave, in *The Amiable Humorist: A Study in the Comic Theory and Criticism of the Eighteenth and Early Nineteenth Centuries* (1960), charts the change from unamiable to amiable humor that differentiates the Augustans from the Romantics. Both Patricia M. Ball, first in "Sincerity: The Rise and Fall of a Critical Term" (*MLR,* 1964) and then in *The Central Self: A Study in Romantic and Victorian Imagination,* and Henri Peyre, in *Literature and Sincerity* (1963), view sincerity as the central doctrine of Romantic aesthetics, a doctrine not without ill effects for both the Romantics and their Victorian and modern successors. Peyre's work is largely concerned with the French Romantics, especially Rousseau, but he alludes to their English counterparts, Arnold in particular. David Perkins' *Wordsworth and the Poetry of Sincerity* (1964) treats the general topic of sincerity as well as Wordsworth's effort to realize this new aesthetic value in his poems. Herbert Read, in *The True Voice of Feeling: Studies in English Romantic Poetry* (1953), equates sincerity with organic form, or "the true voice of feeling," which for Read here as elsewhere in his writing on Romanticism is the distinctive quality of modern poetry, a poetry revolutionary in the expanded consciousness it reveals (see "The Romantic Revolution," in *The Tenth Muse: Essays in Criticism* [1957]). Leone Vivante, in *English Poetry and Its Contribution to the Knowledge of a Creative Principle* (1950), explores, in a philosophical way, the possibility of an active principle or original cause, which when expressed in English poetry justifies the poets' claim to speak ultimate truth. He finds the Romantic poets, with their joy in the "one life within us and abroad," exceedingly helpful to his speculations. To Raymond Immerwahr "The First Romantic Aesthetics" (*MLQ*, 1960) is that of landscape gardening, which preceded the aesthetics of poetry but developed from a common root, the medieval popular romance.

The aspect of Romantic aesthetics dearest to the hearts of scholars, however, is the imagination. Of recent years few books, not to mention articles, devoted to the Romantics are not concerned, at least ostensibly, with the imaginative process. The word imagination or some form of it occurs in titles or subtitles with the regularity of an imprimatur. But many books and articles are in fact genuinely preoccupied with the nature and function of the Romantic imagination, some commencing with the theory and working forward to the poetry, some starting with the poems and moving backward to the theory. The greatest number of these quite naturally concentrate on Coleridge, for which see the appropriate chapter. But we have now accumulated an impressive number of studies which treat the Romantic imagination as a general and pervasive phenomenon—an element of the *Zeitgeist*. Of these, C. M. Bowra's *The Romantic Imagination* (1950) is perhaps best known. Chapters on the Romantic imagination and the Romantic achievement frame chapters on single poets ranging from Blake to Christina Rossetti. For the most part studies of major poems or groups of poems, the inner chapters support the Romantics' ideas about imagination, both those held in common and those held in isolation, delineated in the initial chapter. The grace and easy learning of Bowra's writing recommend the book to both beginning and advanced students of English Romanticism. Ernest Tuveson's *The Imagination as a Means of*

Grace: Locke and the Aesthetics of Romanticism (1960) has little to do with the Romantic poets except by implication, but as background to them it is a seminal study. Tuveson develops with meticulous detail his account of how the view of imagination as creative and hence an avenue of grace emerged from the process of reconstructing the mind instigated immediately by the new epistemology of Locke and ultimately by the new cosmology of Copernicus. Another study much concerned with the implications of Locke and other eighteenth-century philosopher-psychologists for Romantic aesthetics is H. W. Piper's *The Active Universe: Pantheism and the Concept of Imagination in the English Romantic Poets* (1962). Working from the thesis that the crucial point in the history of English Romanticism was the meeting of the concept of an active universe with the developing theory of the imagination, especially the Wordsworthian theory of the imagination or "wise passiveness," Piper dwells on Wordsworth and Coleridge, accounting for their differences as pantheists and assessing their mature theories of imagination, in the belief that Wordsworth through *The Excursion* was the chief source of both Shelley's and Keats's concepts of imagination and is thus the key to his subject. Patricia M. Ball is indebted to Robert Langbaum's view of modern poetry as the poetry of experience for the genesis of *The Central Self: A Study in Romantic and Victorian Imagination.* Borrowing Keats's division of the poet into Shakespearean and Wordsworthian types, she explores the two ways in which the Romantics sought to express experience, the "two poles of the Romantic imagination," both valid means of self-realization and both influential in Victorian and modern poetry. Ball's scheme takes her into the forgotten land of Romantic drama, the subject of her most interesting chapter. Alethea Hayter's *Opium and the Romantic Imagination* is a highly specialized study but a welcome addition to the work of M. H. Abrams and Elisabeth Schneider. The author concludes that opium, which does affect the creative imagination, has mixed results: from it the writer may derive unique materials but from it, too, he may lose the will and the power to make effective use of them. Northrop Frye's "The Imaginative and the Imaginary" in *Fables of Identity* is, on the other hand, an urbane account of the Romantic imagination as it differs from earlier imaginations, in particular the Renaissance imagination. Drawing upon the literature, psychology, and history that is familiar to any decently educated person, Frye's piece is a good reminder that the subject, for all its complexity, need not be treated complexly in order to command interest and respect.

With special reference to W. J. Bate's *From Classic to Romantic,* which argues to the contrary, A. S. P. Woodhouse's "Romanticism and the History of Ideas" (*English Studies Today*, 1951) sketches the evolution of the Romantic imagination, a process in four stages, in order to assert that the Romantic Movement was not a rejection of the rationalist tradition but a reconciliation of "the imitation of nature" with "the creative imagination." Something of the same idea appears in N. P. Stallknecht's "On Poetry and Geometric Truth" (*KR*, 1956), a pleasantly speculative essay which presents poetry and geometry, or imagination and understanding, as distinct but complementary modes of truth and suggests that the two seldom come together except in the vision of the philosophical poet, a special breed. D. R. Godfrey, in "Imagination and Truth: Some Romantic Contradictions" (*ES*, 1963), and Harry Blocker, in "Kant's Theory of the Relation of Imagination and Understanding in Aesthetic Judgments of Taste" (*BJA*, 1965), attempt to shed light on some of the contradictions and obscurities that plague Romantic aesthetics, Godfrey by comparing English theories with Goethe's and Blocker by simply exploring one of Kant's remarks. L. A. Willoughby, in "English Romantic Criticism or Fancy and the Imagination" (*Festgabe für Fritz Strich*, ed. Walter Muschg and Emil Staiger, 1952), would distinguish the English Romantics from their German cousins on the basis of their different aesthetic interests, the English preoccupied with the difference between imagination and fancy, the Germans with the antithesis of classical and romantic. Most of the essays on this "English" problem are discussed in the chapters on Wordsworth and Coleridge, for obvious reasons, but it is appropriate to mention here George Watson's short history of the distinction, written in response to Barbara Hardy's "Distinction with Difference: Coleridge's Fancy and Imagination" (*EIC*, 1951), "Contribution to a Dictionary of Critical Terms: 'Imagination' and 'Fancy' " (*EIC*, 1953). An article jointly authored by J. Bullitt and W. J. Bate, "Distinctions between Fancy and Imagination in Eighteenth-Century English Criticism" (*MLN*, 1945), points up possible sources, notably William Duff, of the Romantics' ideas and of their vocabulary for expressing them.

The relation of the Romantics to the literary past is best approached through Walter Jackson Bate's fine essay *The Burden of the Past and the English Poet*. In feeling the past to be burdensome—restricting and inhibiting—the Romantics were, he shows, true offspring of the eighteenth-century writers, the first to experience the problem and to reckon with it; in responding to the burden with honesty and courage, as their immediate predecessors had shown them how to do—in openly admiring the Renaissance masters and deliberately striking out to emulate them, the Romantics discovered the freedom to become great artists in their own right and thereby transformed burden into blessing. A short but provocative essay by Harold Bloom, "First and Last Romantics" (*SIR,* 1970), affirms Bate's ideas. For the most part, books and articles on this subject belong in the chapters subsequent to this, but it is appropriate to mention here R. D. Havens' *The Influence of Milton on English Poetry* (1922), which has important bearings on the greater Romantic poets, and Joseph Wittreich's more restricted *The Romantics on Milton* (1970), which collects the Romantics' criticism of Milton, with a view to presenting a more accurate picture of their knowledge and judgment of the master than has heretofore obtained. Earl Wasserman has recently speculated on whether or not Shakespeare's plays, in the Romantic Period, passed beyond idolatry, their status in the eighteenth century, to become the sources of archetypes ("Shakespeare and the English Romantic Movement," *The Persistence of Shakespeare Idolatry,* ed. Herbert M. Schueller [1964]). He concludes that, though a tendency in this direction can be observed, the Romantics were on the whole too close to Elizabethan England to engage widely in such use of Shakespeare. The important subject of *Dryden and Pope in the Early Nineteenth Century* (1962) is treated by Upali Amarasinghe. Raymond Bentman has argued, in "The Romantic Poets and Critics on Robert Burns" (*TSLL,* 1964), that the Romantics looked upon Burns as a spiritual kinsman and both felt and acknowledged his influence—a point of view not common in twentieth-century criticism.

III E. DEFINITIONS

Though Romanticism would seem to elude definition, for more than a century men have tried to compress its essence into one short phrase or sentence. In 1903 W. D. McClintock's *Some Paradoxes of the English Romantic Movement* protested against such vain attempts; but Paul Kaufman, "Defining Romanticism: A Survey and a Program" (*MLN,* 1925), advocated collecting as large a number of definitions as possible, apparently supposing that in quantity there dwells enlightenment. Twenty-eight of the best-known definitions, selected from many hundreds, were listed in Bernbaum's *Guide Through the Romantic Movement.* Each one, from Goethe's to Saintsbury's, differs from all the others; none has gained general acceptance. Since Bernbaum, and even before him, most other such efforts to collect definitions have had polemical implications and will be introduced in this section as appropriate.

A brief discussion of the earlier definitions, useful for introductory purposes, is David Ash's "Creative Romanticism" (*CE,* 1942). Very early uses of the word "romantic" are mentioned by John Butt, W. E. Ustick, and others in letters to *TLS,* 3 Aug. and 21 Dec. 1933, and 4 Jan. and 8 April 1934. Herbert Weisinger, "English Treatment of the Classical-Romantic Problem" (*MLQ,* 1946), considers the distinctions made by Coleridge, Hazlitt, and De Quincey. Logan Pearsall Smith's *Four Words: Romantic, Originality, Creative, Genius* (1924; rpt. in *Words and Idioms: Studies in the English Language,* 1925) is an intelligent historical sketch. Factually instructive is Fernand Baldensperger, " 'Romantique,' ses analogues et ses équivalents: Tableau synoptique de 1650 à 1810" (*Harvard Studies and Notes,* 1937). E. B. O. Borgerhoff, "*Réalisme* and Kindred Words: Their Use as Terms of Literary Criticism in the First Half of the Nineteenth Century" (*PMLA,* 1938), is valuable on the close relationships between Romanticism and Realism.

Two of the best-known modern "definitions" were not formulated as such, and in their original context are not so rigid and narrow as they appear in isolation—Walter Pater's "the addition of strangeness to beauty," from his *Appreciations* (1889), and Theodore Watts-Dunton's "the renascence of wonder in poetry," from the introduction to Volume III of *Chambers's Cyclopaedia of English Literature* (1901). J. G. Robertson's "The Reconciliation of Classic and Romantic" (*Pubs. Mod. Hum. Res. Assoc.,* 1925), a speculative essay, is attacked by R. S. Crane (*PQ,* 1926). H. J. C. Grierson, "Classical and Romantic," rpt. in *The Background of English Literature and Other Collected Essays & Addresses* (1925), suggests that the classic and the romantic correspond to "the systole and the diastole of the human heart." F. E. Pierce, "Romanticism and Other Isms" (*JEGP,* 1927), stresses four tendencies, two bad, sentimental and aesthetic, and two good, exploratory and mystical-ethical. Lascelles Abercrombie, *Romanticism* (1926), asserts that the real distinction is not between romantic and classic, but between romantic and realistic (contrast Borgerhoff, mentioned in the previous paragraph). F. L. Lucas' sprightly *The Decline and Fall of the Romantic Ideal* (1936), after rejecting scores of definitions by others, insists that it is "the revolt of the unconscious." The leading article, "Rococo to Romanticism" (*TLS,* 23

March 1946), is primarily concerned with architectural terms, but has literary implications.

In the first half of this century the most persistent attempt to define the nature and meaning of Romanticism was made by a historian of ideas, A. O. Lovejoy, in a series of essays spanning twenty-five years: "On the Meaning of 'Romantic' in Early German Romanticism" (*MLN*, 1916 and 1917), "Schiller and the Genesis of Romanticism" (*MLN*, 1920), "On the Discrimination of Romanticisms" (*PMLA*, 1924), " 'Nature' as Aesthetic Norm" (*MLN*, 1927), "Optimism and Romanticism" (*PMLA*, 1927), and "The Meaning of Romanticism for the Historian of Ideas" (*JHI*, 1941). These keen linguistic analyses of many varieties of Romanticism ended in a denial of any real unity among them: "there are *many* Romanticisms." So-called "romantic" ideas are "heterogeneous, logically independent, and sometimes essentially antithetic"; they have no one connection in actual literary history, and therefore cannot be summed up in one term or definition that has objective validity. For a time Lovejoy's studies had a sullying effect upon the term Romanticism among critics and among professors of literature, few of whom were sufficiently interested in metaphysics to see that his method did not permit him to deal with a literary work as an emotional and imaginative structure but only as a logical one—in short, to see that logical positivism and nominalism were unfit for literary interpretation. But refutation did eventually come, first from the philosopher Bernard Phillips, in "Logical Positivism and the Function of Reason" (*Philosophy*, 1948), and then from the literary scholar René Wellek, in "The Concept of 'Romanticism' in Literary History" (*CL*, 1949), an essay which asserted the general coherence and integration of the Romantic Movement by arguing that the Romantics held in common a view of nature as organic, a view of the imagination as creative and thus the source of art, and a view of the method of art as symbolic and mythic.

Like Lovejoy before him, Wellek has reiterated and supplemented his argument in subsequent essays and books. Among the essays two may be especially noted: "Romanticism Re-examined" (see 1 above) and "German and English Romanticism: A Confrontation" (*SIR*, 1964; rpt. in *Confrontations*, 1965). The former expresses Wellek's belief that the scholarship of the last several years points to the same conclusions he arrived at in 1949 and that the argument for the validity of the term Romanticism has in fact been won: "they all see the implication of imagination, symbol, myth, and organic nature, and see it as part of the great endeavor to overcome the split between subject and object, the self and the world, the conscious and the unconscious. This is the central creed of the great Romantic poets in England, Germany, and France. It is a closely coherent body of thought and feeling." At the same time the essay surveys the important scholarly writing on the subject, both in this country and abroad, between 1949 and 1963. The second article confirms Wellek's claim that he is not insensitive to the very real differences within the national literatures of the Romantic Movement by demonstrating the peculiar character of German Romanticism when compared to English Romanticism. The concept of a coherent movement is most expansively elaborated, of course, in Wellek's *History of Modern Criticism 1750–1950, Vol. 2, The Romantic Age* (1955), which in its scope is without peer among modern Romantics studies. To be sure, Wellek has not convinced everyone that Romanticism is a valid literary term—least of all Lovejoy, who in the Preface to *The Reason, the Understanding, and Time* (1961) reiterated his objection to the word Romanticism and even to the question What is Romanticism. There remain latter-day skeptics, and we will come to them shortly. But the definition he champions, because it is not narrowly the product of a single critical method but receives support from the several critical approaches currently most in vogue, is not easily dismissed.

Not far behind Wellek in taking up the challenge of Lovejoy was Morse Peckham, who has been without doubt the liveliest polemicist on the field. For Peckham, the answer to Lovejoy was to be found in the latter pages of Lovejoy's own *The Great Chain of Being,* wherein is implied the very definition of Romanticism that the author had earlier proclaimed impossible. Seeing himself as a reconciler of Lovejoy and Wellek, Peckham claimed, in "Toward a Theory of Romanticism" (*PMLA,* 1951), that the three ideas by which the former argued for the inconsistency of Romantic thought and art (organicism, dynamism, diversitarianism) and the three by which the latter argued for its consistency (organicism, imagination, symbolism) could all be derived from a root-metaphor, the organic metaphor of the structure of the universe, or "dynamic organicism." The values of Romanticism so defined are change, imperfection, growth, diversity, the creative imagination, and the unconscious. In order to comprehend Byron in his definition, however, Peckham was forced to speak of a negative Romanticism and a positive Romanticism, by analogy with Carlyle's Everlasting No and Everlasting Yea, and in doing so provided skeptical readers or those merely offended by his tone and procedure with the opportunity to scoff. In the following year Peckham wrote of "The Triumph of Romanticism" (*Magazine of Art*, 1952), referring to modern art in general as the triumph of nineteenth-century Romanticism. By the 1960's, however, Peckham had become less confident about the theory he had so vigorously proposed. In a sequel to the original article, "Toward a Theory of Romanticism: II. Reconsiderations" (*SIR*, 1961), he retracted the definition that he had formerly assigned to Romanticism and bestowed it instead upon the Enlightenment in its last and highest phase. (These essays and ones discussed below are gathered in *The Triumph of Romanticism: Collected Essays,* 1970.) *Beyond the Tragic Vision* (1962), the culmination of Peckham's efforts, continues this line of thinking and thus prefers "Enlightenment" to "Romanticism." An ambitious attempt to explain the unparalleled change in the mind and thought of Western man that occurred in the eighteenth century—the change that has made so imperative an adequate definition of Romanticism in the first place—the book surveys very generally the old ways by which man oriented himself to the world prior to the modern period and then shows, by ranging widely among the major artists of the nineteenth century, the new way that emerged from the disintegration of the old—the way of the self which projects value upon the world and so creates its own orientations. For his title Peckham draws upon Nietzsche's vision of a joy that is deeper than woe, a vision that indicates the true source of being for the truly modern man, his imaginative mind. Still more recent essays—"Romanticism: The Present State of Theory" (*Pennsylvania Council of Teachers of English Bulletin,* No. 12, Dec. 1965) and "The Dilemma of a Century: The Four Stages of Romanticism," in *Romanticism: The Culture of the Nineteenth Century,* ed. Peckham (1965)—do not represent significant shifts in position. The latter might be described as a condensed version of *Beyond the Tragic Vision,* with some few refinements; the former, while it offers a brief account of Peckham's theory as it evolved from 1951 to 1965, is primarily a quest for allied opinions, of which one is turned up in the recent writing of Earl Wasserman (see below). In the process of the quest Peckham makes it abundantly clear that he is not one of those whose opinions converge with Wellek's or anyone else's. The character of Peckham's writing is not calculated to win wholesale acclaim. Response has ranged from open contempt to keen excitement. But the controversies he has deliberately provoked in what he has called "interim reports" (see "On

Romanticism: An Introduction," *SIR,* 1970) must themselves be accounted contributions toward a theory of Romanticism. Many another scholar has had his wits sharpened by them.

Yet a third scholar whose writing over a period of years has contributed significantly to the effort to validate Romanticism is Northrop Frye, in the minds of many people the chief apostle of archetypal or myth criticism in the last two decades. Frye's brilliant study of Blake, *Fearful Symmetry* (1947), though restricted to that poet, is not unrelated to his more general studies of Romanticism, for Blake is crucial to Frye's interpretation of the Romantic Movement. Nor is his *Anatomy of Criticism* (1957), the widely influential apology of myth criticism, beside the point. But most relevant here are Frye's essays "The Drunken Boat: The Revolutionary Element in Romanticism," in *Romanticism Reconsidered* (rpt. in *The Stubborn Structure: Essays on Criticism and Society,* 1970), and "The Imaginative and the Imaginary," in *Fables of Identity,* and his recent volume *A Study of English Romanticism* (1968). It cannot be said that these and related essays in *Fables of Identity* duplicate themselves, but it is possible to see running through them Frye's belief that Romanticism denotes the beginning of the first major change in the encyclopedic myth derived largely from the Bible that dominated the literature and philosophy of Western Europe for centuries prior to 1800—a change that replaced the old myth, which attributed the projection of reality to God and nature, with a new one, which recovered the projection of reality to man himself, in particular, to his own creative imagination. With special attention to the imagery of poetry, Frye demonstrates the change from an exterior reality to an interior one on the four levels of being in which man has been traditionally framed—heaven, Eden, nature, hell. The new images which convey the new myth are symptomatic of the general transformation of literary genres by which Frye has also defined Romanticism. That he sees Romanticism as having its center of gravity in the creative arts makes more tenable Frye's theory that, though we may have had a post-Romantic movement in the twentieth century, we have not yet, to judge from the imagery of modern poetry, created a new myth or even some new patterns of myth, nor have we reverted to the old one. The problems with Frye's approach to literature are conveniently raised in Irene Chayes's "Little Girls Lost: Problems of a Romantic Archetype" (*BNYPL,* 1963), which, while discussing the Persephone archetype in Blake's Lyca, Wordsworth's Lucy Gray, and Keats's Madeline, poses the larger question of what her method can contribute to the understanding of a literary period such as the Romantic.

Chayes's article is fair-minded, recognizing both gains and losses, and it is probably just such temperate use of archetypal criticism as hers that has carried the day against the more violent opponents of Frye, his predecessors, and his disciples. Though there are still too many good scholars ready to convert any and every theme of Romantic art into a myth, few of us would care to be deprived of the insights which Frye and his better students have provided.

In his Preface to a volume of essays entitled *Romanticism and Consciousness* (1970) Harold Bloom suggests that the advanced criticism of Romanticism has increasingly identified Romantic self-consciousness as the most central problem in defining our own relation to the Romantic poets. The impetus for this trend is the writing of certain European scholars variously labeled "the Swiss School," "the Geneva School," or "critics of consciousness." Laurent LeSage provides an introduction to their work and some extracts from it in *The French New Criticism* (1967). Of the many critics he discusses, Georges Poulet is most familiar to scholars this side of the Atlantic because he alone has written about the English Romantic poets, first in the article "Timelessness and Romanticism" (*JHI,* 1954) and then in the book *The Metamorphoses of the Circle* (1967). Like his fellows, Poulet is concerned with describing the consciousness of the poet in its conflict with the phenomenal world as this consciousness can be discerned in his poetry, but from the beginning Poulet has focused on the poet's consciousness of time and space. Thus the article contends, with particular reference to Coleridge, that the Romantics brought Eternity into Time, thereby converting God's Timelessness to man's. Similarly, the book, based on the premise that the circle is the most constant form whereby men have represented their consciousness of time and space, contends, again with special attention to Coleridge, that the Romantics through consciousness of the self (the center or point of the circle) returned to the non-self (the periphery of the circle). Romanticism becomes the "taking possession by consciousness of the fundamentally subjective character of the mind," or the retreat of the mind to its centermost point, from which it returns reinvigorated and in quest of a circle, i.e., of self-realization. J. Hillis Miller, in "The Literary Criticism of Georges Poulet" (*MLN,* 1963), has described Poulet's work in largely favorable terms, but Geoffrey Hartman, in "Beyond Formalism" (*MLN,* 1966), has questioned Poulet's approach, particularly as it postulates a Romantic or period consciousness as opposed, say, to a Coleridgean consciousness. Poulet's results, he finds, are not greatly different from those of an historian of ideas like Lovejoy.

Hartman is not, however, to be construed as hostile to phenomenological criticism, for no American scholar is more closely identified with it than he—so much so that scholars of other literary periods interested in its method have had to brush up on Romantic poetry. Hartman's two books on Wordsworth, appropriately discussed in the next chapter, are his chief contributions to this method, but his essays, especially "Romanticism and 'Anti-Self-Consciousness'" (*CentR*, 1962) which treats of consciousness or imagination as the remedy to self-consciousness, are also valuable. Reviewers and readers have complained of difficulty in reading Hartman, not always it seems a difficulty of thought, but most acknowledge that his work is among the most original and exciting of the last decade.

Because existential philosophy, Jungian psychology, and myth criticism may find a home under the same roof, as Hartman's work demonstrates, the new approach to Romanticism is not always self-apparent. But that it has made considerable inroad into Romantic studies there can be no doubt. Everywhere about us are articles and books concerned with "consciousness." Richard Haven's recent book on Coleridge, with its title *Patterns of Consciousness* (1969), may be taken as a fair sample of the trend, to which the best introduction is probably the Bloom anthology with which we began this discussion, especially Bloom's own essay, reprinted from *The Yale Review* (1969), "The Internalization of Quest Romance," where the idea of Romanticism as a process from Promethean Man to "the real man, the imagination" recalls Peckham's negative Romanticism leading to positive. Bloom's scheme, however, is not motivated by the desire to find a niche for Byron; rather it assumes Byron's Romanticism from the beginning.

The word "self," like the word "consciousness," is much in vogue these days and may be used to organize a group of essays and books that also proffer definitions. Most prominent of the group is probably Wylie Sypher's *Loss of Self in Modern Literature and Art* (1962), a book provocative in its effort to characterize the shifts in the concept of self from the Romantic Period to the present and encouraging in its prophecy of a new humanism that Sypher labels "post-existential," but Romantics scholars may have difficulty in crediting Sypher's premise that the Romantic self is represented by the Byronic man—a shaky foundation which tends to weaken the entire superstructure of his thesis. George Boas' "The Romantic Self: An Historical Sketch" (*SIR,* 1964) seems more sound and, though far shorter, more comprehensive. The theme of Romantic individualism is also the subject of two other articles that do not entirely agree: Peter L.

Thorslev's "The Romantic Mind Is Its Own Place" (*CL*, 1963), a useful essay on the familiar topic of Romantic satanism, which concept Thorslev explains well but does not question; and Frederick Garber's "Self, Society, Value, and the Romantic Hero" (*CL*, 1967), an interesting article that challenges the traditional view of the Romantic mind as autonomous, the Romantic hero as morally and spiritually isolated from society. Similar in point to his earlier article is Thorslev's later "Incest as Romantic Symbol" (*CLS*, 1965), which concludes that incest is the "symbol of the Romantic psyche's love affair with self and of its tragic isolation in an increasingly alien world." By far the most important contribution to the subject—and a seminal interpretation of Romanticism—is Earl Wasserman's "The English Romantics: The Grounds of Knowledge" (*SIR*, 1964). Wasserman asserts that the fundamental problem of Romanticism for the Romantics themselves was to define the relationship between self and nature, subject and object. His essay not only demonstrates the centrality of this epistemological problem to the Romantics and thus to any effort by scholars to define their movement, but it also testifies to the radical diversity of the Romantics as witnessed by their solutions to the problem and thus cautions us against seeking to reconcile all opposites in our anxiety to establish definitions.

Some of the additional efforts to define Romanticism in the last twenty years—though by no means all of them—would suggest that the work of Wellek, Peckham, Frye, and the "consciousness critics" has produced, if no widespread consensus, considerably less disagreement than formerly obtained. It is not uncommon to find, both in this country and abroad, agreement with the ideas of one or another of these writers. Henry H. H. Remak, for example, first in "West European Romanticism: Definition and Scope," *Comparative Literature: Method and Perspective*, ed. N. P. Stallknecht (1961), and later in "A Key to West European Romanticism?" (*CollG*, 1968), as he lists characteristics of Romanticism and suggests a key or common denominator in the Romantics' attempt to "heal the break in the universe" is keenly aware of his proximity to Wellek. Similarly, Albert Gérard in his writing on English Romanticism has come under Wellek's sway. The articles "Sur la logique du romanticisme anglais" (*L'Athénée*, 1956; tr. in *EIC*, 1957) and "Le Romantisme anglais: Orientation récentes de l'histoire et de la critique" (*Revue des Langes Vivantes*, 1959), and the books *L'Idée romantique de la poésie en Angleterre* (1955) and *English Romantic Poetry: Ethos, Structure, and Symbol in Coleridge, Wordsworth, Shelley and Keats* (1968)—all speak of Romantic art as symbolic statement of the cosmic unity which the Romantics experienced by means of their reconciling imaginations. But Gérard's work, if not wholly original in theory, has its own very distinctive merit. The books in particular study Romantic poetry in such a way as to show how the Romantic experience of organic unity is given organic form through imagery, structure, and symbol. Gérard's last volume has the reputation of being the best study of English Romanticism by a European author in recent years. Certainly one comes away from it with considerable respect not only for the author but also for the poetry he so sensitively analyzes. For somewhat less derivative definitions of Romanticism in the last decade one might consult, finally, Herbert M. Schueller's "Romanticism Reconsidered" (*JAAC,* 1962), which argues for a broad definition such as the urge of the human psyche to go beyond the human confines in which it finds itself, and Calvin S. Brown's "Toward a Definition of Romanticism," *Varieties of Literary Experience,* ed. Stanley Burnshaw (1962), which argues for a definition based on genre, the lyric being the characteristic expression of the Romantic set of mind, satire that of the antithetical set of mind. Brown's article is more successful in contrasting lyric and satire than in defining Romanticism.

Opposition to the increasingly intensive quest for a definition is neither meager nor meek. Irving Massey, in "The Romantic Movement: Phrase or Fact?" (*DR,* 1964), recommends that we abandon all preconceptions about Romantic writers and look at what they are and what they say, admitting all the while that we do and must refashion the period in our own image. In the process of mounting his argument Massey provides a good summary of current definitions—those preconceptions he is protesting. George Whalley also rejects Romanticism as a critical term, in "Literary Romanticism" (*QQ,* 1965). Like Massey, he would have us start and end with the poems, not with historical or cultural labels. Whalley's essay, which examines Wordsworth and Yeats, identifies three dominant activities of mind in the poems of these poets. Though they need not be labeled Romantic activities of mind, "The symbolic ring, the dream, and organic form" when differently phrased comprise the core of many a current definition of Romantic consciousness. Scholars of European Romantic literature, especially German literature, have not so much objected to definitions as to those projected and widely accepted. Raymond Immerwahr, in "German Romanticism and the Unity of the Romantic Imagination," *On Romanticism and the Art of Translation,* ed. Gottfried F. Merkel (1956), has dismissed the organic concept of Wellek and Peckham as worthless for defining German Romanticism, which is a part of the European Romantic Movement only because it shares with the other literatures "a unified but complex activity of the imagination." Robert Kahn, in "Some Recent Definitions of German Romanticism, or the Case Against Dialectics" (*Rice Univ. Studies,* 1964), also dismisses Lovejoy, Wellek, and Peckham, all of whom by theorizing from dialectics merely confound the chaos of scholarship in German Romanticism that has resulted from a historical approach predicated upon the principles of polarity and synthesis. (See, however, Ernst Behler's "The Origins of the Romantic Literary Theory," *CollG,* 1968, for a late effort to define by the dialectical method.) A still more recent article by Lilian R. Furth, "Romanticism in Historical Perspective" (*CLS,* 1968), rehearses once again the history of Romanticism in England, Germany, and France in order to demonstrate the lack of a unified movement across national boundaries. Her *Romanticism in Perspective* (1969) elaborates upon the likenesses and differences among the various national literatures but to the same end that she pursues in the article. Finally, Herbert S. Gershamn, "Romanticism Revisited" (*Symposium,* 1969), locates the essence of the Romantic revolt not in Wellek's trinity but in what he calls an "innate Dionysianism." If as John C. Stephens has observed in " 'Classic' and 'Romantic' " (*Emory Univ. Quarterly,* 1959) the twentieth century is an age of criticism, an age of definition, then it may be that those scholars opposed to defining Romanticism are doomed to frustration. Perhaps they can take consolation in his further observation that Romanticism as a critical term is in constant use by people aware of its ambiguities, people who use it with care and discrimination.

III F. JUDGMENTS

Judgments of the Romantic Movement in the first half of the twentieth century, especially adverse judgments, came from several quarters, but the frontal attacks of the "Humanists" (or "New Humanists") and, later, the "New Critics" had the greatest consequences for Romanticism. For the most part, these attacks, though persistent, vigorous, and effective, were delivered in short essays or in books primarily devoted to other subjects. The leaders of the Humanists, Paul Elmer More and Irving Babbitt, whatever the shortcomings of their critical methods or argumentative strategies, rendered a real service to Romantics studies, at a time when critics were either generally appreciative or specifically aesthetic in approach, by insisting on the ethical implications and responsibilities of literature. Alike in their objections to Romanticism, the two men differed sharply in tone and manner. More's attacks in his *Shelburne Essays,* e.g., "Wordsworth" and "Shelley" in the Seventh Series (1910) and "Beckford" and "Definitions of Dualism" in the Eighth (1913), are gentle and philosophical; Babbitt's are characteristically indignant and propagandistic. "The Primitivism of Wordsworth," in *On Being Creative, and Other Essays* (1932), is the most direct application of Babbitt's ideas to an English author; but his general position is best seen in his much earlier *Rousseau and Romanticism* (1919). He regarded Rousseau as the founder of Romanticism, and mistakenly insisted that Rousseau advocated an extreme form of naturalism, primitivism, and democracy. (On that side-issue, see the review by A. O. Lovejoy, *MLN,* 1920; Jeannette Tresnon, "The Paradox of Rousseau," *PMLA,* 1928; and G. R. Havens' reply, *PMLA,* 1929.) Subsequently, Babbitt insisted, Romanticism developed its worst characteristic, the glorification of an uncritical, irresponsibly aesthetic, and centrifugal imagination, uncontrolled by reason or good sense, and encouraging man's impulsive egotism and wishful illusions. The gap and conflict between the natural and the human, both within man and without, was an absolute and unbridgeable dualism which it was vain for Romanticism to try to overcome. To yield to the natural was evil and disastrous; but man had a power, which Romanticism was accused of weakening, namely, "the inner check," to curb his will for his own good.

Two contemporary articles, W. S. Knickerbocker's "Humanism and Scholarship" (*SR,* 1930) and Gorham Munson's "Humanism and Modern Writers" (*EJ,* 1931), reflect on the controversy generated by More and Babbitt when at its height.

Several refutations of the Humanistic indictment of Romanticism are outstanding. C. H. Herford, "Romanticism in the Modern World" (*E&S,* 1922), points out the parallels between the attitudes of the Humanists and those of the discredited neoclassical contemporaries of the Romantics, Gifford and Croker. Hugh I'A. Fausset, "The New Humanism Disputed," in his *The Proving of Psyche* (1929), persuasively argues the Romantic case on psychological, ethical, and aesthetic grounds. Lawrence Hyde in *The Prospects of Humanism* (1931), the most philosophical of the rejoinders, protests that Humanism fabricates too sharp an opposition between the natural and the moral elements in man, and that it is vulnerable because it relies entirely on the "inner check" without calling it a conscience or giving it any religious basis whatever. In "The Practical Results of the Humanistic Theories" (*EJ*, 1931) Ernest Bernbaum suggests that, if the Humanists' literary criteria were applied to other authors, most of the greatest masters of world literature, including Sophocles, Horace, and Shakespeare, would, like the Romantics, be found shockingly unaware of the "inner check" and deplorably given to the freedom of imagination and its visions.

Latter day contributions to the controversy include Albert Gérard's "Prometheus and the Aeolian Lyre" (*YR*, 1944), which sums up the Humanistic case by reiterating that the Romantics' beliefs are nothing more than beautiful "myths," and J. W. Beach's *A Romantic View of Poetry* (1944), which engages in *ad hominem* argument (Beach was Babbitt's student) in order to expose the essentially negative and puritanical aesthetic of the Humanists. A second effort to account for anti-Romanticism by drawing on personal acquaintance with some of the principal players is E. M. W. Tillyard's "The Origin of English Anti-Romanticism," in *Essays Literary and Educational* (1962). Tillyard's thesis is that those who led the attack, both in England and in America, were strongly indebted to the anti-Romanticism rampant in France in the later nineteenth century. Raleigh and Nichol-Smith at Oxford, Hulme while a student at Cambridge, and Babbitt and Santayana at Harvard were all influenced by French academics. The reminiscing tone of Tillyard's essay is sufficient sign that the Humanists have long since passed from the scene; his concluding discussion of Eliot, who had access to all five of the above scholars, brings us to the New Critics, the second line of opponents to Romanticism in this century.

C. D. Thorpe and N. E. Nelson, in "Criticism in the Twentieth Century: A Bird's-Eye View" (*CE*, 1947), provide a good introduction to the New Critics as they appeared to academic scholars in their heyday. More narrowly literary in interests and temperament than the Humanists, the New Critics were concerned first of all with expounding and applying a theory of literature which would interpret and defend their own school of poetry and only secondly with evaluating Romantic poetry, which they treated at random and at widely scattered intervals in their writings. For this reason Richard Harter Fogle's thoughtful and well-documented studies, "Romantic Bards and Metaphysical Reviewers" (*ELH*, 1945) and "A Recent Attack upon Romanticism" (*CE*, 1948), once the source of considerable comfort to the faithful, remain valuable surveys of the New Critics' pronouncements on the Romantic poets. (His later "A Note on Romantic Oppositions and Reconciliations," in *The Major English Roman-*

tic Poets, while locating the source of Romantic poetry in the reconciliation of opposites, turned the tables on the New Critics, who in Fogle's eyes were Romantics despite themselves.)

On occasion the New Critics could admire a Romantic work, but in the main they were hostile to Romanticism both as philosophy and as art. Their sharpshooting was chiefly aimed at Shelley (a poet of adolescent ideas for readers of adolescent enthusiasms) and Wordsworth, though Coleridge, whose aesthetics were a major source of their own, fared little better. Only Keats escaped their fire virtually unharmed. The trouble with the Romantics was their ability to detect intimations of immortality or to create myths which enabled them to wander in gladness. The New Critics spoke for a generation which was world-weary, materialistic, and skeptical; which regarded the human situation as a hopelessly perplexing existence in a barren, wasted land; and which despised any literature that envisages it otherwise. Hence they asserted that Romantic literature as a whole (including Shakespeare) is too emotional, too soft (not "dry, hard, and classical"), too hopeful that the good in man's nature may overcome the evil, too desirous of simplifying human experience into intelligible designs, too credulous in sensing a harmony in the apparent discords of the universe, and, above all, too certain that Imagination, cooperating with Reason, can reveal such truths through the beautiful. In the opinion of the New Critics, the best poetry stresses everything that is not Romantic—the unemotionally intellectual, the heterogeneous, the paradoxical, the witty, the ironical, the irreconcilable complexities, the nonsensicality of human life and therefore its wretchedness—and stresses it in a style that is part Metaphysical, part Classical.

T. E. Hulme, *Speculations: Essays on Humanism and the Philosophy of Art,* ed. Herbert Read (1924), was the detonator of the New Criticism, with his frank "I object even to the best of the Romantics" and his famous "Romanticism then, and this is the best definition I can give it, is spilt religion." Next came T. S. Eliot, major poet and brilliant critic, with *The Use of Poetry and the Use of Criticism . . .* (1933), a series of lectures given at Harvard 1932–33. Eliot's reputation as a slayer of Romantic poets rests chiefly on his severe handling of Shelley; Wordsworth and Coleridge emerge from the fray in fair shape, and Keats comes out quite well, especially in his letters. A third Englishman, I. A. Richards, *Principles of Literary Criticism* (1924) and *Coleridge on the Imagination* (1934), gave the New Critics their bases in psychology and aesthetics. Less important but characteristic of the new fashion were William Empson, *Seven Types of*

Ambiguity (1930; 3rd rev. ed., 1963), which regards the Romantics as escapist or childish; Edmund Wilson, on T. S. Eliot in *Axel's Castle* . . . (1931); and Riding, Graves, and Reeves, *Epilogue: A Critical Summary* (1936), which calls the Romantics tradition-ridden, spiritually hermaphroditic, predominantly sexual, etc. The most thoughtful and effective American attacks on Romanticism are found in John Crowe Ransom's *The World's Body* (1938), which asserts that the "modern poet has performed a work of dissociation and purified his art," and *The New Criticism* (1941); in Cleanth Brooks's *Modern Poetry and the Tradition* (1939) and *The Well Wrought Urn: Studies in the Structure of Poetry* (1947; see his article "Irony and 'Ironic' Poetry," *CE*, 1948); and in Allen Tate's *Reason in Madness: Critical Essays* (1941), which assails Coleridge as the source of all erroneous modern criticism, psychological or historical, condemns "the poetry of communication" of intelligible sentiments and ideas, and desiderates a poetry which has "perfect inutility." The dominance of the New Critics throughout the 1940's, and the corrosive effects of their anti-Romanticism, were summed up in David Daiches' statement, "The school that maintains that the essence of poetry is paradox, and that Keats must be proved paradoxical before he can be shown to be a great poet, is the ascendant critical school in the United States today" (*TLS*, 29 July 1949).

The early opponents of the New Critics were such literary scholars as: the author of a *TLS* review (4 April 1935) of Richards' Coleridge book, who called attention to his impoverishment and perversion of Coleridge's principles; G. Rostrevor Hamilton, who in *Poetry and Contemplation: A New Preface to Poetics* (1937) attacked Richards' notion that "the function of the arts is to increase the activity and promote the health of the nervous system"; D. G. James, who in *Scepticism and Poetry: An Essay on the Poetic Imagination* (1937) refuted Richards' interpretation of Coleridge and defended the poetics of Wordsworth and Keats; the author of a *TLS* article, "Romanticism in the Dock: A Plea for a Reprieve" (8 Jan. 1938), who spoke out against both the Humanists and the New Critics; Eric R. Bentley, a pragmatist, who in "Romanticism: A Re-Evaluation" (*Antioch Review*, 1944) criticized Eliot and Tate because of their rigid dogmatism and praised the Romantics for their encouragement of individualism and for their sense of historical development; Lorna Reynolds, who in "In Defence of Romanticism" (*Dublin Magazine*, 1946) rejected Eliot's strictures, using chiefly Wordsworth in refutation; C. S. Lewis, who in *The Abolition of Man* . . . (1947) attacked Richards' "appetencies" and "satisfactions"; E. E. Stoll, who in "Symbolism in Coleridge" (*PMLA*, 1948) showed how preposterously the New Critics sometimes misinterpreted Romantic works; R. S. Crane, who in "Cleanth Brooks; or, The Bankruptcy of Critical Monism" (*MP*, 1948) exposed the weakness of the philosophical assumptions on which the criteria of the New Critics rested and in "I. A. Richards on the Art of Interpretation" (*Ethics*, 1949) proceeded to demolish Richards as he had formerly demolished Brooks; David Daiches, who in *A Study of Literature for Readers and Critics* (1948) fairly but firmly condemned the New Critics; and Douglas Bush, who in "The New Criticism: Some Old-Fashioned Queries" (*PMLA*, 1948 Proceedings) turned the ironic wit so much admired by the New Critics against their own superficiality, dogmatism, and aestheticism.

Bush's essay might be said to mark the end of heat and the beginning of light. Though some scholars continued from time to time to assail the New Critics (see, for example, Newell F. Ford's "Empson's and Ransom's Mutilation of Texts," *PQ*, 1950; and, for references to other such attacks, Murray Krieger's "After the New Criticism," *Mass. Review*, 1962), others began to see that Romantics studies were much the better for having gone through the fire of battle. Articles and books started giving the New Critics their due, with the result that most scholars in the field today look quite charitably on the once terrible New Critics. Indeed, most of us are in some part "new critics" ourselves and thankful for it. Characteristic of the more balanced perspective that commenced in the 1950's and continued through the 1960's is Frederick A. Pottle's "The New Critics and the Historical Method" (*YR*, 1953). More extensive are the writings of Murray Krieger, Richard Foster, and Frank Kermode, all of whom, while assessing the New Criticism or relating it to the Anglo-American critical tradition, turned up unmistakably Romantic elements in the principles and attitudes of the New Critics. Indeed, in various ways they have demonstrated the essentially Romantic roots of the school. The writings of these men, though not strictly relevant to this chapter, deserve brief notice. Krieger's essay "The Ambiguous Anti-Romanticism of T. E. Hulme" (*ELH*, 1953), which reveals in Hulme's writing an uncompromising prejudice against Romanticism coupled with a constant invocation of Coleridgean precepts, anticipates his book *The New Apologists for Poetry* (1956), which in turn reveals the New Criticism as a whole to be a Romantic criticism in its philosophy. Foster's *The New Romantics: A Reappraisal of the New Criticism* (1962), based on a series of essays published in various journals in 1959, is concerned with the sensibility of the New Critics, which the author sees as Romantic in kind, and is intended to complement Krieger's work. (For a dissenting view of Foster's theory as it involves Richards, see Gerald E. Graff's 1967 article for *Criticism*, "The Later Richards and the New Criticism.") Kermode's *Romantic Image*, discussed earlier in this chapter, places Hulme, Pound, and Eliot in the full Romantic tradition of art as Kermode defines that tradition.

A very late contribution to the subject is Ernest J. Lovell's essay for the memorial volume to William H. Marshall, *Romantic and Victorian . . .* (1971): "The Heretic in the Sacred Wood; Or, the Naked Man, the Tired Man, and the Romantic Aristocrat: William Blake, T. S. Eliot, and George Wyndham." Lovell is primarily concerned to expose the moral and intellectual failure of Eliot's criticism of the Romantics, especially Blake, and to suggest the reasons for it, but in the course of his essay he repeatedly demonstrates the Romantic origins of Eliot's aesthetic theory, not to mention his aesthetic tastes. But one should note G. Ingli James's "The Unexplored Romanticism" (*Criticism*, 1959), for the view that Kermode and others who are anxious to make Romantics of the New Critics are blind to the emotive theory of poetry, which in the nineteenth century shared the stage with the organic theory but in the twentieth century lost out to it, thanks to the New Critics who rejected it soundly. Also noteworthy is Frank Lentricchia's *The Gaiety of Language: An Essay on the Radical Poetics of W. B. Yeats and Wallace Stevens* (1968), which attempts to show that the symbolists cannot be explained or defined by reference to Romantic aesthetics except as those aesthetics contrast with the symbolists' theories and practices of poetry. Taken as a whole, these and other discussions of the New Critics are sympathetic in approach and respectful in tone. In the long run the New Criticism, in spite of itself, served the Romantic Movement well.

Needless to say, the negative judgments of the Humanists and the New Critics and the positive judgments of their antagonists do not exhaust the evaluations of the Romantic Movement in the twentieth century; they are simply the most conspicuous. Other writers have examined the Romantic poets from other perspectives and made their assessments accordingly. One such is Myron F. Brightfield, *The Issue in Literary Criticism* (1932), a radical attack on Romanticism in the name of "the scientific method"; another is E. B. Burgum, "Romanticism" (*KR,* 1941), an indictment of the movement as an ideology arising out of the "antagonisms between the middle and lower classes." Several studies, some wittingly, some not, have tended to denigrate Romanticism for its bent toward the extreme and the sensational. The Romantic faith that love, on the human level, is an incarnation of the unity of the universe is studied in its literary exaggerations in Albert Mordell's *The Erotic Motive in Literature* (1919; rev. ed., 1962). A more favorable view of the subject is Gerald Enscoe's in *Eros and the Romantics* . . . (1967), where he suggests that in the poetry of Coleridge, Shelley, and Keats sexual love is the means of psychic regeneration and not, as in the literature of the past, the means of spiritual degradation. Mario Praz's *The Romantic Agony* (discussed above), while not condemnatory, gives the impression that the Romantics were excessively erotic. F. L. Lucas' lively and amusing *The Decline and Fall of the Romantic Ideal* (also discussed above), which on the whole is hostile to the Romantics and especially so to Coleridge, also concentrates on the emotional, and therefore the sensational, extremes of the movement; it calls them "the crocodiles of the unconscious." In a class by itself is F. R. Leavis' *Revaluation: Tradition and Development in English Poetry* (1936), a perplexing but provocative book. Leavis admires aesthetic and moral sensibility, but only when it is united with critical intelligence. He is observant and usually judicious, though in the opinion of Ernest Bernbaum mistaken about Milton and Shelley. He undervalues Coleridge; but, so far as his secularism permits, he appreciates Wordsworth and, especially, Keats.

In contrast to these adversaries, there has been a small group of non belligerent admirers, who sensed the power of the Romantics to lift the spirit of man to new heights of perception and faith, who responded to that power, and gave their testimony as to its immense value. This group is distinguished by an unusually sympathetic insight into the spirit and intent of the Romantics, by a delight in the beauty of their styles, and by a responsive sympathy with their religious, mystical, and imaginative tendencies. Most of these enthusiasts are poets, or creative men of letters. An introduction, elementary and clear, to their attitude of mind, is found in Ernest Earnest's "Infinity in the Palm of Your Hand: A Study of the Romantic Temper" (*CE,* 1941). The more important essays in this subdivision may be divided into those that are chiefly concerned with the *beauty* of the Romantic works, and those that also admire their *substance* and try to estimate its significance. The first group is exemplified by Arthur Symons' *The Romantic Movement in English Poetry* (1909; 4th ed., 1924); Charles Williams' *The English Poetic Mind* (1932), which sympathetically describes how the souls of all great poets grow through experience, and are recurrently clouded by disillusionment, as in the cases of Shakespeare, Milton, Wordsworth, and Keats; Walter De La Mare's *Behold, This Dreamer* . . . (1939); and Edith Sitwell's *A Poet's Notebook* (1943). Among those who admire the Romantics for what they say as well as for how they say it, there is usually a strong devotion to religion (though not necessarily to any particular church or sect). Mrs. Olwen Ward Campbell's "Some Suggestions on the Romantic Revival and Its Effects," in her *Shelley and the Unromantics* (1924), though it recognizes the weaknesses of Romantic literature, is an admirable appreciation of its faith in the greatness of man's soul. J. Middleton Murry, with his *Keats and Shakespeare* . . . (1925) and *Heroes of Thought* (1938), belongs here, with his emphasis on the democratic character of the Romantic faith; and also Hugh I'A. Fausset, *The Proving of Psyche* (1929) and his *Studies in Idealism* (1923), with his stress upon the agreement between Romanticism and liberal Christianity. The friendly attitude of Roman Catholicism toward some features of Romanticism is indicated in Christopher Dawson's "The Origin of the Romantic Tradition," *Mediaeval Religion—the Forwood Lectures, 1934—and Other Essays* (1934). But by far the most valuable, if controversial, of the studies in this group are those of G. Wilson Knight. His *The Christian Renaissance* (1933) lays the religious foundations, a Hellenized non-ascetic kind of Christianity. His *The Burning Oracle: Studies in the Poetry of Action* (1939), largely devoted to Byron, is a fervent eulogy of those emotional and imaginative audacities that abash rationalistic and prosaic critics; and his *The Starlit Dome: Studies in the Poetry of Vision* (1941) is the most eloquent appreciation of the prophetic insights into the meaning of life given us by Wordsworth, Coleridge, Keats, and Shelley. Another outspoken admirer is Charles du Bos in *What Is Literature?* (1940), a book which is based on Thomas Aquinas' idea that beauty is life becoming conscious of itself. Du Bos maintains that the three greatest poets are Shakespeare, Dante, and Keats. Less weighty but stimulating is Dorothy Sayers' *The Mind of the Maker* (1941), which draws parallels between the Creator's work and that of the Romantics.

It is tempting to say that in this age of hyper-criticism the appreciative book of the kind just discussed is an extinct species. But any such remark would be half true at best. Rather what seems to have happened, at least in Romantics studies, is a reconciliation of the two approaches. Certainly the major contributions of recent years have increasingly wedded the critical and the appreciative perspectives. It is no longer bad form for the scholar-critic to show his enthusiasm along with his talents for research and explication; similarly the man of letters need no longer apologize for his erudition. To cite examples here would be only to repeat authors and titles already discussed above, particularly in these last two sub-sections but generally throughout the chapter, or to engage in "the relevance game" by observing, for example, that Paul Goodman, hero of the "counter-culture," seldom passes up the opportunity, whatever his subject, to pay tribute to Wordsworth. (On the subject of relevance, see Karl Kroeber's witty and provocative essay, "The Relevance and Irrelevance of Romanticism," *SIR*, 1970.) Suffice it to say that some see in this trend the Romantic consciousness come into its own. If this should be the true state of affairs, then Romantics studies are not merely holding their own or making satisfactory progress but are indeed "stepping westward."

II
WORDSWORTH

Ernest Bernbaum

James V. Logan, Jr.

Ford T. Swetnam, Jr.

I. BIBLIOGRAPHIES

The nearest approach to a full bibliography of books, manuscripts, and Wordsworthiana is George Harris Healey's *The Cornell Wordsworth Collection: A Catalogue of Books and Manuscripts Presented to the University by Mr. Victor Emanuel, Cornell 1919* (1957). The catalogue lists 3206 items, and includes very full bibliographic descriptions of works published by Wordsworth during his lifetime. Other sections include Writings of Wordsworth in Book Form, 1851–1955; Writings of Wordsworth in Early Periodicals (not complete); Writings of Wordsworth in Early Anthologies and Other Books; Wordsworthiana (the largest section); Coleridge and His Family; The Lake District; Books of Associative Interest (from Wordsworth's library, presentation copies, etc.); Manuscripts; and Miscellaneous Items. Healey's volume supersedes L. N. Broughton's earlier bibliographies of the Cornell Wordsworth Collection (1931, supplemented 1942). Other bibliographies include Cornelius Howard Patton, *The Amherst Wordsworth Collection: A Descriptive Bibliography* (1936), William Hale White's *Description of the Wordsworth and Coleridge Manuscripts in the Possession of Mr. T. Norton Longman* (1897), which describes manuscripts now in the Yale University Library, and two bibliographies by Thomas James Wise, which describe books now in the British Museum: *A Bibliography of The Writings in Prose and Verse of William Wordsworth* (1916) and *Two Lake Poets: A Catalogue of Printed Books, Manuscripts, and Autograph Letters by William Wordsworth and Samuel Taylor Coleridge* (1927; rpt. 1965), which, although they are generally quite reliable, contain at least one forgery (of "To the Queen, 1846"; see J. E. Wells, *PQ,* 1942). The admirable section on Wordsworth in the *New CBEL,* compiled by W. J. B. Owen, lists criticism through 1967.

Among the miscellaneous bibliographical studies are David F. Foxon's "The Printing of *Lyrical Ballads, 1798*" (*The Library,* 1954) and E. L. McAdam's "The Publication of *Lyrical Ballads, 1800*" (*Yale University Library Gazette,* 1933); two articles by J. E. Wells, *"Lyrical Ballads,* 1800: Cancel Leaves" (*PMLA,* 1938) and "Wordsworth's *Lyrical Ballads, 1820*" (*PQ,* 1938); Helen Darbishire's *Some Variants in Wordsworth's Text in the Volumes of 1836–7 in the King's Library* (1949), which is a discussion of some of Wordsworth's revisions; two discussions of "The Barberry Tree," one by Jonathan Wordsworth, "The New Wordsworth Poem" (*CE,* 1966), the other by Mark Reed, "More on the Wordsworth Poem" (*CE,* 1966); Jonathan Wordsworth's "A Wordsworth Tragedy" (*TLS,* 21 July 1966), an account of what is known about the *Somersetshire Tragedy,* the text of which was destroyed by Gordon Wordsworth; and some speculations by Fritz W. Schulze on "Wordsworthian and Coleridgian Texts (1784–1822) Mostly Unidentified or Misplaced" in *Strena Anglica,* ed. Gerhard Dietrich and Fritz W. Schulze (1956).

Bicentenary Wordsworth Studies in Memory of John Alban Finch (1970), ed. Jonathan Wordsworth, contains several articles of bibliographical interest. Finch's own "On the Dating of *Home at Grasmere:* A New Approach" proposes that much of the poem was done in 1806, not 1800; needless to say, acceptance of this dating would bring about important changes in the critical view of the evolution of Wordsworth's ideas. Also in the volume are "Wordsworth's Two-Handed Engine," in which Finch argues that the opening lines of *The Prelude* were composed 18 November 1799, and *"The Ruined Cottage* Restored: Three Stages of Composition, 1795–1798," which originally appeared in *JEGP* (1967). These essays suggest what remarkable things John Finch would have done had it not been for his early death. In addition to Finch's work, *Bicentenary Wordsworth Studies* contains essays by Stephen Parrish, who gives a text of the "ballad-*Michael*" in *"Michael* and the Pastoral Ballad"; by Stephen Gill, whose "The Original *Salisbury Plain*: Introduction and Text" opens up new critical insights about the poem as well as printing a stage of the poem that is difficult to recover from the de Selincourt-Darbishire text; by Carol Landon, who shows how Wordsworth drew on some of his school and college notebooks in "Some Sidelights on *The Prelude*"; by

G. H. Healey, who tells the story of "Cynthia Morgan St. John and Her Collection"; and by Beth Darlington, the assistant editor of the volume, who prints "Two Early Texts: *A Night-Piece* and *The Discharged Soldier.*"

The bibliography of the early years is quite complex, partly because of Coleridge's practice of submitting poems by Wordsworth to the newspapers. Jane Worthington Smyser, in her important article "Coleridge's Use of Wordsworth's Juvenilia" (*PMLA,* 1950), lists some of these appearances, as does Carol Landon in "Wordsworth, Coleridge, and the *Morning Post:* An Early Version of 'The Seven Sisters'" (*RES,* 1960). The most comprehensive account of these dealings is R. S. Woof's "Wordsworth's Poetry and Stuart's Newspapers: 1797–1803" (*SB,* 1962), which lists more than forty appearances of Wordsworth's poems in the *Morning Post* and *The Courier.* Stephen M. Parrish and David V. Erdman discuss one of the *Morning Post* poems in "Who Wrote *The Mad Monk?* A Debate" (*BNYPL,* 1960).

Invaluable bibliographies of criticism have been provided by James V. Logan, Elton F. Henley, and David H. Stam. Logan's *Wordsworthian Criticism: A Guide and Bibliography* (1947; rpt. 1961) has a selected list of major criticism from 1850 to 1899, and a comprehensive list for the period from 1900 to 1944. There are helpful annotations to the entries for each section. The first part of the book is an excellent survey of the main trends of criticism to 1944. Logan's work has been carried on by Henley and Stam, whose *Wordsworthian Criticism 1945–1964* (rev. ed. 1965) catalogues the great burst of Wordsworth scholarship in those nineteen years. Stam's revised edition of this bibliography will carry the story through 1970. Henley has also done *A Check List of Masters' Theses in the United States on William Wordsworth* (1961), which covers the period from 1887 through 1959. Finally, there is at long last a newsletter, *The Wordsworth Circle,* which, besides printing articles and reviews, lists work in progress. *The Wordsworth Circle* is published quarterly by the Department of English at Temple University. Its Fall 1970 issue contains a checklist of the Wordsworth collection at the Huntington Library prepared by Paul Zall. Subscribers to *TWC* have also received a brief account of the Indiana Wordsworth Collection by Russell Noyes (*Lilly Library Publications,* IX).

Reviews of Wordsworth's poetry may be found in Donald Reiman's collection *The Romantics Reviewed* (1972), in Elsie Smith's *An Estimate of Wordsworth by his Contemporaries, 1793–1822* (1932), which condenses much of its material, and in John Wain's *Contemporary Reviews of Romantic Poetry* (1953), which reprints essays by Jeffrey, John Wilson, and Lamb. For more on the reviews, see William S. Ward, "Wordsworth, the 'Lake' Poets, and Their Contemporary Magazine Critics, 1798–1820" (*SP*, 1945) and Jack C. Barnes, "A Bibliography of Wordsworth in American Periodicals through 1825" (*PBSA*, 1958). Thomas M. Raysor's observation in "The Establishment of Wordsworth's Reputation" (*JEGP*, 1955) that Wordsworth's poetry sold rather well until Jeffrey's damaging review of 1807 is corroborated and amplified by W. J. B. Owen in "Costs, Sales, and Profits of Longman's Editions of Wordsworth" (*Library*, 1957). For further information on Wordsworth's dealings with his publisher, see Owen's "Letters of Longman & Co. to Wordsworth, 1814–36" (*Library*, 1954). Russell Noyes has studied Wordsworth's most famous battles against hostile criticism in *Wordsworth and Jeffrey in Controversy* (1941); Owen suggests in "Wordsworth and Jeffrey in Collaboration" (*RES*, 1964) that Wordsworth borrowed some of his best points from his opponents. Herbert Lindenberger's "The Reception of *The Prelude*" (*BNYPL*, 1960) deals with that poem's failure to attract wide interest in 1850. Later developments may be seen in J. Dover Wilson's lecture, *Leslie Stephen and Matthew Arnold as Critics of Wordsworth* (1939); in W. A. Jamison, *Arnold and the Romantics* (1958), and Leon Gottfried, *Matthew Arnold and the Romantics* (1963); and in C. H. Patton, *The Rediscovery of Wordsworth* (1935; rpt. 1966). R. H. Fogle's two defenses of Romanticism against the New Critics, "Romantic Bards and Metaphysical Reviewers" (*ELH*, 1945) and "A Recent Attack Upon Romanticism" (*CE*, 1948), are reprinted, much changed, in *The Imagery of Keats and Shelley* (1949). There is an interesting interplay of attacks and defenses in *Wordsworth: Centenary Studies Presented at Cornell and Princeton Universities,* ed. Gilbert T. Dunklin (1951).

II. EDITIONS

Primarily because of the unstinting efforts of Ernest de Selincourt and Helen Darbishire, Wordsworth has been the most carefully and fully edited of the Romantic poets. Their standard edition, *The Poetical Works of William Wordsworth, Edited from the Manuscripts, with Textual and*

Critical Notes (5 vols.; rev. ed., 1952–59), follows the six-volume edition of 1849–50, the last one supervised by Wordsworth. The *apparatus criticus* provides a record of the growth of the poems, and the appendices give poems and fragments which Wordsworth either left in manuscript or expunged from his works. The notes that Wordsworth dictated to Isabella Fenwick are also included. *The Prelude, or Growth of a Poet's Mind, Edited from the Manuscripts with Introduction, Textual and Critical Notes* by Ernest de Selincourt, second edition revised by Helen Darbishire (1959), prints, on the right-hand page, the text that was published in 1850, and on the left, the text which Wordsworth read to Coleridge in 1807. The notes and apparatus of this edition are very full, and the introduction is critically sound. For the second edition, Miss Darbishire was able to include a transcript of MS. JJ, the earliest substantial draft of what was to become *The Prelude.*

The de Selincourt-Darbishire edition is a splendid work of scholarship; few poets are so fortunate in their editors. Yet there remain textual problems in Wordsworth scholarship, as Jonathan Wordsworth's remark that most poets "are known by the best versions of their works: Wordsworth is almost exclusively known by the worst" might indicate (*The Music of Humanity,* p. xiii). The difficulty stems from Wordsworth's extensive revisions, carried out over a long period of time during which his philosophical views changed, and from his arrangement of his poems into groups illustrative of various faculties of the mind and stages of the mind's growth. De Selincourt's editorial practice is of course sound, and Wordsworth's arrangement is not without its logic, as James Scoggins has shown in his critical study, *Imagination and Fancy: Complementary Modes in the Poetry of Wordsworth* (1966). Nonetheless, the chronological pattern of Wordsworth's works, the integrity of his individual volumes and even of his individual poems may be sacrificed by following Wordsworth's last corrected edition, as de Selincourt recognized when he printed two reading texts of *The Prelude.* Despite the excellence of the standard edition, then, there is a real place for editions of individual volumes of Wordsworth's poetry and for the one-volume chronological edition of the poems which Jonathan Wordsworth and Stephen Gill are preparing.

There is a fine edition of the *Lyrical Ballads,* the volume most obviously requiring separate treatment, by R. L. Brett and A. R. Jones (1963; rev. ed., 1965). The editors give the original texts of the poems printed in 1798 and 1800, with variants from the 1802 and 1805 editions. There are tables to show the various arrangements of the poems, and good notes. The

Lyrical Ballads of 1798 has been edited most recently by W. J. B. Owen (1967; 2nd ed., 1969). Helen Darbishire's edition of the *Poems in Two Volumes, 1807* (2nd ed., 1952) has excellent notes on Wordsworth's remin'scences of older poetry. There are editions of the *Ecclesiastical Sonnets* by Abbie F. Potts (1922) and of *The White Doe of Rylstone* by Alice P. Comparetti (1940). The poem which perhaps gains the most from a separate edition is *The Ruined Cottage.* Before it was published as the first book of *The Excursion,* Wordsworth had obscured the bare lines of the original narrative. Jonathan Wordsworth's *The Music of Humanity: A Critical Study of Wordsworth's* Ruined Cottage *Incorporating Texts from a Manuscript of 1799–1800* (1969) restores this important document of Wordsworth's attempts to come to terms with human suffering. The associated text of *The Pedlar,* in which Wordsworth develops the new philosophical ideas first seen in the Alfoxden fragments, is also given, and there is a full critical discussion of both poems. Additional material on the growth of the poem may be found in Helen Darbishire, " 'The Ruined Cottage' and 'The Excursion',", in *Essays Mainly on the Nineteenth Century Presented to Sir Humphrey Milford* (1948); Thomas M. Raysor, "Wordsworth's Early Drafts of *The Ruined Cottage* in 1797–98" (*JEGP,* 1956); and John A. Finch, " 'The Ruined Cottage' Restored: Three Stages of Composition, 1795–1798" (*JEGP,* 1967; rpt. in *Bicentenary Wordsworth Studies*).

The most elaborate of the specialized editions will be the Cornell Wordsworth, a series in which de Selincourt's editorial principle will be reversed. Wordsworth's longer works will be presented in their earliest completed form, rather than their latest; all variant readings will also be given. The general editor of the series, Stephen M. Parrish, reports that for some poems, as many as four different kinds of text will be presented: a) the published texts of the poems concerned, b) photographic reproduction of some of the pages in the manuscripts, c) full transcriptions of the manuscripts, with the type arranged, as far as is practical, to reflect the appearance of the manuscript page, and d) simplified "reading" versions of the underlying basic texts of the manuscripts. The first volume in the series, *Salisbury Plain,* ed. Stephen Gill, will present three distinct poems: *Salisbury Plain,* completed about 1794, *A Night on Salisbury Plain,* completed and transcribed by 1799, and *Guilt and Sorrow,* the version Wordsworth finally published, which was completed about 1841. Each of these poems will be presented in full with all variant readings. Anyone who has ever tried to reconstruct the earlier texts from de Selincourt's edition, which follows the final version of *Guilt and Sorrow,* will appreciate the need for this new series, in which at least ten other volumes are projected.

Among the one-volume editions of Wordsworth's poems, Thomas Hutchinson's *Poetical Works* (1895; rev. ed., 1950) is still satisfactory for most purposes. It may be supplemented with the Oxford edition of the 1805 *Prelude* (1933; 2nd ed., 1970). The *Concordance to the Poems of William Wordsworth,* by Lane Cooper (1911), is based on Hutchinson's edition and therefore does not analyze such important works as the 1805 *Prelude.* Nevertheless, it is quite useful within its limits. *The Critical Opinions of William Wordsworth,* by Markham L. Peacock, Jr. (1950; rpt. 1969), is a useful compilation of Wordsworth's remarks on various literary subjects (poetic diction, purpose in writing, etc.), on other authors and their works, and on his own writings. There is a good index, and the entries are cross-referenced. Karl Kroeber has been working on a computer concordance to the 1805 *Prelude.*

The prose writings are at last being issued in a truly scholarly edition by W. J. B. Owen and Jane Worthington Smyser. They will be printed in chronological order, with each work having both a critical introduction and a textual introduction. In the case of a work published by Wordsworth, the text is based on his own final edition; the textual apparatus preserves all the verbal variants from earlier editions as well as all the variants from extant manuscripts. In the case of a work not published in Wordsworth's lifetime, the text is the final manuscript version, with variant readings from earlier drafts recorded in the textual apparatus; the variants also preserve deletions. The critical commentaries seek to gloss all quotations and allusions, and to make the appropriate cross-references to the prose, poetical works, and letters. The appendices preserve documents related to Wordsworth's prose writings, such as the Letter of "Mathetes" by John Wilson. The editors have omitted the prose notes Wordsworth attached to various poems, as well as the notes he dictated to Isabella Fenwick, because they are available in the *Poetical Works.* This edition will replace those of A. B. Grosart (3 vols., 1876) and William Knight (2 vols., 1896). I am most grateful to Mrs. Smyser for her advance description of the new edition.

Some of the prose has been separately edited: Paul M. Zall's *Literary Criticism of William Wordsworth* (1966) is perhaps more widely available than the older edition by Nowell C. Smith (1905); *Wordsworth's Tract on the Convention of Cintra* has been edited by A. V. Dicey (1915).

De Selincourt has edited *Wordsworth's* Guide to the Lakes (1926); another edition of the *Guide* (1952), which also follows the text of 1835, has an introductory essay on "Wordsworth and the Picturesque" by W. M. Merchant, but has no notes. De Selincourt's slightly inaccurate transcription of the important preface to *The Borderers* is most conveniently found in the first volume of the *Poetical Works.* Wordsworth's uncompleted essay upon the moral habits is transcribed, with commentary, by Geoffrey Little (*REL,* 1961).

The writings of Dorothy Wordsworth, which provide a crucial record of the events in the Wordsworth household, have been edited by Ernest de Selincourt in *Journals of Dorothy Wordsworth* (2 vols., 1941; rpt. 1959), which includes Dorothy's accounts of the Scottish and Continental tours; by Helen Darbishire in *Journals: The Alfoxden Journal, 1798; The Grasmere Journal, 1800–1803* (1958), whose text is better than de Selincourt's, though her edition is less comprehensive; and by Mary Moorman (1971).

The Letters of William and Dorothy Wordsworth, which de Selincourt published in six volumes (1935–39), are being re-edited to include the many Wordsworth letters that have come to light subsequently. The revised edition also has more comprehensive and helpful notes than its predecessor. The letters of *The Early Years, 1787–1805* have been issued (1967) by Chester L. Shaver, who was able to include forty letters not in the first edition. Mary Moorman and Alan G. Hill have revised the letters of *The Middle Years, 1806–1820* (2 vols., 1969–70). These volumes include the numerous letters written to Henry Crabb Robinson, which were formerly available only in Edith J. Morley's edition of the *Correspondence of Henry Crabb Robinson with the Wordsworth Circle* (1927) and the letters published by L. N. Broughton in *Some Letters of the Wordsworth Family* (1942). There are also about 150 previously unpublished letters from Wordsworth to William, Earl of Lonsdale, and to the Earl's son, Viscount Lowther. Alan G. Hill will edit the letters of *The Later Years, 1821– 1850.* These letters will be spread over four volumes, and will include those published by L. N. Broughton in *Wordsworth and Reed: The Poet's Correspondence with His American Editor, 1836–1850* (1933). There will also be, at the very least, two hundred letters previously unpublished. The final volume will have an appendix of letters from Wordsworth's early and middle years which turned up too late to be included in the appropriate volume, and a comprehensive index to the whole series. Mr. Hill, to whom I am indebted for this information, expects the edition to be completed in five to ten years. This work of revision is extremely useful, as it reduces the need to consult a multitude of separate editions. Broughton's volume, because it prints Reed's letters as well as Wordsworth's, will not be completely replaced, and the letters of Wordsworth's other correspondents, particularly those of Coleridge, Lamb, Crabb Robinson, and De Quincey, whose correspondence with the Wordsworths has been edited by John E. Jordan in *De Quincey to Wordsworth: A Biography of a Relationship* (1962), remain indispensable to the close study of any episode of Wordsworth's life. There are three notable editions of the correspondence of members of Wordsworth's family: Kathleen Coburn has edited *The Letters of Sara Hutchinson from 1800 to 1835* (1954), Mary E. Burton has made a selection of 178 *Letters of Mary Wordsworth, 1800–1855* (1958), and fifty-one surviving *Letters of John Wordsworth* have been edited by Carl H. Ketcham (1969).

III. BIOGRAPHICAL STUDIES

The many discussions of Wordsworth's life and character published before the appearance of Christopher Wordsworth's official *Memoirs of William Wordsworth* in 1851 have been described by Walter E. Swayze in "Early Wordsworthian Biography" (*BNYPL*, 1960). Christopher's biography of his uncle, which stresses his orthodoxy and slights his youth, is discreet, pious, and largely uninformative. Some of the limitations of the *Memoirs* were deliberate, as Christopher intended neither a full-scale biography nor a commentary on the poetry, but illustrations of Wordsworth's life and character. The *Memoirs* do contain Wordsworth's own Autobiographical Memoranda.

Some later biographers perhaps overemphasized the qualities that Christopher played down, giving us a "Byronic Wordsworth" instead of "Daddy Wordsworth," as H. W. Garrod remarked of George McLean Harper's *William Wordsworth: His Life, Works, and Influence* (2 vols., 1916; rev. and abridged, 1929). Some of Harper's emphases were indeed doubtful; his lack of sympathy with Wordsworth's later years and his minimizing of the spiritual crisis of 1793–95 have been criticized as weak spots. His biography was nevertheless a good one, and a solid accomplishment in literary criticism as well. It was also Harper who made public Wordsworth's relationship with Annette Vallon, which he described in *Wordsworth's French Daughter* (1921); Emile Legouis added considerable information to Harper's account in *William Wordsworth and Annette Vallon* (1922).

In the years since the publication of Harper's biography, much more material, particularly about the poetry, has come to light. Mary Moorman's *William Wordsworth: A Biography* (2 vols., 1957–65), a comprehensive and sympathetic narrative which is now the standard life, takes advantage of such crucial documents as the early drafts of *The Prelude,* the Godwin diaries, the Lonsdale papers, and the de Selincourt-Darbishire editions of the poems and letters to present a great deal of information very lucidly. Mrs. Moorman has no special case to plead, and her biography is consequently free of the distortions and overemphases of some of her predecessors. Her assessment of Wordsworth's relationship with Annette is generally sane; while she may underestimate the strength of Wordsworth's attachment and the qualities of Annette herself, she does not metamorphose the affair into a guilty and tormenting passion, as had been done by Sir Herbert Read in *Wordsworth* (1930) and Hugh I'Anson Fausset in *The Lost Leader* (1933). Mrs. Moorman presents Wordsworth's feelings about Annette as a contribution to his spiritual crisis, but not the cause of it. The friendship with Coleridge and the eventual estrangement are both handled fairly. Perhaps the collaboration between the two partners of *Lyrical Ballads* was not as close as they themselves sometimes allege it to have been, and perhaps Wordsworth's part in the quarrel was more regrettable than Mrs. Moorman indicates, but, particularly in the latter case, she makes a careful presentation of the evidence. The account of Wordsworth's politics, early and late, is also judicious; his acceptance of the office of Distributor of Stamps is defended, and the late conservatism, which is often difficult to make attractive, is at least made understandable. Mrs. Moorman relies heavily but intelligently upon *The Prelude* to suggest the quality of Wordsworth's life, and consequently stresses the visionary side of Wordsworth's youth and early manhood. Unfortunately, her book is not distinguished as literary criticism, though it uses the poems very well as biographical documents. The great virtues of this biography lie in its wealth of information, in its careful organization, and in its fair-mindedness.

In following *The Prelude,* Mrs. Moorman takes the path first marked out by Emile Legouis, whose *La Jeunesse de Wordsworth, 1770–1798* (1896; English trans. by J. W. Matthews, 1897; 3rd ed., 1932) was the first major study to emphasize the importance of that poem; indeed,

Legouis subtitled his book *A Commentary on* The Prelude. It is still quite a readable account, having particularly useful critical material on Wordsworth's poetry up to the publication of the *Lyrical Ballads*. Where Legouis and Moorman follow *The Prelude,* George Wilbur Meyer, in *Wordsworth's Formative Years* (1943), did not consider the poem a valid source for biography, arguing that it is a rhetorical work whose value as fact is distorted by the gloss the older Wordsworth wished to put on his earlier experiences. There is a good deal of common sense to Meyer's position; any autobiography involves the mediating efforts of its author, and Wordsworth was neither particularly scrupulous about facts nor concerned with giving an exact record of his growth. To this extent, then, *The Prelude* is unreliable. But Meyer certainly overstates his case at a number of points, and his psychological readings of the poems are sometimes rather crude. There is much to be said for his procedure, however; it has certainly influenced the care with which Mrs. Moorman uses *The Prelude.* Meyer's perception that Wordsworth was not always completely certain about some of the higher points of his faith is also valuable, as it is a point of view which is basic to much modern criticism.

For really detailed work, such as tracing the growth of a poem or following the daily movements of Wordsworth, the best source is Mark L. Reed, *Wordsworth: The Chronology of the Early Years, 1770–1799* (1967) and its succeeding volumes. Reed presents a sequential account of the basic factual information of Wordsworth's life, selected for its relevance but still more abundantly given than elsewhere. Naturally, the chronology also records the important movements of Dorothy, Coleridge, and other people whose lives touched Wordsworth's at many points. More speculative information, references to scholarly debates, and incidental material are given in the footnotes, and the appendices and prefatory matter provide careful arguments about such points as Wordsworth's early travels in Wales and the 1798 visits of Hazlitt and Cottle. There is also a convenient General Chronological List of Wordsworth's Writings, which includes manuscript work, and extensive material on the composition of such important works as *The Borderers, Salisbury Plain, The Ruined Cottage,* and "Nutting." There will be two more volumes of this valuable research tool: the second, which will be published in 1972, will cover the period from 1800 to 1815, and the third, which will understandably be more selective than the first two, will cover the last thirty-five years of Wordsworth's life.

Among the more specialized studies, F. M. Todd's *Politics and the Poet* (1957) is a careful and unbiased account of Wordsworth's developing political opinions. Zera S. Fink's *The Early Wordsworthian Milieu* (1958), a study of a notebook of the poet's brother Christopher in which William also made some entries, throws light on the kinds of literary influence the boys felt in their school days. Ben Ross Schneider's *Wordsworth's Cambridge Education* (1957) has much useful information on the course of study followed at St. John's College and on the way of life of students there in the last years of the eighteenth century.

Additional studies of Wordsworth's youth include Ernest de Selincourt's *The Early Wordsworth* (1936), an address which is reprinted in *Wordsworthian and Other Studies* (1947). De Selincourt discusses Wordsworth's juvenile poetry, and argues that Mary Hutchinson was more important in the poet's early life than was Annette Vallon. Carol Landon's article on "Wordsworth's Racedown Period: Some Uncertainties Resolved" (*BNYPL*, 1964) has material on some of Wordsworth's early poems. David V. Erdman's two-part essay on "Coleridge, Wordsworth, and the Wedgwood Fund" (*BNYPL*, 1956) discusses a visionary scheme for the reform of education, Wordsworth's reaction to which, Erdman argues in the second part of his article, helped to form the ideas on the growth of the child's mind which got into *The Pedlar* and, ultimately, *The Prelude*. Wordsworth's relationship with his longtime friend James Losh has been described by Paul Kaufman in "Wordsworth's 'Candid and Enlightened Friend' " (*N&Q*, 1962).

The relationship with Coleridge is one of the most complex and problematical episodes in Wordsworth's early life. Even the circumstances of their meeting are unclear, as Reed's *Chronology* and Robert Woof's essay "Wordsworth and Coleridge: Some Early Matters" in *Bicentenary Wordsworth Studies* demonstrate. What happened after the meeting is subject to conflicting interpretation. E. L. Griggs, in "Wordsworth through Coleridge's Eyes" (*Wordsworth: Centenary Studies*), maintains that Wordsworth's coldness and indifference to Coleridge's poetical powers discouraged and helped to deaden them. His self-centered attitude and later impatience with Coleridge were a heavy blow to Coleridge's sensitive nature. A. M. Buchan takes a similar point of view in "The Influence of Wordsworth on Coleridge (1795–1800)" (*UTQ*, 1963), which argues that Wordsworth's unwillingness to confront the darker elements in Coleridge's poetry contributed to Coleridge's despair. In *Wordsworth and*

Coleridge, 1795–1834 (1953), H. M. Margoliouth takes a gentler and more traditional view of the celebrated friendship, presenting it basically as an ennobling interchange in which both friends found something they needed to fully develop their talents. Three literary studies cast doubt on accounts, including Coleridge's, of close collaboration between himself and Wordsworth. Mark L. Reed's "Wordsworth, Coleridge, and the 'Plan' of the *Lyrical Ballads*" (*UTQ*, 1965) argues that there was little coherent sense of purpose in the publication of the volume, whose contents were determined by "a late decision among a variety of choices they had been exploring." Max F. Schulz, in "Coleridge, Wordsworth, and the 1800 Preface to *Lyrical Ballads*" (*SEL*, 1965), proposes that far from being a shared enterprise, half a child of Coleridge's brain, the Preface was put together by Wordsworth after Coleridge failed to write it, and therefore contains the seeds of the later critical disagreement. Stephen M. Parrish, in "The Wordsworth-Coleridge Controversy" (*PMLA*, 1958), sees the controversy arising even earlier, in the attempts at collaboration on "The Three Graves," "Cain," and "The Ancient Mariner." William Heath has devoted a book to a crucial year in the relationship in *Wordsworth and Coleridge: A Study of their Literary Relations in 1801–1802* (1970). Heath presents the year as a turning point in the lives of both men. He sees important changes in the stance and language of the poetry, with Wordsworth moving towards an objective way of expressing emotion and Coleridge towards the subjective language of the first version of "Dejection." These changes, which were perhaps not as dramatic as Heath considers them to have been, were brought about in response to the extraordinarily complex emotional demands on Wordsworth and Coleridge during this period. For Wordsworth, the attitude expressed in "Resolution and Independence," which Heath sees as the climactic poem of the year, meant survival both as a man and as a poet.

The great problem of the later years is Wordsworth's decline. The effect of the death of John Wordsworth has been explored by E. L. McAdam, Jr., in "Wordsworth's Shipwreck" (*PMLA*, 1962) and by R. C. Townsend in "John Wordsworth and His Brother's Poetic Development" (*PMLA*, 1966). E. H. Hartsell's "The Date of the 'Ode to Duty'" (*TLS*, 30 May 1935) and Nowell Smith's supplementary letter of 20 June demonstrated that the Fenwick note which gave the date of composition of that somber poem as 1805 was inaccurate, and that the "Ode" must have been composed rather early in 1804. Therefore, this poem cannot have been affected by the death of John Wordsworth, and William's increasing austerity must have had other causes. In *Wordsworth's Anti-Climax* (1935), a study of the whole question of Wordsworth's decline, Willard Sperry demonstrated that the many simplistic explanations for the falling-off are insufficient, but his contention that Wordsworth simply exhausted his reservoir of childhood memories is similarly inadequate. A. L. Strout, in "Wordsworth's Desiccation" (*MLR*, 1940), also weighs many possible causes of the decline, and attempts to allow for both continuity and change within Wordsworth's work. The later poetry has no lack of defenders; Edith C. Batho, in *The Later Wordsworth* (1933), argues that Wordsworth's abilities, though differently directed, were essentially undiminished, and that Wordsworth himself was not as unattractive as he has been made out to have been; Mary E. Burton, in *The One Wordsworth* (1942), maintains that Wordsworth's revisions of *The Prelude* show that his powers in later life were still great. Both sail against the tide, and have heavy going of it, although Miss Batho's book is a useful corrective to Harper's emphasis on Wordsworth's youth and liberalism. John Jones writes well of Wordsworth's later Christian poetry in *The Egotistical Sublime* (1954), and Bernard Groom asserts its consistency with the themes and techniques of Wordsworth's earlier work in *The Unity of Wordsworth's Poetry* (1966).

Wordsworth's activities in support of the Lonsdale interest in the 1818 election in Westmorland have been described by J. E. Wells, "Wordsworth and De Quincey in Westmorland Politics, 1818" (*PMLA*, 1940); in an addendum to Wells's article by L. N. Broughton (*PMLA*, 1941); and by W. W. Douglas in "Wordsworth in Politics: The Westmorland Election of 1818" (*MLN*, 1948). His dedicated support of the Copyright Act of 1842 has been traced by Paul M. Zall (*PMLA*, 1955; see the addendum by Russell Noyes, *PMLA*, 1961). J. E. Wells has recorded Wordsworth's agitation over unwelcome political and economic events in "Wordsworth and Railways in 1844–45" (*MLQ*, 1945), and de Selincourt has described some agitation over the unwelcome Quillinan in "Wordsworth and His Daughter's Marriage" in *Wordsworth and Coleridge*, ed. E. L. Griggs (1939). H. D. Rawnsley's "Reminiscences of Wordsworth among the Peasantry of Westmorland" (*Transactions of the Wordsworth Society*, No. 6) is a colorful account of Wordsworth's later years. Most of this information is now, happily, found in Moorman.

Among the other biographies, Frederika Beatty's *William Words-*

worth of Rydal Mount (1939) and *William Wordsworth of Dove Cottage* (1964) are both enthusiastic and essentially popular works; Amanda M. Ellis' *Rebels and Conservatives* (1967) is a study of the relationships among the Wordsworth circle; W. W. Douglas' *Wordsworth: The Construction of a Personality* (1967) is a protest against the sentimentalization of Wordsworth's life, which Douglas believes Wordsworth fostered. All through his youth, Wordsworth's was a nearly disintegrating personality, making a mother image both of Nature and of Dorothy. Douglas' method has much in common with that of G. W. Meyer in *Wordsworth's Formative Years,* but his book is of less critical value than Meyer's. Douglas has also written on "The Problem of Wordsworth's Conservatism" (*Science and Society,* 1948) and on "Wordsworth as Business Man" (*PMLA,* 1948).

Wordsworthians who wish to see their man plain may do so in Frances Blanshard's *Portraits of Wordsworth* (1959), which includes reproductions of sixty-three portraits of the poet.

There are two biographies of Dorothy Wordsworth; one by Ernest de Selincourt (1933), which is standard, and one by Catherine M. Maclean (1932). John Wordsworth's life and death are described in *Wordsworth's Mariner Brother* (1966), by Frank Prentice Rand, but the introduction to Ketcham's edition of John's letters is far superior.

Information about Wordsworth's reading may be found in the *Rydal Mount Catalogue* of his books in *Transactions of the Wordsworth Society,* No. 6, which, since it lists only those books which the Wordsworth family did not wish to keep, must be used with caution. Other studies include Kurt Lienemann's *Die Belesenheit von William Wordsworth* (1908); the references to other authors in Peacock's compilation of Wordsworth's critical opinions; and C. N. Coe's *Wordsworth and the Literature of Travel* (1953). There is a manuscript catalogue of Wordsworth's books in the Widener Collection at Harvard.

Scholars of Wordsworth, then, are in the happy position of having sound texts, edited from a variety of points of view; excellent bibliographies of criticism; a first-rate biography, which provides a fair and comprehensive history of Wordsworth's life and works; and a chronology which provides more detailed information about his movements and activities. Biographical and textual problems do remain, but we may feel quite confident about the authority of the basic materials of Wordsworth scholarship.

IV. STUDIES OF IDEAS, CHIEFLY PHILOSOPHICAL, POLITICAL, AND RELIGIOUS

Every age creates its own Wordsworth. The Victorian debate between Leslie Stephen and Matthew Arnold over whether Wordsworth could be considered a philosopher at all was begun by Stephen's essay on "Wordsworth's Ethics" (*Cornhill Magazine,* 1876; rpt. in *Hours in a Library*). Arnold, who elevated the lyric poet over the thinker, and argued in the enormously influential introduction to his selection of the *Poems of Wordsworth* (1879) that the poet's business had been with nature, not with ideas, could nonetheless speak feelingly of Wordsworth's "healing power." Despite their differences, Arnold and Stephen were in underlying agreement that what was philosophically worthwhile in Wordsworth had to do with ethics, rather than with epistemology or, perish the thought, metaphysics. Wordsworth was the poet whose ability to lay us on the cool flowery lap of earth or to inspire fortitude and patient cheer could resolve a mental crisis like that of John Stuart Mill or of Stephen himself. This view of Wordsworth did not disappear in the twentieth century; it figures prominently in the writings of such Wordsworthians as Ernest Bernbaum and Bennett Weaver. But questions of ethics have generally given way to the study of the great problem in Wordsworth's thought, the relationship of the mind with nature, and the conception of Wordsworth as the poet able to allay the doubts and fears of others must be set against the recent view that Wordsworth could not resolve his own inner conflicts.

The first important modern contribution to the study of Wordsworth's philosophy was Arthur Beatty's *William Wordsworth: His Doctrine and Art in their Historical Relations* (1922; rev. ed., 1927), which presented the case for the strong influence of David Hartley's associationist psychology upon Wordsworth's work. Beatty's book was conceived as a defense of Wordsworth as a philosophical poet against those who, following Arnold, rigorously separated the poetry and the philosophy, and certainly such an argument needed to be made. But Beatty bound Wordsworth rather too tightly to the English Associationist tradition; Wordsworth did not for long believe the mind was merely passive, for example, and his theory of human development is far from identical with Hartley's.

In *Presiding Ideas in Wordsworth's Poetry* (1931), which was one of the first detailed comparisons between the 1805 and 1850 texts of *The*

Prelude, Melvin M. Rader corrected Beatty's emphasis by showing the continuing presence of transcendental ideas in Wordsworth's writings. Rader's later book, *Wordsworth: A Philosophical Approach* (1967), is very closely based upon his earlier monograph; the book takes advantage of some, but not all, of the relevant recent scholarship in advancing essentially the same argument. Rader finds that Hartley's influence on the poetry was transitory. He shows that it was Hartley's emphasis upon the growth of the moral sense and his binding together of present and past by the law of association that attracted Wordsworth, who nonetheless shied away from Hartley's mechanistic necessitarianism. Rader establishes that Wordsworth was influenced by a good deal more than associationism, but he does not delineate very exactly what Wordsworth did know. He finds that Wordsworth's ideas resemble those of Shaftesbury, Rousseau, Spinoza, Kant, and Plato, among others, and he takes Coleridge's great knowledge of these philosophers to imply Wordsworth's, but the precise nature of the influence remains unclear. Rader concludes that Wordsworth became more of a transcendentalist as he grew older, coming to believe that "The base of the world is God" and that the "highest faculties" in man and the world revealed by the senses alike arise from this base. The function of sense is to call the inner faculties into play, rather than into being, and to sustain them with the conviction that the external world is exquisitely fitted to the mind. "The mightiest life is to be achieved by combining the empirical and transcendental factors into a most potent unity."

Newton P. Stallknecht's *Strange Seas of Thought: Studies in William Wordsworth's Philosophy of Man and Nature* (1945; 2nd ed., 1958), like Rader's books, is in part an argument against Beatty's emphasis upon Locke and Hartley, but his chapter on "Hartley Transcendentalized by Coleridge" does attempt to give Hartley due place. Stallknecht's chief interest, however, is in Wordsworth as a mystic, whose theory of the imagination was heavily influenced by Jakob Boehme and whose ethics owe much to Spinoza. To advance these arguments, Stallknecht, like Rader, relies heavily upon Coleridge's well-documented dealings with philosophy to suggest the tendencies of Wordsworth's mind, though he does bring to bear many parallels between Wordsworth's poetry and the philosophy to which it is compared. For Stallknecht, the chief characteristic of Wordsworth's philosophy is its emphasis on freedom. The imagination, which grows freely and organically rather than by "laws of association," confers freedom upon those who live imaginative lives; it reconciles "emotion, intelligence, and volition, and frees the soul from conflict." In his chapter on "The Tragic

Flaw in Wordsworth's Philosophy," Stallknecht suggests that Wordsworth's mind was unable to bear the freedom with which his philosophy endowed it, and he retreated to the concept of duty, which supplied him with metaphysical and moral imperatives. Here, Stallknecht anticipates the recent concern with the existential consequences of Wordsworth's philosophical beliefs.

Part of the contention among Beatty, Rader, and Stallknecht involves Wordsworth's theory of the growth of his own soul. Beatty first made popular the theory that Wordsworth believed in three ages of man: childhood, the age of sensation; youth, the age of "aching joys and dizzy raptures"; and maturity, the age of the philosophic mind. As R. D. Havens pointed out in *The Mind of a Poet* (1941), such a system is not much more than a commonplace, and Wordsworth's poetry does not in any case conform to it. Rader's scheme is more elaborate than Beatty's, having five stages, essentially adding a stage of fancy and a stage of reason as an analytical faculty to Beatty's three ages. It, too, has a mechanical air about it, and it is difficult to apply to any poem but *The Prelude,* from which it is drawn. A recent article by Robert Langbaum, "The Evolution of Soul in Wordsworth's Poetry" (*PMLA,* 1967), stresses, as Stallknecht had done, the organic nature of this growth, and shows, without reference to stages, how impulses from within and without combine to bring the soul to maturity.

Other important influences on Wordsworth's philosophy have been proposed by Ellen D. Leyburn in "Berkeleian Elements in Wordsworth's Thought" (*JEGP,* 1948) and by Joseph Warren Beach, whose chapter on Wordsworth in *The Concept of Nature in Nineteenth-Century English Poetry* (1936) contains considerable material on the Cambridge Platonists as well as on most of the other possible sources. In *Wordsworth and the Great System: A Study of Wordsworth's Poetic Universe* (1970), G. H. Durrant has argued that Newton, who is another of the sources Beach considers, was tremendously important to Wordsworth's way of perceiving the world and organizing his perceptions into poetry. According to Durrant, Wordsworth's mathematical and scientific interests made him less concerned with particular objects than with their place in the great system described by Newton. No one would deny that Wordsworth seeks to describe relationships rather than things, but whether those relationships are in any meaningful way Newtonian is another question. In *The Active Universe: Pantheism and the Concept of Imagination in the English Romantic Poets* (1962), H. W. Piper argues that Wordsworth's "religion of Nature" was drawn from English Unitarian and, particularly, French radical sources, both of which in turn drew upon scientific theories "in which the system of inert matter was replaced by a system of forces, of which matter itself might be only an effect." With this system of forces, Piper connects the Romantic doctrine of the life in things. He points to the lines Wordsworth added to *An Evening Walk* at Windy Brow in 1794, soon after his return from France, as evidence that the poet's mature philosophy was formed before his meeting with Coleridge, and was influenced by such works as d'Holbach's *Système de la nature* and Volney's *Les Ruines . . . des empires.*

Piper's case is weak in several important particulars. His interesting account of the circles in which he presumes Wordsworth to have moved in Paris and London is vitiated by several errors in fact and by the generally inferential quality of the argument, and the lines written at Windy Brow, while they may be taken as an extrapolation from Unitarian, Deist, or quasi-scientific thought, may be less epochal in the development of Words-worth's thought than Piper and G. W. Meyer have taken them to be. No similar ideas appear in Wordsworth's verse for more than two years after the stay at Windy Brow, so it seems unlikely that Wordsworth's philos-ophy had been formed by then. Piper does have some interesting material on the pantheistic tendencies of late eighteenth-century science, though he pushes some of his texts to the limit, and on the influence of *The Excursion,* whose effect we are inclined to underestimate even though Keats found it full of "mighty workings."

Elizabeth Sewell's *The Orphic Voice: Poetry and Natural History* (1960) has an extensive section on "Wordsworth and Rilke: Toward a Biology of Thinking," in which the vitalist ideas with which Piper is working are discussed with reference to the survival and mutation of the Orpheus myth. *The Orphic Voice,* like *The Active Universe,* is concerned with the ways in which science sought to escape the constrictions of its method, to approximate the "postlogic" of myth or poetry; Erasmus Darwin, for example, figures prominently in both books. The correspon-dences between Piper's book and Sewell's wider-ranging study are remark-able indeed, particularly when the difference in their methods is considered.

As Piper's book suggests, the distinction between materialism and transcendentalism is sometimes hard to draw; most recent commentators, including Rader in his later book, have concluded that Wordsworth combined elements of the two systems in a sometimes precarious way. Certainly neither Hartley nor the transcendentalists, in themselves, can account for Wordsworth's beliefs, which were in any case constantly developing and changing. In discussing Wordsworth's idea of the relationship between the poet's imagination and the external world, René Wellek observes that "Wordsworth disconcertingly vacillates among three epistemological conceptions." Sometimes imagination is "purely subjective," sometimes it is "an illumination beyond the control of the conscious mind," and most often it implies some kind of collaboration between what is within and what is without (*A History of Modern Criticism*, Vol. II, 1955). Similar multiplicity of conception is evident in most of Wordsworth's philosophical views, and critics have necessarily come to concentrate on the paradoxes and potential conflicts in his thought.

Paradox is, in a sense, the subject of E. D. Hirsch, Jr., in *Wordsworth and Schelling: A Typological Study of Romanticism* (1960) and of C. C. Clarke in *Romantic Paradox: An Essay on the Poetry of Wordsworth* (1962). Both admire the equipoise Wordsworth found between regarding the mind as creator and regarding it as perceiver. Their methods of proceeding are different: Hirsch compares Wordsworth's poems with parallel passages in Schelling, while Clarke studies three words, "image," "shape," and "form," as a means of coming at Wordsworth's paradoxical attitude towards the natural world. Hirsch's book is perhaps the more traditional of the two, for it treats Wordsworth's "both-and" logic, which argues that there is no radical separation between thing and thought or life and death, in an almost entirely optimistic light. For Hirsch, the mind may occasionally be blocked or baffled in its drive for unity, but that is no really desperate crisis—"Striving never ceases, but in striving itself man fulfills his nature." Such, at any rate, is the state of affairs up until the shock recorded in "Elegiac Stanzas," when Wordsworth's denial of contrary states of being is itself denied. For the most part, however, Hirsch emphasizes the underlying identity between such supposed opposites as time and eternity and God and the world as it is seen in "The Two April Mornings," "Tintern Abbey," *The Prelude,* and, most particularly, the *Immortality Ode.* Clarke's brief but suggestive treatment views the relationship between mind and nature as a more problematical one: there is a good deal of dramatic tension in the poetry because Wordsworth's "conviction that the natural world is solid, and substantially 'other' than the mind that contemplates it, had to come to terms with his conviction that what we perceive is inevitably mind-dependent." Clarke finds that the bond of union between life and joy, although sundered in the *Immortality Ode,* is generally successfully forged, and the epistemological ambiguities contribute "to rich and noble effects."

In *Coleridge and Wordsworth: The Poetry of Growth* (1970), Stephen Prickett is concerned with some of the same material and reaches some of the same conclusions as Hirsch and Clarke. Prickett analyzes images like Coleridge's Brocken-spectre or Wordsworth's rainbow to show how they imply a creative interaction between the eye and the object. Both this interaction and the experience of sudden desolation lead to the affirmation of mental growth which Prickett sees as central to the romanticism of Coleridge and Wordsworth. The focus of the book is more on Coleridge than on Wordsworth, about whom there are some errors (he did not give *The Prelude* its title or subtitle), but there are some useful comparisons between the two poets.

The proposition that the conflict between the mind and the external world could only temporarily be resolved is central to the interpretations offered by F. W. Bateson in *Wordsworth: A Re-Interpretation* (1954; 2nd ed., 1956) and John Jones in *The Egotistical Sublime: A History of Wordsworth's Imagination* (1954). For Bateson, Wordsworth's poetry has "Two Voices," the "Augustan," realistic, objective poetry of the ballad and narrative class; and the subjective, reflective, "Romantic" type. The best poetry occurs when the "Two Voices" combine "as positive and negative poles between which the spark of his genius plays." But psychological disturbances kept breaking this balance, splitting Wordsworth's personality, and throwing him into one or the other extreme. To explain this, Bateson's book soon becomes a psychological biography. He exploits to the full Wordsworth's allegedly unhappy boyhood and his somewhat neurotic "ecstatic, terrified absorption in natural scenery." Bateson goes further into biography in postulating three crises that disturbed the balance between objectivity and subjectivity, with almost schizophrenic results, ending with the poet's final complete retreat within himself. One of these crises has to do with the hypothetical Mary of Esthwaite Water, one of them involves Annette, and the third of them was stimulated by passion for Dorothy. Bateson builds his case upon doubtful, or at best disputed, biographical data, and the psychological motivations stemming from them are mostly assumptions. There is a good deal of perceptive reading and entertaining writing in Bateson's book, but it is unfortunately overshadowed by the dubiousness of his basic arguments. For Jones, whose book is the more successful of the two, Wordsworth's confident poetry of "solitude and relationship," in which the reciprocity between the self and the outer world has its most perfect expression, was replaced by "the poetry of indecision" as Wordsworth began to lose his vivid touch with outside reality, and as his confidence that the mind and nature are exquisitely fitted to one another wavered. *The Prelude* is shown to have an inner conflict between the faith in nature and nature's purposes of 1798–99 and the belief that the mind of man is a thousand times more beautiful than the earth on which he dwells, which is characteristic of the sections of the poem composed after 1804. Similar indecision about the value of nature pervades *The White Doe of Rylstone*. The later poetry is dedicated to separating what had once been blended, to splitting man off from nature. The cultivation of naturalness in the earlier poetry is replaced by the cultivation of artifice in the later. Wordsworth "can assent no longer to the literalness of the natural order and its moral-poetic power: he cannot strive, with effort unparalleled in English poetry, to see things as they are. He is trying to write transcendental poetry, to tell tales of the invisible world." This is the offering of "the baptised imagination," and Jones demonstrates that it deserves considerable respect. His readings, both of the poems of relationship and those of artifice, are full of insight. He has an exemplary section on the workings of Wordsworth's favorite metaphors for the interrelatedness of reality, the images of winds, echoes, and water, and his epilogue is a brief but important essay on Wordsworth's incarnational concept of language. As these topics suggest, Jones deals with Wordsworth as a philosophical poet, but his emphasis is not on Wordsworth as a thinker, but as one who had deep feelings connected with certain philosophical problems.

For Edward E. Bostetter, Wordsworth's philosophy of the blending of man and nature was ultimately a piece of self-deception which could not protect him against the doubts it had been designed to allay. In *The Romantic Ventriloquists* (1963), Bostetter attacks the belief that romantic poetry is fundamentally confident in spirit and sure of its own vision. Centering his discussion on important unfinished poems by the major romantics, he argues that what was formerly seen as "triumphant affirmation" should instead be regarded as "a desperate struggle for affirmation against increasingly powerful obstacles." Bostetter finds that Wordsworth was unable to complete *The Recluse* because of an irreconcilable internal conflict, the two poles of which are embodied in the Wanderer and the Solitary in *The Excursion*. The skeptical Solitary is not converted by the Wanderer's arguments that the divine purpose, by which human suffering is justified, is revealed in or through the medium of nature, because Wordsworth had come to share his skepticism. Bostetter writes that the myth of interchange between man and nature, which figures in the poems of 1797 to 1800 and on which the arguments of the Wanderer are founded, was based upon Wordsworth's purely subjective happiness at that time. Such happiness could stand up neither to the persistence of suffering nor to the presence of hostility in nature, as it was most strongly manifested in the death of John Wordsworth. Bostetter's argument parallels Jones's in recording the evolution of Wordsworth's belief that whatever was benign was not in, but beyond nature, but he differs from Jones in finding that the withdrawal destroyed Wordsworth's powers rather than eventually refocussing them in an intellectually valid Christian belief. Bostetter also differs from Jones in seeing Wordsworth's disillusionment with nature to have set in quite early; "Resolution and Independence" is a poem of resolve to be independent of nature. A similar withdrawal from humanity marked Wordsworth; the compassion of *The Ruined Cottage* is replaced as early as "The Old Cumberland Beggar" by the distant moralizing characteristic of *The Excursion,* Book VI. Unable to rationalize or to alleviate human suffering, Wordsworth simply refused to see it, except as an object of contemplation. Wordsworth's philosophy, far from bringing comfort out of despair as so many in the nineteenth century thought it did, was simply whistling in the dark. "The possibility that man might accept responsibility for human suffering and live usefully without despair in an indifferent universe was inconceivable to him," so he continued to publish facile complacency like the Wanderer's, unable to believe it but even less able to confront the consequences of not believing it.

Bostetter's argument incorporates the frequent charges of earlier critics that Wordsworth stripped nature of its savagery in order to make it conform to his desires and that he averted his eyes from half of human fate, and it is liable to some of the same objections. Bennett Weaver's reply to some of these earlier critics, "Wordsworth: The Property of Fortitude" (*SP,* 1940), still has considerable validity in its implication that Wordsworth's wishes about man and nature were not father to his thoughts as consistently as Bostetter makes them out to have been. Moreover, Bostetter's device of assuming Wordsworth's failure from the start leads to an underplaying and, at times, a distortion of the accomplishment of the earlier poetry. It seems unfair to associate Wordsworth's complacency about the estate of Cumberland Beggars and Leech-gatherers with the decline in his powers; Wordsworth was not for long the humanitarian of

The Ruined Cottage, but he could write good poems without the feelings Bostetter desires him to have had. But *The Romantic Ventriloquists* establishes the presence of doubt at the very heart of Wordsworth's beliefs, and demonstrates the tremendous emotional importance of the philosophical issues in his poems.

Concentration upon Wordsworth's problems in constructing a philosophy, rather than upon the philosophy itself, is not particularly new. Basil Willey's brilliant essay "On Wordsworth and the Locke Tradition," in *The Seventeenth-Century Background* (1934), adumbrates much of the recent concern in its argument that the Locke tradition was important to Wordsworth because it left him in a demythologized world, in which he had to create value out of his own unaided dealings with the visible universe. Although Willey emphasizes Wordsworth's accomplishment, he finds that it was the effort of continually having to redeem the world by his mental powers that finally wore Wordsworth out, and he finds that Wordsworth had to make that effort from his very earliest poetry. The general currency of the picture of the romantic poet as one who must forge a new reality because the old "cosmic syntax," as Earl Wasserman calls it in *The Subtler Language* (1959), no longer applies, is partly due to Willey's essay.

Geoffrey H. Hartman's *The Unmediated Vision: An Interpretation of Wordsworth, Hopkins, Rilke, and Valéry* (1954) is similar to Willey's essay in its presentation of Wordsworth as a turning point, perhaps the first poet of the demythologized imagination. In a discussion of "Tintern Abbey" which ranges widely over Wordsworth's other works, Hartman shows how Wordsworth found revelation in the natural world without the mediation of traditional religion. But while *The Unmediated Vision* recognizes Wordsworth's ability to present pure representations of the visible world and to find manifested in the world an overarching principle of generosity which unites man and nature, it also suggests that there is conflict. The imagination cannot be true to itself and true to nature; each seeks to impose its categories upon the other. This conflict between the world and the imagination is the subject of Hartman's major study of Wordsworth, *Wordsworth's Poetry 1787–1814* (1964).

Hartman's is the most comprehensive attempt to argue that Wordsworth's poetry, good and bad, arises from internal conflict; in place of the poet of the "ennobling interchange," Hartman gives us "the most isolated figure among the great English poets." Wordsworth's poetry is seen as a struggle to reconcile a radical opposition between the imagination, "consciousness of self raised to an apocalyptic pitch," and nature, which the "supervening consciousness" of imagination seeks to obliterate or go beyond. Hartman sees this conflict not only in works of the middle or later years, as, for example, Jones had done, but in the very earliest of Wordsworth's poetry as well. He differs also in his contention that nothing, not even baptism, could keep Wordsworth's imagination from seeking autonomy; the things which have been taken as constants in Wordsworth, "Nature, time, memory, and poetry itself, can only fitfully bind an imagination which is radically in excess of nature as of every socializing principle." But Wordsworth could not simply be William Blake, and declare his autonomy and have done with it; he both courted and feared the moments when his absolute self would stand alone. For although nature is inadequate to the mind's conceptions, its attractions are very great, and the mind is unwilling to assume the terrible burden of self-consciousness, particularly when self-consciousness seems inevitably to involve a violation of nature. Therefore, writes Hartman, Wordsworth created the myth that Nature seeks to make the mind independent, the myth of the *via naturaliter negativa.* "The child grows from a stage in which it walks *with* nature, to one in which it is in search *of* nature, and finally to a crisis when nature no longer suffices. This crisis is overcome when it is seen that Nature itself taught the mind to be free of nature and now teaches the mind to be free of mind and mingle with nature once more." Assent to the myth is a defense against the alienation of the mind, which is now seen not as violating nature's being, but as fulfilling it. So great, however, is the apocalyptic power of imagination that even when the mind gives free assent to the myth, as it does in *The Prelude,* the conflict breaks out from time to time. Nature seems to rise up against the poet, but, in fact, the poet's own consciousness, projected through the medium of nature, is rebuking him for being content with his homely nurse. These promptings finally forced Wordsworth to flee from his own vision. His withdrawal, however, was not into peace but into isolation and fear that man and nature were soon to be separated forever.

Hartman's closely reasoned argument is difficult to summarize adequately, and this account of his main thesis does not do justice to his exposition of Wordsworth's successful attempts to embrace nature. But it is not the temporary resolutions of the conflict that Hartman stresses, though he reads the resulting poetry very well; it is the conflict itself which concerns him. Wordsworth as nature poet did seek to show that the service of nature was perfect freedom, but he did so partly to convince himself of that; he did not want to be alone with his own consciousness. Hartman thus gives full credit to much that has been said about the gravitational bond between man and nature, but he sees the bond as something in which Wordsworth desperately wanted to believe, despite continuing doubts.

As his useful critical bibliographies, which are filled with generous acknowledgments, demonstrate, Hartman has had many predecessors in his emphasis upon the apocalyptic tendencies in Wordsworth's work. A. C. Bradley's brilliant *Oxford Lectures on Poetry* (1909), D. G. James's description of the "visionary dreariness" in *Skepticism and Poetry* (1937), G. Wilson Knight's "The Wordsworthian Profundity" in *The Starlit Dome* (1941), and Harold Bloom's comparisons of the treatment of nature by Blake and the other romantics in *The Visionary Company* (1961) have all helped to define the qualities of Wordsworth's moments of vision, when the visible world is suspended and the invisible one revealed. The growing critical concentration on Wordsworth's self-doubts and internal conflicts has already been documented. But in his combination of these two tendencies, and in his comprehensive application of his thesis to the poems both early and late, Hartman is most original. No one has located the apocalypse so squarely in Wordsworth's own consciousness; no one has gone so far in denying any ultimate value to nature. The boldness of the argument sometimes leads to overstatements of the case, but Hartman has convincingly shown how complex a mixture of desire and fear any relationship between consciousness and nature must be.

Fine sections on individual poems occur throughout the book; *The Prelude,* which is the ideal poem with which to demonstrate the thesis, is handled with particular care and insight, but there are also important chapters on the *Lyrical Ballads,* the major lyrics, and *The Excursion.* Perhaps because they have seldom been so intensively analyzed, the earlier poems, from "The Vale of Esthwaite" through *The Ruined Cottage,* best repay Hartman's scrutiny. His description of their recurring figures, such as the "spot-fixation" which is transmuted into the spots of time in *The Prelude,* of such issues as the conflict between the intellect and the moral order in *The Borderers,* and of Wordsworth's innovative use of traditional genres and themes all help to demonstrate that the early poems are more closely related to the main body of Wordsworth's work than has previously been thought. The neglected fragments written at Alfoxden are shown to be crucial documents in the evolution of Wordsworth's beliefs and style. But the book should be read for its challenging argument about all of Wordsworth's poetry, rather than for its local insights, however fine they may be. *Wordsworth's Poetry, 1787–1814* is a major work of criticism, and as Robert Langbaum points out in his useful review "Magnifying Wordsworth" (*ELH,* 1966), it has caused important changes in the way we must see Wordsworth.

The theme of the retrospective eighth book of *The Prelude,* if we are to believe Wordsworth's title, is "Love of Nature Leading to Love of Man." Recent critics, however, have found Wordsworth's love of man to be as complex and ambivalent as they have considered his dealings with nature to be.

Since Legouis and Harper, Wordsworth's biographers have emphasized the importance of the radical culture of the 1790's in the formation of Wordsworth's creed of philosophical benevolence. The central problem has been the nature and extent of the influence of William Godwin's political and moral philosophy. Was Wordsworth as thorough a Godwinian as Hazlitt, in *The Spirit of the Age,* said he had been? Does *The Borderers* record Wordsworth's rejection of Godwin's philosophy? And what was the effect of this intellectual ferment upon Wordsworth's poetry?

Godwin's diary, upon which Mary Moorman was able to draw, makes it plain that Wordsworth saw a great deal of the philosopher in the months following their first meeting in 1795. Although the earlier influence of Godwin cannot have been as important as Harper supposed it to have been, it is possible that Godwin's *Political Justice* or *Caleb Williams* influenced Wordsworth before he met their author. F. M. Todd, in *Politics and the Poet,* sees Godwin's ideas in Wordsworth's *Letter to the Bishop of Llandaff,* which he never published, and in *Salisbury Plain,* but, as other writers have pointed out, the supposedly Godwinian ideas in the former work could have come from virtually any radical political tract of the times. The key text in the debate, of course, is *The Borderers.* Emile Legouis saw the play as a rejection of Godwin's trust in the "independent intellect," a spirit which he considered embodied in the ruthless Oswald. H. W. Garrod (*Wordsworth,* 1923) replied that the entire play is Godwinian, because the characters are not rational and benevolent, but anarchic. The play illustrates the problems that Wordsworth thought Godwin could answer. Later critics have seen the truth to lie some where between these two positions. Alan Grob's recent article, "Wordsworth and Godwin: A Reassessment" (*SIR,* 1967), reviews the whole controversy, analyzes all the available documentary evidence, and concludes that Wordsworth was reacting to an ethics based on pure self-interest, which is not characteristic of Godwin, and on rationality rather than feelings and experience, which is. Grob's article generally amplifies the middle position taken by R. D. Havens in *The Mind of a Poet.* He finds that other influences have been confused with Godwin's, and that Wordsworth's reaction against mechanical moral philosophy was directed against utilitarian doctrines, as exemplified in Paley, as well as against Godwin. The best sketch of the philosophical background against which Wordsworth tried to work out his ideas is in the opening chapters of Herschel Baker's *William Hazlitt* (1962), which show young Hazlitt grappling with some of the same problems a few years later. Helen Darbishire has distinguished Wordsworth's idea of the perfectibility of man from Godwin's in "Wordsworth's Belief in the Doctrine of Necessity" (*RES*, 1948). Thomas J. Rountree has argued unconvincingly for the continuing influence of Godwinian ideas in *This Mighty Sum of Things: Wordsworth's Theme of Benevolent Necessity* (1965).

Another early influence upon Wordsworth, the eighteenth-century School of Sensibility and the related cult of "virtue in distress" as a means of moral regeneration, has been studied by O. J. Campbell in *Sentimental Morality in Wordsworth's Narrative Poetry* (1920) and "Wordsworth's Conception of the Esthetic Experience" in *Wordsworth and Coleridge,* ed. E. L. Griggs; and in essays by Campbell and Paul Mueschke on *Guilt and Sorrow* (*MP*, 1926), *The Borderers* (*MP*, 1926), and "Wordsworth's Aesthetic Development, 1795–1802" (Univ. of Michigan Pubs. in Lang. and Lit., 1933). The value of some of these essays is impaired by a good deal of speculation about Wordsworth's remorse over his affair with Annette, but Campbell and Mueschke do demonstrate the importance of the concept of the sympathetic imagination in Wordsworth's early poetry. Roger Sharrock in "Wordsworth and John Langhorne's 'The Country Justice'" (*N&Q,* 1954), Bishop C. Hunt, Jr., in "Wordsworth and Charlotte Smith" (*TWC,* 1970), and E. H. King in "James Beattie's *The Minstrel* (1771, 1774): Its Influence on Wordsworth" (*SSL,* 1970) discuss important literary sources of this poetry.

Wordsworth's own testimony in such documents as the Preface to *The Borderers* and "Lines left upon a Seat by a Yew-tree" confirms the basic necessity for sympathy; isolated from others, man is a tragic and potentially evil figure, cut off from the joy which is reserved for the benevolent and lowly of heart. Newton P. Stallknecht's chapters on ethics in *Strange Seas of Thought* and his essay on "Wordsworth and the Quality of Man" in *The Major English Romantic Poets: A Symposium in Reappraisal,* ed. C. D. Thorpe, Carlos Baker, and Bennett Weaver (1957), explore this point of view, pointing out that the Romantics and the existentialists, whether or not they share the same idea of heaven, "agree heartily enough on the subject of hell." For Stallknecht, whose essay makes frequent comparisons between Wordsworth and twentieth-century philosophy, even nature is incomplete unless it is joined to the whole community of man by the imagination, and Wordsworth, unlike Coleridge, is consistently able to effect this great consummation.

Such optimism as Stallknecht's has been challenged by several recent critics, most notably by David Perkins in *The Quest for Permanence: The Symbolism of Wordsworth, Shelley, and Keats* (1959) and David Ferry in *The Limits of Mortality: An Essay on Wordsworth's Major Poems* (1959). Perkins sees the poetry of the romantics as an attempt to overcome the instability, "the jostle and constant change which seemed to them the leading principles both of their own psychology and of the life around them." Wordsworth found the permanence to offset this instability in the natural world, the home of "holy calm," and as long as man could be linked to the permanence of nature, all was well. But Wordsworth saw man as a being full of restless and aggressive passions, an intruder who continually violates the calm of nature. The failure of relationship, then, is essentially a failure in man, though nature is seen to fail in "Elegiac Stanzas"; Wordsworth feared that it might be impossible for man to reduce the demands of his ego, and to harmonize with other men or the natural world. From this standpoint, Perkins is able to study both Wordsworth's images of isolation and the images of relationship with which he sought to counteract his fears. Perkins has defined an important source of Wordsworth's figurative language. W. J. B. Owen has shown the importance of the idea of permanence in the *Lyrical Ballads* Preface in the commentary on his edition (*Anglistica*, 1957) and in "The Major Theme of Wordsworth's 1800 Preface" (*EIC*, 1956). In "Wordsworth and Glitter" (*SP*, 1943) Josephine Miles showed how deeply the opposition between the permanent and enduring and the quick, the restless, and the glittering was embedded in Wordsworth's mind. Perkins explores this opposition nicely; his descriptions of Wordsworth's ambivalence about man and of his fears about the possible inadequacy of poetic language, which will be discussed in the next section, have helped to reveal Wordsworth's affinities with twentieth-century poetry.

Ferry goes even further than Perkins in asserting Wordsworth's radical distrust of man. He writes that the essential Wordsworth is not the poet of the human heart and primal sympathy, but a poet whose "yearning for an uncorrupted experience of the eternal is so intense and powerful that it ends in the devaluation of our ordinary experience, even in the desire for its destruction . . . Wordsworth is not a great lover of man but almost a great despiser of him." The human figures Wordsworth approves—the Leech-gatherer, Lucy, the Discharged Soldier—are all essentially unearthly, and Wordsworth cares not for their humanity, but for their distance from humanity. They have come to share the eternal aspect of Nature, rather than the temporal aspect of man. In a long section on *The Prelude,* Ferry presents Wordsworth's experience in the human world as exile, and his retirement as his spiritual home.

Ferry's book has been influential in the creation of the recent conception of Wordsworth as a poet hedged about by ambiguities and conflict. *The Limits of Mortality* anticipates Hartman in seeing a radical opposition between nature and human consciousness; man is aware of change and death, nature is not, and man's intrusion of his consciousness into nature is an act of violence. Although Ferry feels that Wordsworth was able to find value in nature more consistently than Hartman will allow, he too argues that Wordsworth's love of nature had conflicting sides. On the one hand, there is the sacramentalist concept in which the natural world provides symbols of eternity; on the other, there is the mystical concept, in which Wordsworth was impatient with symbols for standing between himself and eternity. Finally, there is the conflict in which Wordsworth's ostensible love of mankind is actually something close to hatred.

Ferry would seem to have drawn some of these oppositions too neatly The basic conflict in his book, between Wordsworth's desire for eternity and his imprisonment in time, ignores some of the means, most notably memory, by which Wordsworth was able to transcend time. Hirsch's book is relevant here, as is Bennett Weaver's essay "Wordsworth's *Prelude*: The Poetic Function of Memory" (*SP,* 1937). The best contrast with Ferry, however, is Christopher Salvesen's *The Landscape of Memory: A Study of Wordsworth's Poetry* (1965). For Salvesen, Wordsworth was not a prisoner of time; he used memory to suggest a multi-temporal existence. Memory does not completely overcome the sense of loss, nor can it allow Wordsworth, until relatively late in his career, to reach the passiveness in time of the old man traveling, for example. But memory can lead Wordsworth "out of the linear flux of human life into the continuous repetitions of Nature." Salvesen's terms here suggest that his argument is not too different from Ferry's in acknowledging the tensions between time and eternity, but he does not see the opposition as radical; different orders of being can be fused. *The Landscape of Memory* contains some illuminating comparisons between Wordsworth's sense of time and that of other writers, especially Rousseau and Hazlitt, which, together with the similar comparisons by Herbert Lindenberger in *On Wordsworth's Prelude* (1963), are helpful in elaborating upon Ferry's somewhat oversimplified account of Wordsworth's consciousness of time. It should be added that Ferry's formula serves him very well in his analysis of the double consciousness of time and eternity in the poems, and that his emphasis upon Wordsworth's impatience with temporality catches an important quality in the poet's mind. But there is still a problem of interpretation, for the same simultaneous awareness of time and eternity which, to Ferry, generates anxiety has been seen by other readers as producing comfort.

In "Wordsworth's *Nutting*" (*JEGP*, 1962), Alan Grob has protested against the readings of that poem by Perkins and Ferry, both of whom see in it evidence of an abiding conflict between man and nature. Grob concedes that the boy in the poem is indeed a wild and passionate being, but points out that the boy has grown into a gentle man. The whole idea behind the poem, as Grob sees it, is that the boy's experience tempered his wildness. Nature is violated, but only so that a lesson which leads to reverence for her can be learned. In Grob's reading, the conflict is temporary, the love permanent.

Again, however, there is much truth to Ferry's argument. His description of Wordsworth's aloofness from humanity recalls Coleridge's remark that Wordsworth's proper title was *Spectator ab extra,* though Coleridge was careful to add that while Wordsworth could not feel with his characters, he could feel for them. Aloofness is also one of the reasons for Hazlitt's portrayal of Wordsworth's intense egotism in his brilliant essays on *The Excursion.* Wordsworth was not, however, always aloof. *The Ruined Cottage* may be an exception, but Jonathan Wordsworth is surely correct, in *The Music of Humanity,* in pointing to the deep compassion of that poem, which "shows in Wordsworth a humanity, an insight into emotions not his own, that is wholly convincing." Jonathan Wordsworth's book traces the evolution of Wordsworth's views about human suffering through his early poetry, with extensive comparisons between Wordsworth's work and poems by Bürger, Southey, Langhorne, and others. He examines, as Jones had done, most of Wordsworth's solitaries, and concludes that Wordsworth's aloofness is partly a question of date. In the poems of 1797–1800, man may often have been presented as an abstraction, as in "The Old Cumberland Beggar," but he was still man. The humanity of "Michael," "The Brothers," and "The Idiot Boy" reveals a side of Wordsworth which Ferry's argument cannot encompass. And on

the strength of *The Ruined Cottage,* Jonathan Wordsworth ranks Wordsworth among the few great English tragic writers.

Among the other works which bear upon this question are James
Smith's "Wordsworth: A Preliminary Survey" (*Scrutiny,* 1938); Cleanth
Brooks's essay, "Wordsworth and Human Suffering" in *From Sensibility
to Romanticism: Essays Presented to Frederick A. Pottle,* ed. F. W. Hilles
and H. Bloom (1965), which deals with "The Old Cumberland Beggar"
and *The Ruined Cottage,* and finds Wordsworth's Olympian perspective
troublesome; Stephen C. Gill's "Wordsworth's Breeches Pocket: Attitudes
to the Didactic Poet" (*EIC,* 1969), which is concerned with "The Old
Cumberland Beggar" and the 1793–95 *A Night on Salisbury Plain,* and is
in part a reply to Brooks; Michael Irwin's "Wordsworth's 'Dependency
Sublime'" (*EIC,* 1964); and John F. Danby's *The Simple Wordsworth*
(1960), a fine study of some of Wordsworth's most compassionate poems
which will be discussed in the next section.

The recent questioning of Wordsworth's commitment to what were
previously thought to be his most fundamental beliefs has overshadowed
earlier controversies about the validity and nature of those beliefs. Contention was particularly hot about Wordsworth's philosophy of nature, which
was attacked as a touching sentimental illusion, at best unrealistic and
outdated and at worst immoral, and defended as a scientifically sound basis
upon which to build a personal faith. Paul Elmer More, in *Shelburne
Essays,* Seventh Series (1910), and Irving Babbitt, in *Rousseau and
Romanticism* (1919) and "The Primitivism of Wordsworth" in *On Being
Creative* (1932), charged that Wordsworth cultivated an unhealthy trust in
spontaneity and passion, and ascribed to nature virtues that nature cannot
give. Aldous Huxley's famous essay "Wordsworth in the Tropics," in *Do
What You Will* (1929), alleged that Wordsworth misrepresented nature
by "pumping out the dangerous unknown" and ignoring the savagery.
Salvador de Madariaga wrote in "The Case of Wordsworth" in *Shelley and
Calderón* (1920) that Wordsworth was not, properly speaking, a nature
poet at all, for his meddlesome intellect prevented him from seeing what
nature was about. Most of these attacks read a bit oddly now that the
grounds of the argument have shifted; if, as David Perkins believes,
Wordsworth distrusted human passion, the charges of the "New Humanists" are pointless. Some of the attacks, however, have survived nicely;
Bostetter uses a version of Huxley's argument in *The Romantic Ventriloquists,* though he sees Wordsworth's attribution of benevolence to nature

as a deep psychological need, rather than as a result of Wordsworth's good fortune in living in what is misleadingly called a temperate climate.

The writings of the "New Humanists" and others helped to stimulate an impressive group of attempts to define precisely what Wordsworth's beliefs about nature had been. Joseph Warren Beach's *The Concept of Nature in Nineteenth-Century English Poetry* (1936) and his "Reason and Nature in Wordsworth" (*JHI*, 1940) carefully explored the sources of Wordsworth's naturalism, and dispassionately discussed the interrelationship between Nature and God. Raymond Dexter Havens, in *The Mind of a Poet,* gave a similarly fair-minded account of Wordsworth's animism and his beliefs about nature and religion, although he tended to underplay the importance of sense-perception and took a generally transcendentalist line. Basil Willey's *The Eighteenth Century Background* (1940), a study of the idea of nature through the whole century, culminating in Wordsworth, also helped to show that nothing could be further from Wordsworth's beliefs than facile pastoralism. Willey relates the growth of Wordsworth's faith in nature to the loss of his faith in politics.

Other writers went further, and asserted the enduring viability of the Wordsworthian attitude. A. N. Whitehead's important and influential discussion of Wordsworth in *Science and the Modern World* (1925) contrasted Wordsworth's ability to see things whole with science's ability to see only parts and emphasized the importance of intuition as a complement to reason. Ernest Bernbaum's essay "Is Wordsworth's Nature-Poetry Antiquated?" (*ELH,* 1940) argued that, far from having been outmoded by science, Wordsworth had anticipated many of its more recent discoveries. This whole debate has been overshadowed by the questioning of whether Wordsworth was able to assent to his own myth and believe in nature at all.

Since his own time, Wordsworth's political and religious ideas have been a source of controversy. Harper's elaboration of the "lost leader" theory had plentiful antecedents in the nineteenth century, including Browning's resentful poem from which the phrase comes, and ranging in tone from the fierce attacks of Byron and Hazlitt to the usually private doubts of the faithful Henry Crabb Robinson. F. M. Todd's *Politics and the Poet,* which does an admirable job of placing Wordsworth's ideas in their contemporary context, has laid many of these ghosts to rest. Todd argues that Wordsworth's early liberalism was in some respects superficial; certainly it was at odds with what liberalism came to mean in the nineteenth century. Most of these principles, by whatever name they are to be called, were never abandoned. Nor does Todd find any relationship between Wordsworth's poetic decline and the supposed change in his politics, as Harper, Hugh I'Anson Fausset in *The Lost Leader* (1933), and others have done. Although Todd claims his book is not a defense of Wordsworth, he does gloss over some of the less-appealing pronouncements of the later years. Still, his much-needed study serves its purpose well.

Carl Woodring's *Politics in English Romantic Poetry* (1970) is the best general discussion of the ways in which Wordsworth's political ideas figure in his poetry. Woodring observes that historians of literature have usually regarded romanticism as revolutionary, while social scientists have considered it conservative. He argues that both schools of thought are in a sense correct; the poets themselves felt an inconsistency between the empirical assumptions and reforming zeal of liberalism on the one hand and the romantic ideals of organicism and imaginative unity on the other. Woodring surveys Wordsworth's poems chronologically, showing that their political vision is wider than labels like "liberal" or "conservative" indicate. *The Borderers* is not an attack on reform, but on the narrow basis from which reformers argue; in the late poetry, in which Wordsworth accepts that men are naturally unequal, he nonetheless does not lose sight of the way society distorts and magnifies that inequality. Woodring shows, as he had done in his essay "On Liberty in the Poetry of Wordsworth" (*PMLA*, 1955), the analogies between Wordsworth's political beliefs and his landscapes, which are read as allegories of unassuming freedom. Woodring discusses *The Prelude* in considerable detail, dealing both with its political material and with the question that material raises: can a poet enter the world of power and action without violating himself? Woodring feels that Wordsworth in particular could not maintain the reformer's agony and inability to rest.

Other studies of Wordsworth's politics include G. K. Thomas' *Wordsworth's Dirge and Promise: Napoleon, Wellington, and the Convention of Cintra* (1971) and David R. Sanderson's "Wordsworth's World, 1809: A Stylistic Study of the Cintra Pamphlet" (*TWC*, 1970). F. H. Langman, in "Wordsworth's Patriotism" (*Theoria*, 1962), discusses the link between patriotism and domestic love which is prominent in "I travelled among unknown men." Kenneth MacLean's *Agrarian Age: A Background for Wordsworth* (1950) examines Wordsworth's ideas in light of the vast changes in agriculture, and their consequences for the rural population, at the end of the eighteenth century. E. P. Thompson's *The Making of the English Working Class* (1963), while seldom explicitly concerned with Wordsworth, is a brilliant history of radical agitation, urban and rural, from the 1790's on, which makes Wordsworth's milieu seem very immediate. E. H. Hartsell's "Wordsworth's 1835 'Postscript': An Advanced Program for Labor" (*SP*, 1945) argues that Wordsworth was ahead of his time in considering the needs of the workingman. Zera S. Fink's "Wordsworth and the English Republican Tradition" (*JEGP*, 1948) documents Wordsworth's imaginative identification with the line of democratic prophets which includes Algernon Sidney and James Harrington, the men who called Milton friend, as well as Milton himself. H. J. C. Grierson's *Milton and Wordsworth* (1937) explores the similarities between the two poets, but much more can be done with the philosophical implications of Wordsworth's Miltonizing. Alfred Cobban's *Edmund Burke and the Revolt Against the Eighteenth Century: A Study of the Political Thinking of Burke, Wordsworth, Coleridge, and Southey* (1929) and Crane Brinton's *Political Ideas of the English Romanticists* (1926) both supply useful comparisons with other writers, and Cobban particularly has influenced later writers. However both books are somewhat outdated.

There are a number of appreciations of Wordsworth's political views. A. V. Dicey, writing during the first World War, found in Wordsworth an eloquent expression of the best principles of English political thought (*The Statesmanship of Wordsworth*, 1917); the sonnets, particularly, are praised as "Psalms of England." Nettie S. Tillett in "Poet of the Present Crisis" (*SR*, 1944) and B. Ifor Evans in "Wordsworth and the European Problem of the Twentieth Century," in *Wordsworth: Centenary Studies,* both discuss Wordsworth's continuing relevance. V. G. Kiernan praises the democratic side of Wordsworth and his hope for a society without artificial distinctions in "Wordsworth and the People," in *Democracy and the Labour Movement,* ed. John Saville (1954).

The persistence and importance of religious patterns of thought, not only in Wordsworth but in the romantic movement as a whole, is the subject of M. H. Abrams' *Natural Supernaturalism: Tradition and Revolution in Romantic Literature* (1971). Abrams seeks to define the spirit of the age by describing parallels in form and idea in the works of the poets and philosophers of the period, whose most significant common preoccupation was "with the secularization of inherited theological ideas and ways of thinking." The book is organized around the lines which Wordsworth used as Prospectus to *The Recluse* ("On Man, on Nature, and on Human

Life"), which are seen as a concise statement of the romantic beliefs that only in the actual world can man find a paradise that will justify mortal good and evil, and that this state of bliss will be brought about by human powers rather than exclusively divine ones. In discussing Wordsworth, Abrams draws on two significant earlier essays, "The Correspondent Breeze: A Romantic Metaphor" (*KR*, 1957; revised in *English Romantic Poets*, ed. M. H. Abrams, 1960) and "English Romanticism: The Spirit of the Age" in *Romanticism Reconsidered*, ed. Northrop Frye (1963). The first of these essays shows how such figures as Wordsworth's correspondent breeze and Coleridge's aeolian lute preserve the imagery of divine inspiration in order to suggest both the unity of the cosmos and the divinity of the creative mind. The new book derives from the second essay in its discussion of the apocalyptic expectations generated by the French Revolution, and of the way in which images associated with the apocalypse were applied to a revolution in the mind after the failure of political revolution. This process is most familiar in the works of Blake, but Abrams demonstrates its pervasive presence in Wordsworth as well. He traces the impulse behind the *Lyrical Ballads*, with their "proud humility," to the New Testament conviction that "the last shall be first," and concludes that the young Wordsworth, "semi-atheist" though he may have been, was full of the spirit of primitive Christianity. There is a full discussion of *The Prelude* as a crisis-autobiography whose pattern comes ultimately from St. Augustine, and both *The Prelude* and *Home at Grasmere* are illuminated by comparisons with Milton. Even the theory of poetry Wordsworth elaborates in the 1815 Preface is shown to depend upon the concept of the incarnation of the word. Abrams' subject is wider than Wordsworth, of course. He is trying to define romanticism despite the objections of A. O. Lovejoy that romanticism is too diverse to be defined, he is trying to re-emphasize the optimistic character of romanticism, and he is trying to show the ways in which the twentieth century has inherited romantic preoccupations. That Abrams chooses to organize his book around Wordsworth is an indication of the importance of the poetry, both in its time and ours.

Other works on the influence of religion on Wordsworth include Hoxie N. Fairchild's *Religious Trends in English Poetry* (1939–68), which, despite its tendentiousness, has in its second volume a good general introduction to the religious climate into which Wordsworth was born. The treatment of Wordsworth in the third volume, however, consists mainly of an attack upon the subjectivity and unorthodoxy of his religion, and is of extremely limited value. Alan G. Hill's *Wordsworth and the Church*

Tradition: Studies in the Mind and Poetry of William Wordsworth, which is forthcoming, will be a more objective survey of the poet's thinking about history and religion, with particular reference to the ecclesiastical movements of the nineteenth and twentieth centuries. James Benziger's *Images of Eternity: Studies in the Poetry of Religious Vision from Wordsworth to T. S. Eliot* (1962) is concerned with the ways in which Wordsworth found religious meaning through the apprehension of nature in the absence of traditional belief. Benziger concerns himself with Wordsworth's shift from naturalism to transcendentalism, but his treatment is too brief to really settle the issues he raises. John Jones's chapter on "The Baptised Imagination" in *The Egotistical Sublime,* though also brief, deals provocatively with the ways in which Wordsworth's Christianity influenced the structure of his imagery. Geoffrey Hartman, who characterizes Wordsworth as a "radical Protestant" or as a latter-day Puritan, has many penetrating but scattered remarks in *Wordsworth's Poetry 1787–1814,* and discusses the importance of Biblical imagery in Wordsworth's writings in *The Unmediated Vision.* Jane Worthington [Smyser], in *Wordsworth's Reading of Roman Prose* (1946; rpt. 1970), deals with the influence of Stoicism on Wordsworth's beliefs. Lionel Trilling's "Wordsworth and the Iron Time," in *Wordsworth: Centenary Studies* and, with revisions, in *The Opposing Self* (1955), is a discussion of Wordsworth's quietism, which is both Christian and similar in tone to the sententiae of the *Pirke Aboth.* Alice P. Comparetti's introduction to her edition of *The White Doe of Rylstone* discusses Wordsworth's sympathetic understanding of other varieties of religious experience than his own. Also in the *Centenary Studies* is Willard L. Sperry's sensible account of "Wordsworth's Religion." Other studies which touch upon the problem include J. D. Rea, "Coleridge's Intimations of Immortality from Proclus" (*MP,* 1928); W. A. Claydon, "The Numinous in the Poetry of Wordsworth" (*HJ,* 1930); S. G. Dunn, "A Note on Wordsworth's Metaphysical System" (*E&S,* 1933); J. Crofts, *Wordsworth and the Seventeenth Century,* a Warton lecture of 1940; Elizabeth Green, "The Concept of Grace in Wordsworth's Poetry" (*PMLA,* 1943); Melvin G. Williams, "A New Look at Wordsworth's Religion" (*Cithara,* 1962), and F. X. Shea, S.J., "Religion and the Romantic Movement" (*SIR,* 1970).

Wordsworth said that he wished to be remembered as a teacher or as nothing, and the Victorians took him at his word. The calm assurance of his poems, and his quiet evocation of virtues that seemed increasingly to be lost, were immensely appealing to a generation which felt its isolation, its distance from the springs of feeling, and its divided consciousness. But at the same time, the feeling that Wordsworth was irrelevant to the modern predicament grew. The world in which Wordsworth had lived was seen as circumscribed or as utterly changed, and his poetry, depending upon one's viewpoint, as beautiful but outmoded or as simply windy moralizing. Both attitudes were present quite early in the history of Wordsworthian criticism, and both persisted well into the twentieth century. E. E. Bostetter has detected the presence of the first point of view in the essays contained in *The Major English Romantic Poets*; and Douglas Bush's "Wordsworth: A Minority Report" in *Wordsworth: Centenary Studies,* which argues that the poetry is limited by an insufficient awareness of evil, is an intelligent example of the second argument. Both of these viewpoints generally assume that Wordsworth's ideas were clearly defined and firmly held. H. W. Garrod's statement about the effect of Wordsworth's youthful *Sturm und Drang* upon his poetry was considered true in a wider sense; the best poetry grew, not out of conflict, but out of resolution. Recently, of course, the emphasis has shifted. The work of Perkins, Ferry, Bostetter, and Hartman has presented Wordsworth not as "a man in mental repose, one whose principles were made up, and so prepared to deliver upon authority a system of philosophy," as Coleridge said the speaker of *The Recluse* should be, but as a man who continually grappled with the difficulties of forging a philosophy. Wordsworth has been shown to be one of the crucial forerunners of the modern consciousness.

V. STUDIES OF POETRY AND POETICS

Among the best brief general introductions to Wordsworth's work are Walter Raleigh's *Wordsworth* (1903); A. C. Bradley's two important essays in *Oxford Lectures on Poetry* (1909); H. W. Garrod's sensible *Wordsworth* (1923), some of whose material on the composition of *The Prelude* and the relationship with Godwin has been corrected by later scholars; C. H. Herford's *Wordsworth* (1930); C. H. Patton's *The Rediscovery of Wordsworth* (1935; rpt. 1966); Helen Darbishire's excellent introduction to the poetry of the great decade, *The Poet Wordsworth* (1950); Lascelles Abercrombie's *The Art of Wordsworth* (1952); Carl Woodring's *Wordsworth* (1965), which is especially good on the *Lyrical*

Ballads; G. H. Durrant's *William Wordsworth* (1969); and George L. Nesbitt's *Wordsworth* (1970).

The indispensable criticism of Wordsworth by his contemporaries is by Coleridge, primarily in the *Biographia Literaria,* but also in the letters; there are a few fine fragments in the *Table Talk* as well. Hazlitt's essay in *The Spirit of the Age* emphasizes the revolutionary character of Wordsworth's early writings, and his essays on *The Excursion* in *The Round Table* are brilliant discussions of Wordsworth's self-consciousness, his "intense intellectual egotism." The reminiscent "My First Acquaintance with Poets" is among the most vivid pictures of Wordsworth we have, and makes a remarkable comparison with Carlyle's picture of the aged Wordsworth in *Reminiscences.* Hazlitt's essays are best consulted in the *Collected Works,* ed. P. P. Howe. Lamb's perceptive review of *The Excursion,* written for the *Quarterly,* was mutilated by Gifford and is abridged by Elsie Smith; a complete text may be found in E. V. Lucas' standard edition of the works of Charles and Mary Lamb. Keats's grapplings with the spirit of Wordsworth are recorded in his superb letters, particularly those of 3 February and 3 May 1818. De Quincey's *Literary and Lake Reminiscences* and "On Wordsworth's Poetry" have important insights. John Wilson's letter to Wordsworth, which provoked Wordsworth's defense of "The Idiot Boy" in his "Letter to John Wilson," is printed in the memoir by Mary Gordon, *Christopher North* (1863); for Wilson's other essays, see the excerpts in the collections by Elsie Smith and John Wain. A. L. Strout has described Wordsworth's relationship with Wilson (*PMLA,* 1934). *Jeffrey's Literary Criticism* has been edited by D. Nichol Smith (1910). Shelley's *Peter Bell the Third* has a few shrewd hits.

In addition to the exchange between Arnold and Stephen and Mill's remarks on Wordsworth in the *Autobiography,* there are important nineteenth-century critical essays by Wordsworth's friend Sir Henry Taylor, "Essay on the Poetical Works of Mr. Wordsworth" (*Quarterly Review,* 1834); Walter Bagehot, "Wordsworth, Tennyson, and Browning," a discussion of Wordsworth's "pure" style reprinted in *Literary Studies* (1879); J. C. Shairp, "Wordsworth, the Man and the Poet," in *Studies in Poetry and Philosophy* (1868); R. H. Hutton, "The Genius of Wordsworth" in *Literary Essays* (1871); Stopford Brooke, *Theology in the English Poets* (1874) and *Naturalism in English Poetry* (1902); Walter Pater's acute "Wordsworth" in *Appreciations* (1889); Edward Caird, "Wordsworth," reprinted from *Fraser's* (1880) in *Essays on Literature and Philosophy* (1892); A. C. Swinburne, "Wordsworth and Byron" in *Miscellanies* (1886); and John Morley's Arnoldian introduction to his *Complete Poetical Works of William Wordsworth* (1888).

The basic documents for dealing with Wordsworth's aesthetics are M. H. Abrams' *The Mirror and the Lamp: Romantic Theory and the Critical Tradition* (1953) and René Wellek's chapters on Coleridge and Wordsworth in the second volume of *A History of Modern Criticism* (1955), both of which give excellent general overviews of the critical theory. For Abrams, eighteenth-century criticism had been dominated by the mimetic theory of art, in which the poet is said to hold the mirror up to nature; Wordsworth's criticism is based on an "expressive" theory, which makes the feelings of the poet, rather than his reflection of reality, the center of critical reference. Despite his originality and his opposition of nature and art, Wordsworth's links with the eighteenth century are shown to have been particularly strong; he appeals consistently to the standard of the common nature of man, and shares many of the attitudes of eighteenth-century primitivism. The controversy concerning poetic diction was essentially a disagreement about where the common nature of man could best be seen; Wordsworth found it in the Cumberland dalesmen, and the whole decorum of poetry had perforce to be scrapped.

Abrams' influential discussion has been modified somewhat by other writers, but not in its basic propositions. W. J. B. Owen, in his edition of the Preface to the *Lyrical Ballads* (*Anglistica,* 1957), emphasized that Wordsworth was neither completely hostile to art nor completely on the side of nature; for Owen, "selection" is the crucial word in the phrase "a selection of the real language of men." The poet, in other words, always mediates. Abrams' study is quite naturally concentrated on Wordsworth's earlier critical writings, rather than on the growth and development of his ideas. Here Wellek's book, which draws heavily upon such later works as the Essays upon Epitaphs, provides a rich complement to *The Mirror and the Lamp.* Wellek tends to doubt the importance of the antithesis between "simple passionate 'nature' poetry" and " 'art' and the artificial," observing that Wordsworth assimilated "Spenser, Milton, Chaucer, and Shakespeare to his concept of 'nature' without making them over into primitives." Both Abrams and Wellek consider Wordsworth a turning point, a combination of old and new ideas about literature, and both place him in the context of his times. The organization of Abrams' book is topical, and in support of his main thesis, he gives a masterly survey of the mutations, from the eighteenth to the twentieth century, of such crucial critical ideas as the psychology of literary invention, science and poetry, the truth of poetry to nature, and literature as a revelation of personality. Wellek's book concentrates more on elucidating the critical position of each author it considers. Both books are indispensable.

Another general survey of Wordsworth's critical position by a distinguished critic is Albert Gérard's *L'Idée romantique de la poésie en Angleterre* (1955), which is also concerned with Coleridge, Keats, and Shelley.

Recent studies of Wordsworth's criticism have tended to emphasize the development of his ideas, partly because the general tendencies of the early criticism have been so well covered, and partly because of the way in which the later criticism strikes new directions. In *Wordsworth as Critic* (1969), W. J. B. Owen gives a close account of the growth of Wordsworth's critical theory, including what is virtually a line-by-line commentary on the various Prefaces to the *Lyrical Ballads*. Owen finds that, to borrow Abrams' terms, Wordsworth's theory in 1800 was essentially mimetic, that he was interested in the real language of men, but that by 1802, he had moved to an expressive theory of poetry, in which the mind of the poet takes pleasure in its own processes. The real language of men, which had served as a norm, was now replaced by the language of prose, a significant shift in the direction of art. Owen then shows how the Essays upon Epitaphs clarify the ideas of the 1802 Preface, partly by simplifying them and partly by pursuing the implications of the expressive theory in the discussion of the necessity for the sincere emotional involvement of the poet. The Essays in turn adumbrate a theory of imagination upon which Wordsworth elaborates in the Preface and Essay Supplementary to the Preface of 1815. Thus one concern creates another, and Wordsworth's critical theory is not complete until he has given a full description of "the poetics of his own verse." In *Wordsworth's Theory of Poetry: The Transforming Imagination* (1969), James A. W. Heffernan moves even further than Owen towards an emphasis on the later criticism. Heffernan's book, essentially, contests Abrams' view that Wordsworth made "the transition from the eighteenth-century view of man and nature to the concept that the mind is creative in perception" only in his poetry, and not in his criticism. Heffernan finds the *Lyrical Ballads* Preface to be essentially at odds with itself, having two voices, a major voice denouncing "art" in favor of "elementary feelings" and a minor voice which "enunciates the value of a discerning sensibility and meditative emotion." As Wordsworth's criticism developed, Heffernan believes, the minor voice came to dominate the major one. Wordsworth adopts a more subjective, less matter-of-fact point of view, emphasizing what Heffernan calls the supernaturalizing powers of the imagination; Wordsworth's defenses of *The White Doe* would have done very nicely to defend "The Ancient Mariner" against his own attacks in the 1800 Note to the poem. Heffernan's book, then, is in accord with much modern criticism in seeing a drift to transcendentalism in belief and symbolism in art in Wordsworth's later period, and gives the theoretical justification for the kind of poetry described by John Jones in the last part of *The Egotistical Sublime* or by Seymour Lainoff in "Wordsworth's Final Phase: Glimpses of Eternity" (*SEL,* 1961). However, Heffernan underplays the importance of the early documents, emphasizing the confusion which, he argues, only the theory of the transforming imagination could resolve.

Wordsworth's theory of the imagination has seldom been thought to have been as well developed as that of Coleridge; Abrams, for example, seems to accept Coleridge's contention that his friend's theory was essentially associationist. Heffernan, who wishes to demonstrate that Wordsworth's terminology too often failed to distinguish between perception and association, argues that the general lines of his theory are nonetheless clear, particularly in the distinction between imagination and fancy in the 1815 Preface. The basic distinction is in the kind of unity created; imagination fuses essences, fancy fuses accidents. Heffernan, in other words, does not find Wordsworth and Coleridge to have been in fundamental disagreement about imagination and fancy, although, because of the slipperiness of Wordsworth's vocabulary, they did not realize their agreement. Clarence D. Thorpe's "The Imagination: Coleridge *versus* Wordsworth" (*PQ,* 1939) examines the apparent differences between the two theories, and finds them less easily reconciled. In *Wordsworth as Critic,* Owen points out that there seem to be two kinds of imagination, one in which the mind reorders nature and one in which the mind is more transformed than transforming. This second class, which is exemplified in poems like "There Was a Boy," usually records the breaking in of imagination upon the ordinary consciousness, rather than the coadunating operations of the poet's mind. James Scoggins' *Imagination and Fancy* (1966) is an attempt to define the two modes by looking at the poems Wordsworth placed in those groups in the edition of 1815 and after. Scoggins offers a detailed analysis of Wordsworth's difficult arrangements of the poems, which were at various times supposed to signify a progression from youth to age or a progression in the degree of imagination or fancy expressed. Scoggins' interpretations differ in detail from those of Owen—they disagree about whether fancy is able to modify its materials, for example—but their conclusions are not fundamentally opposed. More basic is the difference with Heffernan, who acknowledges the importance Wordsworth placed in the fancy but generally treats it as a distorting power that has to be outgrown. Scoggins does much to show the importance of the poems of the fancy, which to him are basically expressions of confidence; nature always makes subjects available, and the mood of spontaneous joy which the poems celebrate is the complement to the explorations of the unknown, tinged with the possibility of failure, represented by the poems of imagination.

Coleridge's regretful remark that the Preface to the *Lyrical Ballads* had caused most of the controversy about Wordsworth has been borne out by time, although few writers agree with his contention that the doctrine of the Preface is foreign to Wordsworth's genius. The question of poetic diction has drawn most of the attention since Coleridge. Some of the noteworthy studies include Marjorie L. Barstow, *Wordsworth's Theory of Poetic Diction: A Study of the Historical and Personal Background of the* Lyrical Ballads (1917); Alexander Brede, Jr., "Theories of Poetic Diction," in *Papers of the Michigan Acad. of Science, Arts, and Letters* (1931); T. S. Eliot, "Wordsworth and Coleridge" in *The Use of Poetry and the Use of Criticism* (1933); George McL. Harper, "Wordsworth's Poetical Technique," in *Literary Appreciations* (1937); T. M. Raysor, "Coleridge's Criticism of Wordsworth" (*PMLA,* 1939); E. B. Burgum, "Wordsworth's Reform in Poetic Diction" (*CE,* 1940); G. S. Fraser, "Common Speech and Poetic Diction in Wordsworth" in *Tribute to Wordsworth,* ed. Muriel Spark and Derek Stanford (1950); John E. Jordan, Jr., "De Quincey on Wordsworth's Theory of Diction" (*PMLA,* 1953); Roger Sharrock, "Wordsworth's Revolt against Literature" (*EIC,* 1953); M. H. Abrams, "Wordsworth and Coleridge on Diction and Figures" (*EIE: 1952;* 1954); John Crowe Ransom, "William Wordsworth: Notes Toward an Understanding of Poetry" in *Wordsworth: Centenary Studies;* Stephen Maxfield Parrish, "Wordsworth and Coleridge on Meter" (*JEGP,* 1960); and Donald Davie's two studies, which have as much to do with Wordsworth's practice as with his theory, "Diction and Invention: A View of Wordsworth" in *Purity of Diction in English Verse* (1952) and "Syntax in the Blank-Verse of Wordsworth's *Prelude*" in *Articulate Energy: An Inquiry into the Syntax of English Poetry* (1955).

Wordsworth said that he had at all times endeavored to look steadily at his subject, and Coleridge came to believe that he had looked so steadily as to fall into matter-of-factness. Frederick A. Pottle's superb essay "The Eye and the Object in the Poetry of Wordsworth" in *Wordsworth: Centenary Studies* showed how Wordsworth modified the merely matter-of-fact in "I wandered lonely as a cloud," and suggested that Wordsworth's fidelity is to the mental image, and his reality is the reality of the mind. John E. Jordan, Jr., has made the same point in a study of Wordsworth's revisions of certain passages from *The Prelude,* "Wordsworth's 'Minuteness and Fidelity'" (*PMLA,* 1957). In "Preface to *Lyrical Ballads:* A Portent" (*UTQ,* 1956), George Whalley has argued that such literalness as Wordsworth is supposed to have practiced actually constricted his genius. Whalley here takes a line adumbrated by Harper, who similarly felt that the literalness of many of the *Lyrical Ballads* had to be outgrown before the greater poetry of vision could be written.

The implications of Wordsworth's belief that the poet had to confer pleasure have been studied by Lionel Trilling in "The Fate of Pleasure: Wordsworth to Dostoevsky" in *Romanticism Reconsidered.* Roger Sharrock has discussed Wordsworth's hopes for science and the possible influence of Humphry Davy in "The Chemist and the Poet: Sir Humphry Davy and the Preface to *Lyrical Ballads*" (*Notes and Records of the Royal Society of London,* 1962). A distilled version of this essay is printed as "Wordsworth on Science and Poetry" (*REL,* 1962). Sharrock suggests that a lecture given by Davy in January 1802 was instrumental in changing Wordsworth's view of science. H. W. Piper's *The Active Universe,* however, indicates that Wordsworth was aware of scientific theories about the activity of matter before any possible influence from Davy.

The problem of Wordsworth's relationship with his audience has been studied from a number of points of view. It is central, of course, to *The Mirror and the Lamp.* The early reviews are also relevant here, as are the articles by Samuel Holt Monk, "Anna Seward and the Romantic Poets," in *Wordsworth and Coleridge,* ed. E. L. Griggs, and R. S. Woof, "Coleridge and Thomasina Dennis" (*UTQ,* 1962), which have some interesting material on the taste of the times. Patrick Cruttwell has discussed "Wordsworth, the Public, and the People" (*SR,* 1956). A more systematic discussion of the same topic may be found in W. J. B. Owen's "Wordsworth, The Problem of Communication, and John Dennis" in *Wordsworth's Mind and Art,* ed. A. W. Thomson (1969). Owen delineates Wordsworth's successive conceptions of his audience and explanations of why his poetry was not popular. The critical vocabulary of John Dennis is visible in Wordsworth's distinctions among the different kinds of passion which poetry may communicate, and, consequently, in the different kinds of audience which it may reach. David Perkins, in *Wordsworth and the Poetry of Sincerity* (1964), treats the failure of communication as a rhetorical problem for Wordsworth, rather than as a sign of deficiency in his audience. Perkins sees the conflict between art and nature as having persisted through Wordsworth's career. On the one hand, there are the demands of art, which Wordsworth increasingly felt; on the other, there is the criterion of sincerity, which he never abandoned, and which works against art. Another problem for Wordsworth was his growing sense that language is inadequate to carry belief live into the heart. With this last point in particular, Perkins amplifies his earlier remarks in *The Quest for Permanence*. There, he had written that Wordsworth chose to communicate by image and symbol, rather than by abstract discourse, because symbol, rising directly from the imagination, is more trustworthy than any other mode. But symbol, too, may be arbitrary, or its meaning private, and the poet comes to distrust his own materials. Part of the difficulty, as Basil Willey pointed out, lies in Wordsworth's having lived in a demythologized world. It is traditionally difficult to write poetry, at least "Things unattempted yet in prose or rhyme," but the difficulties are multiplied when there is no generally accepted body of symbols upon which to draw. The poet is at every turn forced back upon himself. Perkins' book, then, takes up a major dilemma of poetry since Wordsworth, using Wordsworth as an example. His argument, which produces some good readings of the poems, should be contrasted with such studies as Abrams' essay on "The Correspondent Breeze" and Hartman's *The Unmediated Vision,* which show how Wordsworth was able to adapt traditional symbols to his own purposes. Douglas Bush's *Mythology and the Romantic Tradition in English Poetry* (1937), which pictures Wordsworth as the poet who recreated classical myth for the nineteenth century, also suggests that Wordsworth's resources were not as limited as Perkins considers them to have been. *Wordsworth and the Poetry of Sincerity* does lay out the rhetorical problems nicely, though the analysis of Wordsworth's rhetoric receives less stress than the problems it was shaped to overcome, despite the presence of two chapters on "Resources of Style and Expression." Perkins also provides plausible explanations for the long fallow periods which Wordsworth had, but his emphasis upon the embattled poet will trouble readers who remember Wordsworth's confidence in the power and permanence of the written word.

The originality of the *Lyrical Ballads* has been disputed by Robert D. Mayo, whose article "The Contemporaneity of the *Lyrical Ballads*" (*PMLA*, 1954) shows the presence of themes, techniques, and attitudes supposedly characteristic of Wordsworth and Coleridge in the magazine verse of the 1780's and 1790's. But, as Charles Ryskamp shows in "Wordsworth's *Lyrical Ballads* in their Time," which appears in *From Sensibility to Romanticism* (1965), similarity does not make identity. Ryskamp shows the novelty of Wordsworth's evocation of feeling by comparisons with the poetry of Cowper. John E. Jordan's "The Novelty of the *Lyrical Ballads*" in *Bicentenary Wordsworth Studies* also examines the contemporary context of Wordsworth's poems. Another attempt to define Wordsworth's originality, James Scoggins' "The Preface to *Lyrical Ballads*: A Revolution in Dispute" in *Studies in Criticism and Aesthetics, 1660– 1800,* ed. Howard Anderson and John S. Shea (1967), maintains that the early critics of Wordsworth sensed and reacted hostilely to the revolutionary proposition that the poet is an autonomous creator who endows all things, even the trivial, with enormous significance. To make his case, Scoggins relies heavily upon criticisms of the 1807 *Poems.*

The most consistent attempt to define the originality of the *Lyrical Ballads* has been by Stephen Maxfield Parrish, who has argued in a series of articles that it is dramatic technique, which, since Hazlitt, Wordsworth has been supposed to have lacked, that differentiates Wordsworth's poetry from what came before it. In " 'The Thorn': Wordsworth's Dramatic Monologue" (*ELH*, 1957), Parrish took Wordsworth's 1800 Note to the poem as a fair statement of its purpose, which was to describe the narrator's reactions to Martha Ray, rather than the mysterious woman herself. In answer to Mayo's article, Parrish argued generally that while "low" characters and unfortunate women were indeed commonplace in popular verse, they were not commonplace as narrators. In "The Wordsworth-Coleridge Controversy" (*PMLA*, 1958), Parrish suggested that the essential theoretical disagreement between the two poets was over precisely this point; Coleridge wanted a synthesis of nature and art which a poem written from a "natural" point of view could not provide. Parrish extended his thesis to other poems in "Dramatic Technique in the *Lyrical Ballads*" (*PMLA*, 1959). Parrish's work parallels that of Robert Langbaum, whose study of *The Poetry of Experience: The Dramatic Monologue in Modern Literary Tradition* (1957) virtually begins with Wordsworth. Langbaum points out that Wordsworth believed that to have the feeling give "importance to the action and situation, and not the action and situation to the feeling" was a revolutionary departure in poetry, and demonstrates how that departure has conditioned poetry since.

In "Dionysius in *Lyrical Ballads*," in *Wordsworth's Mind and Art*, Donald Davie denies any dramatic talent to Wordsworth. For Davie, the central quality of the *Lyrical Ballads* is "glee," the wondering and immobile joy which spreads out to encompass feelings normally not joyful at all. Death and life, as Hirsch and others have pointed out, can be equally part of glee, because glee seeks out what is normally painful and so works upon it as to allow it to be contemplated with perfect equanimity. This point is developed in a remarkable reading of "The Brothers." Davie associates the principle of glee with Nietzsche's description of the Dionysiac spirit, and with the Aristotelian concept of wonder, or *admiratio*, which he sees in the Preface. Wordsworth, then, moves far beyond the sentimental principle of mingling contrary emotions; he fuses them, and his originality lies in having done so.

Sometimes, however, it is precisely dramatic technique that allows Wordsworth to fuse contrary emotions. John F. Danby's *The Simple Wordsworth* has demonstrated how complex Wordsworth's persona is in such poems as "The Idiot Boy" and "Simon Lee." Danby shows in these poems what he calls the "irony of loving-kindness," in which the enormous and unalterable passions of the Mad Mother or the Idiot are balanced by the "perdurable ordinariness and faulty comprehension" of the narrator. The dramatic construction of the poems allows Wordsworth to avoid both condescension and idealization, and also to draw the distinction between "literary" pathos, which the narrator mocks, and real human feeling, whose mystery he tries clumsily but genuinely to express.

The concentration of Parrish and Danby on Wordsworth's experimental poems has helped to stimulate other studies. Mary Jacobus' discussion of "The Idiot Boy" in *Bicentenary Wordsworth Studies* shows how the humor of the poem both concedes the story's absurdity and undermines the attitude which makes it absurd. Albert Gérard has discussed the relative importance of the thorn itself, the narrator, and the tale of Martha Ray in "Of Trees and Men: The Unity of Wordsworth's 'The Thorn'" (*EIC*, 1964). John E. Jordan, Jr., has done a valuable study of "The Hewing of *Peter Bell*" (*SEL*, 1967) which traces the poem's growth and Wordsworth's purposes. G. H. Durrant has discussed the poem's mockery of established literary values in "Wordsworth's 'Peter Bell'—A *Pons Asinorium* for Critics" (*Wascana Review*, 1966). Frederick Garber's essay, "Wordsworth's Comedy of Redemption" (*Anglia*, 1966), concentrates on the poem's balance of comedy and potential tragedy, as had Jordan in his article on "Wordsworth's Humor" (*PMLA*, 1958), which isolated a quality in Wordsworth's style that is important to many of the *Lyrical Ballads*. Carl Woodring's *"Peter Bell* and 'The Pious': A New Letter" (*PQ*, 1951) also suggests the importance of comedy in the poem. Melvin R. Watson's "The Redemption of Peter Bell" (*SEL*, 1964) pursues the comparison with "The Rime of the Ancient Mariner." Alun R. Jones, in "The Compassionate World: Some Observations on Wordsworth's *Lyrical Ballads* of 1798" (*English*, 1970), describes Wordsworth's ability to enter the feelings of others; Paul Edwards, in "The Narrator's Voice in 'Goody Blake and Harry Gill' " (*English*, 1970) applies Danby's method to that poem more thoroughly than Danby himself had done. The "curse poems," as Thomas Hutchinson called them, have been studied by Charles J. Smith in "Wordsworth and Coleridge: The Growth of a Theme" (*SP*, 1957); by Kathleen Coburn, who argues in "Coleridge and Wordsworth and 'the Supernatural' " (*UTQ*, 1956) that Wordsworth was actually more reliant upon the supernatural than was Coleridge; by Parrish in "Dramatic Technique"; and by Hartman in *Wordsworth's Poetry, 1787–1814.*

Some of the best stylistic studies of Wordsworth show how his imagery reflects his philosophical beliefs. De Quincey long ago noticed Wordsworth's deft blending of the physical and mental worlds (*Literary Reminiscences*), and many writers since have explored the "rhetoric of interaction," as Herbert Lindenberger calls it. This body of criticism owes a great deal to W. K. Wimsatt's "The Structure of Romantic Nature Imagery" in *The Verbal Icon* (1954), which demonstrated the constant presence of the poet's consciousness in romantic nature metaphors. Wordsworth's habits of blending the perceiver and the perceived and of blurring the outlines of things have been discussed by F. R. Leavis in *Revaluation* (1936) and by William Empson in *Seven Types of Ambiguity* (1930), although Empson in particular considers Wordsworth's language a symptom of philosophical vagueness. Leavis takes the Arnoldian view; Wordsworth gave us poetry by blurring the thought. Carl Robinson Sonn, in "An Approach to Wordsworth's Earlier Imagery" (*ELH*, 1960), sees the blurring too; Wordsworth's images are too unified to answer to the terminology of vehicle and tenor, and new terms adequate to Wordsworth's language must be found. M. H. Abrams' "The Correspondent Breeze" is an examination of one of Wordsworth's most important images of relationship. Kenneth MacLean's "The Water Symbol in *The Prelude*

(1805–6)" (*UTQ*, 1948) surveys another. Florence Marsh, in her study of *Wordsworth's Imagery* (1952), shows the way in which recurrent images, like wind and water, reinforce each other and grow into symbols. Wordsworth's metaphors are not bold, but they build up great effects through a series of gentle shocks of mild surprise. *Wordsworth's Imagery* contains a discussion of Wordsworth's theory of imagery, as well as detailed looks at particular images. C. J. Smith's "The Contrarieties: Wordsworth's Dualistic Imagery" (*PMLA*, 1954) discusses the many pairs of images that occur in the poems. Donald Wesling discusses the prosody of Wordsworth's meditative style in "The Inevitable Ear: Freedom and Necessity in Lyric Form, Wordsworth and After" (*ELH*, 1969). Helmut Viebrock discusses the versification of "Written in March . . ." in *Versdichtung der englischen Romantik,* ed. Teut Andreas Riese and Dieter Riesner (1968). Roger N. Murray's *Wordsworth's Style: Figures and Themes in the Lyrical Ballads of 1800* (1967) is a useful rhetorical analysis of the poetry.

It is almost a commonplace that Wordsworth's later imagery is more abstract than his earlier because Wordsworth could no longer maintain the belief that nature was valuable in herself. Seymour Lainoff's "Wordsworth's Final Phase: Glimpses of Eternity" (*SEL*, 1961) takes this point of view, as does Stewart C. Wilcox in "Wordsworth's River Duddon Sonnets" (*PMLA*, 1954), which reads the whole sequence as an allegory of human life for which the river is but the flimsiest of pretexts. Donald Wesling, in *Wordsworth and the Adequacy of Landscape* (1970), traces, as many have done, Wordsworth's growth away from picturesque description to the creation of meditative landscape. Wesling goes on to argue that meditative landscape was itself inadequate, as it did not give an adequate image of man, and he discusses the ways in which Wordsworth filled his landscapes with symbols of human activity. A most sophisticated treatment of Wordsworth's tendency towards symbolism may be found in Paul de Man's essays "Structure intentionelle de l'image romantique" (*Revue Internationale de Philosophie,* 1960; trans. in *Romanticism and Consciousness,* ed. Harold Bloom, 1970) and "Symbolic Landscape in Wordsworth and Yeats," in *In Defense of Reading,* ed. R. A. Brower and R. Poirier (1962), which show Wordsworth's balance between direct and imagined vision in analyses of passages from *The Prelude* and "Composed by the Side of Grasmere Lake."

Emblematic imagery is not confined to Wordsworth's later period; James Kissane has seen "A Night-Piece," written at Alfoxden, as an emblem of the mind similar to the vision from Snowdon (*MLN*, 1956). However, Jonathan Wordsworth draws clear distinctions between the treatment of the two episodes in "The Climbing of Snowdon" in *Bicentenary Wordsworth Studies*. James R. Baird, in "Wordsworth's 'Inscrutable Workmanship' and the Emblems of Reality" (*PMLA*, 1953), has shown the way in which Wordsworth builds up greatest truths from least suggestions. Frederick Garber's "Wordsworth at the Universal Dance" (*SIR*, 1969) discusses the movement from a perception of daffodils to a vision of cosmic harmony in "I wandered lonely as a cloud." Both Jones, in *The Egotistical Sublime*, and Perkins, in *The Quest for Permanence*, have much to say about Wordsworth's images of blending and his attempts to redeem nature from flux by means of symbol. Ellen D. Leyburn has described the symbolic "Radiance in *The White Doe of Rylstone*" (*SP*, 1950); her essay should be compared with Martin Price's "Imagination in *The White Doe of Rylstone*" (*PQ*, 1954), which argues that the poem has less to do with the supernatural than with the imagination. Mary Lynn Woolley, in "Wordsworth's Symbolic Vale as it Functions in *The Prelude*" (*SIR*, 1968), sets out the nexus of symbols that serves as a norm for the experiences described in the poem. R. A. Foakes, in *The Romantic Assertion* (1958), and Bernard Blackstone, in *The Lost Travellers* (1962), have discussed Wordsworth's use of that inevitable symbol the journey-plot. Blackstone's reading of Wordsworth is under the influence of Blake; Wordsworth's figures wander about in a postlapsarian universe in which nature and man have been separated. It may be doubted whether *The Waggoner* portends that much.

In addition to the studies of imagery, there are several interesting studies of words and of syntax. Josephine Miles's "Wordsworth: The Mind's Excursive Power" in *Eras and Modes in English Poetry* (1957) and *Wordsworth and the Vocabulary of Emotion* (1942) do much to recover the force of such Wordsworthian words as "breath" and "spirit." The later book has useful tables which compare Wordsworth's use of the different parts of speech, and hence his apprehension of reality, with that of other poets of other eras. William Empson has traced Wordsworth's use of "Sense in *The Prelude*" in *The Structure of Complex Words* (1951). See also Ellen D. Leyburn's "Recurrent Words in *The Prelude*" (*ELH*, 1949) and Clarke's discussion of Wordsworth's use of "image," "form," and "shape" in *Romantic Paradox*. Both Frances O. Austin in "Time, Experience, and Syntax in Wordsworth's Poetry" (*NM*, 1969) and Robert M. Maniquis in "Comparison, Intensity, and Time in 'Tintern Abbey' "

(*Criticism,* 1969) wish to defend Wordsworth's syntax as functional, not vague or flabby.

One of the most important recent studies of Wordsworth is Herbert Lindenberger's *On Wordsworth's* Prelude (1963), a series of essays considering the poem from several points of view. Lindenberger has much to say about Wordsworth's various styles, which range from the most common to the most elevated, and from private utterance to public statement. Lindenberger's chapter on *"The Prelude* and the Older Rhetoric" draws upon the work of Klaus Dockhorn, whose two papers, "Wordsworth und die rhetorische Tradition in England" and "Die Rhetorik als Quelle des vorromantischen Irrationalismus in der Literatur und Geistesgeschichte" (*Nachrichten der Akademie der Wissenschaften in Göttingen,* 1944 and 1949) showed the influence of classical rhetoric in the formation of Wordsworth's poetic theories. In particular, Lindenberger applies the distinction between pathos and ethos to Wordsworth's poem, to account thereby for its variety of style. The poetry of ethos, he feels, has been relatively neglected; he shows, for example, the annoyance of reviewers at the alternate soaring (pathos) and sinking (ethos) in *The Prelude.* His own readings of the non-visionary books of the poem, together with those by Ferry in *The Limits of Mortality* and Hartman in *Wordsworth's Poetry, 1787–1814,* show what a crucial part of the whole they are.

Lindenberger also devotes attention to Wordsworth's more visionary rhetoric, discussing the images of interaction and analyzing the structure of several of them to show how, as F. R. Leavis put it, they both describe and create the experience which is their subject. This second technique is used in Lindenberger's discussion of the "spots of time," for which he seeks to define a common structure. He finds it in Wordsworth's creation of a movement from the simple and precise to the extraordinary. Earlier, Jonathan Bishop in "Wordsworth and the 'Spots of Time' " (*ELH,* 1959) had found a common psychological pattern to these visionary moments; the poet, off by himself, performs some prideful act with guilty overtones, and is then checked and chastened by the sudden appearance of power from without. Geoffrey Hartman, to whom the whole idea of spots, both in space and time, is crucial, also presents the spots of time as a trial of strength against nature, one whose implications are not fully realized until the older Wordsworth, writing of the experience, sees that the power he had assigned to nature truly belongs to the mind. The spots of time have their beneficent aspect, as well as their frightening one. Lindenberger's discussion of the refraction of emotion shows how the spots create a diversity of feeling, and Hartman suggests that the conception of the spot of time is associated with the tradition of the *genius loci,* whose ministering virtue is now seen to reach through time.

R. D. Havens' *The Mind of a Poet* (2 vols., 1941) is an important book in the history of Wordsworthian criticism. Although it is now somewhat dated, it is still a useful and basic text for the study of *The Prelude.* Havens' first volume is a study of Wordsworth's philosophy, primarily as it is seen in *The Prelude,* though it draws upon and applies to other poems as well. The second volume, a detailed commentary on both the 1805 and 1850 versions, shows an excellent sense of the relationships among different parts of the poem and a keen awareness of Wordsworth's tone, and provides as well a biographical and historical gloss to the text.

The literary influences on Wordsworth have been carefully catalogued by Abbie Findlay Potts in *Wordsworth's* Prelude: *A Study of its Literary Form* (1953) and *The Elegiac Mode* (1967). The former book discusses the influence of virtually everyone but Coleridge upon the form and language of *The Prelude;* the material on Bunyan is perhaps most helpful. Miss Potts's later study connects Wordsworth's practice in the "Lucy" and "Matthew" poems with the techniques of the classical elegists. Charles N. Coe's *Wordsworth and the Literature of Travel* (1953) records Wordsworth's borrowings from travel books, which, although extensive, are not crucial to the poetry.

There are numerous studies of Wordsworth's relationship with other literatures, other poets, and other arts, though, particularly in the latter case, much remains to be done. Margery Sabin has distinguished between the conceptions of "Imagination in Rousseau and Wordsworth" (*CL,* 1970). Geoffrey Hartman's *The Unmediated Vision* considers Wordsworth with Rilke, Hopkins, and Valéry; Karl Kroeber's *The Artifice of Reality* (1964) compares him with Foscolo, Keats, and Leopardi. Kroeber is interested in defining the spirit of the age by seeing what his four writers have in common, a method which does not allow him to break much new ground. The chapter on "The Temporalization of Space," however, is nicely done, and Kroeber is certainly successful in his attempt to widen the audience of the Italian poets.

Kroeber's earlier book, *Romantic Narrative Art* (1960), examines Wordsworth's use of traditional genres, the literary ballad and the epic. Kroeber concentrates mainly on "Michael," which he considers Wordsworth's finest short narrative, and on *The Prelude,* whose debt to and difference from the epic tradition he defines. Lindenberger compares

Wordsworth's practice in his long poem with that of his contemporaries, and Brian Wilkie explores the whole matter of the relationship of *The Prelude* to epic convention in *Romantic Poets and Epic Tradition* (1965). Hermann Fischer's *Die romantische Verserzählung in England: Versuch einer Gattungsgeschichte* (1964) is concerned with the development of epic, romance, and ballad during the period. Fischer gives special attention to the *Lyrical Ballads* and *The White Doe of Rylstone*. On the ballad, in addition to Kroeber and Fischer, see C. W. Stork, "The Influence of the Popular Ballad on Wordsworth and Coleridge" (*PMLA*, 1914), Paul G. Brewster, "The Influence of the Popular Ballad on Wordsworth's Poetry" (*SP*, 1938), a much more detailed article, and Irving H. Buchen's "Wordsworth's Gothic Ballads" (*Genre*, 1970). Charles Tomlinson's brief review of *The Common Muse: An Anthology of Popular British Ballad Poetry XV–XXth Century*, ed. V. de Sola Pinto and Allan Rodway (*Poetry*, 1958), identifies the anapestic meter common in the 1800 *Lyrical Ballads* with that used by street singers of Wordsworth's time. On Words-worth's use of pastoral, see Lindenberger on "true pastoral"; L. N. Broughton, *The Theocritean Element in . . . Wordsworth* (1920); E. K. Knowlton, "The Novelty of Wordsworth's *Michael* as a Pastoral" (*PMLA*, 1920); D. L. Durling, *The Georgic Tradition in English Poetry* (1935); and Renato Poggioli's "The Pastoral of the Self" (*Daedalus*, 1959), a brief survey of tendencies in the genre with important implications for Wordsworth. There are two important essays on Wordsworth's use of genre in *From Sensibility to Romanticism*. Geoffrey Hartman's "Wordsworth, Inscriptions, and Romantic Nature Poetry" shows how Wordsworth modified the inscription, a form which derives ultimately from the *Greek Anthology*, to include a more direct and more extensive perception of the natural scene. Ernest Bernhardt-Kabisch's "Wordsworth: The Monumental Poet" (*PQ*, 1965) also bears on Wordsworth's creation of memorials. The second essay in *From Sensibility to Romanticism*, M. H. Abrams' "Structure and Style in the Greater Romantic Lyric," is concerned with the transmutations of the eighteenth-century loco-descriptive poem effected by Coleridge in his conversation poems and Wordsworth in "Tintern Abbey." Abrams discusses the growing interpenetration of thought and nature as the genre developed, and relates romantic practice to the analogism of seventeenth-century meditative poetry. Earl R. Wasserman's "The English Romantics: The Grounds of Knowledge" (*SIR*, 1964) also examines the way in which moral value is seen to inhere in a landscape. Wasserman's essay explores the different attitudes of the romantic poets towards the relative primacy of mind and landscape; Wordsworth is a subjectivist for him, Keats is Wordsworth's antithesis, and Coleridge, appropriately enough, is a synthesizer of subjective and objective. Paul de Man has recently questioned the assumptions of Abrams and Wasserman in "The Rhetoric of Temporality" in *Interpretation: Theory and Practice,* ed. Charles S. Singleton (1969). De Man argues that the dialectic between nature and the self, with nature being read symbolically, is not really the characteristic romantic attitude; nature is instead read allegorically, it is a construct of the mind, which gains no real knowledge but what it imposes on such an alien order. De Man, like Bostetter and Hartman, finds the real problem to be the conflict between knowledge of the self seen in its "authentically temporal predicament" and a wish to flee from this "negative self-knowledge." The creation of symbols in the natural world is part of this attempt to evade solitude. The second part of de Man's essay is a discussion of romantic irony, which, like allegory, is seen as a mode which defines the temporal predicament, though it does so from a different point of view. This definition involves an analysis of the time-consciousness in "A Slumber did my spirit seal." Despite the theoretical differences between de Man on the one hand and Abrams and Wasserman on the other, they are agreed in finding Wordsworth's relationships with older modes of thought, particularly those which flourished in England in the sixteenth and seventeenth centuries, to be crucial in the formation of his poetry.

Wordsworth's relationships with the other arts have been studied by Russell Noyes in *Wordsworth and the Art of Landscape* (1968), which brings together much earlier material on Wordsworth's taste in gardening and ideas about landscape; by Martha H. Shackford in *Wordsworth's Interest in Painters and Pictures* (1945), which includes a chronological record of Wordsworth's references to painters and painting; and by Alec King in *Wordsworth and the Artist's Vision* (1966), a comparison of Wordsworth's ways of seeing and reordering the physical world with the theoretical statements and the works of various painters and sculptors. For a psychological account of Wordsworth's way of seeing, one may consult Gerhard Hensel, "Das Optische bei Wordsworth" (*Archiv für die gesämte Psychologie,* 1930). Wordsworth's familiarity with the aesthetic terminology of the sublime, the picturesque, and the beautiful is writ large in a number of studies. Irene P. McKeehan has defined some meanings for such terms in "Some Observations upon the Vocabulary of Landscape Description among the Early Romanticists," in *Elizabethan Studies and Other Essays in Honor of George F. Reynolds* (1945); John R. Nabholtz, in

"Dorothy Wordsworth and the Picturesque" (*SIR*, 1964), "Wordsworth and William Mason" (*RES*, 1964), and "Wordsworth's *Guide to the Lakes* and the Picturesque Tradition" (*MP*, 1964), has shown the considerable influence of theorists of the picturesque; James Benziger's *Images of Eternity* makes use of the aesthetic categories to explain Wordsworth's religious vision; James Scoggins has associated imagination with the sublime and fancy with the beautiful in *Imagination and Fancy*; and Noyes provides a succinct discussion of the whole matter in *Wordsworth and the Art of Landscape.* Wordsworth's own fragmentary essay on the sublime and the beautiful is included in the new edition of his prose. The best information on this topic, however, is in the major studies by Samuel Holt Monk, *The Sublime: A Study of Critical Theories in XVIII-Century England* (1935); Christopher Hussey, *The Picturesque* (1927); Walter J. Hipple, *The Beautiful, the Sublime, and the Picturesque* (1957); and Ernest Lee Tuveson, *The Imagination as a Means of Grace* (1960). Marjorie Hope Nicolson, in *Mountain Gloom and Mountain Glory* (1959), relates Wordsworth's feeling for mountains to that of his contemporaries.

There are many comparisons of Wordsworth and Constable. The biographical facts have been given by J. R. Watson in "Wordsworth and Constable" (*RES*, 1962). Sir Kenneth Clark pointed to the similarities between poet and painter in *Landscape into Art* (1949); D. S. Bland, in "Wordsworth and Constable" (*English*, 1950), finds Keats, with his refusal to moralize, a better parallel with Constable. The real difficulty is the same that afflicts King's study: finding an adequate terminology for comparison. The large bibliography in aesthetics on this problem has had little practical effect upon Wordsworthian criticism. Morse Peckham, in *Beyond the Tragic Vision* (1962), makes a noteworthy attempt to compare Wordsworth's philosophical orientation with that implied in Constable's paintings. R. F. Storch, in "Wordsworth and Constable" (*SIR*, 1966), has tried to deal in a systematic way with the means by which poet and painter suggest "something far more deeply interfused." Despite these efforts, more remains to be done, both in the formulation of an adequate method and in the study of Wordsworth's iconography. Wordsworth's relationship with Sir George Beaumont, who was Constable's patron as well as his own, is described well in Moorman. For different views of Beaumont's role as an artist and critic of art, compare Van Akin Burd, "Background to *Modern Painters*: The Tradition and the Turner Controversy," (*PMLA*, 1959), which disparages Beaumont, with Graham Reynolds, *Constable* (1965), which gives him qualified praise. The most notable connection between

Beaumont and Wordsworth, Beaumont's painting of Peele Castle, has been fruitfully compared with the poem by J. D. O'Hara, "Ambiguity and Assertion in Wordsworth's 'Elegiac Stanzas' " (PQ, 1968).

VI. STUDIES OF INDIVIDUAL WORKS

This is a very selective guide to the critical issues surrounding some of Wordsworth's major poems. The more general works listed in the previous sections are not always discussed here; they should of course be consulted.

The Borderers is the earliest of Wordsworth's works about which much critical controversy has grown up. The question of Wordsworth's relationship with William Godwin, described in Section IV of this bibliography, has been extensively debated; more recent studies have concentrated on the broader moral questions raised by the play. Legouis, in La Jeunesse de William Wordsworth, treated the play as a purgative rendering of Wordsworth's pessimism. There is in the play no plausible alternative to the intellectual pride of Oswald or the ignorance of Marmaduke, no means by which the good man can find moral certitude. Garrod, on the contrary, believed that Wordsworth had an answer to the problems posed by the play. He argued that the tragedy was designed as a rejection of anarchy, in which rational benevolence was shown to be the only fit standard of moral judgment (Wordsworth, 1923). Ernest de Selincourt's commentary on "Wordsworth's Preface to The Borderers" in Oxford Lectures on Poetry (1934) reiterated the position of Legouis, stressing the traditional problem of pride. G. W. Meyer, in Wordsworth's Formative Years, sought, like Harper, to deny that Wordsworth experienced any spiritual crisis between 1793 and 1795; consequently, he found The Borderers optimistic. Marmaduke welcomes the healing power of remorse, which comes to him for having acted as though man were evil; the play reveals the possibility of good. In Meyer's treatment, then, as he himself observed, The Borderers "ceases almost to be a tragedy." Earlier, Campbell and Mueschke (MP, 1926) had found the remorse to be the tragedy, not the catharsis. D. G. James's Skepticism and Poetry (1937) identified Wordsworth with Oswald, rather than with Marmaduke. This line of reasoning was followed up in G. Wilson Knight's "The Wordsworthian Profundity" in The Starlit Dome (1941), an essay which contains many of the themes of later criticism. Knight argues that the problem of the play is how to act rightly in a random universe. He suggests that Oswald acts not from reason but from passion; in Oswald, Wordsworth is exploring the consequences of his own recurrent commitment to feeling. Knight presents Marmaduke as caught between those Wordsworthian opposites, action, in this case dangerously free, and passiveness, in this case dangerously vulnerable. The play itself cannot resolve these issues; it is an exploration of energies beyond good and evil, an evocation of "nakedly spectral powers," out of which Wordsworth tried to build a more positive doctrine. Knight's argument here anticipates that of Geoffrey Hartman, except that Hartman redefines the "spectral powers" which Wordsworth had to domesticate as self-consciousness. In *Wordsworth's Poetry, 1787–1814* (and in his essentially identical treatment of the play in *JEGP*, 1963), Hartman presents Oswald as an intellectual murderer who forces Marmaduke to pass into "a new and isolating consciousness." The problem of the play lies in whether this new, basically modern consciousness, created in violation of the natural order, can ever have a moral function. To this problem the play offers no solution, because when Marmaduke comes to the point of self-consciousness, he is offered only unpalatable choices. He can embrace remorse, or he can live in radical exile from humanity, accepting complicity with Oswald. Marmaduke obviously rejects complicity, rightly seeing Oswald's independence as illusory; Hartman feels that he also rejects remorse, and possible suicide, on the strength of Oswald's arguments. Instead, he chooses romantic exile, a "spiritual rather than moral" position, thus evading the issue. Like Knight, Hartman sees the play ending in a moral standoff, its questions unanswerable. Robert Osborn's "Meaningful Obscurity: The Antecedents and Character of Rivers" in *Bicentenary Wordsworth Studies* discusses the ambivalent conception of Rivers (later Oswald), who is both the man of experience in a drama of initiation and the villain. Osborn does not feel that the natural order is violated, arguing instead that there is no natural order evident in the play, and that the crimes are in fact misguided attempts to create order.

Roger Sharrock's *"The Borderers:* Wordsworth on the Moral Frontier"* (*Durham University Journal*, 1964) associates Wordsworth's border region with the Terror, as Legouis had done; for Sharrock, the basic questions are whether force is justified to bring about social amelioration, and whether individualism is justified at all. R. F. Storch, in "Wordsworth's *The Borderers*: The Poet as Anthropologist" (*ELH*, 1969), is, like Knight, aware that the emphasis upon Oswald's rationality is misleading, because Oswald argues almost invariably from the passions. Storch disagrees with Knight's statements about the sexlessness of Wordsworth's world. For him, the play turns upon sexual energy, with Oswald's willingness to abandon Herbert a result of sexual jealousy over Idonea, which overcomes the taboo on parricide. The play explores the conflict between the individual and society, expressed in terms of desire and taboo. Other criticism includes Donald Hayden's "Toward an Understanding of Wordsworth's *The Borderers*" (*MLN,* 1951), which finds the play ambivalent about Godwin; John Jones's discussion in *The Egotistical Sublime,* which contrasts the kinds of solitude experienced by Oswald and Marmaduke, and sees evidence of a right guide to moral action in nature; Irving H. Buchen's "Wordsworth's Exposure and Reclamation of the Satanic Intellect" (*University Review,* 1966), which treats Oswald and Marmaduke as fragmentary halves of a whole being, each having qualities which the other lacks; and Peter L. Thorslev's "Wordsworth's *Borderers* and the Romantic Villain-Hero" (*SIR,* 1966), which examines the Gothic originals of Oswald. The Shakespearean parallels have been frequently noted; Enid Welsford's *Salisbury Plain: A Study in the Development of Wordsworth's Mind and Art* (1966) is a recent comparison of the universe of Wordsworth's play with that of *Othello* and *King Lear.* On the chronology of *The Borderers,* see J. R. MacGillivray, "The Date of Composition of *The Borderers*" (*MLN,* 1934), which argues from the date that the play is unlikely to be Godwinian in spirit, and Reed, *Chronology,* Appendix x, a careful account of what is known about the growth of the play.

The "Lucy" and "Matthew" Poems: There has been a great deal of speculation about who "Lucy" was, most of it, since Coleridge's remark that Wordsworth had possibly imagined the death of his sister, centered upon Dorothy. Herbert Hartman's "Wordsworth's 'Lucy' Poems: Notes and Marginalia" (*PMLA,* 1934) has a selective bibliography of scholarship up to that point; Hartman points out that "Lucy" was a common literary name. F. R. Leavis has an analysis of "Strange fits of passion have I known" in *Revaluation* (1936). F. W. Bateson's famous thesis that the poems are a symbolic killing of an incestuous love for Dorothy has somewhat obscured the care which he brings to "She dwelt among the untrodden ways." Bateson sees the poem as one which breaks down the usual beliefs about language and life to hint at a higher reality. There has been considerable debate about Wordsworth's attitude toward nature and human life in such poems as "A slumber did my spirit seal." Cleanth Brooks, in "Irony as a Principle of Structure" in *Literary Opinion in America,* ed. M. D. Zabel (1951), argued that the poem is ironic, with the end being an

utterly shattering vision of void and nothingness. Numerous other writers
have seen the ending as a version of the traditional elegiac consolation.
David Ferry sees it both ways in *The Limits of Mortality.* Lucy is made
part of nature in an ironical sense, but at the same time, she is ennobled by
being made "one with the natural processes which made her die." The
speaker's idealization of her in the first stanza was right, for "she had
nothing to do with humanity or mortality." Ferry reads the whole group of
poems as a paradigm of Wordsworth's equivocal beliefs about human life
and the imagination. There is no place within the limits of mortality for
Lucy's mystical identification with nature; the speaker, by contrast, remains
alive but in the flux of time, able to have only a symbolic relationship with
eternity. Life, and the poetic imagination, are shown to be limited. In
Wordsworth and the Great System, G. H. Durrant argues that the effectiveness of the poems arises from the polarity between Lucy's individual
identity and "her dependence on and ultimate subjection to the physical
universe." There is considerable discussion of the imagery of the group in
Durrant's attractive readings. Geoffrey Hartman sees the poem in terms of
self-consciousness, with Lucy dying before she becomes fully human; the
speaker, however, is self-conscious. See also the exchange between Hugh
Sykes Davies and R. F. Storch in *EIC,* 1965. Sacvan Berkovitch associates
Lucy with the creative principle in "Lucy and Light: An Interpretation of
Wordsworth's Lucy Poems" (*English,* 1966); James G. Taaffe has dis-
cussed a "plot" in the poems in "Poet and Lover in Wordsworth's 'Lucy'
Poems" (*MLR,* 1966), arguing that the lover acquires a poet's vision.
John F. Danby in *The Simple Wordsworth* and Anthony Conran in "The
Goslar Lyrics" in *Wordsworth's Mind and Art* have discussed the poems as
a group; both find the "Matthew poems" as fine as the more celebrated
poems about "Lucy." E. D. Hirsch, Jr., has a detailed reading of "The
Two April Mornings" in *Wordsworth and Schelling;* he finds that in spite
of all apparent change, the poem affirms that nothing is lost. Anne
Kostelanetz has examined the dramatic dimension of two "Matthew"
poems in "Wordsworth's 'Conversations': A Reading of 'The Two April
Mornings' and 'The Fountain' " (*ELH,* 1966).

Tintern Abbey: On the biographical issues, see John Bard McNulty's
"Autobiographical Vagaries in *Tintern Abbey*" (*SP,* 1945) and Charles
Harold Gray, "Wordsworth's First Visit to Tintern Abbey" (*PMLA,*
1934). Most writers on Wordsworth's philosophy consider the poem the
high point of his faith in nature, though recent writers have emphasized
the more tentative qualities of the poem. C. Clarke shows in "Loss and

Consolation in the Poetry of Wordsworth (1798–1805)" (*ES*, 1950) that Wordsworth both welcomed and feared the change from attachment to nature to attachment to the human world. Albert Gérard, in "Dark Passages: Exploring *Tintern Abbey*" (*SIR*, 1963), provides a study of the rhythm of the poem's construction, which he finds similar to the "systolic rhythm" he identified in Coleridge's conversation poems; the recoil from vision and the diffidence of the speaker balance the passages of affirmation. Harold Bloom's reading of the poem in *The Visionary Company* suggests also that man and nature are not always intimately combined; man is absorbed into nature in his youth and in his extreme old age, but in middle life he is separated, having to create as well as perceive, which is "his freedom and his grief." Bloom finds the end of the poem marked by desperation and waning faith; Gérard reads the last lines as a basis for Wordsworth's future beliefs. The play of faith and doubt in the poem is also illuminated by Eudo C. Mason's discussion, in *Versdichtung der englischen Romantik*, of such problems as the sufficiency and trustworthiness of nature and man's ability to establish continuity with himself. The function of the opening lines has been discussed in various ways by James Benziger in "*Tintern Abbey* Revisited" (*PMLA*, 1950), Geoffrey Hartman in *The Unmediated Vision*, and by Gérard in "Symbolic Landscape in Wordsworth's *Tintern Abbey*" (*Publ. de l'Univ. de l'Etat à Elisabethville*, 1962).

Resolution and Independence: Some of the best practical criticism of the poem is in Wordsworth's discussion of its figures in the 1815 Preface. Wordsworth's letter of 14 June 1802 and Dorothy's journal entry of 3 October 1800, which records the actual meeting with the Leech-gatherer, are also relevant. More biographical information may be found in George W. Meyer's "*Resolution and Independence*: Wordsworth's Answer to Coleridge's *Dejection: An Ode*" (*TSE*, 1950). Recent criticism of the poem has explored the conflict between the two sides of Wordsworth's experience, the visionary life and the prosaic life about which the speaker comes to worry. W. W. Robson's essay in *Interpretations*, ed. John Wain (1955), treats "Resolution and Independence" as a poem of maturity, in which the speaker eventually realizes that there is life independent of his own fears, which can help him to ward off "the encroachments of fantasy." In *Wordsworth and Coleridge*, William Heath treats the poem as a crucial event in Wordsworth's life, seeing it as the culmination of the search for a new way of dealing with experience in which he was engaged in 1801–02. Albert Gérard, in "Resolution and Independence: Wordsworth's Coming of Age" (*ESA*, 1960), concentrates on the alternation between concern with the self and concern with the not-self in the poem's formal design; he sees the Leech-gatherer as the symbol of a new moral interest in mankind, as distinct from the interest in nature which had marked the period when life was a summer mood. Florence G. Marsh is also concerned with the dialectical play of the inner and outer worlds in *"Resolution and Independence* Stanza XVIII" (*MLN*, 1955). Anthony E. M. Conran, in "The Dialectic of Experience: A Study of Wordsworth's *Resolution and Independence"* (*PMLA*, 1960), like Gérard and Marsh, finds that Wordsworth has to be drawn out of an unhealthy self-absorption; this is accomplished by the sudden comedy of the end of the poem. Conran suggests that "Resolution and Independence" has a pattern similar to that of medieval dream-allegory; it opens with Wordsworth at the mouth of the Romantic hell of wasted imagination, and it closes with his awakening from the dream, thanks to the revelation of the Leech-gatherer. David Eggenschwiler is also concerned with the dialectical interplay of styles in the poem in "Wordsworth's *Discordia Discors"* (*SIR*, 1969). A. W. Thomson has also explored the poem's reminiscences of allegory, particularly Spenser's, in his article in *Wordsworth's Mind and Art*. Alan Grob, in "Process and Permanence in *Resolution and Independence"* (*ELH*, 1961), and E. E. Bostetter, in *The Romantic Ventriloquists,* both point out that nature has nothing to do with the resolution of the poem; indeed, Bostetter finds nature associated with improvidence and eventually threatening, and Grob believes that the unsteadiness of the moods nature inspires precipitates the speaker's despair. Both see the poem as a significant turn toward the Christianity of the later works. The Leech-gatherer's soul sings the louder for every tatter in its mortal dress, demonstrating that while nature may not endure, spirit does.

Ode: Intimations of Immortality: Modern study of the *Ode* begins with Lionel Trilling's essay on the poem in the *English Institute Annual* (*1942*); reprinted in *The Liberal Imagination* (1950). Trilling's argument is that the poem is not about growing old, but about growing up. It is not at all about the loss of poetic power, but about the onset of philosophical maturity, and it is about immortality only in a limited sense. The lost glory is not imagination, but the glad illusion of perfect union between the self and nature; poetry comes with the sense of personal identity, not with the edenic early life. Cleanth Brooks's "Wordsworth and the Paradox of the Imagination," in *The Well Wrought Urn* (1947), is an important examination of the imagery of the poem, which argues that Wordsworth treats the imagination both as projectionist and as naturalist. Brooks also denies that the loss in the poem is absolute; the vision of childhood is only one aspect of the primal sympathy, and when the vision has gone, the sympathy, which is associated with the synthesizing imagination, remains. E. D. Hirsch, Jr., extends Brooks's contention that the dominant mode of the poem is paradox in his chapter on "Both-And Logic in the Immortality Ode" in *Wordsworth and Schelling.* For Hirsch, the statements of loss in the poem are consistently balanced by paradoxical statements of gain, even in the first four stanzas. Stuart M. Sperry's "From 'Tintern Abbey' to the 'Intimations Ode': Wordsworth and the Function of Memory" (*TWC,* 1970) and Kenneth R. Johnston's "Recollecting Forgetting: Forcing Paradox to the Limit in the 'Intimations Ode'" (*TWC,* 1971) are both concerned with the meaning that emerges from Wordsworth's paradoxes. T. M. Raysor's "The Themes of Immortality and Natural Piety in Wordsworth's Immortality Ode" (*PMLA,* 1954) contests Trilling's naturalist reading and A. C. Bradley's assertion in *Oxford Lectures on Poetry* (1909) that Wordsworth did not believe in personal survival after death. Raysor adduces evidence from other works of Wordsworth, and from the canceled reference to the grave as "A place of thought where we in waiting lie," to argue his point. His conclusions have been disputed by Robert L. Schneider in "The Failure of Solitude: Wordsworth's Immortality Ode" (*JEGP,* 1955), which sees a growing dualism in the *Ode,* and reaffirmed by David Rogers, in "God and Pre-Existence in Wordsworth's *Immortality Ode"* (*Durham University Journal,* 1969). In "Wordsworth's *Ode*: Obstinate Questionings" (*SIR,* 1966), Florence G. Marsh has tried to see whether the theme of immortality outlined by Raysor coheres with the theme of growth and recompense described by Trilling. Marsh takes a somewhat darker view of the loss than Trilling does, finding that Wordsworth's loss of mystical insight is a personal loss, not one that is common to humanity; Wordsworth's confusion of these two losses damages the poem. Like G. Wilson Knight, Marsh finds that the child is the center of the poem, analogous in meaning to the landscape of "Tintern Abbey," but she finds also that Wordsworth's turning away from the divine immanence revealed in the child to the idea of transcendence implied in the last stanzas leaves the poem confused. Alan Grob's "Wordsworth's *Immortality Ode* and the Search for Identity" (*ELH,* 1965) relates the growth of the poem to the changes in Wordsworth's philosophy. Grob compares the different stages of the poem to other poems contemporary with them, as H. W. Garrod had done, and argues that it was only the "adoption of an enlarged metaphysical framework" in 1804 that allowed Wordsworth to resolve the questions he had posed two years earlier. Wordsworth's growing dualism gave him a way of seeing contradictory evidence of loss and gain not as contradictory, but as referring to different levels of being. Moreover, the theme of immortality was suggested naturally, because if the search for identity is concentrated in "the ideal and changeless," there must be "a component of self whose being must extend beyond life's temporal boundaries." Grob, then, sees the poem as essentially unified, a record of conversion from doubt to faith.

The Prelude: It has been so central to our interpretation of Wordsworth since the publication of Legouis' biography that many of the important studies have already been mentioned. The narrative voices of the poem have been studied by Mark Reed in "The Speaker of *The Prelude*" and Ford T. Swetnam, Jr., in "The Satiric Voices of *The Prelude*," both of which essays appear in *Bicentenary Wordsworth Studies*: by Jonathan R. Grandine in *The Problem of Shape in 'The Prelude': The Conflict of Private and Public Speech*, a Harvard Honors essay; and by R. J. Onorato in his comprehensive psychoanalytic study *The Character of the Poet: Wordsworth in 'The Prelude'* (1971). The excellent work of Lindenberger and David Ferry on the non-visionary books may be supplemented by two essays on Book v: Jane Worthington Smyser, "Wordsworth's Dream of Poetry and Science: *The Prelude*, v" (*PMLA*, 1956), and Evelyn Shakir, "Books, Death, and Immortality: A Study of Book v of *The Prelude*" (*SIR*, 1969). R. F. Storch has a discussion of "Wordsworth and the City: 'Social Reason's Inner Sense' " (*TWC*, 1970). Richard Stang, in "The False Dawn: A Study of the Opening of Wordsworth's *The Prelude*" (*ELH*, 1966), and John F. McCarthy, in "The Conflict in Books I–II of *The Prelude*" (*MLQ*, 1969), have discussed the poem's problematic opening. E. A. Horsman's "The Design of Wordsworth's *Prelude*" (conveniently reprinted in *Wordsworth's Mind and Art*) is a good discussion of the poem's structure. Charles Williams centered his important essay on Wordsworth in *The English Poetic Mind* (1932) on *The Prelude*. C. Clarke's "Nature's Education of Man: Some Remarks on the Philosophy of Wordsworth" (*Philosophy*, 1948) discusses *The Prelude* and "Tintern Abbey." Frances Christensen's "Creative Sensibility in Wordsworth" (*JEGP*, 1946) and "Intellectual Love: The Second Theme of *The Prelude*" (*PMLA*, 1965) throw valuable light on Wordsworth's philosophy of the imagination and man.

The Excursion: The best criticism is by Bostetter in *The Romantic*

Ventriloquists and Hartman in *Wordsworth's Poetry 1787–1814*. Both see the poem as a record of Wordsworth's flight from his own vision. Judson Stanley Lyon's *The Excursion: A Study* (1950) is a full-length treatment of the poem's genesis, reputation, content, and imagery. Enid Welsford, in *Salisbury Plain: A Study in the Development of Wordsworth's Mind and Art*, devotes considerable space to the structure and symbols of the poem, showing how it reflects Wordsworth's emblematic view of nature. The biographical and historical background has been explored by M. Ray Adams, "Joseph Fawcett and Wordsworth's Solitary" (*PMLA*, 1933); Alfred C. Ames, "Contemporary Defense of Wordsworth's 'Pedlar' " (*MLN*, 1948); and B. Bernard Cohen, "William Hazlitt: Bonapartist Critic of *The Excursion*" (*MLQ*, 1949).

III
COLERIDGE

Thomas M. Raysor
Max F. Schulz

I. BIBLIOGRAPHIES

The student of Coleridge will find satisfactory bibliographical tools at his hand so far as the original texts are concerned. Thomas J. Wise's *Bibliography* (1913) has not been appreciably diminished in value by the forgeries of first editions of which he has been convicted by John Carter and Graham Pollard; but George Whalley shows in "The Publication of Coleridge's 'Prometheus' Essay" (*N&Q,* 1969) that Wise was not above careless ascription on occasion. This bibliography is inclusive up to the date of publication, listing items first published in periodicals, memoirs, etc., and listing collected editions of the works of Coleridge. Wise's own collection of Coleridge first editions, as described bibliographically in his *Catalogue of the Ashley Library* (1922) and in *Two Lake Poets* (1927), has gone to the British Museum, so that it is accessible to students. The British Museum *General Catalogue of Printed Books* covers Coleridge in Volume XL (1947); and the *Catalogue of Additions to the Manuscripts* of the British Museum lists the successive accumulations of Coleridge manuscripts. The Ottery Collection is described by T. C. Skeat (*British Museum Quarterly,* 1952). Both Kathleen Coburn in her edition-in-progress of the *Notebooks* (1957, 1961) and Donald Sultana in *Coleridge in Malta and Italy* (1969) have supplemented this list with descriptions of additional Coleridgeana mainly associated with his years in the Mediterranean area and housed in Victoria College Library, Toronto; Public Record Office; National Maritime Museum, Greenwich; Royal Malta Library and Palace Archives, Valletta. William Hale White provides a *Description of the Wordsworth and Coleridge Manuscripts in the Possession of Mr. T. Norton Longman* (1897), now in the Yale University Library, whose acquisitions of the manuscript of *Lyrical Ballads* (1800) and of an incomplete set of sheets used as printer's copy for the 1802 edition are noted by Cornelius H. Patton and Frederick A. Pottle in *Yale University Library Gazette* (1934, 1966). Roberta Florence Brinkley lists the Coleridge holdings at the Huntington Library (*HLQ,* 1945), supplemented by P. M. Zall (*The Wordsworth Circle,* 1971); and Fran Stephens describes the Coleridge Family Papers at the University of Texas (*Library Chronicle of the Univ. of Texas,* 1970).

There are two other bibliographies of continuing value, by John Louis Haney (1903) and by Virginia Kennedy and Mary Barton (1935). Both books were criticized bibliographically, but they have been useful because of their lists of marginalia by Coleridge and lists of critical references, in which the later Kennedy and Barton volume supplements Haney. Both bibliographies analyze their reading lists, Kennedy and Barton very fully. Haney has added twice to his list of books with annotations by Coleridge, in *Schelling Anniversary Studies* (1923) and in *Coleridge* (ed., Edmund Blunden and E. L. Griggs, 1934); while Whalley gives an excellent account of Coleridge's habits of annotation, his library, its dispersal after his death, and a checklist of the books, in "Portrait of a Bibliophile" (*BC,* 1961), in "Coleridge Marginalia Lost" (*BC,* 1968), and in "The Harvest on the Ground: Coleridge's Marginalia" (*UTQ,* 1969). Newly revised and updated, Volume III of *CBEL* (1969) has an analyzed list of successive authoritative editions of Coleridge compiled by Whalley.

An annotated bibliography of all the published references to Coleridge through 1840 and of all but passing and trivial allusions since 1840 is being prepared by Richard Haven, with Walter Crawford, Edward Lauterbach, and Maurianne Adams (see *Victorian Periodicals Newsletter,* 1968). Until it is completed, one must make do with the selective bibliographies in Volume III of the Old *CBEL* (1941) compiled by T. M. Raysor, supplemented in Volume V (1957) and revised and updated in Volume III of the New *CBEL* by Whalley; and with the annual reviews of Coleridge scholarship and criticism in the bibliography for the Romantic Movement in *ELH* (1937–49), *PQ* (1950–64), and *ELN* (1965–). "A Check List of Coleridge Criticism" (*BB,* 1968, in three parts) by Thomas Hall, extending from 1790 to 1965 but alphabetically arranged, is of limited value despite the effort at inclusiveness. It is capriciously incomplete and occasionally inaccurate. Most irritating is its inconsistent practice of citing a journal with volume number but without date of publication. Richard Harter Fogle's *Romantic Poets and Prose Writers* (1967) in the Goldentree Bibliography series, while idiosyncratically selective, conveniently organizes many entries by individual work.

For additional information on the contemporary response to Coleridge, one should consult William S. Ward's "The Criticism of Poetry in British Periodicals, 1798–1820" (Duke Univ. diss., 1943; microcards, Univ. of Kentucky, 1955) and his articles published in the 1940's, cited later; John O. Hayden's *The Romantic Reviewers, 1802–1824* (1969); and J. R. de J. Jackson's *Coleridge: The Critical Heritage* (1970), which reprints 114 reviews of Coleridge's publications during his lifetime and thus supersedes the previously circumscribed usefulness of Walter Graham's "Contemporary Critics of Coleridge, the Poet" (*PMLA*, 1923) and *Contemporary Reviews of Romantic Poetry* (ed. John Wain, 1953). Finally, for the current response to Coleridge, one has Miss Coburn's introductory survey to *Coleridge: A Collection of Critical Essays* (1967), a gathering of previously published views, more than half concentrating on critical, philosophical, aesthetical, economic, and political aspects of Coleridge; and the journal *The Wordsworth Circle,* edited by Marilyn Gaull and Charles Mauskopf, which began in 1970, publishes notes and queries, and reports among other items on papers, meetings, research in progress, auctions, exhibits, library holdings and special events of importance to Coleridge studies. At present no formal bibliography or book review section is planned.

II. EDITIONS

The important activity of the past twenty-five years has been the editing of Coleridge's works, notebooks, and letters. He left so much unpublished, R. H. Fogle has remarked ("The Romantic Movement," *Contemporary Literary Scholarship,* ed. Lewis Leary, 1958), that the problem of texts "has made the work of his editors peculiarly important." Much of Coleridge's writing, difficult or impossible to obtain and of a scattered and fragmentary nature, is being brought together for the first time, and offers, as G. Whalley has succinctly phrased it in "Coleridge Unlabyrinthed" (*UTQ*, 1963), a chance "to study the mind of genius in its activity rather than in its products."

The *Collected Coleridge* under the general editorship of Kathleen

Coburn, with Bart Winer as associate editor, is the most important continuing event in Coleridge studies of the 1970's, and a fitting memorial to the bicentenary (1972) of Coleridge's birth. Sponsored by the Bollingen Foundation, this critical edition comprises sixteen titles in about twenty-four volumes. The specific works being prepared for the collection, and their editors, are (1) *Lectures 1795: On Politics and Religion*, ed. Lewis Patton and Peter Mann; (2) *The Watchman*, ed. L. Patton; (3) *Essays on His Times*, ed. David V. Erdman; (4) *The Friend*, ed. Barbara E. Rooke; (5) *Lectures 1808–1819: On Literature*, ed. Reginald A. Foakes; (6) *Lay Sermons*, ed. R. J. White; (7) *Biographia Literaria*, ed. M. H. Abrams; (8) *Lectures 1818–1819: On the History of Philosophy*, ed. Thomas McFarland; (9) *Aids to Reflection*, ed. J. B. Beer; (10) *On the Constitution of the Church and State*, ed. John Colmer; (11) *Shorter Works and Fragments*, ed. E. E. Bostetter; (12) *Marginalia*, ed. G. Whalley; (13) *The Logic*, ed. J. R. de J. Jackson; (14) *Table Talk*, ed. Carl R. Woodring; (15) *Opus Maximum*, ed. G. N. G. Orsini; (16) *Poetical Works*, ed. G. Whalley.

Three titles have appeared so far, *The Friend* (2 vols., 1969), *The Watchman* (1 vol., 1970), and *Lectures 1795: On Politics and Religion* (1 vol., 1971). The next two titles to be published should be *Lay Sermons* (1 vol.) and *Essays on His Times* (2 vols.). *The Logic* (1 vol.), *On the Constitution of the Church and State* (1 vol.), and *Marginalia* (probably 4 vols.) are also in advanced stages of editing.

The condition of much of this material—fragmentary and multiple manuscript drafts, marginalia, transcriptions, and shorthand reports of talk—poses difficult questions of editorial policy, which are being handled in the critical apparatus with great care for detail. Considering that over 150 years elapsed before the first collected edition of Coleridge's works materialized, these volumes will unquestionably provide the standard text for the next century or more. Consequently we are fortunate in being served so well by the meticulous scholarship of Miss Coburn and her fellow editors.

For the edition of *The Friend*, B. E. Rooke prints both the three-volume 1818 *rifacimento* and the original 1809–10 periodical. In footnotes she gives Coleridge's revisions of the 1809–10 text for the 1812 publication, as well as his emendations, cuts, and marginal comments noted in copies of the work, plus manuscript deletions and additions. In appendixes Miss Rooke analyzes the colophons of the 1809–10 and 1812 versions; describes folio by folio the partial manuscript of 1809–10 to indicate content, break in continuity, and handwriting; describes known annotated copies of the 1809–10, 1812, and 1818 versions; collates in parallel columns the folios of the manuscript and the pages of the 1809–10, 1812, and 1818 *Friend* and the 1837 (HNC) and *Collected Coleridge* reprints; lists the known subscribers to *The Friend,* their addresses, and their connections with the Coleridge circle; and prints letters (mostly unpublished) concerning *The Friend,* particularly the lengthy correspondence of Daniel Stuart and interested readers' responses. The index of 167 double-columned pages will be of incalculable aid to all who study this work of Coleridge's; it should provide accessibility to many ideas of Coleridge hitherto embedded in a lengthy and difficult prose that tended to put off students and critics alike. The Introduction gives a full history of *The Friend* from inception to the posthumous edition of 1837 of Henry Nelson Coleridge, detailing "the mundane problems of paper, stamps, and subscribers" that Coleridge struggled with, summarizing the revisions Coleridge made for the 1812 and 1818 publications, and analyzing Coleridge's organization (his "method") of the 1818 *rifacimento.* The editorial care that Miss Rooke has lavished on this work is everywhere apparent. She has provided the text; now students of Coleridge may furnish us with the rest of the story: an analysis of his philosophical antecedents; an exposition of his political, moral, and religious principles as they are initially set forth in the 1809–10 periodical and evolve into the 1818 statement; an account of how each version "is a civil libertarian tract for the times"; and a history of what the writing of *The Friend* meant to Coleridge and to the middle decades of the nineteenth century. A qualified start toward realizing some of these goals had been attempted, but with limited results, prior to Rooke's edition. Both E. L. Griggs in *"The Friend*—1809 and 1818 editions" (*MP,* 1938) and Dudley Bailey in "Coleridge's Revision of *The Friend"* (*MP,* 1961) give accounts of the differences in the three editions, although they disagree over whether Coleridge significantly changed his ideas from 1809 to 1818 or merely clarified his expression of them.

L. Patton prints the ten issues of *The Watchman,* from 1 March to 13 May 1796, with a table of contents analytical of the matter of each issue. In footnotes he gives the original source of each item, manuscript fragments, textual variants, Coleridge's annotations on two copies of the periodical, and the political and literary background to the various essays, reviews, and news items. In a succinct Introduction, Patton sketches the shifting political climate of Whiggish opinion which forms the inception and demise of *The Watchman,* rehearses the efforts of Coleridge and his friends to enlist subscribers, summarizes the potpourri that as a provincial periodical and eighteenth-century miscellany comprised its contents, identifies contributors, and analyzes the complex question of Coleridge's journalistic skills and evolving intentions. There is an analytical subject index of eighty-four double-columned pages. This is the first complete edition of *The Watchman* since its original issuance, the partial reprinting in Sara Coleridge's edition of *Essays on His Own Times* (1850) having attempted to exclude those items not by Coleridge, and these occupied more and more of the periodical as it proceeded. S. F. Johnson comments on this increase of Coleridge's borrowings, in "Coleridge's *The Watchman*: Decline and Fall" (*RES,* 1953).

Two other publications-in-progress of primary importance carrying over from the past decade are Miss Coburn's edition of the *Notebooks* and Griggs's of the *Collected Letters.* Close to seventy notebooks have survived—those "confidantes who have *not* betrayed me" as Coleridge alluded to them. For over thirty years Miss Coburn has been engaged in the self-imposed task of editing, dating, and annotating these notes, in performing what Whalley (*UTQ,* 1963) has called a "scholarly work of great daring, skill, and insight." Supported by the Bollingen Foundation, two large volumes covering the years 1794 to 1807 of the *Notebooks* of a projected five have appeared (1957, 1961), each bound in two parts, one text and the other notes on the text. Each double-volume contains chronological and notebook tables of dates for the entries that appear in it, and a mammoth triple index of names of persons, selected titles, and place names (130 pages in Volume I and 95 pages in Volume II). Users of the *Notebooks* will have to wait until the final volume in the collection for a subject index. The companion volumes of textual notes give detailed descriptions of each notebook. There are also informative appendixes (to Volume I) on Coleridge's knowledge of German and on his marginal notes on Thomas Taylor's *Proclus,* and (to Volume II) on Coleridge's knowledge of Italian, on his official duties in Malta, on his construction of a cryptogram, on the account in the Maltese political journal *Il Cartaginese* of the sinking of Captain John Wordsworth's ship *The Earl of Abergavenny,* on the contents of Wordsworth MS. M which accompanied Coleridge to Malta, and on Coleridge's reorganization of Nicholson's observations on weather. Needless to say Miss Coburn's notes are an incalculable aid in grasping the often profound but highly condensed records of Coleridge's thought and observation. In a pioneering scholarly effort of such complexity and monumentality, errors and omitted or overlooked facts are certain to have

occurred. Correcting dates, supplementing sources, and elaborating interpretations are sure to occupy scholars for years. Already D. Sultana in
"Coleridge's Autographs" (*TLS*, 15 February 1963) and in *Coleridge in
Malta and Italy* (1969) has challenged Miss Coburn's disposition of some
documents, notebook entries, and events associated with Coleridge's Maltese and Italian years. Earlier excerpts from the notebooks, which Miss
Coburn's edition reduces in effectiveness but which still offer resonances of
scholarly acumen and of historical perspective, are found in Ernest Hartley
Coleridge's *Anima Poetae* (1895), which E. Blunden (*REL*, 1966) considers still one of the "best collections of miscellaneous observations and
speculations in English since Boswell's Johnson"; Alois Brandl's inaccurate
transcription of the Gutch Notebook in Herrig's *Archiv* (1896); the Rev.
G. H. B. Coleridge's publication of a "picturesque tour" of the Lakes in
Wordsworth and Coleridge (ed. E. L. Griggs, 1939); and K. Coburn's
collection of Coleridge's prose *pensées* in *Inquiring Spirit* (1951). Then
there is R. F. Brinkley's *Coleridge on the Seventeenth Century* (1955), a
collection of everything which could be found of Coleridge's writings on
seventeenth-century philosophy, religion, science, and literature.

Prior to Griggs's edition of the *Collected Letters,* scholars had to
resort to scattered sources for Coleridge's letters: early memoirs such as
Cottle's (1837; 1848 version rpt. in 1970) or Allsop's (1836); the
Biographical Supplement to the 1847 edition of *Biographia Literaria,*
edited by H. N. Coleridge and Sara Coleridge; *Memorials of Coleorton*
(1887), edited by William Angus Knight; *Thomas Poole and His Friends*
(1888), by Mrs. Henry Sandford; *Letters from the Lake Poets to Daniel
Stuart* (1889), edited by Mary Stuart and E. H. Coleridge; *Tom Wedgwood, the First Photographer* (1903), by Richard B. Litchfield; the *Biographia Epistolaris* (1911), edited with a biographical commentary by
A. Turnbull, which however contains no letters not already printed earlier;
the two volumes of *Letters* (1895), edited with significant omissions by
E. H. Coleridge; and the supplementary two volumes of *Unpublished
Letters* (1932), edited by Griggs largely from transcripts made by E. H.
Coleridge; as well as (in Griggs's words) "a long succession of miscellaneous publications—memoirs, biographies, magazines, and newspapers." In
the *Collected Letters* Griggs has gathered all this correspondence together
for the first time but has wherever possible transcribed directly from holographs, thus correcting the numerous liberties taken with the manuscripts
by all nineteenth-century editors. Approximately one-third of the letters
have not been previously printed. The first four volumes covering the

correspondence from 1785 to the end of 1819 appeared in 1956 and 1959. The final two volumes were issued in 1972. The critical apparatus is Spartan but adequate. The Introduction to Volumes III and IV contains a biographical overview of the years covered by the letters in that two-volume set, concentrating on the progression of Coleridge's opium addiction, his brief association with Byron in 1815–16, and his vicissitudes with the writing and publication of *Biographia Literaria*. Coleridge's letters are not to be compared in literary value with the letters of Byron or Keats, and they do not contain a large body of literary criticism, as one might expect. But they are sometimes excellent illustrations of Coleridge's power in psychological introspection, and they are invaluable records of his life for the biographer.

When the monumental task of editing Coleridge's writings is completed, with the sheer number and size of the volumes telling at a glance how assiduously Coleridge kept to his desk, no one again will be able to confuse the fact of his unfinished work with the myth of his indolence. Only then, also, can we begin to assess how much our insight into his genius has suffered from lack of adequate texts. It appears clear that our conception of him as a poet needs to be revised. The prose bulks too large in his lifetime output for us much longer to consign it a secondary position in our considerations of its author.

The new editions of Coleridge's works have already born fruit of another sort: extensive and systematic searches by the editors of the *Collected Coleridge* and by fellow Coleridgean scholars in the periodicals of the times have uncovered unsuspected evidences of Coleridge's publishing activities and of the inadequacies of previous editings of Coleridge's poetry and prose. These discoveries have also stimulated a spirited re-assessment of the uses of external and internal evidence for establishing authorship of unsigned publications, chiefly in a series of articles in *BNYPL*, some of which were read at a symposium of the English Institute at Columbia University in 1958, and eventually collected in *Evidences of Attribution* (ed. David V. Erdman and Ephim Fogel, 1966). Much discussion centers on twenty-five newly identified essays. The case for considering Coleridge the author of six of these is made by Charlotte Woods Glickfield in "Coleridge's Prose Contributions to the *Morning Post*" (*PMLA*, 1954); of two, by Erdman in "Coleridge on George Washington: Newly Discovered Essays of 1800" (*BNYPL*, 1957); of one, by J. Colmer in "Coleridge on Addington's Administration" (*MLR*, 1959); and of several, by Erdman in "The Case for Internal Evidence (6): The Signature of Style" (*BNYPL*,

1959), in which there is also a valuable elucidation of the "editorial family" of the *Morning Post* in 1800, with the stylistic and intellectual traits of each as distinguished from Coleridge's. As for new poems assigned to Coleridge, the most important discussion is Erdman's "The Case for Internal Evidence (3): Newspaper Sonnets Put to the Concordance Test: Can They Be Attributed to Coleridge?" (in three parts, *BNYPL*, 1957, 1958), which considers seven sonnets, and differs with Griggs ("Notes Concerning Certain Poems by Coleridge," *MLN*, 1954) on the authenticity of two sonnets "To Stanhope." For other attributions, see S. F. Johnson's "An Uncollected Poem by Coleridge" (*BNYPL*, 1957); J. R. MacGillivray's discovery of the earliest known published Coleridge poem, "The Abode of Love," in the *Cambridge Chronicle* for 26 July 1790 (*BNYPL*, 1959); Erdman's fascinating story of "Lost Poem Found ["The Snow-Drop"]: The Cooperative Pursuit and Recapture of an Escaped Coleridge 'Sonnet' of 72 Lines" (*BNYPL*, 1961), which also prints in parallel columns holograph and newspaper versions and is one more confirmation of the truth in spirit if not entirely in letter of Coleridge's anecdotes about himself; and two installments of the continuing study by Lucyle Werkmeister and P. M. Zall of Coleridge's contributions to London newspapers prior to 1798, "Coleridge's 'The Complaint of Ninathóma' " (*N&Q*, 1969) and "Possible Additions to Coleridge's 'Sonnets on Eminent Characters' " (*SIR*, 1969). Finally, there are two important lists of conjectural attributions, new discoveries, and uncollected variant readings of poems already in the canon compiled by Erdman in "Unrecorded Coleridge Variants" (*SB*, 1958); and by Erdman, Werkmeister, and R. S. Woof in "Unrecorded Variants: Additions and Corrections" (*SB*, 1961), which attempt a collation of all Coleridge's known periodical publications of verse through 1820.

The question of Coleridge's contribution of reviews to the periodicals has aroused some controversy in the last two decades. In *A Wiltshire Parson and His Friends* (1926), Garland Greever reprinted four essays from the *Critical Review* (on Lewis's *The Monk*, Mrs. Radcliffe's *The Italian* and *The Mysteries of Udolpho*, and Mary Robinson's *Hubert de Sevrac*, all in the late 1790's) that he claimed were Coleridge's. While C. I. Patterson was questioning "The Authenticity of Coleridge's Reviews of Gothic Romances" (*JEGP*, 1951), accepting only the essay on *The Monk* as Coleridge's, Whalley was discovering and reprinting from the *Critical Review* an essay, "Coleridge on Classical Prosody: An Unidentified Review of 1797" (*RES*, 1951). A few years later Derek Roper in "Coleridge and the 'Critical Review' " (*MLR,* 1960) reconfirmed all but the essay on *The Mysteries of Udolpho,* and added another review of slight substance. Finally, in a comprehensive tripartite article, "Immoral Acts of a Library Cormorant: The Extent of Coleridge's Contributions to the *Critical Review*" (*BNYPL,* 1959), Erdman gives a brief history of the changing policy and political orientation of the *Critical Review* and of the styles of the regular contributors, re-authenticates all the reviews attributed at one time or another to Coleridge, and advances evidence for believing that Coleridge wrote five additional articles for the *Critical Review* between 1796 and 1798, which he reprints. Erdman seems to be expanding the Coleridge canon at an alarming rate; yet his sensitivity to Coleridge's turn of phrase and movement of mind as well as his submission to the rigorous discipline of requiring a conjunction of both internal and indirect external evidence give an authority to his attributions that cannot be dismissed lightly. Despite the recent activity in searching out his periodical contributions, Coleridge's work-a-day as a journalist remains still a partly explored chapter in his life.

Although the *Collected Coleridge,* the *Notebooks,* and the *Collected Letters* will become the standard texts, they will not supersede all earlier editions, which will continue to serve useful, if drastically limited, purposes. G. Whalley has proposed in "Coleridge's Poetical Canon: Selection and Arrangement" (*REL,* 1966) that, because "the exclusiveness of *Poems* of 1797, of *Sibylline Leaves,* and the 1828 edition [are] more typical of Coleridge's taste than the inclusiveness of *Poems* 1796 or the *Poetical Works* of 1834," therefore the canon in the *Poetical Works* for the *Collected Coleridge* should be purified of poems printed in periodicals and not collected by Coleridge, juvenilia not printed after 1797, and poems composed after 1815 and included only in the 1834 edition. Hence, students and scholars should find it convenient still to refer to both *Poetical Works* (1893), edited by James Dykes Campbell, and *Complete Poetical Works* in two volumes (1912), the previous standard edition, edited by E. H. Coleridge, not only because of the former's critical notes and biography and the latter's collation of manuscripts and previous printings, even though faulty, and appendix of first drafts and early versions of poems, but also because of the inclusion in both editions of verses, epigrams, and poems culled from Coleridge's notebooks and papers and from the files of newspapers and periodicals, which he had never seen fit to include in the collected editions of his poetical works in his lifetime. For the same reasons, E. H. Coleridge's facsimile edition of one of the manuscripts of

Christabel (1907), with full critical notes and with an account of the history and sources of the poem, will probably not be entirely superseded by the new *Collected Coleridge.* And of course there have been countless elaborate editions of "The Ancient Mariner" which need not detain us here. Given Whalley's preference for the selectivity of the 1828 edition of poems, Coleridgeans are fortunate in that an edition of the *Poetical Works and Drama* based on the comprehensiveness of the 1834 *Works,* like that of the 1912 edition, is being prepared by Griggs for Clarendon Press. Under contract since 1958, it will include an exhaustive collation of manuscript and published poems.

Similarly, the Shawcross and the Watson editions of the *Biographia Literaria* will continue as valuable adjuncts to the *Collected Coleridge* text. For over sixty years the Shawcross two-volume edition (1907), which included Coleridge's aesthetical essays, furnished students and scholars with the standard text. It was based on the 1817 publication and its notes on the 1847 reissue of H. N. Coleridge. One of its adornments is an Introduction which deals with Coleridge's aesthetic speculations on the distinction between the fancy and the imagination, the indebtedness of Coleridge to Kant and Schelling, and his ultimate divergence from both. The notes amplify the analysis of the introduction greatly and deal with the chapters upon Wordsworth with equal fullness. These latter notes defend Wordsworth and attack Coleridge, and have in their turn been questioned in an article by T. M. Raysor on "Coleridge's Criticism of Wordsworth" (*PMLA,* 1939). A dispassionate discussion of some aspects of the controversy appears also in W. J. B. Owen's critical edition of the *Preface to Lyrical Ballads* (1957) and in his *Wordsworth as Critic* (1969), which reprints "slightly reduced in length" the introduction to the earlier book. In 1956 George Watson issued a one-volume edition of *Biographia Literaria* in Everyman's Library, minus Satyrane's Letters and the critique of "Bertram." Fully annotated, it reprints Coleridge's footnotes, cites the sources of his borrowings, corrects his errors of detail, and translates his Greek and Latin quotations. The Introduction locates the origin of the book in discussions by Coleridge and Wordsworth about language and poetry for tne Preface to *Lyrical Ballads,* questions its genesis as a "Preface" to *Sibylline Leaves,* and narrates the difficulties Coleridge encountered in the completion and publication of the work. Without questioning the traditional story of its genesis, Whalley in an article on "The Integrity of *Biographia Literaria"* (*E&S,* 1953) singled out with slightly different emphasis Coleridge's long and hard thought about Wordsworth's poetry as the thread on which all the other considerations of *Biographia Literaria*—the theories of diction, meter, and association—are strung.

Coleridgean and Shakespearean scholars alike have for more than forty years been indebted to T. M. Raysor for his two-volume edition of *Coleridge's Shakespearean Criticism* (1930; reissued in Everyman's Library, 1960), edited from manuscripts and from reports of Coleridge's public lectures, with notes and an introduction on Coleridge as a critic of Shakespeare. The marginalia and manuscripts that form the basis of the first volume of this edition had in the main been included first in H. N. Coleridge's edition of *Literary Remains* (1836–39), which was edited more freely than is now acceptable. Raysor, of course, followed Coleridge's unrevised manuscripts faithfully. Most recently, R. A. Foakes has re-examined these manuscripts and reports preparatory to his edition of them for the *Collected Coleridge*, in "The Text of Coleridge's 1811–12 Shakespeare Lectures" (*ShS*, 1970) and in *Coleridge on Shakespeare: The Text of the Lectures of 1811–12* (1971), which publishes John Payne Collier's previously unprinted longhand transcripts of his shorthand notes and his relevant diary entries, from which Collier produced his 1856 edition of Coleridge's *Seven Lectures on Shakespeare and Milton*. The *Miscellaneous Criticism* (1936), also edited by Raysor, is a less ambitious edition, since manuscripts and marginalia for a new text were not available for a large proportion of the critical notes, which had to be edited according to the text of *Literary Remains*. Both of these editions collect scattered criticism from various sources which were not available to H. N. Coleridge.

Several editions of Coleridge's philosophical and political prose which have served scholars reliably and well will now give way to the *Collected Coleridge*, although because of their historical importance they will not vanish wholly from sight. First in sentimental importance as well as in scholarly integrity is Sara Coleridge's edition of her father's *Essays on His Own Times* (1850). For more than a century it was the only text in which one could conveniently study Coleridge's early lectures at Bristol and his political articles in the *Morning Post* and *Courier*. Then there is the edition of the publications of the Highgate period—the *Complete Works* (1853) issued by W. G. T. Shedd—which is, of course, not complete, in spite of its title, but was for over one hundred years serviceable. There are two excellent editions by Alice D. Snyder: *Coleridge on Logic and Learning* (1929) and *Coleridge's Treatise on Method* (1934). The first volume includes extended excerpts from the two-volume manuscript "Logic" in the

British Museum (with the argument of the whole), and other philosophical manuscripts. The *Treatise on Method* from the *Encyclopaedia Metropolitana* is a venture into popular philosophy which was repeatedly reprinted, as one of the most successful of Coleridge's works. In its later form, in *The Friend,* Coleridge himself regarded it with more pride than any other part of his prose except the long Wordsworth chapters in *Biographia Literaria.* G. N. G. Orsini describes the manuscript, its appearance, history, and commentators, in "Coleridge's Treatise on Logic" (*The Disciplines of Criticism: Essays in Literary Theory, Interpretation, and History,* ed. Peter Demetz, Thomas Greene, and Lowry Nelson, Jr., 1968). Additional memorabilia associated with the *Encyclopaedia Metropolitana,* an unpublished fragment of the *Treatise,* and a history of the venture and its aftermath are reported by Miss Snyder in "Coleridge and the Encyclopedists" (*MP,* 1940); by Lore Metzger in "Coleridge's Vindication of Spinoza: An Unpublished Note" (*JHI,* 1960); and by Robert Collison in "Samuel Taylor Coleridge and the *Encyclopaedia Metropolitana*" (*Cahiers d'Histoire Mondiale,* 1966). While his volume of selections published as *The Political Thought of S. T. Coleridge* (1938) is composed of so many unrelated bits from all of Coleridge's political writing that it is not very useful, R. J. White has also published *The Statesman's Manual* and the second *Lay Sermon* in *Political Tracts of Wordsworth, Coleridge, and Shelley* (1953). In 1949 Kathleen Coburn edited Coleridge's *Philosophical Lectures,* on the history of philosophy rather than on his own system, although the lectures were critical and interpretative, and thus largely expressive of Coleridge's own point of view. The text is a skillfully edited transcription of shorthand reports and represents Coleridge's attempt to adapt a difficult subject to a popular audience. Thomas McFarland is re-editing these lectures for the *Collected Coleridge.*

Over the years there have been countless printings of Coleridge's marginalia, which the *Collected Coleridge* will reduce in importance. Fragmentary and diffuse by the nature of the material, they were nevertheless peculiarly important for filling gaps in our knowledge of Coleridge's mind, given his predilection for the privacy of the margin of a book. Since at their best the aim was more than a transcription of Coleridge's words, the labors of Henri Nidecker, A. Snyder, R. F. Brinkley, K. Coburn, C. Seronsy, and W. Schrickx, especially, deserve mention. For their and other important recoveries one should consult the listings in Volume v of *CBEL* (1957) and in Volume III of the New *CBEL* (1969). The *Con-*

cordance (1940) to the poetry compiled by Sister Eugenia Logan will continue to serve critics' needs, although it is hoped that someone will turn out a new computerized concordance based on the *Collected Coleridge*.

III. BIOGRAPHIES

With the notebooks, letters, and complete writings of Coleridge available in their entirety, we have the materials for a mature and definitive biography, at least as regards the facts of Coleridge's life and works. The paradoxes of the man's inner life may continue to elude us, for there is an unfathomable human element at the core of his emotional and intellectual contradictions that allows us, like his contemporaries, to register symptoms, seldom to locate first causes. In his own lifetime he had become legendary, the focus of recollections of such men as Lamb ("Christ's Hospital Five and Thirty Years Ago," 1820, and "The Two Races of Men," 1820), Hazlitt ("My First Acquaintance with Poets," 1823, and "Mr. Coleridge" in *The Spirit of the Age*, 1825), De Quincey (*Tait's Magazine*, 1834–35 and 1839), and Carlyle (in *Life of John Sterling*, 1851). Indeed, almost every literary man of Coleridge's time testified in some form to his central position in letters. Such personal reminiscences as those of Joseph Cottle (*Early Recollections* . . ., 1837), Thomas Poole (*Thomas Poole and His Friends*, by Mrs. Henry Sandford, 1888), Daniel Stuart ("Anecdotes of the Poet Coleridge and His Newspaper Writings," *Gentleman's Magazine*, 1838; and *Letters from the Lake Poets* . . ., 1889), Thomas Allsop (*Letters, Conversations, and Recollections of S. T. Coleridge*, 1836), and James Gillman (*Life of S. T. Coleridge*, 1838) represent a multitude of records from writers of less intellectual endowments but with sufficiently intimate contact with Coleridge to give invaluable if not always accurate information regarding his life. And allusions to him in letters, diaries, and journals are almost endless. One can only cite here some of the most famous and important: Keats's Sunday morning walk in Highgate with Coleridge, memorably recounted in a letter of 14 February–3 May 1819, Crabb Robinson's record of conversations with him, available in editions by Thomas Sadler (1869) and Edith Morley (1922), and H. N. Coleridge's specimens of his uncle's *Table Talk* (1835) in the last years of Coleridge's life. An article by Paul Kaufman on James Losh, "Wordsworth's 'Candid and Enlightened Friend' " (*N&Q*, 1962), most recently has called our attention to yet another of Coleridge's fellow Unitarian and social liberals, whose thirty-three manuscript volumes of diary extending from February 1796 to September 1833 contain portraits of Coleridge in 1800 and 1810. Though the bare lists of titles in Haney or Kennedy and Barton would be sufficient to indicate the nature of Coleridge's complicated intellectual relationships, the R. W. Armour and R. F. Howes compilation of records of *Coleridge the Talker* (1940) is impressive evidence. Since Coleridge did not live in seclusion like Wordsworth, and since he had unparalleled powers of social conversation, he was constantly exposed to public observation and record.

Based in part on these records, James Dykes Campbell's biographical introduction to his edition of the *Poetical Works* (1893), published as a separate volume the next year, provided the first half of this century with the standard life of Coleridge. Campbell devoted a large part of ten years to his study of Coleridge, and this brief biography has not lost its value with the passage of time. An accumulation of published material since Campbell's research, however, particularly the Griggs edition of *Unpublished Letters* (1932), justified the new biography of *Samuel Taylor Coleridge* (1938) by E. K. Chambers. The book, unfortunately, is marred by an inadequate index and by an unsympathetic attitude, which caused Chambers to echo drearily the previous century—particularly the Oxford Hegelianism of the seventies and eighties, as Graham Hough notes in "Coleridge and the Victorians" (*The English Mind,* ed. Hugh Sykes Davies and George Watson, 1964)—in his estimation of Coleridge's philosophical writings ("a will-o-the-wisp light for bemused thinkers") and in his moralistic disapproval of Coleridge's character.

The record has been happily righted by Walter Jackson Bate's one-volume biography of *Samuel Taylor Coleridge* (1968). Magisterially paced and proportioned, this biography touches on all the controversial aspects of Coleridge's life, both literary and personal, with fresh perspective: the poet-metaphysician dichotomy, the plagiarism, the unsystematized philosophy, the fragmentary theory of imagination, the opium addiction, the psychic dependency, the unfinished "Kubla Khan" and "Christabel," and the medical history of the man. For the first time we get a serious treatment of the second half of Coleridge's life, the years when he functioned as critic, philosopher, and religious thinker. Bate sees Coleridge as both blessed and cursed with a comprehensive mind. The most gifted psychological intelligence of his time, "one of the half-dozen greatest critical interpreters in the history of literature," and an innovative and farsighted religious thinker, he was forever getting trapped by the largeness of his vision, by his sympathetic openness to ideas, his eagerness to include rather than exclude. Both the glory and the failure of Coleridge's intellectual pilgrimage, accordingly, lie in his persistent effort to accomplish *all* things at once. Coleridge's was a lifelong search (or at least from roughly 1802 to his death) for the means philosophically by which the mystery of creation could be answered to the satisfaction of the claims of (1) traditional Christian theology, (2) modern epistemology and logic, and (3) "dynamic philosophy" with its inclusion of the discoveries of science and philosophy.

The rigid economy of a one-volume biographical narrative points up the need of a larger scale for the definitive biography of Coleridge, to allow for interpretative criticism of the details of his personal life and of his mental and literary development, and to set his life against the background of intellectual history. If Wordsworth, like many others, could call Coleridge "the most wonderful man I have ever known," the definitive biography, if it is ever written, should show something of the reason for such a judgment from one of the most cautious of men; for the most excellent biographies presenting the external facts of Coleridge's life can only result in showing the frustration and ruin which exasperate so many students, and arouse in some not pity, but unjustified contempt.

Although it requires correcting and updating in details, an excellent account of *The Life of S. T. Coleridge: The Early Years* (1938), to 1800, by Lawrence Hanson takes such a broad view of biography. It interprets, for instance, the early relationship of Wordsworth and Coleridge, discusses the attitude of both toward the French Revolution, gives something of the historical and intellectual background of their opinions, criticizes their poetry, and in general follows the traditions of literary biography, as Campbell and Chambers do not. Unfortunately, Hanson did not continue his account of Coleridge's life in subsequent volumes. Nor has anyone, as yet, had the courage to perform the task. Although his aim is to give us a comprehensive history of *La Formation de la pensée de Coleridge, 1772–1804* (1964), Paul Deschamps likewise breaks off the narrative with half of Coleridge's life of mental striving still before him.

Coleridge was involved with so many different people and in such varied enterprises in his lifetime that scholars have preferred to pursue narrow and special facets of the Coleridge enigma rather than attempt the difficult full-scaled comprehensive survey. Hugh I'Anson Fausset has written a psychological interpretation in *Samuel Taylor Coleridge* (1926), which is primarily a critical essay cast into a biographical form, giving no references, frequently summarizing events, and interpreting Coleridge's life and works in terms of a thesis—his inability to cope with reality. Stephen Potter in *Coleridge and S.T.C.* (1935) develops the hypothesis that there were two Coleridges: the poet whose spontaneity, imagination, and joy won the hearts of the Wordsworths, and the theologian whose Pecksniffian righteousness and self-pity alternately bored and embarrassed his auditors. The distinction, of course, is far too facile and simplistic to explain the psychological complexities, or to convey the sensitivity and range, of Coleridge. Another critical biography which may be compared with Fausset's and Potter's is Malcolm Elwin's book *The First Romantics* (1948), which studies Coleridge in his personal relationships with Wordsworth and Southey, and, to some extent, with other members of his group, as far as the year 1802. Elwin has the advantage over Fausset and Potter of willingness to look steadily at the qualities which made Coleridge great rather than at his psychological abnormalities. He is hostile to Wordsworth and Southey, sympathetic toward Coleridge, but without sentimental piety. H. M. Margoliouth's *Wordsworth and Coleridge, 1795–1834* (1953) is a safer guide than Fausset, Potter, or Elwin and is quite as readable. With marvelous compactness, Margoliouth manages to introduce excellent literary criticism as part of his factual narrative of the two men's friendship. An example of the useful exact details that Margoliouth provides (outside the book in this case) is the diary of dates in which Margoliouth follows Wordsworth and Coleridge day to day from 13 May to 2 July 1798 (*N&Q,* 1953). For Coleridge's associations with Wordsworth from the time of his first meeting with the older poet, probably in August 1795 to the end of 1799, the student should also consult Mark L. Reed's *Wordsworth: The Chronology of the Early Years* (1967); and, for a sense of place, Berta Lawrence's *Coleridge and Wordsworth in Somerset* (1970).

Much has been written on Coleridge's relationships with the writers of his generation with whom he felt closest. Griggs has interpreted the new information in his collection of unpublished letters concerning Coleridge's friendships with Southey, Poole, Wordsworth, Lamb, and Hazlitt. These articles include a brief but deft survey of "Coleridge and His Friends" (*CLSB,* 1956); a summary of "Robert Southey's Estimate of Samuel Taylor Coleridge: A Study in Human Relations" (*HLQ,* 1945); a discussion of "Hazlitt's Estrangement from Coleridge and Wordsworth" (*MLN,* 1933) as set forth between 1814 and 1816 by Wordsworth, who expressed moral disgust at a purportedly scandalous affair of Hazlitt's during a visit to the Lakes in 1803 (see in this regard a letter of Wordsworth's published by W. M. Parker in *TLS*, 21 December 1941); and an analysis of "Wordsworth Through Coleridge's Eyes" (*Wordsworth: Centenary Studies*, ed. G. T. Dunklin, 1951) suggesting the detrimental effect that Wordsworth's self-centered habits of mind must have had on the sensitive, less secure Coleridge. Robert S. Newdeck in "Coleridge on Hazlitt" (*Texas Review*, 1924) finds the two men still friendly in 1811 but no longer so in 1815, and examines the political and temperamental reasons for their rupture. G. Whalley has contributed two studies of Southey's and Lamb's beneficial influences on Coleridge's poetic development in "Coleridge and Southey in Bristol, 1795" (*RES*, 1950) and "Coleridge's Debt to Charles Lamb" (*E&S*, 1958). And Jonathan Wordsworth, in an analysis of *The Ruined Cottage* and "The Pedlar" (*The Music of Humanity*, 1969), argues for Coleridge as the source of Wordsworth's conceptualization of the One Life theme.

Although not formally biographical, two books surveying Coleridge's lifelong concern with the exercise of civil and social authority are John Colmer's *Coleridge: Critic of Society* (1959) and Carl R. Woodring's *Politics in the Poetry of Coleridge* (1961). Both books concur in their insistence that the time is past when a Crane Brinton (in *Political Ideas of the English Romanticists*, 1926) could indict Coleridge for betraying the revolutionary ardor of his youth with the conservative fears of his old age. Both insist that Coleridge was always motivated more by his humanitarian response to the sufferings of the poor, the enslaved, and the economically exploited than by abstract promises of political theory, a view shared by R. W. Harris in "Coleridge and the Philosophy of Conservatism" (*Romanticism and the Social Order 1780–1830*, 1969) and reiterated by Woodring in his broader study *Politics in English Romantic Poetry* (1970). In an earlier article, "Coleridge and the Communication of Political Truth" (*ESA*, 1958), as well as in his book, Colmer presents an astute estimate of the vexing problem of Coleridge's inability to establish a satisfactory relationship with his readers, and of his lifelong preoccupation with the responsibilities of the political writer to the public he addresses. The central concern of Colmer's book, however, is a survey of Coleridge's political and social conscience as it is expressed in his prose writings from *The Watchman* and early Bristol lectures through the *Morning Post* and *Courier* leaders to *The Friend*, the *Lay Sermons*, and *On the Constitution of the Church and State*. Woodring reviews "the variety of ways by which . . . political ideas, feelings, and dilemmas" provide "an important impulse" in Coleridge's poems and in this respect his study is complementary to Colmer's. Although politics engaged the intellectual earnestness of Coleridge the practicing journalist, they never released his imagination as wholly as did his obsession with the "one Life within us and abroad." Woodring necessarily then attends less to the central canon of "The Ancient Mariner," "Christabel," "Kubla Khan," and the Conversation Poems, than to the plays, the "Sonnets . . . to eminent Contemporaries," and the occasional newspaper squibs, *jeux d'esprits,* and lampoons, which he interprets within the context of the political events of the day and of the partisan commitments of Coleridge.

The necessarily general nature of Colmer's survey and the special poetic focus of Woodring's still leave for some future scholar the history of Coleridge's place in the grub-street world of London. D. V. Erdman in "Coleridge as Editorial Writer" and E. P. Thompson in "Disenchantment or Default? A Lay Sermon" (*Power and Consciousness,* ed. Conor Cruise O'Brien and William Dean Vanech, 1969) have contributed in this regard studies of the political and journalistic state of affairs in the 1790's and first few years of the new century, as well as offering fresh reasons for Coleridge's and Wordsworth's sudden decision to go to Germany in 1798. Besides narrating Coleridge's evolution from inflammatory anti-administration radical to reluctant pro-war advocate, Erdman has also analyzed Coleridge's three stints at parliamentary reporting for the *Morning Post* in 1800. In "Coleridge in Lilliput: The Quality of Parliamentary Reporting in 1800" (*Speech Monographs,* 1960), he formulates rules-of-thumb for gauging the reliability of the parliamentary speeches, as reported in the newspapers, and as compiled by John Debrett in the *Parliamentary Register* (1781–1801) and by John Wright in the *Parliamentary History* (edited from the reports of Cobbett and Hansard). He collates Coleridge's renderings in the *Morning Post* of Pitt's speeches on 3 and 17 February and of Sheridan's on 10 February 1800, with Coleridge's on-the-spot notes, other newspaper reports, and Debrett's and Wright's compilations. His conclusion is that Coleridge "managed to outdo other newspaper reporters by being simultaneously more faithful and more splendidly creative."

For the record, as much as for the special but cautionary uses they may still have, two earlier biographies and chapters of a third should at least be mentioned. Joseph Aynard's *Vie d'un poète: Coleridge* (Paris, 1907) is another interpretative biography, which comments on Coleridge's political views. Still earlier is the unreliable biography by Alois Brandl, *Samuel Taylor Coleridge und die englische Romantik* (Berlin, 1886). In spite of its frequent errors, which are multiplied in the English translation by Lady Eastlake, this book has still some value in its references to German influences on Coleridge. There are also several chapters in existence of Ernest Hartley Coleridge's projected life of Coleridge, which were published by the Rev. G. H. B. Coleridge in *Coleridge* (ed. Blunden and Griggs, 1934). These deal with Coleridge's family (Ch. i), the year of *The Watchman* (Ch. v), and the year of political journalism and translation after returning from Germany (Ch. ix).

Then there are those episodes in Coleridge's life such as his school-day escapades, his army enlistment, his Pantisocratic and Jacobin enthusiasms, his Wedgwood annuity, his German adventures, and his library cormorancy, that have attracted specific attention from scholars. In the same memorial volume, edited by Blunden and Griggs, is a treatment by Blunden of Coleridge's experience at Christ's Hospital, which may be used as a commentary on Lamb's two essays. Vera Watson in "Coleridge's Army Service" (*TLS*, 7 July 1950) has found in the Public Record Office documents which show that the official pretext for Coleridge's discharge from the Army in 1794 was insanity; and E. L. Griggs (*English*, 1953) has described the whole episode as reflected in the Coleridge letters, eliminating some often repeated legends. On Coleridge's and Southey's scheme to found a utopian settlement on the banks of the Susquehanna River, Hoxie N. Fairchild has discussed the Rousseauistic and Godwinian ideas that influenced their plans, in *The Romantic Quest* (1931) and *The Noble Savage* (1928); Sister Eugenia Logan has considered "Coleridge's Scheme of Pantisocracy and American Travel Accounts" (*PMLA*, 1930); J. R. MacGillivray has reported on "The Pantisocracy Scheme and Its Immediate Background" (*Studies in English by Members of Univ. College, Toronto,* 1931); and L. W. Deen has set forth some of the basic ideals which motivated Coleridge and Southey, in "Coleridge and the Sources of Pantisocracy: Godwin, the Bible and Hartley" (*Boston Univ. Studies in English,* 1961). In his Bristol lectures of 1795, Coleridge presumably spoke out among other subjects about the impending Twin Bills against sedition and unlawful assembly. G. Whalley in "Coleridge and Southey in Bristol, 1795" (*RES*, 1950) analyzes Cottle's vague account of the lectures, and reduces the probable number to eleven, supposing that the six political lectures announced for June and July were not delivered. Only four were published, so far as we know. For updating and correction of this analysis, one should also consult Patton's and Mann's reviews of the evidence in their Introductions to the *Collected Coleridge* edition of the lectures. Coleridge's fear of governmental reprisal for the Jacobinical nature of one or more of his talks leads Lucyle Werkmeister in "Coleridge's *The Plot Discovered*: Some Facts and a Speculation" (*MP*, 1959) to conjecture that Coleridge hurried into print something purportedly his speech to demonstrate to the Pitt government that he had not advocated revolt. And an article by A. J. Eagleston on "Wordsworth, Coleridge, and the Spy" (*Nineteenth Century,* 1908; rpt. in *Coleridge,* ed. Blunden and Griggs, 1934) describes a later run-in with the law, when a spy was sent by the government to watch the young poets at Nether Stowey under the supposition that they were dangerous Jacobins. The story behind Coleridge's acceptance of the Wedgwood's generous offer of an annuity is traced by Erdman in "Coleridge, Wordsworth, and the Wedgwood Fund" (*BNYPL*, 1956, in two parts). And Edith J. Morley contributes an account of "Coleridge in Germany (1799)" (*Wordsworth and Coleridge,* ed. E. L. Griggs, 1939), as portrayed in the journal of George Bellas Greenough, which supplements Clement Carlyon's recollections in *Early Years and Late Reflections* (1836). Coleridge's reading has always been a reliable index of the restless directions taken by his maturing mind. G. Whalley has published a useful list, with full annotation and discussion, of "The Bristol Library Borrowings of Southey and Coleridge, 1793–98" (*Library,* 1944). Alice D. Snyder records those "Books Borrowed by Coleridge from the Library of the University of Göttingen, 1799" (*MP,* 1928). Paul Kaufman in "Coleridge's Use of Cathedral Libraries" (*MLN,* 1960) gives the titles of books Coleridge withdrew from the cathedral libraries of Carlisle and Durham in 1801. And G. Whalley adds to Max H. Fisch's story of "The Coleridges, Dr. Prati, and Vico" (*MP,* 1943–44), a history of Coleridge's response to Vico (*Giambattista Vico: An International Symposium,* ed. Giorgio Tagliacozzo and Hayden V. White, 1969).

The skepticism expressed by Griggs concerning the tradition that Coleridge's association with Wordsworth at least for a few halcyon years was mutually fructifying appears also in the hard look recent scholars have taken at the meeting of minds on matters poetic that supposedly marked the *annus mirabilis,* the German tour, and the first year of Coleridge's relocation near Wordsworth in the Lake Country. This unsentimental scrutiny is epitomized by the title of Ruth I. Aldrich's article "The Wordsworths and Coleridge: 'Three Persons,' but *not* 'One Soul' " (*SIR,* 1962). Coleridge's disagreement with Wordsworth over the function of meter is, of course, well known from his discussion fifteen years later in *Biographia*

Literaria. For a dissent, though, from the conventional assumption that Wordsworth disparaged meter as ornamental and Coleridge elevated meter to high importance as organic, with a not wholly convincing special plea that the reverse is closer to the truth, one should consult Stephen M. Parrish on "Wordsworth and Coleridge on Meter" (*JEGP,* 1960). The picture emerging from a re-examination of the famous collaboration on the first two editions of *Lyrical Ballads* and on the 1800 Preface depicts a Coleridge who never allowed his ardor for Wordsworth to stifle entirely his literary sensibility and philosophical independence of mind. In two articles, "The Wordsworth-Coleridge Controversy" (*PMLA,* 1958) and "Dramatic Technique in the *Lyrical Ballads*" (*PMLA,* 1959), Parrish argues that the issue of dramatic propriety, not poetic diction, underlay their disagreement. The drama of the origin and execution of *Lyrical Ballads,* focusing on the reasons for Wordsworth's dominance in the project and Coleridge's acquiescence in a secondary position, and on the psychological needs and aesthetical preoccupations of the two men at the time, is rehearsed by A. M. Buchan in "The Influence of Wordsworth on Coleridge (1795–1800)" (*UTQ,* 1963); by M. Reed in "Wordsworth, Coleridge, and the 'Plan' of the *Lyrical Ballads*" (*UTQ,* 1965); by Max F. Schulz in "Coleridge, Wordsworth, and the 1800 Preface to *Lyrical Ballads*" (*SEL,* 1965); and by G. Whalley in "Preface to *Lyrical Ballads*: A Portent" (*UTQ,* 1956).

Some indication of "the barrier of taste that Coleridge and Wordsworth were up against" with the experiment of the *Lyrical Ballads,* and hence the need for an explanatory Preface, may be had by reading W. S. Ward on "Some Aspects of the Conservative Attitude Toward Poetry in English Criticism, 1798–1820" (*PMLA,* 1945) and "Wordsworth, the 'Lake' Poets, and Their Contemporary Magazine Critics, 1798–1820" (*SP,* 1945); and R. S. Woof on "Coleridge and Thomasina Dennis" (*UTQ,* 1962–63). For the conventional side of Coleridge's and Wordsworth's poetic efforts, one should read Robert Mayo on "The Contemporaneity of the *Lyrical Ballads*" (*PMLA,* 1954).

The dating of Coleridge's greatest poems continues to be a nagging question. E. K. Chambers has a concentrated and detailed analysis of this problem in "Some Dates in Coleridge's *Annus Mirabilis*" (*E&S,* 1933). There was a postscript on "The Date of Coleridge's *Kubla Khan*" (*RES,* 1935; both essays rpt. in *A Sheaf of Studies,* 1942) in which Chambers carried the study somewhat further. He makes a heroic attempt to date "The Ancient Mariner," "Christabel," and "Kubla Khan," with some lesser poems, more definitely than had hitherto been done, and to clear up the curious confusion of the evidence. The biography of Coleridge by Malcolm Elwin (see above) added an analysis of Coleridge's personal relations with Charles Lloyd that will enable some readers to accept 1798 as the date for "Kubla Khan." This issue of the poem's dating has divided the scholars. Coleridge claimed, in the Preface to the 1816 publication, to have written "Kubla Khan" "In the summer of the year 1797"; in the Crewe manuscript he noted its composition as having taken place "in the fall of the year, 1797." E. H. Coleridge, Lowes, and Hanson settled for May 1798 on the basis of a notebook entry of Coleridge's in 1810 linking the poem to the completion of "Christabel" and to the quarrel with Lloyd, which led them to decide that Coleridge had erred when he wrote summer 1797, meaning 1798. Chambers ultimately decided in his biography in favor of the Crewe manuscript date, and was followed by Wylie Sypher (*PQ*, 1939), Bate, and Griggs in a headnote to Volume I of the *Collected Letters*, all opting in the absence of better evidence for a time prior to 14 October, when Coleridge mentions in a letter to John Thelwall having been absent from home "a day or two." Margoliouth and Reed consider as more likely the early November 1797 walking tour with Wordsworth to the Valley of Stones. Elisabeth Schneider contrariwise argues in *Coleridge, Opium and Kubla Khan* (1953) for 1799 (or perhaps even 1800). She believes also that "Christabel," Part I, may have grown during the period immediately after Coleridge's return from Germany (*PQ*, 1953). And on this conflicting note the issue stands.

Documents for the years 1804–06 which Coleridge spent abroad in search of health were sadly decimated by the vagaries of the postal service and overseas travel during the Napoleonic Wars. Consequently, few of the papers pertinent to a history of Coleridge's movements and thoughts in these years have survived. D. Sultana after diligent search has unearthed government documents and new autograph material, which he incorporates into his study of *Samuel Taylor Coleridge in Malta and Italy* (1969), the most detailed narrative to date of the roughly two years Coleridge spent in the Mediterranean area. Particularly enlightening is Sultana's recital (in Coleridge's words) of "the business, intrigue, form and pomp of a public situation"—for example, the efforts to supply Malta with cheap bread and the continuing exigencies and crises of a naval port in time of war—which form a background to Coleridge's six-month tenure as public secretary to Sir Alexander Ball, the Civil Commissioner of Malta. When it deals directly with Coleridge, however, the book offers a mosaic of quotations and references, not always accurate nor lucidly stitched together (see the exchange of comments in *TLS*, June through October 1969, and Erdman's review in *ELN*, 1970), which unnecessarily complicates the narrative. It is also lamentable that the growth and change of Coleridge's mind is not dealt with, since these were formative years for his theories of government and for his acceptance of Trinitarian Christianity; but Sultana is less able to control his hostility for what he considers Coleridge's "defects of character" than was Chambers. For a sympathetic rendering of the inner man during these years one fortunately can turn to Miss Coburn's inspired insights in the notes to her edition of the notebooks and to her sensitive summary in "Poet into Public Servant" (*PTRSC*, 1960) of Coleridge's fifteen months on Malta, her definition of the Coleridgean movement of mind from outer contemplation of things to inner concern with states of feeling, and her demonstration of how this imaginative process underlay Coleridge's functioning as a civil servant.

In his middle years Coleridge struggled unsuccessfully to control his opium addiction and his love for Sara Hutchinson, the sister of Mrs. Wordsworth. Lydia Wagner has shown (*Psychoanalytic Review*, 1938) that Coleridge's initial experiences with laudanum and opium were connected with his interest in contemporary physiological and medical theories on stimulation and sensation, which she describes. And E. L. Griggs has written a long sympathetic history of Coleridge's addiction in the Introduction to Volume III of the *Collected Letters* (1959) which supplements an earlier account in "S. T. Coleridge and Opium" (*HLQ*, 1954) of Coleridge's use of laudanum at Highgate. Griggs's version of the chronology and extent of Coleridge's opium habits is challenged by Sultana in his book on Coleridge in Malta and Italy. As a consequence of the enervation and apathy caused by his addiction Coleridge was unable during the nadir years 1813 to 1815 to bestir himself on Hartley's behalf. G. L. Little in "Hartley Coleridge, Wordsworth and Oxford" (*N&Q*, 1959) relates the efforts of Southey, Wordsworth, and Coleridge's brothers to provide for Hartley's matriculation at Oxford in 1815. Griggs has written excellent biographies of Hartley Coleridge (1929) and Sara Coleridge (*Coleridge Fille*, 1940), which throw light on Coleridge's wife and children and his last years at Highgate. Mrs. Coleridge speaks for herself in an edition of her letters by Stephen Potter (*Minnow Among Tritons*, 1934). T. M. Raysor has published an article on "Coleridge and 'Asra'" (*SP*, 1929) which gives most of the long record in the notebooks of Coleridge's love for Sara Hutchinson. Since "Love" and "Dejection," as well as "A Day-dream" and

"Recollections of Love," plus other lesser poems between 1799 and 1810 are associated with this frustrated love, the subject has literary as well as biographical implications. These implications have been studied by G. Whalley in *Coleridge and Sara Hutchinson, and the Asra Poems* (1955), which prints Sara's little notebook anthology of poems by Coleridge (and Wordsworth), gives full biographical background for the relationship of Coleridge and Sara, and extends the list of Asra poems greatly by including not only those addressed to or referring to her but also influenced by or associated with her. A. P. Rossiter would enlarge the list of Asra poems even further to include those items, mostly jottings in the notebooks, which were intended for a book-length collection known as "Coleridge's 'Soother of Absence' " (*TLS*, 8 May 1953); but M. F. Schulz argues against this ascription in an attempt to reconstruct the contents of the projected work, in *"The Soother of Absence*: An Unwritten Work by S. T. Coleridge" (*Southern Review*, Adelaide, 1967). Miss Coburn has published a large volume of *The Letters of Sara Hutchinson* (1954). These do not, of course, give us information about her relations with Coleridge; and Sara excludes literary criticism and even literary gossip from these family letters. But she tells us a good deal about herself and her life in the Wordsworth family.

Since the days of Carlyle's and De Quincey's ambivalent tributes, biographers have tended to scant the Coleridge of Highgate Sage fame, although John Charpentier's *Coleridge, the Sublime Somnambulist* (1929) is largely concerned with Coleridge's later years and his philosophical criticism, and Basil Willey has completed an as yet unpublished book studying the growth of Coleridge's mind, especially of his religious thought. There are, however, several articles on special literary efforts of his, for one his writing of *Theory of Life*. As regards the immediate occasion of the essay and the problems of dating it, see A. D. Snyder's two articles on "Coleridge's 'Theory of Life' " (*MLN*, 1932) and "Coleridgeana" (*RES*, 1928). For its intellectual antecedents, see Roy R. Male's "The Background of Coleridge's *Theory of Life*" (*TexSE*, 1954); and, most recently, Sam G. Barnes's "Was *Theory of Life* Coleridge's 'Opus Maximum'?" (*SP*, 1958), which further considers the questions of its authenticity, date, and genesis in a quarrel between two medical colleagues of Dr. Gillman. And in articles from 1927 to 1931 in *RLC*, H. Nidecker argues that *Theory of Life* is closer to Schelling and Steffens than to Kant in its philosophy. During the years after his placing himself in the care of the Gillmans, Coleridge had a resurgence of productivity—the *Theory of Life* is one instance. The two *Lay Sermons* are another, about which D. V. Erdman adds a fascinating footnote in his article "Coleridge on Coleridge: The Context (and Text) of His Review of 'Mr. Coleridge's Second Lay Sermon' " (*SIR*, 1961). After an illuminating survey of Coleridge's condemnations of anonymous reviewing and of his practices as a reviewer, Erdman cites a review article of the Second Lay Sermon, "written by a friend" (Morgan as dictated to by Coleridge) and published 25 March 1817 in the *Courier*, representing Coleridge's effort to correct the false impressions of a review in the *Times* and incidentally to puff his own work. A similar sidelight on Coleridge's uses (or abuses) of Morgan's friendship appears in W. Braekman and A. Devolder's "Three Hitherto Unpublished Letters of S. T. Coleridge to J. J. Morgan" (*Studia Germanica Gadensia*, 1962), which reopens the question of Morgan's role in the critique of *Maturin* published with *Biographia Literaria*. In an article on "Coleridge and the Royal Society of Literature" (*EDH*, 1969), which presents a more favorable side of Coleridge's complex personality, G. Whalley gives a history of Coleridge's association with the Royal Society of Literature from 1824 to 1830. As one of ten Royal Associates with life annuities of £100 made possible by a gift of George IV, which was discontinued by William IV, Coleridge was under obligation to communicate to the Society a paper per year. He read only one, 18 May 1825, "On the *Prometheus* of Aeschylus," reflections about the Promethean myth less literary than metaphysical, which Whalley summarizes and analyzes (*PTRSC*, 1960).

IV. HISTORICAL AND LITERARY CRITICISM OF COLERIDGE'S POETRY

I. GENERAL EVALUATIONS OF COLERIDGE

Thanks in large part to the lifetime labors of Kathleen Coburn and E. L. Griggs, a major re-evaluation of Coleridge is underway. Already signs point to an upgrading of his prefigurative role (and vindication of John Stuart Mill's acumen) in the intellectual ferment of the past century and a half. It becomes increasingly apparent that in addition to critical theory, he still speaks meaningfully to us in the areas of psychology, religion, politics, and philosophy (which Mr. Wellek will give due credit to in his chapter).

At the same time, his standing among the major English poets remains undiminished; if anything our receptivity to the quiet tones of many of his poems has led to an extension of the canon treated with critical seriousness. Not just the "handful of golden poems" that fascinated E. K. Chambers and the late Victorians but the whole garden of Coleridgean poesies of variable hues and scents moves present-day readers.

For decades, John Livingston Lowes's *The Road to Xanadu* (1927) dominated Coleridge studies. It was the first important book dealing with Coleridge since the days of Campbell and E. H. Coleridge. As a study of Coleridge's sources, it is a brilliant culmination of a critical tradition, but time has shown it to have serious deficiencies otherwise. In its concentration on "The Ancient Mariner" and "Kubla Khan," in its timid retreat from coping with the meaning of these poems, and in its stress on the subconscious, Aeolian processes of the poetic imagination, it perpetuated the nineteenth-century fiction that Coleridge was a "Divine somnambulist," the involuntary poet of one miraculous poem and two enchanting fragments. During the past decade the books attempting to set the record straight have multiplied tenfold. The first critic to try for a review more responsive to the processes of Coleridge's creative imagination than previous treatments was Humphry House in the Clark Lectures of 1951–52 at Cambridge, which were published as *Coleridge* (1953). The scope of the lectures is wide. House approaches Coleridge's mind and personality by analysis of characteristic entries from the notebooks and ends with a similar analysis of crucial entries which illustrate Coleridge's views of association as determined by emotion and of the nature of the conscious will in creation. Unfortunately, House limits his sensitive descriptive analyses of poems, besides of course the famous triumvirate, to only "Dejection" and "Frost at Midnight" and to some cursory remarks about "The Eolian Harp." The literary taste and maturity of scholarship of House are admirable and his book has been seminal for Coleridge critics, but it is not intended as a general introduction to Coleridge's poetry.

Several other books better serve this purpose, although none precludes the need of the student to put together for himself the studies of particular poems. William Walsh's *Coleridge: The Work and the Relevance* (1967) is probably too designedly directed toward the general reader to suit most Coleridgeans; but it is incisive, accurate, and comprehensive, although more illuminating on Coleridge's educational theory, for example, than on his poems, where Walsh relies heavily on Eliot's 1933 essay for critical guidance. Both Max F. Schulz in *The Poetic Voices of Coleridge* (1963) and George Watson in *Coleridge the Poet* (1966) insist that Coleridge is a multifaceted poet with a diversity of styles at his command; but they diverge radically in the emphasis they place on Coleridge's origins, directions, and effects. The Coleridge who emerges from Schulz's book is innovative of organic forms, the Coleridge from Watson's is imitative of traditional genres. The two books tend to supplement each other, together providing both forward and backward looking contexts. Bent on counteracting the influence of Lowes's book, Schulz views Coleridge's poems against the background of the late eighteenth century as varied solutions to the problem of ordering the spontaneity of experience into a form which does not sacrifice naturalness of diction and syntax. Although the classifications Schulz institutes are modestly invoked, with recognition of overlapping of voices, he inevitably flattens the peaks of Coleridge's achievement in his advocacy of the low-keyed conversational mode as the true voice of Coleridge's poetry. Whereas Schulz gives a good part of his space over to analysis of the post-1800 Coleridge, Watson excels in his discussion of the pre-1800 schoolboy Coleridge. Insisting that Coleridge's critical genius aided his poetical genius, supplying his creative imagination with the curiosity, acumen, and taste that mastery of poetic languages and metrical experiments and practice of literary kinds demand, Watson contends that "The Ancient Mariner," "Kubla Khan," and "Christabel" achieve their symbolism through their imitative forms, an insight richly suggestive in its allusion to the neoclassical tradition of imitative art but disappointing in its execution, because Watson rejects the prevailing concern with the moral urgencies of Coleridge's poetry, limiting his analyses to equations of the poems with medieval ballad, Gothic horror tale, and neoclassical-romantic modes.

The inference in Lowes's study that Coleridge found his true poetic voice once (twice if we count "Kubla Khan") before losing it forever, by momently ignoring his metaphysical preoccupations, gains few adherents among current Coleridgean critics, most agreeing that Coleridge's inquiring mind and his shaping spirit were equally strong, indeed that his intellectual pursuits were necessary to his poetical visions. This is the Coleridge whom Marshall McLuhan and Miss Coburn celebrate in essays that comprise part of a book-length assessment of the value of the Romantic poets for this century, in *The Major English Romantic Poets* (ed. C. D. Thorpe, Carlos Baker, and Bennett Weaver, 1957); the Coleridge whose unitive thought is admired by Elizabeth Sewell in "Coleridge: The Method and the Poetry" (*The Poet as Critic,* ed. Frederick P. W. McDowell, 1967); the Coleridge whose poetic and psychological models of reality are described by Stephen Prickett in *Coleridge and Wordsworth: The Poetry of Growth* (1970); and the Coleridge whose organic sense of wholeness and dynamic observations of the phenomenal world are acclaimed by Miss Coburn in a Warton Lecture on "The Interpenetration of Man and Nature" (*Proceedings of the British Academy,* 1963). The assumption that Coleridge was a great poet because he was in addition a great philosopher also underlies Paul Deschamps's spiritual biography of the early Coleridge. Similarly Richard Haven in *Patterns of Consciousness* (1969) contends that the universe which Coleridge "tried to define as philosopher was the universe which he experienced as poet," both characterized by patterns of consciousness most comprehensively symbolized in the figures of the Mariner and the Wedding Guest. G. N. G. Orsini registers a minority dissent in *Coleridge and German Idealism* (1969), insisting that Coleridge the poet and Coleridge the philosopher seek different ends with different means, hence the poetry is not a reliable source for Coleridge's philosophy.

Although it is now generally recognized that Coleridge's poetic energies never altogether ceased to function, that they flagged sharply after 1800 is incontrovertible. What caused this decline remains a moot question; yet the phenomenon of a noble mind like Coleridge's seemingly inhibited in strange ways continues to pique scholars and critics. In spite of the difficulty of any one explanation—psychoneurosis, drug addiction, unrequited love, metaphysical preoccupations—winning wholehearted espousal, much recent criticism lured by the promises of anthropology and psychology with their flexible methodologies has been occupied anew with the question. Unavoidably conjectural, these exercises in observation and ratiocination are valuable mainly for the correlative insights that their special perspectives on the workings of Coleridge's mind offer us concerning the stuff of his poetry.

Coleridge's use of occult and mythological material has undergone considerable scrutiny of late. One of the best studies is J. B. Beer's neo-Lowesian *Coleridge the Visionary* (1959). Instead of determining what went wrong with Coleridge's poetic creativity, Beer seeks an explanation for the *annus mirabilis.* For a brief period, Beer believes, Coleridge's imagination seized on a limited myth of the Fall and of redemption vivid enough to provide him with an organizing framework for a poetry which sought to link society and the physical universe in an ultimate spiritual order. The great visionary poems of 1797–98 were the fruit of his effort to place rationalism in a broader perspective of human thought. Between

1799 and 1804, however, Coleridge devoted himself to nature in more empirical fashion and never again succeeded in combining the two worlds. It is not accidental that Beer and Bernard Blackstone (*The Lost Travelers: A Romantic Theme with Variations*, 1962), who casts Coleridge in the role of the lost pilgrim in time bent on a return to Eden by way of self-denying cosmic union with the physical world, have written books on Blake. Their Coleridge is a first cousin of the older poet, as also is that of John Armstrong (*The Paradise Myth*, 1969), who offers a variant on this explanation of Coleridge's inconstant artistic control. Backed by a historical exposition from Sumerian times of what he calls the tradition of a counter ideal to the myth of paradise, Armstrong blames Coleridge's ultimate poetic failure on a divided imagination, which was equally attracted to the unconfined principle of energy and the continuing order of an earthly arcadia, but because of a bias toward appealing seductive torpor was unequal to the dimension of mind necessary to unite these contrary modes of fulfillment.

A critic who would go the route and make Coleridge out to be a misdirected mystic is Marshall Suther in *The Dark Night of Samuel Taylor Coleridge* (1960). Suther argues that Coleridge's failure in love and frustration of poetic activity have a common root: he expected from each experience "something like the beatific vision, a complete presence and union in full knowledge" with the absolute. When he failed to find it in either experience because it is not there to be found, he etherealized love and rejected poetry. Can Coleridge's discovery that the physical world is a perpetual reminder of the sacred nature of life be equated automatically with a mystical sense of the divine presence of God? It is a crucial short-coming of Suther's argument that it too readily assumes so.

Many studies locate Coleridge's poetic inhibitions in the conflict between the conscious and unconscious powers of his mind. Edward E. Bostetter in *The Romantic Ventriloquists* (1963) sees the Romantic poet engaged in a desperate struggle for affirmation of his world against increasingly powerful obstacles to this belief. Desirous of belonging to a living universe of purpose and values, manifest to the imagination, the Romantic poet conceived of himself as a divine ventriloquist projecting the voice of ultimate truth. Unhappily Coleridge was unable to feel what he thought he should feel, unable to write what he thought he should write, his imagination unable to affirm a world too complex for unqualified optimism. Horrified by the "sensual and the dark" that his imagination intuited, and finding it impossible to control, Coleridge in effect gave up writing poetry after 1800 when he could not resolve the moral contradictions of "Christabel." Patricia Adair in *The Waking Dream: A Study of Coleridge's Poetry* (1967) attributes the greatness of Coleridge's poetry to the successful, but temporary, conjunction of his conscious and subconscious thoughts. She contends that Coleridge's creative powers withered when he began to distrust the "terrifying activity of the unconscious" and to quell it in favor of the "conscious will"—not an original view since Bostetter demonstrated that dreams were associated with evil in Coleridge's mind by the date of the second part of "Christabel." Furthermore, stripped of its Coleridgean jargon, Adair's point is in effect that Coleridge's best poetry is the product of the "shaping spirit" of his whole being's response to experience— hardly a revolutionary idea! Not his fear of the unconscious but his dread of adult responsibility defines Coleridge's acute psychoneurosis according to Geoffrey Yarlott's *Coleridge and the Abyssinian Maid* (1967). In Yarlott's view Coleridge was trapped by his emotional immaturity and fear of solitude into a lifelong search for masculine figures of maturity and stability—his brother George, Southey, Poole, and Wordsworth—on whose practical integrity he could lean, and for feminine figures, or Abyssinian Maids as Yarlott exotically terms them—Mary Evans and Sara Hutchinson—in whose serene affection he could find poetic inspiration. After his marriage Coleridge oscillated fatally between this need for emotional security and his antithetical preoccupation with the impulses from a vernal wood. Between 1801 and 1803, guilt over his love for Asra and the accompanying emotional desertion of his wife and children made it increasingly difficult for him to separate his private feelings from his public utterances, and the universalizing capacity of poetry slowly withered in him. Although Yarlott exaggerates the intensity and lasting effect of Coleridge's love for and abandonment of Mary Evans, he wields this not overly original psychological frame of reference with restraint in his reading of the poems—both pre-1797 and *annus mirabilis*.

The psychological ambivalences in Coleridge's nature are almost as plentiful as the contraries with which he was fond of formulating reality. Considerations of how these ambivalences affected his poetry are equally plentiful, although only a few will be mentioned here, the rest reserved for discussions of individual poems. M. F. Schulz in "Coleridge Agonistes" (*JEGP*, 1962) delineates Coleridge's irresolute oscillation most of his life between withdrawal to a place of retirement and dutiful performance in "the World without." The same insecurity of mind, with "a desire to retreat from the world and, no less, from himself," is noticed as the theme of Coleridge's poems, by D. G. James in *The Romantic Comedy* (1948). Identifying the "Verse Letter" to Sara Hutchinson as the moment of truth for Coleridge, William Heath in *Wordsworth and Coleridge: A Study of Their Literary Relations in 1801–02* (1970) argues that the poet recognized his inability (somewhat before the fact!) to unite the universal and the particular in the effort of that poem to "make himself simultaneously the student and the object studied." If the source of poetry is "confusion and mystery," Heath notes, then such self-conscious intellectual solution of the personal problem as one finds Coleridge bent on in the "Verse Letter" spells the end to poetic creativity.

Jungian and Freudian critics find Coleridge an attractive subject, although most employ with a heavy hand the theoretical framework of archetypes, Oedipal conflicts, phallic women, and, in the case of Arthur Wormhoudt (*The Demon-Lover: A Psychoanalytical Approach to Literature,* 1949), Edmund Bergler's theories about breast feeding. Studies which reflect these critical *aperçus* are Douglas Angus' "The Theme of Love and Guilt in Coleridge's Three Major Poems" (*JEGP,* 1960); J. Garth Ware's "Coleridge's Great Poems Reflecting the Mother Image" (*American Imago,* 1961); Arthur Clayborough's *The Grotesque in English Literature* (1965); and Beverly Fields's *Reality's Dark Dream: Dejection in Coleridge* (1967).

Finally, there is increasing temptation among critics to attribute to Coleridge what Miss Coburn has called "pre-Sartrian existentialism." This criticism probably tells us as much about the modern sensibility as about Coleridge's; but it manages to make a case based equally on Coleridge's theological thought which is undergoing renewed scrutiny, on his psycho-aesthetic theorizing, and on the dramatization in his poems of his personal experience of alienation. Most of these critical essays are noted in the discussion of specific poems in later pages of this section; but Patricia M. Ball's discriminating book *The Central Self: A Study in Romantic and Victorian Imagination* (1968) can be mentioned here, although she might justifiably object to her classification among those who reflect the post-war susceptibility to the existential ordering of experience. Her thesis is that the Romantics were committed to a double view of the imagination: as the means of discovering self-identity (which she terms the egotistical element) and as the means of escape from the self (the chameleon element). Thus Miss Ball extends the implications of Robert Langbaum's *The Poetry of Experience* (1957) that "the Romantic quality of mind grows out of a total crisis of personality," the poem becoming the experiential process by means of which the self is realized; and questions the insistence of John Bayley's *The Romantic Survival* (1957) that egotistical self-consciousness dominates the Romantic imagination. Rather, according to Miss Ball, Romantic poetry even when explicitly in one mode manages to include the ends of the other. This book is no less stimulating for its sensitive discussions of the personal and the dramatic modes of Coleridge's poetry than for its larger aim, like Langbaum's and Bayley's books, to show the Romantic quality of imagination which informs the poetry of the rest of the nineteenth century.

Two conceptions of Coleridge, often at submerged levels of articulation, can be discerned in much of this criticism. There are those partisans who impatiently brush aside evidences of Coleridge's personal shortcomings to get at his inquiring spirit and largeness of mind. And there are those advocates, presently in the minority, who respond to the manqué in him. Their search for the key to his failure as husband, father, poet, and man of genius largely sidesteps his positive achievements in favor of an unsentimental understanding of the negative aspects of the man and of the period. This search often displays a covert hostility toward the Romantic impulse. When these scholar-critics turn to consider individual poems the question of Coleridge's psychological maladjustments becomes happily and largely inoperative.

2. CRITICISMS OF THE POEMS: ORIGINS, EARLY INFLUENCES, AND INDEBTEDNESSES

Coleridge's early poems exhibit a high visibility of influence, a "laborious and florid diction" that does not reward critical exegesis with aesthetic and thematic dividends, and a tendency to reflect in successive versions the stages of their author's mental and emotional development. Hence the poetry written before the year of Coleridge's companionship with Wordsworth in Somerset has attracted scholars mainly interested in genesis and development.

In Chapter i of *Biographia Literaria* Coleridge recalls his excitement at the discovery of William Lisle Bowles, whose "style of poetry so tender and yet so manly, so natural and real, and yet so dignified and harmonious," affected Coleridge's own style. Specific attributions of indebtedness to Bowles are made by Garland Greever, *A Wiltshire Parson and His Friends* (1926); by Griggs, *Collected Letters,* i; by A. P. Rossiter (*TLS,* 28 September and 26 October 1951, and in a note in *Collected Letters,* ii);

and by Lucyle Werkmeister (*JEGP*, 1959). The nature and degree of this debt is clarified by Mrs. Werkmeister in "Coleridge, Bowles, and 'Feelings of the Heart' " (*Anglia*, 1960) and by P. M. Zall in "Coleridge and 'Sonnets from Various Authors' " (*Cornell Library Journal*, 1967).

Among the many other eighteenth-century authors and thinkers who stand tall in the pre-Kantian pantheon of Coleridge's enthusiasms can be counted Priestley, Hartley, and Erasmus Darwin. H. W. Piper succinctly traces their footsteps as part of "The Pantheistic Sources of Coleridge's Early Poetry" (*JHI*, 1959). A fuller statement of these influences, including Berkeley, Cudworth, and the whole context of Unitarian thought of the 1790's, appears in Piper's *The Active Universe* (1962). A supplement to this discussion is L. Werkmeister's consideration of the impact of Berkeley and Burke on "Coleridge on Science, Philosophy, and Poetry: Their Relation to Religion" (*HTR*, 1959); and of Plotinus on "The Early Coleridge: His 'Rage for Metaphysics' " (*HTR*, 1961).[1]

Coleridge's indebtedness to the authors of his schoolboy and university days inevitably raises the nagging question of his plagiarisms, which loom so large in his later years. The question is compounded by his compulsion to castigate others for borrowing freely and without acknowl-

---

[1] Coleridge's indebtedness to other writers and related matters of date of composition, first drafts, and later versions are dealt with further by L. Werkmeister in "Coleridge's 'Mathematical Problem' " (*MLN*, 1959) and in "Some Whys and Wherefores of Coleridge's 'Lines Composed in a Concert-Room' " (*MP*, 1963); by R. Mayo in "Two Early Coleridge Poems ['Absence, an Ode' and 'Absence, a Poem']" (*Bodleian Lib. Record*, 1956); by W. Braekman in "The Influence of William Collins on Poems ["Kisses," "The Rose," and "Absence: A Poem"] written by Coleridge in 1793" (*Revue des Langues Vivantes*, Brussels, 1965); and by C. G. Martin in "Coleridge, Edward Rushton, and the Cancelled Note to the 'Monody on the Death of Chatterton' " (*RES*, 1966; with partial retraction in 1967), in "Coleridge's *Line to Thelwall*: A Corrected Text and First Version" (*SB*, 1967), and in "Coleridge ['Lines on Having Left a Place of Retirement'] and William Crowe's 'Lewesdon Hill' " (*MLR*, 1967); by John J. Dunn in "Coleridge's Debt to Macpherson's Ossian," *Studies in Scottish Literature* (1969); by M. F. Schulz in "Coleridge's 'Ode on the Departing Year' and [Thomas Burnet's] *The Sacred Theory of Earth*" (*Concerning Poetry*, 1968); by D. V. Erdman and S. M. Parrish in "Who Wrote *The Mad Monk*? A Debate. I *The Mad Monk*: An Early Ode of Wordsworth's? II *The Mad Monk*: A Voice Heard by Coleridge? III *Rebuttals*" (*BNYPL*, 1960); by Frederick L. Beaty in "Mrs. Radcliffe's Fading Gleam [in 'The Mad Monk']" (*PQ*, 1963); by Warren U. Ober in "Mohammed: The Outline of a Proposed Poem by Coleridge and Southey" (*N&Q*, 1958) and in "Original Versions of Two Coleridge Couplets ['The Homeric Hexameter' and 'The Ovidian Elegiac Metre']" (*N&Q*, 1957); by K. Coburn in "Original Versions of Two Coleridge Couplets" (*N&Q*, 1958); by Werner W. Beyer in "Coleridge, Wieland's *Oberon*, and *The Wanderings of Cain*" (*RES*, 1940), and in "Coleridge's 'Oberon' Translation and 'The Wanderings of Cain' " (*N&Q*, 1956); by W. Braekman in "A Reconsideration of the Genesis of S. T. Coleridge's Poem 'On Taking Leave of ———' ['To Two Sisters']" (*N&Q*, 1964); and by George M. Ridenour in "Source and Allusion in Some Poems of Coleridge" (*SP*, 1963).

edgement of debt, and further complicated in reference to his poems, because Coleridge presented some as his own, translated or adapted others for periodical publication without claiming or intending to claim authorship, and copied others in his notebooks without any intention of publication. Editors have in some cases innocently published as Coleridge's poems which he would never have claimed. The plagiarism involving "Hymn Before Sunrise" is discussed later in this section and that involving the lectures on Shakespeare and the composition of *Biographia Literaria* is reported by René Wellek in the next chapter; but the student will find much information on the poetry in E. H. Coleridge's and J. D. Campbell's notes or appendixes, and the work of identification goes on. In *Englische Studien* (1924) O. Ritter has a series of identifications of epigrams and fragments, of Metrical Experiments No. 4 (Sir John Beaumont) and No. 7 (Parnell), of "Habent Sua Fata—Poetae" (Burns); F. W. Stokoe identified Glycine's song from *Zapolya* as suggested by Tieck's "Herbstlied" (*German Influence on the English Romantic Period*, 1926) and M. F. Schulz (*The Poetic Voices of Coleridge*, 1963) has analyzed the extent of Coleridge's indebtedness; L. Patton (*TLS*, 3 Sept. 1938) identified "To A Primrose" and several epigrams from *The Watchman* as taken from the *Anthologia Hibernica*; E. R. Wasserman (*MLN*, 1940 and 1948) identified the Metrical Experiments No. 7 (Parnell, as Ritter had remarked), No. 10 (Cartwright), and No. 12 (a song of the seventeenth century); John Sparrow (*TLS*, 3 April 1943) identified "A Wish Written in Jesus Wood" as translated from Jortin's "Votum"; de Selincourt's Oxford edition of Wordsworth (1940, 1944) made clear that several poems attributed to Coleridge by his editors were actually juvenilia or at least early poems of Wordsworth: the first draft of "Lewti"; "The Three Graves," Part II, and probably Part I; "Inscription for a Seat"; and "Alcaeus to Sappho." Coleridge's two translations from Catullus should be added. For comments on "Coleridge's Use of Wordsworth's Juvenilia," see Jane W. Smyser (*PMLA*, 1950); and Carol Landon on "Wordsworth, Coleridge, and the *Morning Post*: An Early Version of 'The Seven Sisters' " (*RES*, 1960); and for a table of Coleridge-Wordsworth poems found in the *Morning Post* and *Courier* for 1797 to 1803, with a full consideration of the case for single or joint authorship, date of composition, manuscript variants, and previous errors of transcriptions, see R. S. Woof on "Wordsworth's Poetry and Stuart's Newspapers: 1797–1803" (*SB*, 1962). Most of these identifications are corrections of perfectly natural mistakes of Coleridge's editors, and not evidences of plagiarism. Indeed, Coleridge's own contemporaries and close friends were at times confused by his "merry act[s] of hostility," his cheeky plundering of unpublished efforts of Wordsworth, and his self-mocking lampoons of Lamb and Lloyd, as D. V. Erdman reports in a spirited analysis of Coleridge's "three mock sonnets" of 1797 in "Coleridge as Nehemiah Higginbottom" (*MLN, 1958*).

"The Case History of Coleridge's 'Monody on the Death of Chatterton' " is examined by I. A. Gordon (*RES, 1942*), who isolates the changing styles of its successive versions, each with its specific literary influences. Gordon prints the 1794 version, and the 1796 addition, so that they may be compared with the 1790 and 1829 versions, which are accessible in E. H. Coleridge's edition with textual notes. The minor changes in 1797 and 1803, and the final additions to the poem in 1834, also require some consideration.

"Lewti" is based on Wordsworth's schoolboy poem "Beauty and Moonlight," which de Selincourt first published in Volume I (1940) of the Oxford edition of *Wordsworth's Poetical Works*. The Wordsworth manuscript indicates that the inception of Coleridge's poem could not be earlier than the autumn of 1795, not 1794 as Campbell had conjectured, and almost certainly belongs to the period of Wordsworth's close intimacy with Coleridge after June 1797. T. M. Raysor attempts to date the poem after 6 December 1797 (*PQ, 1953*), in accord with its versification and imagery. The most careful study of "Lewti" is a short monograph by G. L. Joughin (*TexSE, 1943*). The critical judgments and even the problems considered are disturbed a little by the error of Campbell and Lowes in regard to date, for de Selincourt's new evidence on the origin of the poem was first noticed by E. H. W. Meyerstein (*TLS,* 29 Nov. 1941); but Joughin has made a useful historical and critical study of the poem in all its various versions.

3. "THE ANCIENT MARINER," "KUBLA KHAN," AND "CHRISTABEL"

Although Lowes's *The Road to Xanadu* (1927) is often under attack these days, it remains one of the most exciting books of critical detective work of this century. A survey of recent criticism and scholarship on "The Ancient Mariner" and "Kubla Khan" properly begins with it. Following the clues to be found primarily in Coleridge's earliest notebook, Lowes tracked Coleridge through his reading to demonstrate that the actual images from reading (and sometimes from experience) passed from a poet's conscious to his unconscious mind, to merge there with each other and finally reappear in a work of art. In Lowes's hands the book becomes not a study of parallels, as one might expect, but a psychological study of the associative processes of the creative imagination. It is in this theory of creation that the book's greatest shortcoming has with time been shown to lie. J. Armstrong states it well in *The Paradise Myth* (1969) when he complains that Lowes fails to offer a rationale for the selective process that took place in Coleridge's mind and that led to the design of the poem. *The Road to Xanadu* remains, however, that rarity, a beautifully written book of learned scholarship, with over 150 pages in fine print of encyclopaedic notes and a magnificent index.

Lowes sparked a search for the ingredients of "The Ancient Mariner" that continues to the present. The hunt has fanned out from Lowes's trek through travel accounts, Gothic tales, and scientific reports into exotic realms distant probably from even the strange tracts that Coleridge's mind was wont on occasion to roam. The explorers vary from rank amateurs who amaze with their audacious claims to sophisticated investigators who enrich with their discoveries. Obviously they cannot all be named, particularly those giving a source for a single stanza, narrative event, or verbal detail. A representative sampling of those that strive for an inclusive explanation of the poem's origins, ranging from the "lunatic" to the sane, would include Ivor James's *The Source* [*The Strange and Dangerous Voyage of Captain Thomas James*] *of "The Ancient Mariner"* (1890), taken seriously by Lowes but disclosed by Morchard Bishop (*TLS*, 16 Jan. 1959) to have been a hoax perpetrated for the amusement of the Fortnightly Literary Club of Cardiff; C. S. Wilkinson's *The Wake of the Bounty* (1953), which seems to be generating a "Baconian" heresy for Coleridgean studies, as witness Neal B. Houston's extravagant claim for "Fletcher Christian and 'The Rime of the Ancient Mariner'" (*DR*, 1965–66) and Robert C. Leitz's refutation (*DR*, 1970); Rosalina Icban-Castro's claim for the Gospel story of Jesus's crucifixion as the outstanding source of the poem (*Diliman Review*, 1959); Bernard Martin's *The Ancient Mariner and the Authentic Narrative*, by the Rev. John Newton, 1764 (1949), which Malcolm Ware in turn links to an undercurrent of reference to the slave trade in the poem, in "Coleridge's 'Spectre-Bark': A Slave Ship?" (*PQ*, 1961); John R. Moore's "Coleridge's Indebtedness to Paltock's *Peter Wilkins* [, *A Cornishman*, 1751]" (*MP*, 1933); O. Bryan Fulmer's "The Ancient Mariner and the Wandering Jew" (*SP*, 1969), the most recent of the claims for the influence under one guise or another of the archetypal figure of the doomed wanderer, which Armstrong counters in *The Paradise*

Myth (1969) with evidence in favor of Charon in Aristophanes' *The Frogs*; Werner W. Beyer's speculations (*RES*, 1939; *N&Q*, 1956; and *The Enchanted Forest*, 1963) that Wieland's *Oberon* provides the key to the matrix of "The Ancient Mariner"; and Bernard Smith's "Coleridge's *Ancient Mariner* and Cook's Second Voyage" (*JWCI*, 1956), as it relates to William Wales, astronomer and meteorologist on the *Resolution* and Coleridge's mathematics instructor at Christ's Hospital.

Diverging from Lowes's treatment of "The Ancient Mariner," most recent criticism has emphasized a moral interpretation, in an effort to bring the poem into harmony with what is known of Coleridge's early philosophy. This approach originates in the work of intellectual historians, such as S. F. Gingerich on the progress "From Necessity to Transcendentalism in Coleridge" (*PMLA*, 1920; rpt. in *Essays in the Romantic Poets*, 1924), which speaks of the philosophy of unifying love in the poem, stemming from Coleridge's early Unitarianism, from the Gospel of St. John, and from Plato and Plotinus, but which exaggerates the influence of Hartley's necessitarianism; Dorothy Waples on "David Hartley in 'The Ancient Mariner' " (*JEGP*, 1936), which finds too much of Hartley's stages of association in the poem; A. E. Powell (Mrs. E. R. Dodds) on *The Romantic Theory of Poetry* (1926), which deals with Coleridge's early Neoplatonism; and H. N. Fairchild on "Hartley, Pistorius, and Coleridge" (*PMLA*, 1947), which shows that even Hartley, with the aid of the religious editing of Pistorius, seemed to the young Coleridge to vindicate the very elements in his thought now recognized as chiefly Neoplatonic, and on the whole course of Coleridge's religious thought, in Volume III (1949) of *Religious Trends in English Poetry*, which charts the religious tendencies of the Romantics with profound antipathy. Disregarding strictures against the moral sham of the poem lodged by Irving Babbitt (*On Being Creative and Other Essays*, 1932) and by Marius Bewley (*Scrutiny*, 1940), the scholarly effort to place "The Ancient Mariner" in an ethical frame of reference that is recognizably Coleridgean continues most recently with Piper's *The Active Universe* (1962), which attributes much in the poem to the late eighteenth-century Unitarianism and scientific thought of such men as Priestley and Darwin; with John A. Stuart's "Augustine and 'The Ancient Mariner' " (*MLN*, 1961) and with his "The Augustinian 'Cause of Action' in Coleridge's *Rime of the Ancient Mariner*" (*HTR*, 1967), the latter analyzing the poem in terms of Coleridge's theological position on original sin, his view of nature, and his acceptance of unqualified ontological optimism; with Malcolm Ware's " 'The Rime of the Ancient Mariner':

A Discourse on Prayer?" (*RES,* 1960), which rigidly treats the poem as a dissertation on the efficacies of prayer, following the five stages of prayer outlined in the Gutch Notebook; with Maren-Sofie Røstvig's " 'The Rime of the Ancient Mariner' and the Cosmic System of Robert Fludd" (*TSL,* 1967), which arbitrarily finds that the syncretic Neoplatonism of Renaissance thought best explains the Mariner's crime as the sin of ignorance; with Irene H. Chayes's "A Coleridgean Reading of 'The Ancient Mariner' " (*SIR,* 1965), which fits the poem with Procrustean efficiency into the context of Coleridge's later metaphysical cosmos, particularly as set forth in *Biographia Literaria* and *Aids to Reflection* and as it touches upon his interest in Fénelon and the quietistic love of all men; and with Milton Teichman's "The Marriage Metaphor in *The Rime of the Ancient Mariner*" (*BNYPL,* 1969), which elaborates on the wedding celebration as an analogue for the central action of the poem, the knowledge gained by the mariner through his experience about the spiritual foundation of reality.

Early ethical or religious readings of "The Ancient Mariner" tended toward allegory. Such is the case with Gertrude Garrigue's interpretation (*Journal of Speculative Philosophy,* 1880) and with Stallknecht's (*PMLA,* 1932; and *Strange Seas of Thought,* 1945). Others tried to ascertain to what extent the poem has a moral structure. The best of these are George Herbert Clarke's "Certain Symbols in *The Rime of the Ancient Mariner*" (*QQ,* 1933); H. F. Scott-Thomas's "The Ethics of 'The Ancient Mariner' " (*DR,* 1938); Elizabeth Nitchie's "The Moral of *The Ancient Mariner* Reconsidered" (*PMLA,* 1933), which examines the effect of the Mariner's horrible dream experience on the participants in the outer realistic frame of the poem; Gayle S. Smith's "A Reappraisal of the Moral Stanzas in *The Rime of the Ancient Mariner*" (*SIR,* 1963), which considers the ironic significance of the dramatic framework as a whole, when viewed from the vantage point of the reader; and Coleman O. Parsons' "The Mariner and the Albatross" (*VQR,* 1950), which uses methods close to those of Lowes, finding the antecedents to Coleridge's moral outlook in *Osorio* and the notebooks, in Bürger's "Wild Huntsman," and in Longueville's story of shipwreck. W. H. Gardner's "The Poet and the Albatross (A Study in Symbolic Suggestion)" (*ESA,* 1958) is too arbitrarily personal an exegesis to be of use.

G. H. Clarke made a desirable shift from allegory to symbolism in his consideration of the poem, singling out the Sun, Polar Spirit, and First Voice as symbols of Law and the Moon, Hermit, and Second Voice as symbols of Love; but recent symbolist interpretations take their beginning rather from the appearance of the most influential essay after Lowes's on "The Ancient Mariner," Robert Penn Warren's "A Poem of Pure Imagination: An Experiment in Reading" (*KR*, 1946; published in expanded form, with very full critical notes, in an edition of the poem, 1946; and reprinted with additional notes answering House's and Schneider's objections, in *Selected Essays*, 1958). Accepting the fable at its face value as a story of crime and punishment and reconciliation, Warren identifies two thematic levels of reference as functioning in the poem. The primary is the vision of a sacramental universe in which the Christian pattern of Fall and Redemption operates in an endless parable of original sin. The secondary is the concept of creative imagination by means of which the "One Life" of universal love is apprehensible. Warren's discussion casts a wide net, touching on the relationship of the supernatural to the spiritual perceptions of Coleridge's great poetry, on his attitude toward symbolic poetry, on his realization of his experience in poetry, and on other themes related to Coleridge's poems, so that in the end the essay is one of the most stimulating, if also one of the most controversial, interpretations of "The Ancient Mariner." Indeed, few critics since have been wholly free from indebtedness to it.

Warren's interpretation has not gone unchallenged. Early opponents were recruited from the ranks of older scholarly traditions which found symbolical interpretations abhorrent or inexplicable. E. E. Stoll in "Symbolism in Coleridge" (*PMLA*, 1948) accused Warren of critical misdemeanors that read embarrassingly now like anachronisms from another age. Newell F. Ford added to Stoll's criticism in "Kenneth Burke and Robert Penn Warren: Criticism by Obsessive Metaphor" (*JEGP*, 1954); Elder Olson handled Warren's essay even more roughly (*MP*, 1948; rpt. in *Critics and Criticism*, ed. Ronald S. Crane, 1952); and J. W. R. Purser in "Interpretation of *The Ancient Mariner*" (*RES*, 1957) and R. L. Brett in *Reason and Imagination* (1960) further complain about over-interpretations of the poem to the general neglect of the conscious design of Coleridge as indicated in the critical principles he held in 1798 and in the directions he gave in the text and marginal gloss of the poem. Time has shown that Warren's essay is not without defects, its critical methodology, as House (*Coleridge*, 1953) notes, following a "rigid theory of symbolic reference" particularly as regards the deployment of sun and moon in the narrative. But House is in basic agreement with the moral world of "The Ancient Mariner" posited by Warren—as is Beer (*Coleridge the Visionary*, 1959), who sets forth in great detail the occult symbolism of such key images as the sun—and wishes to salvage much of the value of his essay, suggesting that the symbol terminology be replaced with "progressively rich associations" of images. The validity of Warren's symbols was further eroded by Elliot B. Gose's "Coleridge and the Luminous Gloom: An Analysis of the 'Symbolical Language' in 'The Rime of the Ancient Mariner' " (*PMLA*, 1960), which reads inadvertently like a bad parody of Warren's essay in its inversion of the sun-moon symbolism. And most recently, James H. Justus has made the intriguing observation in "The Mariner and Robert Penn Warren" (*TSLL*, 1966) that Warren's Mariner is an analogue of the heroes of his novels, who morally relive the ceremony of confession and aesthetically reenact the process of the artist.

The most telling contradiction of Warren's thesis has come not from the anti-symbolists but from critics employing the same critical procedures as Warren. The world depicted in "The Ancient Mariner" they contend does not conform to a sacramental pattern of fall-redemption nor is there indication that it is sustained by an active vision of creative imagination. Rather, all is nightmarish inconsequence and senseless suffering, expressive of Coleridge's covert fear that we may inhabit an irrational and inhospitable universe. The first critic to delineate this version of the Mariner's tale was E. E. Bostetter in "The Nightmare World of *The Ancient Mariner*" (*SIR*, 1962; reiterated in *The Romantic Ventriloquists*, 1963). He was followed by Daniel McDonald in "Too Much Reality: A Discussion of 'The Rime of the Ancient Mariner' " (*SEL*, 1964); and by A. M. Buchan, who characterizes "The Sad Wisdom of the Mariner" (*SP*, 1964) as Coleridge's recognition of the moral and epistemological dangers inherent in dependence on the dreamlike sensory world of nature. In an essay in *From Sensibility to Romanticism* (ed. F. W. Hilles and Harold Bloom, 1965), James D. Boulger tries to adjudicate between Warren's sacramental vision and Bostetter's nightmare world by characterizing "The Ancient Mariner" as a parable of the uneasy Christian skepticism that has been with us since Newton and Locke. Boulger places much importance on the dreamlike quality and epic journey of the poem for an understanding of the difference between the outside logical world of the Wedding-Guest and the inner prerational world of the Mariner and his voyage. He restates this thesis in his Introduction to *Twentieth Century Interpretations of* The Rime of the Ancient Mariner (1969).

Mythic readings of the poem began with Maud Bodkin's moderate and tactful Jungian "Study of 'The Ancient Mariner' and of the Rebirth Archetype" in *Archetypal Patterns in Poetry* (1934). Other interpretations drawing on a Jungian frame of reference are Mark Littman's *"The Ancient Mariner* and Initiation Rites" (*PLL,* 1968); and Carl Frances Keppler's unpublished dissertation (Univ. of Michigan, 1956) on "Symbolism in *The Ancient Mariner."* Keppler equates the Mariner's voyage into the fearful unknown with the painful and dangerous growth of the psyche into a new reintegrated whole. But Mary Jane Lupton in " 'The Rime of the Ancient Mariner': The Agony of Thirst" (*American Imago,* 1970) rejects such optimistic versions of events (specifically R. P. Warren's and Maud Bodkin's) leading to regeneration and reintegration of the Mariner into the community of men and the harmony of the universe, arguing rather that the emotive emphasis of the poem lies in its negation of life, in its expression of the death wish, oral fantasies, fears of genital sexuality, and totem-mythic rebellion (with fear of the consequences) against the established order. In agreement generally about the pattern of crime, isolation, and redemption or rebirth of the soul, numerous critics have found the voyage symbolic of intrepid mental, moral, or spiritual adventure: W. H. Auden in *The Enchafèd Flood* (1951); E. M. W. Tillyard in *Five Poems, 1470–1870* (1948); R. A. Foakes in *The Romantic Assertion* (1958); and Florence G. Marsh in "The Ocean-Desert: *The Ancient Mariner* and *The Waste Land"* (*EC,* 1959). Implicit in these conceptions of the Mariner (in the words of Northrop Frye, *A Study of English Romanticism,* 1968) as "the alienated man cut off from nature by his consciousness," is the notion that his intellectual adventuring transforms him into a romantic wanderer, an outcast from society. Clearly the poem has much to say to an age preoccupied with the existential condition of man and with the social alienation of the artist.

Almost one hundred years ago Stopford Brooke noted in *Theology in the English Poets* (1874) the striking identification of Coleridge with the Mariner. Coleridge, of course, drew the parallel on his voyage to Malta in 1804. Central to D. W. Harding's discussion of "The Theme of *The Ancient Mariner"* (*Scrutiny,* 1941) is his recognition as a psychologist of the personal emotion of isolation pathological in its intensity conveyed by the poem, an overwhelming desolating loneliness which he compares with the statements of "Dejection" and "The Pains of Sleep." His essay might be associated with a similar interpretation by Louise Boas (*EXP,* 1944) and with an important article by George Whalley, "The Mariner and the Albatross" (*UTQ,* 1947), which presents persuasively the view that "The Ancient Mariner" is a revelation of Coleridge's inner life and the albatross whether consciously or unconsciously a symbol of his creative imagination.

Although the poem was probably not originally intended to be a personal allegory, "that is what in Coleridge's eyes it became later, as prophecy was slowly, inexorably, and lingeringly fulfilled." G. Wilson Knight's comments in *The Starlit Dome* (1941) and Kenneth Burke's Freudian interpretation of the poem as Coleridge's symbolic solution to his marital difficulties, in *Philosophy of Literary Form* (1941), need not be dwelled on; but David Beres's, "A Dream, a Vision, and a Poem: A Psychoanalytic Study of the Origins of *The Rime of the Ancient Mariner*" (*IJP,* 1951) is worth mentioning for its early observation of Coleridge's guilty feelings of love-hate for his mother. Idiosyncratic is the word for William Empson's sprightly but iconoclastic remarks (*Critical Quarterly,* 1964) about Coleridge's ambivalent repugnance for the Christian theory of salvation by suffering and about his desire with "The Ancient Mariner" to write a story of uncaused guilt, a parody of the traditional struggle for atonement.

The mode, revisions, and artistry of "The Ancient Mariner" have not gone unnoticed. In "The Influence of the Popular Ballad on Wordsworth and Coleridge" (*PMLA,* 1914), C. W. Stork compares "The Ancient Mariner" with the narrative method of the folk ballad; and Karl Kroeber, with the quest, in " 'The Rime of the Ancient Mariner' as Stylized Epic" (*Transactions of the Wisconsin Academy of Science, Arts, and Letters,* 1957); but Brian Wilkie in *Romantic Poets and Epic Tradition* (1965) considers the epic impulse in the poem to be minor. Tristram P. Coffin analyzes "Coleridge's Use of the Ballad Stanza" (*MLQ,* 1951); Cecil C. Seronsy, Coleridge's "Dual Patterning" (*N&Q,* 1956) of rhyme, imagery, and syntax; and Alice Chandler, the inversion pattern of narrative, structure, and symbol in the poem (*MLQ,* 1965). C. M. Bowra in his chapter on Coleridge in *The Romantic Imagination* (1949) explores among other things how Coleridge makes the supernatural credible in his concern with a mystery which belongs not to faith but to the imagination; and R. H. Fogle defines "The Genre of *The Ancient Mariner*" (*TSE,* 1957) as a kind of "romantic poem" bent on the hard task of imagining the unimaginable, of giving "to airy nothing a local habitation and a name." In 1932 B. R. McElderry, Jr., studied "Coleridge's Revision of *The Ancient Mariner*" (*SP*) so thoroughly that to this day it remains the standard statement on the subject; but it may be supplemented by Stewart C. Wilcox's consideration of Coleridge's intentions with "The Arguments and Motto of *The Ancient Mariner*" (*MLQ,* 1961); and by Huntington Brown's characterization of the fictional minstrel of the poem and of the antiquarian compiler of "The Gloss to *The Rime of the Ancient Mariner*" (*MLQ,*

1945). As might be expected some critics have resisted conceiving of the Mariner as Coleridge's alter-ego, and have instead portrayed him as a dramatic study in "the psychology of superstition and hallucination" (Lionel Stevenson in " 'The Ancient Mariner' as a Dramatic Monologue," *Personalist,* 1949); or as a study in mistaken anthropomorphic notions of the supernatural (William H. Marshall in "Coleridge, the Mariner, and Dramatic Irony," *Personalist,* 1961); or as a study in the superstitions of a Catholic sailor (Edward E. Gibbons, "Point of View and Moral in 'The Rime of the Ancient Mariner,' " *University Review,* 1969). A corollary approach to the poem argues that its dramatic center is the impact of the Mariner's tale on the Wedding-Guest (Charles A. Owen in "Structure in 'The Ancient Mariner,' " *CE,* 1962); or, following House's lead, not so much a drama of conflicting personalities as of two aspects of reality, the visible world of human beings versus the invisible world of spirits, which have interpenetrated by the end of the poem (Ward Pafford in "Coleridge's Wedding-Guest," *SP,* 1963). Then there is the argument over the concluding moral stanzas of the poem, which continues to wend its tedious way, exacerbated by the considerations of the dramatic tension between the Mariner and the Wedding-Guest, and between their two spheres of activity. Pervasive in most critiques dealing with the ethical theme and structure, it would be pointless to cite all the shades of disagreement, other than to mention T. M. Raysor's analysis of the significance of the two versions of "Coleridge's Comment on the Moral of *The Ancient Mariner"* (*PQ,* 1952). Finally, various aspects of the imagery have been traced: A. C. Bradley has pointed out "Coleridge's Use of Light and Colour" (*Miscellany,* 1929); N. Bøgholm similarly emphasizes the effect of light, shadow, and sound (*Anglia,* 1939); and S. C. Wilcox sets forth the sacramental meaning of "The Water Imagery of *The Ancient Mariner"* (*Personalist,* 1954).

The intensity of Coleridge's senses within certain limits inevitably brings up the subject of opium. The question of its effect on his creative imagination has elicited much controversy. Lowes insisted that "The Ancient Mariner" must, as a work of conscious art, be clearly distinguished from "Kubla Khan," in which the dreams of opium enter according to Coleridge's own account. But M. H. Abrams's study (*The Milk of Paradise,* 1934), of the effects of opium on the works of De Quincey, Crabbe, Francis Thompson, and Coleridge modified Lowes's assumption. His conclusion is that Coleridge's dreams did furnish materials for "The Ancient Mariner," in such vivid images as those of intense light, color, and sound, and of persecution and horror. He is supported by R. C. Bald in "Coleridge and *The Ancient Mariner*: Addenda to *The Road to Xanadu*" (*Nineteenth-Century Studies,* ed. Herbert Davis, 1940). Bald's article studies those notebooks which Lowes did not see and finds passages bearing on "The Ancient Mariner," especially on the revisions or additions, as evidence of Coleridge's conscious accumulation of images for poetry; and it also re-studies Coleridge's use of opium or laudanum, with reference to the dosage permitted by contemporary medicine, studies his comments on various dreams and reveries, and greatly increases the probability that the materials of opium reveries were used for "The Ancient Mariner."

At this point the matter rested until the publication of Elisabeth Schneider's dissent in "The 'dream' of Kubla Khan" (*PMLA,* 1945), which was later developed into an important book, *Coleridge, Opium and Kubla Khan* (1953). Miss Schneider, who is chiefly concerned with "Kubla Khan" rather than "The Ancient Mariner," has studied recent medical literature on the subject even more than Abrams and Bald, and seems at first to controvert their conclusions flatly and completely. Older medical writers tended to depend far too much on De Quincey and Coleridge for their accounts of the effects of opium, which are not supported by the extensive modern case-studies to which she refers. It appears that opium does not cause dreams, she says. Opium addicts are usually neurotics and sometimes already dreamers, like De Quincey and Coleridge; the attempt of an addict to give up opium may produce hysteria, hallucination, or even delirium; and the temporary sense of wellbeing which opium gives neurotics may encourage daydreaming; but it is most doubtful if opium in itself causes dreams, like the dream which is supposed to have been the origin of "Kubla Khan." The question remaining would be whether dreaming under the influence of opium, in sleep or in reverie, would have special characteristics because of the drug. Miss Schneider thinks not: the sense of fear or guilt (especially for the neurotic), the endless extension of space and time, are characteristics of dreams, which require no explanation from opium.

The most recent effort to determine if opium affects the creativity of writers has been made by Alethea Hayter. Her book *Opium and the Romantic Imagination* (1968) contains a lengthy review of the traditional attitudes toward opium, case histories, reports of artistic stimulation, evaluations of opium inspired imagery, and summaries of the effect of the drug on writers from Coleridge and De Quincey to Wilkie Collins and Francis Thompson. The conclusions reached "lie somewhere in between the extremes" of the Abrams and Schneider positions. Opium will not in itself inspire artistic creativity; it only "works on what was already there." If the writer "already has a creative imagination and a tendency to reverie, dreams and hypnagogic visions," then opium may intensify and alter his perceptions—but often at the price of the will and the power to make use of it and of the capacity to execute large imaginative designs.

So much for the opium background. As for the dating and meaning of "Kubla Khan," since 1934 it has been known that there existed a holograph of the poem, the Crewe Manuscript (reported by Alice Snyder in *TLS*, 2 Aug. 1934; reproduced by T. C. Skeat in *British Museum Quarterly*, 1963; and by John Shelton in *REL*, 1966) in which Coleridge had inscribed that the "fragment with a good deal more, not recoverable, [was] composed in a sort of Reverie brought on by two grains of Opium." Miss Schenider considers the probability that this note is earlier in date than the published preface, which speaks of "a profound sleep, at least of the external senses," rather than a reverie; and she comes to the conclusion that the variant phrasing suggests a less marvellous origin for the poem. Like others, she is skeptical of the possibility of semiconscious composition and believes that "Coleridge's original inclination toward day-dreaming, encouraged by the use of opium, had combined with his introspective habit of observing closely his own mental process . . . to make him consciously capture and use . . . the content and perhaps one might say the 'technique' of the day-dream." Consequently, she insists rightly that it is not a meaningless dream. As in the ode "Dejection," the poet longs for the joy necessary for poetry. If he could revive that joy from the vision of the damsel's song, he could recreate the paradise of Kubla and all would hear him as an inspired poet-prophet. She shows that the final figure of the sacred poet is part of one of the oldest traditions of literature and quotes Plato's *Ion* as proof. A study of the "Formal Structure in 'Kubla Khan' " (*SIR,* 1962) by Alan C. Purves, demonstrating that the poetic elements of rhyme, meter, and structure follow tight patterns, supports Miss Schneider's analysis of the formal composition and metrical ordering of the poem. In an effort to show that "Kubla Khan" could have been written as late as October 1799 (or perhaps May–June 1800) after Coleridge's return from Germany, Miss Schneider also examines the relation of Coleridge's poems to the literary tradition of pseudo-Oriental poetry in England and lists an impressive number of parallels of "Kubla Khan" with Landor's *Gebir* and Southey's *Thalaba.* An argument like this from internal evidence cannot be entirely conclusive; yet it establishes another date for the composition of the poem which must be seriously considered with the other dates offered on various occasions by Coleridge and the scholars.

Since the publication of Miss Schneider's book and the furor which it raised, preoccupation with the dating of "Kubla Khan" and with the prefatorial tale of the poem's origin as somehow confirming its fragmentariness and thus influencing the way one is to understand the poem has dwindled in favor of the critical imperative that the poem is either complete as it stands (advanced by E. H. W. Meyerstein in *TLS* as early as 30 October 1937) or if not complete has at least a total meaning that is not fragmentary. Two "standard" interpretations have emerged. Both are symbolist readings and hence implicit rejections of Miss Schneider's contention that Coleridge is basically a non-symbolist poet.

The first, pioneered by G. Wilson Knight in *The Starlit Dome* (1941), reads the description of the garden as containing reference to the mystery of existence in its cycle from birth to death. The dome becomes a symbol of positive meaning and of romantic wholeness, reconciling within its shadow the contraries of sun and ice, heat and cold; while the garden and "deep romantic chasm" with its "woman wailing for her demon-lover" incorporate a seeming inexhaustible range of dualisms—the natural-artificial, indefinite-precise, infinite-finite, sacred-profane, inchoate-structured, etc. For a discussion of these reconcilables see R. H. Fogle's "The Romantic Unity of 'Kubla Khan'" (*CE*, 1951) and Bernard R. Breyer's "Towards an Interpretation of Kubla Khan" (*English Studies in Honor of James Southall Wilson,* ed. Fredson Bowers, 1951). Knight boldly identified Kubla with God. H. House (*Coleridge*) demoted him to Representative Man who is the author of his own paradise. Juxtaposed to Kubla and the pleasure grounds he has decreed into existence is the poet, an analogous creator who looks upon the garden of Xanadu not only as paradisal but also as sacred to the poetic experience.

Several recent critiques of the poem, however, reject this view of the garden and pleasure-dome as representative of the momentary realization of paradise in the natural harmonious forms of a poet-king. Instead, they look upon Xanadu as the contrived artifice of a tyrant (or at best of an eighteenth-century gentleman of understanding) imposing rational order on the universe. For Beer in *Coleridge the Visionary,* Kubla functions as the Eastern priest-king-pontiff-judge-artist who in a time of peace imposes his being upon the world in an effort to recreate a postlapsarian Eden. For Woodring in "Coleridge and the Khan" (*EC*, 1959) Kubla is an instance of the profane potentate who tries to appropriate and incorporate for his pleasure the unencompassable sacred. For Watson in "The Meaning of 'Kubla Khan' " (*REL,* 1961; restated in *Coleridge the Poet,* 1966) Kubla represents the true Augustan disporting in his formal garden. In all three versions, Kubla is a commanding genius, who presides over a fallen world, a faulty, time-bound earthly garden inevitably artificial, mechanical, and transitory. Opposed to Kubla's "erection of an outbuilding," to quote Woodring, is the poet's bardic vision which comprehends a reality beyond the reach of worldly potentates, a reality when recovered in song which is of rarer device than any mere Khan's. W. J. Bate conjectures intriguingly in his biography that "Coleridge's own religious censor had naturally demanded that the song of paradise that he heard ['in a vision once']—the song the poet is inspired to emulate—should not be a song of the true Eden." Fearful of its being misinterpreted as an expression of such poetic hopes, Coleridge put the poem aside for almost twenty years before timidly presenting it to the public "rather as a psychological curiosity, than on the ground of any supposed *poetic* merits."

A division of opinion also occurs over the connection between the garden and the "deep romantic chasm" with its "woman wailing for her demon-lover." Whereas there is general agreement, in the words of Suther (*Visions of Xanadu,* 1965), on the incursion of the supernatural and of potentiality and creativity, there is disagreement over whether garden and chasm are antithetical aspects of a continuous reality, and over whether the elements involved are the natural opposed to the supernatural, the natural to the artificial, or the good (desirable) to the evil (undesirable). In the fullest survey to date of the interpretative questions raised by "Kubla Khan" and of the answers offered by the critics, Suther demonstrates by way of an exhaustive survey of Coleridge's poetry that the natural and the artificial are not mutually exclusive concepts for Coleridge, at least in his poetic references to gardens and domes, but that the two versions of reality are treated as both equivalent and continuous, as one might expect from the high priest of the doctrines of the reconciliation of opposites and of the secondary imagination. Suther does not otherwise radically increase our understanding of "Kubla Khan." The value of his study lies in its dispassionate analysis of the conflicting interpretations, in its conclusive rejection of the view which responds to the world of Kubla negatively, and in its provision of another basis (the symbolizing habits of Coleridge's mind as revealed in his other poetry) for an affirmative reading of the paradise decreed by Kubla.

The second, and pivotal, interpretation is broached not only through symbolic extension of the creation process occurring in the chasm and garden but also through reference to the poet's longing to revive his vision of the Abyssinian maid's song. House, Beer, and Woodring all ultimately consider "Kubla Khan" to be a poem about the workings of the creative imagination. It does not take much more symbolic pressure on the contents of the poem than that applied in the interpretations already summarized to read the fountain, mazy river, and its sudden demise in the "caverns measureless to man" as a map of the conscious and unconscious levels of the mind, from which inspired visions involuntarily emerge, are shaped into harmonious forms, and then as mysteriously disappear. In general, these readings conceive of Kubla's actual arrangement of reality as an instance of *natura naturata,* and the poet's "airy way" as *natura naturans.* The siren's song of this symbolist reading of the poem is that it can lure critics into ever more elaborate allegorical equivalents. Thus Watson, who believes "Kubla Khan" to be specifically about two kinds of poems, perversely argues that the description of Xanadu is not vague and general but factual and fanciful, an unpoetical allusion to Augustan poetry, while the lines depictive of the poet are vatic and imaginative, an evocation of Romantic poetry. Less arbitrary than Watson, J. Shelton in "The Autograph Manuscript of 'Kubla Khan' and an Interpretation" (*REL,* 1966) also eventually succumbs to equations, finding the violent birth of the river and its subsequent meandering course, for example, plus "the caves of ice in the sunny pleasure-palace," as indicative of art's inability ever to capture quite the original force of the vision which inspired it. And Irene H. Chayes in " 'Kubla Khan' and the Aesthetic Process" (*SIR,* 1966) would read the poem as a full demonstration of Coleridge's theory of the imagination, as expounded in Chapters xiii and xiv of *Biographia Literaria,* with the three stanzas of the poem equated respectively with the workings of the memory and fancy, of the primary and secondary imaginations, and of the will and consciousness.

As one might guess, "Kubla Khan" attracts psychoanalytical and myth oriented comments. Most, however, like Robert Graves's in *The Meaning of Dreams* (1924), are either strained Freudian interpretations or inflexible dream-book transferences, emphasizing Coleridge's suppressed sexual desires and frustrations. A responsible instance of this criticism worth mentioning is Eli Marcovitz' argument in "Bemoaning the Lost Dream: Coleridge's 'Kubla Khan' and Addiction" (*IJP,* 1964), which tests its conclusions against the published criticism and scholarship. James F. Hoyle demurs in " 'Kubla Khan' as an Elated Experience" (*L&P,*

1966). Not a psychology of opium addiction but a psychology of elation or hypomania he believes is needed to render the experience of "Kubla Khan" convincing. For a rebuttal see Mabel Worthington's "Comment on 'Kubla Khan as an Elated Experience'" (in the same issue of *L&P*). Maud Bodkin's *Archetypal Patterns in Poetry* (1934) is still probably the best introduction to a Jungian interpretation of the poem. Whereas she emphasizes the Paradise-Hades archetype, S. K. Heninger (*JAAC*, 1960) stresses the individuation process set forth in the poem. More conscious than most psychoanalytical criticism of the pitfalls that the "peculiar ambivalence" of "Kubla Khan" poses in allowing "the widest divergencies of critical interpretation," Yarlott's *Coleridge and the Abyssinian Maid* (1967) sides with those who would identify Xanadu with the refinement of artifice and the claustrophobia of confinement, against which the inspired romantic wildness of the chasm, wailing woman, and fountain are opposed. Read thus, the poem becomes a universalization of Coleridge's private feelings, a projection of his fear that his wife's domesticity would stifle his creative powers. Despite the current critical vogue for these "facts of mind" and despite their being part of the critical record, Suther is likely correct when he dismisses the psychoanalytical readings as not serious contenders for authoritative interpretations.

Most of the countless "sources" advanced for "Kubla Khan," which Lowes's book spawned, can also be dismissed either for not adding to our understanding of the poem or for not observing rudimentary scholarly procedure in the zeal to offer (in the words of Ephim G. Fogel in "The Signature of Style," *BNYPL*, 1959; rpt. in *Evidences of Attribution*, ed. Erdman and Fogel, 1966) *Bruchstücke* rather than *Gestalten* as evidence of influence. For an example of post-Lowesian source-hunting, the student might look into Beyer's *The Enchanted Forest* (1963), which places Wieland's *Oberon* at the inceptive center of an ever-expanding circle of poems, not only Coleridge's but Southey's, Wordsworth's, Byron's, and Thomas Love Peacock's as well. And if the student does not care for the Oberon myth as an analogue, he can check out the alternative myths of Adonis and Cybele, which are advocated in a series of articles by Hans Heinrich Meier ("Ancient Light on Kubla's Lines," *ES*, 1965; and "Xanaduvian Residues," *ES*, 1967) and Richard Gerber ("Keys to 'Kubla Khan,'" *ES*, 1963; and "Cybele, Kubla Khan, and Keats," *ES*, 1965). Meier's conclusion in this exchange is that the aim of his source hunting differs from that of Gerber's and Beyer's. He concentrates on the poem as a finished product and seeks to define the diverse symbolism accruing around one element of it (such as the image of the river or the dome); they are interested in the creative act of the poet and seek to find in one myth the formative motif for the diverse elements of the poem. For additional samplings of exercises in attribution, one may look at Wylie Sypher's "Coleridge's Somerset: A Byway to Xanadu" (*PQ,* 1939), Geoffrey Grigson's "Kubla Khan in Wales" (*Cornhill,* 1947), G. Whalley's "Romantic Chasms" (*TLS,* 21 June 1947); Dorothy F. Mercer's "The Symbolism of 'Kubla Khan'" (*JAAC,* 1953); J. Beer's *Coleridge the Visionary;* W. Ober's "Southey, Coleridge, and 'Kubla Khan'" (*JEGP,* 1959); and Kathleen Raine's "Traditional Symbolism in *Kubla Khan"* (*SR,* 1964).

"The Ancient Mariner" and "Kubla Khan" inevitably attract more attention than the other poems of Coleridge; but there are always readers who find "Christabel" entrancing because of the marvels of its music, because of the mystery of how it might have ended had Coleridge been able to finish it, and because of the moral ambiguities of its theme.

The lyric magic of Coleridge and the versification of "Christabel" specifically, however, were of more interest to literary critics and historians in the nineteenth century and in the early decades of this century than they are at present. Hazlitt in his deservedly famous essay "My First Acquaintance with Poets" (1823) recalled that Coleridge "read aloud with a sonorous and musical voice" and that both he and Wordsworth were remarkable for the *"chaunt"* in their recitation. As the century progressed the praise of Coleridge's lyricism increased in din, becoming a stock response and a standard by which other poets were measured. Henry Nelson Coleridge put an official *imprimatur* on this concept of his uncle and father-in-law in a pioneering essay on "The Poetical Works of S. T. Coleridge" (*Quarterly Review,* 1834). Poets are either painters or musicians, he argued, and Coleridge's "verbal harmony" and "perfection of . . . rhythm and metrical arrangement" mark him as a supreme example of the latter. Leigh Hunt's final assessment in *Imagination and Fancy* (1844) supports this judgment, dramatically reversing his earlier estimates of Coleridge (see George D. Stout, "Leigh Hunt on Wordsworth and Coleridge," *KSJ,* 1957) to call him "the sweetest of all our poets," preferring him even to Spenser and Shelley. Swinburne likewise thought the melody of "Christabel" (and "Kubla Khan") to be "incomparable with any other poet's," though the lyricism of Shelley was nearest. And Rossetti in a sonnet on Coleridge hails him as "the father-songster." On the threshold of the nineties, Arthur Symons reconfirmed the importance that Coleridge had for the Victorian age when he wrote in *Appreciations* (1889) that the distinctive Coleridgean note was "his lucid and liquid melody, his imagery of moving light and the faintly veiled transparency of air, his vague, wildly romantic subject-matter, coming from no one knows where, meaning one hardly knows what; but already a magic, an incantation."

Although there has been difference of opinion over the prosody of "Christabel," the consensus is that it subordinates the syllabic structure of the line to the temporal structure. To use the words of Karl Shapiro in "English Prosody and Modern Poetry" (*ELH,* 1947), "both Hopkins and Coleridge stood for the prosody that sounds in the ear and therefore does not 'scan,' and this is the prosody of nearly all English lyric poetry." Shapiro helps to place Coleridge in the history of versification, but the article is condensed, without illustrations, and refers to Coleridge only in comparison with twentieth-century versification. The most useful essay on "The Meter of 'Christabel' " is still that of Ada Snell in the *Fred Newton Scott Anniversary Papers* (1929), since it corrects mistakes in Saintsbury's *History of English Prosody* (1908; 2nd ed. 1923; rpt. 1961), silently readjusts what should at least be considered a false emphasis in Jakob Schipper's *Englische Metrik* (II, 1888), and gives a clearer statement of the metrical principles involved than Coleridge himself had done. After all, Coleridge had been writing his prefatory note on the versification of "Christabel" for the general reader rather than for specialists, and could not easily have given a full statement of the principles involved without writing something like the essay on meter which he had proposed in a letter to Poole of 16 March 1801, when he still had hopes of completing the poem.

The dependence upon accent (and by implication, time) instead of syllable-counting was new to critics of the day, as T. S. Omond remarks in *English Metrists* (1921), new (in the sense of reviving the lost freedom of Renaissance versification) to nearly all the poets; but its fundamental originality, says Miss Snell, was in the adjustment of musical modulations to mood, which Coleridge emphasized at the end of his preface, and which Schipper partly recognized but Saintsbury denied. Recent considerations of Coleridge on prosody have been made by Whalley in "Coleridge on Classical Prosody: An Unidentified Review of 1797" (*RES,* 1951), by C. I. Patterson in "An Unidentified Criticism by Coleridge Related to *Christabel*" (*PMLA,* 1952), and by Paul Fussell, Jr., in *Theory of Prosody in Eighteenth-Century England* (1954).

Like the myriad efforts to explain the drying-up of Coleridge's poetic creativity, the conjectures about how he planned to complete "Christabel" are inevitably unsatisfactory since they deal with what might have been rather than with what is. This guessing game, however, received almost royal sanction with Gillman's account that Coleridge's conception of "The story of Christabel is partly founded on the notion, that the virtuous of this world save the wicked," corroborated by Derwent Coleridge's note in his 1870 edition of his father's poems that "the sufferings of Christabel were to have been represented as vicarious, endured for her 'lover far away.' " Although these reports of Coleridge's intentions are unverifiable, they have provided the substance for more than one interpretation. A balanced consideration of this evidence as an aid to understanding the poem appears in two articles by B. R. McElderry, Jr., "Coleridge's Plan for Completing *Christabel*" (*SP*, 1936) and *"Christabel,* Coleridge, and the Commentators" (*RSSCW,* 1941). A dissent against the belief that Coleridge could have finished "Christabel," if "bad luck and acute personal problems" had not intervened, is registered by Bate in his biography of Coleridge. The whole concept of the poem—its psychological dramatization of "the subtleties of the human will, the inner debates, the tensions and self-betrayals of the open heart" that Coleridge was trying to understand in himself—"was too great for the vessel of this quasi-Gothic tale, with its admittedly suggestive atmosphere but with its small roster of characters, two of which," the passively virtuous Christabel and her one-dimensional father, "proved [too] limited for further development."

Most interpretations, although there are exceptions, begin with the premise that "Christabel" represents Coleridge's concentrated effort to deal with the problem of evil, its origin, and its ambiguous interrelation with good. But division over the question of whether Geraldine functions as a figure of evil (Gillman's view) or as an agent of ultimate good (Derwent Coleridge's view) continues to be radical. Is she an erring mortal expiating a past sin? or a benign spirit sent to inflict vicarious suffering on the martyr Christabel? or a reluctant vampire? or a demon lover? or a man in disguise? The moral frame of reference by no means exhausts the possibilities. Charles Tomlinson, for example, in an essay contributed to *Interpretations: Essays on Twelve English Poems* (ed. John Wain, 1955) equates Geraldine with the "fatal woman" of the Gothic tale, whose "evil works upon and transforms the innocence" of Christabel, leaving her at the end in pathological isolation. Gerald Enscoe, contrariwise, in *Eros and the Romantics* (1967) argues that Geraldine's baleful presence has a benevolent effect, rescuing Christabel from a deathlike state of innocence and blindness through sexual awakening to the attainment of vision, although he does confess to the indeterminateness of Coleridge's attitude because of the ambivalence of the poetic treatment of this transformation. In short, not just its unfinished form but also the uncertainty of Coleridge's view of the nature of evil at the time of writing "Christabel" leaves the poem dramatically and thematically irresolute. According to Bostetter in *"Christabel*: The Vision of Fear" (*PQ*, 1957; rpt. in *The Romantic Ventriloquists*), and Beer in *Coleridge: The Visionary*, Coleridge arrived at the unacceptable hypothesis that evil may be a necessitarian part of the universe and one of the primary laws of nature identified with the terrifying activity of the streamy nature of the unconscious (which P. Adair iterates in *The Waking Dream*, 1967), destructive of will and hence not redeemable by the conscious exercise of good. Until Coleridge solved the problem of evil in his own life, Bostetter concludes, it is unlikely that he could have finished "Christabel." A footnote to Bostetter's conclusion, analyzing the brilliance and cogency of the poem's imagery and narrative framework of moral ambiguity, is offered in *"Christabel*: A Variety of Evil Experience" (*MLQ*, 1964) by Lawrence D. Berkoben. Macdonald Emslie and Paul Edwards in "The Limitations of Langdale: A Reading of *Christabel"* (*EC*, 1970) sidestep somewhat the issue of moral ambiguity by considering the poem to be a dramatic rendition of Christabel's awakening to the reality of the complex nature of adult life, with its inextricable combination of virtue and evil. The texture of the verse, it is argued, particularly the resort to stereotyped and gauche statements, expresses Christabel's conventional state of mind.

The interpretations of "Christabel" have generally followed one of two approaches. Either they invoke a psychosexual frame of reference or they appeal to the literary conventions of the tale of terror. For the respective values of each see Virginia L. Radley, *"Christabel*: Directions Old and New" (*SEL*, 1964).

Psychosexual readings began with the poem's publication in 1816, when the *Edinburgh Review* hinted at its presumed treatment of aberrant sex. This anonymous review has been traditionally attributed to Hazlitt and/or Jeffrey (see Campbell's biography of Coleridge; and T. Hutchinson, *N&Q*, 1902); but Col. W. F. Prideaux (*N&Q*, 1902) and most Hazlitt authorities (P. P. Howe in *Life of William Hazlitt*, 1922, rev. 1928; Catherine Macdonald Maclean in *Born Under Saturn*, 1943; and Herschel Baker in *William Hazlitt*, 1962) have denied that the writing is Hazlitt's; while P. L. Carver in "The Authorship of a Review of *Christabel* Attributed to Hazlitt" (*JEGP*, 1930) has argued that Brougham was the culprit. Elisabeth Schneider also challenged the Hazlitt ascription in "The Unknown Reviewer of *Christabel*: Jeffrey, Hazlitt, Tom Moore" (*PMLA*, 1955), following a lead of the nineteenth-century bibliographer T. F. Dibdin who identified the author as Tom Moore. Her closely reasoned arguments have not gone unchallenged. Hoover H. Jordan in "Thomas Moore and the Review of *Christabel*" (*MP*, 1956) and Wilfred S. Dowden in "Thomas Moore and the Review of *Christabel*" (*MP*, 1962) defend Moore against her allegations and reiterate the older established tradition that Hazlitt and Jeffrey were the culprits. Miss Schneider's answer in "Tom Moore and the *Edinburgh* Review of *Christabel*" (*PMLA*, 1962) unrecalcitrantly reasserts that "The review, I think quite certainly, could have been written only by Moore." Kathleen Coburn substantiates Miss Schneider's certainty somewhat in "Who Killed Christabel?" (*TLS*, 20 May 1965) with a notebook entry of September–October 1829 in which Coleridge, who had earlier attributed the review to Hazlitt, implicates Moore, although "the wording . . . falls short of an explicit charge." The first judicious analysis of the poem, in terms of Coleridge's critical tenets, was made by John Sterling (*Athenaeum*, 1828), who it is assumed had Coleridge's blessings if not his direct help; but most of the early efforts to deal with the supposed obscenity, obscurity, and unorthodox versification of the poem are crude and libelous stuff in the anonymous atmosphere of partisan nineteenth-century journalism. Allusions to these contemporary reviews are made by Arthur H. Nethercot in *The Road to Tryermaine* (1939); by J. Percy Smith in "Criticism of *Christabel*" (*UTQ*, 1951); by G. L. Little in "Christabess: By S. T. Colebritche, Esq." (*MLR*, 1961); and by J. O. Hayden in *The Romantic Reviewers, 1802–1824* (1969). Another favorable account, besides Sterling's, was found in the London *Times* for 20 May 1816, which Erdman in "A New Discovery: The First Review of *Christabel*" (*TexSE*, 1958) conjectures may have been written by Crabb Robinson; and which Lewis M. Schwartz (*SIR*, 1970) attributes to Lamb.

In the best of recent psychosexual interpretations, the underlying assumption is that "Christabel" is no supernatural poem of fright, even though it relies on the conventions of the Gothic novel and on the machinery of vampirism, witchcraft, and folklore superstition, but as Miss Coburn contends in "Coleridge and Wordsworth and 'the Supernatural' " (*UTQ*, 1955–56) a personal expression of Coleridge's inner experience of desolation, anxiety, fright, love, loneliness, and motherlessness. Roy P.

Basler (*SR,* 1943; rpt. in *Sex, Symbolism, and Psychology in Literature,* 1948) is less concerned with the psychological insight the poem may disclose about Coleridge than with the emotional truth it contains about the human condition. He bases his interpretation on the theory that the folk tale, fairy tale, and medieval romance are preoccupied with the "mystery of sex as a powerful and inscrutable force which drives men and women into irrational emotional situations and strange actions almost beyond human comprehension." Taking his cue from Coleridge's statement, reported in Allsop (1836), that he had Crashaw's *Hymn to Saint Teresa* in mind while writing "Christabel," Basler argues that Christabel does not go into the forest, in emulation of Teresa's self sacrifice to the Moors, to offer herself to preternatural powers as requite for her absent lover (as Gillman and Derwent Coleridge claimed), but is meant to effect the transformation and salvation of Geraldine, by assumption of Geraldine's appearance and entrancement for a time. Only through the magic potency of contact can this rejuvenation be effected, hence the lesbian element. Irene H. Chayes offers a variant of this hypothesis in "Coleridge, Metempsychosis, and 'Almost all the followers of Fénelon' " (*ELH,* 1958), based on Coleridge's fusion of the Platonic concept of pre-existence with the theory of metempsychosis (as expounded by such followers of Fénelon as Andrew Michael Ramsay) that souls born into fleshly existence are degraded intelligences condemned to a period of punishment and purification. Thomas R. Preston in the Duquesne University Philological Series (*Essays and Studies in Language and Literature,* ed. Herbert H. Petit, 1964) instead interprets the psychosexual passion of Christabel in terms of traditional mystical uses of the imagery of profane love, particularly as defined by Boehme. Geraldine thus becomes an agent of God, and her embrace the symbolic instrument by which Christabel participates in the act of suffering and redemption that reunites man with the Divine.

Ultimately, any psychosexual approach must face the problem of the ambivalent love relationship presented in the poem. This neither Basler nor Chayes adequately explains, although Preston passes muster, perhaps too easily, as does Radley (*SEL,* 1964) who cuts through this impasse by contending that the poem is a study in ambivalent love relationships. While this interpretation links the conclusion of Part II with the rest of the poem, it does not explain why Coleridge should be so preoccupied presumably with ambivalent love, other than to suggest weakly that Coleridge saw ambivalence as a natural condition of intense love. G. Yarlott in *Coleridge*

and the Abyssinian Maid supplies a psychoanalytical explanation by interpreting Part II as a symbolic projection of Coleridge's guilt over his wish
for Derwent's death (born September 1800), particularly in the dramatization of Sir Leoline's repudiation of Christabel. In love with Sara Hutchinson, Coleridge could not face squarely his altered feelings toward his
children, the anchors mooring him to his wife. Part II, written in 1800,
reflects this state of mind in "its shifting the center of interest from the
heroine to her father, and introducing psychological complexities which
place it in a different genre altogether from the conventional tale of
terror." The shortcoming of this interpretation is that it has difficulty
accounting for Geraldine, whose function Yarlott ingenuously contends is
never adequately objectified, even though the moral ambivalence of her
person in Part I does give way to unequivocal evil in Part II.

The other approach to "Christabel," as Radley has classified it,
assumes that the ingredients of the poem are based on the logically understood machinery of demonology. The most thorough study of this aspect of
"Christabel" is still *The Road to Tryermaine* by Arthur H. Nethercot.
Building on E. H. Coleridge's edition of the poem, Nethercot gives its
history, and then examines in detail the background of Coleridge's known
or probable reading in demonology and other subjects which contributed to
the poem. He examines Coleridge's knowledge of vampires, lamias, ophi-
ology, ocular fascination, the mark of the beast, the transmigration of
souls, guardian spirits; his use of local names; his attitude toward the
"preternatural"; and makes it clear how these themes appear in "Christabel." Nethercot seems to understate the vague influences upon "Christabel"
of Percy's *Reliques* and the Gothic romances of "Monk" Lewis, Mrs.
Radcliffe, and Mrs. Robinson. This influence is the subject of an article by
Donald R. Tuttle (*PMLA*, 1938) and surely represents at least part of the
background of the poem. But neither Tuttle nor Nethercot is able to find
such convincing and specific parallels in image and phrase between Coleridge's known reading and "Christabel" as those which Lowes had found
in his study of "The Ancient Mariner" and "Kubla Khan."

On a different tack, R. H. Fogle in the climactic chapter to *The Idea of
Coleridge's Criticism* (1962) offers a practical "Coleridgean" demonstration of the utility of Coleridge's insistence on a combination of the particular with the universal, of the occasional with the permanent, and of the
part with the whole. Fogle discusses "Christabel" as a "drama of concealment"—with equal emphasis on both aspects of the phrase—and explores

the ways that the poem dramatizes the perennial epistemological dilemma of appearance and reality, realized here in the struggle between the beauty of innocence and the beauty of evil, with evil assuming endless false guises.

4. CRITICISM OF THE POEMS: CONVERSATION POEMS

Considerable attention has been directed the past twenty years to determining whether Romantic nature poetry exhibits a unique imaginative structure. In an early important article on the subject, W. K. Wimsatt, Jr., in "The Structure of Romantic Nature Imagery" (*The Age of Johnson,* ed. Frederick W. Hilles, 1949; rpt. in *The Verbal Icon,* 1954) locates this uniqueness in a movement of thought which simultaneously focuses on the landscape as a literal object of attention and on it as a metaphor of the spirit which informs it or visits it. In its dual function then nature provides the Romantic poem with both vehicle and tenor, unlike the metaphysical poem which maintains a tension of severe disparity.

The poems often cited as prototypical of the Romantic poem are a group of eight named by George McLean Harper "Coleridge's Conversation Poems" (*Quarterly Review,* 1925, and *Spirit of Delight,* 1928). Until very recently most critics either searched these poems for instances of Coleridge's personal views and early domestic joys (Harper in "Gems of Purest Ray," *Coleridge,* ed. Blunden and Griggs, 1934) or condescendingly dismissed them as "too diffuse and unorganized to make a very decisive total impression" (G. Hough, *The Romantic Poets,* 1953). D. G. James has even suggested (*The Romantic Comedy,* 1948) that the unpretentiousness, a "sort of middle thing," of these poems reflects Coleridge's awareness "of a certain failure of imagination, of something negative arresting the flow of his energies," and hence his " 'affecting' not to write poetry or being excessively 'poetical,' " as a way of concealing the canker at the heart of his capacity for creativity. But beginning with House (*Coleridge,* 1953), who showed that the Conversation Poems enacted attitudes and beliefs central to Coleridge's creative experience, critics have found their complexity of meaning and intricacy of form increasingly central to a measure of Coleridge and of the Romantic sensibility. A distinctly new kind of poem, with low-keyed conversational blank verse in the form of a meditative-dramatic monologue, its structure, while imitating naturalness and spontaneity, is carefully controlled to convey a curving pattern of emotion, circular progression of thought, philosophy of "the one Life within us and abroad," and an imagery expressive of this sense of the totality of experience. A convenient summary of these characteristics is given by Schulz (*Poetic Voices of Coleridge,* 1963). For a thorough historical survey of the literary progenitors of the form—the descriptive-meditative poem of the eighteenth century, the relaxed mock-Miltonic manner of Cowper's *The Task,* and the reflective ease of Bowles's poems—one can go to M. H. Abrams' "Structure and Style in the Greater Romantic Lyric" (*From Sensibility to Romanticism,* ed. Hilles and Bloom, 1965).

Critics generally agree that the Conversation Poems enact an out-in-out movement of mind by means of which the poet repeatedly engages the kaleidoscope of nature in a creative interchange of subject and object. Essays which define this Romantic egoism as a tactical move to confirm the organic link between the self and the world around and above include Albert Gérard's "The Systolic Rhythm: The Structure of Coleridge's Conversation Poems" (*EC,* 1960); R. H. Fogle's "Coleridge's Conversation Poems" (*TSE,* 1955) and his *The Idea of Coleridge's Criticism*; and M. F. Schulz's "Oneness and Multeity in Coleridge's Poems" (*TSE,* 1959). But in a philosophically sophisticated analysis of "Imagination and Speculation in Coleridge's Conversation Poems" (*JEGP,* 1964), J. D. Boulger finds an "underlying power of speculative reason, very strong in Coleridge the poet-philosopher," which achieves in the Conversation Poems as compared to "The Ancient Mariner" and "Kubla Khan" only a limited order of imaginative reality in Coleridge's desperate attempt at poetical "blending of paradoxical heterogeneous ideas of the idealistic, associational, and Christian traditions." Other considerations of the mode and manner of the Conversation Poems can be found in Langbaum's *The Poetry of Experience* (1957), which considers them, specifically "Frost at Midnight," to be forerunners of the dramatic monologue; and in Geoffrey Little's "Lines Written at Shurton Bars: Coleridge's First Conversation Poem?" (*Southern Review,* Adelaide, 1966).

Of individual poems, "The Eolian Harp" and "Reflections on Having Left a Place of Retirement" have attracted most critical attention, in part because of their genesis, their unevenness of style, and their thematic contradictions—all reflective of a transitional state in the development of Coleridge as poet and as philosopher. One of the early attempts to come to grips with the theme and form of the first poem in which Coleridge's poetic genius was truly in evidence is made by H. J. W. Milley in "Some Notes on Coleridge's 'Eolian Harp'" (*MP,* 1939). Though Coleridge knew Wordsworth's early poems, Milley gives reasons for doubt that they could be regarded as an influence upon Coleridge's pure diction, his fluent and musical blank verse, or his fresh feeling for nature, which is rather the result of his first true life in the countryside. Indeed the influence is probably in the reverse direction, not only in the sense of a spiritual presence animating all nature, but in the form of "The Eolian Harp," which anticipates "Tintern Abbey."

The "favorite of *my* poems" Coleridge called "The Eolian Harp" in a letter to Thelwall of 31 December 1796, and again, at some unspecified time after the 1797 edition of his poems was published, "the most perfect poem I ever wrote." Without denying the virtues of the poem, its distinctive structure and its lyrical blank verse, much recent criticism has worried over its thematic inconsistencies. H. House (*Coleridge*) bluntly denounced as intellectually intolerable Coleridge's capitulation in the conclusion to Mrs. Coleridge's "governessy" Christianity, but accepted the poem's questioning expression of doubt as consistent, if the famous "One Life" passage added in 1817 with its eloquent but contradictory idealism were deleted. A. Gérard similarly sees Coleridge engaged in the 1796 version in a dialogue with himself about the distinction between God and nature. In "Counterfeiting Infinity: *The Aeolian Harp* and the Growth of Coleridge's Mind" (*JEGP*, 1961), Gérard reminds us of the hypothetical and diffident nature of the "organic Harps" lines, their pantheism not a firmly held, fully realized idea, but little more than a temptation. In the conclusion to the poem, Coleridge repudiates not the experience he has just had, as House maintains, but his interpretation of that experience. In this respect, the poem reflects a stage in the growth between 1795 and 1797 of Coleridge's concept of the symbol and of his speculation about nature-as-infinity to nature as a counterfeit of infinity. Gérard, however, is unwilling wholly to ignore Coleridge's own artistic intentions with such arbitrary selection of an early version over the final one. In "The Systolic Rhythm: The Structure of Coleridge's Conversation Poems" (*EC*, 1960), he acknowledges an inconsistency of thought and feeling in both "The Eolian Harp" and "Reflections." Both essays, the latter significantly retitled "The Discordant Harp," plus a third, "Clevedon Revisited: Further Reflections on Coleridge's 'Reflections on Having Left a Place of Retirement' " (*N&Q*, 1960), were revised for inclusion in *English Romantic Poetry* (1968).

The unity of the poem has also had its defenders: an overschematized effort by W. H. Marshall in "The Structure of Coleridge's 'The Eolian Harp' " (*MLN*, 1961); a quasi-existentialist reading by E. San Juan, Jr., in "Coleridge's 'The Eolian Harp' as Lyric Paradigm" (*Personalist*, 1967); and an exposition of Coleridge's emancipation from the limitations imposed on the conception of the reason and the imagination by associationist theories of mind and mechanistic explanations of the universe, by Ronald C. Wendling in "Coleridge and the Consistency of 'The Eolian Harp' " (*SIR*, 1968).

There has always been disagreement over the philosophical sources of "The Eolian Harp," A. E. Powell citing Plotinus; House, Neoplatonism; Deschamps, Hartley's "vibrations"; Stallknecht, Boehme; and Piper, Priestley. Orsini (*Coleridge and German Idealism*, 1969) attributes such confusion to Coleridge's philosophical oscillation and to the nature of poetry. The appearance of the first volume of the *Notebooks* has stirred up the controversy anew. Arguing for Ralph Cudworth's *The True Intellectual System of the Universe* as "A Source for 'The Eolian Harp' " (*N&Q*, 1966), C. G. Martin equates lines 39–43 with associationism and 44–48 with Neoplatonism, one a passive and the other, reflecting the impact of Cudworth, an active accounting of the mind. In this light, "The Eolian Harp" exhibits Coleridge's intellectual enthusiasms in transition from one philosophical system to another. The same case for Coleridge's indebtedness to Cudworth is made by W. Schrickx in "Coleridge and the Cambridge Platonists" (*REL*, 1966). More sweeping in his generalizations than Martin, Schrickx overlooks the conventions of descriptive-meditative poeticizing and of landscape painting in his zeal to find instances of Cambridge Platonism in the set scenes of "The Eolian Harp" and "Reflections." H. W. Piper in " 'The Eolian Harp' Again" (*N&Q*, 1968) refutes the ascription of influence to Cudworth.

Two critics have found a complex pattern of Christian analogues in "Reflections." M. F. Schulz in "Coleridge, Milton and Lost Paradise" (*N&Q*, 1959) attributes the ambivalence of focus in the poem to an unresolved interaction of the themes of private retirement and public activism, intensified by the poetic identification of the place of retirement with lost paradise. W. H. Marshall (*N&Q*, 1959) extends this analogy of Coleridge and Sara with Adam and Eve (and their abandonment of Clevedon with the re-enactment of eviction from Eden) to include the promise that the Christian myth holds of a future return to paradise. If man-fallen is identifiable with Adam, man-redeemed partakes of the being of Christ. And in the humanitarian love based on equality and fellowship asserted in the poem's conclusion is prefigured each man's participation in the saving action that will bring on the Millennium. A. Gérard (*N&Q*, 1960), while not denying the Christian analogues, questions Schulz's explanation for the equivocation and obscurity of focus of the poem.

The Conversation Poem that has elicited least positive response, with the exception of "Fears in Solitude," is "The Nightingale," possibly because it comes so close in subject matter to the conventional nightingale poem of the day. Coleridge admitted as much in the doggerel verse epistle which accompanied the poem when he sent it 10 May 1798 to Wordsworth for his perusal. For a brief list of nightingale poems in the magazine verse of the 1790's of the kind Coleridge must have had in mind when he penned his note to Wordsworth, see Mayo's "The Contemporaneity of the *Lyrical Ballads*" (*PMLA*, 1954). In a laudable effort to improve the image of "The Nightingale," R. H. Hopkins makes a case for it as "Coleridge's Parody of Melancholy Poetry" (*ES*, 1968), Coleridge subtly converting the stereotypes of gloom into symbols of joyance.

A. Gérard ranks "This Lime-tree Bower" among the most delicate, the most sensitive of Coleridge's personal poems (*English Romantic Poetry*, 1968). A fine analysis of the poem as an enactment of Coleridge's belief that poetry symbolically repeats nature's essential act, *natura naturans* or realization of the universal in the particular, is R. A. Durr's " 'This Lime-tree Bower My Prison' and a Recurrent Action in Coleridge" (*ELH*, 1959). Durr interprets this essential thrust of poetry as the action of the individual soul realizing its true being in the One Life of God. The "recurrent action" then that Durr locates in Coleridge's poetry is a redemptive process whereby the poet proceeds from an initial state of isolated despondency and disharmony with nature, through an imaginative act of recall or an empathic identification with natural objects, to a state of unitive joy and oneness with God and the world. It is appropriate, given the esteem so many critics have for "This Lime-tree Bower," that A. W. Rudrum has drawn his examples from it, especially the "roaring dell" and the hilltop passages, for his evaluation of the way syntax and metrics combine with sound to support sense in the Conversation Poems (*Southern Review*, Adelaide, 1964).

It is, however, "Frost at Midnight" among the Conversation Poems which has drawn most praise. In his pioneering study of the printed versions of the poem, House (*Coleridge*) shows how "Frost at Midnight" evolved from the playful looseness and domestic shapelessness of Cowper's "divine chit-chat" into a controlled statement about the act of cognition, the perceiving, remembering, projecting mind simultaneously providing the poem with its subject and with its mode of development. Analyses of the thematic and structural progression of the poem, the accrual in meaning of "secret ministry of frost," its identification with the silent processes of life, and the ambience of the poem's aural-visual and change-permanence imagery, have been made by Langbaum in *The Poetry of Experience* and by Schulz in *Poetic Voices of Coleridge*. For those who believe that existential relevance is all, Michael G. Sundell attempts to set forth Coleridge's "Theme of Self-Realization in 'Frost at Midnight' " (*SIR*, 1967).

Coleridge's postmortem on his poetic career, incorporated into his tribute "To William Wordsworth," has been characterized by A. Reeve Parker in "Wordsworth's Whelming Tide: Coleridge and the Art of Analogy" (*Forms of Lyric: Selected Papers from the English Institute*, ed. Reuben A. Brower, 1970) as Coleridge's counter-elegy, a funeral hymn shaped by "Lycidas" and by his response to the eulogy of him in Book x of *The Prelude*.

5. CRITICISM OF THE POEMS: LAST PHASE, DRAMA, AND LOVE POETRY

"Dejection: An Ode" is popularly taken to mark a crisis in Coleridge's poetic energies. He continued to compose at least a few poems every year until his death, some of high quality, but never enjoyed again the profound union of thought and feeling of the poems of the *annus mirabilis*. "Dejection" laments the loss of those qualities which were responsible for his greatest poetry, yet it has an intensity of personal feeling which always attracts attention. It has, moreover, a body of thought which has forced comparisons with Wordsworth's Ode. John D. Rea in "Coleridge's Intimations of Immortality from Proclus" (*MP*, 1928) and Fred M. Smith in "The Relation of Coleridge's *Ode on Dejection* to Wordsworth's *Ode on Intimations of Immortality*" (*PMLA*, 1935) have studied the connection between the two poems. George W. Meyer extends the comparison to include *"Resolution and Independence*: Wordsworth's Answer to Coleridge's *Dejection: An Ode*" (*TSE*, 1950). In a detailed account of the circumstances of 1802 surrounding their composition, he sees the two poets engaged in a continuing dialogue about the nature of the poetic act and about the interaction of the perceiving mind with the physical world. A report by B. Ifor Evans on the "Coleorton Manuscripts of 'Resolution and Independence' and 'Ode to Dejection' " (*MLR*, 1951) would seem to confirm "the close relationship of Wordsworth's poem with that of Coleridge's by their presentation in [the] joint form" of a letter to the Beaumonts. Harold Bloom in *The Visionary Company* (1961) restates the Coleridge-Wordsworth controversy in a trenchant analysis of the dialectical resolutions of "Dejection." Bloom argues convincingly that "To William Wordsworth," written by Coleridge in response to his hearing *The Prelude* read on his return from Malta, is a part of the dialogue which preoccupied the two poets during the years of their close association. S. Prickett (*Coleridge and Wordsworth,* 1970) re-examines the "fruitful tension of ideas" developed by Coleridge and Wordsworth in their poems, and interprets "To William Wordsworth" as a critique of *The Prelude.*

A. O. Lovejoy, who had the combination of philosophy and literature which a student of Coleridge needs, has warned briefly but emphatically in "Coleridge and Kant's Two Worlds" (*ELH,* 1940) that "Dejection" does not embody a transcendental epistemology and metaphysics such as has been suggested by Gingerich, Winkelmann, and others; rather the "joy" which the poet lacks, the "beautiful and beauty-making power," refers quite simply and directly to personal feeling, without which the perception of beauty is abstract and empty. Lovejoy does not cite the earlier argument of Stallknecht in "The Doctrine of Coleridge's *Dejection* and Its Relation to Wordsworth's Philosophy" (*PMLA,* 1934; rpt. in *Strange Seas of Thought,* 1945), which takes up again, as in the article on "The Ancient Mariner," the central Wordsworth-Coleridge conception of imaginative love. His article has the merit of considering the relation of "Dejection" to Wordsworth, to "The Ancient Mariner," and to "The Eolian Harp." As a result of this treatment, however, Stallknecht throws out illuminating suggestions regarding Coleridge without fully developing or justifying them, merely as incident to his study of Wordsworth. The consequence is that a valuable study both of Coleridge and Wordsworth has not been fully incorporated in contemporary research. A qualified response has also greeted Suther's discussion of "Dejection" in *The Dark Night of Samuel Taylor Coleridge* (1960). He considers the poem to be Coleridge's recantation of the belief that his poetic experience of nature was equivalent to the mystical experience of God—hence a key document in Coleridge's spiritual biography. The poignancy of Coleridge's *mea culpa* is recorded for Suther in the continued presence in the poem of a vocabulary characteristic of Coleridge's earlier heralding of nature and of his presumed mistaking of the poetic experience of it as a religious experience, but now contrariwise used to deny flatly to nature any vital capacity to affect the individual. Suther's thesis assumes that Coleridge the "subtle-souled psychologist" and metaphysician could easily confuse the poetic and religious activities of the mind and heart. On this point, however, the evidence is open to more than the one interpretation Suther places on it, so that his argument is less than convincing.

In 1937 the original version of "Dejection," a "Verse Letter" addressed to Sara Hutchinson, was published by de Selincourt in *Essays and Studies,* and later in *Wordsworthian and Other Studies* (1947). The poem is more than twice as long as the version which Coleridge published and gives more knowledge of Coleridge's miserable domestic life than could have been published before the present. Subsequent consideration of "Dejection" has compared it both unfavorably and favorably with the "Verse Letter." Those hesitant to put their seal of approval on "Dejection" are rueful about the final two stanzas, in particular, declaring them an excrescence on the admirable lines about joy and the imagination. In one of the earliest of such plaints, House (*Coleridge,* 1953) concludes that although "Dejection" is brilliantly successful in parts, "it fails to achieve complete artistic unity" and hence is "not a whole poem." House's understanding of "Dejection" is controlled by his belief that its intention is identical with that of the "Verse Letter." If the two poetic statements are thematically the same, then "Dejection" is "not primarily a poem about modes of perception" but a flawed public rendering of a private utterance "about unhappiness and about love and about joy." Charles S. Bouslog in "Structure and Theme in Coleridge's 'Dejection: An Ode' " (*MLQ,* 1963) concurs, accusing Coleridge of being concerned in the revision with concealment of his original state of mind rather than with the aesthetics of the imagination. He also scores the poem for not being self-contained, since it forces the reader to seek information external to it to understand it. Suther faults only Stanza vi for being "completely out of reference with the symbolic structure of the poem," which otherwise is "a poem about the poetic experience and the incapacity for it in which Coleridge found himself." In an analysis of the psychological reasons Coleridge gives for his deadened feelings, Suther finds the "Verse Letter" equally "confused, contradictory, and factually inaccurate."

On the credit side, Stephen F. Fogle admires "The Design of Coleridge's 'Dejection' " (*SP,* 1951), especially Coleridge's use of the storm, which is only a "minor theme" in the verse epistle, to furnish "the framework for the organization of 'Dejection.' " "By letting the physical situation develop to keep pace symbolically with the development of his emotional situation . . . Coleridge has taken what was a useful but subordinate element of a confused and uneven poem and made it of the first importance to the structure of a powerful one." R. H. Fogle in a dissent against the idea that "The Dejection of Coleridge's Ode" (*ELH*, 1950) continues to the end has much to say about the structure of the poem and thus prefigures his brother's conclusion, finding that the ode "reveals a more highly organized, a more rounded and comprehensive experience than investigation of either its biographical or its philosophical elements can uncover." M. F. Schulz in *Poetic Voices of Coleridge* finds, like Bouslog, that Coleridge did not wholly successfully reduce the double theme of his "coarse domestic life" and his deadened spirit to the single theme of dejection over the loss of his creative imagination; Schulz however finds much in the symbolism of "Dejection" to praise, particularly that of the developing storm and of the viper, which are "responsive to every nuance of the poet's mind" and responsible for a " 'unity of impression upon the whole' unknown to the early odes."

The outcome of "Dejection" has also elicited considerable controversy. Is the poet's despair permanent, because his poetic powers are dead and hence incapable of being aroused by the swelling gust and "slant night-shower" of the storm (Suther)? Or is the poet's despair, albeit continuing, startled out of its "stifled, drowsy, unimpassioned grief" into sharply felt agony (Schulz)? Or has the poet's agony lessened to the extent that the enlightening experience through which he has just passed has stirred him for the moment out of the lethargy in which he began, but he continues immobilized in the closing lines waiting for the storm to end, his actual revival still in the future and hence still in doubt, even though he is able now to wish joy for another (I. H. Chayes, "Rhetoric as Drama: An Approach to the Romantic Ode," *PMLA*, 1964)? Or does the poet's mood of dejection give way to joy in the reconciliation and equilibrium that the imagination promises in the second lute song and in the "outward-moving love" expressed for the Lady (K. Coburn, "Coleridge Redivivus," *Major English Romantic Poets*, ed. Thorpe, et al.; and R. H. Fogle)? What Coleridge meant when he wished the storm to "be but a mountain-birth" has also elicited glosses from House, Schulz, and Marsh (*N&Q*, 1955).

Recent psychoanalytical attempts to get at the crux of Coleridge's neuroses have found the "Verse Letter" a fascinating document. According to B. Fields in a long chapter on "The First Draft of *Dejection*: An Explication" in her book *Reality's Dark Dream* (1967), the poem embodies covert expressions of hostility toward Sara Hutchinson and homosexual implications in the references to Wordsworth. The cause of this hostility according to Marcovitz (*IJP*, 1964) and Mary Jane Lupton, "The

Dark Dream of 'Dejection' " (*L&P*, 1968), is the unresolved Oedipal conflict Coleridge was left with at the death of his father. There are gleanings helpful to our understanding of "Dejection" to be gathered from these psychoanalytical exegeses: the emotional implications in the language Coleridge uses and the emotional discrepancies that exist between the two versions; but for the most part the poem is less the goal of these studies than a bridge to the poet. It is probably safe to say that those interested in Coleridge the man and in the biographical facts behind the composition of the poem will prefer the "Verse Letter," while those concerned with literary questions of theme and form will be drawn to "Dejection."

The subject of Coleridge's dejection over the loss of his imaginative genius is taken up again in a study of *Coleridge's "Hymn Before Sunrise"* (1942) by Adrien Bonjour. Over two hundred pages are devoted not only to the poem itself, the various versions of its text, its origin, and its plagiarism from Friederike Brun, but to what Bonjour calls Coleridge's "Dejection crisis." Since the "Hymn Before Sunrise" is associated in date with "Dejection" and the conscious loss of Coleridge's poetic powers, Bonjour makes a thorough analysis of the personal causes of Coleridge's loss of hope, which was a chief cause of his plagiarism. Bonjour accepts Coleridge's version of how the poem was initially inspired: on 5 August 1802 while climbing on Scafell Coleridge had "involuntarily poured forth a hymn in the manner of the *Psalms,*" so he said in a letter of 26 August 1802 to Sotheby. But A. P. Rossiter in *TLS* (28 Sept. and 25 Oct. 1951) rejects Coleridge's claim as "an Estecean myth." Rather, Coleridge wrote "Hymn Before Sunrise" with Bowles' "Coombe Ellen" and Friederike Brun's poem on Mont Blanc lying open before him. Without denying the part the Brun poem plays in the composition of "Hymn Before Sunrise," L. D. Berkoben in "The Composition of Coleridge's 'Hymn Before Sunrise': Some Mitigating Circumstances" (*ELN,* 1966) takes issue with all those critics who would make much of Coleridge's borrowings in the poem and little of his own contribution, demonstrating that Coleridge also drew on his firsthand experience of the Lake country, as verified in his letters and notebook entries of November 1799 and August–September 1802. The design of "Hymn Before Sunrise" has also come under scrutiny. F. R. Leavis sounded the attack in *Revaluation* (1936) when he dismissed the poem as simultaneously striving for sublimity and for sweetness and beguilement. Because it expresses a conflicting attitude toward the mountain, Leavis contends, the poem lacks thematic and tonal unity. Both Bonjour and Schulz (*Poetic Voices of Coleridge*), contrariwise, have defended the integrating act of the poem, which reconciles in the image of the mountain a variety of contraries.

Coleridge was the most successful of the Romantic poets in their sporadic flirtations with the theater. He did verse translations between December 1799 and April 1800 of Schiller's historical dramas *The Piccolomini* and *The Death of Wallenstein,* still standard English versions of these plays; and he wrote two verse dramas, *Osorio* in 1797 which he revised and saw staged as *Remorse* at Drury Lane in 1813 for a run of twenty days, and *Zapolya* in 1815 (rejected by Drury Lane 1816, published 1817). There are also fragments—Act I of *The Fall of Robespierre* written in 1794, less than one act of *The Triumph of Loyalty* written in 1800, scraps of a prose play *Diadeste* conjecturally dated 1812–20 and published by E. L. Griggs (*MP,* 1937), and a sketch for a play about *Michael Scott* projected in 1812 and analyzed by J. M. Nosworthy (*E&S,* 1957)—which can be dismissed without discussion. P. Machule in "Coleridge's *Wallenstein*-Übersetzung" (*Englische Studien,* 1902) and Rudolf Haas in "Zu Coleridges *Wallenstein*-Übersetzung" (*Versdichtung der englischen Romantik: Interpretationen,* ed. Teut A. Riese and Dieter Riesner, 1968) have made long and detailed though unenthusiastic analyses of Coleridge's translation; and Bayard Quincy Morgan, asking "What Happened to Coleridge's *Wallenstein?*" (*MLJ,* 1959), has collated Coleridge's translation of the two plays with the standard German versions, which Schiller extensively revised after preparing the two manuscripts from which Coleridge worked, and with the Bohn Library edition of Schiller's works in English, which uses Coleridge's translation but changes the arrangement of acts and scenes to conform to the German editions and adds its own translations of many lines that Coleridge had not translated because they were not in his copy. For information on the performances of *Remorse,* the acting versions, and the three editions of the play that appeared in 1813, see two notes by Campbell on "Coleridge's 'Osorio' and 'Remorse'" (*Athenaeum,* 1890 and 1892); and one by Woodring on "Two Prompt Copies of Coleridge's 'Remorse'" (*BNYPL,* 1961). In a study of "Coleridge's Unpublished Revisions of 'Osorio'" (*BNYPL,* 1967), P. M. Zall collates three manuscripts and remains of a fourth, which have survived, correcting E. H. Coleridge's collation in the *Complete Poetical Works* (1912) and distinguishing three stages of revisions. Dora Jean Ashe dispels the "apparently accepted belief," perpetuated by Griggs in "Coleridge and Byron" (*PMLA,* 1930), that Byron allegedly had a part in the production of *Remorse* (*N&Q*, 1956). She also cites Coleridge's and Byron's common debt to Schiller's *Der Geisterseher* (*N&Q*, 1956). The most thorough and reliable "measurement of political winds" in the plays is Woodring's review of Coleridge's twenty-year exploration in dramatic form of the tyrannies of power, in a chapter of *Politics in the Poetry of Coleridge* (1961). Arnold B. Fox also surveys somewhat hurriedly the "Political and Biographical Background of Coleridge's *Osorio*" (*JEGP*, 1962), the general set of equivalents that the situations of the play have politically with the repressive events of 1794–96 and psychologically with the ambivalent love-hate feelings Coleridge had for his fatherly older brother George. One might add that in these plays some of Coleridge's most eloquent poetry occurs, which has received cursory scrutiny, along with comments on setting, characterization, and theme, in Bernard Knieger's "Wordsworth and Coleridge as Playwrights" (*CLAJ*, 1962); in Clark Emery's "*Remorse*: Coleridge's Venture in Tragedy" (*Carrell*, 1964); in Patricia M. Ball's "The Waking Dream: Coleridge and the Drama" (*The Morality of Art: Essays Presented to G. Wilson Knight*, ed. D. W. Jefferson, 1969), as well as in her *The Central Self* (1968); and (on *Zapolya*) in the surveys of Rudolf Lutz' *S. T. Coleridge: Seine Dichtung als Ausdruck ethischen Bewusstseins* (1951), Beer's *Coleridge the Visionary*, and Schulz's *Poetic Voices of Coleridge*.

Coleridge's love poems likewise "deserve more attention than they have ever received," so Raysor lamented in his pioneering article "Coleridge and 'Asra' " (*MP*, 1929). The frame of reference for Raysor and for Whalley in *Coleridge and Sara Hutchinson* (1955) is primarily Coleridge's love for Sara. Derek Stanford's short essay on "Coleridge as Poet and Philosopher of Love" (*English*, 1960) is concerned in a larger way with the implications of weakness and personal insufficiency that Coleridge's psychology of love, of sympathy, and of empathy had about himself and with the deleterious impact that it had on such nineteenth-century poets as Clare, Hood, Darley, Beddoes, and Rossetti. And in "The Wry Vision of Coleridge's Love Poetry" (*Personalist*, 1964), Schulz sets forth Coleridge's curious ambivalence towards love as it appears almost motif-like in his poems from 1790 to practically the day of his death: his emphasis on marital love as a pledge of permanence, his identification of sexual and maternal love, his etherealization of the beloved, and his sad acceptance of the ephemerality of unreciprocated love.

The poetry of Coleridge's Highgate years, especially the Indian

Summer resurgence of poetic powers in the second half of the 1820's, has had few defenders, beyond I. A. Richards who comments on the unacknowledged merit of *Coleridge's Minor Poems* in a lecture given at Montana State University in 1960; Schulz who cites "The Improvisatore" as *sui generis* of "Coleridge's Improvisation Poems" (*TSE*, 1960; rpt. in *Poetic Voices of Coleridge*); and Whalley who offers a scholarly comprehensive consideration of the canon—distribution over the years, modes, themes, tone, and technical scope—of " 'Late Autumn's Amaranth': Coleridge's Late Poems" (*PTRSC, 1964*).

Studies of recurrent images and patterns of thought in Coleridge's poetry are less plentiful than with the other Romantic poets. The concentration in this century on Coleridge's criticism and on source hunting for "The Ancient Mariner" and "Kubla Khan" may account in part for this neglect, which is unfortunate since there is indication that Coleridge expressed himself no less than other poets in ways idiosyncratic and recurrent—as is demonstrated by Suther's pursuit of Coleridge's wind, moon, sun, river, dome, and bower imagery through the badlands of the pre-1795 poetry with single-minded devotion in his two books on "Kubla Khan" and "Dejection." Others who have surveyed this terrain are Miss Coburn in "Reflections in a Coleridge Mirror: Some Images in His Poems" (*From Sensibility to Romanticism,* ed. Hilles and Bloom) on the meaning in Coleridge's poetry of the mirror reflection, spider web, fountain, upwelling spring, nursing babe, and sheltering tree with its life-drawing roots; and in "Coleridge and Restraint" (*UTQ,* 1969) on coercion and confinement; Schulz in "Coleridge Agonistes" (*JEGP,* 1962) on parricide-fratricide, the garden dell, song bird, and nursing child; Judson S. Lyon in "Romantic Psychology and the Inner Senses: Coleridge" (*PMLA,* 1966) on inner eyes, ears, light, hearing, and deafness; Alvin D. Alley in "Coleridge and Existentialism" (*SHR,* 1968) on the Cain theme; H. B. de Groot on the emblem of the Ouroboros (*ES,* 1969); and S. Prickett (*Coleridge and Wordsworth*) on the rainbow, aureole, and mirror reflection as images of the experiential operation of the mind. There are also some older essays worth citing: Lane Cooper on "The Power of the Eye in Coleridge" (*Studies . . . in Celebration of . . . James Morgan Holt,* 1910), and C. S. Bouslog on "The Symbol of the Sod-Seat in Coleridge" (*PMLA,* 1945); as well as a gaggle of more recent articles by Japanese critics in *English Quarterly* (Kyoto) and *Studies in English Literature* (Tokyo), and by Indian critics in *Calcutta Review* and *International Journal of English Studies.*

In this year, the bicentenary of Coleridge's birth, the final judgment of the man—the artist and the philosopher—is still not in. It is quite possible at this date to get conflicting testimony, as in two books recently published that explore his thought. G. N. G. Orsini in *Coleridge and German Idealism* (1969) acknowledges somewhat subversively his belief that "Coleridge is primarily a poet, and a great poet. But he wrote splendid prose," while Thomas McFarland in *Coleridge and the Pantheist Tradition* (1969) responds to Kittredge's summing-up ("Coleridge was a great poet, and a considerable critic") with the truculent estimate: "Coleridge was not a great poet, although he wrote one or two great poems and undeniably possessed the abilities to have written more. Nor was he merely a considerable critic . . . [but] the most profound of English critics." And on that unresolved but forward-looking note stands Coleridge's reputation today.

Additional commentaries and interpretations:

J. Beer, "Coleridge at School" (*N&Q*, 1958); P. Kaufman, "New Light on Coleridge as Undergraduate" (*REL*, 1966); W. W. Beyer, "Coleridge's Early Knowledge of German" (*MP*, 1955); M. Bishop, "Notes of Two Coleridges" (*BNYPL*, 1959); D. Stanford, "Coleridge: The Pathological Sage" (*Month*, 1962); B. R. McElderry, Jr., "Coleridge on Blake's *Songs*" (*MLQ*, 1948); L. Werkmeister, "Jerdan on Coleridge" (*N&Q*, 1959).

Ward Pafford, "Samuel Taylor Coleridge" (*Emory University Quarterly*, 1965); Vincent Buckley, "Coleridge: Vision and Actuality" (*Melbourne Critical Review*, 1961); M. F. Schulz, "*The Soother of Absence*: An Unwritten Work by S. T. Coleridge" (*Southern Review*, Adelaide, 1967), "*Comforts and Consolations*: An Unwritten Work by S. T. Coleridge" (*Coranto*, 1967), "Coleridge's 'Apologetic' Prefaces" (*TSE*, 1961); Carol L. Bagley, "Early American Reviews of Coleridge as Poet" (*RS*, 1964). D. F. Rauber, "The Fragment as Romantic Poem" (*MLQ*, 1969); E. Schneider, "Notes on *Christabel*" (*PQ*, 1953); F. Marsh, "*Christabel* and Coleridge's 'Recipe' for Romance Poems" (*N&Q*, 1958); Katherine Garvin, "Snakes in the Grass (with Particular Attention to Satan, Lamia, Christabel)" (*REL*, 1961); W. Edward Farrison, "Coleridge's 'Christabel,' The Conclusion to Part II" (*CLAJ*, 1961); Raymond J. Smith, "The Imagery of 'Christabel'" (*McNeese Review*, 1964), and "Christabel and Geraldine: The Marriage of Life and Death" (*BR*, 1965); C. Woodring, "Christabel of Cumberland" (*REL*, 1966);

Terry Otten, "Christabel, Beatrice, and the Encounter with Evil" (*BR*, 1969).

Alfred Weber, "Samuel Taylor Coleridge: *Dejection: An Ode*" (*Versdichtung der englischen Romantik: Interpretationen*, ed. Teut A. Riese and Dieter Riesner, 1968).

COLERIDGE'S PHILOSOPHY
AND CRITICISM
(*To 1956*)

René Wellek

I. THE SOURCES

The study of Coleridge's thought—his philosophy, theology, political and scientific theory, aesthetics, and literary criticism has advanced greatly in the last decades, as Coleridge is again taken seriously as a thinker, and, for the first time, is studied closely. His important position in the history of English thought is now generally recognized, and many of his ideas (or ideas transmitted by him) excite widespread interest. Still, much remains to be done before we can arrive at a final description, analysis, and evaluation of Coleridge's thought.

Not all the evidence for Coleridge's thought is in. Many of his largest manuscripts have never been published *in extenso,* though they have been described by Alice D. Snyder in *Coleridge on Logic and Learning* (1920), J. H. Muirhead in *Coleridge as Philosopher* (1930), and René Wellek in *Immanuel Kant in England* (1931). There are also two articles which contribute additional information, by Kathleen H. Coburn (*RES,* 1934) and R. Florence Brinkley (*HLQ,* 1945). Many notebooks, marginalia, and letters of philosophical interest are still unpublished. A complete edition of Coleridge's prose is certainly a *desideratum,* but in view of present publishing conditions is not likely. Only *Biographia Literaria* in the Shawcross edition of 1907 and the three volumes of criticism collected by T. M.

Raysor (*Coleridge's Shakespearean Criticism,* 1930, and *Coleridge's Miscellaneous Criticism,* 1936) are available in satisfactory modern editions. Recently (1949) Kathleen Coburn has published a careful, annotated edition of Coleridge's *Philosophical Lectures,* a series on the history of philosophy delivered in 1818–19.

Extracts from unpublished notebooks (as well as selections from published prose-writings) are arranged by topics in Miss Coburn's collection, *Inquiring Spirit* (1952). R. Florence Brinkley has compiled a large volume, *Coleridge on the Seventeenth Century* (1955), which prints all of Coleridge's scattered pronouncements on seventeenth-century philosophers, theologians, poets, and dramatists. Many of the known texts are printed from MSS in a more exact form and Miss Brinkley has added marginalia, letters, and notebook entries from MS sources. To these should be added Alice D. Snyder's elaborate edition of Coleridge's *Treatise on Method as Published in the Encyclopædia Metropolitana* (1934).

Even if we had a complete edition of Coleridge's prose, we would still have to face the question of Coleridge's "plagiarisms." It has been continually discussed in Coleridge scholarship since the time shortly after his death when De Quincey, in *Tait's Magazine* (1839), and J. F. Ferrier, in *Blackwood's* (1840), drew attention to the passages from Schelling which Coleridge used at crucial points of the *Biographia Literaria.* Coleridge's daughter, Sara, in her edition of the *Biographia* (1847), surveyed rather fully the evidence for the relation with Schelling, giving the actual text of Coleridge's sources. Her introduction made the defense which even today can be made for Coleridge: there are psychological reasons for Coleridge's plagiarisms; they are rarely reprehensible, since Coleridge makes general or specific acknowledgments; and frequently they are rather legitimate borrowings in support of his own argument. One may take as ethically lenient as possible a view of Coleridge's borrowings, but still one cannot deny the central fact that, on many crucial issues and at many important points of his writings, Coleridge adopts the words and terminology of other men and that many of his ideas are verbally dependent on other thinkers. The exact degree of this indebtedness, the relative importance of different writers for Coleridge, presents us with a large variety of historical questions of sources and influences which have not been discussed adequately.

Thus we have no competent studies of Coleridge's relation to the thought of antiquity: to Plato, Aristotle, and Plotinus. Claud Howard's little book, *Coleridge's Idealism* (1924), makes much of his indebtedness to the Cambridge Platonists of the seventeenth century, but the argument is

greatly impaired by Howard's unfounded claim that all of Kant is con
tained in the English Neoplatonists, and by his obvious ignorance of the
relevant German texts. In Louis I. Bredvold's introduction to Miss Brinkley's *Coleridge on the Seventeenth Century,* this view is restated in a more
persuasive form. The seventeenth century was his spiritual home and his
philosophical position was that of Cambridge Platonism. We have no
study of Coleridge's relations to Bacon or Spinoza (see, however, W. H.
White, "Coleridge on Spinoza," *Athenaeum,* May 1897), Leibniz or
Berkeley, though all of these thinkers engaged him deeply in various
periods of his career. We have some articles which treat some aspects of
Coleridge's relations to Swedenborg, to Boehme, to Bruno and Hartley,
and which clear up his relation to Vico: Benjamin P. Kurtz, "Coleridge on
Swedenborg" (*Essays and Studies by Members of the Dept. of English,
Univ. of California,* 1943); A. D. Snyder, "Coleridge on Böhme"
(*PMLA,* 1930); "Coleridge and Giordano Bruno" (*MLN,* 1927); Hoxie
N. Fairchild, "Hartley, Pistorius, and Coleridge" (*PMLA,* 1947); Max
Fisch, "The Coleridges, Dr. Prati and Vico" (*MP,* 1943).

Coleridge's indebtedness to Kant has been studied most fully. There
are two full-length studies, one by René Wellek in *Immanuel Kant in
England,* the other by Elizabeth Winkelmann, *Coleridge und die Kantische
Philosophie* (Leipzig, 1933. Palaestra, 184). The second book is dependent in its arguments and conceptions upon the first, though it adds much
detail. It differs in laying a greater stress on Coleridge's relation to Jacobi,
and in taking a more favorable attitude towards Coleridge's use of Kant.
Wellek's book analyzed the Kantian elements in the published writings
and in the manuscripts preserved in the British Museum, and attempted to
show that Coleridge, while reproducing even the most mechanical features
of Kant's architectonics and terminology, criticized Kant from a point of
view and with arguments substantially derived from the early Schelling.
While Coleridge envisaged a philosophical ideal very close to Schelling's,
he fell back into a sterile dualism of the head and heart, knowledge and
faith, intellect and intuition. Though the chapter contains some *lacunae*
and a few errors, its conclusions still seem substantially accurate. Since
then, A. O. Lovejoy, in a paper on "Coleridge and Kant's Two Worlds"
(*ELH,* 1940; rpt. in *Essays in the History of Ideas,* 1948), has stressed the
rôle of Kant's ethics for Coleridge's philosophy and theology and has come
to the conclusion, similar to that of Wellek, that "Kant opened for him the
gate back into the emotionally congenial fields of evangelical faith and
piety."

Elio Chinol's *Il pensiero di S. T. Coleridge* (Venezia, 1953) reopens the question of Coleridge's indebtedness to Kant. Signor Chinol uses unpublished notebooks and the MS. "Logic," giving a careful though brief exposition of Coleridge's logic, metaphysics, and ethics. His main thesis is a sharp periodization of Coleridge's thought, which after 1801 is supposed to have first passed through a Kantian phase, then through a short Schellingian stage from 1815 to 1818, and finally to have returned to Kant in 1818. Only the last phase—and especially *Aids to Reflection*—represents Coleridge's true position. It is an attempt to supersede Kant by combining him with Platonizing Christianity. The little book is sensible and accurate: Chinol recognizes the close dependence of the MS. "Logic" on the very words of Kant and traces the many Kantian elements in Coleridge's reflections on metaphysics and ethics. He rightly rejects the extravagant claims for Coleridge's philosophical greatness but sees his importance in a history of English idealism. The chronological scheme, in its very neatness, is however, untenable: even the latest writings of Coleridge are full of Schellingian echoes (see Wellek, *History of Modern Criticism,* 1955, II, 153–54) and Kant is, even in Coleridge's last MSS, criticized with the arguments of Schelling.

The question of Coleridge's relation to Fichte and Schelling, while incidentally studied in Wellek's book and in Miss Winkelmann's, still needs investigation. H. Nidecker has shown that the *Theory of Life* is largely drawn from Schelling and Steffens (*Bericht der philosophisch-historischen Fakultät der Universität Basel. 5. Heft.* Basel, 1927); W. K. Pfeiler has described the use Coleridge makes of Schelling's speculations on the Samothracian Deities (*MLN,* 1937); and J. W. Beach has pointed to further passages of Schelling, in his *The Concept of Nature in Nineteenth-Century Poetry* (1936, especially pp. 573, 598) and "Coleridge's Borrowings from the German" (*ELH,* 1942).

The relationship to Jacobi, originally suggested by Shedd and further developed by Wellek and more fully by Miss Winkelmann, was examined by J. H. Muirhead in an essay, "Coleridge: Metaphysician or Mystic?" in *Coleridge: Studies by Several Hands,* a volume edited by E. Blunden and E. L. Griggs (1934). Muirhead minimizes the relationship, since Coleridge's ideal was that of a speculative philosopher and not of a mystic, and since Coleridge's comments on Jacobi show disagreement. J. Lindsay's publication of marginalia to Jacobi's *Werke* (*MLN,* 1935) clinches this last point. But Muirhead proposed too simple a dilemma between Coleridge as mystic and Coleridge as metaphysician. Nobody has ever argued that Coleridge was a genuine "mystic" but merely that he abdicated his grandiose speculative pretensions in favor of the acceptance of traditional faith, which he came to defend *in toto,* including the Trinity, original sin, redemption, personal immortality, etc. Jacobi himself was not a mystic in any strict sense, but a philosopher of faith whose thought has been found to anticipate some of the positions of Dilthey's *Lebensphilosophie* and of existentialism (Otto Friedrich Bollnow, *Die Lebensphilosophie F. H. Jacobis,* 1933).

The relations to Kant, Fichte, Schelling, and Jacobi do not, however, exhaust the many influences which Germany had on Coleridge's thought. Miss Snyder has shown the use Coleridge made of Moses Mendelssohn's speculations (*JEGP,* 1929). Miss Coburn has studied the extensive use Coleridge made of Tennemann's *Geschichte der Philosophie* (*RES,* 1934, and in her edition of *Philosophical Lectures,* 1949). Alois Brandl, *Samuel Taylor Coleridge und die englische Romantik* (1886, pp. 335–426), was the first to discuss the details of Coleridge's use of an obscure book on Imagination by J. G. Maass (though Sir William Hamilton was the first to point out that the history of association psychology in the *Biographia Literaria* comes from Maass, *Versuch über die Einbildungskraft,* 1797). Miss Broicher, in the *Preussische Jahrbücher* (1912), has drawn, unconvincingly to my mind, a parallel to Fries. A. C. Dunstan has established Coleridge's use of Schiller's *Über naïve und sentimentalische Dichtung,* in an important context (*MLR,* 1922, 1923), but has totally failed to establish any significant relationship to Herder. He is surely mistaken too in dismissing the importance of Schelling and A. W. Schlegel. Coleridge's relation to Herder is discussed very thoroughly in Henri Tronchon's *Le Jeune Edgar Quinet* (1937), a book which contains a history of Herder's early reputation in England and tells us a good deal about other German contacts. J. M. Moore, *Herder and Coleridge* (1951), adds little except tenuous parallels and extravagant claims for the affinity between the two thinkers. G. A. Wells, in two essays, "Man and Nature: An Evaluation of Coleridge's Rejection of Herder's Thought" (*JEGP,* 1952) and "Herder's and Coleridge's Evaluation of the Historical Approach" (*MLR,* 1953), contrasts Herder's naturalism and historical relativism with Coleridge's belief in absolute principles of knowledge, beauty, and religion.

For Coleridge's critical thought the borrowings from August Wilhelm Schlegel's lectures *Über dramatische Kunst und Literatur* are crucial. The passages can be found conveniently printed in parallel columns in Anna von Helmholtz's (Mrs. Phelan's) thesis on *The Indebtedness of*

S. T. Coleridge to A. W. Schlegel (1907). T. M. Raysor's edition of Coleridge's *Shakespearean Criticism* lists also all the references and, in the introduction, re-examines the whole question most cautiously and fairly. Coleridge read many other German authors of philosophical importance: Lessing's works; Jean Paul's *Vorschule der Aesthetik*; some of the writings of Solger, who formulated most strikingly the romantic aesthetics of poetry as irony and paradox, and, of course, many writings of the *Naturphilosophen*, such as Oken and Schubert and scientists such as Ritter. T. M. Raysor has published Coleridge's notes to Solger's *Erwin* (1815) in "Unpublished Fragments on Aesthetics by S. T. Coleridge" (*SP*, 1925). An interesting marginal note on Oken is quoted in Alice D. Snyder's "Coleridge's Cosmogony: A Note on the Poetic World-View" (*SP*, 1924). There are marginalia on Schubert and Steffens in the series published by Nidecker in *RLC* and further comments in Nidecker's thesis, quoted above. On all of these questions detailed studies would be welcome.

There are several general treatments of the question of Coleridge's relations to the Germans. Alois Brandl's biography has been somewhat discredited by a grossly inaccurate translation, but it is still valuable, though it was written at the height of the fashion for parallel-hunting and indulges in many strained and even absurd analogies which do not withstand critical examination. Brandl was the first to survey the question with anything like a good firsthand knowledge of German literature and philosophy. The thesis by John Louis Haney, *The German Influence on Samuel Taylor Coleridge* (1902), has no value except for a few minor corrections of Brandl. J. Shawcross' introduction to his edition of *Biographia Literaria* surveyed Coleridge's thought especially in relation to Kant and Schelling, with special stress on Coleridge's theory of imagination. The careful chronological order of the survey makes the study especially valuable, though Shawcross, I think, overrates Coleridge's originality considerably. Helene Richter's article in *Anglia* (1920) is, as a description of Coleridge's philosophy, hardly more than a mosaic of quotations with no regard for chronology or context. But her survey of Coleridge's relations to Kant, Fichte, and Schelling seems substantially correct, for instance, in the stress on the differences between Coleridge and Kant, and Coleridge's affinities with Neoplatonism. Miss Richter seems only mistaken in her emphasis on the place of Shaftesbury in Coleridge's intellectual ancestry. The two general surveys of the question by L. A. Willoughby (*Pubs. of the English Goethe Society*, 1934; *Germanisch-romanische Monatsschrift*, 1936) are mostly occupied with Coleridge's personal relations and visits to Germany, and treat the intellectual relations only scantily. A new examination of Coleridge's "Borrowings from the German," by Joseph Warren Beach (*ELH*, 1942), raises the ethical issues involved and treats them with some severity. Beach rightly objects to the way in which many discussions shirk these issues and ignore the overwhelming evidence for literal borrowings from Schlegel, Schelling, Steffens, and others. Kathleen Coburn's edition of Coleridge's *Philosophical Lectures* (1949) raises new problems about Coleridge's sources which are solved only partially in her elaborate introduction and notes. She overrates Coleridge's originality on almost every point but has done much to explore a very difficult, badly preserved text.

Still, in spite of the number of studies, the question of Coleridge's relation to German thought seems far from being answered in a comprehensive and systematic manner. The task could be done only by a scholar who had a thorough knowledge of the enormous body of German speculative thought of the time, and who could use the huge literature which has accumulated around such figures as Kant, Fichte, and Schelling. He would have to pay considerable attention to the vexed question of chronology in Coleridge's thought, and could not be satisfied with the usual textbook conceptions of such complicated thinkers as Schelling, who passed through many stages in his very varied development and himself underwent the most divers influences, from Boehme, Bruno, and Leibniz, who, in part, were also among Coleridge's own intellectual ancestry.

One question of Coleridge's intellectual milieu has hitherto been almost totally neglected. Coleridge knew and read his contemporaries and obviously could not have been as isolated in his time as it is sometimes assumed he was. The strangely parallel figure of Thomas Wirgman, studied in Wellek's *Kant in England,* is a case in point. Coleridge certainly had many contacts and sympathies with contemporary scientific and medical theoreticians: with Hunter, Abernethy, Sir Humphry Davy, Richard Saumarez, and others. The usual assumption that in the relationship between Wordsworth and Coleridge, Coleridge was intellectually always the benefactor, needs reexamination. Certainly, Coleridge's criticism is related to the immediately preceding English tradition of aesthetics and criticism. R. W. Babcock, in *The Genesis of Shakespeare Idolatry, 1766–99* (1931), has argued for Coleridge's knowledge of the Shakespearean characters of the later eighteenth century, though Babcock produced little concrete evidence. W. J. Bate and J. Bullitt in "Distinctions between Fancy and Imagination in Eighteenth-Century Criticism" (*MLN,* 1945) and Earl R. Wasserman in "Another Eighteenth Century Distinction between Fancy and Imagination" (*MLN*, 1949) have pointed out anticipations in English eighteenth-century writers of Coleridge's distinction of fancy and imagination. Wilma Kennedy has published a study of *The English Heritage of Coleridge of Bristol, 1798* (1947) and has argued that the roots of Coleridge's distinctions between fancy and imagination are in Berkeley and Reynolds, and that Coleridge is also anticipated by Blake. Her book, however, is quite uncritical, and dismisses the German question far too lightly. Undoubtedly, much of the aesthetic, philosophical, and political thought (not to speak of the theology) of eighteenth-century England must have impinged on Coleridge's mind. The influence of Burke on Coleridge's political thought is too central to be ignored. It is touched upon in all discussions of Coleridge's politics. But the whole English ancestry of Coleridge's ideas needs closer examination.

II. ANALYSES AND EVALUATIONS

The study of sources and the actual analysis and evaluation of Coleridge's thought are, of course, inextricably connected. Some of the books mainly devoted to the study of sources go further in the critical analysis of Coleridge's thought than many more general discussions. Among the older discussions there is still value in J. S. Mill's sympathetic appraisal (*Westminster Review*, 1840; rpt. in *Dissertations and Discussions,* 1857), in the essay by F. L. Hort which stresses the theology (*Cambridge Essays,* 1856), and in Walter Pater's sensitive and understanding pages on Coleridge's philosophy (*Appreciations,* 1889). This is a combination of two articles of which one, first published in the *Westminster Review* (1866), is devoted to Coleridge's thought. The part Pater dropped in the final version was reprinted under the title "Coleridge as Theologian" in *Sketches and Reviews* (1919). Two unsympathetic reviews done from the point of view of nineteenth-century rationalism still deserve attention: Alfred Benn's full treatment in his *History of English Rationalism* (1907) concludes that Coleridge was really a pantheist and that it is absurd to think of him as an apologist of orthodox Christianity; J. M. Robertson in *New Essays towards a Critical Method* (1897) goes to the extreme of seeing in Coleridge only a "master in verbalism," an "obscurantist," "generally a convert to the last philosopher he has read." There are some excellent pages in the opening portion of Norman Wilde's paper "The Development of Coleridge's

Thought" in the *Philosophical Review* (1919), though the detailed work-ing-out of his thesis regarding Coleridge's Platonism is disappointingly thin. S. F. Gingerich's article, "From Necessity to Transcendentalism in Coleridge" (*PMLA*, 1920; rpt. in *Essays in the Romantic Poets*, 1924), stresses the early poetry and the revolt against necessitarianism, but is unsatisfactory in the discussion of the later thought.

J. H. Muirhead's *Coleridge as Philosopher* (1930) is the only book which gives a reasoned survey of the whole of Coleridge's thought. Its values are obvious: it is written by a professional philosopher of standing in the Neo-Idealist movement, it is full of quotations from manuscript sources, it gives a conspectus of Coleridge's ideas which bears out the claim that Coleridge's ideas "formed in his mind a far more coherent body of philosophical thought than he has been anywhere credited with." But the book suffers from the excessive claims made for Coleridge's originality and importance. Coleridge is called the founder of "the voluntaristic form of idealist philosophy, of which . . . [he] remains to this day the most distinguished representative." At times Muirhead does not recognize close paraphrases from Schelling, and ignores the fact that literally all the formulas and concepts which he considers central for Coleridge's philos-ophy, such as the primacy of will and individuation, come from Schelling. The chapter on the Theory of Fine Arts is disappointingly thin, and makes hardly any effort to relate Coleridge's aesthetics to his criticism. In spite of these shortcomings Muirhead's book is still basic and has not been super-seded.

The study of Stephen Potter, *Coleridge and S. T. C.* (1935), is a psychological sketch based on a crude dichotomy between the great Cole-ridge and the small S. T. C. It shares Muirhead's view of Coleridge as "the first exponent of Modern Voluntary Idealism" and even calls him the "Father of modern psychology." But in spite of this, the book contains a number of genuine insights and a candid exposition of the less familiar and less reputable aspects of Coleridge's thought.

Recently other general treatments of Coleridge's thought have stressed different aspects. Hervé Marcoux's series of articles in *Revue de l'Univer-sité d'Ottawa* (1948) give a descriptive, rather commonplace account of Coleridge's thought with some final criticism from a Neo-Thomist point of view. Basil Willey, in his *Nineteenth-Century Studies* (1949), devotes the first chapter to a lucid and skillful exposition of the main features of Coleridge's thought, the distinctions of Reason and Understanding, Imagi-nation and Fancy, his views of the Bible and of Church and State. The chapter is, however, content to ignore the historical questions and the technical philosophical issues in favor of a general endorsement of Coleridge's distinctions and his position as an enemy of eighteenth-century rationalism and religious fundamentalism. There is still little work devoted to specific aspects of Coleridge's philosophy. A German dissertation, Georg Gerdt's *Coleridges Verhältnis zur Logik* (Berlin, 1935), is of slight value.

The theology of Coleridge, though it is central in importance for his thought and for its effects on his contemporaries and successors, has not been studied very closely. Josefine Nettesheim in "Die innere Entwicklung des englischen Romantiker S. T. Coleridge" (*Literaturwissenschaftliches Jahrbuch der Görresgesellschaft,* ed. G. Müller, 1930), has interpreted Coleridge's evolution purely in terms of a religious conversion paralleling those of the German Romantics such as Friedrich Schlegel. Her sensitive study is rather psychological than ideological. Short descriptions of Coleridge's theological position are in V. F. Storr's *Development of English Theology in the Nineteenth Century, 1800–1860* (1913) and in Herbert Stewart's "Place of Coleridge in English Theology" (*HTR,* 1918), which defines Coleridge's position very well but is rather perfunctory on the details. The fullest account of Coleridge's theology is C. R. Sanders' *Coleridge and the Broad Church Movement* (1942). It gives an intelligent digest of Coleridge's opinions, both philosophical and theological, with little attempt at analysis or interpretation. Sanders, in accordance with the general aim of his book, stresses Coleridge's "humanitarian liberalism," which, in his opinion, was "vigorously practical," Coleridge's disbelief in verbal inspiration, his arguments for the catholicity of the English Church —in short, all the elements which entered into the thought of Maurice and Sterling.

There are two recent discussions of Coleridge's religion. In D. G. James's elaborate treatment of Coleridge's theology, his *Romantic Comedy* (1948), Coleridge appears as a romantic thinker who is still a good Christian, a parallel and forerunner to Newman, with whom James compares Coleridge much more carefully than anybody had done before. Coleridge and Newman are approximated but also distinguished as Protestant versus Catholic, Gothic versus Romanesque. All the emphasis falls on the late writings of Coleridge, with the result that his German relations are minimized as a passing or preparatory phase. Hoxie Neale Fairchild, in a special chapter of the third volume of *Religious Trends in English Poetry* (1949), comes to almost the exactly opposite conclusion from James. Fairchild's chapter is not a systematic treatment of Coleridge's philosophical theology but rather a spiritual biography of Coleridge with stress on the early years and the evidence of the poems. But it contains also a review of Coleridge's later religion, which is judged very severely from the point of view of Christian orthodoxy. Fairchild concludes that Coleridge "although ostensibly a metaphysical absolutist, was at bottom an extreme sentimental pragmatist." One may not share Fairchild's particular frame of reference but will have to acknowledge that it helps to make Coleridge's pantheistic and naturalistic elements stand out much more clearly than before. James's and Fairchild's treatments, in their opposition, demonstrate how much interpretations of Coleridge's thought may still differ even at this stage of our knowledge: Fairchild's view is better documented but more rigidly doctrinaire; James's is frequently fanciful in its sweeping generalizations and arbitrary associations but full of imaginative sympathy and independent speculative power.

Coleridge's social and political thought appears today more interesting than it seemed to nineteenth-century liberals. We have an anthology, mostly of brief excerpts, from Coleridge's political thought, by R. J. White, *The Political Thought of S. T. Coleridge* (1938); and several fairly extensive discussions. Of these, Alfred Cobban's in *Edmund Burke and the Revolt against the Eighteenth Century* (1929) is clearly the best. There are also brief studies which are much slighter and say little that is new: Crane Brinton, *Political Ideas of the English Romanticists* (1926); Robert Henry Murray, *Studies in the English Social and Political Thinkers of the Nineteenth Century* (1929); Keith Feiling, *Social and Political Ideas of Some Representative Thinkers of the Age of Reaction and Reconstruction, 1815–65* (1932); F. J. C. Hearnshaw, "Coleridge, the Conservative" (*Nineteenth Century,* 1934), Harold Beeley, "The Political Thought of Coleridge" (in *Coleridge,* ed. Blunden and Griggs). Charles Cestre's treatment of Coleridge in his book *La Révolution française et les poètes anglais* (1906) is more biographical and far too inclusive to be sharply focussed on its topic, but is still of some value. In German there is a detailed thesis by W. Wünsche, *Die Staatsauffassung S. T. Coleridges* (Leipzig, 1934), which is pedestrian but full of useful materials: it is vitiated by its Nazi tinge and the excessive eagerness to find in Coleridge a propounder of the "organistic" view of society. Cobban, much more sensibly, points rather to the surprisingly utilitarian features in Coleridge's political thought, and to his conception of the state as a moral unity, an idea rather than an organic whole.

Coleridge's speculations on natural science have also received some attention. A paper by the biologist Joseph Needham, "S. T. Coleridge as a Philosophical Biologist," in *Science Progress* (1926), finds interest in Coleridge's panpsychism and his use of the polarity principle, and sees anticipations of the principle of "emergent evolution" in him. Reuben Potter in "Coleridge and the Idea of Evolution" (*PMLA*, 1925) more soberly considers Coleridge to be hostile to evolution in a modern sense, though his biological speculations contain many evolutionary ideas. Both these papers, though they touch on the question of Coleridge's sources, go astray in their judgments as they fail to recognize that Coleridge's ideas of natural science are not original with him and are frequently literally lifted from Steffens, Schelling, Ritter, and possibly others. Nidecker's unpublished thesis, available in a short abstract, has not attracted sufficient attention. Only J. W. Beach, in his *Concept of Nature,* has studied Coleridge's ideas on nature, mostly in relation to Emerson. G. A. Wells's "Coleridge and Goethe on Scientific Method in the Light of Some Unpublished Coleridge Marginalia" (*German Life and Letters,* 1951) points out the difference between Goethe and Coleridge: Goethe seeks to achieve the interpenetration of the universal and the particular by starting with the particular, whereas Coleridge's point of departure is the universal. Goethe's method is inductive, Coleridge's deductive, speculative (and, I should add, derived from *Naturphilosophie*).

On the whole, I am convinced that Coleridge's thought cannot claim a high position in the history of philosophy. It is true that Coleridge discusses many more questions and issues, possibly more systematically and coherently, than was thought when his philosophy was dismissed as mere "Romantic moonshine." One must recognize the considerable historical importance of his mediatory rôle between Germany and England, and I would be the last to deny the fascination of the many historical problems which are raised by his eclectic use of sources, his gift of phrasing, and the psychological issues raised by his whole intricate development. But I have still to be convinced that Coleridge deserves a place among independent and original speculative philosophers.

III. AESTHETICS AND LITERARY CRITICISM

He does obviously deserve such a place in the history of criticism. It is not extraordinary now to see claims that Coleridge "is, with the exception of

Aristotle, certainly the most important progenitor of modern criticism" (Stanley Edgar Hyman, *The Armed Vision,* 1948). Long ago G. Saintsbury had hailed him as one of the greatest critics of all times, and Arthur Symons called *Biographia Literaria* "the greatest book of criticism in English." However, the reasons for this praise vary considerably. One could distinguish two main views: one which values Coleridge's practical criticism most, and does not see any close relationship which it bears to his speculative aesthetics; the other which stresses the value of the speculations and sees the criticism as subordinate to them. The first point of view, which prevails in Saintsbury and Symons, seems now less widely accepted. It has, however, a few proponents. J. Middleton Murry in "Coleridge's Criticism" (*Aspects of Literature,* 1920) dismisses Coleridge's theories but praises some aspects of his practice. F. R. Leavis in a very grudging essay on "Coleridge in Criticism" (*Scrutiny,* 1940; rpt. in *The Importance of Scrutiny,* 1948) takes a similar position. Leavis dismisses Coleridge's aesthetics as a "nuisance" and comes to the conclusion that his "currency as an academic classic is something of a scandal," though he recognizes the value of selected reflections on meter and imagery, and the novelty of many of his literary opinions. The most coherent exposition of this view is T. M. Raysor's in the introduction to his edition of *Coleridge's Shakespearean Criticism.* He dismisses Coleridge's "unfortunate," "eccentric" theory of imagination and thinks that "a good case may be made out to show that Coleridge lost rather than gained from the German influence." The German influence, Raysor shows convincingly, is, at least in the Shakespearean criticism, confined to aesthetic generalities, to the use of the polarities such as Romantic and Classical, Sculpturesque and Picturesque, Mechanical and Organic, while the most valuable of Coleridge's insights are rather individual critical perceptions of characters, on the art of Shakespeare, etc. "As an aesthetician, Coleridge . . . was unfortunately derivative, mediocre, and, in a subject which requires system, fragmentary." As Raysor is thoroughly familiar with Coleridge's sources and ideas, his opinions should carry weight.

The earliest full treatment of Coleridge's aesthetics and criticism, by Laura Wylie in *Studies in the Evolution of English Criticism* (1894), ignores the most fruitful ideas, is completely vague in its conceptions, and is dependent on Brandl in the matter of sources. The effective study of Coleridge's aesthetics begins only with Shawcross' excellent introduction to his edition of the *Biographia,* which, though largely devoted to sources, brings out the interest of Coleridge's thought on those matters. But Enrico

Pizzo in a good article in *Anglia* (1916) first expounded the intimate connection between Coleridge's theory and practice, and the central tension between his stress on the universal and the individual, the whole curious blend of classicism and romanticism in his theories. The article is introduced by a superficial sketch of eighteenth-century aesthetics, and the implied Crocean view may appear unacceptable to many readers; but it is a good piece which has been unduly neglected. Alice Snyder's thesis on the *Critical Principle of the Reconciliation of Opposites as Employed by Coleridge* (Ann Arbor, Mich., 1918) tried to show how closely Coleridge's theory and practice are integrated and how fruitful this metaphysical principle was in Coleridge's hands, especially in the details of the Shakespearean criticism. Today Miss Snyder seems needlessly apologetic about Coleridge's principle, which she tried to assimilate to a logic acceptable to John Dewey. But she perceived the essential unity of Coleridge's critical thought, and also has the merit of quoting, I believe for the first time, the passage on the imagination which T. S. Eliot later quoted in his essay on Marvell (1921) and which has since become a crucial text in modern criticism (T. S. Eliot, *Selected Essays*, 1932; I. A. Richards, *Principles of Literary Criticism*, 1924).

Like Pizzo, A. E. Powell (Mrs. Dodds), in her *Romantic Theory of Poetry* (1926), approaches Coleridge from the Crocean point of view: she ably traces his development, and discusses the question of sources, deciding in favor of Neo-Platonism. She makes large claims for Coleridge's supposedly epochmaking discovery of art as the "free activity of the mind," a view hardly unknown to Kant or Schiller. She criticizes Coleridge, however, for what from her Crocean point of view she considers a confusion of intuition and reason. "Coleridge's attempt to find universals in intuition wrecked the theory," she declares. But Coleridge, of course, could not abandon the claim that poetry is a way of knowledge and hence contains a universalizing element.

Elizabeth Raab, *Die Grundanschauungen von Coleridges Aesthetik* (1934), made a successful start in clearly and simply expounding some of the basic notions of Coleridge's aesthetics.

The most influential discussion of Coleridge's aesthetics is I. A. Richards' book, *Coleridge on Imagination* (1934). The book is not primarily a historical study of Coleridge, but rather an original elaboration of Richards' own theories, which uses Coleridge frequently only as a springboard or pretext. The point of view is definitely that of a member of a different philosophical tradition: Richards writes "as a Materialist trying to interpret . . . the utterances of an extreme idealist." In practice, Richards cuts off Coleridge very frequently from his philosophical moorings and misunderstands his terminology. For instance, he quotes a letter in which Coleridge expresses the hope by a work on poetry to "supersede all the books of metaphysics and all the books of morals too." But this does not mean, as Richards takes it to mean, that Coleridge hoped by semantics to show metaphysical problems to be pseudo-problems, but rather that Coleridge uses here the term "poetry" in a grandiose sense in which *Dichtung* and *Kunst* were used by Schelling and Schlegel, who wanted to absorb metaphysics and ethics into a crowning philosophy of art. Coleridge was no Bentham or Carnap, and would have repudiated a philosophy refusing to face ultimate problems. His view was exactly opposed: he regarded poetry as an access to reality, a way of knowing. But in spite of such lapses of misrepresentation, Richards shows a considerable sympathy with Coleridge's thought, or rather with the thought of Schelling, as the central dialectical passages in Coleridge are derived from him. Richards explains the beginnings of the dialectical process, the identity of subject and object, and accepts the principle of the activity of the soul. But he combines such an activist psychology with a metaphysical materialism which assumes that mental activity is only an aspect of physical activity. He does not see that the "act" in Schelling, Fichte, and Coleridge is not merely a psychological fact, but an epistemological principle, creating reality. The activity of the mind is the starting-point for Coleridge's rejection of association psychology and for the acceptance of the distinction between Fancy and Imagination, as fancy is related to association and imagination to creative act. Richards interprets the distinction as merely the distinction between the mental processes which result in two types of imagery. There is a type of image such as Samuel Butler's

> *And like a lobster boil'd, the morn*
> *From black to red began to turn,*

where the relation between the morning and the lobster turns only on one point of similarity, and another type such as Coleridge's favorite from *Venus and Adonis*

> *Look, how a bright star shooteth from the sky*
> *So glides he in the night from Venus' eye,*

where it is possible to discover many interconnections, in the manner of Empson's *Seven Types of Ambiguity*. Richards uses the distinction of Fancy and Imagination also in order to justify the romantic interpretation of nature, but it appears to him merely as another poetic mythology while Coleridge, of course, considered it a true rendering of reality. Richards' analysis of the concept of nature is an analysis of the word, as all thinking is to him linguistics—that is, reflection on the meaning of words. He expects tremendous revolutions and revelations from this linguistic analysis, of which he professes to see Coleridge as an ancestor. "With Coleridge we step across the threshold of a general theoretical study of language capable of opening to us new powers over our minds comparable to those which systematic physical inquiries are giving us over our environment." We need not pause to inquire here whether semantics has justified or can justify such highpitched expectations. But Coleridge cannot be claimed as an ancestor of this creed, though, no doubt, he was highly conscious of words and language, and very much interested in terminology, in "de-synonymization," in etymology and general theories of language. Though his views on language have been studied in several papers, it is impossible to see in what respects Coleridge strikingly differs from his many contemporaries indulging in linguistic speculations: J. H. Hanford, "Coleridge as a Philologian" (*MP*, 1919); L. A. Willoughby, "Coleridge as a Philologist" (*MLR*, 1936); Joshua H. Neumann, "Coleridge on the English Language" (*PMLA*, 1948). Richards' book should be supplemented by his introduction to *The Portable Coleridge* (1950), which is in part devoted to biography and the poetry but contains also an interesting analysis of the definition of the Imagination.

Two articles on terms used in Coleridge's criticism are closely related to the treatments of his interest in language. J. Isaacs' article, "Coleridge's Critical Terminology," in *Essays and Studies* by members of the English Association (1936), is most valuable. In some cases, Isaacs does not see the German models for Coleridge's terminology (e.g., potence). P. L. Carver's article, "The Evolution of the Term *esemplastic*" (*MLR*, 1929), proved that the term 'esemplastic' appears as early as 1802. It thus is not necessary to think of *In-eins-Bildung* as Coleridge's model. He formed his term by misinterpreting the etymology of *Einbildungskraft*, in which the *ein* has nothing to do with *in-eins*. Coleridge's theory of imagination is also treated in D. G. James's *Scepticism and Poetry: An Essay on the Poetic Imagination* (1937). It is used there only as a point of departure in the author's own theory. Incidentally Richards' view of Coleridge is discussed "to show

how impossible is his effort to eat his Coleridge and have him too."
Stephen Potter's *Coleridge and S. T. C.* also disagrees with Richards' interpretation in an appendix.

Richards' book, which gives such a personal interpretation of Coleridge, has impressed many modern critics and must have done much to
draw attention to Coleridge's speculations. A paradoxical situation has
developed: the modern anti-romantic critics appeal constantly to the highly
romantic, dialectical thought of Coleridge, which, in the passages which
interest them most, is really the thought of Schelling. The specific distinction between symbol and allegory was first elaborated by Goethe, as Curt
Richard Müller clearly demonstrated in *Die geschichtlichen Voraussetz-
ungen des Symbolbegriffs in Goethes Kunstanschauung* (1937). One may
compare also Julien Rouge, "La Notion du symbole chez Goethe," in
*Goethe, Etudes publiées pour le centenaire de sa mort . . . sous les
auspices . . . de l'Université de Strasbourg* (1932). Other crucial critical
concepts have come from Germany through the mediation of Coleridge and
have profoundly influenced modern anti-romantic English and American
criticism: "organistic" aesthetics (whatever its antecedents in Aristotle),
the view of imagination as a reconciliation of opposites, the use of irony,
paradox, and tension as poetic principles. But in contemporary criticism
these terms are shorn of their metaphysical implications and are taken out
of their context, which, in Coleridge and Schelling, is that of a justification
of art as the mediator between man and nature. This difference is well
brought out in Ronald S. Crane's attack on Cleanth Brooks, "The Bankruptcy of Critical Monism" (*MP*, 1948), which was reprinted in *Critics
and Criticism: Ancient and Modern* (1952). The discussion of Coleridge's
concept of poetry there is one of the clearest expositions of his central
critical ideas which I know.

The philosophical context is excellently explained in Gordon Mc-
Kenzie's *Organic Unity in Coleridge* (Univ. of California Pubs. in English, 1929). The many interconnections between Coleridge's theory and
practice are analyzed very skillfully. But mistakenly, I think, too sharp a
distinction is drawn between the principle of the reconciliation of opposites
and the principle of organic unity. McKenzie errs also in his reflections on
the historical background. He considers Coleridge the anticipator of the
organic view developed only much later by Bernard Bosanquet. But the
organic point of view is clearly much older than Coleridge, and can be
found fully developed in Goethe, Schelling, and the Schlegels. The dialectical reconciliation of opposites is a development of the organic principle,

of the concept of polarity which is so prominent in Goethe and Schelling, both in their aesthetic and scientific thought, and not the other way round. The continuity of the organic conception from Leibniz onwards is well described in James Benziger's "Organic Unity: Leibniz to Coleridge" (*PMLA*, 1951).

There are other good general discussions of Coleridge as aesthetician and critic. Clarence D. Thorpe, in "Coleridge as Aesthetician and Critic" (*JHI*, 1944), surveyed Coleridge's thought lucidly, stressing especially the continuity with classical theories, the empirical psychology, the application of such old criteria as probability and unity.

Herbert Read's lecture, "Coleridge as Critic" (*SR*, 1948; also in *Lectures in Criticism*, ed. H. Cairns, 1949, and in *The True Voice of Feeling*, 1953; and independently 1952), focuses on the premises of Coleridge's criticism: his introduction of a philosophical method of criticism, his conception of art "as a dim analogue of creation" and the close interrelation between his theory and practice. Read recognizes Coleridge's dependence on Kant and Schelling on these central points and shows a rare sympathy with Coleridge's and Schelling's point of departure, in which he finds anticipations of existentialism and the Jungian "collective unconscious." Read's lecture is a skillful sketch which would need much elaboration.

Walter J. Bate (in *Perspectives of Criticism*, ed. Harry Levin, 1950) conceives of Coleridge's critical theories as a "long series of spasmodic attempts to harmonize the traditional rationalistic precepts of classicism with romantic vitalism," the organic view of nature. Bate acutely criticizes the view that the theory of imagination is central in Coleridge's criticism. He considers it rather as a "roundabout psychological justification of his conception of the mediating function of art." Bate is, however, mistaken in claiming that Coleridge's position is unique; Goethe, Schelling, the two Schlegels, Solger, and Hegel were concerned with the same problem and were, like Coleridge, in the tradition of Neoplatonism in aesthetics. Coleridge, in turn, is closely dependent on Schelling and the Schlegels: but Bate is right in stressing that Coleridge cannot be labeled a "subjectivist romantic without grave reservations."

E. L. Stahl's "S. T. Coleridges Theorie der Dichtung in Hinblick auf Goethe" (in *Weltliteratur: Festgabe für Fritz Strich*, 1952) compares Coleridge's and Goethe's theories of poetry, emphasizing the differences in their conception of imagination, symbol, metaphor, etc. Howard H. Creed's "Coleridge's Metacriticism" (*PMLA*, 1954) is a general article which says nothing new or challenging. Another lucid, though somewhat too streamlined exposition of "Coleridge's Critical Principles" by Richard H. Fogle is in the *TSE* (Vol. 6, 1956). The emphasis on the role of genre concepts in Coleridge's theories is particularly striking.

Frederick B. Rainsberry, in "Coleridge and the Paradox of the Poetic Imperative" (*ELH*, 1954), makes another attempt to show the basis of Coleridge's aesthetics in his metaphysics. In a closely reasoned article which draws also on Coleridge's poetry, Rainsberry excellently expounds the dialectics of object and subject which justifies Coleridge's aesthetic. Still, it would be hard to find any text in Coleridge which would support Rainsberry's central thesis: i.e., that "Coleridge insists upon the existence of an aesthetic self as a kind of poetic imperative which urges all creative wills towards expression." Like Muirhead, Rainsberry makes excessive claims for Coleridge's philosophical originality: finding "anticipations" of Hegel in passages of Coleridge written long after the *Phenomenology of the Spirit* (1806). Coleridge knew little of Hegel but he used Fichte and Schelling, who invented the dynamic and voluntaristic dialectics which recent students extol as Coleridge's greatest achievement.

In recent years two elaborate discussions of Coleridge's criticism have surveyed the whole problem. In M. H. Abrams, *The Mirror and the Lamp, Romantic Theory and Critical Tradition* (1953), a general book on the change from imitation theory to theories of expression, there are many passages and several chapters expressly devoted to Coleridge. Mr. Abrams excellently discusses and analyzes Coleridge's theories of imagination and diction and, less fully, takes up other aspects of Coleridge's criticism, such as his concept of the objective poet, his views on personification and myth. An article by Abrams, "Wordsworth and Coleridge on Diction and Figures" (in *EIE: 1952*, 1954), supplements the large book. Mr. Abrams sees Coleridge in a wide perspective but minimizes his dependence on German sources, unduly to my mind (see Wellek's review in *Comparative Literature*, 1954).

René Wellek's *History of Modern Criticism 1750–1950* (4 vols.; first 2 vols. published 1955) contains a lengthy chapter on Coleridge in the second volume: *The Romantic Age* (1955). It follows a detailed treatment of all the German classical and romantic critics and aestheticians and, with this background established, argues that Coleridge's originality has been greatly overrated. After a discussion of the problem of sources, Wellek analyzes the main strands of Coleridge's aesthetics, the scheme of his theory of literature, and his practical criticism. He comes to the conclusion that Coleridge as an aesthetician is fragmentary and derivative. His theory of literature is his most impressive achievement: an attempt to fuse many elements into a unity. On the one hand we have the holistic arguments about structure and his symbolist view of the poet, and on the other the incompatible pleasure principle and emotionalism which Coleridge tries to preserve in spite of everything. The poet as philosopher and "knower" (the principle of imagination) cannot, however, be combined with the poet as the man of passion aiming at immediate pleasure. Fancy, talent, the mechanical, the separate, and the like are all concepts in Coleridge designed to disparage what has survived from associationist psychology, but Coleridge refuses to cast them out: he tries to preserve everything in an all-embracing eclectic scheme. Coleridge's very eclecticism was of the greatest historical importance. He served as a transmitter of German literary ideas and carried enough of the Aristotelian and empirical tradition to make the idealistic elements palatable today. Wellek's chapter is the fullest, most detailed, and systematic survey and criticism of Coleridge's aesthetics, literary theory, and opinions. The notes contain a bibliography and complete references.

Details of Coleridge's criticism have more and more attracted scholarly attention. Clarence D. Thorpe discussed the differences between Coleridge's and Wordsworth's theories of the imagination and expounded Coleridge's conception of the sublime in "The Imagination: Coleridge vs. Wordsworth" (PQ, 1939) and in "Coleridge on the Sublime," in Wordsworth and Coleridge: Studies in Honor of George McLean Harper (ed. Earl L. Griggs, 1939). T. M. Raysor made a convincing defense of "Coleridge's Criticism of Wordsworth" (PMLA, 1939). In a different context, R. Wellek argued in favor of Coleridge's conception of poetic diction and meter, which, on several points, anticipates modern "formalist" views ("Wordsworth's and Coleridge's Theories of Poetic Diction" in Charisteria Guilelmo Mathesio . . . Oblata, Prague, 1932). P. L. Carver, in "Coleridge and the Theory of Imagination" (UTQ, 1940), has tried to show that the distinction of Fancy and Imagination is due to Coleridge's rejection of Associationism. Imagination, according to Coleridge's later idealism, should be identical with Reason, but this was recognized by Coleridge only in "Poesy and Art," while the bafflement in the twelfth chapter of Biographia was due to his lack of recognition of this identity. The point remains doubtful, however, because Carver refuses to discuss the relation to Schelling which is surely crucial for these passages. Among other discussions of Imagination versus Fancy one must mention Irving

Babbitt's article on "Coleridge and Imagination" in *The Nineteenth Century and After* (1929; rpt. in *On Being Creative and Other Essays*, 1932), a well-known attack on Coleridge's imagination. It is, however, largely concerned with the *Ancient Mariner* and the vices of spontaneous romantic imagination in general. Its discussion of Coleridge's theory is quite perfunctory: it formulates the view that there is a sharp contrast between the Aristotelian chapters on Wordsworth and the foggy metaphysics of the Imagination which precedes them. The sympathetic discussions of Imagination and Fancy by Margaret Sherwood, *Coleridge's Imaginative Conception of the Imagination* (1937), and Basil Willey, *Coleridge on Imagination and Fancy* (Warton Lecture, *Proceedings of the British Academy*, 1946), do not add appreciably to our knowledge or insight. Miss Sherwood quotes Plotinus as the main source of Coleridge's aesthetics. Basil Willey, in a well-phrased, lucid lecture, defends Coleridge's distinction. R. L. Brett's "Coleridge's Theory of Imagination" (*English Studies by Members of the English Association*, 1949) adds little. The paper emphasizes Neoplatonic influence and dismisses the question of German sources, completely ignoring the ample evidence to the contrary.

Barbara Hardy, in "Distinction without Difference: Coleridge's Fancy and Imagination" (in *EIC*, 1, 1951), argues again that the two faculties cannot be distinguished, as it is impossible to discriminate between the success of Fancy and the failure of Imagination. George G. Watson, "Contribution to a Dictionary of Critical Terms: *Imagination* and *Fancy*" (*EIC*, 3, 1953), comes to the odd conclusion that the result of Coleridge's distinction was "an unworthy one, an immense heightening in the prestige of imagination." But the preceding history of the terms is quite thin: it ignores all Italian and German developments.

There are a number of papers on individual points in Coleridge's criticism. Among them, Roberta Morgan's piece on the "Philosophical Basis of Coleridge's *Hamlet* Criticism" (*ELH*, 1939) deserves special attention: it shows that there are two distinct versions of Coleridge's interpretation of Hamlet's character, of which the earlier can be related to Associationist psychology, while the later makes use of the Kantian concept of the Idea. Dorothy J. Morrill discusses "Coleridge's Theory of Dramatic Illusion" (*MLN*, 1927). Charles Patterson's "Coleridge's Concept of Dramatic Illusion in the Novel" (*ELH*, 1951) comments acutely on Coleridge's remarks on a forgotten novel, *The Provost* by John Galt. Alice D. Snyder in "A Note on Coleridge's Shakespeare Criticism" (*MLN*,

1923) finds all sorts of anticipations of modern psychological insights in Coleridge's criticism of Shakespeare's characters. Howard H. Creed discusses the conceptions of "Coleridge on 'Taste' " (*ELH,* 1946).

A student of Coleridge should know the worst and read F. L. Lucas' indictment of Coleridge's criticism in his *Decline and Fall of the Romantic Ideal* (1936). Lucas collects Coleridge's absurdities, sentimentalities, and evidences of his moralistic and nationalistic prejudices, but shows no insight into the theoretical issues or sympathy with the real merits of Coleridge's critical practice.

Surveying all these writings on Coleridge as aesthetician and critic, one cannot help concluding that the case for the interdependence of Coleridge's theory and practice is well-established. But still it would be hard to deny that Coleridge's main theoretical ideas are derivative and secondhand, and that his specific merit as a critic is in the practical application of his principles. Paradoxically, these derivative principles are those which are now most admired. In a history of European criticism, Coleridge can claim a high position only in virtue of his novel critical opinions and the considerable merit of being the transmitter of many aesthetic ideas from Germany to England.

IV. INFLUENCE AND REPUTATION

Only a few aspects of the complex story of Coleridge's influence and reputation have been studied hitherto. Sanders examined the Broad Church movement in relation to Coleridge. Miss Broicher discussed the relation of Coleridge and Newman, especially the *Grammar of Assent,* in "Anglikanische Kirche und deutsche Philosophie" in *Preussische Jahrbücher* (1910). There is a slight German thesis on Coleridge's influence on the social teachings of Carlyle by Nikolaus Schanck, *Die sozialpolitischen Anschauungen Coleridges und sein Einfluss auf Carlyle* (Bonn, 1924). More can be found on Coleridge in America. Alice D. Snyder studied early American reactions to Coleridge in "American Comments on Coleridge a Century Ago" (in *Coleridge,* ed. Blunden and Griggs); Marjorie Nicolson showed how warmly Coleridge's ideas were welcomed by James Marsh, President of the University of Vermont, in "James Marsh and the Vermont Transcendentalists" (*Philosophical Review,* 1925). There are papers which barely begin the study of Coleridge's influence on Emerson and Poe:

F. T. Thompson, "Emerson's Indebtedness to Coleridge" (*SP*, 1926), and Floyd Stovall, "Poe's Debt to Coleridge" (*TexSE*, 1930). The best discussion of Coleridge's influence on Emerson is in Beach (*Concept of Nature*). There are frequent references to Coleridge's influence in *The Development of American Literary Criticism* (ed. Floyd Stovall, 1955), especially in Richard H. Fogle's chapter "Organic Form in American Criticism: 1840–1870." But we still are very far from being able to trace Coleridge's effect on posterity with any clarity and detail. His influence as a thinker and critic, which seemed to have completely waned around the middle of the last century, is now again discernible. One can today even speak of a Coleridge revival.

COLERIDGE'S PHILOSOPHY
AND CRITICISM

(*From 1956*)

I. THE SOURCES AND INTELLECTUAL RELATIONSHIPS

Since the revised edition (1956) of this review of research on Coleridge's philosophy and criticism new studies and new discussions have proliferated at an amazing rate. Some of the new interest is due to the increased availability of hitherto unpublished or partly published texts, particularly to the publication of Kathleen Coburn's edition of *The Notebooks* and Earl Leslie Griggs's *Collected Letters* and soon also to the *Collected Coleridge* recently begun by an edition of *The Friend* and *The Watchman*. Besides, unpublished materials in the British Museum and at Toronto have become accessible to scholars. But part of the enormous expansion of Coleridge scholarship is due to a genuine new interest in romantic philosophy and religion of which Coleridge is, in many ways, the most articulate spokesman. In the English-speaking world Coleridge is the only great literary figure who invites discussion of the issues posed by German idealist philosophy and the only great critic in the remoter past who escaped the prevalent tradition of Aristotelian classicism and thus can speak to our contemporary needs more clearly than Dryden, Dr. Johnson, or even Matthew Arnold.

The preceding section includes a discussion of the sources of Coleridge's poetry which, in the nature of the question, cannot pose the same problems as the prose. The unacknowledged translations or paraphrases could be dropped from Coleridge's canon without much hurt to the body of his work. Sources in the poetry are, as John Livingston Lowes showed so brilliantly, transformed within the configuration of a poem even though Coleridge may use the exact words of a travel-book or scientific treatise. The situation is, however, very different in the case of philosophical or critical prose which claims truth or insight, coherence, and even system. One cannot ignore the fact that, in many crucial passages in Coleridge's most quoted writings, we are confronted with either word-by-word translations or with close paraphrases, mainly of German writers. Many scholars, however, prefer to shut their eyes and ears either ignoring the evidence or, confronted with it, dismissing it as irrelevant. Thus Kathleen Coburn, the editor of the *Notebooks* and the *Philosophical Lectures,* editions which assemble much evidence for Coleridge's sources, can say blandly that the "question is anyhow irrelevant and unimportant except for its historical interest" ("Coleridge redivivus" in Thorpe-Baker-Weaver, *The Major English Romantic Poets,* 1957) or that "we are no longer primarily interested in whether Coleridge had his ideas from the German transcendentalists or whether they were original with him" (*Coleridge: A Collection of Critical Essays,* 1967). R. H. Fogle, in *The Idea of Coleridge's Criticism* (1962), appeals to an unpublished dissertation which "decisively rejects the claim to any substantial indebtedness" and proceeds to ignore it almost totally. In a chapter on "The Romantic Movement" in *Contemporary Literary Scholarship,* ed. Lewis Leary (1958), Fogle rejected my view of the derivativeness of Coleridge's philosophy by saying that "this verdict is opposed by most English and American scholarship." But this appeal to majority opinion merely states the fact that many English and American scholars have no firsthand knowledge of German philosophy and aesthetics to lend weight to their opinions about this issue. George Watson, in *The Literary Critics* (1962), says that "the question of Coleridge's plagiarism from Schlegel" [is left] "for ever uncertain" and W. J. Bate in his fine biography of *Coleridge* (1968) minimizes the extent of Coleridge's borrowing, never alluding to the chunks of Kant in the MS. "Logic" or "The Principles of Genial Criticism," rehearsing all the mitigating circumstances, and when discussing "Coleridge as Critic," quotes as "the essence of Coleridge's critical thought" a phrase literally translated from Schelling (cf. Bate, p. 146, with *Bio. Lit.,* ed. Shawcross, II, 253, and with Schelling, *Werke,* I, VII, 292). J. A. Appleyard, in *Coleridge's Philosophy of Literature* (1965), thinks that "little has been added to our understanding of the value or meaning of Coleridge's thought itself" by a study of his borrowings though he recognizes that Coleridge "regularly cannibalized the works and ideas of others."

George Whalley, in "Coleridge Unlabyrinthed" (*UTQ,* 1963), draws a useful distinction between the "public" Coleridge of the nineteenth century and the "internal" Coleridge of the notebooks, letters, marginalia, and fragments, describing the task of the new edition in glowing terms. He rightly protests against the view that Coleridge is a Kantian. "I reply that Coleridge was Coleridge," a simple way of cutting the Gordian knot. In a comic "idiot's guide" "that sounds like a sight-translation from an untractable central European dialect," (what could that be?) Whalley makes the invented author say: "His philosophical writing sometimes derives from Unacknowledged transcendental sources," but he makes no attempt to refute the only correct statement in that mock biography. He merely postpones consideration to the time when all of Coleridge's writings will be edited. Coleridge's "philosophy and psychology—and even his theology" "have scarcely been touched yet," Whalley concludes, dismissing thus the whole enormous literature on these topics.

Three new books will, however, make it impossible to ignore or to minimize the question of Coleridge's dependence on sources, which is not merely a question of historical curiosity or an ethical puzzle but profoundly affects our judgment of Coleridge's position in the history of philosophical thought and literary criticism. Gian N. G. Orsini's *Coleridge and German Idealism* (1969) reexamines the question of Coleridge's relation to Kant, Fichte, and Schelling thoroughly and conclusively. The clarity of exposition and argument, the command of evidence, the fair-minded and level-headed attitude implied or displayed on every page are beyond cavil.

Orsini has opted for an unusual way of exposition: he starts with a chapter on Coleridge's intellectual biography tracing his early beliefs and speculations up to the year 1799 but abandons then a chronological examination of Coleridge's writings and pronouncements and shifts to an exposition of the teachings of Kant, Fichte, Schelling, and Hegel, insofar as they are relevant to Coleridge, with constant documented reference to his use of either direct quotations, paraphrase, or assimilation of the ideas of the German philosophers. Only one last chapter is devoted to a specific piece of Coleridge's writings: the MS. "Logic," still resting, largely unpublished, in the Library of the British Museum. The method fulfills its purpose if we assume, as we must, that most students of Coleridge, particularly professional students of English literature, are largely ignorant of German philosophy and thus need to be presented with a clear and systematic account of what are the main sources of Coleridge's philosophical ideas: the writings of Kant, Fichte, and Schelling. Orsini demonstrates, with concrete examples, ample quotations, and references, that Coleridge expounded Kant and Schelling, the two German philosophers who attracted him most, adhering closely not only to their general arguments but following often the very phrasing and vocabulary. On occasion, Coleridge criticized Kant with arguments derived from Schelling or distanced himself from Schelling as a pantheist and even (quite unjustly) as a Roman Catholic obscurantist (cf. *Philosophical Lectures*, 1949, pp. 390–91, a passage mercifully ignored by Orsini). As Orsini rightly emphasizes, "in spite of strong leanings toward absolute idealism, Coleridge in the end always returned within the fold of orthodox theism" and in practice engaged in his later years mainly in Anglican apologetics.

Orsini marshals his evidence so well, documents every detail so carefully, that it will be impossible to challenge his general argument. His book should lay the ghost of theories asking us to believe that Coleridge found all these ideas in the Cambridge Platonists or even in antiquity (as Coleridge, on occasion, claimed when he blithely substituted the name of Plato for Kant). Orsini demonstrates conclusively that Coleridge accepted the epistemology of the *Critique of Pure Reason* in all its details, reproducing the Transcendental Aesthetic, the doctrine of the categories, the Transcendental Unity of Apperception, and the Transcendental Dialectic, while, on other occasions, he quoted or paraphrased central passages from Schelling's philosophy of identity and drew from him the basic ideas about the relation between art and nature. I am gratified that, on the whole, Orsini corroborates, sometimes with new materials and new interpretations, my examination of the relationship between Coleridge and Kant (and incidentally Schelling) in a chapter of my early book, *Immanuel Kant in England* (1931), even though the chapter today needs supplementing and emending in the light of new evidence.

Surprisingly, in view of the evidence marshaled in the book, Orsini assumes a hesitant and sometimes contradictory position as to the ultimate value of Coleridge's philosophical thought, postponing judgment till the complete publication of the MS materials, though the MSS have been described and quoted from sufficiently for us to know that they contain mainly theological and obsolete scientific speculations which will not change our judgment on the stature of Coleridge as a philosopher. (More on this in my review in *CL,* 1970.) Orsini's papers "Coleridge, Fichte, and 'Original Apperception' " in *Friendship's Garland, Essays Presented to Mario Praz,* ed. V. Gabrieli (1966), and "Coleridge's Manuscript Treatise on Logic" in *The Disciplines of Criticism,* ed. P. Demetz, T. Greene, and Lowry Nelson, Jr. (1968), are absorbed into the book. As a supplement to Orsini, attention should be drawn to Gisela Shaw's *Das Problem des Dinges an sich in der englischen Kantinterpretation* (1969), which contains a few acute pages on Coleridge's view of Kant's thing-in-itself, particularly on a marginal note which tries to build a bridge to theology on the basis of a supposed etymological relation between *Noumenon, Nomen* and *Numen.*

The second book, Thomas McFarland's *Coleridge and the Pantheist Tradition* (1969), differs from Orsini's in scope. It is wider since McFarland examines not only Coleridge's relations to Kant and his followers but includes discussions of his relations to Plato, Plotinus, Bruno, Boehme, Descartes, Spinoza, the Cambridge Platonists, Leibniz, Swedenborg, and Jacobi. But McFarland's book is also more narrow than Orsini's in scope. McFarland focuses on the one question indicated in the title: Coleridge's attitude toward pantheism, his long struggle with it and his final acceptance of a "trinitarian solution." There are only incidental discussions of Coleridge's aesthetics and criticism, particularly of the imagination in relation to Kant and Boehme, and there is an Excursus on "Coleridge's Indebtedness to A. W. Schlegel." Within these limits McFarland gives an extremely erudite, well-documented account of Coleridge's relations to the main figures of the history of philosophy. The sections on Spinoza, Leibniz, and Jacobi are particularly fresh. For example, a learned passage in *Biographia Literaria* (Shawcross, I, 169–70) is shown to be a translation from an obscure pamphlet of Leibniz. McFarland discusses the problem of Coleridge's philosophical originality and of his plagiarisms at length recognizing that "it is difficult to credit seriously any defense, however well intentioned, that in any way glosses over or attempts to extenuate the fact of Coleridge's borrowings." Coleridge's borrowings, many of them still unidentified, "are not only real, but so honeycomb his work as to form virtually a mode of composition." Coleridge "squirrel-like, stockpiled terminology, phrasings, concepts from other thinkers." McFarland argues that "the very multiplicity of instances (of Coleridge's borrowings)—far more than at first charged, and by no means as yet all identified—suggests the explanation, bizarre though it may seem, that we are faced not with plagiarism, but with nothing less than a mode of composition—composition by mosaic organization rather than by painting on an empty canvas." Mosaic technique, honeycomb of quotations, squirrel-like stockpiling, all these are phrases for what I called eclecticism and confirm my view that Coleridge cannot claim a high position in a history of philosophy. McFarland ascribes however great significance to Coleridge's trinitarian solution, though he admits that the *magnum opus* was a "poignant illusion." (More on McFarland in my review, *CL,* 1970.)

The third book, Norman Fruman's *Damaged Archangel* (1971), differs from Orsini's and McFarland's in taking a stern view of the ethics of Coleridge's procedures. He accumulates an array of facts showing Coleridge's deliberate misdatings, misstatements, and concealments of sources and elaborate covering up of traces which might lead to their discovery. Fruman shows also in detail how uncharitable and often unfounded Coleridge's views of plagiarism in others were: thus he accused Locke and Hume quite unjustly. The common theory that Coleridge quoted from memory or on the basis of old notes is, Fruman argues, untenable, as in most cases he must have been translating with the printed original in front of him. Fruman comes to agree with Charles Lamb that Coleridge was "in the daily and hourly habit of quizzing the world by lies" (*Letters*, ed. E. V. Lucas, I, 172) and thus doubts most of Coleridge's statements about his early reading, his claim for precocity and anticipation of other thinkers' ideas, and the whole account of his intellectual development. Fruman presses the evidence sometimes very hard and uncharitably allows little for oversights or lapses of memory. The discussion of Coleridge's ideas or rather of the ideas borrowed by Coleridge is somewhat vitiated by Fruman's unsympathetic attitude toward post-Kantian idealism and *Natur-philosophie* which, whatever its value may seem today, engaged such great minds as Goethe, Schelling, and Hegel. Fruman must be thanked for stating the case against Coleridge's candor so frankly and forcefully. The question cannot be glossed over even though we may come finally to a more lenient view of the ethics of Coleridge's behavior.

Many more specialized contributions to a study of Coleridge's sources have been made in recent years. A series of articles by W. Schrickx—"An Unnoticed Note of Coleridge on Kant" in *Neophilologus* (1958); "Coleridge Marginalia in Kant's *Metaphysische Anfangsgründe*" in *Studia Germanica Gadensia* (1960); "Coleridge, Ernst Platner and the Imagination" in *English Studies* (1959); "Coleridge and F. H. Jacobi" in *RBPH* (1958); "Unpublished Coleridge Marginalia on Fichte" in *Studia Germanica Gadensia* (1961); "Coleridge and the Cambridge Platonists" in *REL* (1966)—are particularly valuable as Schrickx presents his evidence with meticulous care and knows the history of philosophy. Lore Metzger published an important note on Spinoza ("Coleridge's Vindication of Spinoza," *JHI*, 1960). Walter Greiner ("Deutsche Einflüsse auf die Dichtungstheorie von Samuel Taylor Coleridge," in *Die neueren Sprachen*, 1960) quotes anticipations of Coleridge's distinctions in the faculty of imagination from Tetens' *Philosophische Versuche über die menschliche Natur* (1777). Orsini, in "Coleridge and Schlegel Reconsidered" (*CL*, 1964), shows—not for the first time—that Coleridge's definition of organic form is not a condensation but a word-for-word translation from A. W. Schlegel and traces the background of the definition in the general history of the organism concept. McFarland in an excursus of his book took exception to Orsini's argument, showing that Coleridge knew of organic form prior to quoting the passage from Schlegel. Daniel Stempel ("Coleridge and Organic Form: The English Tradition," in *SIR*, 1967) shows that the difference between mechanical and organic form was known to Kames and David Hume as well as to Kant. But the point raised by Orsini is not the history of the idea of organic form, which is as old as Aristotle, but its use in aesthetics and the specific formula devised by Schlegel.

Robert Marsh, in an appendix of his *Four Dialectical Theories of Poetry: An Aspect of English Neoclassical Criticism* (1965), suggests that Coleridge's poetic theories are related, in methods and aims, to the four "dialectical" theorists (Shaftesbury, Akenside, Hartley, and James Harris) he discusses in the body of the book. The term "dialectical," which in Marsh's use has nothing to do with Hegel or Marx, conceals a discussion of what is usually called the Platonic tradition: the emphasis on poetry as knowledge of the true nature of the world, on the poet's inspiration, and on the resemblance of the poet's art to divine creation. In this very wide sense Coleridge's theory is, no doubt, Platonic, though Marsh has to point out that, e.g., in contradistinction to Hartley, Coleridge's theory "is framed in terms of innate human spirituality and creative power," a distinction which makes all the difference in the world.

P. W. K. Stone, in *The Art of Poetry 1750–1820: Theories of Poetic Composition and Style in the Late Neo-Classic and Early Romantic Periods* (1967), comes to an opposite conclusion. He sees a complete sudden break in theories of composition and style with the arrival of Wordsworth and Coleridge, denying any value to the concept of "pre-Romanticism." He ascribes the change to the influx of Kantian ideas on imagination and genius but is frankly puzzled by Wordsworth's independent formulations. Coleridge is, however, only one of the many writers discussed.

A large amount of discussion has been devoted to the intellectual allegiances of the early Coleridge before his intensive study of Kant in 1801. Orsini, Appleyard (see below), J. B. Beer (discussed in the preceding section), and many other writers examine Coleridge's relations to Plato, Plotinus, Boehme, the Cambridge Platonists, Berkeley, Priestley, Hartley, Erasmus Darwin, etc. They often assume what would need proof: that Coleridge in these early years had definite philosophical allegiances and that one can, in the texts preserved, distinguish clearly between Platonism, Neoplatonism, and even the Hartleian "materialism" capped by theology. Nor am I convinced that Coleridge's poetry and individual lines and expressions can be taken as evidence of philosophical beliefs. Besides, the problem is made difficult by Coleridge's later attempts to claim amazing precocity and at the same time to minimize his concern for what later seemed to him aberrant or heretical ideas. Nor can the chronology of these presumed allegiances be made so neat as to distinguish sharply between different periods and subperiods.

The fullest account is Paul Deschamps, *La Formation de la pensée de Coleridge* (*1772–1804*) (1964), a diffuse French *Thèse* which displays, mainly in French translation, all the evidence from the Letters, Notebooks, poems, and prose writings of the time, paying attention to Coleridge's reading, tracing Coleridge's psychological and political views and interests as well as his philosophical development. Deschamps stresses Coleridge's Platonism or rather Neoplatonism but sees the turn toward Kant after 1801. In spite of all his care Deschamps draws often uncritically on Coleridge's much later pronouncements and marginalia or often lacks decisiveness or clarity of point of view. The whole idea of Coleridge's "Platonism" remains vague and undefined.

H. W. Piper, in *The Active Universe: Pantheism and the Concept of Imagination in the English Romantic Poets* (1962), a book largely concerned with Wordsworth, discusses Coleridge as a "Unitarian poet, between 1794–6," stressing his allegiance to Priestley, an argument he had before presented in "The Pantheistic Sources of Coleridge's Early Poetry" (*JHI*, 1959). Leonard W. Deen in "Coleridge and the Radicalism of Dissent" (*JEGP*, 1962) emphasizes Priestley but rather within the context of social and political ideas: "Coleridge's belief in the efficiency of religion as a political instrument separated him from the more purely secularist strain of English radicalism" is Deen's sensible conclusion. Deen also discussed "Coleridge and the Sources of Pantisocracy: Godwin, the Bible, and Hartley" (*Boston University Studies in English*, 1961). Lucyle Werkmeister, in "Coleridge, Science, Philosophy and Poetry: Their Relation to Religion" (*HTR*, 1959), argues that Coleridge derived suggestions for a theology from the combined teachings of Burke and Berkeley. There is no evidence, to my mind, that Burke was important for Coleridge in these early years or that his views can be described as "a synthesis of the positions of Burke and Berkeley." In "The Early Coleridge: His 'Rage for Metaphysics' " (*HTR*, 1961), she attempts to reconcile the recollections of Coleridge with the juvenilia. The "rage for metaphysics" could have been only a rage for Neoplatonism. She finds definite traces of Plotinus in Coleridge's early poems. Lucyle Werkmeister made also an odd discovery. In "Coleridge and Godwin on the Communication of Truth" (*MP*, 1958) she pointed out that the essay of that title in the 1809 *Friend* copies long passages from Godwin's *Political Justice* without acknowledgment. Richard Haven, in "Coleridge, Hartley and the Mystics" (*JHI*, 1959), argues that the early influence of the Platonists and Boehme has been exaggerated. "It is a mistake to see Coleridge's early years as a sort of Battle of Books from which Plotinus or Boehme or Cudworth emerges as victor, and Hartley, Priestley and Berkeley as losers." Rather Coleridge read the mystics for "facts of mind" but did not accept their systems. Coleridge's reading of Boehme, Haven shows in "Coleridge and Jacob Boehme: A Further Comment" (*N&Q*, 1966), dates from 1817–18. A supposedly Boehmean passage in "The Eolian Harp" (1795) was not published until 1817. Irene H. Chayes, in "Coleridge, Metempsychosis, and 'Almost all the followers of Fénelon'" (*ELH*, 1958), has traced a puzzling allusion to the Chevalier Ramsey's *Philosophical Principles of Natural and Revealed Religion* (1748–49).

E. M. Wilkinson, "Coleridge und Deutschland, 1794–1804," in *Forschungsprobleme der vergleichenden Literaturwissenschaft* (II, 1958), surveys Coleridge's early contacts with Germany and German thought. Because she is the editor of the German items in the first volume of *The Notebooks* and a lifelong student of German aesthetics her views of Coleridge's affinities with Goethe and particularly with Schiller deserve hearing.

Roy Park's "Coleridge and Kant: Poetic Imagination and Practical Reason" (*BJA*, 1968) is not a source study. It ignores the mass of evidence but points out correctly that Coleridge uses Practical Reason "in ways far beyond the ethical" and that imagination, in Coleridge, is interpreted as a constitutive rendering of Reason, in a very un-Kantian manner. Art becomes an expression of the artist's own intuitive insight into ideas as real. Park sees that Coleridge's demand for unification and harmony entailed the conversion of the poetic into something other than the poetical, its subordination to philosophy and ultimately to religion. "Fortunately," says Park, "this 'constitutive' theory remains only a bias in the period of Coleridge's greatest critical activity." Park sees that Coleridge rejected Kant in favor of orthodoxy but does not see that the interpretation of Kant is identical with Schelling's even though Coleridge distanced himself from what he considered to be Schelling's pantheism.

II. ANALYSES AND EVALUATIONS

Park's paper, as well as many pages in the books of Orsini, McFarland, and Deschamps, goes far beyond source study or even discussions of Coleridge's relationships to other thinkers. These studies analyze and evaluate Coleridge's philosophy. Most general books on Coleridge devote at least a section to his thought. Thus Virginia L. Radley's *Coleridge* (1966) expounds Coleridge's philosophy with no attention to its sources, heavily relying on quotations from other scholars. The tone is disarming: "to keep all of these definitions and distinctions in mind is rather a chore."

William Walsh's *Coleridge* (1967) discusses Coleridge's educational theory perceptively but shows little interest in his philosophy or theology. "Nothing is gained by making claims for Coleridge as a great philosopher," he says, as Coleridge "used philosophic ideas as symbols for his reading of life." The famous passage on Imagination is dismissed because "Coleridge's criticism has to modern nostrils a distasteful, philosophic air." "Modern" presumably means "British empirical" or even Leavisite as Walsh approves of Leavis' dismissal of Coleridge's thought. Still, the book claims much for Coleridge "as the first modern consciousness."

W. Jackson Bate's *Coleridge,* though mainly a biography, makes running comments on Coleridge's prose, his plans for a *magnum opus,* and sketches the final Christian philosophy besides reprinting the earlier article on Coleridge as Critic. Bate accepts the most extravagant claims for Coleridge's biological speculations and finds that his theology "has a familiar ring to readers acquainted with present-day Christian existentialism" but finally decides that Coleridge's political philosophy is "in many ways the most finished and . . . perhaps the most satisfying aspect of his thought."

There are several papers which sketch aspects of Coleridge's philosophy. Joan Larsen ("S. T. Coleridge: His Theory of Knowledge," *Transactions of the Wisconsin Academy,* 1959) points to Coleridge's blurring of the distinction between daydreaming, mystical experiences, and blind sense perception, and states clearly Coleridge's need for faith and belief in a God known intuitively through Reason. "Coleridge could and did calmly reconcile Plato and Bacon in a new synthesis."

Nicholas Brooke, in "Coleridge 'True and Original Realism' " (*Dur-*

ham University Journal, 1961), expounds Coleridge's realism. He sees Coleridge's difficulty with the idea that we know objects as dead only by a deliberate abstraction, by a failure of the imagination. Brooke does not see that Coleridge's "realism" is that of Schelling who aimed at a philosophy of identity which would allow a reconciliation of realism and idealism. Much more systematic and thorough is David Keppel-Jones's long paper "Coleridge's Scheme of Reason" (*Literary Monographs,* 1957), which digests Coleridge's late philosophy around key terms: Understanding, Imagination, Will, Reason, emphasizing the late definition of Reason as one with the absolute Will. In a conclusion Keppel-Jones surveys some of Coleridge's sources and suggests a particular affinity with Philo, though the evidence for Coleridge's knowledge and interest, he recognizes, is very tenuous.

Wendell V. Harris, in "The Shape of Coleridge's 'Public' System" (*MP,* 1970), makes the excellent point that we must distinguish between Coleridge's thought known through his publications and lectures and the thought newly reconstructed on the basis of manuscripts and marginalia. Harris summarizes the "public" thought of Coleridge, focusing on his concept of method, on the distinction of Reason and Understanding, commenting on the divergence from Kant; on Coleridge's empirical view of politics; on the way he absorbs morality in religion. Imagination, Harris argues, is not transcendent in Coleridge, even though at times, under the influence of Schelling, Coleridge was induced to make such claims. While Harris sees Coleridge's lack of method and knows that, "unable to begin from the beginning, he begins anywhere," he concludes that Coleridge's "brilliance as a commentator results from his constant philosophical endeavor."

There are a few good pages on Coleridge in Frederick Copleston, S.J., *History of Philosophy.* Vol. VIII: *Part I British Empiricism and the Idealist Movement in Great Britain* (1966), incidentally the only recent history of philosophy that pays any attention to Coleridge. Bertrand Russell and Lord Passmore with their anti-idealist orientation barely mention him. Father Copleston knows only a few texts but knowledgeably points out that Coleridge in discussing the theory of knowledge "asks Schelling's question, then supplies Schelling's answer, namely that we must postulate an original identity of subject and object, and finally switches to Fichte's idea of the ego." Later he tends to speak as though the transcendental ego were the absolute *I am that I am* of Exodus. "All this is obviously cloudy and imprecise," he concludes.

Two writers see the unity of Coleridge's thought in method. Kathleen Coburn in several papers emphasizes Coleridge's "method of going about the business of thinking and formulating" ("Poet into Public Servant," *PTRSC*, 1960). She insists on the unity of Coleridge's endeavors—poetry, philosophy, and theology were his concerns all his life long. His sense of "the interpenetration of man and nature" (the title of a paper, in *Proceedings of the British Academy,* 1963) is not, she argues, pantheism or mysticism but "a dynamic organic sense of wholeness, of the relation of man to the natural world, of the necessity of physical and intellectual reconciliations in one system." "Fields, rivers, mountains, the Bible, *Paradise Lost,* are for Coleridge all books to be read." In our age of dissociation Coleridge appears as the total man. Kathleen Coburn's concern is with Coleridge as a person or with the psychologist and moralist. She can quote to show Coleridge's vivid sense of nature or his sensitive introspection but she does not succeed in defining his method in any but the most general way. Elizabeth Sewell ("Coleridge: The Method and the Poetry" in *The Poet as Critic,* ed. F. P. W. McDowell, 1967) brings together a passage of self-description in allegorical terms with Coleridge's insistence on method, which she interprets as "self-imagining or mythologizing," a whimsical idea which has no support in Coleridge's text.

Richard Haven, in *Patterns of Consciousness: An Essay on Coleridge* (1969), argues in a well-written and sensitive book that Coleridge should not be judged as a philosopher but rather considered "a born psychologist trying to write as a metaphysician." His attempts to construe a system should, like his poetry, be seen "as a projection, an 'elaborated transformed symbol,' for his own psychological experience." Haven assumes that Coleridge was a "visionary" though not a mystic and that his philosophy is an attempt to find formulas for this vision. "The Ancient Mariner" represents "the sense of experience as a continuum between extremes of alienation and communion" and this very pattern underlies also Coleridge's abstract thought as "the fundamental structure of consciousness was the same as the fundamental structure of the external universe." Haven interprets Coleridge's assimilation of German philosophy as an "attempt to find a language, a set of symbols in terms of which he could describe and make intelligible his own experience of himself in the universe." Kant and Schelling are quoted but Coleridge "did not 'mean' merely the works from which he borrowed." He was rather concerned to justify "the movement from the 'normal' to communion, from discursive consciousness to what might be called 'unitive' consciousness." Haven pays close attention to

Coleridge's scientific speculations, partly derived from German *Natur-philosophie,* and partly parallel to concerns of such English scientists as Sir Humphry Davy. All aspects of Coleridge's thought are explained by his psychological need. "The notion of imagination looks to the philosophy of mind for its definition, that of symbol, to theology, and that of organic form, to the philosophy of nature. But all these refer ultimately to the problem of expressing in language an intuitively known structure of experience." This underlying pattern constitutes Coleridge's real originality more than his position in intellectual history as Haven recognizes that "his philosophy as philosophy has little value today." But this explanation by genesis in Coleridge's mind—for which there is no real evidence—is a reduction of Coleridge's thought to a psychological "case" or even "oddity." Ideas have to be judged by their truth value or by their historical importance or efficacy. "Motivation" does not change their meaning.

One point in Coleridge's psychology is illuminated in a paper by Judson S. Lyon, "Romantic Psychology and the Inner Senses: Coleridge" (*PMLA,* 1966). Terms like "inner sense," "inner eye" create a kind of parallel inner world. Lyon also pays intelligent attention to the sources.

Two recent books take Coleridge's late thought (in practice, his theology) seriously, expound it carefully and make great claims for its significance. James Boulger's *Coleridge as Religious Thinker* (1961) argues that Coleridge tries to maintain a balance between intellect, will, and emotion in his religious thinking. Coleridge's chief polemical targets were rational theology and Unitarianism. Boulger defends Coleridge's combination of mysticism and rationalism, his concept of "higher reason" identified with faith, which he considers an "existential" concept similar to Schleiermacher's or Kierkegaard's. Boulger describes Coleridge's attempt to combine the methods of Schelling's identity philosophy with Christian dualism, his repudiation of what he considered the pantheist implications of Schelling's thought and his ultimate acceptance of authority which included an "existential and volitional basis for Christian thinking." Boulger considers this as an important anticipation of Kierkegaard and the neo-orthodox movement in Germany and the United States. Still, he recognizes that "Coleridge straddled too many fences, was aware of too many contradictory trends, and lacked the profound power of integration necessary to launch a true theological movement." Boulger studies and quotes the late unpublished *Notebooks* full of theological speculations and makes a valiant effort to find coherence and novelty in them. The fact that these ideas were buried in unpublished notebooks made them ineffective in their time and they can hardly become important today in competition with new formulations in totally different contexts. Coleridge's published theological writings had a demonstrable effect on the Latitudinarian movement which has, needless to say, no touch of Kierkegaard. Historically, Coleridge's theology was an apologetics for Anglican orthodoxy liberalized on such points as the literal inspiration of the Bible. If one judges Coleridge as a philosopher one must agree with Karl Jaspers "that a philosophy which is drawn from Revelation, which submits to the authority of Revelation, ceases to be philosophy" (*Schelling,* 1955).

J. Robert Barth, S.J., in *Coleridge and Christian Doctrine* (1969), differs from Boulger by attempting a synoptic systematization of Coleridge's doctrines according to a scheme modeled on a handbook of dogmatics. We are informed of Coleridge's conception of the nature of faith, the nature and role of Sacred Scripture, the one and tri-une God, Creation and sinful man, Redemption and justification, Church, sacraments and prayer, and finally Coleridge's view of death, the Last Judgment, Heaven, and Hell. The evidence is carefully digested (also from the unpublished *Notebooks*) and confronted mainly with modern Roman Catholic doctrine and studies of the history of these doctrines. Father Barth frequently shakes his head over Coleridge's "theological blunders" and draws attention to gaps in Coleridge's assumed system. An Epilogue sees Coleridge as analogous to Pierre Teilhard de Chardin. "Both are profoundly Pauline in their theology: both see Christ as the final cause and matrix of the whole created world; both focus on the evolutionary movement of the world as a progressive development toward ultimate perfection, culminating in union with the Godman." The first chapter sketches Coleridge's theological development as a conflict between "dynamic philosophy" (i.e., Schelling's) and Christian Faith. Father Barth lumps Kant, Herder, Fichte, and Schelling (not to speak of René Wellek) together as "rationalists" though at least Herder and Schelling disparaged reason. Schelling wrote a *Philosophy of Revelation* and figures, for instance, prominently in Georg Lukács' *Zerstörung der Vernunft.* The simple dichotomy between orthodoxy and rationalism obscures Coleridge's painful conflict between head and heart.

Like Boulger, Hugh Parry Owen, in "Theology of Coleridge," *Critical Quarterly* (1962), considers Coleridge's affinities with Kierkegaard remarkable. They both repudiate pantheism and rational theology, they both consider religious truth personal truth, truth *for me,* and faith to be an act of will. Coleridge, Owen points out, differs from Schleiermacher in not recognizing a special religious experience and differs from recent Christian existentialists in not succumbing to irrationalism. Owen does not consider the filiation Schelling-Kierkegaard-Tillich (and Tillich was also a close student of Schelling) nor does he consider the fact that Coleridge's Reason is, at least in his later thinking, simply another term for faith. Owen's final comparison of Coleridge with St. Augustine seems even more far-fetched. H. Jackson Forstman's "Samuel Taylor Coleridge's Notes toward the Understanding of Doctrine" (*Journal of Religion*, 1964) expounds Coleridge's views of the doctrine of election on the basis of *Aids of Reflection*. Forstman emphasizes Coleridge's interest in theological language: in a description of what is involved in faith, in the question of what a doctrine means rather than whether it is true. He concludes that Coleridge "anticipates something like the approach to theology on the part of Bultmann." Benjamin Sankey's "Coleridge and the Visible World" (*TSLL*, 1964) discusses Coleridge's view of the visible world as a system of symbols, to be interpreted in Christian terms. "Coleridge's theory of knowledge takes for granted a Fall with the possibility of Grace and Revelation and it presupposes a theological tradition." Even "Imagination" is called "a theological notion." But these suggestions remain undeveloped and the final page referring to Charles Darwin's scientific work "as a successful application of Coleridge's methodological program" cannot convince.

Coleridge's scientific speculations were also discussed again. Sam G. Barnes, in "Was 'Theory of Life' Coleridge's *Opus Maximum?*" (*SP*, 1958), argues that this little treatise follows the order of the projected *Opus Maximum* though Barnes has to admit that religion is missing in the scheme. Organic development and polarity are the main principles of Coleridge's philosophy. But this emphasis on an occasional paper derived largely from German *Naturphilosophie* and referring to a specific debate is surely unconvincing. The *Opus Maximum* was an illusion but the notebooks, the MS. "Logic," and the three volumes of theological speculations called *Opus Magnum* adumbrate it far more systematically than *Theory of Life*.

Craig W. Miller, in "Coleridge's Concept of Nature" (*JHI*, 1964), expounded Coleridge's concept of nature systematically: his essential dualism, the null point of indifference, the quadrants and hemispheres, totally ignoring the fact that all these ideas come from Schelling and his followers. Coleridge, though an avid reader, had no direct experience of science and used it merely for his theory of knowledge and theology. The claim Miller makes for his evolutionary conception is quite unfounded: all these ideas were debated by biologists and speculative scientists in Germany much more concretely. A glance at the introduction and notes to M. J. Petry's edition of Hegel's *Philosophy of Nature* (1970) should suffice. Louis Bonnerot's graceful lecture "The Two Worlds of Coleridge: Some Aspects of His Attitude to Nature" (*EDH*, 1956) makes good observations on Coleridge's key-words, the little and the vast, linking the outward world with the inward world.

Coleridge's ideas on society and his political journalism have been studied much more thoroughly than before. There is a good chapter in Deschamps on his early period. D. V. Erdman has made Coleridge's political journalism his specialty. Some of his papers are listed in the preceding section. An excellent discussion of Coleridge's contributions to the *Morning Post* (1798–1803) called "Coleridge as Editorial Writer" is in *Power and Consciousness*, ed. Conor Cruise O'Brien and William Dean Vanech (1969). Erdman discovered the review which Coleridge wrote of his own *Second Lay Sermon*; see "Coleridge on Coleridge: The Context (and Text) of His Review of Mr. Coleridge's *Second Lay Sermon*" (*SIR*, 1961). Donald Sultana (*Samuel Taylor Coleridge in Malta and Italy*, 1969) throws much light on Coleridge's ideas and attitudes during his stay at Malta. John Colmer's *Coleridge: Critic of Society* (1959) gives a clear, chronological account of Coleridge's writings on political and social questions. Colmer admires "Coleridge's profound understanding of individual and group psychology," and finds "imperishable wisdom" in his ideas of church and state and in the foresight of his political attitudes, for instance, toward Napoleon. He deplores—and this is a recurrent theme of his sober instructive book—Coleridge's inability to find a proper intimate relation to his public. "He thus failed to produce an immediate effect on the minds and behavior of his readers."

David P. Calleo's *Coleridge and the Idea of the Modern State* (1966) is a political scientist's attempt not only to make sense of Coleridge's concept of a national state and the British Constitution but also to see the relevance of these ideas in a present-day context. While Calleo's exposition of Coleridge's "conservativism with a strong radical impulse" and the emphasis on Coleridge's good sense and feeling for particular circumstances is convincing, the attempt, in the last chapter, to see Coleridge's ideas as compatible with the ideal of a European federation and even the Common Market, strikes me as forced.

William F. Kennedy, in *Humanist versus Economist* (1958), shows that Coleridge's views on government spending, taxation, and the national debt were similiar to those held by Malthus and were prior in publication. Kennedy draws attention to Sir James Steuart's *Inquiry into the Principles of Political Oeconomy* (1767) as the main source of Coleridge's ideas on economics, which ran counter to those of the then prevailing views of Adam Smith.

III. AESTHETICS AND CRITICISM

Coleridge's aesthetics is clearly bound up with his philosophy and can hardly be discussed apart from it. Also the practical criticism is, at least in ambition, influenced by Coleridge's philosophy and aesthetic thought, as is recognized by all the new books and articles under review. These books and articles often seem to stress the coherence and implications of the philosophy, aesthetics, and criticism excessively.

Coleridge's theory, besides, must be seen in the context of the theories of the other English poets of the time and in their European setting. Three new books on the Romantic theory of poetry, all from the Continent, deal with Coleridge prominently, interweaving a discussion of his ideas with treatments of Wordsworth, Shelley, Keats, Hazlitt, and others, and comparisons with German and French developments. Albert Gérard's *L'Idée romantique de la poésie en Angleterre: Etudes sur la théorie de la poésie chez Coleridge, Wordsworth, Keats et Shelley* (1955) makes a judicious and careful survey of the theories of poetry using Coleridge frequently as the crown witness. The chapter headings—"The Poetic Experience, Romantic Spiritualism, Creative Imagination, *Anima Poetae,* The Poetic Form"—indicate the main topics. The main effort of the book is directed to a synthesis of the theories of Coleridge, Wordsworth, Shelley, and Keats, with the result that Coleridge's peculiar position is obscured. The effort to make the teachings of these four poets homogeneous and to set them off from Continental developments seems sometimes mistaken. Thus Coleridge's concept of the symbol is supposed to differ from that of the Germans, largely on the basis of Fritz Strich's much later and quite idiosyncratic interpretation of the differences between German classicism and Romanticism (in *Deutsche Klassik und Romantik,* 1922) though Coleridge exactly shares Goethe's, Schelling's, and Creuzer's views. In a later book, *English Romantic Poetry: Ethos, Structure, and Symbol in Coleridge,*

Wordsworth, Shelley and Keats (1968), Gérard interprets poems very successfully and only incidentally discusses theory. There no such claim for uniqueness is made. "If Coleridge borrowed from his German contemporaries for his definition of the symbol, that can only be because their ideas corresponded to a need in his own mind."

Cornelis de Deugd's Dutch thesis, *Het Metafysisch Grondpatron van het romantische literaire Denken: The Metaphysical Pattern of Romantic Criticism* (1966), contains a sixty-page summary in English. The book tries by a purely descriptive method (which the author calls phenomenological) to survey and digest the romantic theories of the poet as prophet, of poetry as divine and eternal, of the identification of poetry with religion and philosophy, on an international scale. Coleridge is considered to belong to a separate group: the Schlegels, Schelling, Solger, Hugo, and Joubert, i.e., the group which took the step from "viewing the infinite in the finitude of poetry to the unity of finite and infinite." (Precisely the idea Gérard reserved for Coleridge only.)

The third book, Herbert Mainusch's *Romantische Ästhetik: Untersuchungen zur englischen Kunstlehre des späten 18. und frühen 19. Jahrhunderts* (1969), is the most learned and most independent of these books. Mainusch reaches far into the past and consistently uses German, French, and Italian authors to illuminate the English developments. He is mainly interested in the role of art in the hierarchy of the mind: its emancipation as "romantic" art. Coleridge is discussed only incidentally, in spite of numerous references. Still, the pages on Coleridge's views of the Romantic, of Fancy and Imagination, of the function of philosophy in art, of the unities, of beauty and taste belong to the best I know as they are nourished by a wide knowledge of the background. Thus we get a clear history of the distinction between *imaginatio* and *fantasia* since Ficino. Mainusch considers this distinction a survival from the past and the formulas about primary and secondary imagination "mystification." He rejects my view that Coleridge had merit as the transmitter of many aesthetic ideas from Germany to England. "One could," he says, "rather argue that Coleridge by an unsystematic and unintegrated accumulation of gleanings from his reading of German authors has substantially contributed to their discredit with the English public." But this seems an uncalled-for cultural nationalism.

W. K. Wimsatt's and Cleanth Brooks's *Literary Criticism: A Short History* (1957)—it runs to 755 pages—contains two excellent chapters concerning Coleridge: one on Poetic Diction centered on the criticism

Coleridge made of Wordsworth's pronouncements and one on "Imagination: Wordsworth and Coleridge." Both chapters are skillfully expository and interpretative, and pay attention to the German background discussed in an intermediate chapter.

James Volant Baker's *The Sacred River: Coleridge's Theory of Imagination* (1957) asks the question "to what extent did Coleridge allow for unconscious as well as conscious processes at work in poetic creation." Baker dismisses the views of the early Coleridge as "temporary wobble" and then traces Coleridge's pronouncements on imagination to the conclusion that Coleridge saw a "balance of conscious and unconscious powers" in imagination, an insight which Baker considers "Coleridge's signal achievement." But Baker's own interest is in the role of the unconscious. Though he knows of the unconscious in Leibniz or Schelling he makes Coleridge anticipate Freud because Coleridge found significance in dreams, as if this were news at any time. Baker can exclaim, quoting Coleridge on Pan: "No, we are not dreaming, this is not D. H. Lawrence but S. T. Coleridge!" Coleridge is also supposed to have had an "uncanny anticipation" of *Gestalt,* e.g., in accounting for Martin Luther's hallucination of the devil at the Wartburg. Baker is unaware that Coleridge was merely translating a German travel book by one Jonas Ludwig von Hess, as pointed out by M. Eimer in *Englische Studien* (1913–14). Baker's claims for anticipation, his profuse references to any writer he can think of, his breezy style, calling Thelwall "comrade," for example, or saying that the Germans "licked the frosting off Spinoza's system," should not obscure the merits of the book which gives a good account of the theory of imagination with proper regard to its sources, in the English tradition (Dugald Stewart in particular) and the Germans.

Richard Harter Fogle's *The Idea of Coleridge's Criticism* (1962) expounds rather the ideal of Coleridge's criticism of which the actual corpus is an imperfect and incomplete appearance. Fogle outlines Coleridge's theories with a clear realization of their implications: what they should have been rather than what they were in all their fragmentariness and contradictoriness. The reconciliation of opposites is for him "the Archimedes lever of Coleridge as criticism." Fogle elaborates the key concepts of organic unity, polarity, beauty, taste, and art as the mediatress between nature and man, streamlining Coleridge's thought, ignoring or minimizing the survivals of empirical and neoclassical doctrines. Most interestingly Fogle argues that Coleridge's criticism of Wordsworth—which in its listing of faults and beauties seems to contradict his ideal of criticism—agrees with his fundamental principles: the standards of harmony, keeping, congruity. The same is true, Fogle argues, of Coleridge's Shakespeare criticism: particularly in its grasp of the nature of dramatic illusion.

J. R. de J. Jackson's *Method and Imagination in Coleridge's Criticism* (1969) explores the link between Coleridge's theory of method and his theory and practice of criticism. Jackson accepts the stress on Coleridge's method first voiced by Alice Snyder and since by Kathleen Coburn. It amounts, however, to little more than the principle of "unity with progression," a concern for system and principles. In the study of the poetic process, it means a theory of imagination. Jackson discusses the famous passage identifying Primary Imagination with Reason itself, and he shows the relevance of Coleridge's theory of imagination to his practice. Coleridge's turn to theology is described as an abandonment of method which Jackson surprisingly considers "an attempt at a new scepticism." He concludes that "we should avoid mistaking the philosophical background of Coleridge's criticism for his special contribution." Rather, the application of the techniques and conclusions of philosophy to the discussion of literature is Coleridge's peculiar achievement. Though Jackson's book contains many acute observations and shows some awareness of Coleridge's sources, the general thesis does not convince as "method" is too empty and general a term to make Coleridge's application anything distinctive: even Kames had his method, not to speak of the Germans. It seems impossible to accept Jackson's interpretation of Primary and Secondary Imagination and Fancy. Primary Imagination is not Reason itself, nor can it be taken, as Jackson does, self contradictorily, as "the literary term for the unconscious"; nor is Fancy "derived from the objects around us." Rather, in accordance with Schelling's scheme, Coleridge calls Primary Imagination the agent of all human Perception (*Anschauung* in Schelling's terminology), which is not at all "literary"; while the secondary imagination, though continuous with the primary, is co-existing with the conscious will. Fancy is not derived from the objects around us but plays with them arbitrarily according to the laws of association.

J. A. Appleyard's *Coleridge's Philosophy of Literature* (1965) seems more satisfactory as he does not press a limited thesis as Jackson does. Father Appleyard gives a careful chronological account of Coleridge's philosophical development with emphasis on his theory of literature. The early stage of empiricism is considered an episode, while the concept of "a symbolical, mighty alphabet" echoed from Berkeley, in "The Destiny of

Nations" (1796), is singled out as the anticipation of Coleridge's mature view, later based, however, "on a more realistic metaphysics and a concept of analogy." The Imagination-Fancy distinction is rightly seen as preceding the Reason-Understanding dichotomy. Imagination-Fancy was formulated first in 1802 while Reason-Understanding becomes prominent only in 1806. Father Appleyard argues that, under the influence of Schelling, the concept of Imagination became inflated in the later formulation at the end of the first volume of *Biographia Literaria*. "Coleridge could not really give that importance to imagination." Coleridge's later formulations about the nature of poetry (between 1815 and 1819) with their emphasis on illusion and pleasure seem to Appleyard "more authentic." Surprisingly, in view of the low opinion Father Appleyard has of Chapters xii and xiii of *Biographia Literaria* as derivative and confused, he sees, ultimately, the most significant contribution of Coleridge to a theory of literature in the idea of art as mediating between man and nature and his exposition of the concept of symbol. The first doctrine occurs almost exclusively in the essay "Of Poesy or Art" which is a paraphrase of Schelling's Oration before the Munich Academy; it had been a commonplace idea since Schiller, while the concept of symbol in Coleridge is derivative of statements by Goethe, Schelling, and Creuzer. Both these doctrines remained isolated and unassimilated: Coleridge, for example, confuses symbol and synecdoche and does not make any attempt to give a symbolic interpretation of literature except in the essay on the *Prometheus* of Aeschylus which again is closely dependent on Schelling, Creuzer, Welcker, and possibly others. Though Father Appleyard sees that Kant is "behind a good many arrases" on such points as the theory of taste and genius, he ignores the evidence for the derivativeness of "Of Poesy or Art" or the formulas on the symbol, and construes a conflict between the theory of imagination, which, he assumes, has pantheist implications Coleridge could not accept, and the theory of the identity of subject and object grounded in divine creativity, though both theories are easily reconciled in Schelling. Still, Father Appleyard recognizes Coleridge's *volte-face* into orthodoxy about 1819 which entailed the abandonment of interest in a theory of literature. While the general thesis seems doubtful, the book has the merit of allowing space for many acute analyses and for a chronological exposition distinguished for lucidity. Roy Park, in "Coleridge: Philosopher and Theologian as Literary Critic" (*UTQ*, 1968), discusses Coleridge's concept of imagination and his conception of the philosophical poem. He shows well that Coleridge wavered between an experiential and constitutive rendering of poetic reality. "The ambiguity of Coleridge's theory of poetry as ideal or as symbol, combining experiential and constitutive facets, finds its counterpart in the basic ambiguity within his theory of poetic imagination itself." Park reformulates what I have several times described as the basic disparity in Coleridge's theory between an organistic, idealistic superstructure and an empiricist psychological groundwork.

Robert D. Hume, in "Kant and Coleridge on Imagination" (*JAAC*, 1970), thinks that Coleridge's theories "are fragmentary and his borrowings seem ill amalgamated." It is a waste of time to discover what Coleridge meant in the definition of the Imagination in Chapter xiii of the *Biographia*. Still, he draws a picture with an elaborate diagram of Coleridge's concepts and comes to the conclusion that Coleridge "failed to justify beyond question the truth of imagination." Kant's and Coleridge's speculations are old-fashioned faculty psychology of purely historical interest. D. B. Lang, in "Point Counterpoint: The Emergence of Fancy and Imagination in Coleridge" (*JAAC*, 1958), propounds the thesis that the power which Hume designated "imagination" reappears in Coleridge under the name of "Fancy." In Coleridge "the strength of imagination is no other than the self," a view which could not have been Hume's. While the contrast to Hume is obvious, Lang does not establish the relevance of his observations to the "emergence of fancy and imagination in Coleridge," promised in the subtitle of his essay.

These discussions of Coleridge's criticism have been largely concerned with his theory of imagination. Two articles pay special attention to Coleridge's concept of symbol. Patricia Ward's "Coleridge's Critical Theory of the Symbol" (*TSLL*, 1966) sketches the German background with emphasis on the role of Schiller (rather than Goethe and Schelling) and rehearses Coleridge's pronouncements. She sees that Coleridge "as a practical critic appears to fail to realize the implications of his statements on the symbol. He rather emphasizes the negative aspect in his view of allegory, and thus seems far removed from the main stream of German romanticism." Coleridge quoted or adapted statements from Schelling, Goethe, and Creuzer which he did not apply in practice.

Mary Rahme, in "Coleridge's Concept of Symbolism" (*Studies in English Literature*, Leeds, 1969), takes the opposite view. Symbol seems to her central to Coleridge's aesthetics and creation. She gives an explication of the view that symbol is a part of the reality it represents and thus defends Coleridge's identification of synecdoche with symbol. She argues, besides, that Coleridge "can think of physical nature as analogous to spiritual nature and at the same time regard it as symbolic of the spiritual, thinking of the totality as being comprised of both." Elinor S. Shaffer, in "Coleridge's Theory of Aesthetic Interest" (*JAAC,* 1969), draws on marginalia to R. P. Knight's *Analytical Inquiry into the Principles of Taste* to show that Coleridge successfully reconciled Kant with Burke, German idealism with British empiricism. Even if one grants that Coleridge suggests a way to modify Kant's view of the sublime (one of the weakest points of his aesthetic) with arguments drawn from empirical psychology I remain unconvinced that the pleasure principle is not opposed to a symbolic function of art or to a structural conception of it. In any case, the reconciliation concerns only a small point.

Another article by Elinor S. Shaffer, "Coleridge's Revolution in the Standard of Taste" (*JAAC,* 1969), shows that Coleridge equated the beautiful with the sublime and made the sublime the single aesthetic category while still calling it the beautiful. She argues that this is an original achievement. Schelling hesitated on this point because he persisted in defending classical beauty. But the Schlegels and possibly others had rejected the distinction earlier. A. W. Schlegel says condescendingly of Schelling's definition of beauty as the "infinite represented finitely" that it includes the definition of the Sublime, "as it should be" (*wie es sich gehört,* Berlin Lectures, Minor ed., 1, 90). Besides, it seems doubtful that the limitation of beauty to the sublime is such an achievement or had any discernible influence. The sublime disappeared from aesthetics in the nineteenth century all over Europe without Coleridge.

Emerson R. Marks, in "Means and Ends in Coleridge's Critical Method" (*ELH,* 1959), argues persuasively that the distinction between ends and means parallel to that between the rules and the permanent aims of literature survives, in Coleridge, from the neoclassical tradition though it contradicts the organistic and symbolist view in which the boundary separating part and whole is abolished. Coleridge, Emerson Marks concludes, "could not possibly succeed in joining two radically opposed critical schools into a coherent system" but the older view connecting means and ends served as a "salutary correction of extreme organicism."

Coleridge's Shakespeare criticism continues to be studied. There is a reprint of *Coleridge's Writings on Shakespeare,* ed. Terence Hawkes (1959). A. Harbage in the introductory essay dismisses the questions of Coleridge's indebtedness to A. W. Schlegel and the reprint drops all references to parallels listed in Raysor's standard edition. R. A. Foakes describes the MS of J. P. Collier's notes in the "Text of Coleridge's 1811–12 Shakespeare Lectures" (*Shakespeare Survey*, 1970) and comes up with interesting corrections and changes. Sylvan Barnet's "Coleridge on Shakespeare's Villains" (*SQ*, 1956) shows that Coleridge had trouble with Shakespeare's villains as he believed in the purity of Shakespeare's morals and in the identification of a poet with his figures. Coleridge therefore either argues that the villains are not so villainous after all or that they remain externally conceived characters based on observation. Iago is the one exception: Shakespeare resembles him in the powers of his mind. Barnet takes Coleridge's pronouncement "to know is to resemble" (*Bio. Lit.* II, 259) far too literally. Barnet's other paper "Coleridge on Puns" (*JEGP*, 1957) comes to the obvious conclusion that Coleridge's approval of puns in Shakespeare as expressions of agitated minds is "no longer a safe foundation for modern study." L. D. Berkoben's paper, "Coleridge on Wit," in *Humanities Association Bulletin* (Canada), 1964, has a wider scope; it surveys Coleridge's views on Wit and discusses examples of Coleridge's own wit perceptively. M. M. Badawi's "Coleridge's Formal Criticism of Shakespeare's Plays" (*EIC*, 1960) makes the point that Coleridge did not pay exclusive attention to Shakespeare's characters, but also considered the interrelations of the parts of the plays, the incidents, characters, and images. For example, Coleridge analyzes the plot of *The Tempest* and remarks on the role of the comic scenes and the songs. J. R. de J. Jackson wrote three articles arguing similar points: "Coleridge on Dramatic Illusion and Spectacle in the Performance of Shakespeare's Plays" (*MP*, 1964) shows that Coleridge had no prejudice against the theater but objected to the spectacular effect of contemporary productions of Shakespeare as they tended to impede the appeal to the imagination of the audience. Coleridge believed that theatrical illusion is neither delusion nor complete awareness of the act of staging but "a semblance of reality" somewhere in between. "Coleridge on Shakespeare's Preparation" (*REL*, 1966) shows that Coleridge studied Shakespeare's methods of achieving the requisite dramatic illusion, particularly in comments on the first scenes of *Hamlet, King Lear,* and *Timon of Athens.* "Free Will in Coleridge's Shakespeare" (*UTQ*, 1968) argues that one must look for the motivation behind some of Coleridge's apparently strange judgments. Coleridge's preoccupation with the nature of moral responsibility and the nature of free will explains such statements as that there is no change in Macbeth or that Othello is not jealous.

Elinor S. Shaffer in "Iago's Malignity Motivated: Coleridge's *Opus Magnum* Unpublished" (*SQ*, 1968) uses some unpublished passages on the self from the *Opus Magnum* to show that Coleridge conceived of Iago as thoroughly alienated from his true self, as a mere intellect without morals.

I find Stephen Maxfield Parrish's discussion of the "Wordsworth-Coleridge Controversy" (*PMLA*, 1958) particularly striking. Coleridge, more so than to Wordsworth's diction, objected to his dramatic method: he looked for the voice of the poet. In *Table Talk* (21 July 1832) Coleridge stated bluntly: "a great philosophical poet [and surely Coleridge thought of Wordsworth in these terms] ought always to teach the reader himself as from himself." Roy Park, in "Coleridge's Two Voices as a Critic of Wordsworth" (*ELH*, 1969), argues, more conventionally, that Coleridge criticized Wordsworth for lack of ideality "in accordance with the constitutive facet of his late theory of poetry as symbol."

Benjamin T. Sankey, Jr., in "Coleridge on Milton's Satan" (*PQ*, 1962), discusses the parallel Coleridge drew between Satan and Napoleon and tries to make an obscure linkage with the Kantian distinction between phenomenon and noumenon. Elizabeth T. McLaughlin in "Coleridge and Milton" (*SP*, 1964) has carefully collected and digested all references to Milton. She contrasts Coleridge's opinions on every point with Milton's modern detractors: Eliot, Leavis, and others. R. H. Fogle, in "Johnson and Coleridge on Milton" (*Bucknell Review*, 1966), confronts Coleridge's view rather with Johnson's, showing that Coleridge considered Milton's egocentrism "a positive and creative quality."

George Whalley pays close attention to "Coleridge on the *Prometheus* of Aeschylus" (*PTRSC*, 1960), describing the lecture in detail. He considers it surprisingly as "an example of the Coleridgian method-in-action, an example drawn unpurified and unshriven from 'the foul rag-and-bone shop of the heart.' " He totally ignores the fact that parts of the lecture are drawn from Schelling's "Über die Gottheiten von Samothrace" and that the other parts also betray their source in the obsolete learning of such classical philologists as Heyne, Welcker, and Creuzer, and have nothing to do with Coleridge's heart. The elucidations Whalley draws from "Of Poesy or Art" are again quotations from Schelling. The same ignorance of the sources vitiates the discussion of the lecture on Aeschylus in Jackson's book *Method and Imagination* though Jackson recognizes that it "differs from the rest of Coleridge's literary criticism."

IV. INFLUENCE AND REPUTATION

The influence and reputation of Coleridge has still not been studied very fully. Sanders' book remains the most substantial contribution. J. R. de J. Jackson has collected as *Coleridge: The Critical Heritage* (1970) a large volume reprinting reviews of Coleridge's writings up to the time of his death. The introduction is most instructive. John O. Hayden, *The Romantic Reviewers, 1802–1824* (1969), pays attention to the reception of Coleridge. There is a short sketch of Coleridge's reputation in the book by William Walsh. Graham Hough, in "Coleridge and the Victorians" (*The English Mind: Studies Presented . . . to Basil Willey*, 1964), surveys rapidly Coleridge's appeal to religious liberalism, to the Apostles group in Cambridge, to Thomas Arnold, to Newman, and to Disraeli down to Matthew Arnold's *Literature and Dogma* (1873). Robert Preyer in *Bentham, Coleridge and the Science of History* (1958) gives a brief exposition of Coleridge's historical thought emphasizing that Coleridge escaped the deification of the state common among the Germans as he held firmly to the traditional Protestant (and English) emphasis on the freedom of the individual. Preyer shows that some of Coleridge's ideas remained alive in Julius Hare and Thomas Arnold, and, more tenuously, in the histories of George Grote and Connop Thirlwall. G. F. McFarland has devoted a well-documented paper to "Julius Charles Hare: Coleridge, De Quincey, and German Literature" (*Bulletin of the John Rylands Library*, 1964) describing Hare's relations to Coleridge and his defense of Coleridge against De Quincey's charge of plagiarism in 1835.

Everyone acknowledges the great role which Coleridge played in the revival of modern English and American criticism. T. S. Eliot quoting the passage on the reconciliation of opposites in the essay on Andrew Marvell (1921) seems to have been decisive. Later Richards' book *Coleridge on Imagination* (1934) gave a great stimulus to what can be described as the Coleridge revival. He is often regarded as the Father of the New Criticism, though Frank Lentricchia, in the *Gaiety of Language* (1968) and again in "The Place of Cleanth Brooks" (*JAAC*, 1970), correctly draws a distinction between the "contextualist" theory of the New Critics, ultimately derived from Kant, and the organic aesthetic derived from Schelling via Coleridge. Sir Herbert Read would be the closest disciple of Coleridge as G. S. Fraser points out in *Vision and Rhetoric: Studies in Modern Poetry*

(1959). Frank Kermode in the *Romantic Image* (1957) considers Coleridge the originator of the whole conception of the romantic image which he, however, considers "a great and in some ways noxious historical myth." Richard Foster, in *The New Romantics: A Reappraisal of the New Criticism* (1962), boldly considers the New Critics as disguised Romantics, coming to the conclusion that "the flight from Arnold has ended, ironically, not in the Church's but in Coleridge's bosom, redolent with the auras of laudanum and German idealism." R. S. Crane, who is very critical of the New Critics as monists, also considers Eliot, Brooks, Ransom, and Tate along with Richards as "Coleridgian" ("Two Essays in Practical Criticism," *The University Review*, 1942). M. H. Abrams, "Coleridge, Baudelaire, and Modernist Poetics" in *Immanente Ästhetik: Ästhetische Reflexion*, ed. Wolfgang Iser (1966), shows convincingly that there are radical differences between Coleridge's theories and those of the Symbolists and New Critics. Coleridge's organic vitalism, his worship of Nature as the source of joy cannot be reconciled with the anti-naturalism of Baudelaire. Though Coleridge believes in the fall of man the consequences he draws from it are entirely different from those drawn by T. E. Hulme or T. S. Eliot. Most of these discussions move on a very general level: Coleridge is simply taken as the representative for the turn of critical interest to the poetic process, to imagination and organic unity—attitudes widespread all over Western Europe, demonstrably without Coleridge's influence. Only very rarely is the relationship to Coleridge documented concretely. Murray Krieger's *The New Apologists for Poetry* (1956) has perceptive comments particularly on T. E. Hulme's relation to Coleridge.

Emerson Marks in "T. S. Eliot and the Ghost of Samuel Taylor Coleridge" (*SR*, 1964) shows the change in Eliot's attitude from his earlier (1923) calling Coleridge a "corrupter of taste" to his later sympathy for his "organic" social theories. Pasquale DiPasquale, Jr., in "Coleridge's Framework of Objectivity and Eliot's Objective Correlative" (*JAAC*, 1968), tries to establish an analogue between Coleridge's "framework of objectivity" used in 1808 in a lecture, his scattered uses of the term "correlative" and Eliot's objective correlative. But Eliot has much more obvious antecedents in Santayana and possibly Washington Allston. Incidentally, DiPasquale argues that Coleridge did not disparage plot or story and clearly distinguished between them. There is also a sketch of Coleridge's recent reputation in Kathleen Coburn's introduction to *Coleridge: A Collection of Critical Essays* (1967) but much needs further exploration and more precision.

IV
BYRON

Samuel C. Chew
Ernest J. Lovell, Jr.

I. BIBLIOGRAPHIES

The section on Byron, compiled by H. G. Pollard, in *The Cambridge Bibliography of English Literature* (1941), is still a ready guide to editions of the poet's works and to biographies and criticism.[1] It is carefully selective rather than exhaustive. A disadvantage in making use of it—inherent in the general plan of the *CBEL*—is that items are arranged, for the most part, not alphabetically but chronologically; consequently for quick reference one must know the date of the book or article sought for. The corresponding advantage is that this arrangement provides, as it were, a panoramic historical view of the course of Byron's life and achievement as estimated by successive generations of critics. The *Supplement* (London, 1957) adds a fifth volume to the original *CBEL,* follows the arrangement of the earlier volumes, attempts to be effective through 1954, lacks an index, but contains entries not to be found in the Byron section in Volume III of *The New Cambridge Bibliography of English Literature* (London, 1969), revised by H. G. Pollard. This volume follows the basically chronological arrangement of entries in the original *CBEL,* the publica-

---

[1] Only the most minor stylistic substitutions have been made in the discussions of the late Professor Samuel C. Chew, such as the change in the opening sentence above from "the readiest guide" to "still a ready guide." However, a great many sentences and paragraphs have been deleted, chiefly Chew's negative judgments of publications that contributed little to knowledge or have been now superseded. Limitations of space did not permit a survey of even the most important recent articles: my additions to Chew's chapter of 1956, itself a revision, have been confined almost wholly to book-length accounts of Byron, although a certain number of distinguished monographs, chapters, and published lectures have been noticed, along with a few articles. Chew's remarks may usually be distinguished from my own by the fact that he does not give a book's place of publication; I do. An asterisk following a book's second date of publication is used to identify a reprint of the original edition.—E. J. L., Jr.

tions of a single scholar or critic being grouped together at that point determined by the date of his earliest publication listed. Thus the arrangement is neither strictly chronological nor alphabetical. The effective terminal date for Byron entries may be set at 1963, although a few later publications are listed. There are thus some important omissions and, disturbingly, several obvious typographical errors. Volume III has its own index. The list of editions, translations, biographies, critical works, and miscellaneous Byroniana in the new *British Museum General Catalogue of Printed Books* (London, 1959–66), effective to 1955, is of course limited to the Museum's very extensive holdings. The system of cross-references is such that full information on all authors save the poet himself must be sought under the author's name; however, this massive work is of immense value and usefulness. The Byron section here supersedes that by J. P. Anderson, in the old Museum *Catalogue,* reprinted as an Appendix to Roden Noel's *Life of Byron* (1890), as well as that in the 1939 edition of the *Catalogue.* In 1968 a *Ten-Year Supplement* to the new *Catalogue* was published, listing acquisitions between 1956 and 1965, and in 1971 a *Five-Year Supplement* appeared. The student may also wish to consult the various British Museum publications listing its manuscript holdings.

E. H. Coleridge's edition of Byron's *Poetry* (see below) is rounded out with an admirable bibliography of editions of the collected Poetical Works, of individual poems and groups of poems, and of translations. Collations, though not so meticulously detailed as the collector of rare books desiderates, are sufficient to meet the requirements of the student who wishes to identify a particular edition. Coleridge's lists are not quite complete for the period before 1904, and stand in need of a supplement for the period since that date. More particularly designed for the collector is Thomas James Wise's *Bibliography of the Writings in Verse and Prose of George Gordon Noel, Baron Byron* (2 vols., privately printed, 1932–33, 1963*). Fortunately Byron did not come within the compass of Wise's notorious activities as a fabricator of "rarities"; consequently this bibliography, apart from a few omissions, is fairly reliable in so far as it covers the poet's own works; but the catalogue of Byroniana in Volume II is very incomplete, for notwithstanding Wise's arrogant assertion that it contains everything of importance, much is omitted. Covering much the same ground is the Byron section in Wise's catalogue of the *Ashley Library* (privately printed, 1922–36). The "Ashley Library," Wise's own magnificent collection, was purchased by the British Museum after his death; in the Museum *Catalogue* of 1939 items from this source are labeled

"Ashley." Another great collection, devoted wholly to Lord Byron, is that formerly in the possession of the late Herbert C. Roe of Nottingham, England, which was bequeathed by Roe to the City of Nottingham and is now appropriately housed in the poet's ancestral home, Newstead Abbey. On the occasion of the formal dedication of this library in its permanent home the Corporation of Nottingham issued an elaborate catalogue entitled *The Roe-Byron Collection, Newstead Abbey* (1937). This covers not only Byron's works in first and later editions and many original autograph manuscripts but also a large collection of Byroniana and many mementoes and other objects associated with the poet. The accompanying commentary is of some value. The Library of the University of Texas contains a rich collection of Byron rarities. On the occasion of the centenary of his death R. H. Griffith and H. M. Jones compiled *A Descriptive Catalogue of an Exhibition of Manuscripts and First Editions of Lord Byron Held [at] the University of Texas* (1924). Consult also Willis W. Pratt's compilations, *Lord Byron and His Circle: A Calendar of Manuscripts in the University of Texas Library* (1947) and "Lord Byron and His Circle: Recent Manuscript Acquisitions" (*Library Chronicle of the Univ. of Texas,* 1956). The hundred and fiftieth anniversary of the poet's birth was celebrated at the Henry E. Huntington Library with an exhibition which is recorded by Ricardo Quintana in *Byron: 1788–1938* (1938), an attractive little brochure. The largest list of English Byroniana, with "a representative selection from the Byroniana of other countries," is in Samuel C. Chew's *Byron in England: His Fame and After-Fame* (1924, 1965*). This list could be much amplified, for though little of any consequence is omitted of English authorship, the foreign items, which were restricted in number for reasons of space, stand in need of considerable expansion. A valuable supplement to more formal bibliographical aids, recording moreover a few items of excessive rarity omitted from one or another of the compilations already mentioned, is *Byron and Byroniana: A Catalogue of Books* (1930). This was issued by a scholarly London bookseller, Elkin Mathews. The studious attention for long devoted to Byron in Germany resulted in the assembling of fine collections in various public and university libraries. One such has been separately catalogued in a work of composite authorship: *Byroniana und Anderes aus dem englishchen Seminar in Erlangen* (1912). A brief, selective, annotated bibliography, useful to the student beginning the subject, is that in Ernest Bernbaum's *Guide through the Romantic Movement* (1930; 2nd ed., 1949).

More recently, in 1952, Ernest Bernbaum's bibliographical article on

"Keats, Shelley, Byron, and Hunt: A Critical Sketch of Important Books and Articles Concerning Them Published in 1940–1950," four pages of which are given to Byron, appeared in the *Keats-Shelley Journal*. In the same year Leslie A. Marchand's "Recent Byron Scholarship" was published in *English Miscellany*. An expanded and updated version of Marchand's article was included in *Essays in Literary History Presented to J. Milton French,* ed. Rudolph Kirk and C. F. Main (New Brunswick, N.J., 1960). It is effective through 1957, although two publications of a later date are discussed. Willis W. Pratt's discussion of "A Decade of Byron Scholarship: 1946–1956, A Selective Survey" (*KSJ,* 1958) is equally valuable and tries to avoid retreading the ground covered by Bernbaum and by Marchand in his earlier article. All these essays may be enthusiastically recommended. Ian Jack's selective and annotated bibliography, which includes first editions of Byron as well as modern studies, appears in his *English Literature 1815–1832* (Oxford, 1963) and is effective through 1960, although a few titles of later date are included. Richard Harter Fogle's Goldentree Bibliography of *Romantic Poets and Prose Writers* (New York, 1967), "intended for graduate and advanced undergraduate students," although not annotated, has an excellent section on Byron which possesses the advantage of listing critical discussions under the names of Byron's individual poems. Of the approximately 130 titles in the current edition, seven were published later than 1963. Fogle also lists such annual bibliographies as "The Romantic Movement: A Selective and Critical Bibliography," *ELH* (1937–49), *PQ* (1950–64), *ELN* (since 1965); and those which appear in *YWES* (since 1919), *PMLA* (since 1922), and *KSJ* (since 1952). The latter is especially valuable because it lists reviews of books, as does *ELN*.

Selected or specialized bibliographies appear in many of the larger volumes or works discussed below. Particularly recommended are those by Ernest J. Lovell, Jr., *His Very Self and Voice: Collected Conversations of Lord Byron* (New York, 1954); Robert Escarpit, *Lord Byron: Un Tempérament littéraire* (Paris, 1957); Leslie A. Marchand, *Byron: A Biography* (New York, 1957); Peter L. Thorslev, *The Byronic Hero: Types and Prototypes* (Minneapolis, Minn., 1962); M. K. Joseph, *Byron the Poet* (London, 1964); Leslie A. Marchand, *Byron's Poetry: A Critical Introduction* (Boston, 1965); and Truman Guy Steffan's edition of *Cain* (Austin, Texas, 1968). The second edition of Steffan's and Willis W. Pratt's variorum *Don Juan* (Austin, Texas, 1971) contains a bibliographical "Appendix: *Don Juan* in the Sixties," as well as the earlier "Survey of Commentary on *Don Juan,*" both by Pratt. Not yet published except in

Dissertation Abstracts, 29 (1969), 2227A (Baylor), is Oscar J. Santucho's "A Comprehensive Bibliography of Secondary Materials in English: George Gordon, Lord Byron."

II. EDITIONS AND SELECTIONS

The standard edition is that published by John Murray (1898–1904, 1966*), the *Poetry* in seven volumes edited by Ernest Hartley Coleridge, and the *Letters and Journals* in six volumes edited by Rowland E. Prothero (afterwards Lord Ernle). This superseded the edition of 1832–33, which was the only one of earlier date with claims to be considered "definitive." Coleridge was not able to enlarge considerably the corpus of Byron's poetry; the only notable item now published for the first time was the fragmentary beginning of the seventeenth canto of *Don Juan.* But a feature of immense value in Coleridge's work was the recording for the first time of a great number of *variae lectiones* existing in the manuscripts (for the most part in the collection of John Murray, the grandson of Byron's publisher). The most important editorial problem was that of punctuation; and here Coleridge, inexplicably, followed the texts in the edition of 1831 instead of those in the edition of 1832–33, which are undoubtedly better. Coleridge's elaborate annotation is always interesting and informative and sometimes brilliant, but occasionally somewhat erratic and disproportionate to the significance of the subject. The editor of the *Letters and Journals* had an even more rewarding task than that of the editor of the *Poetry,* for Prothero had access to many letters and some other documents which had never hitherto seen the light, and in many other cases was able to give the complete texts of letters which had been printed only in part by Thomas Moore in the *Letters and Journals of Lord Byron, with Notices of His Life* (1830). A large number of documents supplementary to the correspondence and diaries may be found in Prothero's appendices: the texts of Byron's parliamentary speeches; the texts in the controversy with William L. Bowles on the merits of Pope's poetry; the texts on both sides of the quarrel with Robert Southey; and much other valuable material. The texts of the letters are not always reliable (for many are from printed sources), but Prothero's notes are full, accurate, and entertaining, in fact a model of what such editorial apparatus should be.

A few letters ascribed to Byron were rejected by Prothero because he doubted their authenticy, and a great many were not included by him because they were inaccessible. Of such some were first published in the Earl of Lovelace's *Astarte* (1905); others in the revised edition, by the Countess of Lovelace, of that work (1921); and many more in *Lord Byron's Correspondence* (2 vols., 1922). These publications are discussed below. Frequently other letters which were unknown to Prothero turn up in a bookseller's catalogue or elsewhere; one such, for example, is printed in *The Nation* (N.Y.), CVI (1918). Three hitherto unprinted letters of Byron have been published by David B. Green (*KSJ*, 1956). Scores of Byron's letters that have been quoted in sales catalogues are not in any public collection and have disappeared from view.

The Marchesa Iris Origo's *Byron: The Last Attachment* (1949, 1962*) contains the text of 156 letters and notes written by Byron to Teresa Guiccioli as well as much other new material from the Gamba papers, other Italian sources, the Murray archives, the Pierpont Morgan Library, and elsewhere. On the basis of these hitherto unpublished documents the Marchesa has told the whole story of Byron and La Guiccioli. Translations of the letters and other documents are woven into her narrative (which is in English), and the complete Italian text of the letters is given in an appendix. This work enriches greatly our knowledge of Byron's life in Italian society and of his relations with conspiratorial patriots; and its publication was an event of major importance in the history of Byron studies. For an estimate by Samuel C. Chew see the New York *Herald Tribune Book Review*, 6 November 1949. Supplementary to the Marchesa Origo's work with regard to one personal association is Leslie A. Marchand's article "Lord Byron and Count Alborghetti" (*PMLA*, 1949).

Byron: A Self-Portrait, edited by Peter Quennell (2 vols., 1950), a selection from his letters with the complete text of his diaries and "Detached Thoughts," draws its material from the archives of John Murray and from other collections, private or public, in England or America. The editor's prefatory statement that fifty-six letters are here published for the first time requires correction. In a footnote he makes the correction himself with regard to two letters which appear in the Marchesa Origo's book; but several others are to be found in Prothero's edition of the *Letters and Journals.* Quennell notes also that one of his "new" letters is a forgery; there are reasons to believe that another is also a forgery. In about a score of cases the texts are taken from inaccurate printed sources, though the original manuscripts are accessible. There are numerous errors in transcription. See further the notices of Quennell's book by Leslie A. Marchand in the *New York Times Review of Books,* 4 June 1950, and by Samuel C. Chew in the New York *Herald Tribune Book Review,* 16 April 1950.

Of the numerous one-volume editions of the *Poems,* three only need be singled out for mention: those published by John Murray, by Houghton Mifflin (in the "Cambridge Poets"), and by the Oxford University Press. The advantage of the first of these is that it contains a small amount of material still under copyright. The second named has a valuable introduction by its editor, Paul Elmer More. The chief differences among the three are to be found in matters of punctuation and capitalization. In particular, More discarded the old declamatory pointing in favor of a modern system as strictly grammatical as possible. Samuel Chew preferred the older style as more characteristic of Byron and of his period. (On More's "valuable introduction," see K. B. Newell's "Paul Elmer More on Byron," *KSJ,* XII, 1963.)

One of the most important events in the world of Byron scholarship during the 1950's was the appearance of *Byron's "Don Juan," A Variorum Edition,* edited by Truman Guy Steffan and Willis W. Pratt (Austin, Texas, 1957). Although there is important textual information in it, the introductory volume, *Byron's "Don Juan," The Making of a Masterpiece,* by Steffan, is discussed with other critical studies in Part IV of this essay. Using the first edition as the basis of their text, which comprises Volumes II and III, the editors have printed immediately below each stanza all the available variants. These were drawn chiefly from "sixteen first drafts, one for each canto; several first draft fragments; the first draft of the unfinished seventeenth canto; and fair copies of the first eight cantos." In addition, the first edition was collated with five later editions. It is thus now possible to examine Byron's thousands of deletions, additions, and revisions. In the text established, each line or phrase annotated in the fourth volume, *Byron's "Don Juan," Notes on the Variorum Edition,* by Pratt, is marked conveniently with an asterisk. The quantity and variety of these notes reflect the various splendor of the poem itself, as it reaches out into all phases of existence in the early nineteenth century—political, literary, scientific, and artistic—displaying fully the varied panorama of the life and culture of the time. The second edition contains numerous corrections and additions. The extent of these changes is suggested by the fact that the index has been largely reset. This text, with modernized spelling and capitalization, will also be published in the Penguin series with selected variants and notes by Steffan and Pratt. The critical essays accompanying Steffan's massive edition of *Cain* (Austin, Texas, 1968) are discussed below, with other critical works. The text, based on a manuscript at The University of Texas at Austin, has been collated with seven editions and differs from the text of earlier editions chiefly in the use of capitalization, punctuation, and italics. "There are a few deviations in words from the 1821 text," the editor states, and at such points he has used the manuscript version. Variants are recorded in the notes. The manuscript, in Byron's hand, appears to be the one sent to Murray, who probably had a press copy made from it. More recently, Leslie A. Marchand has discovered in Athens six hitherto unpublished stanzas by Byron, in ottava rima, presumably written in Venice in 1819 (*The Griffon* of the Gennadius Library, Summer 1970); but these are less interesting than the witty mock review of Rosa Matilda's epic on the Prince Regent (including forty lines of supposedly quoted verse, in rhymed couplets) which David V. Erdman attributed to Byron in the *Keats-Shelley Journal,* 1970.

The Byronic world eagerly awaits the appearance of a new edition of the complete poems and plays, now being prepared by Jerome J. McGann for the Oxford English Texts series. The editor's principal purposes are, first, to remove the numerous and quite often serious textual corruptions; second, to set more accurate limits upon the actual corpus. A few poems will be dropped, but more than fifty new poems will be added to the canon. These poems have either never been published or have never been collected in the definitive editions. Ancillary purposes will be a complete apparatus, excluding only indifferent readings of various sorts; a coherent accidental system based upon the evidence of the contemporary editions; and a list, as complete as possible, of all extant manuscripts and their location. The edition will have a commentary of the kind usually found in the OET series.

Two of these editions have been made more useful by the recent appearance of two concordances. Ione Dodson Young's *Concordance to the Poetry of Byron* (Austin, 1965) is based upon the Cambridge Edition of P. E. More (Boston, 1905). *A Concordance to Byron's "Don Juan,"* edited by Charles W. Hagelman, Jr., and Robert J. Barnes (Ithaca, N.Y., 1967), uses the *Variorum* edition of the poem and refers to sixteen rejected stanzas and 634 complete-line variant readings.

There are, it is almost unnecessary to remark, more volumes of Selections than can be here enumerated. Two of the older books still possess not only antiquarian interest but a place of their own in the history of English literature. One of these is *A Selection from the Works of Lord Byron* (1866) which was compiled by Algernon Charles Swinburne and contains the eloquent preface that is reprinted in Swinburne's *Essays and Studies* (1875). The other is *Poetry of Byron* (1881), chosen and edited by Matthew Arnold; its celebrated preface, which occasioned much controversy, is reprinted in Arnold's *Essays in Criticism, Second Series* (1888). Of similar anthologies of later date several may be named. *Poems of Lord Byron* (1923), selected and arranged by H. J. C. (later Sir Herbert) Grierson, contains a preface in which Byron is interpreted (not very originally) as the poet of "actuality" and the distinction is drawn (as by various other writers) between Byron and "Byronism." *The Best of Byron* (1933) is tastefully selected and competently introduced and edited by Richard A. Rice. In the Odyssey Press Series in Literature (originally the Doubleday-Doran Series in Literature) two volumes are devoted to Byron; as evidence of the range of his achievement it is worth remarking that no other poet, save Milton, is represented by more than one volume. *Don Juan and Other Satiric Poems* (1935) is edited by Louis I. Bredvold; *Childe Harold's Pilgrimage and Other Romantic Poems* (1936) by Samuel C. Chew. These two books are provided with introductions, bibliographies, and extensive notes. More recently, there have been other selections from the complete works edited by Roy Fuller, *Byron for Today* (London, 1948); E. E. Bostetter, *Byron: Selected Poetry and Letters* (New York, 1951); Leslie A. Marchand, *Selected Poetry* (New York, 1954) and *Don Juan* (Boston, 1958); Peter Quennell, *Byronic Thoughts: Maxims, Reflections, Portraits from the Prose and Verse of Lord Byron* (New York, 1961); W. H. Auden, *The Selected Poetry and Prose of Byron* (New York, 1966); and William H. Marshall, *Byron: Selected Poems and Letters* (Boston, 1968), a selection of generous proportions and variety, with introduction, notes, and bibliography, but omitting *Don Juan*.

Supplementary to Prothero, as was remarked above, are the two volumes of *Lord Byron's Correspondence* (1922), edited by John Murray with the assistance of Lord Ernle and Richard Edgcumbe. Those who have examined the manuscripts of these letters deplore the carelessness of the editorial work. There are omissions without indications, and other liberties, including actual bowdlerizing, are taken with the manuscripts. The letters fall roughly into three categories, representing three phases of the poet's life: those from Greece between 1809 and 1811 (of quite secondary interest); those, chiefly addressed to Lady Melbourne, written during the "years of notoriety," 1811–16, of utmost consequence because in the opinion of most biographers and critics they furnish the proof of the validity of the charges brought against Byron by Lord Lovelace; and those, to and from Byron, written in Italy after his final departure from England. In this last category are some of the poet's most brilliant letters. There are also letters from Shelley and Mrs. Shelley. For a detailed estimate by Samuel Chew of the significance and value of the *Correspondence* reference may be made to a review in *The Nation* (N.Y.), 12 April 1922.

A good anthology, affording a short cut to the student who is not a specialist and may not have time to master the entire immense corpus, is *Lord Byron in His Letters* (1927), edited by V. H. Collins. The selection is excellent, the introduction informative, and passages from the journals are also included. A somewhat similar compilation is *Letters of Lord Byron* (1933; rev. ed. 1962) selected by R. G. Howarth. This contains an introduction by André Maurois. *The Selected Letters of Lord Byron,* edited by Jacques Barzun (New York, 1953, 1957*), has an excellent introduction. Elizabeth Drew discusses the poet's letters in *The Literature of Gossip: Nine English Letterwriters* (New York, 1964).

Very much needed is a definitive edition of all Byron's letters in which the material now dispersed through Prothero, *Astarte,* the *Correspondence, The Last Attachment, The Late Lord Byron, Lord Byron's Wife,* and elsewhere shall be brought together in chronological order, with an authoritative text (so far as possible), editorial apparatus, and a commentary in accordance with modern standards of scholarly practice. This work has been undertaken by Leslie A. Marchand, author of the distinguished three-volume *Byron: A Biography* (New York, 1957), who has a contract with John Murray in England and Harvard University Press in the United States to compile an edition of all the letters, published and unpublished, that can be assembled. Mr. Marchand has a check list in excess of 2,700 letters, 1,500 more, startlingly, than appear in the Prothero edition, the last attempt at a collected edition. Marchand is now engaged in gathering copies of manuscript letters here and abroad, and would appreciate hearing from anyone who knows of Byron a.l.s.'s in private or little-known library collections. He estimates that the edition will include about 200 letters hitherto unpublished and 400–500 published earlier with errors or bowdlerizations. The first two volumes of this projected work of eight volumes should appear in 1972 or 1973.

III. BIOGRAPHIES

To separate the study of Byron's work from that of his character and career is difficult—perhaps impossible; it has, in fact, often been remarked that moral judgments of the man and criticism of the poetry have been persistently fused and confused. Most biographies contain a certain amount of literary criticism; and there are few works of literary criticism before 1950 (other than studies of special topics) that are wholly divorced from consideration of the man behind the work.

No biography of Byron was ever "authorized" by his surviving relatives. The nearest approach to an "official" *Life* was the series of "Notices" which Thomas Moore interwove with the letters and journals published in 1830. Modern biographers must take their start from Lord Lovelace's *Astarte, A Fragment of Truth concerning . . . Lord Byron* (privately printed, 1905). In his famous but so nearly unreadable book— unreadable because the "fragment of truth" is so thickly swathed in inappropriate erudition, unnecessary digression, and angry prejudice—the poet's grandson revived the charge of incest which Harriet Beecher Stowe had made against Byron and Augusta Leigh, and buttressed this accusation with new documentary evidence. The new edition of *Astarte,* which Lady Lovelace issued in 1921, is an improvement upon the original slovenly and pretentious book. Passages not germane to the subject were omitted and thirty-four hitherto unpublished letters of Byron (thirty-one to his sister, three to his wife) were added. Lord Ernle was convinced that the Lovelaces had established their case; see his article, "The End of the Byron Mystery," in *The Nineteenth Century and After* (1921). (More recently, Frederick L. Beaty has suggested an identification in Canto i, *Don Juan,* of Augusta Leigh with Julia and of Byron with Juan. See "Byron and the Story of Francesca da Rimini," *PMLA,* 1960.)

It was obvious that the many biographies published during the nineteenth century were all incomplete and some of them badly distorted, and that the way was open for a new full-length narrative of the poet's entire life. In 1912 Ethel C. Mayne published her *Byron,* a biography composed upon an ample scale and the work of a serious, conscientious, and judicious writer. Mrs. Mayne was the first biographer to accept the evidence in *Astarte* as establishing the charge of incest. Throughout her long book she displays a fine and discriminating insight into her subject's character, in its strength as well as in its weakness. What holds her attention, and the attention of her readers, is Byron's "enthralling humanity." There is candor and tolerance and, on the whole, sympathy in her delineation and analysis. Mrs. Mayne does not wholly divorce the narrative of Byron's life from comment upon his poetry; and the incidental literary criticism, though somewhat impressionistic and occasionally naïve, is generally acute. In 1924 she abridged her original two volumes into one and revised the work in the light of the new evidence in the *Correspondence.* Use was now also made of fresh material in the Countess of Airlie's *In Whig Society, 1775–1818* (1921), a collection of hitherto unpublished letters from members of the Holland House circle in which Byron moved. Mrs. Mayne altered her earlier judgment in several important particulars—for example, on the character of Edward John Trelawny and on the old charge against Byron of having suppressed Mrs. Shelley's letter to Mrs. Hoppner. This revised edition, timed in appearance to coincide with the centenary, is still on the whole a satisfactory life of Byron. It must be said, however, that Mrs. Mayne's documentation is inadequate and her chronology loose and vague; and students may be repelled by her too gushing style and sentimental tone.

Another centennial publication, Harold Nicolson's *Byron: The Last Journey: 1823–1824* (1924), was obviously written under the influence of Lytton Strachey and belongs to the "depedestalizing" school of biography which was the mode of the nineteen-twenties. This literary affiliation is apparent not only in the cold brilliance of the style but in a detached objectivity that is distrustful of all sentiment. Yet the narrative, which in its initial stages resembles a cynical comedy of society, gradually changes in tone as Byron's bearing and conduct during "the last phase" win the sympathy and even the admiration of this cautious, clever skeptic. Whatever the intentions with which Nicolson began his story, there is very little distortion in the picture. The abundant contemporary testimony as to the events in Cephalonia and at Missolonghi is carefully weighed. Literary criticism scarcely comes within this biographer's range, since, apart from the famous lines written on his birthday in 1824, Byron almost entirely abandoned the writing of verse during his last months in Greece. To a new edition (1940) Nicolson added a supplementary chapter in which he summarized Hobhouse's marginalia in a copy of Moore's *Byron.* This material had already been used by Quennell and Maurois (see below).

Yet another biography called forth by the centenary is J. D. Symon's

Byron in Perspective (1924)—in distorted perspective, one is constrained to remark, for there is a disproportionate emphasis upon the poet's childhood in Aberdeen and upon the influence of this early Scottish environment on his imagination and poetry. This emphasis was in part due to the fact that Symon was himself a Scot and in part to the opportunity to make use of a small amount of hitherto unpublished documentary material in the Library of the University of Aberdeen, which sheds some light upon the troubles which Byron's mother experienced with her wayward husband and upon her financial strains and stresses. The narrative is conducted in a fairly adequate way till April 1816; but after Byron's final departure from England it proceeds in a very hit-or-miss fashion. One may note a curiously misplaced sketch of the "fluctuations" in the poet's fame; a desultory chapter on *Don Juan* with some discussion of the elements of comedy and burlesque in his poetry; and an account of the expedition to Greece which needs some modification in the light of Nicolson's narrative. Here it may be remarked that the Scottish influence which Symon emphasizes is proclaimed as a new discovery, argued for, and exaggerated in T. S. Eliot's essay on Byron in *From Anne to Victoria,* edited by Bonamy Dobrée (1937). It may be further noted that the most striking illustration of this influence is to be found in Byron's love of, and intimate acquaintance with, the ballads of the Border country. These he constantly quotes and echoes and occasionally imitates. The indebtedness has been exhaustively investigated by A. P. Hudson in an article on "Byron and the Ballad" (*SP,* 1945).

Sir John C. Fox, whose father had come to the defense of Mrs. Stowe in 1869 and who therefore came by inheritance to his interest in the "problem," chose the centenary year to publish *The Byron Mystery* (1924). Here the case is reviewed by a mind trained in the law of evidence, and the verdict of guilty is handed down against Byron and Augusta Leigh. This little book should have settled the question once for all, but it did not. In passing it may be noted that Fox corrects on several points of detail the account of the Stowe "revelations" given in *Byron in England.*

When John Drinkwater undertook to tell the story of Byron's life and to delineate and analyze his character he brought to his task the intuitive sympathy of a poet and dramatist and the experience of a critic of poetry. *The Pilgrim of Eternity: Byron—A Conflict* (1925) is based upon original sources of information and contains admirable characterizations of each original informant—Hobhouse, Shelley, Dallas, Moore, Hunt, Lady Blessington, Galt, and Trelawny, and the other companions of Byron in Greece who after his death rendered accounts of their experiences. It must be said, however, that when their testimony does not harmonize with Drinkwater's conception of the poet's character (for example, when Shelley writes of his debauchery at Venice, or Hunt of his behavior at Pisa, or Lady Blessington of his appearance and mood at Genoa, or Trelawny of his conduct of the Greek expedition) it is often dismissed as prejudiced or incredible. At each such point in the narrative Drinkwater makes out a plausible case against the witness, but not without exhibiting his own bias. Drinkwater confronts the Byron "problem" in his opening chapter and essays a refutation of *Astarte,* at any rate to the degree of demanding the "Scotch verdict" of "not proven." The fact is that Drinkwater was himself so "normal" a man that he did not firmly grasp the problem of abnormality. Doomed from the first to failure, or at best to inconclusiveness, was the task of portraying Byron as a normal personality while leaving in suspense the problem of abnormal guilt. As part of a determination—understandable and perhaps praiseworthy—to avoid the sentimental and sensational, Drinkwater presents a portrait of the poet as favorable as any possible interpretation of the records permits. Much attention is necessarily devoted to the subject of Byron's relations with women, but the treatment is serious and restrained. The taint of vulgarity in his character and poetry is admitted, but it is denied that there is affectation in the Byronic melancholy. The settings of the narrative, both in England and on the Continent, are excellently arranged; and against these varied backgrounds Byron's friends, acquaintances, and enemies move with convincing vitality. But the great value of this biography is found in the firm integration of Byron's character and career with his achievement as a poet. Critical judgments of the poems are incidental to the principal narrative purpose of the work; but (with exceptions to be noted presently) they are felicitous, sensitive, and authoritative, the pronouncements of one who was himself a poet and wrote with dignity and understanding. These comments center upon the range and mass of Byron's achievement and upon his energy. There is perhaps a tendency to set too high a value upon the historical tragedies, *Marino Faliero, The Two Foscari,* and *Sardanapalus;* but this is what one would expect from a writer who had himself won conspicuous success in this department of drama. Conversely, the significance of *Cain* is not completely brought out, and *Manfred,* notwithstanding its implicit importance as in part autobiographical, is almost entirely ignored. This violation of proper proportion is probably due to Drinkwater's hostility to the distortions and exaggerations of extreme "Byronism." Altogether, this is a richer and more rewarding biography than Mrs. Mayne's; there is more of "saturation ' in the subject. But its value is lessened, because of the irremediable flaw that the central motive of the entire story is misinterpreted.

Albert Brecknock's *Byron: A Study . . . in the Light of New Discoveries* (1926) is by a resident of Nottingham who writes informatively on the topography of the Byron country. He had long since issued a smaller work, *The Pilgrim Poet: Lord Byron of Newstead* (1911), which has still some small value for its excellent illustrations. What the "new discoveries" were which impelled him to return to the subject is not apparent. His book is superficial and injudicious, a mere piece of hero-worship.

During these years a scholar thoroughly trained in the rigorous methods of the German seminars was preparing yet another full-length biographical and critical study. Helene Richter's *Lord Byron: Persönlichkeit und Werk* (1929) is one of the most reliable and authoritative of all books on the subject, superseding such earlier German biographies as Karl Elze's and rivaling the best that have been produced in England. With an almost unique dispassionateness and objectivity the author seeks to disentangle the truth from the web of conflicting, prejudiced partisanship and to present it with calm impartiality. In tone it somewhat resembles Mrs. Mayne's work, if one discounts a certain Teutonic heaviness in style and method. But as a work of literary criticism it handles thoroughly and effectively a part of Byron scholarship which Mrs. Mayne had touched very lightly. Richter makes much of the conflicting elements of classicism and romanticism in Byron's character, tastes, and writings, a dichotomy which she had already studied in an article, "Byron, Klassizismus und Romantik" (*Anglia,* 1924), and which, as we shall see, was at a later date to be the central theme of a volume by an American scholar. In the skillful weaving together of a narrative of the poet's life, an analysis of his character, and an estimate of his work lies the value of this fine biography. An English translation is long overdue.

By a somewhat odd coincidence no less than three French writers were about this time engaged upon the study of Byron. No three compatriots could be less like one another than were Charles Du Bos, André Maurois, and Maurice Castelain, and their books reflect the dissimilarity.

Charles Du Bos has been called by Edith Wharton "the biographer of Byron"—as though *par excellence.* His *Byron et le besoin de la fatalité* (1929, rev. ed. 1956) is certainly to be classified among biographies rather than critical studies devoted primarily to the poetry, but actually Du Bos, in the preface to his book, disclaims any intention to write either. His object, he says, is "exclusivement psychologique, et même . . . serait-il plus exact de dire: zoologique, car ce qui me requiert, ce n'est point la *psyché,* mais *l'espèce:* Byron est à mes yeux avant tout un animal humain de la grande espèce." Du Bos had the advantage of being half-English, with a perfect command of his mother's tongue. He possessed also what some people may consider the disadvantage of being an intense admirer of Henry James and a friend of Mrs. Wharton. His concern is to probe the secret workings of the conscience and to extract the ultimate drop of significance from every situation. His method involves sinuosities and complexities of style with— and in this he constantly reminds one of Henry James—a deliberate avoidance of simplification and as deliberate a choice of involution and abstruseness. The result is a difficult, subtle, sometimes profound, and never altogether convincing study of Byron as *l'homme fatal.* Much is made of the delineations of the "Byronic hero," most notably in the portrait— which Du Bos holds to be a self-portrait—of Lara. Disregarding the rationalistic, critical, and satiric side of Byron's nature Du Bos emphasizes the element of predestinarianism inherited from the Calvinism which Byron tried to reject but could not wholly rid himself of. The chief concern is to explore the condition of mind which impelled Byron to write poetry in order to cleanse his bosom of perilous stuff. The work was originally a series of lectures delivered to a group of intellectuals who were much occupied with psychoanalytic theory. To say this serves as an explanation— and a warning. The style is as abstruse as the thought; and many students may prefer to acquaint themselves with the book in Mrs. Mayne's competent English version, *Byron and the Need of Fatality* (1932).

André Maurois published his *Byron* in 1930, and an English translation by Hamish Miles appeared in the same year (rpt. 1964). It is on an ampler scale and is a more serious piece of work than the same author's better known *Ariel ou la vie de Shelley.* Unlike that work, it is not "fictionized" biography; but though elaborately documented and making use of a small amount of hitherto unpublished information it must be used with caution. For the sake of dramatic effect liberties are occasionally taken with chronology. Subjects of importance are passed over with the easiest unconcern, for no better reason, it would seem, than that their introduction would have occasioned digressions interrupting the lucid flow of the narrative. For example, we hear nothing whatsoever of the quarrel with Robert Southey; and *The Vision of Judgment,* the finest though not the grandest flowering of Byron's genius as a satirist, is not so much as mentioned. Maurois' psychology is of course sharp and clever, but he seldom sees beneath the surface of character. To read him after reading Du Bos is to turn from a river, turgid but deep, to a shallow, sparkling brook. He has an eye for the comedy of human situations but little sense of pathos and none of tragedy. Byron's moral delinquencies are neither ignored nor deplored but are treated with Gallic wit as part of the human comedy. This point of view is of value as a corrective to the usual over-emphasis upon the poet's moral turpitude and as a recognition of standards of conduct tolerated in Regency society. Into a revised version of the French (but not the English) text Maurois inserted some entertaining or sensational matter from the Marchesa Origo's book and from Quennell's collection of letters. Supplementary to this biography is Maurois' *Byron et les femmes* (1934).

On a smaller scale, not so rich in the detail of personalities and not so amusing but more critical and trustworthy, is Maurice Castelain's *Byron* (n.d., 1930), which is one of the best brief biographies. It has not been translated into English.

Peter C. Quennell's *Byron: The Years of Fame* (1935, 1954*) was followed by *Byron in Italy* (1941, 1957*). The first installment—reprinted in 1954 as a Penguin Book—takes its title from Byron's life in London during the four years between the appearance of *Childe Harold* in March 1812 and his final departure from England in April 1816. It is, one ventures to remark, misnamed, for these were the years of notoriety rather than of the substantial and lasting fame which grew to European proportions during his remaining eight years on the Continent. Quennell begins with the morning upon which Byron awoke and found himself famous, the narrative folding back to embrace the years of childhood and immaturity. Into the well-worn story a small amount of new material is inserted. Quennell had access to John Cam Hobhouse's copy of Thomas Moore's biography (that is, the edition of the letters and journals, with "Notices" of the poet's life); but, judging from the excerpts from Hobhouse's marginalia which he quotes, the comments of this closest friend are not very significant save for the support they give to the suspicion (for which there are other grounds) that there was an element of homosexuality in Byron's complex nature. From the Byron archives in Murray's publishing house in Albemarle Street Quennell was permitted to select and print some specimens of the "fan mail" which Byron received during these years. They reveal nothing that we did not know, or at any rate have reason to suspect, about his life during the years when he was the spoiled darling of the fashionable West End and the idol of the vast middle class. In an interesting but very debatable digression Quennell argues that in the latter circle of readers Byron was responsible for the taste for shoddy, flashy, and sensational verse which was in turn responsible for the ugly and grotesque exoticisms of Victorianism. It is difficult to reconcile this opinion with the fact that the decline of the Byronic vogue about the middle of the century coincided with the triumph of Victorian vulgarity and pretentiousness. Quennell has really very little that is new to relate. The setting is vivid; the narrative sparkling; and the "psychology" clearcut though not very original or profound. But little critical insight into the poetry is evidenced; in fact, in his first volume Quennell elected to tell the story of Byron's years of notoriety with the primary cause of that notoriety—*Childe Harold,* the Oriental Tales, and other poems—almost wholly left out of consideration. In the second installment there is a somewhat better adjustment of values, but even so the poetry is often lost sight of in the picturesqueness of Byron's personality. Supplementary to this work is *To Lord Byron: Feminine Profiles* (1939), which Quennell edited in collaboration with "George Paston" (Emily M. Symonds). This is a selection of letters from the Murray archives, addressed to the poet by thirteen women associated with him. There is an accompanying commentary. R. Glynn Grylls (Lady Mander), in *Claire Clairmont, Mother of Byron's Allegra* (1939), made use of hitherto unpublished passages in Miss Clairmont's journal and of other fresh material. In manner, though not in substance, the narrative is, unfortunately, "fictionized." The episode of the unhappy affair with Byron is the high point in the story; but this is a biography of Claire, and it contains much that is not immediately pertinent to the study of Byron. Grylls is also the author of biographies of Mary Shelley (1938) and of Trelawny (1950), both of which deal significantly with Byron.

Austin K. Gray's *Teresa or Her Demon Lover* (1945) deserves no more than bare mention. This narrative of Byron and the Countess Guiccioli is not "fictionized," but it is vulgarized in a fashion of which the flashy title gives an indication. Yet Gray was a good scholar and his book is based upon careful research, though, like Quennell, he did not have access to the Gamba papers. In the English edition (1948) the title is changed to *Teresa: The Story of Byron's Last Mistress.*

Several monographs illuminate to a greater or less degree one or another period or episode in the poet's life. In *Byron at Southwell: The Making of a Poet* (1948) Willis W. Pratt worked, so far as fresh material is concerned, within the limitations of the manuscripts in the Library of the University of Texas, but though the monograph is in large part a repetition of familiar facts regarding Byron's holidays from Harrow and Cambridge there are some hitherto unpublished verse and a number of new letters, including a series to William Harness which had previously been printed in garbled form by Prothero.

William A. Borst's *Lord Byron's First Pilgrimage* (1948) enlarges our understanding of the first two cantos of *Childe Harold* by placing the poem in the context of records of contemporary travel in the Iberian Peninsula, the Mediterranean, and the Near East. The beginnings of Byron's cosmopolitanism—his reaction from British insularity—and of his sympathy with the aspirations of the Greeks for independence are carefully traced.

On the love-affair with Lady Caroline Lamb some fresh light is shed in two books not primarily about Byron. Lord David Cecil in *The Young Melbourne* (1939) devotes a chapter to the liaison, drawing fresh material from hitherto unpublished family papers. Michael Joyce, in *My Friend H: John Cam Hobhouse* (1948), makes use of some letters from Hobhouse to Byron in the Murray archives and also of some hitherto unpublished portions of Hobhouse's diary. From the latter source comes a full narrative of how Hobhouse prevented the poet from eloping with Lady Caroline.

Without altering in essentials a familiar story, C. L. Cline, in his *Byron, Shelley, and Their Pisan Circle* (1952), has filled in gaps in our knowledge and has placed this new information against the background of Byron's life in Tuscany. Patient research in the public archives of Pisa, Lucca, and Florence has been rewarded by the discovery of letters addressed by Byron to the Chargé d'Affaires of the British Legation in Florence and of various manuscripts of John Taaffe's. We now know more about Byron's friendship with Taaffe and about the fracas with the dragoon. Cline's book is careful in scholarship and is a valuable supplement to other biographies. See also *Shelley and Byron in Pisa* (Turin, 1961), by Vera Cacciatore, the curator of the Keats-Shelley Memorial House in Rome.

For other details of the Pisan sojourn one may turn to the *Journal* of Edward E. Williams, edited by Frederick L. Jones (1951). This complete text is printed from the manuscript in the British Museum and supersedes Richard Garnett's abridgement of 1902. It makes apparent that the friendship between Byron and Williams was closer than used to be assumed. Jones's editions of Mary Shelley's *Letters* (1944), her *Journal* (1947), and Shelley's *Letters* (1964) contain, it is almost needless to say, much matter of significance to the student of Byron.

On the periphery of biographies is *Lord Byron: Christian Virtues* (1952) by G. Wilson Knight. With the possible exception of Teresa

Guiccioli's *Recollections of Lord Byron* (a record which Knight admires whole-heartedly and in which he places entire trust) it is safe to say that no other book has ever been written so extravagant in its praise of our poet. Beginning with the assertion that in his opinion Byron is "our greatest poet in the widest sense of the term since Shakespeare," before the close Knight has more than once hinted at an analogy between Byron and his companions in Greece and Christ and His disciples. The work is a sort of anthology of passages from Byron's poems, letters, and journals and from the testimony of those who knew him, set forth with comment and interpretation. Evidence is assembled of the poet's love of animals, his courage, benevolence, asceticism, self-discipline, humility, endurance, energy, courtesy, tact, forgiveness of wrongs, gratitude, unselfishness, tenderness, sweetness of disposition, hatred of tyranny and oppression, opposition to war save in the cause of freedom, qualities of statesmanship and leadership. Byron is a "superman," a Socrates, a St. Paul, a Zarathustra, a Gandhi, a Messiah; he is "Shakespearean drama personified"; he is "poetry incarnate." There is no tampering with the evidence that is quoted and very little special pleading from the evidence. Yet obviously something is wrong. It is disconcerting but necessary to remember that this portrait has not been drawn by a poet's mistress long after her lover's death but by a scholar and critic of wide reputation.

Not a biography but very useful to the student of Byron's life, character, and opinions is *His Very Self and Voice* (1954) in which Ernest J. Lovell, Jr., has assembled in chronological order the recollections and impressions of some hundred and fifty men and women who had the privilege of listening to Byron as he talked on all manner of subjects, from grave to gay, from lively to severe. Lovell left aside the two principal records of Byron's conversations: those made by Thomas Medwin and Lady Blessington, edited later, in 1966 and 1969, and noticed below. Byron's own records of, and comments upon, his talk are not included on the ground that they are easily accessible in editions of his letters and journals. The compilation extends from his first recorded words, at the age of five, when, overhearing a woman comment to his nurse upon his misshapen foot, he lashed out "Dinna speak of it!" to the last incoherent mutterings which Fletcher, his faithful servant, could not understand as Byron lay on his death-bed at Missolonghi. Whatever the subject and whatever the tone and temper of his talk, those who set it down generally thought it worthwhile to note also the setting and the circumstances in which it was heard. Often, indeed, few words, or none, remain, and we have merely a general impression of the poet's manner and his theme. The fact that by no means all who listened approved of the speaker or of what they heard adds to the convincing verisimilitude of their experiences. Not all were friends or admirers of the poet. Leigh Hunt is here with his bitter memories as are Byron's wronged wife and her partisans. But over against these must be set the recollections of such men as Hobhouse and Shelley and Thomas Moore. For a more detailed account of this valuable and entertaining compilation by Samuel Chew see the New York *Herald Tribune Book Review,* 28 November 1954.

The stage was now set for a definitive biography: it would be written, in three volumes, by Leslie A. Marchand, *Byron: A Biography* (New York, 1957). The immensity of Marchand's task is suggested by the fact that Byron's life was already one of the most fully documented in all literary history. One begins with the eight volumes and more of the poet's own published letters and journals. In addition, a most remarkable number of major informants who knew Byron personally had published memoirs or biographies, and in the twentieth century at least ten full-length biographical studies dealing with selected periods of Byron's life had appeared. It was thus possible, before Marchand's definitive work, to survey in some fashion the life of Byron, period by period, in accounts written by those who knew him and by scholars of the present century. The most important early accounts may be briefly described here. John Galt's *Life of Byron* (London, 1830) incorporates the author's first-hand impressions of Byron, chiefly in 1809–12, the period of the poet's first tour and the early months of his return to England. Robert C. Dallas' *Recollections of the Life of Lord Byron, From the Year 1808 to the End of 1814* (London, 1824) is entitled somewhat misleadingly, for the intimacy of the two men reached its peak in 1812, and Dallas did not see Byron on his tour of 1809–11. Thomas Moore (whose *Letters,* London, 1964, were edited by W. S. Dowden), author of *Letters and Journals of Lord Byron, With Notices of his Life* (London, 1830), collected first-hand accounts of Byron wherever he could find them, but his own friendship with Byron began in November 1811 and ended only with Byron's death, although Moore saw Byron only once for a few days on the Continent. John Cam Hobhouse's diary, edited by his daughter, Lady Dorchester, as *Recollections of a Long Life* (London, 1909–11), records impressions of Byron on his first tour, his life following in London, and his travels abroad, but it is especially full on Byron at the time of his marriage and separation. Lady Byron's side of the quarrel emerges from her accounts published in *Astarte,* noticed above, and from Ethel C. Mayne, *The Life and Letters of Anne Isabella, Lady Noel Byron* (London, 1929), which uses the Lovelace Papers and quotes, it seems, from 580 letters. The diary of John William Polidori, Byron's traveling physician in 1816, was edited by William Michael Rossetti (London, 1911). His accounts of this period are to be supplemented by those in the letters and journals of Shelley and Mary Shelley, noticed above, who also knew Byron later in Italy. (The journals of Claire Clairmont, mother of Byron's Allegra, born in January 1817, have been edited by Marion Stocking [Cambridge, Mass., 1968]). Teresa Guiccioli, who met Byron in April 1819 and remained his mistress until he left Italy for the last time, assembled her adulatory *Recollections of Lord Byron* (New York, trans. 1869). Marchand also had a microfilm of her long and unpublished "La Vie de Lord Byron en Italie." Thomas Medwin, who knew Byron between November 1821 and March 1822, published his *Conversations of Lord Byron* in 1824; it was edited by Ernest J. Lovell, Jr., *Medwin's "Conversations of Lord Byron," Revised with a New Preface by the Author . . . and Annotated by Lady Byron, John Cam Hobhouse, Sir Walter Scott, Sir Charles Napier, John Murray, John Galt, William Harness, Robert Southey, Lady Caroline Lamb, Leigh Hunt, Mary Shelley, E. J. Trelawny, William Fletcher, Countess Teresa Guiccioli, and Others Who Knew the Poet Personally* (Princeton, 1966).

The diary of Edward E. Williams, who knew Byron at Pisa and was drowned with Shelley, has been noticed above. Edward John Trelawny met Byron on 15 January 1822 and sailed to Greece with him. In 1858 he published his *Recollections of the Last Days of Shelley and Byron*, more recently edited by J. E. Morpurgo (New York, 1952, 1960*). This and Trelawny's *Records of Shelley, Byron, and the Author* (London, 1878, 1968*) should be read in the light of Anne Hill's article, "Trelawny's Family Background and Naval Career" (*KSJ*, 1956), which demonstrates Trelawny's remarkable talent for fabrication. His letters were incompletely and inaccurately edited by H. Buxton Forman (London, 1910). Leigh Hunt knew Byron in London, but he and his family lived in Byron's house for some months in 1822, and six years later he published the most hostile book on Byron ever written by one who knew him: *Lord Byron and Some of His Contemporaries* (London, 1828). During the last days of Byron in Italy he talked rather regularly with one of the most beautiful hypocrites of the age, Lady Blessington, and in 1834 she published her *Conversations of Lord Byron*. Ernest J. Lovell, Jr., in his edition of her book (Princeton, 1969), utilizes substantial material not previously published, and his introduction explores more fully than any other account the relations that existed between Byron and Lady Blessington. Byron on his voyage to Cephalonia was described by James Hamilton Browne in two articles in *Blackwood's Edinburgh Magazine* (1834), and there on the island of Cephalonia he met a young Scottish army doctor, James Kennedy, who wrote *Conversations on Religion with Lord Byron and Others* (London, 1830), one of the most reliable of the book-length accounts of the poet's conversation. This period was also recorded by the young Pietro Gamba, brother of Teresa Guiccioli, in *A Narrative of Lord Byron's Last Journey to Greece* (London, 1825). Of the remaining major witnesses of Byron's last days in Greece—Leicester F. C. Stanhope, *Greece in 1823 and 1824, to which are added Reminiscences of Lord Byron* (London, 1825), also including recollections by George Finlay, the historian of Greece; Dr. Julius Millingen, *Memoirs of the Affairs of Greece, with Various Anecdotes of Lord Byron* (London, 1831), who attended Byron during his last illness; and William Parry, *The Last Days of Lord Byron* (London, 1825)—Parry is the best, being blunt, humorous, and sympathetically understanding of his subject. Estimates of the reliability of all these informants, and others, appear in Lovell's *His Very Self and Voice,* discussed above. (A recent note in *KSJ,* 1970, casting serious doubt on Parry's authorship of *The Last Days* reaches conclusions not wholly justified by the evidence presented and ignores the facts that Fletcher, Bowring, and Stanhope, hostile witnesses in a libel suit initiated by Parry against the *Examiner,* are ridiculed or otherwise attacked in Parry's book. Parry had also quarreled with Stanhope in Greece. Although Parry's publisher testified that Parry's manuscript was prepared for the press by Thomas Hodgskin, which may mean no more than that Hodgskin was copy editor, the jury awarded damages of £50 to Parry, no small sum. The problem is further complicated by the fact that the defendant, the *Examiner,* was one of two newspapers to report the case at length, and present knowledge must rely heavily on these reports. More recently, the author of the note in *KSJ,* William St. Clair, has asserted, "Parry is one of the best of the contemporary accounts" [*That Greece Might Still Be Free,* New York, 1972, p. 281].)

In addition to these older books, the specialized scholarly studies of selected periods of Byron's life by Pratt, Borst, Quennell, Mayne, Fox, Lovelace, Cline, Origo, Nicolson, and others, noticed above, had all appeared before the date of Marchand's *Byron: A Biography.*

With such a mass of biographical matter already published, it is especially noteworthy that Marchand could look at Byron with a fresh and unbiased eye, for the poet lives again in his pages, which draw upon an immense quantity of hitherto unpublished material, brought alive by Marchand's own pilgrimage in the footsteps of Byron. In Europe alone he "gathered between five and six thousand microfilm frames of manuscript material," with the result that "the problem of selection" became "a difficult one." See his acknowledgments in the Preface and the list of his unpublished sources at the end of Volume III. But this abundance effectively removed any temptation to give undue importance to a document or letter merely because it had not before been published. The result is a sane, scholarly, and balanced view of the poet's life. Not least among the virtues of this book are the perceptive comments on the poems, the publication for the first time of the correct text of many of Byron's letters, and its scrupulous accuracy throughout. Although Marchand, who was unaccountably denied access to the Lovelace Papers, does not solve finally the question of Medora Leigh—surely the evidence no longer exists, if it ever did—the answers to all the other major questions are here (short of a full-scale psychological analysis in depth, the necessary evidence for which not being available either), and Marchand's is now above all others the first biography which should be consulted by Byron scholars. There are forty-eight pages of magnificent illustrations, a map of Byron's Greece, a bibliography of fifteen pages, and a remarkably complete index of eighty-six pages. Marchand's one-volume *Byron: A Portrait* (New York, 1970), containing considerable new material, is based on his three-volume *Byron: A Biography* and like the earlier work is divided into thirty chapters, but it moves at a less leisurely pace, understandably, and it utilizes recent discoveries made by the author himself as well as by others. This is not a mere abridgment. Handsomely printed and bound, this volume has fifty-six illustrations, two maps, and helpful genealogical tables not found in the earlier work.

Eliza M. Butler's *Byron and Goethe: Analysis of a Passion* (London, 1956) appeared too late for Marchand to use in his *Biography,* but its contribution to Byron studies, however interesting, is essentially marginal, for Byron had no German, Goethe spoke no English, and the two men never saw each other. Based on J. G. Robertson's study of the subject in 1924, it uses "some unpublished material connected with Goethe" in the Murray archives and also letters from Kinnaird and Murray to Byron. There are some interesting pages on Byron's opinion of the Germans and the work of Goethe, on Goethe's confusions concerning Byron (deriving from Caroline Lamb's *Glenarvon* and from a misreading of *Manfred* as autobiography), and on the story of Byron's several attempted dedications to Goethe, the imbroglio ending finally with the dedication of *Werner* and the second edition of *Sardanapalus* to the German poet. Part II discusses Thomas Medwin's role in securing Goethe's tribute to Byron, published in Medwin's *Conversations of Byron,* and Goethe's reaction to Medwin's book and to William Parry's *Last Days of Byron.* Part III analyzes Byron as Euphorion in *Faust* II and the continuing influence of Byron on Goethe and through him on the later history of the world.

Byron's relations with a number of other persons more and less central to his life are touched upon or discussed at some length in ten books published since 1952: Willard Connely, *Count D'Orsay: The Dandy of Dandies* (London, 1952), deals with the life of Lady Blessington's companion, who knew Byron at Genoa; Caroline M. Duncan-Jones, *Miss Mitford and Mr. Harness: Records of a Friendship* (London, 1955), includes material on Byron and his early friend William Harness; Richard Findlater, *Grimaldi: King of Clowns* (London, 1955), is concerned with Byron's relations, early in life, with the famous comedian; Dorothy Margaret Stuart, *Dearest Bess: The Life and Times of Lady Elizabeth Foster, Afterwards Duchess of Devonshire* (London, 1955), notes several points of contact with Byron; the Marchesa Iris Origo, in *A Measure of Love* (London, 1957), has revised her earlier *Allegra* (London, 1935) and added a sketch of Byron's Italian friend, the Countess Marina Benzoni; Louis F. Peck, *A Life of Matthew G. Lewis* (London, 1961), makes many references to Byron; Stendhal's *Correspondence I: 1800–1821,* edited by Henri Martineau and V. del Litto (Paris, 1962), is concerned with Byron in Milan, October 1816; Anne Treneer, *The Mercurial Chemist: A Life of Sir Humphry Davy* (London, 1963), discusses Byron's relations with Sir Humphry both in London and in Italy; *New Letters of Robert Southey,* edited by Kenneth Curry (New York, 1965), contains references to Byron; and Byron is also treated in Warren Derry's biography of Byron's old Cambridge professor, *Dr. Parr: A Portrait of the Whig Dr. Johnson* (Oxford, 1966). H. W. Häusermann, *The Genevese Background* (London, 1952), is excellent on Byron's Geneva of 1816.

G. Wilson Knight's *Lord Byron's Marriage: The Evidence of Asterisks* (London, 1957) may be safely disregarded by the student unless he is interested in an account with generous quotations of the two rare *Don Leon* poems, here attributed to George Colman the Younger and treated as major evidence of the cause of Byron's separation from his wife. Knight concludes that the poet had "only one failing: homosexuality, together with its extension into the marriage-relationship . . .," and that the cause of the separation was Byron's unnatural or unconventional sexual relations with Lady Byron, which were carried on, presumably, for the year that they lived together, before she realized what was happening to her. The book is drawn wholly from published sources.

Specialized biographical studies of Byron continued to appear in the 1960's. William H. Marshall's *Byron, Shelley, Hunt, and "The Liberal"* (Philadelphia, 1960) opens with a survey of the relations between the three writers prior to Hunt's arrival in Italy and of the speculations in England concerning the forthcoming *Liberal*. Susequent sections deal, one by one, with each of the four numbers of the journal and the reaction to it, followed by a discussion of the "Aftermath: 1823–1828." Marshall's book is the standard work on its subject and traces an interesting and important chapter not only in the lives of those concerned but also in the history of publishing.

Doris Langley Moore's *The Late Lord Byron: Posthumous Dramas* (London, 1961) is a rich storehouse of hitherto unpublished materials, drawing upon the Lovelace Papers, the Hobhouse diaries, the great archives of John Murray, the Lord Abinger collection, and other manuscript collections. Hers is the first book-length study of the intricate twistings and windings, "the dramas, tensions, feuds, frauds, and blunders," that characterized the lives of Byron's friends, relatives, and acquaintances, as they tried to deal with or were themselves responsible for the events that followed the poet's death. But much also is revealed about Byron, as he lived on in the minds of those who knew him. No one can ever again write about Byron the man without first consulting her book. (For further details, see Lovell's article, *KR,* 1962.) It may be noticed here, however, that Mrs. Moore's chapter on Thomas Medwin, which passes severe moral judgments, offers a much less sympathetic or understanding view of its subject than that which appears in *Captain Medwin: Friend of Byron and Shelley* (Austin, 1962; London, 1963), by Ernest J. Lovell, Jr., who utilizes substantial new material and explores at length for the first time the literary and other accomplishments of Medwin, an important member of the Pisan circle of Byron and Shelley.

Lord Byron's Wife, by Malcolm Elwin (New York, 1963), is now the definitive account of its announced subject and of the poet's relations with Annabella. It also draws heavily upon the rich hoard of the Lovelace Papers (reduced, amazingly, by the second Earl of Lovelace, grandson of the poet, to no less than 170 volumes of typewritten transcripts of letters and other documents in his possession). It is especially valuable because it corrects the bias and inaccuracies evident in Ethel C. Mayne's *Life and Letters of Lady Byron*. Elwin clearly demonstrates the increasing unreliability of Annabella's deliberately composed accounts of Byron's words and actions, establishing their dates of origin and contrasting with telling effect her earlier and later reports of the same episode or conversation with Byron. Elwin has quoted with great generosity from his original sources, which comprise perhaps one-half of his book. This is in line with his stated policy: "I have avoided controversy and concentrated on presenting the evidence."

Although John Buxton in his *Byron and Shelley: The History of a Friendship* (London, 1968) thanks Lord Abinger, John Murray, and others for permission to quote hitherto unpublished letters and other documents, his notes at the end of the volume are limited to a scant four pages, and only three of these notes refer to unpublished material. One quotes a letter by Thomas Medwin which had been published in 1962; two others seem to correct dates in F. L. Jones's editions of Mary Shelley's *Journal* and Shelley's *Letters*. It thus appears that there is very little hitherto unpublished material in this book, and the scarcity of notes makes it difficult to determine sources for statements made in the text. Nor is it necessary to assert, in order to enhance the obviously important subject of the book, that "the friendship between Byron and Shelley was the most important relationship in the experience of either." They saw each other on intimate terms, at various times and places, for a total period of about twelve months. Despite these objections, the book is quite readable, and the author, unlike some others who have written on Byron and Shelley, does not take sides: he likes both his poets. Although he states that he has dealt only "briefly" with the effect of the friendship upon the nature of the poetry written by the two poets, the pages discussing this subject are among Buxton's best. Inevitably, much familiar ground is covered, but Buxton, who has written several books on Renaissance themes and figures, brings a fresh eye to the lives and poems of Byron and Shelley. Those chapters dealing with periods when the two poets were separated focus more directly on Shelley than on Byron.

Derek Parker's *Byron and His World* (New York, 1968) is the nearest thing we have to an iconography of Byron, with 128 pages of pictures, many pages with more than one illustration of the poet, his family, friends, enemies, and the places where he lived or with which he was otherwise associated. The biographical commentary, although seldom concerned directly with the illustrations, is informative and gracefully written. Unfortunately, it has not always been possible to date the pictures, which are, inevitably, of unequal quality and reliability, some postdating Byron by a good many years. In view of the fact that this book is the last full-length biographical study of any importance to appear in the 1960's (aside from Marchand's one-volume recension in 1970 of his earlier three-volume *Biography*), it would appear that studies of Byron's life have for the present achieved a kind of high plateau and must now await the appearance of Marchand's edition of the collected letters, before going on to other or greater heights.

IV. CRITICISM

Interest in Byron's life, as distinct from his poetry, was very great indeed during the first half of the twentieth century. One book, however, stands out conspicuously as an attempt to study the poet in his work, not in his personal career. This is William J. Calvert's *Byron: Romantic Paradox* (1935, 1962*). The problem which he suggests is that of the permanent value of the great mass of Byron's poetry apart from the autobiographical, self-revelatory significance which may, or may not, be implicit in much of it. A book which sets forth the historical significance of Byron's "place" in English poetry without the distracting record of his "iniquities" was well worth writing; and Calvert wrote his with good sense and enthusiasm and wit. On its appearance it was welcomed as a refreshing counterbalance to the over-subtle and somewhat morbid psychoanalytical probings of Charles Du Bos. It was well to hear again from a critic and historian of literature. The "paradox" which Calvert set before the reader is in some of its manifestations a familiar one; it had been recognized to some extent by Byron himself. Fundamental is the vacillation between loyalty to eighteenth-century classicism and adherence to the new romantic fashions in thought, emotion, and poetry. "Classic principles," says Calvert, "were relegated to the position of his conscience—basic but subdued." He cannot be understood unless he is set against the background of the classical and reasonable tradition of the preceding age of which, paradoxically, he was the direct heir and the convinced champion, for if on one side of his nature he had his share in Werther's sorrows, on the other he was an intellectual descendant of Voltaire. Spontaneous and emotional in temperament, he was intellectually sophisticated and obedient to tradition. This is the essential dichotomy which Calvert studies and displays. Calvert traces Byron's growing interest in problems of formal excellence; he observes, as have other recent critics, the gradual abandonment of insincerity and affectation in favor of an increasing seriousness of purpose; and he comments upon the curious intermixture of vulgarity and refinement in his art as in his character. These and other strains—so runs the argument—meet ultimately and harmonize in *Don Juan*. To that masterpiece this critic devotes a final appreciative chapter. One wishes that he had elected to analyze also the minor masterpiece *The Vision of Judgment,* which is as characteristic and as powerful as any single episode in the longer poem.

As a supplement to Calvert's discussion the student will do well to read a suggestive essay of earlier date by G. R. Elliott on "Byron and the Comic Spirit" (*PMLA,* 1924; rpt. in *The Cycle of Modern Poetry,* 1929). The argument which Elliott develops is that Byron in his last years was moving towards "a Stoic acceptance of life" and was near to the attainment of "the balance and poetic comeliness of the true comic spirit."

Upon the religious aspect of the "paradox" Calvert did not dwell. This problem is studied in detail in E. W. Marjarum's monograph *Byron as Skeptic and Believer* (1938, 1962*). Baffling contradictions remain after any inquiry along these lines, for this intellectual child of the age of Bayle and Hume and Voltaire was also the heir of a darkly Calvinistic tradition and was yet receptive to currents of religious and metaphysical thought and emotion of his own age. Apart, however, from such a temporary distraction as that of Wordsworth and Shelley in the summer of 1816, the position maintained with the nearest approach to consistency is that of the eighteenth-century Deists, with attendant doubts as to the immortality of the soul. Even so, Byron's emotional instability separates him from the cool rationalism of Voltaire. The attraction which the Roman Catholic Church exerted upon him was due merely to his curiosity and sense of the picturesque; he never seriously considered an acceptance of its dogmas. Marjarum's work surveys the ground covered long ago by Manfred Eimer in *Byron und der Kosmos* (*Anglische Forschungen,* 1912) which is, however, still of value for the thoroughness with which the evidence is gathered, organized, and appraised.

When allowance has been made for fundamental differences in point of view, it may be held that the best consideration of Byron's opinions on matters of religion is in Hoxie N. Fairchild's *Religious Trends in English*

Poetry, Vol. III (1949), Chapter vii. This scholar's treatment of the problem is on the whole unavoidably unsympathetic (since he is a convinced Anglo-Catholic), but none the less valuable for that as serving to correct other estimates. He remarks that Byron's sense of the limitations of human nature and his sense of the evil in human nature combined with his superstitiousness to prevent him "from denying that Christianity, which he was unable to accept." In an earlier, briefer consideration of the same problem, in *The Romantic Quest* (1931), Fairchild had characterized Byron's mind as "too idealistic to refrain from blowing bubbles, and too realistic to refrain from pricking them." There was a "certain desperate integrity" of intellect which rendered him unable to "dupe himself" when faced with the "toughness of facts."

Related to these studies is E. J. Lovell, Jr.'s *Byron: The Record of a Quest* (1949, 1966*), a survey of the poet's concept and treatment of nature. Among the subjects considered in this thoughtful book are the tradition of the picturesque and Byron's handling of it; the conflict between the urban and the rural; the theme of the beauties of nature lost upon a mind temperamentally disinclined to absorb them; the "rejection of feigned emotion" as a fundamental element in Byron's temperament; and the persistence, with many fluctuations, of deistic thought in the poems and prose writings. Noteworthy is Lovell's postscript on "The Contemporaneousness of Byron."

These four treatises—Marjarum's, Eimer's, Fairchild's, and Lovell's—penetrate to those profounder levels of the poet's thought which are so often hidden beneath the glittering surface. From another angle of approach the attempt is made to reach these levels in G. Wilson Knight's "The Two Eternities: An Essay on Byron," which is the sixth chapter in his volume *The Burning Oracle* (1939). Knight's well-known technique is warmly applauded by some scholars and firmly rejected by others. His claims to recognize metaphysically significant themes beneath the surface of "symbols" have never been more disconcertingly illustrated than in his interpretation of Byron—the least "symbolic" of our major poets. But his investigations have this value, that they serve as one corrective, albeit not a very reliable one, to the oft-repeated strictures against Byron's "shallowness."

Knight discovers the "symbolic" meaning of Byron's imagery in both departments of the poet's work but more richly (as one would expect) in the romantic than in the satiric. He thus recalls to notice poems that have passed into comparative neglect, for present-day criticism and appreciation of Byron generally emphasize the value of the satiric poems at the expense of the romantic and personal. On the romantic, Byronic *Heldentypus* there are informative discussions in E. M. Sickels' *The Gloomy Egoist* (1932), in Mario Praz's *The Romantic Agony* (1933), especially Chapter ii (on the descent of the Byronic hero from the Miltonic Satan), and in Eino Railo's *The Haunted Castle* (1927), especially Chapters vi and viii. See also Carl Lefevre's article, "Lord Byron's Fiery Convert of Revenge" (*SP*, 1952), a study of the renegade aristocrat as a type of the Byronic hero. (More recent studies are discussed below.) An attempt to readjust the balance of appreciation is made in Samuel C. Chew's introduction to his edition of *Childe Harold's Pilgrimage and Other Romantic Poems* (1936), where, however, it is not argued that the poetry of this kind possesses the appeal which the satires make to the modern intelligence. For a corresponding and complementary brief estimate of his work in the other kind the student may turn to Louis I. Bredvold's introduction to the companion volume, *Don Juan and Other Satiric Poems* (1935). A longer survey of earlier date is Claude M. Fuess's *Lord Byron as a Satirist in Verse* (1912, 1964*). Fuess recognizes Byron's satiric power (as who could not?) but he maintains, surprisingly and mistakenly, that his "philosophic satire" is "shallow and cynical" and that "he took no positive attitude towards any of the great problems of existence." This monograph is of more usefulness as a historical survey than as criticism. The subject is reviewed in both its general aspects: Byron's place in the tradition of formal English satire descended from the Augustan Age, immediately from Gifford and ultimately from Pope; and Byron's Italianate satire in the mock-heroic tradition which derives from Pulci and Berni and was immediately suggested by John Hookham Frere's English imitation of the Italian masters. For an account of the English imitations of the Italian comic epics reference may be made to R. D. Waller's introduction to his edition of Frere's *The Monks and the Giants* (1926) and to an older, more extensive study by Albert Eichler, *John Hookham Frere, sein Leben und seine Werke, sein Einfluss auf Lord Byron* (1905). That Byron took only the externals of the manner from the Italian poets and applied them to *Beppo* and *Don Juan* and that he is really in the line of succession from older English writers is well argued by Ronald Bottrall in "Byron and the Colloquial Tradition in English Poetry" (*Criterion*, 1939). This tradition Byron revitalized by introducing into his verse the colloquial force of his prose. Bottrall asserts that *Don Juan* is "the greatest long poem in English since *The Dunciad*." This opinion may be put beside the more cautious but more surprising praise in the essay by T. S. Eliot to which reference has been made above. Eliot is severe upon Byron's stylistic ineptitudes but he recognizes in *Don Juan* an emotional sincerity, a hatred of hypocrisy, and a "reckless, raffish honesty." Much more guarded is Mark Van Doren's estimate in *The Noble Voice* (1946). He holds that though Byron "flounders brilliantly" in *Don Juan* he misses the heart of comedy. Yet "we never quite decide that he is wasting our time." Along the same lines as Bottrall's article is one by Marius Bewley entitled "The Colloquial Mode of Byron" (*Scrutiny,* 1949). Here it is shown that in this mode Byron follows a tradition traceable back to the seventeenth century in English poetry. An authoritative account of the origins and different versions of the great story to which Byron's masterpiece is so loosely attached is still Georges Gendarme de Bévotte's *La Légende de Don Juan* (1906). This is supplemented, however, by Armand E. Singer, *The Don Juan Theme, Version and Criticism: A Bibliography* (1965).

There are two extended studies of *Don Juan,* undertaken independently of one another and consequently to some degree overlapping, though not to a serious extent; to a greater degree each supplements the other. One is P. G. Trueblood's *The Flowering of Byron's Genius: Studies in Don Juan* (1945, 1962*); the other, E. F. Boyd's *Byron's Don Juan: A Critical Study* (1945, 1958*).

Trueblood's monograph is not an exhaustive treatment but is limited to three themes or aspects of the subject. The first is the inception and growth of the poem; and here two points are emphasized—in fact, over-emphasized: the influence of the Countess Guiccioli and the example of Henry Fielding. Teresa's persuasiveness and Fielding's humanitarianism had their effect, he believes, in the evolution of *Don Juan* from mere "sportive satire" into the profound and wide-ranging social criticism of the later cantos. Trueblood's second subject is a survey of contemporary reviews and notices of the poem in the English periodicals and newspapers. He confines himself to these because, as he explains, the "pamphleteer criticism" is covered in *Byron in England.* The generally unfavorable reception of the early installments had its influence in reorienting Byron's plans and purposes and consequently in the change which came over *Don Juan* as it progressed. This change is the theme of the third part of the book in which the significance of the satire is studied and the development is carefully traced as Byron's interest shifted from light social satire and the "mannerly obscene" to the cosmopolitan criticism of the latter part, surveying the European world in general and England in particular. The general tenor of Trueblood's argument and the conclusion at which he arrives are that Byron's satiric genius did not find expression in mere negation, as contemporary hostile reviewers so often charged, but that on the contrary his fiercely witty attacks upon hypocrisy and cant form the obverse to the idealism that is always implicit and sometimes explicit in *Don Juan*. The epic-satire gradually deepened and expanded. Trueblood catalogues and examines the different objects of Byron's satire, both personal and social, and also in the realm of ideas. An account of the poem's "sources"—the sources not only of its many and so startlingly contrasted subjects and moods but also of its far-descended style—did not come within Trueblood's design.

Meanwhile one of the most valuable portions of Miss Boyd's monograph is her survey of Byron's *Belesenheit* and of the literary background of *Don Juan*. In that background she discerns not only the Italian poets from Pulci to Casti and their English imitators Frere and Rose, but also parallels and analogues (not always necessarily direct "sources") ranging from ancient and medieval tales of romance and adventure to contemporary fiction of such contrasting kinds as the Gothic romance and the "discussion-novels" of Thomas Love Peacock. The resemblances which Miss Boyd indicates between *Don Juan* and Wieland's *Oberon* (which Byron knew in William Sotheby's translation) are particularly interesting in view of W. W. Beyer's demonstration of the influence of the same poem upon the imagination of John Keats. Miss Boyd has also a good deal to say regarding possible indebtednesses to Thomas Hope's *Anastasius,* a problem long since handled by Anton Pfeiffer in his monograph *Thomas Hopes "Anastasius" und Lord Byrons "Don Juan"* (1913). She makes the novel suggestion that for the Russian episode Byron may have owed something to Casti's *Poema Tartaro* (1797). There is no direct evidence that Byron knew this work, but he did know and admire Casti's *Gli Animali Parlanti* and the parallels adduced by Miss Boyd, though not very numerous, are sufficiently striking. There is no space here to report upon other results of these *Quellenstudien*. Other portions of Miss Boyd's book have to do with Byron's concept of "epic satire," with the essential characteristics of "Don Juanism," and with the wide horizons of the poet's experience, observation, and comment, embracing not only "Love—Tempest—Travel—War" but a great variety of topics touched on in the characteristic digressions. Miss Boyd's work is reviewed noteworthily in *TLS,* 1 September 1945.

T. G. Steffan, in "The Token-web, the Sea-Sodom, and Canto I of *Don Juan*" (*TexSE,* 1947), is concerned not with literary sources but with the contribution which Byron's own experiences in Venice made to the beginning of the poem.

In connection with *Don Juan* it is appropriate to notice A. L. Strout's reprint (1947) of *John Bull's Letter to Lord Byron* (1821). Strout has produced documentary proof that the author was John Gibson Lockhart, has annotated the text voluminously, and in his introduction set the piece against the background of the contemporary great periodicals and their interest in Byron. In a long appendix all the references to Byron in *Blackwood's Magazine* between 1817 and 1825 are brought together.

An interestingly novel approach to the study of Byron's masterpiece is made in E. D. H. Johnson's article "Don Juan in England" (*ELH*, 1944). Here it is argued that Byron's strictures upon the English moral and social code and his indictments of English hypocrisy originated in a misunderstanding of contemporary ethical standards which was in turn due to his limited experience of English society. The attacks upon hypocrisy covering moral degradation were valid for the entourage of the Prince Regent at Carleton House and for certain other circles of the Whigs but were not with justice to be leveled against English society as a whole. The unfavorable reception of the poem was in part at least owing to an indignant repudiation of these satiric accusations; and this reception merely served in turn to confirm Byron in his convictions. Johnson argues his case well, but it may be suspected that he underestimates both the breadth of Byron's observations and the extent of British cant. It is to be remembered, however, that Byron's personal experiences of English society were "dated" by several years by the time he came to write *Don Juan*. However broadly or narrowly, the poem reflects conditions prevalent in 1812–16 rather than those characteristic of 1819–23. In more general terms and less pointedly Sir Herbert Grierson has written of "Byron and English Society" in a chapter of his *Background of English Literature* (1925). R. W. Chambers, in a brochure entitled *Ruskin (and Others) on Byron* (English Assoc. Pamphlets, No. 62, 1925), after discussing Byron as Ruskin's master, proceeds to an interesting and lively defense of that post-Waterloo reactionary society against which the poet directed his satire.

More specific are three articles by D. V. Erdman, "Lord Byron and the Genteel Reformers" (*PMLA*, 1941), "Lord Byron as Rinaldo" (*PMLA*, 1942), and "Byron and Revolt in England" (*Science and Society*, 1947). During his years in London the poet had moved in the anti-governmental milieu whose center was Holland House. Erdman studies the effect of this environment upon his political and social opinions. In the first article it is demonstrated that Byron's attitude towards reform is that which was assumed in Whig circles; in the second it is shown that the political views of Lady Oxford had an appreciable influence upon his activities in Parliament; and in the third Erdman estimates Byron's influence upon the social and economic disturbances in England following the defeat of Napoleon, and the poet's attitude towards these manifestations of a revolutionary spirit. That attitude and those activities, as reflected in his poetry, form the subject of an article by Bertrand Russell on "Byron and the Modern World" (*JHI*, 1940), in which Byron, "the aristocratic rebel," is contrasted with the "proletarian rebel" of our own day and it is argued that the poet's essential function was to liberate the human personality from social convention and social morality. This essay, somewhat condensed, reappears in Russell's *History of Western Philosophy* (1945). See also D. V. Erdman's analysis of Byron's highly ambivalent response to the spirit of the new democratic age, "Byron and 'The New Force of the People' " (*KSJ*, 1962).

In an article on "Byron's *Hebrew Melodies*" (*SP*, 1952) Joseph Slater shows that in these poems Byron was not concerned with religious problems but voiced a sympathy with Jewish nationalistic aspirations which foreshadowed his devotion to the cause of liberty in Italy and Greece. (Long ago Nahum Sokolow, in his *History of Zionism*, 1919, Chapter xviii, discussed Byron's influence upon the movement.) The obvious truth that Byron, whatever his self-contradictions along other lines, never wavered or faltered in his hatred of oppression is developed by W. S. Dowden in an article on "The Consistency of Byron's Social Criticism" (*Rice Inst. Papers*, xxxvii, 1950).

For a general survey of the aspect of Byron's achievement with which Erdman is concerned from a restricted point of view, reference must be made, for want of anything better, to Dora Neill Raymond's *The Political Career of Lord Byron* (1924), where the material is gathered together but not subjected to any thorough examination. On the particular instance of Byron's opinions of Napoleon Bonaparte there have been two separate monographs. P. Holzhausen's *Bonaparte, Byron, und die Briten* (1904) is supplemented and largely superseded by Gerhard Eggert's *Lord Byron und Napoleon* (*Palaestra*, CLXXXVI, 1933). A comparison of the many allusions to Napoleon in the poems, letters, and journals leads to the conclusion at which every attentive reader must arrive: that the poet was of two minds, admiring the hero and individualist while denouncing the conqueror; in sympathy with the supreme anti-dynastic offspring of the French Revolution while satirizing the low ambition which sought to establish his own dynasty; and after Waterloo keenly aware of the fact that the fall of the Emperor was not the triumph of liberalism but the restoration of reactionary despotism. The related larger problem of the influence of French revolutionary thought upon Byron has not been the subject of detailed, separate investigation since the time, long ago, of Dowden's and Hancock's well-known but now somewhat outmoded studies of that influence upon the English poets.

The problem of Byron's relations with Germany is purely one of reciprocal literary influence, for the poet was in that country but once and for a short time only (when he made the journey up the Rhine in 1816) and seems to have taken no interest in German public affairs. Such debt as his imagination owed to Germany is examined in the seventh chapter of F. W. Stokoe's *German Influence in the English Romantic Period* (1926).

The subject of Byron's relations with Greece is of course treated extensively in every biography. Harold Spender's *Byron and Greece* (1924) contains a short introduction but is in the main a convenient and well-arranged anthology of verse, letters, and journals. The records of the "Greek Committee," which was organized in England to promote Philhellenism and possibly intervention in the Greek War of Independence and to which Byron was attached, have been examined and published by Esmond S. De Beer and W. Seton in "Byroniana: The Archives of the London Greek Committee" (*The Nineteenth Century and After*, 1926). A short critical survey is Karl Brunner's "Griechenland in Byrons Dichtung" (*Anglia*, 1936). On the relation of Byron's travels and oriental poetry to the contemporary vogue of oriental travel-books reference may be made to W. C. Brown's article, "Byron and the English Interest in the Near East" (*SP*, 1937). Brown has published two other articles dealing with this vogue in *PQ* (1936, 1937), but these do not bear directly upon Byron.

There is an old but fairly good anthology compiled from the poems and prose, *With Byron in Italy* (1906), edited by Anna B. McMahan. The abundant illustrations will be of value to students who have not had the opportunity to follow in Byron's footsteps through Italy. In the light of contemporary public affairs in Italy as well as in England E. D. H. Johnson has offered "A Political Interpretation of Byron's *Marino Faliero*" (*MLQ*, 1942), arguing that in the person of the Doge who is party to a conspiracy against the social class to which he himself belongs Byron reflects his own position as an aristocrat in sympathy with movements of revolt. Johnson's article is one of several studies in which Byron's dramas have been subjected to fresh scrutiny. R. W. Babcock's "The Inception and Reception of Byron's *Cain*" (*SAQ*, 1927) supplements the chapter on that "Mystery" in Chew's *Dramas of Lord Byron* (1915) and the chapter on "The Reception of *Cain*" in *Byron in England*. T. H. V. Motter's critical essay, "Byron's *Werner* Re-estimated," in *Essays in Dramatic Literature*, edited by Hardin Craig (1935), puts a higher value upon that play—principally upon the score of its fitness for presentation on the stage—than does Chew. The subject of D. V. Erdman's "Byron's Stage Fright: The History of His Ambition and Fear of Writing for the Stage" (*ELH*, 1939) is indicated in its title. Bertrand Evans, writing on "Manfred's Remorse and Dramatic Tradition" (*PMLA*, 1947), develops in patient and convincing detail an idea suggested long since by Chew, that the literary forerunners of *Manfred* are to be discovered not so much in the Gothic novel as in Gothic drama. (For a different view, see Ernest J. Lovell, Jr., *Byron: The Record of a Quest*, "The Literary Tradition: Sources and Parallels of the Zeluco Theme.") An impressive number of parallels in characters and situations is indicated, and Evans makes it evident that Byron, who in his earlier years was a devotee of the theatre, was steeped in memories of Gothic plays. The articles noted in this paragraph, with others that will doubtless be written, must one day be brought together and summarized in a fresh general survey of Byron's work as a dramatist which will supersede Samuel Chew's monograph of 1915, 1966.*

Any study of Byron's "regular" tragedies must be closely related to a consideration of his critical pronouncements, formal and informal, in verse as well as in prose, and any study of those opinions is bound to put the emphasis upon the "Augustan" elements in his disposition and taste and practice. His opinions of, and relations with, the few poets (such as Samuel Rogers) in whose verse the earlier mode survived are studied in Heinrich Hartmann's *Lord Byrons Stellung zu den Klassizisten seiner Zeit* (1932). The only extended piece of literary criticism which Byron wrote was his reply to the Rev. W. L. Bowles's strictures on the poetry of Pope. This is the subject of a monograph by J. J. Van Rennes, *Bowles, Byron, and the Pope-Controversy* (1927, 1966*); but all the essential documents in the case (from which the student can draw his own conclusions) had already been assembled by Prothero in the fifth volume of *Letters and Journals*. More general surveys, drawing together the *obiter dicta* in the letters, journals, poems, and prefaces to poems, are C. T. Goode's *Byron as Critic* (1923, 1964*) and M. Eisser's *Lord Byron als Kritiker* (1932). Neither is very illuminating.

A small batch of Byroniana had best be considered together. In 1912 funds for an annual "Byron Foundation Lecture" were raised by public subscription at University College, Nottingham. Among those lectures published, *Byron and Switzerland* by Heinrich Straumann of the University of Zurich (1948–49) traces the poet's movements and emotions during the summer of 1816; there is a useful little map of his travels in the Alps. *Goethe and Byron* by Miss E. M. Butler (1949–50) is a most illuminating discussion. *Byron and Shelley* by D. G. James (1951) argues that "Shelley was not what Byron needed" when in 1816 there was "a chance that he might escape from the poison of Romanticism." *Byron's Dramatic Prose* by G. Wilson Knight (1953) considers, with sensitively selected excerpts, the qualities of the poet's prose in the letters and journals and "Detached Thoughts." Graham Hough, *Two Exiles: Lord Byron and D. H. Lawrence* (1956), is interesting but not essential reading. T. J. B. Spencer, *Byron and the Greek Tradition* (1959), reminds us that E. H. Coleridge's edition of Byron's *Poetry* omits the long essay on modern Greek attached to *Childe Harold* in 1812. (It appears in the Oxford Standard Authors edition of Byron's *Poetical Works*.)

It does not fall within the bounds of this brief survey to give any extended account of the many "appreciative" articles on Byron with which the centennial was celebrated in 1924. The flood subsided almost as suddenly as it rose, and since that year little of this kind has appeared. Some brief comments upon the most noteworthy of these "occasional" pieces will serve to continue the story of Byron's reputation since an account thereof was rendered in the last chapter of *Byron in England.* In that book Oliver Elton's chapter in the *Survey of English Literature, 1780–1830,* was recommended as "of all the critiques on Byron produced in the twentieth century . . . on the whole the most satisfactory." Supplementing that survey is Elton's estimate of "The Present Value of Byron" (*RES*, 1925), in which the need to winnow carefully the good from the bad in the lyrics and satires is emphasized and much is made of Byron's power in narrative verse. Other distinguished university professors offered their tributes. A well-weighed appraisal by C. H. Herford is in the *Holborn Review* (1924). A lecture by W. P. Ker, first published in the *Criterion* (1925) and reprinted in Ker's *Collected Essays* (1925), possesses surprisingly little of that great scholar's massive authoritativeness but is suggestive in its remarks on Byron's prosody and on some literary affiliations of which students of Byron are not always aware. R. W. Chambers' *Ruskin (and Others) on Byron* (1925) has already been mentioned. H. J. C. Grierson

was one of the contributors—another was Viscount Haldane—to a volume
of tributes and other essays and addresses of varying value (ranging in date
from 1897 to 1924), entitled *Byron the Poet* (1924), edited by W. A.
Briscoe. As Professor of Poetry at Oxford it was H. W. Garrod's duty to
deliver an official centenary lecture; but *Byron: 1824–1924* (1924) is not
one of Garrod's best efforts; the only novelty in it is a suggestion concerning the element of superstition ("the nightmare of my own delinquencies") in the poet's disposition. At Cambridge the Right Rev. H. Hensley
Henson's *Byron* (1924) was the Rede Lecture for the year; it is a moral
judgment of the man rather than a criticism of his work. Lord Ernle
(R. E. Prothero) wrote with the authority of specialized researches on
"The Poetry of Byron," in the *Quarterly Review* (1924). In the *Edinburgh
Review* (1924) tribute took the form of an essay on "The Personality of
Byron" by C. E. Lawrence. Prince D. S. Mirsky, an expatriated Russian
who was admirably acquainted with English literature, wrote on "Byron'
in the *London Mercury* (1924). The only noteworthy critique called forth
by the occasion in this country was by Howard M. Jones, who wrote on
"The Byron Centenary" in the *Yale Review* (1924). The list could be
extended almost indefinitely, for there was scarcely a newspaper or other
periodical that did not have its say at the time of the centenary. But the
critiques named in this paragraph are sufficient in number for any student
save the most determined specialist.

In the two decades following 1949 (the year of the latest critical
volume discussed by Professor Chew), there has been a most remarkable
resurgence of critical interest in the poetry of Byron, so great as to signal a
rather thorough reversal of earlier estimates. Although Sir Harold Nicolson in a lecture on *The Poetry of Byron* (London, 1943), concerned chiefly
with *Childe Harold,* recognized that interest in the poet's personality and
biography had "almost banished interest in his poetry," he was also aware
that "the expression of this personality has a universal and not merely
particular importance" and that when Byron reacts against the "discontent
and disillusion" of his own time and sings his "central theme of frustration," he speaks directly to the mind of 1943, the year when the tide of
World War II was beginning to turn in favor of the Allied Forces. The
problems discussed by Nicholson, including those of Byron's sincerity and
conviction, have been of increasing importance to critics of more recent
years. Leonard C. Martin, in his somewhat disappointing lecture on
Byron's Lyrics (Nottingham, 1948), asserts that his best lyrics transcend
mere personality and, because of their great and noble style, deriving from

the Greek or Roman classics and from the Bible, "can be called classical."
Although other critics will instruct us more persuasively and clearly in the
nature of Byron's lyrical achievement, Martin concludes, in the words of
Swinburne, that Byron possessed "the excellence of sincerity and strength,"
confessing nevertheless that he is "not one of the subtlest of lyrical poets."
Sir Herbert Read's short monograph on *Byron* (London, 1951), with a
good selective bibliography, continues the tradition of psychological analysis (early experiences produced "a permanent psychological trauma" that
led finally to a nihilistic philosophy) and represents a late flowering of the
disparaging critical school (Byron's mind was "not in the most fundamental sense poetic" and lacked "essential discipline"). These issues will
continue to be debated. Although Read found "at the base of all Byron's
work an essential sanity" (despite the trauma and the nihilism), he thought
that the only poems read in 1951 were the three mature satires and *Childe
Harold,* which, curiously, he regards as a satire. W. W. Robson's lecture on
Byron as Poet (London, 1957) is more rewarding and in effect constitutes both a reply to some of the questions discussed by Nicolson, Martin,
and Read, and also a statement of positions that will be explored further by
the critics of the 1960's. He understands that "No clear line . . . can be
drawn between discussion of 'the man,' and discussion of 'the work':
Byron's personality is as much the subject for a critical essay on Byron, as it
is for a biography." Recognizing that Byron is read quite "as much . . .
as any other English poet," he points up problems that will be considered
repeatedly: there seems to be little "determination to define his peculiar
qualities as a poet." What does Byron's poetry have "to offer to us here and
now in the twentieth century"? After conceding Byron's frequent "lack of
verbal distinction," he writes of the Dying Gladiator passage in *Childe
Harold* iv, "No living poet could write this kind of verse with that degree
of strength and conviction; poetry which is both good, and popular, in the
way this is, I cannot imagine appearing in the twentieth century. Byron
speaks here in the accents of a great European tradition of the public style."
Further, "in admitting a fresh range of feelings into his [more interesting]
poetry, he introduced new shades and inflexions of the speaking voice."
Excellence without obscurity in the colloquial mode is now a recognized
virtue of Byron. After sensitively appreciative comments on "Lines on
hearing that Lady Byron was ill" and "Epistle to Augusta," Robson concludes, the style is not Regency but "dateless." *Don Juan* he sees as "a
triumph of personality," its life a "dialectic" of "contrasting attitudes," its
distinguishing characteristic a "temporary stabilization of conflicting emo-

tions." It has "an internal control which is lacking in other semi-serious poetry, W. H. Auden's for example." Alas, however, although *Don Juan* is "the work of a mature mind," it is "not one with an integral vision," and thus the poem cannot be ranked "very high among the great creative works of literature."

It is difficult to do justice to the usual subtlety of Robert Escarpit's two-volume study of *Lord Byron: Un Tempérament littéraire* (Paris, 1956–57). Early pages discuss the "prestiges byroniens" and "la lecture de Byron," surveying and evaluating in the process a good deal of scholarship and criticism and setting forth the author's own aims. Escarpit effectively rejects the simplistic notion that Byron wrote only to relieve himself of feelings of guilt, a motive which obviously fails to explain why he also published what he wrote. Chapter iii argues that Byron found his true vocation at last as a man of action in Greece, and thus his voluntary exile in 1816 is viewed as "en réalité un retour"—an odyssey of some years leading him finally back again to Greece, "pour y 'engager' son existence," in an effort to achieve "l'affranchissement de sa personne."

Examining next Byron's changing attitudes toward the career of letters, Escarpit recognizes the resemblances between Childe Burun and Don Juan and the way in which the two poems are a "mélange des genres," alternating passages which are comic, violently satiric, melancholy, or meditative. He recognizes also the attention that Byron paid to the opinion of his public and to the advice of Murray, although periodically renouncing authorship. In short, Byron regularly looked upon the publication of each poem as an experiment with his popularity, an adventure or experience in which he risked a reputation.

Rejecting the oversimplified concept of Byron as satirist and Byron as romanticist, Escarpit discerns three Byronic modes, frequently overlapping in the same poems—lyrical, rhetorical, and narrative—and devotes the final three-quarters of his book to them. Thus he can discuss the lyrical element not only in Byron's short poems but also in almost all his other works. Escarpit concludes, however, that for Byron the man of action the narrative form—both dramatic and non-dramatic—was the superior form and that no matter which modes he seems to adopt, his poetic output is a form of action.

Part II opens with an introductory survey of Byron's contemporaries, his literary ideas and affinities, and his paradoxical lyrical realism, the latter discussion relying on Byron's pronouncements in his controversy with Bowles, followed by a brief survey which classifies three types of Byronic lyrics: the traditional poetry of national events, songs intended for music, and poems expressive primarily of personal feeling. Although there are interesting discussions of the problem of "sincerity" and "le moi et le monde," the author's interests do not normally lead him to analyze at length any one lyric poem. Curiously, he translates almost all Byron's English into French. The chapter on lyric form makes much of Byron's habit of painstaking revision, beginning with his early poems, but frankly recognizes his typical stylistic weaknesses. The discussion of Byron's versification sometimes lacks sophistication.

The second volume opens with a survey of Byron's prose, "surtout une prose d'idées," introductory to a discussion of his "rhetorique en vers": the "classical" satires, *Childe Harold,* and the great satires in ottava rima, the intent or design of which is summarized under three heads—"offensive, contemplation, humour"—each of which is then given a chapter. The first of these groups of poems is expressive of Byron's duel or war with the world. The contemplative poetry of *Childe Harold,* far from being merely melancholy, is "active, vivante, et comporte . . . sa part d'esprit offensif." This is contemplative rhetoric. Although the ottava rima stanza excludes "eloquence," it retains the capacity for humorous "rhetoric," chiefly in the digressions. Harold and Juan are thus seen as essentially the same characters, however different their "disguises" may be.

Chapter ii, "L'offensive," begins with a consideration of the psychological origins of the "classical" satires, "la haine réfléchie," moves on to discuss "la technique offensive," basically frontal and simple—epigrammatic defamation, invective in the form of apostrophe, prosopopoeia, antiphrasis, black irony, without gaiety. But Byron's black comedy is not an expression of pessimism or negation: the desire for action is the great reality of his temperament, a confidence that things can be changed.

It is then argued, in a subsection of Chapter iii entitled "La Contemplation du monde: Le Reportage méditatif," that Byron in *Childe Harold* achieves the illusion of a confrontation between external reality and certain intellectual "données." One looks in vain for objective description or evocation of place: everything in Cantos iii and iv is seen through the lens (or lenses) of Byron's reading, which has become part of him. In effect, all Byron's art tends toward a dualistic equilibrium or balance, a double affirmation of the world and himself, though in the last two cantos, unlike the first two, a portion of Byron's private life has become a public thing, and it is the world, now, which "se rattache au moi."

However, because Byron as traveller was seeking always some human experience, some human agony or certitude which had conditioned some aspect of his own existence, the contemplation of things in *Childe Harold* is also at the same time a contemplation of self. Thus it is, as the poem progresses, that the distance between the "fictionnel" time of the poem and the "réel" or psychological time of the poet becomes less and less, for the poem becomes increasingly an account of an interior voyage, elaborated and interpreted for a certain kind of audience. In Canto iv a process of mutual absorption has taken place—of character by author and author by character, with the paradoxical result that increasingly Byron sees himself and knows himself "de l'extérieur," a free and autonomous observer.

It is this achievement that makes possible Byron's humor, allowing him to "sketch your world exactly as it goes," without regard for public opinion, at least in appearance, and affecting a complete contempt for artistic arrangement. Such a reduction to the absurd has certain limits, however; the poet must never paint the picture in colors too somber or too bright and must always sustain it in light of a gaiety that prevents the melancholy from becoming cruel, protected alike from pathos and from preaching.

Central to Byron's satiric humor is the digression, which substitutes psychological time for time fictive and constitutes an intrusion of the present into the literary chronology. In *Don Juan* the digression takes the form of a conversation pure and simple—its tone disengaged, even flippant, and perfectly suited to the role that Byron could now assume with ease— that of the gentleman-author who has seen everything and easily adapts his style to his audience, the digression opposing its "bavardage" to cant on every level and unmasking it.

Part iv, the last, deals with the narrative mode of Byron's poetry, opening with an introductory chapter "Du mythe au récit," in which a startling comparison is made between the secret life of Walter Mitty and Byron's own secret life. Despite all, however, Escarpit is forced to the familiar conclusion that Byron failed in the drama, and in his climactic chapter, containing more plot summary than necessary, he considers the non-dramatic narratives. Indeed, those pages dealing with *Beppo* and *Don Juan* are disappointing, being too often heavily descriptive, and the new sources suggested for *Juan* are merely asserted, not demonstrated.

The portrait of the Byronic literary temperament which emerges finally is by no means always a familiar one, but it is one that demands consideration. Escarpit's Byron engages in the act of writing as a refuge against chaos, including that within himself, and so organizes or creates both self and his world, by an act of combative will almost military in its disciplined thrust. Thus even when Byron wrote, he was a man of action, finding his equilibrium in the gesture of writing rather than in the thing written or in any indestructible image of his agonies. Thus Escarpit sees Byron as a "popular" writer, in the most contemporary sense of the word: he came to love "la canaille" and wrote for it.

There are appendices on Byron's lameness and last illness, the question of incest, his marriage and separation, and his habits of composition. The long bibliography of fifty-one pages is annotated and helpfully divided into sections dealing with criticism of individual poems, Byronic influence in individual countries, and other matters of interest.

The only full-length treatment in English of Byron's poetry to appear in the 1950's is Truman Guy Steffan's introductory volume to the variorum *Don Juan,* entitled *The Making of a Masterpiece* (Austin, 1957). His study is divided into three main parts and five appendices. Part I, "Chronicle," places the poem in its biographical setting, tracing chronologically the circumstances of its composition and quoting generously from Byron's letters. Part II, "The Anvil of Composition," analyzes "Byron's writing as it progressed through his nine hundred manuscript pages" and "speculates about the artistic and psychological motivations for the accretive stanzas, summarizes the facts about the quantity of manuscript correction, sketches the interests and purposes that emerge from the various foci of revision, and . . . defines and illustrates abundantly the major principles that account for Byron's many verbal changes." Part II is the most interesting and valuable of the three parts and is essential to any study of the poem. Part III, "An Epic Carnival," a canto by canto "holiday tour" of the poem is somewhat less satisfactory, intended to "introduce" Byron's poem "to less special readers and to quicken their admiration." Indeed, Steffan sometimes writes as if he is addressing readers who have not read the poem. The long discussion is confessedly and deliberately repetitious; there is much paraphrase, summary, and forthright character analysis, until finally the massed detail becomes almost overwhelming. Nor can we always agree with the critical judgments expressed. For example, the complexity of Julia's character goes unrecognized as Steffan concludes that Byron "has not fully reconciled the three Julias," before, during, and after the bedroom scene. After a clear and convincing description of the artful symmetry of Canto ii, he states that the controlling principle is a "crude dichotomy," the "main doctrine" of the Canto "the dominion of the body." Lambro is "a mixture of unassimilated qualities and scarcely credible as a whole personality. We stare at him as a literary curiosity, a quaint novelty." Henry and Adeline "are the most valid and credible individuals in the epic. They have less paradoxical caricature in them" than any of the other major characters. Or, finally, in the English cantos, Byron becomes "uncomfortably self-conscious about his writing," and most of them "do not leave so strong an impression as do the best of the first eight. . . . improvisation often becomes excessive and capricious. . . . the material for the most part controlled him." Among the appendices, however, are a most useful and detailed "Chronology" of composition and publication, and "A Reference List of Accretive Stanzas," canto by canto. "Stanzas Showing the Full Process of Manuscript Composition" prints twenty-four stanzas just as Byron wrote and revised them line by line, with interesting editorial and critical comment by Steffan.

The decade of the 1960's produced a rich harvest of sixteen full-length critical studies of Byron, introduced with great originality by George M. Ridenour's *The Style of* Don Juan (New Haven, Conn., 1960), which explores the poem in terms of "two organizing themes, the Christian myth of the Fall and the classical rhetorical theory of the styles"; there is also "a third, non-thematic mode of organization, the continuing presence of the speaker or *persona*," which "in its relations with the protagonist, makes it possible for the poem to move," that is, gives to it "a developing dramatic action," from a state of innocence to experience. (Ridenour confesses a debt to Harold Bloom.) Chapter i, "Honest Simple Verse," provides a sensitive, subtle, and enlightening examination of the "Dedication" of *Don Juan* in the light of Augustan satiric theory and practice (and their classical predecessors), to distinguish between Byron's use of the plain, middle, and high styles and to demonstrate his debts and triumphs of tone. The "Dedication" is shown to be "an elaborately traditional satire in the Augustan manner," in which Byron speaks "from behind the traditional satiric mask." Chapter ii, "A Waste and Icy Clime," introduces "the Christian doctrine of the Fall [as] a *metaphor* which Byron uses to express his own personal vision," asserted to be "elaborately coherent." Thus, if his view of human nature "is not remarkably optimistic, neither is it broodingly grim." (Contrast Robert F. Gleckner, seven years later, discussed below.) No one who has read Ridenour can ever again read Byron's Haidée episode in the old simple way. Chapter iii, "The Unforgiven Fire," derives its title from Canto i, stanza 127, which associates "first and passionate love" with Adam's fall, describes it as an "ambrosial sin" but still a sin, and identifies it with "the unforgiven / Fire which Prometheus filched for us from Heaven." In terms of the Haidée episode this means that "The most powerful force undermining the paradisal relationship is the very force that made it a paradise in the first place." Chapter iv, "My Poem's Epic," defines the "action" of *Don Juan* as a "process of gradually narrowing the gap between speaker and protagonist." As Juan "falls from innocence, . . . he rises to the level of the speaker. The gain is not unequivocal . . .," as Byron's poem confronts the problem of becoming an honest epic satire of an age without heroes. This chapter may leave some lingering doubts in the mind of the reader. Chapter v, "Carelessly I Sing," is concerned with "the specifically rhetorical aspects of the art of *Don Juan*," and it is boldly asserted that "Lord Byron had a real genius for the handling of rhythm." Unfortunately, the stanza chosen for analysis (ii.27) is unrelievedly prosaic. Elsewhere Ridenour is more convincing in his demonstration of Byron's mastery of such traditional elements as alliteration, assonance, consonance, internal rhyme, puns, zeugma, metaphor, conceit, and tone, the latter of "special importance." There are two appendices, one on the relation between *Childe Harold* and *Don Juan*.

In the degree of hostility expressed toward Byron's poetry, Paul West's *Byron and the Spoiler's Art* (New York, 1960) is unique among modern critical studies. The book is also remarkable for the contradictory positions it assumes, intemperately stated. Although West is scornful of the biographical approach to Byron and of those who employ biography as an aid to critical analysis, he repeatedly makes biographical assertions himself, many of them related only indirectly to the poetry. He writes, for example, "The more repudiated he [Byron] was, . . . the more he had to resort to sour grapes." Or, still psychologizing simplistically, he asserts, ". . . fearful of derision, he derided first." West takes as his text one of Byron's more melodramatic confessions, and he takes it literally and quite uncritically: "if I don't write to empty my mind, I go mad." So, West believes, all Byron's writing is what he calls "release writing," a "spontaneous overflow." This is supposed to explain the poet's "abdication from the deeper pity, from the final and purposeful language it entails." The limitations of this kind of criticism were pointed out by William H. Marshall (*KSJ*, 1962).

West's curiously ambiguous position concerning Byron's greatest masterpiece may well be explained by one of the most startling statements he makes: "His style does not develop, does not improve between *English Bards* (1809) and *Don Juan*." This represents a fundamental failure of critical sensitivity or understanding, and not untypically it takes the form of assertion rather than reasoned argument. Elsewhere, West praises *Don Juan* repeatedly, and Byron "remains a great comic poet," but West also believes that ". . . choppy absurdities . . . are the essence of the poem," an expression of Byron's "grasshopper mind," insensitive to "the subtler means of articulation." For West, *Don Juan* is merely "a rag-bag of interesting exhibits," and it is therefore understandable, I suppose, why the only sustained discussion of the poem is limited to pages 66–73.

In addition, we are told, Byron "was not a literary critic." He "only rarely made up his own mind about problems of form." "Byron was simply too unimaginative to compose drama." Even so, Byron is compared favorably to Chaucer, Gide, Milton, Verlaine, Landor, T. S. Eliot, Blake, and Villon. Elsewhere there are extended comparisons of Byron with Hemingway and, more remarkably, with Baudelaire. West's cultivated weakness for exaggeration is well-illustrated by his statement, Byron is "unread in England and canonized abroad." There are, to be sure, occasional insights in West's book, even of some brilliance, and they suggest that the author has not found his true subject in Byron, of whom he is essentially contemptuous. One is left with the impression of a mind forcing itself to write of what it does not like, to come up with a very small book.

Andrew Rutherford's *Byron: A Critical Study* (Stanford, 1961, 1966*) is of a different and higher order: always clear, usually convincing, free of arcane critical jargon and of vague abstractions far removed from the poem's concrete world of universal particulars, and respectful of the poem's evidence. Rutherford's criticism is rooted in the reality of Byron's life and personality, but uses these only to throw light on the poems, which he normally reads with both common sense and sensitivity. Rutherford divides his attention about equally between the romantic and satiric poems, excludes the plays, and orders his chapters chronologically. He understands that the "central weakness" of the first two cantos of *Childe Harold* "lies in his [Byron's] failure to establish any significant relationship" between the title character and the narrator. "They co-exist but do not interact." The six verse tales which Byron wrote before leaving England in 1816 Rutherford discusses under the title "Romantic fantasy." Of their heroes he concludes, "it is impossible to take them seriously, either as symbolic figures or as representations of human nature." The protagonist of *Childe Harold* iii "shows a marked advance," for narrator and hero have here become essentially one, and everything is seen in relation to one or another of his four main concerns,—"his own wrongs and sorrows, the fate of genius, the liberty of peoples, the value and significance of Nature"—thus giving to the poem an admirable unity, although there are flaws of tone and consistency in the character of the protagonist, whom Rutherford finds to be "unsatisfactory," finally. The canto is described as "extremely good bad poetry," and on the next page, surprisingly, it is asserted that *The Prisoner of Chillon* is "indeed the best" of Byron's non-satiric work. This view is argued with some persuasiveness, and it is one of the virtues of Rutherford that he stimulates the reader repeatedly to re-examine his own judgments of these poems. The importance and interest of *Manfred* are recognized, but it is judged to be a "failure." The variety of moods and the various levels of style in *Childe Harold* iv, Rutherford observes, permit Byron "to express [more] adequately his own complex nature" and point to the achievement of the mature satires. The origins and triumphs of *Beppo,* allowing Byron to achieve "a new integration of the dandy and the poet," are fully described and its uniqueness recognized: it is "a great satire based not on morality but immorality—on a hedonism which asks us to disapprove only of bores," and "more than any other poet . . . Byron [here] conveys the *fun* of being alive and sinning." *Don Juan* is given five of Rutherford's thirteen chapters, and in them he discusses the composition of the poem, resurveying ground covered by Steffan and agreeing with Steffan that the English cantos possess certain weaknesses and that the unifying theme of the entire poem is in some way illusion or appearance versus reality. *Don Juan* is judged to be a "triumph of self-revelation," its "greatness" dependent in important part on its recognition of "the coexistence in real life of discordant elements"; it is "a very great poem, but a flawed one," marred by a "fundamental ambiguity of outlook," the product of the author's "intellectual and psychological confusions." In short, the poem's "strengths and weaknesses are both related to the poem's inclusiveness." A final chapter argues that *The Vision of Judgment* has "the characteristic excellences of *Don Juan,* with none of the longer poem's faults, just as it has the artistic perfection of *Beppo* without any of its triviality." It is Byron's "masterpiece, aesthetically perfect, intellectually consistent, highly entertaining, and morally profound."

William H. Marshall's *The Structure of Byron's Major Poems* (Philadelphia, 1962) is concerned, as its title suggests, not with style in the limited sense but with the larger organization of a selected number of the poems, many of which Marshall reads as increasingly successful dramatic monologues; thus he analyzes plot structure, characterization, motivation both conscious and less than conscious, and, most centrally, dramatic irony. There is also some theological or philosophic criticism, as well as psychological. Marshall's typical analysis of a poem begins with an introductory statement of his position and moves on through the poem as it develops, with a reasonable amount of quotation and paraphrase, yielding a substantial number of valuable critical insights. After dealing in two early chapters with Byron's work before 1816, Marshall considers the productions of his "Middle Phase," 1816–18, and finds that in these (and later) poems Byron "demonstrated his growing acceptance of imperfection in man's capacities and of disorder in human affairs as the basis for subli-mational order in art: in his major poems of the Middle Phase Byron dramatized the ironic situations of those who were essentially unable to reconcile themselves to imperfection." *Manfred* is read as "essentially a sustained soliloquy," in which the title character, like Childe Harold of Canto iii, fails in his attempts to remake his vision of the world and thus ceases "to struggle toward resolution." The structure of *Childe Harold,* Canto iii, is seen to reveal "a nonmechanical symmetry of which the Rhine Journey is obviously the center and the opening and closing addresses by the speaker to his daughter are the bounds. The second half of the poem mirrors the first half, and the total poem possesses organic wholeness rather than merely an accidental sequence of personal passages." Perhaps the most valuable of Marshall's discussions appears in Chapter vi, which deals with *The Lament of Tasso, Mazeppa,* and *The Prophecy of Dante,* poems which have suffered from relative critical neglect. *Beppo* and *Don Juan* are dealt with briefly in a final chapter, and of the latter poem an original view is proposed: "It is not satire, for it ultimately offers, in its description of the absurdities of the real, no suggestion of the ideal. Its irony is terminal rather than instrumental; this is achieved and sustained principally through a complex of individual monologues . . . ," delivered by "an apparently indefinite number" of speakers. *The Vision of Judgment* is not discussed. George M. Ridenour in a reply to Marshall, "The Mode of Byron's *Don Juan*" (*PMLA,* 1964), demonstrates the existence of a single narrating voice capable of speaking in a variety of tones to express a variety of coherent attitudes; clarifies the various values or ideals that this voice admires and champions, and thus denies that the various ironies of the poem ever "collapse into absurdity." He asserts convincingly that the poem "is in fact a satire in the real sense. . . . It is important to resist the notion that all skepticisms are alike, all ironies equally corrosive."

András Horn's monograph, *Byron's "Don Juan" and the Eighteenth Century English Novel* (Bern, 1962), concerned with Fielding, Sterne, and Smollett, demonstrates first that the influence of Fielding upon Byron's poem is clear but that the extent of it is not overwhelming, nor does Horn press his thesis excessively or generalize beyond his evidence, recognizing that the three novelists whose influence on Byron he explores represent only a small part of Byron's total experience. However, Horn recognizes in Don Juan the same "amorous frailty" that is characteristic of Tom Jones, along with the latter's "passivity, goodness, and harmlessness," and these qualities, in both Byron's and Fielding's major works, are linked with an "active humanitarianism." Sterne's influence is seen in the form of an intrusive first-person narrator, whose presence repeatedly creates the illusion that he is destroying the artistic illusion, and in the relative formlessness of both *Tristram Shandy* and *Don Juan*. (Horn, however, does not seem to understand the two time schemes of Byron's poem—that of the narrator and that of the title character.) Smollett's influence exerts itself in the form of the tradition of the picaresque novel, which tends to create a "conglomerate," achieving great variety of reality, an illusion of totality, but with little interest in unity of plot. Horn recognizes also that "the inner logic of *Don Juan* governed Byron quite independently of Smollett's influence and the picaresque tradition."

Bonamy Dobrée's lecture on *Byron's Dramas* (Nottingham, 1962), although far from uncritical, provides a calm and sensible antidote to Paul West's somewhat hysterical discussion of the plays, arguing that Byron's verse, "eminently sayable," is "admirable stage speech." He states that Byron's plays, if properly pruned, can be most effectively staged.

Peter L. Thorslev in *The Byronic Hero: Types and Prototypes* (Minneapolis, Minn., 1962) deals with a subject of great importance for as the author states, ". . . the figure with the most far-reaching consequences for nineteenth-century Western literature was the Byronic Hero." Somewhat defensively he asserts that there has been "no definitive study of the Byronic Hero's antecedents in the literature before Byron, or of the hero in Byron's poetry itself." However, Thorslev in his introduction alone discusses five books on this subject, and his study closes with a useful, five-page "Bibliographical Appendix of Hero Types." It includes nine pages of notes, chiefly bibliographical. The subject is, in fact, a much studied one, as the author confesses later: "Most of the heroes in this list [to be discussed at length in Chapters ii–viii] have been typed and classified before, and some of them . . . have been the subjects of detailed scholarly studies."

"The main point . . . is that all the elements of the Byronic Hero existed before him in the literature of the age." The author has three "main purposes": "to seek out the origins of the Byronic Hero, not in Byron's personality, but in the cultural and especially the literary milieu of the age in which he lived. Second, . . . to define and briefly to trace the Byronic Hero's development in . . . *Childe Harold,* the four first . . . romances, and . . . *Manfred* and *Cain.* Finally, . . . to place the Byronic Hero in the Romantic tradition." The first of these purposes is the chief one, and the satires are referred to only incidentally or not at all.

The main prototypes are listed in the chapter titles: The Child of Nature; The Hero of Sensibility: Man of Feeling or Gloomy Egoist; The Gothic Villain; The Noble Outlaw; Faust; Cain and Ahasuerus; Satan and Prometheus. The author, then, is concerned with large areas and broad generalizations, and such classification, he admits, "entails a great deal of oversimplification." He denies that his study is a *Quellenstudie* (although there is occasional source hunting): "Whether or not Byron read the works in question is . . . not of great importance in this study." Such an approach, of course, makes it very difficult to consider the ways in which Byron shaped the materials that he inherited, although it is useful "in the organization of literary history," and only the last seventy-two pages, in fact, are concerned directly with Byron's heroes. Elsewhere, references to Byron's poetry are few; in Chapter ii, for example, Byron is referred to only briefly on the last page.

The central chapters (ii–viii) are clearly and interestingly written, however, even though they do not always add greatly to existing knowledge, nor does Thorslev make any very great claims to originality, his notes often failing to clarify the difference between his treatment and that in earlier studies. But these chapters are valuable as wide-ranging summary, the product of immense reading, often emphasizing the relationships between types, and valuable also because here literary history is rewritten from the point of view of the early 1960's.

Chapter ix, on *Childe Harold,* is not convincing in its discussion of the number of main characters in Cantos i and ii, but it is clearly demonstrated that the early Harold is kin to the Child of Nature, the sentimentalized Gothic Villain, the Gloomy Egoist, the Man of Feeling, Cain, and the Wandering Jew. Chapter x points out that the Giaour is "primarily a sensitive Gothic Villain." Selim "is almost pure Hero of Sensibility," but he is also a "fully developed" Noble Outlaw, like Conrad the Corsair, who has the features of the Gothic Villain. There are plot summaries and pages of character description for the sake of establishing relationships. Chapter xi makes the point that "Manfred stands as the culmination of a long tradition of heroes. He is representative of almost every one of the hero-types of the Romantic movement." Parallels are again described, one by one. Thorslev believes that Manfred exists in a "godless universe," but, even so, "like Manfred, Cain remains defiant to the end toward both Lucifer and God." The book closes with a discussion of "The Byronic Hero and Heroic Tradition."

The chapter on Byron in *The Romantic Ventriloquists: Wordsworth, Coleridge, Keats, Shelley, Byron* by Edward E. Bostetter (Seattle, Wash., 1963) is one of the most reasonable and readable accounts of *Don Juan,* its backgrounds and origins. Bostetter discusses such topics as Byron's ideas concerning man's relation to the deity and the universe, man's physical nature, Byron's motives for writing, the development of Byron's heroes, existential elements in Byron's view of human existence, man's insignificance in the universe, the remarkable similarity of *Cain* and *The Vision of Judgment*—and the ways in which all these elements or developments made possible the writing of *Don Juan* and fashioned that poem. Byron is here viewed as the only one of the Romantic poets discussed to come to terms successfully with the complexities of the early nineteenth century and to refuse to retreat into an illusioned world view.

Byron: A Collection of Critical Essays, edited by Paul West (Englewood Cliffs, N.J., 1963), demonstrates again that the critical revolt against Byron and his poetry has run its course. Of the fourteen essays selected by West (one from the 1920's, three from the 1930's, one from the 1940's, six from the 1950's, three from the 1960's), only one is undisguisedly hostile, West's essay on the plays, and one perhaps is of mixed tone, Mario Praz's chapter from his *Romantic Agony,* which seems dated and unconvincing today. The tone of the other twelve is complimentary, often overwhelmingly complimentary. Byron, it seems, often wrote much better than he knew, in terms of fertility symbols and archetypal situations, or, if we read West on the plays, much worse than he thought. M. H. Abrams has pointed out elsewhere "the apparent difficulty of saying unobvious things about his [Byron's] poetry." In these essays, however, one is often struck not so much by obvious things as by a painful or violent straining to avoid the obvious, even to deny it. The results may be most extravagant, as the critic is drawn to see reflections of his own thought on other, less Byronic poets. Among the worst of such offenders are G. Wilson Knight the Shakespearean in "The Two Eternities: An Essay on Byron" (1939) and Bernard Blackstone the Blake scholar in "Guilt and Retribution in Byron's Sea Poems" (1961). But Helen Gardner is excellent on *Don Juan,* in a review-article (1958) of the variorum edition of Steffan and Pratt, as she recognizes Byron's "intellectual vitality and vivacity" and his "intellectual toughness and temperamental resilience." Gilbert Highet in "The Poet and His Vulture" (1954) contemplates Byron's "unrelenting pessimism. It is not hysterical, or revolutionary, nor is it the pessimism of the isolated intellectual. It sounds like the considered verdict of an educated, experienced, reflective man," one whose mind "moulded the minds of Heine, Lamartine, De Musset, Leopardi, Pushkin; yes, and Berlioz." "Probably he is the last of the great satiric poets writing in English." Bertrand Russell and John Wain also call attention to Byron's immense influence on the Continent. Here, then, in this collection one may find a startling variety of Byrons—Byron the schizophrenic and the paranoic, the Shakespearean Byron, Byron the symbolist, Satanist, and surrealist, the Augustan Byron, Byron the careless craftsman as well as the diligent reviser, Byron the mythical force, and several other Byrons—but as one might expect from such a varied collection, no coherent image of the poet emerges from the volume.

Northrop Frye's essay on Byron in *Fables of Identity* (New York, 1963) appeared originally in an anthology of English literature intended for use in college courses. Frye finds that "the main appeal of Byron's poetry is in the fact that it is Byron's," "a consistently interesting person" who wrote "incredibly readable" poems. "He proves what many critics declare to be impossible, that a poem can make its primary impact as a historical and biographical document." Byron is thus viewed as "a tremendous cultural force that was life and literature at once," and his influence is found upon Delacroix, Berlioz, Pushkin, Nietzsche; Balzac, Stendhal, Dostoevsky; Melville, Conrad, Hemingway, A. E. Housman, Thomas Wolfe, D. H. Lawrence, W. H. Auden. All these writers "Byronize." "Modern fiction would be miserably impoverished without the Byronic hero," for he was "a portent of a new kind of sensibility," which dramatically denied the old "hierarchy of nature with a moral principle built into it."

Andrew Rutherford, in his lecture on *Byron the Best-Seller* (Nottingham, 1964), explains the reasons for the poet's popular success in his own day, summarizing the opinion of many of his famous contemporaries. The original *Childe Harold* offered "a fascinating blend of the picturesque . . . ; of current affairs . . . ; of private meditations . . . ; of the ancient and classical . . . ; and of the romantic and exotic." It is "a kind of plain man's poetry, which a plain man can appreciate without difficulty." In addition, Harold "the pilgrim without a faith" and the heroes of the early verse tales, "rebels without a cause," functioned like "projections, symbols, 'objective correlatives' of the deep frustration and disillusion of a generation" growing up amid the evils deriving from the French Revolution. Harold-Byron, the traveler without a destination, is also engaged in a journey within, exploring the self. Thus the Byronic theme of the alienation of the artist spoke to a growing sense of the alienation from society of every sensitive individual. But Byron was also "satisfying a taste that had already been created," and these early works "have certain kinds of appeal characteristic of bad art in any age," related to "certain archetypes of romantic experience." The discussion of *Don Juan,* with brief remarks also on *Beppo* and *The Vision,* is both enlightening and amusing.

Although M. K. Joseph in his *Byron the Poet* (London, 1964) observes that "even now the field of Byronic critical studies appears more lightly tilled than that of any other comparable English poet," his bibliography lists twenty-five full-length critical studies of Byron's poetry and over eighty shorter critical studies. Joseph has done his homework well but he has not been overwhelmed by his critical predecessors and he regularly comes up with insights both original and convincing, expressed with clarity, grace, and precision. Surveying the whole poetry of Byron, Joseph emphasizes the original variety of the early *Childe Harold,* its combination of sentiment and satire or burlesque, and the clear separation of hero and narrator, the former intended as "a negative moral example." Joseph has a gift for quoting the best of the early Byron (for example, *Childe Harold* ii.5–6, on the ruined temple of the skull) and providing a fresh and imaginative analysis of it. He also considers the nature of the description in that poem and its relation to the eighteenth-century topographical poem. Of the early tales he observes, "The journey to the East is also a journey into the past, and both are blended with the atmosphere of the Gothic tales of terror," validated by Byron's personal experiences and authenticated by his careful concern for accurate detail. There are interesting short discussions of the heroes of the tales and of Byron's search after form and variety of meter, along with an essay on *The Island,* which does not deal with the problem of the comic Ben Bunting. Chapter iii, "The Later *Childe Harold,*" opens with a brief section on "Byron as Tourist," moves on to consider "The Author and the Pilgrim," "Nature and Man," "Art and Man," etc. The criticism is not thesis ridden or forced into any preconceived rigid structure, nor is it limited to purely verbal or other textual concerns. It is the expression of an intelligent, sensitive, educated mind reacting to the poems on all possible or reasonable levels. The fourth canto in its "original shape" is seen as "quite firm and symmetrical, ... a kind of debate between art and Nature." There is an enlightening discussion of the later additions to Canto iv and of the thematic conflict and resolution, reminding us that the canto is "as much a political as an antiquarian poem." The chapter on the dramas emphasizes Byron's originality and departures from the melodramatic rant and complexity of most of the plays of his day.

The discussion of *Don Juan,* occupying about half the volume, summarizes briefly the "composition" of the poem, surveys Byron's use of his sources (including non-literary sources), and considers his models in the Italian comic epic, the picaresque novel, improvisation, and conversation. There is a subtle, enlightening, and always interesting consideration of the poem's narrator and related problems, as well as one of the very best discussions in print of the imagery and diction of the poem. Following is an account of the themes of the poem—"love and war, . . . Nature, the poem itself and its moral intention"—and of the function and kinds of scene or setting and characters. Another chapter discusses the morality of *Don Juan,* chiefly in terms of Byron's treatment of love and war. "The Age of Cant" considers the implications of the terms "enthusiasm," "system," and "cant," in the political, poetical, religious, and moral realms. This chapter, however, is centrifugal and often moves away from the poem. A concluding chapter deals with the irony of *Don Juan,* and an appendix provides a table showing the proportion of narrative to comment and digression in each canto. Joseph is aware of the prevailing views of Byron the poet, reflects them reliably and accurately, but also provides a number of important critical insights of his own.

Byron's Poetry: A Critical Introduction by Byron's great biographer, Leslie A. Marchand (Boston, 1965), is, as its title implies, addressed to students and general readers and promises "no startling revelations." It provides, however, a useful poem-by-poem account, chiefly descriptive in nature, written "in the light of what is now known of the life, character, and psychology of the poet, and of the intellectual and literary milieu in which he wrote." About one-third of the book is devoted to *Don Juan,* and an opening and a closing chapter consider Byron's meaning and value for us in our time. There is an excellent selected, annotated bibliography of ten pages.

It is difficult to decide whether to discuss G. Wilson Knight's *Byron and Shakespeare* (New York, 1966) under the heading of biography or criticism (or neither). Although similarities or correspondences between the two great poets of Knight's title often throw unexpected light on Byron, Knight's intellectual excesses are frequent: "Byron *was* Shakespearean drama incarnate." He "was by turns or simultaneously Hamlet, Puck, Macbeth, Falstaff, Antony, Timon and Prospero." The chapter called "Sonnets and Seraphs" attempts to demonstrate that "Byron's life and writings bear evidence of a sexual balance close to Shakespeare's." Both writers express a "horror of sexual lust"; both inveighed against female falsity to vows of love; both sang of homosexual love, etc., etc. There are frequent references to the earlier publications of Knight in place of clearly reasoned argument, as he builds upon himself. When the argument touches upon astral travel or projection and the seraphic experience, it soars out of sight. "A Regency Hamlet" establishes that Byron also had a difficult mother, was "by nature lonely and melancholy," lost his father, and saw ghosts. Byron's *Cain* is said to be "patterned closely on *Hamlet*," both plays being dominated by the idea and presence of death. Mary Anne Chaworth rejected Byron, "as Ophelia rejected Hamlet." Both Byron and Hamlet delighted in acting. The obvious conclusion is that Byron was capable at times of a tragic vision of life, at times with himself as tragic hero. The evidence is swept up, uncritically, from every possible source, often without serious regard for chronology or allowance made for circumstance or the recipient of a letter or the reliability of the reporter of a conversation. The next chapter, "Falstaff and Comedy," underlines the method. Into one bin went all the notes (made fifteen years before the writing of the book and by then somewhat cold) on Byron as Hamlet, into another bin all the notes on Byron as Falstaff. Needless to say, Knight cannot put Byron-Falstaff back together again, although the analysis of Byron's Falstaffian qualities is made somewhat easier by the fact that one may distinguish a variety of Falstaffs. It is also true that stage comedy influences what is called life and that there are certain Shakespearean qualities in Byron (as in almost every man), but these qualities are not to be found significantly in Byron's poetry. Perhaps the chief value of this discussion is the repeated juxtaposition of passages from both poets, which reveals how well Byron stands up beside the master. This chapter also has an interesting biographical discussion of Byron's relations with William Parry at Missolonghi. But the great flaw of the book lies in its mad or immoral treatment of evidence. The thesis is that Byron *lived* Shakespeare's plays; biographical parallels are drawn with the plays; and because in Knight's view the man and his poetry cannot be separated, it is demonstrated that Byron also *wrote* like Shakespeare. What is clear is that Byron spent many hours reading Shakespeare, remembered much of this reading, and quoted repeatedly from Shakespeare, as the indexes to Byron's *Works* demonstrated long ago. Knight can also move directly from the poetry to establish biographical fact: *Childe Harold* iv.5–6 is quoted to demonstrate that "Byron enjoyed experiences of a clairvoyant kind." The last chapter argues that Byron "is a great royalist poet." Perhaps no more need be said about G. Wilson Knight.

Much thought and reading has gone into Robert F. Gleckner's *Byron and the Ruins of Paradise* (Baltimore, Md., 1967), which focuses chiefly on the poems written before Byron left England in 1816, to which about 214 pages are given, in an effort to make a "case" for the quality of these poems, supply a critical need ("most modern critics perpetuate the fashion of disdaining to comment" on them), and provide a firm or extended base for the author's argument that Byron contemplated, consistently and from the first, "a frighteningly dark and coherent vision . . . of the human condition," which "develops gradually into the myth of man's eternal fall and damnation in the hell of human existence, the myth of what I choose to call the ruins of paradise and the consequent human condition." Byron, then, is relentlessly depicted as a peculiarly modern poet-prophet of doom. To support this thesis, 314 pages are given to the non-satiric poems and plays, leaving only twenty-eight pages for *Beppo* and *Don Juan*. (Gleckner is not much interested in the Byronic comedy of love.) *The Vision of Judgment* receives only passing mention. The use of quotation, especially from the letters and journals, is uncritical and highly selective, designed to support the thesis, and the author frequently fails to consider the self-dramatizing qualities of Byron's mind. There are also difficulties in the discussion of the poetic "I" (Byron-the-poet), the narrator, and the title character of *Childe Harold*.

Although Gleckner's book calls us back repeatedly to Byron's non-satiric poetry, especially that of the earlier years, and so performs a service, perhaps its greatest flaw is that it attempts to claim for Byron both too much and too little. He reads Byron through a pair of very dark glasses, which filter out much of the light and deny the balance of Byron's vision. This is an incomplete view. It is too much to claim that the poet of *Childe Harold* iii is "Everyman" or that Manfred, on whom Gleckner is especially unsatisfactory, "is the human condition" or that in *Childe Harold* iv "the particulars of his [Byron's? the narrator's?] little span on earth become human history and *la condition humaine*." Gleckner's Introduction distinguishes between his positions and those of West, Ridenour, Rutherford, and Marshall, discussed above.

In Truman Guy Steffan's *Lord Byron's* Cain: *Twelve Essays and a Text with Variants and Annotations* (Austin, Texas, 1968), brief accounts of the composition and publication of the play are followed by discussions of "Byron's Views of the Play," "*Cain* in Chancery," and Byron's dramatic theory. All this is clearly written and useful to have in one place, but it adds little to what was already known. "The God of This World" considers thirteen numbered ideas which are of interest to the play, and "The Orthodox Family" describes the conformist characters. An analysis of Cain, Lucifer, and Adah follows. Somewhat more interesting are the accounts of Byron's "Re-creation of Genesis," the imagery of the play, the medley of language (not always successfully blended), and the metrics of the play (remarkably free). A description of the manuscript, owned by The University of Texas at Austin, precedes the text and variants. Following the notes, seven-eighths of them concerned with analogues, there is "A Survey of *Cain* Criticism" (160-odd pages), extending from the opinions of members of Byron's circle to the comments of twentieth-century critics. A bibliography of twenty-three pages and a full index close this definitive edition.

The opening chapter of W. Paul Elledge's *Byron and the Dynamics of Metaphor* (Nashville, Tenn., 1968) provides an introduction to his subject and sets forth his conclusions. The author has excluded the satires and limited his analysis to six romantic poems and three plays, but he has defined his topic broadly. The term "metaphor" is "almost always used interchangeably" with the terms "image," "figure," and "configuration," "to suggest the general principle of comparison in Byron's poetry: that is," he continues, "similarities, analogies, correspondences among two or more ostensibly disparate objects, concepts, or experiences are distinguished by the poet for the purpose of illuminating afresh some facet of human existence." Thus the author can discuss stylistic or structural matters as diverse as similes and contrasted characters.

In the poems and plays considered, he discovers four dominant ' metaphorical vehicles for illuminating the paradoxical composition of human nature" · these are fire and clay, light and darkness, "organic growth and mechanical stasis," and "the image of the counterpart (or the *Doppelgänger* motif)." Elledge observes further, "in each of these image patterns, polarities are juxtaposed; and . . . the thematic purpose of the juxtaposition is twofold. Byron means first of all to figure forth the essen tial dichotomy of human nature, and second, to dramatize the pathos and tragedy of mortality, precipitated by man's efforts to reconcile the antithetical impulses of his being. That such a reconciliation is finally impossible is suggested again and again by Byron's antipodal imagistic construct." With the main outlines of this study, then, we can agree. The three central chapters deal with *The Corsair, Lara,* and *Parisina* (1813–15); *The Prisoner of Chillon, Childe Harold* iii, and *Manfred* (1816–17); and *Marino Faliero, Sardanapalus,* and *Cain* (1820–21).

The discussion of *Childe Harold* iii, illuminating as it often is, suffers occasionally from imprecision. For example, "the terms 'Harold,' 'narrator,' and 'speaker' are used interchangeably." Nor is Elledge wholly convincing in his effort to refute the "erroneous notion that the narrator is a static figure," arguing that he is "partially successful" in his "search for spiritual equilibrium." But Elledge is also aware that "Harold has protested too much," is capable of an "exercise in self-deception," and one might wish that this dramatic irony had been explored further. This critic is at his best, perhaps, in his treatment of Cain, whose fire and clay are analyzed most impressively in terms of Cain's impassioned pursuit of knowledge (balanced against his murderous temper) and of his loving care of the earth (balanced against his contempt for the clay-like bonds of merely human limitations), with the devil as *Doppelgänger* throughout.

Fiery Dust: Byron's Poetic Development (Chicago, 1968) by Jerome J. McGann is one of the most important books about Byron to appear in the twentieth century. Using a number of approaches or methods—critical, textual, and biographical—neglecting neither the intellectual nor the psychological elements in Byron's artistic development, McGann addresses himself directly to the problem of the poet's expression of self in his works, a "poetry of sincerity" (however different from Wordsworth's). He is concerned most centrally with *Childe Harold's Pilgrimage,* in all its cantos, dealing with it in a way not customary, as a single poem, to reveal the clear development of the narrator from the first through the fourth canto and to establish this poem as the normative foundation of the argument following, which points out the basic continuity of a developing self in all Byron's poetry, through his last great masterpiece. Thus McGann is most seriously concerned with the problem of biography in art, as Byron explores and creates his own personality as he writes. As the narrating poet is the true hero of *Childe Harold,* so also Byron is the narrator of *Beppo,* the norm of the civilized man, citizen of the world, in that poem. Similarly, the narrator of *Don Juan* is not to be understood as a "persona" in any usual sense of the word, but as a "person," the historical Byron, with the result that if we are to appreciate either poem "not only fully, but properly, we must be familiar with Byron's life." This is still bold argument today, but *Fiery Dust* is a bold book, and its argument is most persuasive.

All of this clearly goes back to *Childe Harold* (and to earlier poems). McGann is the first scholar, to my knowledge, to give a reasonably complete account of the manuscript versions of this great threefold or fourfold poem and of the way in which it grew in length and in artistry. He has, furthermore, learned to write (from Byron, surely), and the felicity of his style is such that it succeeds in making the first two cantos of *Childe Harold* much more interesting than most readers today have ever found them to be. His pages should draw many a reader back even to a reperusal of *Hours of Idleness.*

Perhaps the best way in this brief space to suggest the scope and organization of the book is to quote McGann: ". . . the first two sections [on *Hours of Idleness* and *Childe Harold's Pilgrimage*] and the final section [chiefly on *Beppo*] define certain crucial events in the development of Byron's art, and the second section in particular provides a sustained analysis of poetic development in the case of a single, and fundamental, work. . . . Sections three and four are developmental studies of Byron's tales and plays. These sections contain analyses of certain basic themes in Byron's work, with an emphasis upon the relation of the particular works to the corpus as a whole. The two sections parallel each other insofar as they each carry the analysis of Byron's fundamental ideas well into his *Don Juan* period. In this way they supplement the study of *Childe Harold's Pilgrimage* and prepare even more particularly for the concluding essay on *Beppo*. . . . My concern is primarily with the development of Byron's styles and themes, and with presenting studies of a number of particular works and crucial ideas which have been somewhat neglected." The four tales and five plays discussed are *The Giaour, The Prisoner of Chillon, Mazeppa,* and *The Island*; and *Marino Faliero, The Two Foscari, Sardanapalus, Cain,* and *Heaven and Earth.*

Paul G. Trueblood describes his *Lord Byron* (New York, 1969) as a "modest book" (it is one of the Twayne series) addressed to "the student and general reader." It provides a useful, eclectic, non-controversial summary of a number of dominant critical views up to the early 1960's and gives "considerable attention to Byron's life," upon the assumption, shared with Bernard Blackstone, Edward E. Bostetter, Jerome J. McGann, and others, that an understanding of Byron the man "is prerequisite to a critical assessment" of Byron's poetry. For his biographical account, Trueblood relies chiefly (and inevitably) upon Leslie A. Marchand's definitive life of Byron, and for his discussion of *Don Juan* upon Elizabeth F. Boyd's *Critical Study* of the poem and upon Trueblood's own *Flowering of Byron's Genius*. The author states, "I have dealt with the genesis of each [major] work, its subject matter, structure, style, and relationship to the poet's total poetic production. Likewise, I have endeavoured to present some of the most pertinent and perceptive critical views of Byron now current among scholars. I have concluded the book with a brief summary of Byron's contribution to literature and society." There is a useful selected, annotated bibliography of two and a half pages.

Michael G. Cooke, in *The Blind Man Traces the Circle: On the Patterns and Philosophy of Byron's Poetry* (Princeton, N.J., 1969), arguing that "Byron's poems transcend a collection and exist as a body of poetry," discovers common stylistic and philosophic features in poems and genres remarkably diverse, early and late. In Chapter i an examination of a handful of Byron's lyrics suggests that their "plain, cryptic exterior" will reveal, upon close examination, "finely wrought personal positions on time, memory, nature, will, culture, knowledge, and essential being," all concealed by romantic rhetoric, with its "ostensibly naive surface of form and language." In the words of Earl R. Wasserman (*The Subtler Language*), we are called upon to give to these poems an "intensive metaphysical reading." Chapter ii, "The Fragmented Shapes of Order," argues that "agnosticism is what *Childe Harold* [iii] asserts," contradicting itself repeatedly in its assertions about a transcendental spirit of Nature and revealing to a close reading "the central disarray of Byron's experience." (Cooke believes that Byron's juvenile tribute "To Edward Noel Long, Esq." is "his most accomplished transcendental piece.") The main character of Canto iii is "reconnoitering avenues to emotional and moral security when he knows he contains in himself the insuperable barrier to success," but Cooke does not discuss the irony of this situation. Chapter iii, "The Fatal Bounds of the Will," not always clear or convincing, is concerned chiefly with *Manfred, Cain,* and "Ode to Napoleon Buonaparte." It concludes, "the outstanding common element in the portraits may be taken to be the evocation of a state of antinomy," and complains that Byron's "fictive persons question whether Manfred is sanctified [entitled to respect?] or damned" and that "the enlightened Cain has no viable fruit."

Chapter iv, "Byron and the World of Fact," explains that "the question of knowledge . . . occup[ies] a central position in Byron's work. . . . To study the apparent confusions of imagery and structure in his work, and the apparent rootlessness of his attitudes toward characters, actions, and ideas is to see them as strategies, as means to a comprehensive end which, paradoxically, perhaps, exchanges the hieratic finality of 'I affirm' for the profane unpredictability of 'I would affirm.' Hence . . . the imagery of contradiction in *Don Juan*, 'Mazeppa,' and *Childe Harold* III–IV," poems which are then examined from this point of view, with repeated or numerous references to Cooke's disagreements with other critics and the consistent misspelling of the name of Haidee (sic). This, then, is a study of ambivalence in Byron's poetry, its "readiness to face up to duality," and its "extraordinary accuracy in rendering the simultaneity of plural states."

Chapter v, despite its cumbersome title, "A Sad Jar of Atoms? Antidromic Order in *Don Juan*," is perhaps Cooke's best. It opens with a survey of recent criticism of the poem, moves on to discuss the influence of Restoration comedy on it, and argues that *Don Juan* is "a multiform statement of obligatory irresolution," aiming toward "a state of disequilibrium" in "reader and society," to create "a universe of the unpredictable" and the "recognition of disorder where it has been blinked or denied." In short, "the primary bent of his [Byron's] philosophy must be termed skeptical." This chapter, like the book as a whole, deals only briefly with *Beppo* and *The Vision of Judgment.*

The last chapter, "The Limits of Skepticism: The Byronic Affirmation," is somewhat disappointing. It ringingly asserts that there is a "viable option in Byron's thought, the peculiar form of humanism and stoicism that may be called counter-heroic." But the following discussion turns out to be somewhat more obvious than this statement might suggest: the "typical bête noire" of "counter-heroic humanism" is "Glory, or war," and "It is repeatedly made clear throughout the cantos on the Siege of Ismail that Byron inveighs against war as the epitome of man-made ills." Presumably no reader of these cantos has ever doubted this. And despite the affirmation discussed in this chapter, there is also a curious and disturbing reference to "the peculiarly defeated, even defeatist attitude of the mature satires." As quotations here may suggest, Cooke's style is often dense or labored. However, this book, tightly argued as it often is, has the virtue of frequently forcing the reader to pause and re-examine his own positions. There is a bibliography of seven pages and an index of topics and proper names.

As this discussion nears its end, it is appropriate to notice here *Twentieth Century Interpretations of* Don Juan: *A Collection of Criti-*

cal Essays (Englewood Cliffs, N.J., 1969), edited with an excellent introduction by Edward E. Bostetter, whose discussion of *Don Juan* in *The Romantic Ventriloquists* might have been included. This volume of sixteen essays, nine of them originally published in the 1960's, makes possible a retrospective view of some of the critics noted above and also permits reference to eight other essays not yet considered. Here, then, we find selections from the works of Eliot, Boyd, Steffan, West, Ridenour, Rutherford, Joseph, and Gleckner, already described. In addition, there are excerpts from the comments of Virginia Woolf, William Butler Yeats, Ernest J. Lovell, Jr., W. H. Auden, Karl Kroeber, Brian Wilkie, Alvin B. Kernan, and E. D. Hirsch, Jr. Bostetter's introduction, which deserves careful reading, traces the changing circumstances in Byron's life which influenced the composition of *Don Juan* and thus its form and style, surveys the shifting critical reception of the poem in our time, and explores the reasons for its continuing and increasing popularity. Virginia Woolf, writing in her diary in 1918, concluded, "It is the most readable poem of its length ever written," its "method . . . a discovery in itself. It's what one has looked for in vain—an elastic shape which will hold whatever you choose to put in it." Yeats, writing to H. J. C. Grierson in 1926, found in the poem examples of "perfect personal speech," an ideal which Yeats achieved increasingly in his own poetry. Byron was "the one great English poet—who sought it constantly." (Although James Joyce wrote no extended comment on Byron, Byron was one of Joyce's favorite poets and lives on in *Finnegans Wake*: see Robert F. Gleckner's essay in *Twelve and a Tilly,* ed. J. P. Dalton and Clive Hart [London, 1966].) Ernest J. Lovell, Jr., in "Irony and Image in *Don Juan*" (1957) finds the unifying principle of the poem in "the basically ironic theme of appearance versus reality" and explores "the consistently organic relation between episode and theme" as a prelude to a discussion of style. W. H. Auden, reviewing Marchand's *Byron: A Biography* in 1958, observes that in description of "the motion of life, the *passage* of events and thoughts," Byron is "a great master." (Auden, who was significantly influenced by Byron, discussed *Don Juan* in *The Dyer's Hand and Other Essays,* New York, 1962, and more recently in the *New York Review of Books,* 18 August 1966; he has stated that *"Don Juan* is the most original poem in English.") Karl Kroeber, in a chapter from his *Romantic Narrative Art* (1960) which does not always throw a great deal of light on Byron's poem, views it "as a precursor of a new kind of novel writing," anticipating "later novels rather than rework[ing] earlier models." Brian Wilkie, in pages selected from

"Byron and the Epic of Negation," a chapter in his *Romantic Poets and Epic Tradition* (1965), assumes that Byron "wanted to show life itself as ultimately without meaning," "emptying *Don Juan* of meaning" to produce "a sad and frightening poem" that expresses a view of existence "similar to [that of] many twentieth-century existentialists." Wilkie is more rewarding when he deals directly with epic structures in *Don Juan*. Taking a hint from Auden, perhaps, Alvin B. Kernan, in the excellent climactic chapter of his *The Plot of Satire* (1965), argues persuasively that Byron's "sense of life as endless movement and change" determined the "central rhythm," the "controlling concept of the poem, its basic action," a pattern which "comprehends and is made up of the movements of all the component parts, characters, events, metaphors, settings, stanza form, rhythms, and rhymes." This being true, it then follows that "In every case, what he holds up to ridicule is some attempt to restrain life, to bind and force it into some narrow, permanent form." Finally, E. D. Hirsch, Jr., in "Byron and the Terrestrial Paradise," an essay in *From Sensibility to Romanticism*, ed. Frederick W. Hilles and Harold Bloom (1965), extends and revises Ridenour's views on the metaphorical centrality in *Don Juan* of a Fall from Eden: it is "predicated on the periodic recurrence of a Redemption," translating man back again to a condition of "Edenic purity and perfection," the most important form of which is a "vision of a totally selfless and totally fulfilling love relationship. That is the principal earthly paradise. . . . These recurrent visions of an earthly perfection bear witness to the power of Byron's persistent faith in the possibilities of life. It was a faith that suffered from attacks launched continually by his own invincible honesty, but it also prevailed to the end."

The complex nature and the pervasive presence of that faith as it expressed itself in political terms in Byron's poetry is dealt with learnedly and authoritatively by Carl Woodring, *Politics in English Romantic Poetry* (Cambridge, Mass., 1970), who analyzes the political elements in all Byron's major poems and many of the lesser ones. David V. Erdman has surveyed the "Life and Works" of Byron in Volume III of *Shelley and His Circle,* ed. Kenneth Neill Cameron (Cambridge, Mass., 1970), as an introduction to twelve letters and literary manuscripts there published. This essay also emphasizes Byron's political interests. The account of " 'Fare Thee Well'—Byron's Last Days in England" in Volume IV, which publishes the first draft of the poem, with facsimiles and variants, adds to our knowledge of the newspaper attacks upon Byron at the time and their complex political motivation. There are shorter essays providing the necessary background for each of the ten letters and the two poems published.

For those who may believe that the great critical issues concerning Byron's poetry approached solution only during the last half-century or less, with the advent of "modern" criticism, it will be salutary to turn to *Byron: The Critical Heritage,* edited by Andrew Rutherford (New York, 1970), which reprints critical comments ranging from Brougham's attack on *Hours of Idleness* in the *Edinburgh Review* of 1808 to Arthur Symons on Byron in 1909, in *The Romantic Movement in English Poetry*. In between, constituting the first half of the book, are examples of criticism written by Byron's contemporaries, almost all of it during Byron's lifetime. Here we find, among others, Coleridge, Scott, Wordsworth, Jeffrey, Gifford, Jane Austen, Keats, Leigh Hunt, Croker, Hazlitt, John Wilson, and Shelley. These are helpfully organized or grouped in terms of Byron's individual poems or of genres such as the Turkish tales and the dramas. The second half of the volume reprints major documents of Victorian and Edwardian criticism, by such writers as Carlyle, Macaulay, Newman, Thackeray, George Eliot, Swinburne, Ruskin, Arnold, Saintsbury, and Paul Elmer More. This collection is limited almost wholly but not exclusively to English critics. The editor's introduction is excellent, and brief headnotes preface the selections. "Material has been selected on various grounds—for its intrinsic value as criticism, for its historical interest, for the light it throws on other authors through their response to Byron's works, for its impact on Byron himself, and for its representative quality."

V. REPUTATION AND INFLUENCE

For the history of the vicissitudes and fluctuations of the poet's reputation in his own country reference should be made to S. C. Chew's *Byron in England: His Fame and After-Fame* (1924). Based upon this, supplementing it in some particulars, and containing interesting illustrations is Mario Praz's *La Fortuna di Byron in Inghilterra* (1925). R. A. Rice's *Lord Byron's British Reputation* (Smith College Studies, v, 1924) is an excellent brief survey of the subject. For this country we have W. E. Leonard's *Byron and Byronism in America* (1905, 1965*), which reveals less indebtedness than might have been expected. Leonard's monograph is summarized and to a slight degree supplemented by S. C. Chew in "Byron in America" (*American Mercury,* 1924). Byron was for long interested in the United States and the other countries of the Western Hemisphere and persistently toyed with the idea of emigration. See B. R. McElderry, "Byron's Interest in the Americas," *Research Studies of the State Coll. of Washington,* v (1937), and J. J. Jones, "Lord Byron on America," *TexSE* (1941). For France a thorough piece of investigation which has maintained its authority is Edmond Estève's *Byron et le romantisme français: Essai sur la fortune et l'influence de l'œuvre de Byron en France de 1812 à 1850* (1907). The initial discussion of what may be called "pre-Byronic Byronism," especially in the writings of Chateaubriand, is of much interest and value. The story—not precisely of Byron's influence but of his "fortune"—is carried far beyond Estève's temporal limits in an article by E. P. Dargan on "Byron's Fame in France" (*VQR,* 1926), and in a monograph by W. J. Phillips, *France on Byron* (1941). For Germany we have L. M. Price's *The Reception of English Literature in Germany* (1932), in which Byron has his place. Cedric Hentschell's *The Byronic Teuton* (1939) is disappointing, for this is chiefly concerned with an aspect of the German temperament. Beyond the linguistic range of most of us are two large monographs in which the influence in Holland is demonstrated: T. Popma, *Byron en het Byronisme in de Nederlandsche Letterkunde* (1928), and U. Schults, *Het Byronianisme in Nederland* (1929). There have been similar studies for Spain and for Scandinavian and Slavic countries.[2]

---

[2] Thanks are due to Professors Marchand, Pinto, and Trueblood for information and suggestions used in the revision of this chapter.—S. C. C.

V

SHELLEY

Bennett Weaver
Donald H. Reiman

I. BIBLIOGRAPHY

Although there is no exhaustive list of all Shelley criticism and significant allusion, the student will find competent guidance whether he wishes to study the general contours of Shelley's reputation as a man, a poet, and a thinker or whether he needs to search out all the important studies of one of Shelley's major works or ideas.[1] The standard enumerative bibliography is G. M. Matthews' excellent chapter on Shelley in George Watson's *New Cambridge Bibliography of English Literature*, III (1969), 309–43, which gives publication data on books and articles through 1967. Supplementing information of the succinct entries in *NCBEL* and keeping the enumeration up-to-date are the annual bibliographies in *Keats-Shelley Journal* (*KSJ*) and *PMLA* (both of which list dissertations, as well as

[1] Aimed at the graduate student of English, this chapter should also serve the needs of the undergraduate writing a term paper or honors thesis on Shelley or the non-specialist college teacher preparing to teach Shelley. I have commented upon and given the original publication dates for all useful books dealing with Shelley that might reasonably be found in substantial college or university libraries or metropolitan public libraries. In an age when photofacsimile reprints both in paperback and hardcover are appearing daily from a variety of publishers and reprint specialists, it can be given as a general though not inviolable rule that almost any worthwhile scholarly book will reappear in *Books in Print* or *Paperback Books in Print*. I have added an asterisk to the date of publication of books that I know to have been reprinted in substantially unaltered form. If the book has been substantially revised, I have added a second date to indicate this fact. I mention selectively articles in periodicals that would be similarly available and a few significant English-language articles in journals of more limited circulation. In the languages traditionally associated with graduate study in English literature—particularly French, German, and Italian—I treat a number of books useful to the advanced student, pleading my own limitations and the difficulty of access for not discussing the publications on Shelley in Japanese, Dutch, Russian, Czech, Bengali, and other languages.

In updating Professor Weaver's account of Shelley scholarship since the 1956 edition, I have left his opinions of earlier studies wherever this was possible under the altered situations and exigencies of space caused by the proliferation of Shelley scholarship during the subsequent fifteen years.

published books and articles) and *English Language Notes* (*ELN*), which since 1965 has published "The Romantic Movement: A Selective and Critical Bibliography" that had previously appeared in *ELH* (1937–49) and *PQ* (1950–64). A collected volume of the earlier bibliographies in this series is in prospect, comparable to that edited in 1964 by David Bonnell Green and Edwin Graves Wilson collecting the first twelve annual bibliographies from *KSJ* (covering July 1950–June 1962). For those who need listings of earlier British and American criticism of Shelley not treated by the annual periodical bibliographies, four studies supply the want: Newman Ivey White's *The Unextinguished Hearth* (1938*), which lists, discusses, and reprints the bulk of published comment on Shelley during his lifetime; Willis W. Pratt's unpublished Ph.D. thesis (Cornell, 1935) "Shelley Criticism in England: 1810–1890"; Julia Power's *Shelley in America in the Nineteenth Century* (1940*); and Sophia Phillips Nelson's unpublished Ph.D. thesis (Pittsburgh, 1950) entitled "Shelleyana: 1935–1949." See also Kenneth Neill Cameron's excellent critical account of "Shelley Scholarship: 1940–1953" (*KSJ*, 1954). Those seeking lists of studies of Shelley's major poems or important aspects of his thought can find them in specialized studies listed elsewhere in these pages. The leading earlier French studies of Shelley are listed in Henri Peyre's *Shelley et la France* (1935) and Hélène Lemaitre's *Shelley, poète des éléments* (1962) There has been no good study centering on German criticism since Solomon Liptzin's *Shelley in Germany* (1924), but there have been useful articles on Shelley studies in the Netherlands by L. Verkoren (*Levende Talen,* 1950; in Dutch) and in the Soviet Union by Boris Gilenson (*Soviet Literature,* 1963; in English). There have been numerous studies of Shelley in Japanese and in various languages in Europe and India, but unfortunately, the original contributions in these languages must find their way into the English-speaking critical tradition through English-language writings by scholars from these countries. Dissertations, published and unpublished, that treat Shelley are included in Lawrence F. McNamee's *Dissertations in English and American Literature* (1967; Supplement One, 1969). Finally, a brief but useful paperback bibliography for undergraduates is Richard H. Fogle's *Romantic Poets and Prose Writers* (1967).

The best *descriptive* bibliography of the first editions and other early editions of Shelley's own works is still Harry Buxton Forman's *The Shelley Library* (1886). Supplementing Forman's descriptions are those by Ruth S. Granniss in her catalogue of the Grolier Club's centennial exhibition *A*

Descriptive Catalogue of the First Editions in Book Form of the Writings of Percy Bysshe Shelley (1923) and by Thomas James Wise in *A Shelley Library* (1924); both these volumes contain many facsimiles of title pages and manuscripts. Wise's fine collection, also described in his *Catalogue of the Ashley Library* (1922–36), is still basically intact in the British Museum. *The Early Collected Editions of Shelley's Poems* by Charles H. Taylor, Jr. (1958), centers on Shelley's *Posthumous Poems* of 1824 and the pirated editions that appeared between that date and Mary Shelley's four-volume *Poetical Works of Percy Bysshe Shelley* (1839). Other bibliographical points are to be garnered from critical editions of Shelley's works or of individual poems.

Important manuscripts relevant to Shelley, besides those recorded in Forman's and Wise's collections, have been enumerated or described in various publications; Forman wrote a three-volume account of three rough-draft *Note Books of Percy Bysshe Shelley . . . in the Library of W. K. Bixby* (1911*), now in the Henry E. Huntington Library. Another important Huntington manuscript, Edward Williams' transcript of *Hellas* corrected by Shelley, is described by Bennett Weaver in an essay published in Volume VIII of the University of Michigan's Publications in Language and Literature (1932). The fair-copy notebook of Shelley's poems now known as the *Harvard Shelley Notebook* has been reproduced in facsimile with notes by George Edward Woodberry (1929). Unfortunately, in some instances Woodberry confused the handwriting of Shelley and Mary Shelley, and the work requires reediting. Another, slighter Shelley notebook now in the Library of Congress has been discussed by Frederick L. Jones (*SP,* 1948). The Shelley manuscripts at the University of Texas have been enumerated in *An Account of an Exhibition of Books and Manuscripts of Percy Bysshe Shelley* (1935), Willis W. Pratt, *Lord Byron and His Circle: A Catalogue of Manuscripts in the University of Texas Library* (1948), and Pratt's "Lord Byron and His Circle: Recent Manuscript Acquisitions," *Library Chronicle of the University of Texas* (1956). Those at Texas Christian University have recently been published in full by Lyle H. Kendall, Jr., in *A Descriptive Catalogue of the W. L. Lewis Collection. Part One: Manuscripts* (1970). The holdings of the Pierpont Morgan Library were briefly sketched by George K. Boyce (*PMLA,* 1952, p. 21) and those in the Huntington Library by H. C. Schulz in his account of "English Literary Manuscripts in the Huntington Library" (*HLQ,* 1968). A complete *Catalog of Books and Manuscripts at the Keats-Shelley Memorial House in Rome* appeared in 1969.

At present the three largest and most important collections of manu-scripts of Shelley, his family, friends, and acquaintances are owned by Lord Abinger, by the Bodleian Library, Oxford, and by The Carl H. Pforzheimer Library, New York. James Scarlett, Eighth Baron Abinger, inherited the bulk of letters and manuscripts relating to William Godwin, Mary Woll-stonecraft, and Mary Wollstonecraft Shelley that once formed part of the collection assembled by Shelley's son Sir Percy Florence Shelley at Bos-combe Manor. (Large portions of the Boscombe collections were tran-scribed and printed—though not especially accurately—in the privately printed, limited edition entitled *Shelley and Mary*, 1882.) Lord Abinger's collection has been twice microfilmed, once for Duke University (copies of these films have been deposited in the Bodleian Library, Oxford, and various American university libraries, including the University of Texas) and once for the late Carl H. Pforzheimer for the private use of the staff of his library. Portions of the Duke microfilms have been described by Lewis Patton in an article in *Library Notes* (Duke Univ., 1953). In 1893 the Bodleian Library, Oxford, received certain Shelley manuscripts as a bequest from Lady Jane Shelley, widow of Sir Percy Florence Shelley. Portions of this bequest were described in three publications: C. D. Locock, *An Examination of the Shelley Manuscripts in the Bodleian Library* (1903), which concentrated on the poetic texts; A. H. Koszul, *Shelley's Prose in the Bodleian Manuscripts* (1910); and R. H. Hill, *The Shelley Correspon-dence in the Bodleian Library* (1926). In 1948 and 1962 the Bodleian received two additional bequests of manuscripts once at Boscombe Manor from Sir John Shelley-Rolls and from his widow. The first of these be-quests was described by Neville Rogers in *TLS*, 27 July, 3 August, and 10 August 1951, and at greater length in *Shelley at Work* (1956; 2nd ed. 1967). Parts of these twentieth-century bequests of Shelley manuscripts have been examined by a number of scholars: James A. Notopoulos has discussed Shelley's tranlations and quotations from Plato in *The Platon-ism of Shelley* (1949*) and in *KSJ* (1966); Irving Massey has edited one of the copybooks in which Mary Shelley transcribed texts for her collected editions of Shelley's poetry (*Posthumous Poems of Shelley*, 1969), at the same time collating the texts of these poems with Shelley's drafts scattered through the Bodleian and Huntington manuscripts; G. M. Matthews, Donald H. Reiman, Joseph Raben, Jean de Palacio, R. B. Woodings, and Judith Chernaik have studied various special problems within the manuscripts in books and articles cited later in this chapter. Their publications provide incidental guidance to various parts of the

Bodleian's collections, which have been microfilmed for Duke University, the University of Wisconsin-Milwaukee, and various Shelley scholars.

The Carl H. Pforzheimer Library, the third major repository of Shelley manuscripts, has undertaken systematic publication of its major holdings. *Shelley and his Circle, 1773–1822* includes a diplomatic text and bibliographical description of each manuscript, besides discursive commentaries and essays, and many illustrations, maps, and facsimiles of manuscripts. Though generally chronological in arrangement, the catalogue-edition has been expanded through new acquisitions as the work progressed. Kenneth Neill Cameron was the general editor of the first four volumes that cover the period through November 1816 (Vols. I–II, 1961; Vols. III–IV, 1970); Donald H. Reiman is editing the succeeding volumes. Volumes V–VI, covering Shelley's life through the end of 1819, are scheduled for publication late in 1972.

Finally, F. S. Ellis' *Lexical Concordance to the Poetical Works of Percy Bysshe Shelley* (1892*) is a most useful reference book; though not quite as accurate, perhaps, as the recent computer-printed concordances, it has the virtue of being much more legible, especially in its handsome first printing. Unfortunately, its titles are keyed to Harry Buxton Forman's two-volume edition of Shelley's poetry (1882), which is not now widely available. Because it lacks reference to Shelley's poems and variant readings published since 1882, a new concordance will have to be done after there is a standard, complete edition of Shelley's poetry.

II. EDITIONS

The text of Shelley is now in flux. Fresh examination of the manuscript sources of the texts of Shelley's poems, prose works, and correspondence has stimulated an interest in editing his works unmatched since the 1860's and 1870's. These efforts will probably continue until there are new collected editions of Shelley's poetry, prose, and letters that can stand up under the scrutiny of the best modern textual critics. This section will review the earlier critical editions of Shelley's poetry, prose, and letters, discuss the present state of the various texts, and mention the principal editions known to be in progress.

Besides the texts published during Shelley's lifetime and Mary Shelley's volume of his *Posthumous Poems* (1824), Mary's collected editions are of primary importance. Her four-volume *Poetical Works of Percy Bysshe Shelley* (1839) has valuable notes and comments on the poems, though as Taylor has shown in his *Early Collected Editions of Shelley's Poems,* Mrs. Shelley carried over some errors from two early pirated editions that she used as copy texts. Her one-volume second edition of the *Poetical Works* (1839–40) added several poems—including *Peter Bell the Third* and *Swellfoot the Tyrant*—but she made no substantive corrections in the texts of the poems published earlier. The one-volume collected edition was reprinted for years, sometimes bound with a similar reprinting of the prose and letters contained in Mary Shelley's edition of Shelley's *Essays, Letters from Abroad, Translations and Fragments* (2 vols., 1840). Mary Shelley's three-volume edition of Shelley's poetry (1847; the last edition during her lifetime in which type was completely reset) corrects some errors in the earlier collected editions but basically derives from the 1839–40 texts, besides introducing additional errors.

William Michael Rossetti's two-volume edition of *The Poetical Works of Percy Bysshe Shelley* (1870) addressed itself to many of the difficulties in Mrs. Shelley's editions and corrected a number of errors. But Rossetti was somewhat too confident of his own judgment in the absence of corroborating objective evidence, and many of his shrewd guesses turned out to be merely guesses. His methods were challenged and Shelley's text corrected by Harry Buxton Forman, whose four-volume edition of the *Poetical Works* (1876–77) was joined with a four-volume edition of Shelley's prose and letters (1880) to form the Library Edition of his works. Rossetti profited from Forman's suggestions to revise his rival edition of the poems in 1878 (3 vols.), and in three volumes or one (Moxon's Popular Poets) Rossetti's text of Shelley's poetry challenged Forman's (revised in two volumes, 1882, and in five volumes as the Aldine Edition, 1892). New competition arose in England from Edward Dowden's one-volume text (1890) and in America from George Edward Woodberry's variorum Centenary Edition (4 vols., 1892; condensed in one volume as the Cambridge Edition, 1901). Dowden's editing was conservative, following Forman as his basic text; Woodberry had the advantage of using Shelley manuscripts in the collection of Charles W. Frederickson, the first important American collector of Shelley, and in the Centenary Edition he also recorded the substantive variants between his text and other editions.

C. D. Locock entered Shelley studies with his *Examination of the Shelley Manuscripts in the Bodleian Library* (1903), in which he presented variants from the accepted printed texts that he had culled from the MSS. Following that exploratory exercise, Locock went on to edit *The Poems of Percy Bysshe Shelley* for Methuen (2 vols., 1911). Locock's interest in the Bodleian holographs (none of which contained texts that Shelley had actually polished for the press) had given him a rather too easy acceptance of all manuscripts as authoritative over the printed first editions. Like Rossetti, however, Locock had acute logical sense and poetic sensitivity. His text is radical in the number of conjectural emendations it introduces, but his notes—giving reasons for his conjectures—are extremely valuable to the critic. Locock's edition will remain useful to students and critics, though its text can never be trusted without consulting other editions.

In 1904 the Oxford University Press published Thomas Hutchinson's edition of Shelley's poetry. In 1905 this text was reset as the Oxford Standard Authors Edition; in 1934 it was reset again, and after many printings it has recently been reissued in an edition slightly corrected and updated by G. M. Matthews (1969). As Matthews states in his preface, the basic text is that of Hutchinson; its strengths are that Hutchinson had the good sense to use as his principal copy text Forman's carefully done, conservative edition. The chief weakness of the OSA text for the modern student is that it fails to include most poetic texts and information about them that have been discovered or accepted since 1904. For example, it lacks the final three-and-a-half lines of "The Triumph of Life" (first published by C. D. Locock in 1911), as well as the dozens of substantive textual corrections of that poem derived from the manuscript by Matthews himself and by Donald H. Reiman in the 1960's. Much the same criticism can be directed at the poetic texts in the Julian Edition (10 vols., 1926–30*), edited chiefly by Roger Ingpen, though nominally the joint work of Ingpen and Walter E. Peck. In addition to being outdated by recent scholarship, the Julian Edition exhibits some strange twists in its search for novelty as it accepts dubious authorities, changes copy texts without reason, and occasionally introduces conjectural emendations without necessity. Yet, because the Julian Edition conveniently collects most of Shelley's writings in one edition, it and the readily-accessible Oxford Standard Authors edition remain the two texts most often quoted and cited by students and critics and from these editions derive—with or without acknowledgment— the texts of Shelley used in most selections and anthologies intended for the student and general reader. Thus most readers have access only to incomplete and corrupt texts of some of Shelley's most discussed poems.

Few editors of selections from Shelley's poetry have made any attempt to update their texts and notes to accord with recent scholarly findings. G. M. Matthews' earlier *Shelley: Selected Poems and Prose* in the New Oxford English Series (1964) contains freshly edited texts of the poetry it includes and helpful notes as well; unfortunately the narrow space-limitations of the series restricted Matthews to 114 pages of poetry, making *Adonais* the longest poem to be included entire. In the United States M. H. Abrams included a recent text of "The Triumph of Life" and excellent notes on Shelley's thought and art in the revised edition of the *Norton Anthology of English Literature* (1968). Abrams' space is also restricted (though not quite so severely as Matthews'), and neither of these selections really serves the need for a Shelley text in an upper-level undergraduate or post-graduate course on the Romantics.

The Shelley texts in the series that usually fill these needs are at the time of this writing inadequate. Carlos Baker's Modern Library College Edition (1951) has a text based on the first-editions, but contains no notes. Kenneth Neill Cameron's Rinehart Edition (1951) bases its text on the Julian Edition, prints selections from the poems, prose, and letters in arbitrary order based on thematic categories, and includes only portions not only of *Queen Mab* (as does Baker) but even of *Julian and Maddalo*. Cameron's notes and study helps, though brief, are usually helpful. Not so those in Neville Rogers' Riverside Edition (1968), which besides selecting only from Shelley's poetry in texts basically those of Thomas Hutchinson's 1904 edition, contains numerous factual errors and misquotations in the Introduction and notes. (Rogers' volume was reprinted without correction in England in 1969.) Harold Bloom's Signet Classic edition (1966) glosses over its textual limitations with a plea for eclecticism; it provides a stimulating essay on Shelley in its Introduction but has few notes. Ellsworth Barnard's Odyssey Press edition (1944) stands apart from most of the selections in the amount of original work the editor put into his student edition. Barnard drew texts of generous selections from Shelley's poems, essays, and letters from a variety of authorities and annotated them fully and with originality. Yet the very independence of Barnard's work and its inability to reflect the scholarship and criticism of the last quarter-century combine to make it, like Locock's edition, most useful as a supplementary study aid. None of the Shelley editions, complete or selected, contain any of the early poetry from the Esdaile Notebook, first published in 1964 (see below).

After pointing out the limitations of all these collected and selected editions of Shelley's poetry, it would be pleasant to announce that the ideal editions for the novice and for the advanced student, teacher, and specialist that overcome them are about to be published. But no quick or easy solution is in sight. Projected critical editions of Shelley's complete poetry have been announced by Neville Rogers (in four volumes for Oxford University Press) and G. M. Matthews (in one volume for Longman's), but neither has indicated a target date for publication. At least one students' edition of textual integrity is also in progress for Norton Critical Editions, but no such selection of Shelley's works will fully serve the advanced student or teacher.

Nor are the collected editions of Shelley's prose and letters complete or up-to-date. After Mary Shelley's, only three collected editions of Shelley's prose have any claim to attention—Volumes v–viii of Harry Buxton Forman's Library Edition, Volumes v–vii of Ingpen's and Peck's Julian Edition, and David Lee Clark's one-volume edition entitled *Shelley's Prose* (1954*). Forman's edition is incomplete, not including Shelley's longest prose work, "A Philosophical View of Reform"; the value of Clark's edition is vitiated by the editor's lack of interest in ascertaining his textual authorities and by numerous typographical errors, as well as by the editor's egregious, misguided theories on the dates and—consequently—the purposes of Shelley's surviving prose. By default, therefore, the best collective text of Shelley's prose is that in the Julian Edition. But, as with Shelley's posthumously published poetry, there are numerous corrections of the published texts to be made from Shelley's holograph manuscripts. Those selections of Shelley's prose useful to the student include *Shelley's Literary and Philosophical Criticism,* ed. John Shawcross (1909), *Political Tracts of Wordsworth, Coleridge, and Shelley,* ed. R. J. White (1953), *Prose of the Romantic Period,* ed. Carl R. Woodring (1961), *A Defence of Poetry and The Four Ages of Poetry,* ed. John E. Jordan (1965), *Shelley's Critical Prose,* ed. Bruce R. McElderry, Jr. (1967), and *Shelley's Political Writings,* ed. Roland Duerksen (1970).

Frederick L. Jones's *Letters of Percy Bysshe Shelley* (2 vols., 1964) claims to be complete except for the unpublished letters in The Carl H. Pforzheimer Library that are to appear in *Shelley and his Circle*. Actually it is something less carefully wrought, including two letters certainly not by Shelley—Jones's numbers 413 (by an unidentified contemporary of Shelley) and 454 (a forgery)—and omitting a large number of checks, promissory notes, and other relevant items. Jones worked primarily from photocopies and in some instances introduced new errors into texts that were relatively accurate in earlier editions (including the Julian Edition). As Jones's editions of *The Letters of Mary W. Shelley* (2 vols., 1944) and *Mary Shelley's Journal* (1947)—the latter based on the corrupt text in *Shelley and Mary*—stand in need of reediting, so there will be material for a new edition of Shelley's letters as soon as *Shelley and his Circle* is completed. Until then the scholar and advanced student will do well to compare Jones's text with other printings of the letters—especially those based on the holographs, such as *Shelley and his Circle* and Lyle Kendall's *Descriptive Catalogue of the W. L. Lewis Collection* (see Part I above).

Individual portions of Shelley's works have been reedited, though with mixed success: the early poems contained in the so-called Esdaile Notebook have been printed in three texts—by Kenneth Neill Cameron in *The Esdaile Notebook* (1964), by Neville Rogers in *The Esdaile Poems* (1966), and again by Cameron in Volume IV of *Shelley and his Circle* (1970), where the collective ideas of the two earlier editions and their reviewers are used to help establish the substantive text. Similar interaction by two editors has marked the reediting of Shelley's last major poem, "The Triumph of Life." In articles entitled "The 'Triumph of Life' Apocrypha" (*TLS*, 5 August 1960), "'The Triumph of Life': A New Text" (*SN*, 1960), and "Shelley and Jane Williams" (*RES*, 1961), G. M. Matthews presented new texts of "The Triumph" and some late lyrics associated with it. Donald H. Reiman challenged Matthews' *RES* article in "Shelley's 'The Triumph of Life': The Biographical Problem" (*PMLA*, 1963) and presented his own text of the poem (utilizing Matthews' work) in *Shelley's "The Triumph of Life": A Critical Study* (1965), which Matthews, in turn, reviewed in detail in *JEGP* (1967).

Lawrence John Zillman's two major attempts to edit *Prometheus Unbound* show a kind of schizophrenic self-rivalry wherein an editor lacking fixed principles of textual criticism is corrected for pursuing one false extreme and promptly rushes to its opposite. In his *Shelley's* Prometheus Unbound: *A Variorum Edition* (Univ. of Washington Press, 1959) Zillman reprinted the error-ridden first edition (1820), not even correcting obvious typographical errors; in his *Shelley's* Promotheus Unbound: *The Texts and the Drafts* (Yale, 1968) Zillman "corrects" far more than the full textual evidence warrants, depending far too heavily on three surviving Bodleian notebooks which contain an intermediate fair copy of the poem, but not the text as Shelley (or Mary under Shelley's supervision) finally prepared it for the press. If the reader of Zillman's editions has some sense of editorial principles, he can evaluate the textual problems of

Shelley's longest poem out of the raw material scattered through Zillman's texts, collations, and notes. But even Zillman's latest text marks no significant advance over earlier critical editions like Forman's, Hutchinson's, Locock's, or the Julian Edition, though it does provide improved readings of some individual cruxes. Until a sounder text is published, both the student and the scholar should be careful not to spin an interpretive point on *Prometheus Unbound* so finely that it can exist only on the basis of a particular reading in a single textual authority.

On the texts of a number of Shelley's other poems—particularly those lyrics and translations that first appeared after Shelley's death—similar problems exist and similar caution should be exercised. Shelley's translations from Plato are in a better state than some other texts because James A. Notopoulos in *The Platonism of Shelley* reedited them from the Bodleian MSS, updating his work in *KSJ,* 1966. More recently Timothy Webb has undertaken a study of the texts and significance of Shelley's translations of Greek poetry—the first visible fruit of his efforts being a new text of the Homeric "Hymn to Venus" (*RES,* 1970). *The Lyrics of Shelley* by Judith Chernaik (1972) offers readings of a number of Shelley's shorter poems—from "Hymn to Intellectual Beauty" and "Mont Blanc" through the lyrics to Jane of 1822, all newly edited from the manuscripts and first printings. Many of the smaller textual studies published in journals await confirmation of their authors' theories by later students of Shelley's texts. To return to the statement at the outset of this section, Shelley's text is in flux.

III. BIOGRAPHY

Mary Shelley herself, by the dictates of Timothy Shelley, was restrained from publishing any significant biographical comment on Shelley. For her thinking we turn to her Preface to *Posthumous Poems,* her notes to Shelley's *Poetical Works,* and her letters and journal. But toward the middle of the century Lady Jane Shelley and four men who had known the poet wrote on his life. In his article, "The Beautiful Angel and His Biographers" (*SAQ,* 1925), Newman Ivey White pointed out that by 1887 there were fourteen biographies of Shelley, no one of which agreed with the other thirteen. Like Sappho, thought White, Shelley had an "almost irrecoverable personality." And the scholar who was to write the master biography of Shelley concluded that such a biography could not be written. The student who wishes an authoritative comment on earlier biographers should turn to White's article. He deals with Shelley biography from the beginning down through André Maurois's *Ariel: A Shelley Romance* (1924).

Let us list the five early biographies, adding brief evaluative notes.

1. Thomas Medwin, *Life of Shelley* (2 vols., 1847; ed. H. B. Forman, 1913, "From a copy copiously amended and extended by the Author"). In dealing with the Oxford days, Medwin draws from Hogg's articles in the *New Monthly Magazine* (1832–33; see Hogg's *Shelley at Oxford*, ed. R. A. Streatfeild, 1904). Medwin, though sometimes factually inaccurate, gives valuable information about Shelley's literary interests.

2. Thomas Jefferson Hogg, *The Life of Percy Bysshe Shelley* (2 vols., 1858; ed. Edward Dowden, 1906). Again the first word is "unreliable," and the second, "the work must be read." See Edward John Trelawny, *The Relations of Percy Bysshe Shelley with His Two Wives Harriet and Mary* (1920), and Walter Sidney Scott, *Harriet and Mary* (1944). See also Henry S. Salt, *Hogg's "Life of Shelley"* (Shelley Soc. Papers, Ser. 1, No. 1, 381 ff.), and Elizabeth Nitchie's "Shelley at Eton: Mary Shelley vs. Jefferson Hogg" (*KSMB*, 1960).

3. Lady Jane Shelley, *Shelley Memorials* (1859). This book is not so much wrong in what it says as misleading through its intentional omissions. It provided the earliest texts of many letters to and from Shelley, but tended to gloss over incidents that reflect badly on Shelley or Mary.

4. Edward John Trelawny, *Recollections of the Last Days of Shelley and Byron* (1858; revised as *Records of Shelley, Byron and the Author*, 2 vols., 1878). Edward Dowden, who edited *Recollections* in 1905, wrote: "It is the record of a direct, competent and sympathetic witness," but Dowden did not know the full extent of Trelawny's penchant for fictionalized narration, and we may hesitate over the word "direct" (see Leslie Marchand, "Trelawny on the Death of Shelley," *KSMB*, 1952, and Anne Hill, "Trelawny's Family Background and Naval Career," *KSJ*, 1956).

5. Thomas Love Peacock, *Memoirs of Shelley* (1858–62; new edition, H. F. B. Brett-Smith, 1909). On 12 May 1858 Peacock wrote Claire Clairmont commenting on the review he had prepared for *Fraser's Magazine* (see Thomas J. Wise, *A Shelley Library*, pp. 118 ff.). Part 1 of the *Memoirs*, which appeared in the June number of the magazine, was a review of three works: Charles S. Middleton, *Shelley and His Writings* (1856); Edward J. Trelawny, *Recollections* (supra, 1858); Thomas J. Hogg, *The Life of Percy Bysshe Shelley* (1858). Part II appeared in

January 1860, Part III in March 1862. Peacock provides a clear, accurate, and just statement of the part of the truth he felt should rightly be public record.

These, then, are the five seminal biographies which the student must know. All are friendly to the poet. From William Michael Rossetti's "Memoir" (1870) to Edmund Blunden's *Shelley, A Life Story* (1946), the friendliness continues, with two exceptions. The first, John Cordy Jeaffreson's *The Real Shelley* (1885), attacks the poet. The book, which because of its astringency might have been healthful, is made ineffectual by irritated assertion and slanting accusation. The second, Robert Metcalf Smith's *The Shelley Legend* (1945), has been repudiated by N. I. White, F. L. Jones, and K. N. Cameron in *An Examination of the Shelley Legend* (1951). Among the minor friendly biographies of the last century are Denis Florence MacCarthy's *Shelley's Early Life* (1872), which, though doing excellent pioneer work in presenting the Irish episode, is not well organized and gives way easily to grateful enthusiasm; Felix Rabbe's *Shelley: The Man and the Poet* (in French, 1887; English, 1888); and *Shelley: A Monograph* (1888; revised as *Percy Bysshe Shelley, Poet and Pioneer*, 1896) by Henry S. Salt who, having examined the facts of the poet's life, acclaims him as an intellectual and social pioneer.

Rossetti's "Memoir" (first published with Rossetti's edition of Shelley's *Poetical Works* in 1870, revised, 1878, 1886) aims to transmit "a compact cento of facts." This it does. And the work deserves the characterization "scrupulous." The student, then, may well follow chronology, and having read the basic biographical works written by the friends of Shelley, read the "Memoir" by Rossetti. Rossetti will impress upon the student the fact that in biography the wisest friendliness is of the kind which stays closest to the truth. John Addington Symonds in his *Shelley* (1878; revised, 1887) carried on the friendly but fair tradition of Rossetti. His little work was soon overshadowed by Edward Dowden's *Life of Percy Bysshe Shelley* (1886), and the *Life of Percy Bysshe Shelley* (1887) by William Sharp was brought out in that shadow. The aim of this work was as far as practicable to narrate the incidents of Shelley's life impartially. Sharp proposed to write no more than "an introduction to the study of Shelley's life and work"; this purpose he satisfied sensibly and well. But for half a century the influence of Dowden's work remained dominant.

Dowden, like Hogg, was given access to materials in the possession of the Shelley family, but he betrayed no confidence. His favored position gave him all the advantage he desired. In fact, his work was one of impressive scholarship, dignity, and magnitude. Dowden failed, in deference to the insistence of Shelley's heirs, to tell the whole truth which he knew. (See Louise S. Boas, "Edward Dowden, the Esdailes and the Shelleys," *N&Q*, 1965.)

Arthur Clutton-Brock in *Shelley, the Man and the Poet* (1910), fearing to turn people against Shelley by disguising his faults, insisted too much on the faults themselves. Biographically more successful, although limited to the earlier years of the poet, is A. H. Koszul's *La Jeunesse de Shelley* (1910). Believing with Keats that "a man's life of any worth is a continual allegory," Koszul brought to his task the freshness of a mind skilled in another literature, and he was a thorough workman.

Roger Ingpen's *Shelley in England* (1917) is more valuable than is Koszul's book. Charles Withall, successor to William Whitton, lawyer for Sir Bysshe and Sir Timothy Shelley, discovered in Whitton's files twenty-nine letters, some pamphlets, and other documents dealing with Shelley. In order to utilize these materials, Ingpen decided to retell the story of Shelley's early years and to incorporate the materials at the proper places. He succeeded in writing an accurate book free of all moralizing. And since he was not interested in the criticism of the poet's works, he achieved objective biography.

Edmund Blunden's *Shelley, A Life Story* (1946*) has as its only serious weakness a failure to take into account all new information of Newman Ivey White's *Shelley*. In such earlier work as "Shelley Is Expelled," published along with essays by Gavin de Beer and Sylva Norman in *On Shelley* (1938), Blunden had proved himself a capable writer. In his biography, he added freshness and a sense of immediacy to the record. Such critical comments as he offered are generous and aged in careful appreciation.

Through the century of Shelley biography there runs a general trend toward the objective. Associated with this tendency is the drift toward the separation of the biographical and the critical. Walter E. Peck's two volumes, *Shelley: His Life and Work* (1927), learned but often inaccurate, had as a distinguishing characteristic the separation of the biographical and the critical. Having presented the biographical data pertinent to a given period of Shelley's life, Peck then wrote a critical inter-chapter treating Shelley's work during that period. In separating the one from the other, Peck made it possible to see what each is and to see clearly the relationships between them. *Shelley* (1940; revised, 1947) by Newman Ivey White is a masterwork. Facts here are gathered with great patience and presented with honesty. Critical evaluations are vitally related to the poet's life, yet White attempts to avoid forcing poetry into unnatural relationships with biographical facts. White, writing with both common sense and sympathy, explores the relationship between Shelley's family background and early life and the growth of his political and literary interests. Concerned as he is with Shelley's reputation, he brings to bear all the contemporary descriptions of Shelley and reactions to his personality and writings in an attempt to present an honest, rounded account of the man and the poet. White's chief discovery—the birth and death records of Elena Adelaide Shelley, the "Neapolitan child"—is treated within the context of Shelley's entire life and interests and given the most generous possible explanation. Though White occasionally introduces a factual error or draws an unwarranted inference, his picture of Shelley is both fair and full, so far as evidence was available in 1940. Should the student be interested in the work stripped of the trappings of scholarship, he should read White's *Portrait of Shelley* (1945*).

The biographical studies which have appeared since White's books have all been more limited in their scope, most examining one period or aspect of Shelley's life. Shelley's entire early career is most carefully reexamined by A. M. D. Hughes in *The Nascent Mind of Shelley* (1947) and, especially, by Kenneth Neill Cameron in *The Young Shelley* (1950), *Shelley and his Circle*, Vols. I–IV (1961, 1970), and his notes to *The Esdaile Notebook* (1964). Aspects of Shelley's associations with the Eton-Windsor-Marlow region were explored by W. G. Bebbington (earlier under the name "Noel Scott") in short studies published since 1949 in *N&Q, KSMB,* and *KSJ*. The most substantial of these are "Charles Knight and Shelley" (*KSJ*, 1957) and "A Friend of Shelley: Dr. James Lind" (*N&Q,* 1960). Desmond King-Hele, apparently unaware of Bebbington's work, also sketched Dr. Lind in *KSMB* (1967). Shelley's adventures in Wales including the Tanyrallt episode came under the scrutiny of H. M. Dowling in five pieces for *N&Q* (1954–55) that he to an extent summarizes in *KSMB* (1961); the same story is set in a larger context in Elisabeth Beazley's *Madocks and the Wonder of Wales* (1967). Shelley's first marriage and separation are examined from the bride's perspective in *Harriet Shelley: Five Long Years* (1962) by Louise Schutz Boas, who had earlier unravelled a minor mystery of 1815 in " 'Erasmus Perkins' and Shelley" (*MLN*, 1955). Samuel Joseph Looker's *Shelley, Trelawny and Henley: A Study of Three Titans* (1950) is interesting mainly because of its illustrations from the Worthing region.

Moving to Shelley's life after his elopement with Mary, we can add Shelley's *Letters* (ed. Jones) and *Shelley and his Circle* to the basic reference sources of *Mary Shelley's Journal* (1947) and *Letters of Mary W. Shelley* (2 vols., 1944), edited by Frederick L. Jones, and *The Journals of Claire Clairmont*, ed. Marion Kingston Stocking (1968). One can also consult books on Mary by R. Glynn Grylls (1938), Elizabeth Nitchie (1953), and Jean de Palacio (1969) and on Claire by R. Glynn Grylls (1939) and Iris Origo (*A Measure of Love*, 1957). Aspects of Shelley's two visits to Switzerland, earlier surveyed by Charles I. Elton (1894), are studied authoritatively by Sir Gavin de Beer in a variety of publications, including *KSMB* (1958) and Volumes III and IV of *Shelley and his Circle* (1970). A primary document for the second visit (1816) is *The Diary of John William Polidori*, edited in 1911 by William Michael Rossetti (Polidori's nephew). See also H. W. Häusermann, *The Genevese Background* (1952). John Buxton's *Byron and Shelley* (1968) promises more than it delivers in examining the long interaction of the two but it succeeds in reminding us that biographical material on Byron's later career is often useful for Shelley studies. Two books centering on Byron are especially important: C. L. Cline's *Byron, Shelley, and Their Pisan Circle* (1952) depicts Shelley as the center of the Pisan group and sketches for the first time John Taaffe, a minor associate of Shelley there (see also Cline's study of the threatened *auto-de-fé* at Lucca in 1821, *TSLL*, 1968); William H. Marshall's *Byron, Shelley, Hunt and the "Liberal"* (1960) deals with Shelley himself only in its early chapters but shows his spirit influencing the course of the periodical, including its hostile reception in England. Other aspects of Shelley's life in Italy are examined from the perspectives of his friends and acquaintances there—Elizabeth Nitchie, *The Reverend Colonel Finch* (1940); Edward C. McAleer, *The Sensitive Plant: A Life of Lady Mount Cashell* (1958); Ernest J. Lovell's *Captain Medwin* (1962); *Maria Gisborne and Edward E. Williams, Shelley's Friends: Their Letters and Journals,* ed. Frederick L. Jones (1951; for corrections to the Gisborne portions, see the review by George H. Ford, *MP*, 1952).

Ivan Roe uses Shelley's "last sixty-nine days" as a center for perspective on the poet's entire life in *Shelley: The Last Phase* (1953). Shelley's mood in this period has been examined by G. M. Matthews in "Shelley and Jane Williams" (*RES*, 1961) and by Donald H. Reiman in "Shelley's 'The Triumph of Life': The Biographical Problem" (*PMLA*, 1963). Reiman also examines a number of biographical matters in the 1816–19 period of Shelley's life in Volumes V–VI of *Shelley and his Circle*.

IV. CRITICISM

A. GENERAL CRITICAL STUDIES, 1900–1970

As Cameron has noted, until the mid-1930's there was no full scale critical book on Shelley, but there were a number of earlier books on him that aimed less at giving an account of his life than a conception of his thought and commentary on his works. The nineteenth-century studies of this kind have all been treated under "Biography," but a few in the first four decades of the twentieth century deserve mention here.

Henry Noel Brailsford's *Shelley, Godwin, and Their Circle* (1913; revised, 1951), though instructive in pointing out the importance of Godwin's (then) all-but-forgotten ideas in Shelley's thinking, reduced all of Shelley's poetry to versified Godwinism, overlooking the symbolic patterns that William Butler Yeats had already called attention to in his important essays entitled "The Philosophy of Shelley's Poetry" (1900; rpt. in *Ideas of Good and Evil,* 1903*). In 1924 Mrs. Olwen Ward Campbell evaluated Shelley's character and applied her conceptions to extended criticism of *Alastor, Prometheus Unbound,* and some of Shelley's lyrics in *Shelley and the Unromantics.* Carl Grabo's study of Shelley's interest in the science of his day, *A Newton Among the Poets* (1930*), led him first into detailed analyses of *Prometheus Unbound* and *The Meaning of 'The Witch of Atlas'* (both 1935) and finally to *The Magic Plant* (1936), which Cameron cited as the first full-scale critical book on Shelley. In spite of its overemphasis of Grabo's unsubstantiated theory that many of Shelley's ideas and images derive directly from the Neoplatonist philosophers, *The Magic Plant* is still useful and eminently readable.

The other significant critical books on Shelley in the 1930's dwelt less on close analysis of his poetry than on his general psychic and philosophical orientation. Floyd Stovall's *Desire and Restraint in Shelley* (1931), Bennett Weaver's *Toward the Understanding of Shelley* (1932), Benjamin P. Kurtz's *The Pursuit of Death* (1933), and Ellsworth Barnard's *Shelley's Religion* (1937*) are all books with a thesis, either tracing a systematic chronological pattern of development in Shelley's thinking or else examining thematically a pattern seen in static terms. Stovall argues that Shelley learned to modify his impulsive actions in deference to the realities of his physical and social environment. Kurtz also finds Shelley growing wiser as he comprehends the greatest of all wisdom—that all life teaches the acceptance of death. Bennett Weaver's book emphasizes Shelley's knowledge and use of the Bible and portrays Shelley in the tradition of the Old Testament prophets of social justice. Barnard passionately defends the modernity of Shelley's ideas finding his religious beliefs to be parallel to Christianity in many respects but more relevant to the questionings of the modern spirit. These four books, like Grabo's studies, constitute an indirect answer to contemporary critical hostility towards Shelley epitomized by T. S. Eliot in *The Use of Poetry and the Use of Criticism* (1933*) and F. R. Leavis in *Revaluation* (1936*), as well as in the novels of Aldous Huxley, the poetry and criticism of John Crowe Ransom and Allen Tate, and such academic criticism as Sister M. E. Mousel's "Falsetto in Shelley" (*SP*, 1936). A more direct answer came from C. S. Lewis, who in his biting and brilliant essay "Shelley, Dryden, and Mr. Eliot" (*Rehabilitations*, 1939*) fairly demolished Eliot's ranking of Dryden's poetry above Shelley's, while purporting at least to accept Eliot's basic criteria of judgment.

The sting of the attacks on Shelley was felt for a generation, however, imparting a defensive tone to much Shelley scholarship and criticism of the 1940's and 1950's. Typical responses by critics friendly to Shelley were Frederick A. Pottle's "The Case of Shelley" (*PMLA*, 1952) and the essays on Shelley by Raymond D. Havens, Carlos Baker, Stewart Wilcox, and Herbert Read in *The Major English Romantic Poets: A Symposium in Reappraisal* (ed. C. D. Thorpe, Carlos Baker, and Bennett Weaver, 1957*). Such defenses of Shelley's poetic and intellectual viability were paralleled by a defense of the integrity of his personality from attacks by psychologists, professional or otherwise. Carl Grabo's *Shelley's Eccentricities* (1950) recounts in eighty-four pages the unusual and unconventional features of Shelley's personality and activities with a view to showing that the poet was abnormal only in the sense that "men of genius" are "the only sane or relatively sane beings in a half-mad world." Grabo's evidence is generally accurate, but unfortunately undocumented; the essay depends for effect substantially on Grabo's rhetoric and his sympathy for Shelley's ideas. In this respect, Grabo's monograph resembles the Princeton undergraduate prize essay *Mad Shelley* (1930) by James Ramsey Ullman, whose flair for writing, here precociously exhibited, later made him a successful novelist (*The White Tower*, etc.). Grabo takes special pains to contest the views of Edward Carpenter and George Barnefield (*The Psychology of the Poet Shelley*, 1925) and Herbert Read, who in his essay entitled *In De-*

fence of Shelley (1936) accepted currently fashionable psychological theories to label Shelley neurotic, paranoid, and latently homosexual.

A different and stronger line of defense was being built by those who worked to clear up critical misunderstanding of Shelley by recovering and documenting what he actually had written and explaining what that meant. A number of his patterns of imagery were elucidated by Oscar W. Firkins' *Power and Elusiveness in Shelley* (1937), and in Estonia by Ants Oras' *On Some Aspects of Shelley's Imagery* (*Acta et Commentationes Universitatis Tartuensis,* 43; 1939). After World War II this kind of study was supplemented by a series of books that strove to understand the intellectual and aesthetic bases of Shelley's art. A. M. D. Hughes's *The Nascent Mind of Shelley* (1947) and Kenneth Neill Cameron's *The Young Shelley: Genesis of a Radical* (1950*) both confine their focus to the early ideas and writings of Shelley up through *Queen Mab.* They show Shelley as a relevant thinker firmly grounded in his historical and intellectual milieu, though rising above it. Their demonstration was supported by David Lee Clark's edition *Shelley's Prose; or, The Trumpet of a Prophecy* (1954*), the introductory and critical notes to which emphasized Shelley's debts to Hume and other leading eighteenth-century philosophers. On quite a different plane, James A. Notopoulos' massive and very valuable study of *The Platonism of Shelley* (1949*) explores at length Shelley's direct and indirect "Platonism" (a word that Notopoulos, a professor of classics rather than philosophy, never defines with precision). He looks very hard for Platonic influence in everything Shelley wrote and is not disappointed. Joseph Barrell, who in *Shelley and the Thought of His Time* (1947*) approached Shelley with a broader (but admittedly shallower) perspective, had denied any direct Platonic influence on "Hymn to Intellectual Beauty," for example, writing: "the poem has been dubbed Platonic with a frequency that suggests either that the term has no meaning or that the critics of the poem have written from general recollection, without . . . rereading Plato and Shelley" (p. 126). Barrell explores Shelley's radicalism and his Platonism as a continuous intellectual development growing out of two conflicting strains of seventeenth- and eighteenth-century thought—(1) the rational empiricism of the French *philosophes* and (2) the emotional reaction epitomized in Rousseau. Barrell sees these two elements forming an unstable union in Godwin's *Enquiry concerning Political Justice,* and he analyzes Shelley's development to an extreme monistic idealism in *Hellas* as the natural result of a continuous struggle to reconcile the two schools of thought. Plato, whose influence Barrell finds strongest in Acts I–III of

Prometheus Unbound, gave Shelley a way "to explain man's freedom in an idealistic world," but Shelley's ethical thought differed from Plato's in having an emotionalist (subjective) rather than an intellectual (objective) basis.

Though *Shelley and the Thought of His Time* is now outdated on certain facts and ideas, it is a useful corrective to critics like Notopoulos who see Plato (or Berkeley) as the source of all Shelley's ideas. Barrell's greatest error was to dismiss Sir William Drummond's *Academical Questions* (1805) as a Berkeleian "textbook" rather than seeing it as an original exposition of "academic skepticism" deriving from classical sources as well as from Hume. C. E. Pulos corrected this misconception in *The Deep Truth: A Study of Shelley's Scepticism* (1954*), which remains in some ways the best introduction to Shelley's thought. For Pulos, Shelley's skepticism about man's capacity for understanding ultimate reality found expression in poems and essays that postulate various alternative solutions to the human predicament. These alternatives arise, however, from a consistent context of ethical norms based on the probabilities that derive from the application of reason to experience. In other words, reason and experience unite both to show their respective limitations *and* to suggest ethical norms sufficiently probable to guide everyday conduct. According to Pulos, apparent inconsistencies in Shelley's thinking are explained not in terms of a struggle among inconsistent elements in his intellectual heritage, but as explorations of different possibilities and a refusal to assert one dogmatic viewpoint. Pulos' interpretation not only harmonizes with Shelley's own repeated acknowledgment of his debt to Drummond, but it shows Shelley's poetry and prose to be intellectually consistent as no other explanation has succeeded in doing.

If Pulos may be said to have discovered the philosophical center of Shelley's writings, Carlos Baker's *Shelley's Major Poetry: The Fabric of a Vision* (1948*) was an important attempt to find the center of Shelley's literary method. Treating each longer poem from *Queen Mab* through "The Triumph of Life" as an integral work of art having its own pattern of imagery, Baker emphasized Shelley's debts to earlier English literature—especially the works of Edmund Spenser. Baker attempts to minimize the role of Shelley's own life as a source of material for his poetry, a viewpoint he had earlier expressed most forcefully in "Shelley Ferrarese Maniac" (*EIE,* 1946), where he argued that the madman in *Julian and Maddalo* was based on Shelley's conception of Tasso, rather than on his own experience. Baker's book, though mistaken on individual points, represents a salutary tendency to deal with Shelley as a serious poet working consciously in a poetic tradition rather than as a revolutionary lover who merely happened to versify his uppermost thoughts and most recent experiences.

Richard Harter Fogle's useful comparative study of *The Imagery of Keats and Shelley* (1949*) examines recurring patterns of poetic imagery in the two poets to generalize about their respective psychic and philosophical orientations. This kind of study is carried further in Peter H. Butter's *Shelley's Idols of the Cave* (1954). Butter takes up Yeats's suggestion that the source of Shelley's imagery lies deep within a mythic memory and attempts to show both what some of those fundamental patterns are and how Shelley works them out in particular ways in his individual poems. Butter's work exhibits so much common sense and fundamental intelligence that even where he is (in the opinion of later critics) mistaken, he has aided in the solution of problems by pointing up the crucial difficulties and their various resolutions. *Shelley's Idols of the Cave* is an excellent example of a newer attitude toward Shelley in which the critic does not attempt to judge the value of Shelley's life or to pontificate on every obscurity in Shelley's works or thought, because he recognizes that Shelley may have known more (or had different information) on a question than any or all modern scholar-critics.

The same undogmatic spirit characterizes Neville Rogers' *Shelley at Work: A Critical Inquiry* (1956; rev. ed., 1967). Besides exploring patterns of imagery in Shelley's works as indexes to his thought, Rogers also analyzes the method—or lack of it—evidenced by Shelley's rough-draft notebooks. Anyone who has ever looked at these notebooks will testify that, had Shelley never published his poems, few as we know them could have been derived from his confused and fragmentary drafts. Rogers concludes, quite naturally from his perspective, that not only was Shelley a Platonist in all the ways explored by Notopoulos (whose conclusions Rogers accepts), but that he was also "Platonic" in lacking an interest in the details of diction, punctuation, grammar, or syntax that are of concern to less impetuously creative poets. Rogers' examination of the Bodleian manuscripts provided the impetus for the revival of textual study surveyed in Part II above.

Among recent books, three that treat the full range of Shelley's writings are designed specifically as guides for the student or nonspecialist beginning to study Shelley: Desmond King-Hele, author of *Shelley: His Thought and Work* (1960), is a British scientist; he describes his book as "a new appreciation of Shelley's poetry, both lyrics and longer poems, for readers who have no special knowledge of the subject." On those poems that King-Hele *appreciates,* his comments are balanced and intelligent, and he brings his special professional knowledge to bear on a few poems like "Ode to the West Wind" and "The Cloud." But on those occasions when King-Hele falls out of sympathy with his subject (e.g., on *Epipsychidion*) he becomes needlessly condescending. Seymour Reiter's *Study of Shelley's Poetry* (1967) avoids the tendency to deprecate what it cannot fully explain. The difficulty here is more in the format of the book, which instead of having footnotes integrates long argumentative and informative digressions into the text (though set off by brackets). Reiter's explications are sane and incorporate some interpretations more recent than King-Hele's, but he scants his discussion of such major poems as "The Witch of Atlas" and *Adonais.* The third (and shortest) of the general introductions is Donald H. Reiman's *Percy Bysshe Shelley* (1969). The most recent such study and the only one written by a specialist familiar with both the primary materials and current scholarship, it contains—though in a condensed, over-simplified form—an original reading of Shelley's works that can be used by the advanced student as well as the novice.

It was once the fashion for a fledgling scholar to write a dissertation on Shelley, publish all or part of it, and then move into some other special interest—e.g., Stovall, Pulos, and Baker into American literature. Following in this tradition have been the Canadian scholars Milton Wilson and Ross Woodman. Each published an excellent book growing out of his dissertation on Shelley but has since withdrawn, for the most part, from Shelley studies. Wilson's *Shelley's Later Poetry* (1959) uses *Prometheus Unbound* as its "organizing center" to study the ideas and techniques in the poetry Shelley wrote in Italy. Though Wilson does not systematically explicate Shelley's longer poems, he illuminates many crucial passages as examples of recurring problems in Shelley's method. Wilson's study is balanced and intelligent throughout. Ross Woodman's *The Apocalyptic Vision in the Poetry of Shelley* (1964) is a more venturesome study than Wilson's; it contains proportionately more errors of fact and interpretation because Woodman pursues his study of the "mythological mode" of Shelley as an "apocalyptic poet" rather too relentlessly at some points. But the reader with wide knowledge of Shelley's writings and Shelleyan criticism—or even the novice who reads skeptically—will profit greatly from Woodman's detailed readings of Shelley's major poems.

Those scholars who have already written extensively on Shelley and are continuing to do substantial work in the field include Kenneth Neill Cameron, Neville Rogers, G. M. Matthews, Earl R. Wasserman, Harold Bloom, and Donald H. Reiman. Some of their books and articles have been or will be mentioned individually under other headings and can be located by means of the index. Cameron's published work on Shelley includes *The Young Shelley*, a large number of specialized articles that will be mentioned under various categories later in this chapter, the Rinehart edition of Shelley, four volumes of *Shelley and his Circle*, and *The Esdaile Notebook*. He has recently completed the manuscript of a major critical study that will cover the period from *The Young Shelley* to the end of Shelley's life. Cameron's scholarship is consistently accurate and up-to-date and his critical judgments careful and balanced.

Neville Rogers' critical efforts have been *Shelley at Work*, the Riverside edition of Shelley, and brief articles in *KSMB*. Rogers' critical position follows Notopoulos in tracing much in Shelley to Plato or to derivative Platonism. He finds Shelley's poetic language often imprecise but mystically meaningful. He does not discuss the eighteenth-century British philosophers and political writers or recent scholarship that has emphasized Shelley's debts to them. Rogers is best when pointing up the kinship between Shelley's thought and spirit and those of such major European literary figures as Euripedes, Calderón, and Goethe. He is weakest on theoretical matters pertaining to the texts of Shelley's poems and on the accuracy of factual details.

Harold Bloom, like Rogers, is strongest on literary resemblances, but in Bloom's case the emphasis is on the Anglo-American tradition from Spenser and Milton to Yeats and Wallace Stevens. Bloom's *Shelley's Mythmaking* (1959) was notable for its intelligent enthusiasm for Shelley (somewhat warped by irrelevant comparisons with Martin Buber) and its denigration of all earlier Shelleyans; in *The Visionary Company* (1961), Bloom muted his rhetoric and condensed his insights into effective readings of a representative selection of Shelley's poems. In numerous books, lectures, and articles, Bloom has made revealing remarks about Shelley while comparing him with Keats, Yeats, Stevens, and other poets.

G. M. Matthews, whose important bibliographical and textual scholarship on Shelley is discussed elsewhere in this chapter, is also an influential critic. Besides critical comments in his textual studies, the introduction and notes to his *Shelley: Selected Poems and Prose* in the New Oxford English Series, and his brief sketch of Shelley's career in Longman's *Writers and Their Work* series, Matthews has written several important critical articles. The best known is "A Volcano's Voice in Shelley" (*ELH*, 1957), in which Matthews interweaves an account of the literature on volcanic activity during Shelley's time with an explication of the poet's use of volcanic imagery in *Prometheus Unbound* and other poems and a discussion of its symbolic significance. In his later critical essays such as those on "The Triumph of Life" and *Julian and Maddalo* (*SN*, 1962, 1963), Matthews has utilized his detailed researches into Shelley's texts (in the Bodleian and elsewhere) to illuminate critical cruxes. This is true also in his important essay "Shelley's Lyrics" in *The Morality of Art: Essays Presented to G. Wilson Knight,* ed. D. W. Jefferson (1969); there Matthews argues that some of Shelley's posthumously-published lyrics that seem most personal, when their manuscript sources and literary genetics are examined, appear to be either conventionalized set-pieces or fragments intended for longer dramatic works, and hence may be far from personal.

The critic most fully committed to the impersonality of Shelley's art is Earl R. Wasserman, the author of an original and important approach to Shelley's poetry and prose. Beginning with an essay on *Adonais* in *ELH* (1954) and two notes in *MLN* (1954, 1955), Wasserman rose to prominence among critics of Shelley with the publication of *The Subtler Language: Critical Readings of Neoclassic and Romantic Poems* (1959). In that book he moved from detailed analyses of poems by Dryden, Denham, and Pope to a chapter on the breakdown of the accepted neoclassic world-view, and thence into an analysis of Shelley's private symbolic mode as exemplified in "Mont Blanc," "The Sensitive Plant," and *Adonais*. Wasserman continued to explore that poetic universe in *Shelley's "Prometheus Unbound": A Critical Reading* (1965), and he rounds it out in *Shelley: A Critical Reading* (1971). Wasserman brings to his study of Shelley a keen intellect, extensive knowledge of Restoration and eighteenth-century literature and philosophy, and an unparalleled ability to evolve from a unified conception of Shelley's thought a tightly-organized, original interpretation of all of Shelley's writings. His chief weakness is a tendency to overemphasize the philosophical and intellectual aspects of Shelley's work, while relatively slighting the contributions to Shelley's art of both the poet's own experience and purely artistic and literary concerns. (For example, his study of *The Cenci* all but disregards that drama's five-act structure and other features that reflect the history of tragedies acted on the English stage.)

Donald H. Reiman has published the Twayne's English Authors

SHELLEY

Series' *Percy Bysshe Shelley* (1969), *Shelley's "The Triumph of Life": A Critical Study* (1965), and critical articles on specific works noted below. He is Cameron's successor as editor of *Shelley and his Circle,* and he has undertaken two other brief books on Shelley. Reiman views his work as eclectic and undertakes textual criticism, studies of Shelley's philosophical perspective and his literary heritage, and the occasional application of biography to criticism.

A few other recent critical books that treat Shelley are of smaller scope or usefulness. Glenn O'Malley's *Shelley and Synesthesia* (1964) moves beyond the subject of its title to reinterpret *portions* of most of Shelley's major poems in the light of a recurring pattern of imagery, but O'Malley never fully succeeds in integrating his contributions into a total reading of any single poem. The book usefully supplements other general books and should certainly be consulted on specific passages in Shelley's poetry that involve synesthesia. The sections on Shelley in D. G. James's *The Romantic Comedy* (1948) and Edward E. Bostetter's *The Romantic Ventriloquists* (1963) show their authors so much out of sympathy with what they conceive to be the tenor of Shelley's life and thought that even those parts of Shelley's poetry that are correctly interpreted are harshly judged. The three chapters on Shelley in David Perkins' *The Quest for Permanence* (1959) rise above the author's apparent distaste for Shelley by usefully summarizing readings developed earlier by Carlos Baker and Wasserman. On the other hand, James Rieger's *The Mutiny Within: The Heresies of Percy Bysshe Shelley* (1967) suffers from a lack of sympathy not with Shelley but with conventional readers. Rieger, positing that Shelley was a latter day gnostic who prized hidden wisdom, argues (against almost all the evidence) that Shelley tried purposely to write obscurely. Rieger's chapter on *The Cenci,* perhaps the best section of his book, had appeared earlier in *SIR* (1965). Ian Jack's chapter on Shelley in his volume *English Literature, 1815–1832* of the Oxford History of English Literature (1963) usefully focuses on Shelley's search for an audience and the variety of forms in which he wrote in an attempt to achieve popular success. But Jack betrays his limited comprehension of Shelley's art by proclaiming Mary Shelley and Peacock, who failed to appreciate Shelley's greatest poetry, the critics "who understood him best." G. Wilson Knight's principal work on Shelley was in *The Starlit Dome* (1941*), which included a long essay on Shelley's symbolism within a study that also analyzed related recurring images in the poetry of Coleridge and Keats. In two more recent books on Byron (q.v.), Knight (mis)reads the madman

353

in *Julian and Maddalo* as a portrait of Byron. On Shelley, as on other subjects, Knight is full of original ideas and can be stimulating even when wrong.

B. STUDIES OF SHELLEY'S THOUGHT

Several important books that treat Shelley's thought have been mentioned above: Shelley's philosophical orientation, his epistemology, ontology, and ethics are discussed by Barrell in *Shelley and the Thought of His Time*, by Pulos in *The Deep Truth*, by Wasserman cumulatively in his books on Shelley, and by Reiman in the first and fourth chapters of *Shelley's "The Triumph of Life."* Shelley's thought in these areas, as presently explicated by literary scholars, has not been examined critically by a professional historian of British philosophy. Such an examination is one of the chief desiderata of Shelley studies, but such a study must be conducted with corrected texts of Shelley's philosophical prose.

Shelley's religious thought has also been studied chiefly by literary scholars who are well-versed amateurs in theology and the history of religious ideas in England. Besides Barnard's *Shelley's Religion* and Weaver's *Toward an Understanding of Shelley,* the following studies of Shelley's religious perspective deserve attention: Edmund G. Gardner, "The Mysticism of Shelley" (*Catholic World,* 1908), Stopford A. Brooke, "Shelley's Interpretation of Christ and His Teaching" (*HJ,* 1918), Archibald Strong's "The Faith of Shelley" in his *Three Studies in Shelley* (1921*), Solomon F. Gingerich's "Shelley's Doctrine of Necessity *versus* Christianity" (*PMLA,* 1918; rpt. in Gingerich's *Essays in the Romantic Poets,* 1924), Arthur C. Hicks's unpublished dissertation "The Place of Christianity in Shelley's Thought" (Stanford, 1932), Hoxie Neale Fairchild's *Religious Trends in English Poetry, Vol. III. 1780–1830: Romantic Faith* (1949), Bice Chiappelli's *Il pensiero religioso di Shelley* (Rome, 1956), and A. S. P. Woodhouse's *The Poet and His Faith: Religion and Poetry in England from Spenser to Eliot and Auden* (1965). The debate as to whether Shelley was "essentially" a Christian or could have been or might be if he were alive today—moot questions central to many of these works—seems now to be dying away. In his own life Shelley left no doubt that he despised the theology and institutions of Christianity (along with other fideistic religions) and—for reasons clearly set forth by Pulos—he probably would never have accepted the historical church as he knew it even had his theological objections withered. This does not mean that

Christians—especially after the impact of revolutionary nineteenth- and twentieth-century theologians—share none of Shelley's beliefs and ideals. There is certainly room for a study of Shelley's religious thought by a competent critic thoroughly grounded, not in Roman or Anglo-Catholic orthodoxy, but in the recent traditions of Protestant liberal and existentialist theologies originating with Shelley's contemporaries Schleiermacher and Kierkegaard.

Although Shelley's ideas on love and interpersonal relationships have been touched on by almost every major critical study, including Frederick L. Beaty's comprehensive *Light from Heaven: Love in British Romantic Literature* (Northern Illinois Univ. Press, 1971), there is no systematic examination of his theory and his practice. Among the studies not hitherto named that treat the problem are Floyd Stovall's "Shelley's Doctrine of Love" (*PMLA*, 1930), Roy R. Male's "Shelley and the Doctrine of Sympathy" (*TexSE*, 1950), Daniel Stempel's "Shelley and the Ladder of Love" (*KSJ*, 1966), Seraphia Leyda's " 'Love's Rare Universe': Eros in Shelley's Poetry" (in *Explorations of Literature*, ed. Rima Drell Reck, 1966), and Gerald Enscoe's *Eros and the Romantics* (1967), which includes a chapter on "The Physical Basis of Love in Shelley's *Alastor* and *Epipsychidion*." Little has been said, except by the biographers in passing, on Shelley's practice of friendship in his relations, for example, with Hogg, Peacock, Byron, Hunt, and Edward Williams, and even less has been written about his ideals of friendship, though some aspects are treated in scattered commentaries and essays of *Shelley and his Circle*, both in the volumes published and those in press.

In the area of Shelley's political thinking, the scholarship has been fuller and the resulting understanding more comprehensive than in the other areas we have mentioned. In 1875 Charles Sotheran read his *Percy Bysshe Shelley as a Philosopher and Reformer* before the New York Liberal Club. As Newman Ivey White has shown in "Shelley and the Active Radicals of the Early Nineteenth Century" (*SAQ*, 1930), Shelley's poetry and thought had long been popular and influential in English radical circles from the journalists Richard Carlile and William Hone in his own day throughout the Chartist movement, and by 1878 Edward Aveling and Eleanor Marx (Karl's daughter) entered the precincts of the Manchester Shelley Society to lecture on *Shelley's Socialism*; in that lecture they formally claimed Shelley as a proto-Marxist. George Bernard Shaw emphasized the socialist tendencies in Shelley's writings in his lively lecture of 1892 "Shaming the Devil about Shelley," printed in Shaw's *Pen Portraits and Reviews* (1932). There is a considerable body of Marxist and Soviet comment on Shelley, and though much of it is not readily accessible, one important essay in English is Manfred Wojcik's "In Defense of Shelley" in the East German periodical *Zeitschrift fur Anglistik und Amerikanistik* (XI, 1963, 143–88) and reprinted, in part, in *Shelley,* ed. Robert B. Woodings (1968). Perhaps the first full English-language academic study of Shelley's political thinking was Daniel J. MacDonald's *The Radicalism of Shelley and Its Sources* (1912*), which contains a useful bibliography of earlier studies. T. W. Rolleston published the first edition of Shelley's important *Philosophical View of Reform* in 1920. Though some of the studies that followed immediately including George Gordon's Warton Lecture entitled *Shelley and the Oppressors of Mankind* (1922) and Crane Brinton's *The Political Ideas of the English Romanticists* (1926*) were disappointingly shallow, the availability of Shelley's longest political essay greatly informed later students of the poet. One useful historical study in the 1920's was A. Stanley Walker's "Peterloo, Shelley, and Reform" (*PMLA,* 1925).

The three scholars with perhaps the greatest impact on present-day understanding of Shelley's political thought have been Carl Grabo (especially in *The Magic Plant*), Newman Ivey White, and—above all others— Kenneth Neill Cameron, especially in *The Young Shelley* but also in important articles and numerous reviews. Cameron set forth briefly his conception of "The Social Philosophy of Shelley" in *Sewanee Review* (1942) and followed this with explorations of the historical contexts of Shelley's economic thinking in "Shelley, Cobbett, and the National Debt" (*JEGP,* 1943), Shelley's relations with the leading radical thinkers and agitators of his day in "Shelley and the Reformers" (*ELH,* 1945), and Shelley's use of political themes in his poetry in "A Major Source of *The Revolt of Islam*" and "The Political Symbolism of *Prometheus Unbound*" (*PMLA,* 1941, 1943). The influence of Cameron's ideas is amply acknowledged by John Pollard Guinn, whose *Shelley's Political Thought* (1969), though pedestrian and riddled with minor errors, can serve the undergraduate as a brief guide to its subject. Cameron also strongly shaped the conceptions of Gerald McNiece's *Shelley and the Revolutionary Idea* (1969), but McNiece contributes a larger understanding of the influence upon Shelley of his readings in particular radical literature. Finally, Carl Woodring—though obviously working within a context of thought generated by Grabo, White, and Cameron—goes beyond the study of sources and analogues that characterized the efforts of scholars to place Shelley in his socio-political milieu. The hundred-odd pages on Shelley in Woodring's *Politics in English Romantic Poetry* (1970) fulfill their author's promise for the book—"treating poems as final, self-authenticating objects of study and admiration." Woodring does not (as his predecessors sometimes do) murder to dissect. *Politics in English Romantic Poetry* sees political ideas and events as integral vital elements within living poems—not as abstract patterns against which poems are measured. Woodring's chapter—remarkably concise and readable, while informed by profound scholarship—gives hope that the patient labors of those who have for the past forty years been recovering bit by bit Shelley's intellectual heritage and aesthetic method are about to be superseded by a series of studies larger in scope that are both based on the improved understanding of Shelley and encompass a vision of his place within the fabric of English poetry and intellectual history.

Shelley's aesthetic theory or theories have also profited from extensive scrutiny in recent years. Most of them center, of course, around Shelley's *Defence of Poetry,* and the editions of that work almost invariably contain some appraisal of Shelley's aesthetic. The most useful of these introductions at present is John E. Jordan's in the Library of the Liberal Arts edition of Shelley's *Defence* and Peacock's *Four Ages of Poetry* (1965). Of the more formal treatments, those in the general histories of criticism—even in René Wellek's admirable *History of Modern Criticism Vol. II, The Romantic Age* (1955)—tend to read Shelley's words Platonically in a way not now in fashion among—or, to assume that viewpoint, now seen as incorrect by—most Shelley scholars. The older tradition of those who read Shelley's *Defence* as merging poetry with other forms of human creativity may be fairly represented by Melvin T. Solve's *Shelley, His Theory of Poetry* (1927*), which for almost forty years remained the standard study of Shelley's aesthetic, and by Joseph E. Baker's inconclusive exploration of the *Defence* and Peacock's *Four Ages* in *Shelley's Platonic Answer to a Platonic Attack on Poetry* (1965). But a number of studies over the years have looked into other aspects of Shelley's intellectual heritage for elements of the *Defence*: for example, Lucas Verkoren's *Study of Shelley's Defence of Poetry* (1937) recounted the parallels with Sidney's *Defence*; Bruce R. McElderry found "Common Elements in Wordsworth's *Preface* and Shelley's *Defence of Poetry*" (*MLQ,* 1944); Cameron saw Johnson's *Rasselas* as "A New Source for Shelley's 'Defence of Poetry' " (*SP,* 1941); and John S. Flagg studied "Shelley and Aristotle: Elements of the *Poetics* in Shelley's Theory of Poetry" (*SIR,* 1970).

In the mid-1960's a number of scholars published independent descriptions or analyses of Shelley's aesthetic that reordered the perspective: Wasserman's important essay on "Shelley's Last Poetics" (*From Sensibility to Romanticism,* ed. F. W. Hilles and Harold Bloom, 1965) and the section on "Style" in Reiman's *Shelley's "The Triumph of Life"* (1965) both pointed to a reported dialogue between Shelley and Byron on *Hamlet* as another document in Shelley's poetics. John E. Jordan's excellent introduction to his text of the *Defence* (1965) clarified Shelley's meaning in the context of the aesthetic theories of his day. Earl J. Schulze's *Shelley's Theory of Poetry: A Reappraisal* (1966) redefined Shelley's aesthetic theory in the light of the previous decade's emphasis on his eighteenth-century philosophical roots. Schulze wrongly attributed to Shelley certain Kantian-Coleridgean principles (such as a psychology of faculties) but he generally opened up Shelley's ideas to fresh comprehension. More recently, John W. Wright—exploring Shelley's *Defence* and his poetic practice from the twin perspectives of the poet's intellectual debts to Hume and Drummond on the one hand and modern phenomenology on the other—has examined *Shelley's Myth of Metaphor* (1970), arguing that Shelley was a forerunner of modern philosophers in grasping the function of metaphor in organizing the random data of human perception. There is yet a need for a synthesizing study of Shelley's poetics that will elucidate both Shelley's theory (as expressed in his prefaces, reviews, letters, and reported conversations, as well as in the *Defence*) and his practice in the light of the recent examination of his intellectual orientation.

Some aspects of Shelley's aesthetic practice, such as his use of recurring symbols, have been studied repeatedly (see the following section), but Shelley's versification has received only passing comment from most critics. The few studies centered on the topic include two monographs, one in German—Armin Kroder's *Shelleys Verskunst* (1903), and one in English—Louise Propst's *An Analytical Study of Shelley's Versification* (1933). Neither is adequate, but each has a bibliography that helps bring together earlier scattered studies of the topic.

C. SYMBOLS AND SOURCES

Shelley's recurrent patterns of imagery that are more than images and deserve the name symbols are becoming increasingly well-known and better understood, though their significance in particular contexts will be established only through continuing study of Shelley's mythologizing method (as sketched by Wasserman) and of the literary and mythic antecedents that he was shaping to the likeness of the archetypal myth that he envisioned. Major studies mentioned above that have contributed markedly to our knowledge of Shelley's basic image-patterns include Yeats's essays, Carl Grabo's books (on Shelley's scientific and Neoplatonic images), Wilson Knight's *The Starlit Dome,* Butter's *Shelley's Idols of the Cave,* Rogers' *Shelley at Work,* Matthews' "A Volcano's Voice in Shelley" (*ELH,* 1957), Wilson's *Shelley's Later Poetry,* Reiman's *Shelley's "The Triumph of Life,"* and O'Malley's *Shelley and Synesthesia.* Other studies that are especially useful in isolating and bringing together such recurring patterns include Carlos Baker's "The Traditional Background of Shelley's Ivy-Symbol" (*MLQ,* 1943), Newell F. Ford's "The Symbolism of Shelley's Nightingales" (*MLR,* 1960) and "The Symbolism of Shelley's Swans" (*SIR,* 1962), Daniel J. Hughes's "Kindling and Dwindling: The Poetic Process in Shelley" (*KSJ,* 1964), and Peter L. Thorslev's "Incest as Romantic Symbol" (*CLS,* 1965). Another class of studies—far more mechanical than those mentioned above—may be exemplified by Lloyd N. Jeffrey's "Reptile-Lore in Shelley" (*KSJ,* 1958) and " 'The Birds within the Wind': A Study of Shelley's Use of Natural History" (*KSJ,* 1969), which take all mentions of a particular class of animal listed in F. S. Ellis' useful *Lexical Concordance to the Poetical Works of Percy Bysshe Shelley* (1892*), hence excluding the Esdaile poems and other newly-edited texts, and try to make sense out of Shelley's varied usage. Jeffrey very often fails to note the dramatic propriety of the image to a particular movement in one of Shelley's poems of progressive revelation or to a specific speaker. One of the most effective studies of Shelley's images in considering these questions is Chapter iv of Stuart Curran's *Shelley's "Cenci"* (1970).

Some essays that are not studies of symbols per se investigate a pattern of language or technique through various works. Among the more useful of these are two by Newell Ford—"Paradox and Irony in Shelley's Poetry" (*SP,* 1960) and "The Wit in Shelley's Poetry" (*SEL,* 1961), Robert Mortenson's "Image and Structure in Shelley's Longer Lyrics" (*SIR,* 1965), William H. Hildebrand's "Shelley's Early Vision Poems" (*SIR,* 1969), and Judith Chernaik's "The Figure of the Poet in Shelley" (*ELH,* 1968).

Approaching Shelley's poetic meaning from another angle have been those scholars and critics who have investigated the effect of Shelley's reading on his thought and art. Two general books on the impact of Shelley's reading are Adolf Droop's *Die Belesenheit Percy Bysshe Shelleys* (1906) and Joseph Barrell's *Shelley and the Thought of His Time*

(1947*), neither of which makes more than a deep scratch in the surface of the subject (though Barrell's book is valuable for its analysis of Shelley's philosophical orientation; see Section IV.A above). The fullest—but by no means complete—lists of Shelley's reading are found in the index to White's *Shelley* and in Appendix VIII of Frederick L. Jones's edition of Shelley's *Letters*. Jones records the authors and titles mentioned in Shelley's and Mary's letters and journal, but not those mentioned or quoted by Shelley in his poems and prose. Medwin, Hogg, and Peacock in their biographies of Shelley and Mary Shelley in her notes to Shelley's poems provide further information on the reading that had such a shaping influence on Shelley's thought and art. Peck's *Shelley* and *Shelley and his Circle* contain information about some books annotated by Shelley.

The most extensive effort in studying the influence on Shelley originating in one author is Notopoulos' *The Platonism of Shelley*, which followed such earlier explorations of the subject as two studies entitled "Platonism in Shelley" by Lilian Winstanley (*E&S*, IV, 1913) and Amiyakumar Sen, *Studies in Shelley* (Calcutta, 1936), and E. M. W. Tillyard's "Shelley's *Prometheus Unbound* and Plato's *Statesman*" (*TLS*, 1932). A number of essays that center on the sources for a particular work by Shelley are mentioned in the next section. Other significant studies that explore the influence of classical and non-English writers on Shelley (or on him and other Romantic poets) include: Stephen J. Rogers, Jr., *Classical Greece in the Poetry of Chenier, Shelley, and Leopardi* (1970); Roy R. Male, "Young Shelley and the Ancient Moralists" (*KSJ*, 1956); Male and Notopoulos, "Shelley's Copy of Diogenes Laertius" (*MLR*, 1959); Mary Rebecca Thayer, *The Influence of Horace on the Chief English Poets of the Nineteenth Century* (1916); Richard Ackerman, *Lucans Pharsalia in den Dichtungen Shelleys* (1896); Paul Turner, "Shelley and Lucretius" (*RES*, 1959); S. R. Swaminathan, "Possible Indian Influence on Shelley" (*KSMB*, 1958); Corrado Zacchetti, *Shelley e Dante* (1922); Oswald Doughty, "Dante and the English Romantic Poets" (*EM*, Rome, 1951); Werner P. Friederich, *Dante's Fame Abroad* (1950); Herbert G. Wright, *Boccaccio in England from Chaucer to Tennyson* (1957); C[harles] P. Brand, *Italy and the English Romantics* (1957); Salvador de Madariaga, *Shelley and Calderón and Other Essays* (1920*), and Eunice Joiner Gates, "Shelley and Calderón" (*PQ*, 1937); Sophie Bernthsen, *Der Spinozimus in Shelleys Weltanschauung* (1900), and Carl Grabo, "Spinoza and Shelley" (*Chicago Jewish Forum*, 1942); Frank W. Stokoe's chapter on Shelley in *German Influence in the English Romantic Period, 1788–1818*

(1926); Francis G. Steiner, "Shelley and Goethe's *Faust*" (*Rivista di Letterature Moderne*, 1951); Hans Meyer, *Rousseau und Shelley* (1934); Donald L. Maddox, "Shelley's *Alastor* and the Legacy of Rousseau" (*SIR*, 1970); Walter E. Peck, "Shelley and the Abbé Barruel" (*PMLA*, 1921); the influence of Volney's *Ruins of Empire* on *Queen Mab* by L. Kellner (*Englische Studien*, 1896) and that of the same work on *The Revolt of Islam* by Cameron (*PMLA*, 1941); Israel J. Kapstein, "Shelley and Cabanis" (*PMLA*, 1937); Amiyakumar Sen, "Shelley and the French Revolution" (in *Studies in Shelley*, 1936). For international influences on particular themes, see also Gerald McNiece, *Shelley and the Revolutionary Idea* (1969), Pulos, *The Deep Truth* (for skeptical philosophy from the New Academy through Cicero to Hume), George K. Anderson, *The Legend of The Wandering Jew* (1965), and Douglas Bush, *Mythology and the Romantic Tradition in English Poetry* (1937*).

There are numerous examinations of the impact of a few major English poets on Shelley, but no study of Shelley's earlier literary taste and its effects. Some hint of the influence of the Gothic tradition may be garnered from Montague Summers' *The Gothic Quest* (1938*) and Bertrand Evans' *Gothic Drama from Walpole to Shelley* (1947). There have been essays on Shelley and Shakespeare by David Lee Clark (*PMLA*, 1939), Sara R. Watson (*PMLA*, 1940), Frederick L. Jones (*PMLA*, 1944), and Beach Langston (*HLQ*, 1949); for the special problem of Shelley's use of Shakespearean echoes in *The Cenci*, see Chapter ii of Stuart Curran's *Shelley's "Cenci"* (1970). A recent essay of value from a different perspective is Earl Wasserman's "Shakespeare and the English Romantic Movement" (in *The Persistence of Shakespeare Idolatry*, ed. Herbert M. Schueller, 1964). The influence of Spenser on Shelley has been noted passim in Carlos Baker's *Shelley's Major Poetry* and Harold Bloom's *Shelley's Mythmaking* and in articles by Carlos Baker (*PMLA*, 1941) and Frederick L. Jones (*SP*, 1942). Shelley's relations with Milton have been treated by the same three authors—by Baker and Bloom in their books (and Baker also in *MLN*, 1940) and at length by Jones in a substantial catalogue of relationships and echoes entitled "Shelley and Milton" (*SP*, 1952). Subtler than Jones's study are Ants Oras' "The Multitudinous Orb: Some Miltonic Elements in Shelley" (*MLQ*, 1955) and Joseph Raben's "Milton's Influence on Shelley's Translation of Dante's 'Matilda Gathering Flowers'" (*RES*, 1963). Raben has also utilized computer technology to study recurrent patterns of diction in *Paradise Lost* and *Prometheus Unbound* ("A Computer-Aided Study of Literary Influence: Milton to

Shelley," *Literary Data Processing Conference Proceedings,* 9, 10, 11 September 1964, MLA Materials Center). In the older tradition are a series of notes by Robert R. Pelletier pointing out parallels between Milton and various works by Shelley (*N&Q,* March and July 1960; *N&Q,* January and December 1961; *KSJ,* 1962, 1965). Finally, Joseph A. Wittreich's *The Romantics on Milton* (1970) collects all of Shelley's remarks on Milton from his letters as well as his Prefaces and critical prose. Of English literary prose writers Sir Francis Bacon undoubtedly exerted the greatest influence on Shelley, the effects of which have been studied by David Lee Clark ("Shelley and Bacon," *PMLA,* 1933) and William O. Scott ("Shelley's Admiration for Bacon," *PMLA,* 1958). Before Pulos' *The Deep Truth,* G. S. Brett's "Shelley's Relation to Berkeley and Drummond" (in *Studies in English,* ed. Malcolm W. Wallace, 1931*) was useful for its subject.

Shelley's English contemporaries obviously affected his writing substantially, but few scholars have undertaken any systematic study of the question. For example, there are no substantial studies of Southey's or Scott's very important literary influence on Shelley. Wordsworth's influence has been noted in passing by many critics, but the most detailed treatment of Shelley's reaction to the elder poet is J. C. Echeruo's thirty-page "Shelley on Wordsworth" (*ESA,* 1966). The most stimulating recent treatment of the Wordsworth-Shelley relationship is that by Harold Bloom in his *Yeats* (1970). See also F. W. Bateson, "Shelley on Wordsworth: Two Unpublished Stanzas from 'Peter Bell the Third'" (*EC,* 1967). A. C. Bradley included an essay on "Coleridge-Echoes in Shelley's Poems" in *A Miscellany* (1929); Joseph Raben treats Shelley's attitude toward Coleridge in "Coleridge as the Prototype of the Poet in Shelley's *Alastor*" (*RES,* 1966). Shelley's relations with Keats are treated best from the viewpoint of Keats in Walter J. Bate's *John Keats* (1963*) and most fully from Shelley's perspective in an essay by Donald H. Reiman in *Shelley and his Circle,* Volume v. A number of books and articles have treated the interactions of Shelley and Byron, John Buxton's *Byron and Shelley: The History of a Friendship* (1968) being the most extended but not always the most perceptive account. There is certainly room for a detailed examination of the interaction of Shelley's and Byron's ideas and art, and at least one is in progress at this time of writing. Among studies of Shelley and lesser English contemporaries is Walter Graham's "Shelley and *The Empire of the Nairs*" (*PMLA,* 1925); Cameron's earlier study of Shelley's use of Peacock's *Ahrimanes* in *The Revolt of Islam* (*MLQ,* 1942) has been in part superseded by an updated account in Volume III of *Shelley and his Circle*. The only American writer who is known (through Peacock) to have had an appreciable impact on Shelley's thinking was Charles Brockden Brown. His influence has been studied by Melvin T. Solve, "Shelley and the Novels of Brown" (in *Fred Newton Scott Anniversary Papers*, 1929), Eleanor Sickels, "Shelley and Charles Brockden Brown" (*PMLA*, 1930), and Rosemary R. Davies, "Charles Brockden Brown's *Ormond*: A Possible Influence upon Shelley's Conduct" (*PQ*, 1964).

Though there are reputed to be in progress several studies of the impact on Shelley of music and/or the visual arts, those now in print merely suggest outlines and methodologies for such research. The pioneering German book by Ilse Köhling O'Sullivan, *Shelley und die bildende Kunst* (1927), was supplemented by the chapter on Shelley in Stephen A. Larrabee's valuable *English Bards and Grecian Marbles: The Relationship between Sculpture and Poetry, Especially in the Romantic Period* (1943*). Neville Rogers' "Shelley and the Visual Arts" (*KSMB*, 1961) treats Shelley's interest in the head of the Medusa attributed to Leonardo da Vinci, and Daniel J. Hughes's "Shelley, Leonardo, and the Monsters of Thought" (*Criticism*, 1970) plays variations on this theme. One of the few examinations of Shelley's use of architecture as well as sculpture in his poetry is Donald H. Reiman's "Roman Scenes in *Prometheus Unbound* III.iv" (*PQ*, 1967). Shelley's interest in music has been treated, though again superficially, by Neville Rogers in "Music at Marlow" (*KSMB*, 1953), by Jean de Palacio in "Music and Musical Themes in Shelley's Poetry" (*MLR*, 1964), and (in passing) by Judith Chernaik in *The Lyrics of Shelley* (1972). To show how rudimentary has been the exploration of the last subject, one need only note that no recent biographer or commentator seems to have been aware that Shelley played the piano and is recorded as playing for his own amusement during his visit to Field Place just before he eloped with Mary.

D. SELECTED STUDIES OF INDIVIDUAL WORKS

In this brief survey of critical books and articles that treat individual works by Shelley, studies of his minor works receive proportionately more attention than those of equal merit that treat his major writings. Recent studies are, similarly, given preference over earlier ones. This section takes up Shelley's writings in a roughly chronological order. The most recent serious study of *Zastrozzi* and *St. Irvyne*, "Shelley's 'Gothic' Novels" by

David G. Halliburton (*KSJ*, 1967), does not supersede earlier commentary on them, including A. M. D. Hughes's "Shelley's *Zastrozzi* and *St. Irvyne*" (*MLR*, 1912), and Frederick L. Jones's brief note *"Alastor* Foreshadowed in *St. Irvyne*" (*PMLA*, 1934). But Halliburton is much more helpful than the English psychologist Eustace Chesser, whose *Shelley and Zastrozzi: Self-Revelations of a Neurotic* (1965) is completely worthless not only because of its dubious methodology but also because Chesser uses the texts of Shelley's letters to Hogg which Hogg had corrupted by interchanging many of the pronouns.

The fullest account of *The Wandering Jew* is still Bertram Dobell's edition in the Shelley Society's Publications for 1887. Harold Orel's "Another Look at *The Necessity of Atheism*" (*Mosaic*, 1969) argues that the pamphlet may be part of Shelley's deistic period; see also Bice Chiappelli's treatment of *The Necessity of Atheism* in *Il pensiero religioso di Shelley* (1956). Cameron's *The Young Shelley* and Hughes's *The Nascent Mind of Shelley*, combined with Cameron's and Rogers' notes to their editions of *The Esdaile Notebook*, provide the best analyses of most of Shelley's works up through *Queen Mab*. Pulos in *The Deep Truth* is especially good on *A Refutation of Deism*, and Cameron treats Shelley's two revisions of parts of *Queen Mab* into "The Daemon of the World" and "The Queen of the Universe" in *Shelley and his Circle*, Volume IV.

Useful notes on Shelley's prose fragment entitled "The Assassins" are embedded in Geoffrey Carnall's article "De Quincey on the Knocking at the Gate" (*REL*, 1961). The best general attempt to date Shelley's fragmentary prose is James A. Notopoulos' "The Dating of Shelley's Prose" (*PMLA*, 1943).

Besides the major books on Shelley, all of which treat *Alastor*, there are a handful of monographs and dissertations devoted to it, as well as numerous articles. Earlier studies of some interest include source studies by L. H. Allen, "Plagiarism, Sources, and Influences in Shelley's *Alastor*" (*MLR*, 1923); Kenneth Neill Cameron, *"Rasselas* and *Alastor*" (*SP*, 1943); Jerome W. Archer, *"Kubla Khan, Queen Mab*, II, 4–79; VIII, 70–103, and *Alastor*, 81–94, 163–172" (*SP*, 1944). A second focus has been the "identity" of the unnamed poet-protagonist in the poem. Paul Mueschke and Earl Leslie Griggs saw "Wordsworth as the Prototype of the Poet in Shelley's *Alastor*" (*PMLA*, 1934), and more recently Joseph Raben has seen "Coleridge as the Prototype of the Poet in Shelley's *Alastor*" (*RES*, 1966); these studies play off against both the biographies and biographical critics, who see the Poet as Shelley's self-portrait, and those literary critics who see the Poet as a created character. Third, there has been a debate about the poem's central theme and consistency carried on between Raymond D. Havens (*PMLA*, 1930, 1931) and Frederick L. Jones (*ELH*, 1946; *SP*, 1947), on the one side, who find *Alastor* inconsistent and, on the other side, by M. C. Weir (*PMLA*, 1931) and Harold Leroy Hoffman (*Alastor: An Odyssey of the Soul*, 1933), who find the poem coherent; this question should have been resolved by Evan K. Gibson's excellent essay *"Alastor*: A Reinterpretation" (*PMLA*, 1947), which demonstrates the poem's thematic unity. Other significant studies have been Arthur E. DuBois' "Alastor: Spirit of Solitude" (*JEGP*, 1936), William H. Hildebrand's seventy-page *A Study of Alastor* (Kent State Research Series II, 1954), and Albert S. Gérard's *"Alastor*, or the Spirit of Solipsism" (*PQ*, 1954; rpt. in Gérard's *English Romantic Poetry: Ethos, Structure, and Symbol in Coleridge, Wordsworth, Shelley, and Keats* [1968]). An important suggestion was made by T. J. Spencer in "Shelley's 'Alastor' and Romantic Drama" (*Transactions of the Wisconsin Academy of Sciences, Arts, and Letters*, 1959), which interprets the self-destruction of the Poet as a variant of the Hippolytus myth. Finally, an entirely new perspective appears in Earl R. Wasserman's *Shelley: A Critical Reading*.

Though Israel J. Kapstein's "The Meaning of Shelley's *Mont Blanc*" (*PMLA*, 1947) raised many pertinent questions, most recent studies of the poem derive from Charles H. Vivian's "The One 'Mont Blanc' " (*KSJ*, 1955) and Wasserman's explication in *The Subtler Language*. Some later contributions like Joan Rees's (*RES*, 1964) and John Kinnaird's (*N&Q*, 1968) notes on the phrase "But for such faith" and E. B. Murray's "Mont Blanc's Unfurled Veil" (*KSJ*, 1969) have confined themselves to sharpening the interpretation of particular passages. Stuart Curran's "Shelley's Emendations to the *Hymn to Intellectual Beauty*" (*ELN*, 1970) examines Shelley's corrections of the text printed in the *Examiner* and then focuses on the meaning of the altered passages. See also Elizabeth Nitchie, "Shelley's 'Hymn to Intellectual Beauty' " (*PMLA*, 1948).

The fullest explications of both "Mont Blanc" and "Hymn to Intellectual Beauty" are by Judith Chernaik in her *Lyrics of Shelley* (1972). Her eclectic discussion absorbs information and ideas from the studies named above, as well as from readings by Harold Bloom in *Shelley's Mythmaking* (1959) and Donald H. Reiman in *Percy Bysshe Shelley* (1969). Mrs. Chernaik also has discovered a new text and provides the most important reading of the poem traditionally known as "To Constantia, Singing." On this last poem and its milieu, see also Neville Rogers' "Music at Marlow" (*KSMB*, 1953).

Brian Wilkie includes an excellent chapter on *The Revolt of Islam* in *Romantic Poets and Epic Tradition* (1965). Ben W. Griffith, Jr., published notes on the manuscripts of *The Revolt* (also known by its original title of *Laon and Cythna*) in *MLN* (1954 and 1955) and in *N&Q* (1954 and 1956); all are based on his unpublished doctoral dissertation on the poem (Northwestern, 1952). Other studies include Wilfred S. Dowden's *Shelley's Use of Metempsychosis in "The Revolt of Islam"* (*Rice Institute Pamphlets*, 1951), Frederick L. Jones's "Canto I of *The Revolt of Islam*" (*KSJ*, 1960) and E. B. Murray's provocative " 'Elective Affinity' in *The Revolt of Islam*" (*JEGP*, 1968), which centers on the significance of the child born to Cythna during her solitary confinement.

Shelley's *Rosalind and Helen* volume has received relatively little attention. Raymond D. Havens wrote on the title poem (*JEGP*, 1931) and Bennett Weaver also treated it in his more general essay "Pre-Promethean Thought in Three Longer Poems of Shelley" (*PQ*, 1950); the other two poems discussed in the latter essay are "Prince Athanase" and *Julian and Maddalo*. Donald H. Reiman's "Structure, Symbol, and Theme in 'Lines Written among the Euganean Hills' " (*PMLA*, 1962) provides the most detailed analysis of that poem. Among the more numerous studies of "Ozymandias," typical discussions of Shelley's sources for the sonnet are those by Johnstone Parr and H. M. Richmond in *KSJ* for 1957 and 1962 respectively; an excellent brief explication is E. M. W. Tillyard's in his *Essays, Literary and Educational* (1962).

Much of the criticism of *Julian and Maddalo* has centered on the identity of the madman. Carlos Baker's "Shelley's Ferrarese Maniac" (*EIE*, 1946) argued, *contra* White (*Shelley*), for Tasso as the prototype of that mysterious character; J. E. Saveson in "Shelley's *Julian and Maddalo*" (*KSJ*, 1961) follows G. Wilson Knight in thinking the madman based on Byron. G. M. Matthews' " 'Julian and Maddalo': The Draft and the Meaning" (*SN*, 1963) gives useful information on the poem's composition and suggests that the Tasso theory may be correct. James L. Hill's "Dramatic Structure in Shelley's *Julian and Maddalo*" (*ELH*, 1968), like Reiman's *Percy Bysshe Shelley*, abandons the search for the source to concentrate on the dramatic interaction of Julian, Maddalo, the madman, and Maddalo's daughter within the poem itself. See also Raymond D. Havens, "*Julian and Maddalo*" (*SP*, 1930).

By far the largest bulk of Shelley scholarship and criticism has been devoted to *Prometheus Unbound*. Following the early survey in Newman Ivey White's "Shelley's *Prometheus Unbound,* or Every Man His Own Allegorist" (*PMLA,* 1925), there is a mammoth bibliography of studies up through the mid-1950's found in Lawrence John Zillman's *Shelley's* Prometheus Unbound: *A Variorum Edition* (Univ. of Washington Press, 1959). Zillman also abstracts principal ideas and interpretive points from dozens of critics (though the unified thought of the better ones loses a good deal during dissection). So Zillman's *Variorum Edition* should be the student's starting point. Among the earlier studies that should be consulted in their original form are Grabo's *Prometheus Unbound: An Interpretation* (1935), Cameron's "The Political Symbolism of *Prometheus Unbound"* (*PMLA,* 1943), Bennett Weaver's *"Prometheus Bound* and *Prometheus Unbound"* (*PMLA,* 1949); the fifth chapter of C. Maurice Bowra's *The Romantic Imagination* (1949*); Richard H. Fogle's "Image and Image-lessness: A Limited Reading of Prometheus Unbound" (*KSJ,* 1952); and—for the best of the earlier accounts—two lectures by William Michael Rossetti printed in Series I, No. I, Part I, of *The Shelley Society's Papers* (1888). Among the more important later studies devoted to this poem and not treated in Zillman's *Variorum Edition* are Weaver's *Prometheus Unbound* (1957), Wasserman's *Shelley's "Prometheus Unbound": A Critical Reading* (1965), and the following which explore detailed aspects of the poem: I. A. Richards, "The Mystical Element in Shelley's Poetry" (*Aryan Path,* 1959; on Demogorgon); Joseph Raben, "Shelley's *Prometheus Unbound:* Why the Indian Caucasus?" (*KSJ,* 1963); Daniel J. Hughes, "Potentiality in *Prometheus Unbound"* (*SIR,* 1963); Frederick A. Pottle, "The Role of Asia in the Dramatic Action of Shelley's *Prometheus Unbound"* (in *Shelley: A Collection of Critical Essays,* ed. George M. Ridenour, 1965); two articles (in French) by G. Faure and Simone Rozenberg (*Langue modernes,* 1966); James R. Hurt, *"Prometheus Unbound* and Aeschylean Dramaturgy" (*KSJ,* 1966); Donald H. Reiman, "Roman Scenes in *Prometheus Unbound* III.iv" (*PQ,* 1967); Priscilla P. St. George, "Another Look at Two Famous Lyrics in *Prometheus Unbound"* (*JEGP,* 1968); Pierre Vitoux, "Jupiter's Fatal Child in *Prometheus Unbound"* (*Criticism,* 1968); and Mildred S. McGill, "The Role of Earth in Shelley's *Prometheus Unbound"* (*SIR,* 1968). What yet remains to be written is a synthesizing book that will draw together the detailed explications of individual passages within a thematically coherent reading of the whole poem that harmonizes with the newly-developing consensus about Shelley's thought and artistry.

There have been numerous incidental comments on "Ode to the West Wind," "The Cloud," and "To a Skylark." Most of the serious analysis of these famous poems has been written or summarized in the major critical books. Earlier separate studies of at least historical value include Israel J. Kapstein's "The Symbolism of the Wind and the Leaves in Shelley's *Ode to the West Wind*" (*PMLA,* 1936), Richard H. Fogle's "The Imaginal Design of Shelley's *Ode to the West Wind*" (*ELH,* 1948), and two publications by Stewart C. Wilcox, "The Prosodic Structure of 'Ode to the West Wind' " (*N&Q,* 1950) and "Imagery, Ideas, and Design in Shelley's 'Ode to the West Wind' " (*SP,* 1950). The best of the more recent studies is by Irene H. Chayes in "Rhetoric as Drama: An Approach to the Romantic Ode" (*PMLA,* 1964); others of interest include C. C. Clarke, "Shelley's 'Tangled Boughs' " (*Durham University Journal,* 1961), Coleman O. Parsons, "Shelley's Prayer to the West Wind" (*KSJ,* 1962), Eben Bass, "The Fourth Element in 'Ode to the West Wind' " (*PLL,* 1967), and Albert Gérard in Chapter viii of *English Romantic Poetry: Ethos, Structure, and Symbol . . .* (1968). "To a Skylark" is treated by E. M. W. Tillyard in *Poetry: Direct and Oblique* (1934), E. Wayne Marjarum, "The Symbolism of Shelley's *To a Skylark*" (*PMLA,* 1937), Stewart C. Wilcox in "The Scientific Bird" (*CE,* 1949) and "The Sources, Symbolism, and Unity of Shelley's *Skylark*" (*SP,* 1949), Newell F. Ford in "Shelley's 'To a Skylark' " (*KSMB,* 1960), Jean H. Hagstrum in "Romantic Skylarks" (*Newberry Library Bulletin,* 1959), and Parks C. Hunter, Jr., "Undercurrents of Anacreontics in Shelley's 'To a Skylark' and 'The Cloud' " (*SP,* 1968). Recent separate studies of "The Cloud"—like those by James E. Cronin (*N&Q,* 1950), Mignonette E. Harrison (*EXP,* 1953), and Allan H. MacLaine (*KSJ,* 1959)—have treated individual images. On other poems published with *Prometheus Unbound,* the only major study outside the major critical books is Priscilla P. St. George's "The Styles of Good and Evil in 'The Sensitive Plant' " (*JEGP,* 1965). There are no separately published studies of "Ode to Liberty"; the reader should consult the major critical books, especially Judith Chernaik's *The Lyrics of Shelley,* and he may find incidental help in A. M. D. Hughes's *Shelley: Poems Published in 1820* (1910*). A prize should be given to the critic, novice or veteran, who first has the courage to offer a detailed explication of "A Vision of the Sea."

The Cenci has generated a large volume of criticism, much of it revolving around the question of whether the play is stageable—a question that has been rendered all but meaningless by repeated successful productions. The earliest academic work was Ernest Sutherland Bate's *A Study of Shelley's Drama "The Cenci"* (1908). In the following year George Edward Woodberry brought out his valuable edition. The interest in the play's performing qualities—debated in the press during the London productions of 1886 and 1922—was reopened by St. John Ervine, drama critic and director, in a paper published in *Transactions of the Royal Society of Literature* entitled "Shelley as a Dramatist" (1936). In *PMLA* Sara R. Watson risked comparison of *The Cenci* with *Othello* (1940). Arthur C. Hicks first described "An American Performance of *The Cenci*" in *Stanford Studies in English Language and Literature* (1941) and then joined R. Milton Clarke in editing *A Stage Version of Shelley's "Cenci"* (1945). The same year Kenneth Neill Cameron and Horst Frenz compiled "The Stage History of Shelley's *The Cenci*" (*PMLA*), and later Bert O. States, Jr., contributed "Addendum" to that stage history (*PMLA*, 1957). For notices of performances of *The Cenci* at Chicago in 1958 and by the Old Vic company in London in 1959, see *KSJ* (1959, 1960). Marcel Kessel tries the question once more in "*The Cenci* as a Stage Play" (*PMLA*, 1960), drawing a rebuttal from Bert O. States, Jr., in the same issue.

More recently studies of *The Cenci* have shifted to the moral logic and psychology of the drama, as in Melvin R. Watson's "Shelley and Tragedy: The Case of Beatrice Cenci" (*KSJ*, 1958), Robert F. Whitman's "Beatrice's 'Pernicious Mistake' in *The Cenci*" (*PMLA*, 1959), and Joan Rees's "Shelley's Orsino: Evil in 'The Cenci' " (*KSMB*, 1961); James Rieger combined analysis of the play's *ethos* with a convincing suggestion as to Shelley's source in "Shelley's Paterin Beatrice" (*SIR*, 1965; rpt. in *The Mutiny Within*, 1967). Paul Smith analyzed the growth of Shelley's conception of the plot and characters in "Restless Casuistry: Shelley's Composition of *The Cenci*" (*KSJ*, 1964), and Truman Guy Steffan investigated various Italian manuscript versions of the Cenci's family story in "Seven Accounts of the Cenci and Shelley's Drama" (*SEL*, 1969). Charles L. Adams, in his excellent paper "The Structure of *The Cenci*" (*Drama Survey*, 1965), exposes the fallacy that the play has severe "structural weaknesses." Finally, Joseph W. Donohue, Jr., has brought to bear historical understanding of the stage in Shelley's day to elucidate "Shelley's Beatrice and the Romantic Concept of Tragic Character" (*KSJ*, 1968). What remained for critics of *The Cenci* was to seize and synthesize the various strands of critical inquiry. This Stuart Curran has done in *Shelley's "Cenci": Scorpions Ringed with Fire* (1970). Curran devotes the first half of his book to an analysis of *The Cenci* as a poem, including study of the theme, characterization, and imagery. The second half—"The Play"— investigates *The Cenci*'s dramaturgy from various perspectives. Well-written and cogently argued, Curran's book will remain a useful study for years. Earl R. Wasserman has developed new moral-psychological perspectives in the detailed analysis that forms one of the best sections of *Shelley: A Critical Reading* (1971).

Three studies of "The Indian Serenade" deserve mention because this lyric was once picked out by a few influential anthologists and critics as an example of bad, sentimental poetry: Chauncey B. Tinker's "Shelley's 'Indian Serenade'" (*Yale University Library Gazette,* 1950), B. A. Park's "The Indian Elements of the 'Indian Serenade'" (*KSJ,* 1961) and, especially, Richard Levin's "Shelley's 'Indian Serenade': A Re-Revaluation" (*CE,* 1963) put the poem in its literary and dramatic context. Conversely, *The Mask of Anarchy*—the one poem by Shelley found praiseworthy by F. R. Leavis in *Revaluation*—has not been seriously scrutinized in recent years, the standard separate essay remaining the background study of "Peterloo, Shelley, and Reform" by A. Stanley Walker (*PMLA,* 1925). In the same manner, studies of Shelley's long satirical-humorous poems of 1819–1820 "Peter Bell the Third" and *Oedipus Tyrannus; or Swellfoot the Tyrant* have been few and, for the most part, very generalized. Important is Newman I. White's "Shelley's *Swellfoot the Tyrant* in Relation to Contemporary Political Satire" (*PMLA,* 1921) and useful for the student are the comments on both these poems by Carlos Baker in *Shelley's Major Poetry* and Seymour Reiter in *A Study of Shelley's Poetry.*

"The Witch of Atlas" is now coming into its own in the general studies and will undoubtedly receive more individual attention in the future. The only book devoted to it is Carl Grabo's *The Meaning of "The Witch of Atlas"* (1935), an avowedly Neoplatonic reading. After Kathrine Koller had pointed out sources for the poem in Herodotus, Pliny, and Greek romances (*MLN,* 1937), John Livingstone Lowes began a controversy with *"The Witch of Atlas and Endymion"* (*PMLA,* 1940), in which he claimed that "The Witch of Atlas" was dramatically influenced by *Endymion* and other poems of Keats. Lowes was answered emphatically by David Lee Clark in "What Was Shelley's Indebtedness to Keats?" and more obliquely in a companion article by Carlos Baker entitled "Spenser and *The Witch of Atlas*" (both *PMLA,* 1941). John E. Jordan followed by demonstrating the nature of Shelley's self-awowed reaction to Wordsworth's *Peter Bell* in the poem ("Wordsworth and 'The Witch of Atlas,' " *ELH,* 1942). In recent years Shelley's poem has received greater attention in the general critical books—particularly from Harold Bloom—and critical explications of specific aspects are just beginning to appear, led by David Rubin's "A Study of Antinomies in Shelley's *The Witch of Atlas*" (*SIR,* 1969).

Studies of *A Defence of Poetry* have been discussed under IV.B above. *Epipsychidion* is, perhaps, the poem of Shelley's that has caused his admirers the most embarrassment. And yet, viewed within the context that Shelley himself provided for it in the "Advertisement," proem, and *envoi* —the analogy of *La vita nuova* of Dante—the poem stands forth as one of Shelley's finest achievements. Donald H. Reiman in the brief account of the poem in his *Percy Bysshe Shelley* (1969) has pointed the way for full explication that takes the Dantesque context of the poem seriously. Reiman argues that the key to *Epipsychidion* is to be found in Section XVIII of *La vita nuova,* where Dante declares to the ladies that, since Beatrice has decided not to respond to his attentions, he has placed his happiness no longer "in the greeting of this lady" but "in those *words that praise my lady*"—no longer in life, but in art. Most previous studies of *Epipsychidion* centered on the biographical questions of what symbols in the poem represented which women in Shelley's life and whether Shelley's love for Teresa Viviani was "pure" and "Platonic" or "erotic" (as though the last two terms were at all contradictory). The best study of the biographical background of the poem is Kenneth Neill Cameron's "The Planet-Tempest Passage in *Epipsychidion*" (*PMLA,* 1948); in the same year the most elaborate reading of the symbolism in the poem to demonstrate that Shelley's feelings for Teresa Viviani were pure and Platonic appeared in Carlos Baker's *Shelley's Major Poetry* (1948); Shelley's "erotic" intentions toward the lady have been explored by Edward E. Bostetter in "Shelley and the Mutinous Flesh" (*TSLL,* 1959; rpt. in *The Romantic Ventriloquists,* 1963) and by Bostetter's student Gerald Enscoe in *Eros and the Romantics* (1967). For an introduction to the poem's confused manuscript drafts, interwoven with those of Shelley's fragmentary poems "Fiordispina" and "Ginevra," see Chapters xiii and xiv of Neville Rogers' *Shelley at Work* (1956; rev. ed., 1967), and for the source of Chaucer's Knight's Tale as an important parallel to Shelley's entire relationship with Teresa Viviani, see Enrica Viviani della Robbia, "Shelley e il Boccaccio" (*Italica,* 1959). An enterprising study of the poem's imagery—D[aniel] J.

Hughes, "Coherence and Collapse in Shelley, with Particular Reference to *Epipsychidion*" (*ELH*, 1961)—is especially useful in showing how Shelley unifies the thematic strands of sexual desire, the process of thought, and the composing of the poem itself. Now required is a synthesizing study that draws together all these strands, adds a detailed study of the manuscript drafts, and shows how Shelley molded personal experience and literary conceptions into a brilliant poem the theme of which is the value of poetry as the most worthy earthly object of man's imaginative aspirations.

Adonais received considerable early attention from students of the elegy and pastoral, who compared the poem with other works in those conventions. This approach can be found in William Michael Rossetti's Introduction and notes to his edition of the poem (1891*), which altogether offers a specimen of the best criticism of that era. Though T. P. Harrison explored "Spenser and Shelley's *Adonais*" (*TexSE*, 1933) and Cameron pointed out the relevance of Shelley's quarrel with Southey to the stanzas on the venal critic ("Shelley vs. Southey: New Light on an Old Quarrel," *PMLA*, 1942), the earliest detailed explications of *Adonais* in periodical essays were Melvin R. Watson's "The Thematic Unity of *Adonais*" (*KSJ*, 1952) and Wasserman's "*Adonais*: Progressive Revelation as a Poetic Mode" (*ELH*, 1954; rpt. in *The Subtler Language*). These unified readings of the poem were followed by a less detailed one by R. A. Foakes in *The Romantic Assertion* (1958), by Eleanor N. Hutchens' supplementary imagery study of "Cold and Heat in *Adonais*" (*MLN*, 1961), and by Patrick J. Mahony's rather lifeless and inconclusive "Analysis of Shelley's Craftsmanship in *Adonais*" (*SEL*, 1964). Ross G. Woodman's chapter on *Adonais* in *The Apocalyptic Vision in the Poetry of Shelley* (1964) is, as has already been mentioned, one of the high points in that book. Richard Harter Fogle described "John Taaffe's Annotated Copy of *Adonais*" (*KSJ*, 1968), in which Taaffe pointed out many parallels between Shelley's poem and Dante's *Commedia*; Fogle also published an essay on "Dante and Shelley's *Adonais*" (*Bucknell Review*, 1967). With Shelley's rough drafts for *Adonais* extant in the Bodleian Shelley notebooks, what is needed next, perhaps, is a study of the poem's genesis and development of its artistic symmetry so forcefully demonstrated by Wasserman in *The Subtler Language* and elaborated by Reiman in *Percy Bysshe Shelley*.

Of Shelley's major poems, *Hellas* is one that has received far less attention than it deserves. Aside from Newman Ivey White's "The Historical and Personal Background of Shelley's *Hellas*" (*SAQ*, 1921) and

Bennett Weaver's account of "The Williams Transcript of *Hellas*" (Univ. of Michigan Pubs. [in] Lang. and Lit., VIII, 1932), there are no substantive studies in English centering on *Hellas* alone. Even several general studies that, under the logic of their own structure, should have discussed the poem—including Baker's *Shelley's Major Poetry*, Bloom's *Shelley's Mythmaking*, Woodman's *The Apocalyptic Vision in the Poetry of Shelley*, and Reiter's *A Study of Shelley's Poetry*—managed to ignore or slight it. Neville Rogers includes some stimulating remarks on the poem in *Shelley at Work*, as does Milton Wilson in *Shelley's Later Poetry*. But the most coherent explications are three too recent to have been tested in the fires of critical controversy. Reiman's *Percy Bysshe Shelley* (1969) outlines the symmetrical structure of the poetic drama and sketches its theme; Carl Woodring's treatment of *Hellas* in *Politics in English Romantic Poetry* (1970) is excellent on its topic and supersedes Gerald McNiece's inadequate study from the same perspective in *Shelley and the Revolutionary Idea* (1969); finally, Earl R. Wasserman provides the fullest and most penetrating analysis in *Shelley: A Critical Reading* (1971).

Shelley's fragmentary drama "Charles the First" has attracted attention for its potentialities as a stage play and because of its historical background. The first two substantial essays were Newman Ivey White's essay "Shelley's *Charles I*" (*JEGP*, 1922) and Walter F. Wright's critique of "Shelley's Failure in *Charles I*" (*ELH*, 1941). Then Cameron explored "Shelley's Use of Source Material in *Charles I*" (*MLQ*, 1945), suggesting that Mrs. Macaulay's *History of England* was one important source for Shelley's projected drama. Recently R. B. Woodings has studied the Bodleian MSS of "Charles the First" and suggested modifications of previous opinions on several important questions. In "Shelley's Sources for *Charles the First*" (*MLR*, 1969), he observes, *contra* Cameron, that Shelley's notes show his sources to have been Hume's *History of England* and Whitelocke's *Memorials of the English Affairs*; and he argues in "Shelley's Widow Bird" (*RES*, 1968) that the poem was not intended as part of "Charles the First," but was the beginning of a personal lyric, possibly associated with Jane Williams. His major critical essay—the most extensive to date—is entitled " 'A Devil of a Nut to Crack': Shelley's *Charles the First*" (*SN*, 1968). Though many of the major critical studies slide over "Charles the First," there are useful commentaries in Woodman's *The Apocalyptic Vision in the Poetry of Shelley* and Reiman's *Percy Bysshe Shelley*, as well as in the two-volume biographies by Walter E. Peck and Newman Ivey White (both of whom make substantive comment on all of Shelley's longer poems and on many of the significant lyrics and fragments).

Donald H. Reiman's *Shelley's "The Triumph of Life": A Critical Study, based on a Text Newly Edited from the Bodleian Manuscript* (1965) did for Shelley's fragmentary final major poem what Zillman's *Variorum Edition* attempted for *Prometheus Unbound* and Curran's *Shelley's "Cenci"* achieved for *The Cenci*—it synthesized the contributions of previous critics and scholars with an original explication of "The Triumph of Life" based on the new text (which also utilized the work of G. M. Matthews). Reiman's extensive bibliography provides a full (though not exhaustive) record of studies of "The Triumph of Life" through 1963. Among those earlier studies that deserve special attention are A. C. Bradley's "Notes on Shelley's 'Triumph of Life' " (*MLR*, 1914) and F. Melian Stawell's "Shelley's 'Triumph of Life' " (*E&S*, 1914); William Cherubini's "Shelley's 'Own Symposium': *The Triumph of Life*" (*SP*, 1942), which argues—mistakenly, I believe,—for an earlier date and different thematic emphasis than most critics give Shelley's poem; Carlos Baker's *Shelley's Major Poetry*; Bice Chiappelli's *Il pensiero religioso di Shelley* (1956); Harold Bloom's *Shelley's Mythmaking* (1959); Kenneth Allott's "Bloom on 'The Triumph of Life' " (*EC*, 1960); G. M. Matthews' "Shelley and Jane Williams" (*RES*, 1961) and "On Shelley's 'The Triumph of Life' " (*SN*, 1962); Peter H. Butter's "Sun and Shape in Shelley's *The Triumph of Life*" (*RES*, 1962); and Reiman's "Shelley's 'The Triumph of Life': The Biographical Problem" (*PMLA*, 1963). Since the writing of Reiman's study, the most important commentaries have been by Ross Woodman in *The Apocalyptic Vision* . . . (1964); A. M. D. Hughes in *KSMB* (1965); Jerome J. McGann, "The Secrets of an Elder Day: Shelley after *Hellas*" (*KSJ*, 1966), which argues surprisingly that "The Triumph" and other late poems indicate that Shelley was reconciling his dualistic tensions into a new poetry of earth like Keats's "To Autumn"; and Neville Rogers, both in his revised edition of *Shelley at Work* (1967) and in an essay (in English) published in the symposium entitled *Versdichtung der englischen Romantik: Interpretationen,* ed. Teut A. Riese and Dieter Riesner (Berlin, 1968).

Shelley's posthumously published shorter poems have been virtually ignored in most recent major critical studies, and as a result have been left to the mercy of editors of anthologies and writers of introductions to poetry. One fact to keep in mind is that, with few exceptions, Shelley not only made no effort to publish these pieces, but often showed them to no one and in several cases probably did not complete them; a few are published only in corrupt or suspect texts. The student (and the critic) must be careful, therefore, not to assign to them more value and importance than they deserve simply because they fit conveniently into anthologies.

Some of the problems of textual integrity in Shelley's lyrics are surveyed in Irving Massey's "Shelley's 'Music, when soft voices die' " (*JEGP*, 1960; see also the explication in an answer by E. D. Hirsch, *JEGP*, 1961) and Massey's *Posthumous Poems of Shelley* (1969), in Joseph Raben's "Shelley's Invocation to Misery: An Expanded Text" (*JEGP*, 1966), and in G. M. Matthews' essay "Shelley's Lyrics" (see page 352 above). Others are discussed by Judith Chernaik in *The Lyrics of Shelley*, which is at once the best critical *and* textual study of Shelley's major lyric poetry. For the poems addressed to Jane Williams, one should first read Mrs. Chernaik's chapter and then turn back to such accounts as those in the biographies of White and Peck. See also Helmut Mertens' "Entsprechung von Form und Gehalt in Shelleys Gedicht 'To Jane: The keen stars were twinkling' " (*Neueren Sprachen,* 1964). An early dissertation on Shelley's lyrics in general, Herbert Huscher's *Studien zu Shelleys Lyrik* (1919), is pretty well outdated, but it reflects the greater reputation of Shelley's lyrics prior to the attacks of the new critics in the 1920's and 1930's. See also "The Lyrics of Shelley" in Stopford A. Brooke's *Studies in Poetry* (1907).

E. REPUTATION AND INFLUENCE

The best accounts of Shelley's search for an audience during his lifetime—his striving for acceptance either as a popular writer or as a guide to the intelligentsia—are Newman I. White's introduction to *The Unextinguished Hearth* (1938*) and Ian Jack's essay on Shelley in *English Literature 1815–1832* (1963; Volume X in *The Oxford History of English Literature*). In Chapter XXX of his *Shelley,* White sketched "Shelley's Posthumous Reputation," chiefly in England and America, to 1940. Accounts of the growth of his reputation in America, France, Germany, and the Soviet Union are found in the works by Julia Power, Peyre, Liptzin, and Gilenson mentioned in Section I above. The best and most readable general account of the growth (and misfortunes) of Shelley's afterfame is Sylva Norman's *Flight of the Skylark: The Development of Shelley's Reputation* (1954), a study that has been supplemented by Carl Woodring ("Dip of the Skylark," *KSJ,* 1960) and Miss Norman's "Twentieth-Century Theories on Shelley" (*TSLL,* 1967).

The specialized aspect of Shelley's afterfame that has received most scrutiny is the impact of his political ideas and expression. The early phase was studied by White in "Shelley and the Active Radicals of the Early Nineteenth Century" (*SAQ*, 1930) and by Kenneth Muir in "Shelley's Heirs" *Penguin New Writing*, ed. John Lehmann (1945). A broader study is Roland A. Duerksen's *Shelleyan Ideas in Victorian Literature* (1966), which treats the fate of Shelley's published ideas among the high Victorians and through Shaw. Duerksen is best on George Eliot and G. H. Lewes (see also *KSJ*, 1965) and Shaw (see his "Shelley and Shaw," *PMLA*, 1963), because he has little sympathy for those like Arnold, Disraeli, and Carlyle who were hostile to Shelley's social philosophy as they understood it. Shelley's impact on Shaw was viewed from the perspective of the later writer in Julian B. Kaye's *Bernard Shaw and the Nineteenth-Century Tradition* (1958), and Donald H. Reiman commented on another evidence of G. H. Lewes' appreciation of Shelley in "Shelley in the Encyclopedias" (*KSJ*, 1963).

Some significant studies of the impact of Shelley on specific later writers include Frederick A. Pottle's *Shelley and Browning: A Myth and Some Facts* (1923; rpt. with new preface, 1965); Phyllis Bartlett's "Hardy's Shelley" (*KSJ*, 1955) and "Seraph of Heaven: A Shelleyan Dream in Hardy's Fiction" (*PMLA*, 1955); Harris Chewning's "William Michael Rossetti and the Shelley Renaissance" (*KSJ*, 1955); and Leon Gottfried's *Matthew Arnold and the Romantics* (1963). In another vein altogether Julia Cluck has explored "Elinor Wylie's Shelley Obsession" (*PMLA*, 1941).

The poet whose relationship to Shelley has been most closely examined is W. B. Yeats. George Bornstein's *Yeats and Shelley* (1970) thoroughly studies Yeats's use of Shelley's poetry and Yeats's reasons for rejecting aspects of Shelley's thought when he reacted against his own early poetry and philosophy. Bornstein is not only fair to Shelley, but has some original observations on "Prince Athanase," Shelley's idea of love (and his "Discourse on the Manners of the Antient Greeks"), and Shelley's theory of history (and "Ode to Liberty"). Some of the general ideas on the relationship between the two poets were first set forth by H. W. Häusermann in "W. B. Yeats's Idea of Shelley" (*The Mint: A Miscellany*, ed. Geoffrey Grigson, 1946), and Häusermann makes several points not included by Bornstein. Finally, Harold Bloom's massive *Yeats* (1970), in tracing "a particular line of poetic influencing that moves from Milton to Wordsworth to Shelley and then on to Browning and Yeats," again and again returns to Shelley's impact on Yeats. Though Bloom's study—operating in a larger context—is less schematized and neat as well as more speculative than Bornstein's, it will obviously have a greater impact on future thinking about Yeats and the Romantics, as well as on influence-study in general. Bloom introduces into the study of these literary relations categories from Northrop Frye's *Anatomy of Criticism,* but he disagrees with Frye to the extent of seeing anxiety on the part of the new poet (Yeats) as the basis for his reinterpretation of his "precursors." Bloom's system would seem to work better in exploring poets of the Romantic and the post-Romantic traditions than for ascertaining the influence, say, of Virgil on Dante or on Milton. But certainly Bloom's system works well in *Yeats,* and the method will undoubtedly bear more fruit in Bloom's projected study of romanticism in modern poetry. The full extent of Shelley's impact on his literary heirs through Yeats and Eliot will certainly not be established (and accepted) for a number of years, but by the time it has been, Shelley's place in the Anglo-American poetic tradition will no longer be a matter of dispute.

VI
KEATS

Clarence D. Thorpe
David Perkins

I. BIBLIOGRAPHICAL MATERIALS

A really detailed bibliography of Keats is still lacking. When a full compilation has been made, it will be uniquely rich in manuscript items; for the number of extant autographs and transcripts is large. The list of editions and of biographical and critical studies will also be long. More attention was paid to Keats in the nineteenth century than might be supposed, and, during the last forty years in particular, scholars and critics have found Keats an especially congenial subject, and their explorations of every aspect of his life and verse have resulted in a steady stream of publications.

J. R. MacGillivray's *John Keats: A Bibliography and Reference Guide* (1949), the most ambitious attempt thus far in Keats bibliography, is a competently executed book, with some 1,250 classified, sometimes annotated entries, covering what is of main importance in edition, biography, and criticism from 1816 to 1946. The compilation is, however, selective rather than inclusive. MacGillivray has deliberately omitted certain classes of material, and he had no thought of listing the Keats manuscripts.

We have, in addition, a number of earlier bibliographies, some specialized, some quite brief, but all useful. For a list of the manuscript holographs and transcripts of the poems, see H. W. Garrod's Introduction to *The Poetical Works of John Keats* (1939; 2nd ed., 1958). As for the letters, H. E. Rollins, in the opening note to each letter in his edition (1958), discussed below in Section II, gives the location of the manuscript or other source, and also provides a detailed list of lost letters (pp. 9–14). Another bibliography of manuscript materials is to be found in Claude L. Finney's *Evolution of Keats's Poetry* (1936; rpt. 1963), valuable for the listing of manuscript items in such storehouses of Keatsiana as the Wood-house books in the Morgan and Houghton libraries. In addition, there is the catalogue of the Dilke Collection in the Hampstead Library, and the list of manuscripts either in holograph or transcript by Keats's family and friends in Hyder E. Rollins' two-volume *The Keats Circle* (1948; 2nd ed. rev., 1965).

Previous to MacGillivray's book, the nearest approach to a complete listing of printed materials was to be found in Maurice Buxton Forman's bibliography in the Hampstead Edition of Keats, and next to that was the list furnished by Ernest de Selincourt for *The Cambridge Bibliography of English Literature,* Volume III (1941). The *CBEL* is useful but not ex-haustive, despite additions in its *Supplement* (1957), ed. George Watson, and in the *New CBEL,* Vol. III (1969), ed. George Watson. Special mention should be made of the section on Keats in *Romantic Poets and Prose Writers* (1967), comp. Richard Fogle, in the Goldentree Bibliog-raphies. An older compilation that should not be overlooked is that of John P. Anderson of the British Museum, included as an appendix in W. M. Rossetti's *Life of John Keats* (1887), which, for 1816–87, mentions out-of-the-way chapters and articles that might otherwise be easily missed. All these bibliographies need to be supplemented by reference, for more recent items, to such annual bibliographies as those published in *ELH* (1936–48), *PQ* (1949–64), and *ELN* (1965–). Of the annual lists by far the most complete is that of *KSJ* (1952–), the first twelve of which (1950–62) have been published as a separate volume (1964).

One additional compilation may be mentioned: "Tributes and Allu-sions in Verse to Keats, During the Years 1816–1920" (*N&Q,* 1947), a collection of some 140 items, made by M. B. Forman assisted by Edmund Blunden, recording recognitions of Keats in verse during the period covered and so furnishing an instructive footnote to the history of Keats's reputation.

II. EDITIONS

The texts of the three volumes of Keats's verse published in his lifetime have all been made available to modern readers in facsimile, in the English Replicas of *Poems of 1817* and *Poems of 1820* (1928) and in the repro-duction of *Endymion,* with an introduction and notes by H. Clement

Notcutt (1927). Collection of the posthumous and fugitive poems was systematically begun by Richard Monckton Milnes, who gave to the public in his *Life, Letters, and Literary Remains of John Keats* (1848) not only the first *Life* and the first view of the letters, but a number of new poems (38). In subsequent revisions (1854, 1867, 1879) he added poems and letters as they came to his attention, paving the way for later, more nearly definitive editions. Milnes (Lord Houghton) has been reprinted so many times that he is still readily available.

Of annotated texts, H. B. Forman's editions were the first. His Library Edition of 1883, revised and enlarged in 1889, and for the most part carried over into *The Complete Works of John Keats,* in five volumes (1900–01), remains of value both for its text and for the range and interest of its other materials. Besides the poems and letters, Keats's miscellaneous prose is here, along with a considerable body of collateral writing —early reviews, letters by Keats's family and friends, and sundry critical comment, the last mostly included in notes.

The Library Edition was reprinted with additions and revisions by Forman's son, Maurice Buxton, in the sumptuous Hampstead Keats (1938–39), a limited edition (1,050 copies) in eight volumes. The additions—besides Forman's own prefaces, an introduction by John Masefield, and a Memoir of George Keats by Naomi Kirk—were chiefly in the way of additional poems and letters by Keats and by his family and friends. There were also liberal increments to the marginalia and to the bibliography. The Hampstead Keats has all the virtues, except that of accessibility, of the original H. B. Forman editions, and some of its own.

But the two editions of Keats's poems that are now of first importance are Ernest de Selincourt's *Poems* (1905; 6th ed., 1935) and H. W. Garrod's *Poetical Works* (1939; 2nd ed., slightly revised, 1958). If a student is interested in textual problems, in variants in manuscript and printed versions, and in information about manuscripts and editions, he will wish to go to Garrod. If, however, he is more concerned with critical problems, he will go to de Selincourt. For though he took pains with textual matters, establishing a text nearer to Keats's manuscripts than that of any of his predecessors, de Selincourt gave special attention to questions of meaning and aesthetic quality. His substantial introduction is penetrating and sound, in many respects in advance of most current criticism of the time, and his notes are scholarly and inclusive.

Complete editions of the poetry, with helpful commentary, include: J. Middleton Murry's *The Poems and Verses of John Keats* (1927, 1940;

rev. in one volume, 1948); G. R. Elliott's *The Complete Poetry of John Keats* (1927); C. D. Thorpe's *The Complete Poems and Selected Letters of John Keats* (1935); the Everyman *Poems and Selected Letters*, with an introduction by Gerald Bullett (1944); Harold E. Briggs's *Complete Poems and Selected Letters* (1951). Murry arranges the poems, including newly-found verse and fragments, in chronological order and has added economical but distinctive notes. In books intended primarily for the college class and the general reader, Elliott, Thorpe, and Briggs also follow the chronological pattern, Elliott supplying an introduction, Thorpe and Briggs both an introduction and notes. Briggs also includes nine papers concerned with the attacks of the reviewers on *Endymion*. Of less value for most readers is *The Poetical Works*, ed. H. W. Garrod in the Oxford Standard Authors series (1956; paperbound rpt., 1960), which is essentially the text of his 1939 *Poetical Works*, mentioned above, but stripped of its annotation. Mention should also be made of collections edited by Gerald Bullett (1961), Carlos Baker (1962), and Stanley Kunitz (1964).

Of the numerous books of selections, some of which also include many of the letters, particular attention should be called to the valuably annotated *Selected Poems and Letters* (1959), ed. Douglas Bush, which evoked from C. D. Thorpe an admiring review that also became a general survey of Bush's career as a scholar-critic of Keats (*KSJ*, 1960). Other selections, in order of publication, include: *John Keats: An Introduction and a Selection*, by Richard Church (1948); *Poems*, ed. Rosalind Vallance, with an Introduction by B. Ifor Evans (1950); *Selected Poems*, ed. Laurence Whistler (1950); *Selected Poetry and Letters*, ed. Richard H. Fogle (1951); *John Keats, A Selection of His Poetry*, ed. J. E. Morpurgo (1953); *Poems and Letters*, ed. James R. Caldwell (1954); *Poems*, ed. Edmund Blunden (1955), in Collins New Classics; *Selected Poetry*, ed. Howard Moss (1959), in the Laurel series; *Selected Poems and Letters*, ed. Roger Sharrock (1964), in the New Oxford English Series; *Selected Poems and Letters*, ed. Robert Gittings (1966); *Selected Poetry*, ed. Paul de Man (1966), in Signet Classic Poetry Series; and *Selected Poems and Letters*, ed. James Reeves (1967) in Poetry Bookshelf. Many of these volumes have ably written introductions, well adapted to their intended function of invitation and orientation.[1]

---

[1] It seems unnecessary here to make an extensive listing of foreign editions of Keats's poetry, but a brief sampling will show something of the attention Keats is receiving from non-English speaking students of literature: in Switzerland, *John Keats, Gedichte und Briefe*, ed. and trans. H. W. Häusermann (1950); *Tendre est la nuit. Florilège des poèmes*

In spite of the work of such editors as de Selincourt, Murry, and Garrod, as additional holographs and early transcripts of Keats's poems turn up or are more thoroughly examined, evidence of deficiencies in existing editions accumulates. For example, Mable A. E. Steele's "The Woodhouse Transcripts of the Poems of Keats" (*HLB,* 1949), "Three Early Manuscripts of John Keats" (*KSJ,* 1952), and "The Authorship of 'The Poet' and Other Sonnets" (*KSJ,* 1956), ably arguing that "The Poet" was written not by Keats but his publisher, John Taylor; William Allan Coles's "The Proof Sheets of Keats's 'Lamia'" (*HLB,* 1954); Hyder Rollins' "Unpublished Autograph Texts of Keats" (*HLB,* 1952); and Jack Stillinger, "The Text of 'The Eve of St. Agnes'" (*SB,* 1963) and "The Text of Keats's 'Ode on Indolence'" (*SB,* 1969), all furnish arguments leading to the conclusion that data could be assembled for more authentic editions of the poems than we now have. Of special value is Stuart Sperry's detailed *Richard Woodhouse's Interleaved and Annotated Copy of Keats's "Poems" (1817),* Univ. of Wisconsin *Literary Monographs,* I (1967).

The letters of Keats have been printed by Lord Houghton (above), John Speed (1883), Sidney Colvin (1891), and others. But the names inevitably associated with the correspondence are those of H. B. Forman, his son, M. B. Forman, and Hyder E. Rollins. For twenty years or more the elder Forman busied himself in a search for Keats's letters. It was he who first published the letters to Fanny Brawne (1878; rev. and enl. 1889) and who gave us the full canon—as then known—of Keats's correspondence, first in the Library Edition, then in *The Complete Works.* When he died, his son carried on this work. In four separate publications (1930, 1935, 1947, 1952), he offered the fruit of their combined labors, each succeeding edition containing added letters or parts of letters and new data by which to relate the correspondence to Keats's life and poetry. Even so there were serious faults: errors in transcription and dating, failure to make revisions and to rearrange the letters in accordance with newly revealed and easily accessible facts, and continued reliance on out-dated authorities. These defects were cogently dealt with by Hyder E. Rollins in his review of the 1947 edition (*JEGP,* 1948) and later articles (*HLB,* 1950, 1953, 1954;

---

de John Keats, ed. Pierre Louis Natthey (1950), and *Poèmes choisis,* trans., with introd. Albert Laffay (1952); in Belgium, *John Keats* (selected poems, with parallels in French trans.), ed. Maurice Wagemans (1945); in Spain, *Poems,* ed. J. Mascaró (1955); in Japan, *Poems,* ed. Takesha Saito (1959). Students interested in foreign editions of Keats will find the bibliography published annually in *KSJ* a useful guide.

KSJ, 1953; and *SB,* 1957). Rollins meanwhile had decided to bring out a new edition.

The Letters of John Keats, 1814–1821, ed. Hyder E. Rollins (2 vols., 1958), became the definitive edition as soon as it appeared, and will almost certainly remain so for at least a generation. Even if new letters are discovered, they will probably be incorporated by a new editor in this edition or published as a supplement. For it is difficult to imagine that the texts of what we now have could be more scrupulously edited, whatever minor revisions or additions might be made. It differs from the Forman edition, previously the standard one, in the following ways: (1) Aside from printing other material from members of the Keats Circle, it provides seven new letters (or other documents) by Keats, and another seven in new and better texts. (2) About sixty have been redated and rearranged. (3) In all cases where it was possible, the texts have been freshly transcribed from originals. (4) Half of the notes are new, and many of the others have been revised and have been credited, when this was known, to their original sources. The capacious introductory material (92 pages) gives full information on the texts, a history of the letters and their editors, a valuable chronology of Keats's life, succinct biographies of the correspondents, and there is a detailed index.

Among selections of the letters, special mention should be given to that of Lionel Trilling (1951; paperbound rev., 1955), primarily because of its discriminating Introduction (rpt., with a few changes, as "The Poet as Hero" in Trilling's *The Opposing Self,* 1955). Other comparable editions are those of Frederick Page (1954), in The World's Classics, Stanley Gardner (1965), and the selections in the volumes, mentioned above, that include both poems and letters, ed. C. D. Thorpe, H. E. Briggs, R. H. Fogle, J. E. Morpurgo, J. R. Caldwell, Douglas Bush, Carlos Baker, Roger Sharrock, James Reeves, and Robert Gittings.

A volume of correspondence, small but important for the sidelights it throws on Keats's life, is *The Letters of Fanny Brawne to Fanny Keats,* ed. Fred Edgcumbe (1937). The thirty-one letters furnish an informative footnote to other accounts of Keats's love affair. On a larger, far more important scale, is the impressive two-volume edition of letters and other documents by Keats's family and friends, *The Keats Circle* (1948) by Hyder E. Rollins; and also, by the same scholar, *More Letters and Poems of the Keats Circle* (1955). A second edition of *The Keats Circle,* corrected and slightly revised (2 vols., 1965), incorporates *More Letters and Poems.* In these two central works intimate and authentic details about

Keats and his friends, hitherto accessible only in manuscript in the Harvard and Morgan Collections, are now made available to all.

It remains to mention a selected list of editions useful for their specialized subject matter. These are, in chronological order: *Keats' Hyperion mit Einleitung,* ed. Johannes Hoops (1899), which contains a study of sources of Keats's diction; *Hyperion: A Facsimile of Keats's Autograph Manuscript with a Transliteration of the Manuscript of the Fall of Hyperion a Dream,* with an introduction and notes by Ernest de Selincourt (1905)—interesting not only for its reproduction of the holograph of *Hyperion,* now in the British Museum, and for the twenty-four additional lines in the *Fall of Hyperion* with a history of the manuscript in which they occur, but for lists of variant readings and for distinguished critical interpretative comment by the editor; *The Keats Letters, Papers, and Other Relics Forming the Dilke Bequest in the Hampstead Public Library, Reproduced in Fifty-Eight Collotype Facsimiles,* ed. George C. Williamson, with forewords by Theodore Watts-Dunton and an introduction by H. B. Forman (1914); *A Concordance to the Poems of John Keats* by Dane Lewis Baldwin, Leslie N. Broughton, and others (1917; rpt. 1963); *Keats's Shakespeare* (1928; 2nd ed., 1929; rpt. 1966), ed. Caroline Spurgeon, with portions of the plays from Keats's favorite edition reproduced for the sake of showing Keats's underlinings and marginal comments; *John Keats's Anatomical and Physiological Note Book* (1934), ed. M. B. Forman from the manuscript in the Hampstead Library; and Robert Gittings' facsimile edition of *The Odes of Keats and Their Earliest Known Manuscripts* (1970).

III. BIOGRAPHY

After Keats's death in 1821 there were various candidates for the honor of first biographer. C. A. Brown expected the assignment, and did in fact write a brief *Life,* which went unpublished until a few years ago (1937) when it was printed, with an Introduction and Notes, by Dorothy Hyde Bodurtha and W. B. Pope. More recently it has been included entire in Hyder Rollins' *The Keats Circle* (1948; rev. 1965 [see above]). Other aspirants were Joseph Severn, John Taylor, and Charles Dilke; and of perennial interest is Charles and Mary Cowden Clarke's *Recollections of Writers* (1878; rpt. 1969, with an Introduction by Robert Gittings). But the task ultimately fell to the lot of Richard Monckton Milnes (Lord Houghton), who in 1848 brought out his now famous *Life, Letters, and Literary Remains of John Keats,* in two volumes.[2] Aided by George Keats, Taylor, and others, Milnes assembled a remarkable mass of evidence, including, besides letters and new poems, a rich miscellanea of information obtained from members of the Keats circle. Milnes's *Life* has been superseded by the work of later biographers; but for both the freshness of its view and the first-hand quality of its materials it is a book not to be neglected. (A reliable and readable life of Milnes himself is that of James Pope-Hennessy [2 vols., 1951, 1955].)

Of the many critical biographies that have followed Houghton's, two were of particular importance before 1963. The first of these in point of time was Sir Sidney Colvin's *John Keats: His Life and Poetry, His Friends, Critics, and After-Fame* (1917, 1925; rpt. 1970), the culmination of a study begun more than thirty years before, when Colvin wrote his short *Keats* (1887; rpt. 1957) for the English Men of Letters series. The second, Amy Lowell's *John Keats* (2 vols., 1925), had the advantage of fuller information, amassed both through her own research and through the process of accretion in previous studies. For substantial critical judgment, for a more sober interpretation of Keats's work and of matters connected with his life, Colvin is the safer guide. Miss Lowell is throughout more personal, less disinterested. She is eager to shield and uphold a beloved poet toward whom she has developed a maternal attitude. She wishes, moreover, to show that he is one of us—one of the moderns.

A third and shorter book, also written before the reconsideration of Keats that followed World War II, is Dorothy Hewlett's *Adonais: A Life of John Keats* (1937; rev. and enl. 1950). Miss Hewlett puts the poet in the Georgian scene, giving us a nearer perspective of the milieu in which he lived. She has at her disposal some new facts, tells a good story, and gives a full summary of the reception of Keats's work by the reviewers. In her criticism of the poetry, however, she is not up to the mark. Her critical comment has virtues—it is more moderate than Lowell's, is touched with warmer sympathy than Colvin's—but it tends to come to nothing, is incon-

---

[2] Hyder E. Rollins has said in *The Keats Circle* that Leigh Hunt published "the first life of Keats" in *Lord Byron and Some of His Contemporaries* (1828) and that in the same year "he wrote the second life of Keats" for John Gorton's *General Biographical Dictionary*. Important as these sketches were, however, Milnes must still be given credit for the first full-length biography of Keats.

clusive, has the habit of gliding off and around crucial problems, and is likely to be thinly impressionistic.

What outdates these biographies, good as they were, is the detailed analysis of Keats's life and writings that began in the late 1930's and immensely increased after 1947. One important contribution was Hyder Rollins' *The Keats Circle,* later followed by his authoritative edition of the *Letters,* both of which are discussed above. There was also energetic exploration by many scholars of every detail or aspect of Keats's life and that of his family and friends. Published chiefly in articles,[3] much of this showed an almost personal identification with Keats as a "modern," as a poet relevant to us in every way. Meanwhile, the critical reconsideration of Keats multiplied. By the 1960's the time was ripe for a major reinterpretation of his life and works. Then three important biographies appeared—a significant tribute to any poet. One attempted a general summation of what had since been discovered about Keats's life, while coalescing it with a balanced criticism of his writing. Two concentrated more exclusively on the events and details of the life itself, the first from a more overtly narrative and the second from a more scrupulously considered point of view.

Certainly the best of these, *John Keats,* by Walter Jackson Bate (1963), is a model of literary biography. Among its many virtues is that it overcomes the split between biography and criticism that has been one of the more deplorable aspects of present-day literary study. Where so many biographers scarcely or inexpertly notice what their subject actually wrote, though this is the sole reason for studying his life, Bate achieves both the most penetrating narrative of Keats's life that we have and the single most satisfying, full-length critical discussion of the poetry. In doing so he combines different approaches to literature that are usually pursued separately—including literary history, the history of ideas, critical theory, psychology, and stylistic analysis. Among the many new or important contributions that should be mentioned, one may single out (1) the constant mindfulness that the "inner life" of a writer—his fears, anxieties, dilemmas, and satisfactions—is likely to center upon his art. This was especially praised by reviewers who are themselves poets and hence in a position to appreciate Bate's awareness of what it is like to be a writer. (2) The shrewd and new understanding of the situation of poetry in the

[3] Many of the articles on special biographical details, dates, etc., that might otherwise be mentioned in this section are omitted since they are now subsumed, in one way or another, by the general biographies of the 1960's, especially Bate and Gittings.

Romantic period as Keats experienced and sought to diagnose it—the growing self-consciousness on the part of the poet, the fear of being un-original, the whole problem of what still remains for the poet to do. (Bate has since elaborated this theme in a more general context in his Alexander Lectures, *The Burden of the Past and the English Poet,* 1970.) (3) The emphasis on the importance for Keats's self-development of the Longinian ideal, and Keats's bold, high-minded response to what Whitehead called "the vision of greatness." (4) The reinterpretation of the sympathetic imagination or empathy in Keats's character and poetry, climaxing a study that began twenty-five years before with Bate's ground-breaking publication while still a college student of *Negative Capability: The Intuitive Approach in Keats* (1939). The topic is here opened up both psychologically and morally as never before. In the discussion of particular poems the "Ode to Psyche" is seen as a commitment to explore the "untrodden regions" of the mind—the next task before the poetry of the future, a poetry that Keats was reluctantly concluding had to be different from the poetry of Shakespeare and Milton. The "Nightingale" and the "Grecian Urn" are seen as a new form of dramatic lyric that explores further the limitations and gains of imaginative identification that arise in "the greeting of the Spirit" (to use Keats's phrase) and its object. The interpretation of *Lamia* stresses that the poem dramatizes the inevitable relativity of point of view; the characters of the poem find in Lamia what they are predisposed to find. The chapter on *Hyperion* dwells not only on the speech of Oceanus and the "dying into life" of Apollo, but also on the unfinished tragic theme, the fall of Hyperion, and views the poem as in part an exploration of different forms of response to tragic event. *The Fall of Hyperion* turns on the use of the entire self for self-transcendence—a deepening in Keats's concept of sympathetic identification that is seen to have immense importance for the greater poetry of the nineteenth and twentieth centuries. Finally the tone and style of the book deserve special mention. One of the most intellectually informative of biographies, it is also one of the most readable. There is none of the usual quarreling with other students over minor details. There are scenes of humor and moving drama. Nothing that would interest the most highly informed reader or critic is neglected. It is easily the most valuable single book on Keats.

Aileen Ward's *John Keats: The Making of a Poet* (1963) was plainly conceived with other premises in mind. Whatever the intentions implied in the subtitle and in her remark "My account . . . is primarily concerned with the development of [Keats's] character as a poet," the book is essentially in the vein of Miss Hewlett's biography, mentioned above: a quasi-popular "life," with comparatively little critical interpretation (usually no more than two or three pages on each major poem). The difference is that, whereas Miss Hewlett tries to place her story in the social setting of the period, Miss Ward's narrative seeks interest and relevance through a more psychologically oriented approach. The use of psychoanalysis, even by broadly trained analysts, is always questionable when the subject is so remote in time and when we have so much less to go on than any trained psychoanalyst would desire. But a more serious objection is that, as Freud himself admitted, psychoanalysis can tell us little about genius and hence about what it is that really leads to "the *making* of a poet." In the case of Miss Ward's book, she is often encouraged by this approach to interpret a work in a naively autobiographical way (Moneta in the *Fall of Hyperion* has "the face of Keats's dead mother, shrouded in her coffin"), rather than to dwell on what is important or valuable about the work. But the book is readable, warm-natured, and enthusiastic; and, with all its limitations, it might still be regarded as one of the best of the middle-length biographies had it not, in effect, been superseded by Gittings. For Gittings is factually more ample and accurate, less speculative, offers somewhat more critical observation, and is equal if not more vivid in narrative style.

The third of the new biographies, *John Keats* by Robert Gittings (1968), naturally profits from the two earlier ones, especially Bate, and adds some more details (particularly in connection with the family background and finances). It shares certain qualities with each of its predecessors. Like Bate's biography, it is a full-scale life of the writer, is carefully researched, and is the product of many years of earlier work on Keats. If it is shorter than Bate (two-thirds the length), it is because, like Ward, it lacks critical substance. That is, it is concerned more exclusively with the external facts of Keats's life, as contrasted with his inner life and spiritual and technical development, is philosophically and critically simpler, and provides far less of a sense of the context and traditions, poetic and intellectual, within which Keats wrote and through which his achievement is ultimately to be evaluated. One has the feeling that he did not wish to rival Bate in these respects, but to concentrate instead on writing a more factually researched and detailed version of Ward, with whom, in footnotes, Gittings carries on a running quarrel. At the start Gittings announces what the book will do (and thus, by implication, what it will not try to do): its merit will be to scrutinize once more every factual detail in the life of Keats, including the dating of incidents and poems. But as Jack

Stillinger pointed out in his sympathetic and authoritative review (*KSJ,* 1969), the claim is not justified except, perhaps, in those pages in the opening part that concentrate on the background of the family, genealogy, finances, the grandmother's will—much of this treated in more detail in Gittings' earlier monograph, *The Keats Inheritance* (1964). When he reaches the period of the major poems, however, Gittings begins to relax his vigilance and becomes either conservative or mellowly speculative. A principal excellence of the book is its grace of style and (usually) manner. In this major effort Gittings is less cantankerous and argumentative than in some of his earlier writings (notably *The Keats Inheritance*), is less inclined to carry on contentious debate with other scholars, and he allows full play to his gift for vivid biographical narrative, already so apparent in his *John Keats: The Living Year* (1954). As a result, the Keats that appears in his biography is a figure of remarkable dash and gusto, on a colorful canvas of human relations and interests.

To turn to the frankly shorter biographies: by far the best—trustworthy, balanced, wise—is Douglas Bush's *John Keats: His Life and Writings* (1966), in the Masters of World Literature Series. It also provides the finest condensed discussion of Keats as a mind and a poet. Completely familiar with the external and personal events of Keats's life, Bush also brings to the interpretation of the poetry as impressive an authority as anyone of our time, drawing upon an imaginative and close study extending over forty years. All of the more specialized approaches to Keats or interests in him (in many of which Bush was already there before others began) are considered and subsumed with freshness, grace, and the lack of ostentation that only genuine authority seems always able to afford. Of particular value for the book is Bush's remarkable range as a scholar and critic (from classical through Renaissance to modern). Hence, while he has all the knowledge of the specialist, he has none of the myopia; and we are constantly aware that Keats's achievement is being seen and evaluated in the context that Keats himself, with his hope to be "among the English poets," most prized.

Superseded by Bush but worthy of mention is B. Ifor Evans' *Keats* (1934), which is readable, generally authoritative, and contains clear and firm critical comment. It is preferable to *The Life of John Keats* (1929)— the French title is *La Vie de John Keats*—by Albert Erlande (pseud. for Albert Jacques Brandenburg). Erlande is appreciative but lacks the balance of Bush and Evans, and appears subjective by contrast. Mention may also be made of W. M. Rossetti's *Life of Keats* (1887), though its interest has long been only minor. Sober but quite outdated is Lucien Wolff's *John Keats, sa vie et son œuvre* (1910), of which his more mature *Keats,* in Les Grands Ecrivains Etrangers (1929), is a considerably abbreviated and modified redaction. Wolff's real strength lies in critical explication, and his book is accordingly discussed below in the section on criticism. Produced by a professor in an American university, but written in Italian and published in Rome, Michele Renzulli's *John Keats, l'uomo e il poeta* (1956) provides a thoughtful life of Keats, with a running critical study of the poetry, supplemented by reference to the letters. A feature of the book is its "Appendice Bibliografica," covering—though admittedly with omissions —the range of scholarly and critical writings on Keats. Professor Renzulli is to be congratulated for making so comprehensive a book available to Italian readers. Other works include Betty Askwith's *Keats* (1941), sympathetic but undistinguished, and Blanche Colton Williams' *Forever Young* (1943), a lively narrative in which Miss Williams uses the letters for a novelistic account of the thought and acts of Keats. Mention should also be made of Claude L. Finney's *Evolution of Keats's Poetry* (discussed above), a book that in the present survey belongs primarily under IV (Criticism), but which is also, in effect, a story of Keats's poetic life; E. V. Weller's so-called *Autobiography of John Keats* (1933), a piecing together in chronological order of Keats's letters and other prose in such a way as to let Keats tell his own story; and Nelson Bushnell's *A Walk After Keats* (1936)—an entertaining narrative, supported by liberal quotations from the letters and journals of Keats and Brown, of an expedition in which the author followed the trail of Keats and Brown on the famous walking trip of 1818. A capsule biography is Edmund Blunden's *John Keats,* published by the British Council and the National Book League as a supplement to *British Book News* (1950). Blunden is here at his best in easy mastery of his subject and in quick-moving, engaging style.

Three works of Robert Gittings, written earlier than the biography mentioned above, deal with biographical or quasi-biographical matters. The most important, as well as most readable, is his *John Keats: The Living Year 21 September 1818 to 21 September 1819* (1954), which discusses the background of the poems of this year, and attracted notice chiefly by certain new facts about Mrs. Isabella Jones and Keats's relations with her (most of the latter wholly conjectural) and by a fuller account of Keats's visit to Bedhampton and Chichester in early 1819 than was hitherto available. Much of the book is a record of relentless source-hunting, in which Keats's day-by-day experiences are treated as origins for idea and image on something like an equality with his day-by-day gleanings from such writers as Burton, Shakespeare, and Dryden. If Gittings' use of sources remains unconvincing, it is in part because of his dubious theory that Keats is a poet who relies on the experience and reading of the moment for his materials; in part because he sees parallels where none seem to exist. Throughout the book one senses an unwitting devaluation of Keats as both poet and man. A thoughtful examination of the book is provided in J. M. Murry's *Keats* (1955; rev. and enl. 1962), a fourth edition of his earlier *Studies in Keats.* In his general biography, discussed above, Gittings dropped many of the more extreme arguments and parallels for which he had been attacked. Hence *John Keats: The Living Year,* though it retains charm and suggestiveness, may be said to have been superseded by Gittings' own later work. The same may be said of his collection of essays, *The Mask of Keats* (1956), and of his monograph, *The Keats Inheritance,* the latter of which is concerned with the financial affairs of the Jennings family (Keats's maternal grandparents), and what the Keats children inherited from them (see the review by John Rutherford, *KSJ,* 1966).[4]

Supplementary fact and discussion of special aspects of Keats's life will be found in Donald Parson, *Portraits of Keats* (1954), with ninety-four plates, which provides full information about all the paintings, busts, and the life-mask; Guy Murchie, *The Spirit of Place in Keats* (1955), a charming book about places that Keats visited or that are associated with him (see the review by Leonidas Jones, *KSJ,* 1956); Neville Rogers, *Keats, Shelley, and Rome: An Illustrated Miscellany* (1961); and Joanna Richardson's pleasant *The Everlasting Spell: A Study of Keats and His Friends* (1963). Mention should also be made of a group of writings having to do with Keats as a medical student (and often with his medical history as well), though these subjects have since been amply discussed in the biographies of Bate, Ward, and Gittings: Sir William Hale White, *Keats as Doctor and Patient* (1938); Walker A. Wells, *A Doctor's Life of John Keats* (1959), speculative but suggestive; and E. P. Scarlett, "John Keats: Medical Student" (*Archives of Internal Medicine,* 1962). B. R.

---

[4] For further discussion on finances and Keats's family, see Jack Stillinger, "The Brown-Dilke Controversy" (*KSJ,* 1962), a searching examination of the question of George Keats's honesty in financial relations with his brother; Phyllis Mann, "New Light on Keats and His Family" (*KSMB,* 1960) and "Keats's Maternal Relations" (*KSMB,* 1964); Jean Haynes, "John Jennings: Keats's Grandfather" (*KSMB,* 1962) and "Keats's Paternal Relatives" (*KSMB,* 1964); and Norman Kilgour, "Mrs. Jennings' Will" (*KSMB,* 1962) and "Keats and the Abbey Cocks Account" (*KSMB,* 1963).

Richardson, "An Esculapian Poet—John Keats" (*Asclepiad,* 1884), is of little more than antiquarian interest. *The Anatomical and Physiological Note Book* (above, II) is of course as much a document in autobiography as it is an edition. Of ancillary interest is E. W. Goodall's account (*Guy's Hospital Gazette,* June 1936) of passages in Keats indicating his medical training; H. Pettit, "Scientific Correlatives of Keats's 'Ode to Psyche' " (*SP,* 1943), suggesting that some of the imagery reflects Keats's knowledge of the interweaving ganglia of the brain derived from his medical study; and the supplementary article by C. W. Hagelman, "Keats's Medical Training and the Last Stanza of the 'Ode to Psyche' " (*KSJ,* 1962).

Of works not about Keats himself but which directly or indirectly shed light on him or his work one would now place at the top of the list Hyder E. Rollins' *The Keats Circle* (see above, Editions). But it is also biography, of the freshest, most authentic sort, and should be read as a supplement to the biographies. Important related writings, by three of Keats's friends, have been authoritatively edited by former students of Rollins: the great *Diary of Benjamin Robert Haydon,* ed. W. B. Pope (5 vols., 1960–63), previously known only in abridged form; *The Letters of Charles Armitage Brown,* ed. Jack Stillinger (1966), with a valuable, condensed Introduction; and *Selected Prose of John Hamilton Reynolds,* ed. Leonidas Jones (1966).[5] Also of biographical interest are Edmund Blunden, *Leigh Hunt* (1930), Louis Landré's biography (in French), *Leigh Hunt, 1784–1859* (1935–36), and two articles by C. D. Thorpe on Keats's relations with two contemporary writers: "Wordsworth and Keats —A Study in Personal and Critical Impression" (*PMLA,* 1927) and "Keats and Hazlitt: A Record of Personal Relationship and Critical Estimate" (*PMLA,* 1947). For Fanny Brawne, aside from the general biographies of Keats, readers may be referred to Joanna Richardson, *Fanny Brawne* (1952), and the chapters on her and Fanny Keats in J. M. Murry's *The Mystery of Keats* (1949; rpt. in *Keats,* 1955). Fanny Brawne also appears in the strange story of the sequestration of the holographs of her correspondence by F. Holland Day, as told by Hyder E. Rollins and Stephen M. Parrish in their *Keats and the Bostonians . . .* (1951). Likewise of interest are Marie Adami's *Fanny Keats* (1937), Naomi Kirk's *Memoir of George Keats* in the Hampstead Keats (1939), Edmund Blunden's *Keats's Publisher: A Memoir of John Taylor* (1936), and that

---

[5] See also Jones's persuasive argument that Reynolds, not Keats, had written the review, "Richard, Duke of York" for the *Champion* (*KSJ,* 1954), and his general article "Reynolds and Keats" (*KSJ,* 1958).

same author's *Shelley and Keats as They Struck Their Contemporaries* (1925)—though this last touches Keats only lightly. Mention should also be made of Sheila Birkenhead's two books on Joseph Severn, *Against Oblivion* (1943) and *Illustrious Friends* (1965).

Four important studies in reputation and influence remain to be mentioned: George L. Marsh and Newman I. White's "Keats and the Periodicals of His Time" (*MP*, 1934), George H. Ford's *Keats and the Victorians: A Study of His Influence and Rise to Fame, 1821–1895* (1944; rpt. 1962); Hyder E. Rollins' *Keats's Reputation in America to 1848* (1946) and his briefer "The Vogue of Keats 1821–1848" (*Elizabethan Studies and Other Essays in Honor of George F. Reynolds,* 1945). Commenting on a total of some eighty-five items, Marsh and White note that, contrary to general impression, critics of Keats were generally friendly rather than inimical. Ford presents Keats as he emerged from comparative obscurity after his death to become the literary model of men like Tennyson, Rossetti, Morris, and many of their minor contemporaries, a less pervasive but still an unmistakable influence on Arnold, and idol of the *fin de siècle*: "By 1895 to deplore Keats was literary heresy." Ford's book is able and useful, especially in dealing with Keats's fame and influence. It still leaves to be done, however, a full-scale study of Keats's reputation in England. Similarly Rollins' book on the reception of Keats in America points to the need of a companion volume on the reputation of Keats in this country after 1848. Rollins shows that Keats enjoyed a relatively hospitable reception at the hands of Americans. By 1848 his fame, at least in the half-dozen cultural centers in the East and South where he was best known, was secure.

IV. CRITICISM

I. GENERAL CRITICAL WORKS

We may begin with a general glance at the critical rating of Keats as a poet during the last half century. In the background was the enormous influence on the Victorians and Edwardians of what we now see as specialized aspects of Keats. As Saintsbury said: "Keats begat Tennyson and Tennyson begat all the rest" (*A History of Nineteenth Century Literature,* 1896). And in even more sweeping terms H. J. C. Grierson has judged that "Keats has been, without any exception, the greatest influence in English poetry for a whole century" (*The Backgrounds of English Literature,* 1925; rpt. 1960). In similar vein Douglas Bush concludes: "Throughout the nineteenth century the dominant influence was that of Keats, though his magic and intensity were subdued by the cooler and more imitable art of Tennyson." George Ford's overall account of the pervasive and important influence of Keats on nineteenth-century poetry from Tennyson on has already been mentioned.

In the reaction against Romanticism and the nineteenth century that began in the 1920's and continued to the 1950's, the reputation of Keats, far from being shaken, continued to rise, and critics continued to think of him not merely in the Romantic context but as among the major English poets generally. This may be attributed to a union of at least three things, no one of which would perhaps have been sufficient alone: (1) The condensed power of phrase and remarkable artistry of his best poetry. (2) The appeal of the letters and the personality they reveal. (3) The drama of his rapid and sure development. The tendency to rank him in one or more respects with our greatest poets had begun well back in the nineteenth century. "He had something of Shakespeare in him," said Landor, "and (what nobody else ever had) much, very much of Chaucer." Arnold hedged his judgment of Keats with qualifications, but, in "word magic" and "natural poetic felicity," could find only Shakespeare with whom to compare him: "He is with Shakespeare." In our own century, what A. C. Bradley (*Oxford Lectures,* 1909; rpt. 1963) calls the "Shakespearean strain" in Keats was increasingly stressed: sometimes in general temper and character of mind (e.g., J. M. Murry, *Keats and Shakespeare,* 1925); sometimes in "power of expression, in concentrated imaginative phrase" (Robert Bridges, "John Keats: A Critical Essay," 1895; rpt. in *Collected Essays,* 1929); and often in both respects, as in T. S. Eliot on the "kind" of poetic greatness in Keats: "In contrast with the kinds we have been reviewing, it seems to me to be much more the kind of Shakespeare" (*The Use of Poetry and the Use of Criticism,* 1933). At the same time critics and poets found themselves agreeing with the verdict of R. D. Havens (*The Influence of Milton on English Poetry,* 1922): Keats was also able, even in the short time he attempted the Miltonic vein, to come closer to it, in grandeur and strength, than any other poet since Milton. "Despite all limitations," said G. W. Knight, "Keats touches the centres of both Shakespeare and Milton; and it would perhaps be churlish to deny that, granted a steadily expanding range of interest and experience, he might finally have outdistanced even his greatest predecessors" (*The Starlit Dome*, 1941; rpt. 1959 and 1960).

The attitudes just summarized both deepened and spread during the general reconsideration of Keats in the generation that followed World War II, and to such a point that they may now be regarded almost as a premise. At the same time this tendency to regard Keats apart from the merely Romantic context, as that context was more narrowly conceived from the 1890's to 1940, and to place him among peers in other traditions, helped to encourage the reconsideration of other major Romantic poets in the same way during the period 1945 to 1970. As we began to see each of them in other lights (including the modern symbolist movement) and not merely through the spectacles of a Victorian and Edwardian notion of the "Romantic," our whole concept of Romanticism itself became enriched, and with it came an awakened appreciation of the multi-faceted relevance of Romanticism to the whole modern effort in the arts.

Classification of critical works as "general," or as concerned primarily with "thought" or "style," is not only arbitrary but reductive. Many of the best treatments of Keats either as "a poet of thought" or as a "literary artist" are to be found in works that could properly be called "general." Style and form are most nearly understood—above all their success is to be rated—as they embody or express significances beyond their own ghostly paradigms. Conversely, the value of insights (imaginative, moral, psychological) in a work of art exists in and through the form. Yet some rough categorization is of obvious help, perhaps a necessity, in the use of bibliographies. We have accordingly, with some modification, kept our earlier method of dividing works for the convenience of students.

The essays of Arnold (1880) and Bridges (1895), mentioned above, still remain classics. But so richly developed has Keats commentary become during the last forty years that, unless one has a special interest in the particular critic, a single essay on Keats in general now commands little attention. In this section we accordingly mention, with a few exceptions, only books of which the whole or a substantial part deals with Keats generally as a poet or with the bulk of his major poems. We must begin by again mentioning some of the biographies, discussed more fully above. Indeed three of the longer ones (Colvin, Lowell, Bate) and one of the shorter ones (Bush) are the only works (with the exception of Finney, discussed immediately below) that attempt to discuss all, or almost all, of Keats's writings. Colvin (1917) presents a thoughtful, long-meditated handling of Keats's work, seen in close relation to his life and from what is essentially a late Victorian and Edwardian point of view. In other words, for the reader of a half-century later both the approach and the resulting insights are impressionistic (though in the best sense of the word); many of the preoccupations and directions of Keats's artistry that we now take for granted remain unnoticed; and there is comparatively little sense of Keats's relation to the English poetic tradition before him (except for the Elizabethans and Milton, viewed in a specialized, quasi-aesthetic way) and, naturally, no sense at all of his relation to later movements except the Victorian and its early twentieth-century aftermath. At the same time, the letters, and with them the "thought" and the personal experience of Keats, are not coalesced with the poetry to the degree that we should now expect.

Aside from the large store of new biographical information that it made available, Amy Lowell's lavish and loving two-volume *John Keats* (1925), attacked with such strange bitterness for ten years by British reviewers and, occasionally, scholars (notably H. W. Garrod), had two important critical effects, appreciated neither by attackers at the time nor students of Keats later. (1) With the help of her friend John Livingston Lowes, that unrivalled literary detective and author of the greatest source-study (on Coleridge) that we have (*The Road to Xanadu*, 1927), she threw into her biography a huge number of possible or probable "sources," thus inspiring another forty years of "source-study," sometimes brilliant (e.g., Bush and Finney, both of them students of Lowes), sometimes pedestrian and picky, but always of potential indirect value. (2) As one of the principal leaders of the Imagist movement, she helped, as much as anyone, to establish the conception of Keats as a "Modern" poet directly relevant to practicing poets now; and though poetic idiom shifted still more radically from the late 1920's to World War II, her attempt to portray Keats as a "modern" hero-of-letters for the twentieth-century poet was completely accepted and simply transposed to another key. These two major effects amply compensated for her own impulsive whims and sprawling self-indulgence of temper, and make her book more important as a document in the history of critical interpretation than even that of her ablest detractor, H. W. Garrod.

Amy Lowell's issue of "modern" relevance, uniting with the interests of her friend John Livingston Lowes, provided the impulse for several further studies of Keats. The most notable in this particular vein (or union of veins) was Claude Finney's *The Evolution of Keats's Poetry* (2 vols., 1936; rpt. 1963). Almost everything known about every poem of Keats's, at the time that this work was written, is painstakingly considered, with special attention to "sources"; it has continued to be a quarry of information for later critical works that refine or develop details first published there. Until the 1950's the writing of no other romantic poet was considered with comparable scrupulosity. Finney is still reliable, except that he followed Amy Lowell's impulsive notion that the second *Hyperion* (*The Fall of Hyperion*) was not the important recast it was but an earlier version.

Of the new biographies (1963 and later) Bate (see above, under Biography) gives by far the most detailed discussion of all the poetry, fitting it into the biography and the letters, pausing to take up individual poems as a unit, discussing both style and thought in each case, while relating the subject not only to other works by Keats, but also to the Romantic effort and to the tradition of English poetry generally. Since it has already been discussed in some detail, we shall not do so here. But we should emphasize that none of the essential critical issues raised about Keats during the period since Colvin and Amy Lowell has been neglected, and that, in addition, many further critical problems are raised and discussed. The other new biographies, by Ward and Gittings, though they do not go into the writings in any detail, take for granted the established importance and relevance of the poetry for the modern reader. Of the shorter biographies, also mentioned above, that of Bush, with complete authority, offers the best distillation available. Here we have subsumed all the qualities we should expect from this "authority to authorities": his unrivalled knowledge of the use of classical myth, of which he is our generation's greatest scholar; his knowledge—again unexcelled by other Keats authorities—of English poetry of whatever period (especially Milton and the sixteenth and seventeenth centuries); philosophical depth, imaginative good-sense, and grace of style. Thirty years before, he had already performed the same feat of distillation, though in a different and more specialized context. His *Mythology and the Romantic Tradition* (1937; rpt. 1969, and discussed under subdivision 2 below) provides a summation of Keats, which scores of students have since used as a springboard. Still of value, though inevitably somewhat dated, is Fausset (see below, p. 411).

Aside from the biographies and analogous books (e.g., Finney) already mentioned, there are several works that discuss Keats's poetry (or at least the major poems) and his achievement as a poet generally from a comprehensive point of view. We should begin with J. M. Murry's influential *Keats and Shakespeare* (1925), followed by other studies that could be described as a series of appendices or after-thoughts to that pioneer and seminal, though in some ways subjective, book. In the earlier version of this bibliography, Murry was discussed under the subdivision concerned with Keats's ideas. But continued reconsideration of Murry's writing by thoughtful students with whatever approach or interest (though much that he was the first to say has since been absorbed, almost taken for granted) resists this particular categorization. His works seem now to form instead a sympathetic, detailed, long-brooded study of a type of human character and personality. To put it another way: Murry's *Keats and Shakespeare* and its attendant studies are a quasi-psychographic portrait of a kind of human being that represents a triumph of the human spirit, an exemplification of what it can do and be at its best. Murry has muddy stretches. There are also the naïvetés, excesses, and general awkwardness of the autodidact whose insights are self-earned. But these are more tolerantly viewed by the generation that began in the 1960's than they formerly were. What moves us in Murry now, more even than in the generation that profited from his insights, is his direct humanity and his sincerity.

Murry's thesis is that Keats is, next to Shakespeare, the exemplar *par excellence* of "pure poetry" in English. Pure poetry, as defined by Murry, is closely interwoven with truth and thought. It is, in fact, the very essence of truth itself. The thought it contains may not be "explicit and recognizable," but it may be most profound. "It is a perception, not a cogitation," and is characterized by utter loyalty to "immediate and unintellectual experiences—to the passions, to the affections, to the intuitions." Murry proceeds to show, through specific analysis of poem and letter, to what extent Keats's poetry answers to the demands of pure poetry, in what respects it sometimes fails, with what effort Keats strove to master the only philosophy he considered worth-while—that which has to do with a comprehension of the mystery of life and the universe—and to achieve "that necessary wholeness in himself" from which alone the greatest poetry can spring. A man of profound religious insight, Keats finally saw that such comprehension and such wholeness are to be attained through a single process: that of an evolving "soul-knowledge," a realization of "unity and harmony" in the self, which "immediately results in a knowledge of the harmony and necessity of the universe," hence in a knowledge of the essential nature of God.

In two important essays in *Studies in Keats: New and Old* (1939), J. M. Murry considers the relationship of Keats to Milton and Wordsworth, principally in connection with *Hyperion* and *The Fall of Hyperion,* but also in broader aspects of temperament and influence. In *The Mystery of Keats* (1949), a revision of *Studies in Keats,* he adds a comparison of Keats and Blake; and in *Katherine Mansfield and Other Literary Essays* of the same year he discusses Keats and Shelley. In a sense all these comparative studies, including the earlier *Keats and Shakespeare,* are part of a larger campaign, intended to set Keats in truer perspective. Reading Murry we early become aware that in contact with Keats he has felt himself in the presence of the mystery of poetic genius and of the personality that embodies it. In his search for the uniqueness of this genius, Murry has been fond of placing Keats alongside first one and then another of the great poets to discover, if it may be, the crucial centers of likeness or difference, the distinctive marks of *poetness* in each pair, the marks of *Keatsness* that may be separated out by such a method. The results are set down here only in barest summary. Murry finds in Keats a poet who in kind of genius is most like Shakespeare, with the same power of negative capability, the same capacity to see and accept all of life—the harsh and evil along with the pleasant and good—and to perceive there the beauty that is truth; he finds a poet who so closely attached himself to Wordsworth in certain respects that it may be said that he "discovered himself in Wordsworth"— in the example the older poet set both in the "re-exploration of human experience" and in the rediscovery of the truth of religion. Murry also finds in Keats a poet who is "more naturally a Christian than was Milton," and who when compared with Shelley "really believed in the One where Shelley only tried to," who "submitted himself to Life where Shelley could not," who "turned away from abstract thought, where Shelley was intoxicated with it," who was versed in that deeper philosophy (of which Murry holds Shelley knew next to nothing) "which is humble before experience and seeks instinctively to make the Mind the servant of Life instead of its master." In the spring months of 1819, Murry believes, Keats's speculations came to a focus in which his heart and mind were finally in harmony, both instruments to the oneness of his poetic personality in its grapplings with realities, both willing to bow before life in acceptance. It is in this self-abnegation, even in opposition to personal desire, that Keats most nearly approaches Blake's philosophy of self-annihilation; in this brave doctrine of self-renunciation through acceptance Murry finds the clue to the meaning of the great Odes—especially of the "Ode on a Grecian Urn"—and of *The Fall of Hyperion,* hence to much of the best in Keats.

Published a year after Murry's *Keats and Shakespeare,* H. W. Garrod's *Keats* (1926), a series of lectures given at Oxford, was in comparison a rather slight work. There are fine, sensitive pages; he writes a witty, lucid style; and he can make penetrating suggestions (notably that Keats developed his ode-stanza from the sonnet). Also no one could doubt Garrod's learning on many details, at least after his edition of the *Poetical Works,* discussed above, under Editions. But his short critical book has not worn well. We are often presented with Garrod's own personality as much as that of Keats; and this carries with it crotchets as well as an occasional huffiness and petulance about other critics that now seem quaintly donnish. Meanwhile his own taste seems to our generation critically thin and impressionistic—often perceptive but at times irritably refined. In particular, as we point out below (IV, 3), the book reveals an impatience with—or incapacity to understand—the value of thought generally in Keats's writing and own experience as a human being: a naive assumption that Keats's attempts to "think" and to write in a philosophical vein sabotaged his own real "genius" and "spoiled his singing." Fundamentally Garrod's book is a delayed manifesto on behalf of late nineteenth-century aestheticism.

The first book to bring together a more sophisticated knowledge of Keats's main intellectual premises and imaginative aims with detailed formal and stylistic explication of particular poems is Earl Wasserman, *The Finer Tone: Keats' Major Poems* (1953; rpt. 1967). The book (hotly quarreled with at first and just as hotly defended) aroused controversy because it was innovative. For it was the first thoroughgoing application to a Romantic poet of techniques of analysis and explication hitherto applied only to poetry in other traditions, particularly that of "metaphysical" poetry. What made the book important is that, to this close analysis (formal, structural, thematic), Wasserman brought not only imaginative perception but an informed knowledge both of Keats as a whole and also of both the poetry and intellectual history of the eighteenth century and the Romantic era. As a result, it is filled with fertile suggestions from which later studies have profited. The book (though closely unified and drawing on the other poems as well as the letters) concentrates on five of the principal poems, each of which is analyzed in terms of the basic thesis of the book: which is, briefly, that in Keats's thought there is an assumption of a realm of the merely human and a realm of the ideal immortal, and that there is a "knife-edge where the two meet and are indistinguishably present," in a "mystic oxymoron"—a resolution of contraries in the highest happiness man may know: "a fellowship with essence." Such a mystic union is the goal of Endymion in his quest for Cynthia; such, too, is the aspiration of the principals of *Lamia,* one of Wasserman's "major poems."

But Lycius and Lamia fail in their experiment in happy living, since their trial is on the human plane, and only gods may enjoy the ideal vision as a permanent reality. Hence the episode of Hermes and the nymph gives point to the subsequent narrative: the nymph is ideal beauty, a kind of Cynthia. Only when Hermes burns with a "celestial heat" can he see and possess the nymph; only then can the "chaste ideal and the transcendently passionate . . . coalesce and become an eternal love." But in contrast, Lycius' dream is not real: "the green-recessed woods into which the mortal lovers flee is an illusion, and they do grow pale." This, says Wasserman, denying all previous interpretations of *Lamia,* "is the only antithesis developed in the poem." If Porphyro, in "The Eve of St. Agnes," succeeds where Lycius fails, the explanation lies in the fact that the series of actions leading to and taking place in Madeline's chamber "constitute an ascent of the ladder of intensities and a formation of the mystic oxymoron" with such imaginative force that, at the end, the lovers are allowed to flee away into a sort of world of permanent visionary bliss. "Art . . . is a mode of representing in its finer tone the life of sensations. And 'The Eve of St. Agnes' is a special enactment of such a life. . . ." Like the earthly lovers in *Lamia,* the knight in "La Belle Dame," limited by human restrictions, is permitted only an illusory glimpse of happiness. And in the "Ode to a Nightingale" the "mystic oxymoron" is never attained (or if at all only tentatively in the first stanza) because in three separate proposals to realize his desire, the poet not only fails to ascend to the ideal world of the nightingale, but also sinks deeper into his mundane sphere. In "The Ode on a Grecian Urn," Wasserman finds a "collocation of contraries"—the "dynamic versus the static"; "the human and mutable on one hand . . . the immortal and essential on the other"; and here oppositions are resolved, mortal and immortal become one without mutual destruction. In effective explication, the author presents the poet "in the act of freeing the self of its identity and its existence in time and space"; and as he moves to a closer, "more self-obliterating relationship with the urn and the figures on it," he finds the apparent oppositions erasing each other, the "unselfed" poet "entering into a fellowship with their vital essence." It is so that the "mystic oxymoron" is achieved, at a point where the human and earthly beauty merge with the ideal—"at heaven's bourne," which is the beginning of Truth. Awareness that in art such an experience is "forever available is the height of earthly wisdom . . . all man needs to know."

E. C. Pettet, *On the Poetry of Keats* (1957), is less comprehensive than its title implies, and is at least partly described in the first sentence of the Preface as dealing with aspects of Keats's poetry "that I happen to find of particular interest." In so far as the book has a general theme, it is a protest against what Pettet considers the "metaphysical" or "philosophical" approach to Keats (i.e., the interest in Keats as a "poet of ideas"). Unquestionably there have been excesses in this approach as in others. But the correction is not to be found in a naive anti-intellectualism that was more forgivable in Garrod's *Keats* than a work thirty years later. One suspects that Pettet has not kept abreast of major scholarship; and he occasionally, with a sense of discovery, discusses a topic (e.g., Keats's use of assonance and vowel-interplay) without seeming to realize—or at least acknowledging—that it has already been carefully treated in earlier commentary. After preliminary chapters on influences, imagery, and verbal and phonetic melody, Pettet devotes two long chapters to *Endymion,* arguing against attempts to read it as allegory. Shorter discussions then focus on "La Belle Dame" and *Lamia,* and on three of the odes (the "Nightingale," "Melancholy," and the "Grecian Urn"). Other poems are only briefly treated. Particularly slighted, presumably because they present problems that would defy Mr. Pettet's thesis, are the two *Hyperions.*

Bernice Slote's *Keats and the Dramatic Principle* (1958) is of broader interest than its title implies. At once perceptive, thoroughly informed, and wisely balanced, Miss Slote brings together everything that relates to Keats's interest in, and varied gifts for, the "drama" in the wider as well as stricter sense of the word. Given the character of Keats's imagination and temperament (objective, concretely realistic, disinterested, empathic), a book on this subject could ideally turn into a general (and major) study of Keats's mind and art; and that is precisely what happens here. The first of Miss Slote's three sections ("The Poet") concentrates on the "Shakespearean" temper in Keats's own mind and sensibility. Though the least novel part of the book, the discussion—indispensable to her theme—is an admirable treatment of a subject of perennial fascination. The second ("The Play") then turns to the actual theater of the time, Keats's interest in and knowledge of it, and his own beginning attempts (*Otho, King Stephen*) to write for it. The third ("The Poem") then reexamines the poetry, freshly and imaginatively, in the light of what has been said (incidentally offering one of the best discussions of *Lamia* that has thus far been written). What distinguishes the book is a combination of qualities not always found together: sensitivity to style and form; a sophisticated knowledge of English poetry generally; sympathetic and informed insight into Keats as a whole; a respect for and informed background in the literary, intellectual, and theatrical history of the time.

David Perkins, *The Quest for Permanence: The Symbolism of Wordsworth, Shelley, and Keats* (1959; rpt. 1965), considers three major Romantics as prototypes of the modern poetic use of symbolism. From this point of view the book might be classified among studies in poetic technique, but it views technique as the effort of each poet to develop a mode adequate to render his own experience, and thus dwells equally on the attitudes and feelings that characterize each of these writers. Here the main general theme is the Romantic and human quest for permanence and stable meaning. Pursuing this interplay of vision and style, the nine chapters fall into three essays in interpretation and evaluation. At the time of publication the approach was seen as uniting two types of criticism: the more traditional methods of scholarly generalization and the then current orthodoxy of close analysis concentrating on form and imagery. The critical method is eclectic in a way that has become somewhat more common since, and the evaluation seeks to be undoctrinaire; for although the study reflects an interest in contemporary poetry, it is not partisan, but stresses continuities from the Romantic period to our own. The three, final chapters on Keats are the longest in the book. In the realm of nature Keats tended to see "not simply flux and decay," as did Shelley, "nor permanence and stability," as did Wordsworth, "but a process in which change is potentially meaningful and orderly." Against this intense, sensuous, and imaginative awareness of process, in which he comes close to Shakespeare, Keats balances the claims of the visionary imagination, which intuits a transcendent, eternal reality, and also gives it concrete representation for human apprehension and feeling. Keats's greater poetry explores this tension—whether fulfillment and truth can be found in the permanence of the imagination, or whether only in the realm of process, which includes both fulfillment and death. The first of the great odes, the "Ode to Psyche," expresses a relative confidence in the visionary imagination: the poet can still be a worshipper of the mythical or visionary realm of Psyche. In the odes "On a Grecian Urn" and "To a Nightingale" the attempt at union with the visionary and eternal by means of a symbol—more exactly, the development of a symbol that seems to promise an immediate, felt knowledge of the state of mind desired—ends in failure. The massive commitment which the poet brings to bear, the honesty and completeness with which he explores the symbol, ends in partly undermining it, and the poet withdraws from it. In these poems, Perkins argues, Keats develops a poetry of "symbolic debate," a mode of poetry in which the poet responds to his symbolism, clarifies his attitudes by means of it, but remains always present in the poem as a protagonist in a drama of human reactions. "La Belle Dame" and *Lamia* express an even more skeptical view, showing the visionary absorbed in his dream and destroyed by it. In all of these poems Perkins notices ambiguities that reflect uncertainties and tensions in Keats himself, but he concludes that "the over-all course of Keats's development might be described as a periodic, though gradually cumulative, loss of confidence in the merely visionary imagination." This was paralleled by an "affirmation of process" as the condition of value, and his interrupted career may have been developing toward "a rejection of the romantic quest for permanence."

Some of the finest pages in Harold Bloom's *The Visionary Company* (1961; rpt. 1963) are devoted to Keats (pp. 354–427) and provide brilliantly searching and condensed explications of the principal poems. Of special value are the discussions of the odes, *Lamia,* and *The Fall of Hyperion.* Because of its range of implication, we should also mention here, rather than in one of the other subdivisions, his important essay "Keats and the Embarrassments of Poetic Tradition," in *From Sensibility to Romanticism,* ed. Frederick W. Hilles and Harold Bloom (1965), pp. 513–26, in which, paralleling and sometimes developing points made by Bate, he discusses the conflicting pressures on Keats of tradition and the expectations of novelty, and stresses Keats's ability (particularly in the odes and *The Fall of Hyperion*) to become independent of the Miltonic tradition through a deepening naturalness. Brief but wise and generous natured, as well as the expression of a modern poet's admiration, is Archibald Mac-Leish's discussion of Keats ("The Arable Land," pp. 173–99) in *Poetry and Experience* (1961). Another short work, important because of its independence, its controversial nature, and the respect in which he is held generally as a critic, is John Bayley, "Keats and Reality" (*Proceedings of the British Academy,* 1962). Bayley makes a fresh and independent argument for a side of Keats that may have been slighted in our own generation. This Bayley expresses, not too happily, by the term "vulgarity." Aware that Keats was a man of many talents, Bayley is forced to stretch his key word, "vulgarity," until it includes not only mawkishness and "lack of refinement" but most of the virtues suggested by a phrase such as "common humanity." Bayley has in mind a healthful robustness very much like that of Dickens: courage, impulsiveness, a fondness for the rich, the direct, and for the "warmly domestic"; a frank sensuality; a lack of fastidiousness (hence Keats's affinities with the "linguistic innocence" of the Elizabethans); and a down-to-earth empiricism, which led him, more than any of his contemporaries, to feel an anxiety about the relation of art to reality that is essentially modern.

Three other fairly short discussions of Keats, and three collections of essays, remain to be cited. The section in Ian Jack, *English Literature, 1815–1832* (1963), the Oxford History of English Literature, Vol. x, provides a succinct, informed, and balanced account, with helpful bibliography, in what is certainly one of the best volumes of the Oxford History. An excellent introduction for the beginning student is provided by Fred Inglis, *Keats* (1966). Less satisfactory, though written with affection and zest, is Norman Talbot, *The Major Poems of John Keats* (1968). Intended as a short introduction, and as something of a rite of homage, it suffers a little from lack of organization and a diffuse impressionism. To be said in its favor is that it repeats in a new context many insights and points made by leading critics of Keats during the last generation, and offers some good observations of its own, particularly on *The Fall of Hyperion* and "To Autumn."

Among collected essays of a general nature are, in chronological order, the volume sponsored by the MLA entitled *The Major English Romantic Poets* (1957; rpt. 1964), ed. Clarence D. Thorpe, Carlos Baker, and Bennett Weaver. In this general reconsideration of the principal Romantic poets, four writers discuss Keats (pp. 217–58): two concentrate on the ideas and on Keats as a thinker generally (Douglas Bush and J. M. Murry), and two discuss the style and artistry (W. J. Bate and Cleanth Brooks). The essays of each are discussed separately in the subdivisions below, as are those in the other collections to be mentioned. A second volume of essays is *John Keats: A Reassessment* (1958), ed. Kenneth Muir, which consists of ten essays from members of the University of Liverpool: three by Muir, and one each by Kenneth Allott, Miriam Allott, Arnold Davenport, R. T. Davies, Clarisse Godfrey, Joan Grundy, and David Masson. A third volume, *Keats: A Collection of Critical Essays* (1964), ed. Walter J. Bate, contains, besides a general introduction, eleven essays: T. S. Eliot's remarks on Keats in his Norton Lectures at Harvard, Douglas Bush's comprehensive chapter on Keats from *Mythology and the Romantic Tradition*, Richard Fogle's discussion of synaesthetic imagery, Bate on "Negative Capability," and critical writings on eight of the major poems by Jack Stillinger ("The Eve of St. Agnes"), Harold Bloom (the odes "To Psyche" and "On Melancholy"), David Perkins (the "Ode to a Nightingale" and *Lamia*), Earl Wasserman (the "Ode on a Grecian Urn"), W. J. Bate ("To Autumn"), and D. G. James ("The Two *Hyperions*").*

2. WORKS CONCERNED PRIMARILY WITH KEATS AS A POET OF THOUGHT

The Victorian tradition of Keats as an exclusively sensuous poet, a literary artist whose interests began and ended with "beauty," has for over forty years been generally superseded by a more balanced view of a poet who loved physical beauty indeed but who had also a respect and remarkable capacity for things of the intellect. Recognition of Keats as a thinker is to be found in various late nineteenth-century writings, the most noteworthy of which are Mrs. F. M. Owen's *Keats, A Study* (1880), with its allegorical interpretation of *Endymion* and its indications of ideas in other poems; Matthew Arnold's essay (1880), where the critic speaks of central ideas in Keats and ventures the judgment that the poet's "yearning passion for the beautiful" was in truth "not a passion of the sensuous or sentimental poet" but "a spiritual and intellectual passion"; and Robert Bridges' "John Keats, A Critical Essay" (1895), which again proposes an allegorical interpretation of *Endymion* and presents a case for the influence of Wordsworth's thought on Keats.

It is not so much to these critics, however, as to the biographer Sidney Colvin and to the editor Ernest de Selincourt that, prior to 1921, students owed their introduction to the intellectual Keats. Neither Colvin nor de Selincourt was primarily interested in Keats's thought; yet together they furnish starting points for much that has since been developed. Both agree with Bridges about the Wordsworthian influence; both interpret *Endymion* as a serious attempt to represent advance through various gradations to attainment of the ideal; both make wide use of the letters as furnishing clues to serious thought in such other poems as *Lamia, Hyperion,* and *The Fall of Hyperion.* De Selincourt was later, in his Warton Lecture (*The*

---

* Jack Stillinger's valuable *The Hoodwinking of Madeline and Other Essays on Keats's Poems* (1971) appeared after our work was in press, and only a short note can be inserted at this point. Some of the essays now collected in this book have been separately discussed (see particularly Section IV, below, on Individual Poems and under "Stillinger" in the Index to this volume). The principal theme that unites these essays is the conflict in Keats between the idealizing tendencies of the imagination and the actual world. The book subsumes a variety of approaches (textual, stylistic, biographical, historical), and presents its results with impressive authority and distilled consideration.

Keats Memorial Volume, 1921), to expand what he had written for the 1905 edition into a more systematic treatment. Some of his statements have become *loci classici* in Keats criticism. The Lecture is as a whole a forthright declaration for a solid core of intellect in Keats as man and poet. The *Memorial Volume* contained other essays speaking decisively for Keats as a thinker. A. C. Bradley, who had previously in his *Oxford Lectures on Poetry* (1909) pointed to trends of thought in Keats's letters, entitles his contribution "Keats and 'Philosophy,' " and undertakes to show how passages in the poems and letters reveal Keats's concern with specific problems of existence, particularly with those aspects of things which enforce upon his mind the sorrows of the world and "the burden of the mystery." Other essays in this vein are those of Arthur Lynch and A. Clutton-Brock.

Since the *Memorial Volume* there have been numerous studies dealing with Keats as a thinker. Some have to do with the subject in general, others with some special phase, such as his aesthetic theory, still others with specific indications of thought in individual poems. In most cases they have regarded Keats's intellectual interests as an asset, a balancing influence in his preoccupation with the sensuous, an indication of a poet of larger view and greater stature; but a few have argued that the tendency to thoughtfulness has either been overrated or that it was hostile to Keats's native bent.

Of the second group, which, since its number is small, may be treated first, an outstanding representative was H. W. Garrod, who in his *Keats* (1926) presents Keats as one whose genius flourished in the fullness of "sensuous experience." Keats did his best work when he shook himself free from thought and followed his natural inclinations.[6] Garrod's view is in general supported by Hoxie N. Fairchild in both *The Romantic Quest* (1931) and *Religious Trends in English Poetry,* Volume III (1949). In his earlier book Fairchild presents Keats as a native-born poet of the sensuously beautiful, who sometimes "mistakenly" tries to be philosophic. In the second, undertaking to discover possible religious trends in the poet's writings, Fairchild tries out J. M. Murry's interpretation of Keats's belief, and concludes that Murry's idea of Keats as a man of profound essential

---

[6] See also G. R. Elliott, "The Real Tragedy of Keats (A Post-Centenary View)" (*PMLA,* 1921; rpt. in *The Cycle of Modern Poetry,* 1929). Elliott believes that addiction to philosophy, with its attending hopeless conflicts, was to Keats a catastrophe, the real cause of his death. Unmitigated skepticism of Keats's interest in thought is expressed in Royall H. Snow's "Heresy Concerning Keats" (*PMLA,* 1928). A prompt reply to Snow's article was made by Mary Evelyn Shipman, in "Orthodoxy Concerning Keats" (*PMLA,* 1929).

religious insight is fallacious. It must be added that Fairchild is thinking of orthodox, organized religion, and is applying his criteria in conventional rather than flexible terms. A qualification of Fairchild's argument is provided by James Benziger, *Images of Eternity: Studies in the Poetry of Religious Vision from Wordsworth to T. S. Eliot* (1962), which argues that, despite the association of religious faith with personal experience, the Romantics are not as "secular and private" in their approach to religious vision as is generally supposed. What the Romantic imagination sought was "corroborative" of traditional Christianity—supplementary rather than conflicting.[7] Benziger is naturally able to apply this thesis best to a poet like Wordsworth. But his argument that Keats's "sensibility" is often close to "basic Christian traditions" helps to balance one's admission of an undeniable strain of skeptical naturalism and distrust of organized religion—ably discussed and attributed in part to the influence of Voltaire in Stuart Sperry's "Keats's Skepticism and Voltaire" (*KSJ*, 1963).

Nothing of significance, since World War II, has appeared as an argument in what one might call the "anti-intellectual" vein. Occasional discussions of particular poems (particularly *Endymion*) may have something of this flavor (see below in the section devoted to particular poems). And one general book, E. C. Pettet, *On the Poetry of Keats* (1957), has something like this as its premise (see Section IV, 1, above). But in general the debate about whether Keats had a "mind" (i.e., was concerned with fundamental problems of life, including art, and was philosophically open and receptive to ideas) seems to us hopelessly out-of-date—as something that raised a false issue, through a naively false dichotomy, and was then continued by the tendency of human beings to fall into the habit of dispute through polarization.

In works after World War I, the first to provide further nuance and direction to what was argued in the *Memorial Volume,* and to stress Keats's awake mind, was Hugh I'A. Fausset, who in *Keats: A Study in Development* (1922; rpt. 1966) tried to show how, in steady advance from early sensationalism to mature idealism, Keats attained an intellectual peerage with our greatest poets and a view in which the opposing forces of life are seen in "ideal reconcilement." Valuable as are the main parts of Fausset's book, his case for consistent progress and final triumph is open to

---

[7] See the discussion of Keats's knowledge of and allusions to the Bible in Lloyd Jeffrey, "Keats and the Bible" (*KSJ*, 1961).

question; for as R. D. Havens points out in "Unreconciled Opposites in Keats" (*PQ,* 1935), some of the main conflicts continued up to the end with no clear evidence of final resolution.

After Fausset came in rapid succession a number of books more or less concerned with Keats as a man of thought: Amy Lowell's *John Keats* (1925), J. M. Murry's *Keats and Shakespeare* (1925), Clarence D. Thorpe's *The Mind of John Keats* (1926), Takeshi Saito's *Keats' View of Poetry* (1929), and J. M. Murry's *Studies in Keats* (1930). Miss Lowell's main concerns, it is true, are elsewhere than with ideas. Even so she is aware that she is dealing with a thinker and in the course of her two volumes presents striking instances of Keats's thought. Her tendency is to decry attempts to read allegory into the poems, however, and in general she is willing to let Keats's words speak for themselves, making no systematic effort to analyze or define Keats's meanings.

More effective than Lowell in helping to change, during the next fifteen years (1925–40), our conception of Keats as a poet of thought were two books published about the same time as that of Lowell: J. M. Murry's *Keats and Shakespeare* (1925) and Clarence D. Thorpe's *The Mind of John Keats* (1926). These two books had the following in common: (1) They were imaginatively "holistic" in their use of both the letters and the poems, viewing them, in their totality, as an expression of a great writer's achievement through the human "adventure of the spirit." (2) Each was based on the assumption that, when the cards are down, what we ourselves most prize in literature, as a record and expression of the adventure of the spirit, is what we prize most in human nature itself: the union of openness and zest with rectitude and stability; of imaginative range and power with the grasp of reality; of skepticism with eagerness for centrality of insight; of compassion with the sternness of fact and moral value; of artistry, unprisoned and released to its full bent, yet subservient and ministrative to the human. Murry's *Keats and Shakespeare* (1925) and his later books have already been discussed. In *The Mind of John Keats* (1926; rpt. 1964), Thorpe provides an analysis of Keats as a thinker, with emphasis on his aesthetic ideas. What Thorpe finds is not a consistent pattern of thought but tentative conclusions wrested from a set of conflicts: as between an impulse toward dream and the claims of the actual, between a leaning toward the merely sensuous in art and life and a craving for knowledge and understanding. Reconciliation of opposing claims was an increasingly conscious aim as the poet saw more clearly the nature and demands of his art and its relationship to the actualities of existence. Thorpe does not assert final reconciliations, but he believes that Keats was making progress toward solutions and that a study of the process reveals a man and poet of broad and deep sympathies, who in greater maturity, without at all surrendering his affection for material beauty, became more and more aware that great poetry—the serious poetry of "character and sentiment" he aspired to write—is never created by unfurnished minds doting merely on fanciful dreams and physical loveliness but can be produced only by an intellect grown wise through knowledge and experience and disciplined by thought and hard work. In what we have just said of Thorpe, we here print *verbatim* his own modest summary from the second (1956) edition of this book. But we should not only stress again the seminal effect of the book but also add that, like J. L. Lowes and Douglas Bush, Thorpe trained a whole generation of scholar-critics of Keats; that many other scholars were indebted to him every year for private counsel and unfailing generosity; and that much of what has since been said of Keats is an extension or ramification of what he himself taught. Finally, it should be added that, like most of the other really great Keatsians, he had some of the essential human characteristics that distinguished the writer he admired and studied: sympathetic imagination, compassion, warmth and kindliness, freedom from littleness of any kind, empirical good-sense, and flexibility and openness of mind. These qualities were reflected not only in his lifetime study of Keats but also in his study of aesthetic theory and criticism generally in which he was constantly interested in relating the subject to direct human experience and human values.

In a comparative study of Keats and Shelley in his "Purgatory Blind" (*The Romantic Comedy,* 1948), D. G. James finds Keats in poems like *Hyperion,* as well as in the letters, occupied with "ultimate metaphysical perceptions." "In *Hyperion,*" he says, "Keats exhibits the eternal informing the finite," giving not only "knowledge of creations and destroyings," but also "knowledge of those events of time and suffering as held and encompassed by an ineffable peace." Keats's mind was complex, filled with an interplay of speculations on ideal values, tempered by a pervading skepticism: a mind too rich and fecund to settle with comfort into a rigid scheme of beliefs and perceptions, a fine humility, an ability to accept and believe in suffering. The "youngest but also the wisest poet" of the Romantic Movement, James calls Keats, the one who more than any other member of his group saw what was required in great poetry: "the flowing out of the imagination to apprehend event and circumstance and to show them creatively."[8]

The view of Keats as evolving into fuller understanding of life and art is further affirmed by such critics as R. D. Havens and B. Ifor Evans. Havens in "Of Beauty and Reality in Keats" (*ELH,* 1950) represents Keats as passing from early sensuous love of beauty to a view of beauty "as including moral and intellectual excellence." In his introduction to *Poems of Keats,* edited by R. Vallance (1950), Evans sees Keats, intent on the problem of discovering what poetry can do, passing from an early tendency to toy with poetry as a dream world to a theory of poetry as an embodiment of the deepest experiences of human life. Taking issue with many of these points is a provocative, closely argued work by N. F. Ford, *The Prefigurative Imagination: A Study of the Truth-Beauty Identification and Its Implications* (1951; rpt. 1966). Closely analyzing all of Keats's uses of the words "truth" and "beauty" and their contexts, as well as related concepts (ethereal, essence, sensations, imagination, etc.), the book argues that Keats in general was conceiving—especially in the earlier letters and poems—the imagination as "prefigurative" (i.e., prophetic) of a reality that can then be actually experienced. On the other hand, says Ford, this does not mean that the mind is being conceived of in any of the usual "transcendental" and "idealistic" ways (Platonic or generally Romantic). The "reality" envisaged by the prophetic, "prefigurative" imagination is literal and sensuous, and the dream of "immortality of passion" is frankly physical. It follows that all attempts to read *Endymion* (on which Ford especially concentrates) as an ultimately "idealistic" or quasi-Platonic allegory are misguided. After *Endymion,* especially after 1818, Keats became more skeptical, at times pessimistic about this concept, though it reappears strongly as a wish, or more than a wish, when Keats is betrayed by "the elevation of the moment" (e.g., notably, at the close of the "Grecian Urn").

Meanwhile, Basil Willey (*Nineteenth Century Studies,* 1949; rpt. 1964) asserts that more clearly than any of his contemporaries Keats was aware "that the concept of nature in the thought of his own time menaces the poet"; was aware, moreover, of nature's "metaphysical—as well as physical—indifference to any conventional ethical view." In "The Meaning

---

[8] See James's earlier discussion of Keats in "Adam's Dream," *Skepticism and Poetry* (1937; rpt. 1960), pp. 170–204. See also Roberta Cornelius (*KSJ,* 1956), who makes a case for Keats as a humanist in whom we find "such wisdom and bland morality" as the Cowden Clarkes attributed to the "myriad-minded humanist Shakespeare."

of *Hyperion"* (*EC,* 1952), Kenneth Muir is perhaps less interested in the presence of thought than in the effect of thought on Keats's poetry. Even leaving the earlier odes and the Hyperions out of account, Keats could never have written "The Eve of St. Agnes" and "To Autumn" if he had not elsewhere attempted to philosophize. As for the meaning of *Hyperion* Muir finds that the real subject of the first version is "human progress; and the new race of men . . . were not stronger and cleverer than their predecessors, but more sensitive and vulnerable." The new parts in the revision show marked advances in thought over the first *Hyperion.* The trend of Muir's case may be inferred from one sentence: "It is very much a purgatorial poem and the steps symbolize, as they do in Dante, the striving of the dreamer towards the truth." Qualifying these interpretations, E. E. Bostetter, in "The Eagle and the Truth: Keats and the Problem of Belief" (*JAAC,* 1958), provides a condensed and provocative discussion of poetry and belief in Keats. "In theory, he severed poetry from metaphysical and ethical responsibilities," but in practice could not accept this division and sought to overcome it. Bostetter's later book, *The Romantic Ventriloquists* (1963), calls into question the whole achievement of the Romantics not because of their individual lack of endowment but because of the situation in which they were placed. He sees Romanticism generally less as the affirmative triumph of the creative imagination it is often said to be than as revealing a despair before loss and disillusion. Bostetter concentrates on major poems of five poets (all the great Romantics except Blake): in the case of Keats, the two *Hyperions.*

The latest discussion of Keats's general cast of mind and of some of his central ideas is John Jones, *John Keats's Dream of Truth* (1969). Jones finds in Romanticism a common trust in feeling, in the truth of the heart, however different other aspects of Romanticism may be from each other. With this as his premise, he focuses on Keats. The peculiar badness of the early verse is itself a by-product of Keats's honesty, his frank and direct sincerity. Jones's theme is the way in which Keats's self-won knowledge, his honest groping, increasingly deepens his perceptions, his "sensual humanism." One senses throughout the book a protest against going beyond the obvious and immediate, in discussing Keats's mental endowment, and also a protest that the obvious and immediate is quite enough. For example, Jones does not see Keats's undeniable gift for sympathetic identification and "negative capability" as leading to any kind of dramatic achievement. Keats, he thinks, is confusing two different things. His narrative poems, and his two short attempts at drama, show no evidence of dramatic ability. "Space and feel is his thing." Though there are many fine insights in Jones's book, it is retreading what is familiar ground for most readers. In doing so, it does not subsume what Keats criticism and scholarship have done, nor discuss the issues they have raised. The result is a thinner book than might otherwise have been the case.

Before turning to more specific aspects or topics, we should mention two important distilled statements of a general character, by Douglas Bush and J. M. Murry, written for *The Major English Romantic Poets*. Bush's "Keats and His Ideas" (pp. 231–45), written by a master of distillation, is the most condensed authoritative presentation of the subject as a whole yet written. J. M. Murry's "Keats's Thought: A Discovery of Truth" (pp. 252–58) is more personal: an expression of confidence, earned by long and affectionate study of the subject, in Keats as an example to the human spirit—transcending egoism through a union of manly integrity and fortitude, an imaginative and informed trust in the "life-wisdom" of the heart, and a capacity for selflessness at once Christian and empathically Shakespearean. Essentially what Bush, Murry, and Thorpe are saying has become a part of our general consciousness of Keats as almost an *exemplum*, with remarkable resonance, of human mind and character. It is with this thought that Lionel Trilling entitled his Introduction to the *Selected Letters* (above) "The Poet as Hero," when he reprinted it as an essay (*The Opposing Self*, 1955).[9] The Keats of the letters especially is seen by Trilling as a human being, as experiencing nature, of masculinity, responsibility, humor, and general health of mind. As such he "has for us a massive importance." With a rare balance of vision and faculties, he accepted the physical world gladly, but had at the same time an overall respect for the intellect: on the one hand an "intense naturalism," on the other a passionate concern with the "mystery of man's nature, reckoning as boldly with pleasure as with pain, giving a generous credence to growth, development, and possibility," responding warmly "to the idea of community." Keats stands, says Trilling, memorably, "as the last image of health at the very moment when the sickness of Europe began to be apparent."

Of special interest, by the late 1920's and the 1930's, was Keats's own view of poetry. Here was a modern (or near-modern) poet who seemed in the vein of Shakespeare, at least in some respects, yet from whom much

---

[9] See W. H. Auden, "Keats in His Letters" (*Partisan Review*, 1951), a review of Trilling's ed. of *Selected Letters;* rpt. in *Partisan Review Anthology* (1962), ed. W. Phillips and P. Rahv.

that we think of as Victorian aesthetic lyricism seemed to descend. A noted Japanese scholar, Takeshi Saito, in his *Keats' View of Poetry* (1929), initiated the more specialized discussion of this subject, except as it had already appeared in more general works on Keats. Saito sees Keats as a seriously reflective poet, who, beginning with a strong inclination towards the luxurious, developed an interest in truth and the realities of life, until toward the end he came to be a thorough "humanitarian idealist." Keats's unique greatness lies not in his power as a sensuous poet but in his neo-idealistic poetry and view of life. The proper wisdom of a poet, Keats thought, is "deep life experience," a grasp of reality. Great poetry is a representation of this reality, or truth, and this also is beauty.

Another study centering on aesthetic theory is Walter Jackson Bate's brief but suggestive monograph, *Negative Capability* (1939), in the series Harvard Undergraduate Theses in English (No. 13). Here Bate analyzes the meaning of Keats's striking phrase "Negative Capability" in terms of Bergsonian intuition. The principle of negative capability embraces implicit trust in the imagination, objective detachment, passiveness, self-annihilation, and sympathetic identification. Its function is to know the real identity of man, the inner beauty and truth of being, and to portray it in language of intensity. Later works by Bate modified, developed, and went into the background of the subject: the treatments of the "sympathetic imagination" in eighteenth-century thought (*From Classic to Romantic,* 1946; rpt. 1961) and in Hazlitt (see the Introductions to Romanticism and to Hazlitt in *Criticism: The Major Texts,* 1952). A central chapter on "Negative Capability" in Bate's *John Keats* (1963) provides a significant reconsideration; and the concept serves as one of the principal themes of the book generally. While we are on the subject of "Negative Capability," we should also mention a variety of later studies that touch on it and the intellectual background (including the influence of Hazlitt). Of special interest are C. L. Finney, "Keats's Philosophy of Negative Capability in its Philosophical Backgrounds" (*Vanderbilt Studies in the Humanities,* 1951); and, though they rather repeat what had come to be taken for granted, J. D. Wigod, "Negative Capability and Wise Passiveness" (*PMLA,* 1952), and R. T. Davies, "Was 'Negative Capability' Enough for Keats?" (*SP,* 1958). In M. A. Goldberg, *The Poetics of Romanticism,* discussed below, "negative capability" and the "sympathetic imagination" are given special prominence (Chapters vii and ix). Among discussions of Keats's debt to Hazlitt, see C. D. Thorpe, "Keats and Hazlitt" (*PMLA,* 1947); Kenneth Muir, "Keats and Hazlitt" (*Leeds Philosophical and*

Literary Society, 1951; rpt. in *John Keats: A Reassessment,* cited above under General Works); Rotrand Müller, *Keats und Hazlitt* (1957), a Freiburg study of parallels and influences; and, of supplementary interest, R. T. Davies, "Keats and Hazlitt" (*KSMB,* 1957), a sort of appendix to Muir's essay without much sense of what preceded Muir, and H. M. Sikes's more comprehensive "The Poetic Theory and Practice of Keats: The Record of a Debt to Hazlitt" (*PQ,* 1959).

Other discussions of Keats's aesthetic values include J. R. Caldwell, *John Keats' Fancy* (1945; rpt. 1965). Caldwell's main purpose is to show that Keats's central poetic theory and practice were modeled on the associational aesthetic of the eighteenth century, brought to its height in Alison, and carried over into the nineteenth century by Wordsworth and Hazlitt. Setting aside ideas that conflict with his theory, Caldwell argues that Keats believed that the way to make poetry is to give a loose rein to a free-ranging fancy, with the mind in a state of half-dream or trance, in composition rapid, spontaneous, and habitually close to the sensuous level. The best parts of Caldwell's book are the analyses of specific poems. The limitations he imposes upon himself result, however, in a partial view of Keats's whole theory of poetry, with a tendency towards oversimplification, a characteristic which Caldwell's book shares with A. E. Powell's (Mrs. Dodds's) chapter in *The Romantic Theory of Poetry* (1926), in which she proposes to identify Keats's more mature aesthetic views with those of Croce. A reflective summary, but of no particular interest to the specialist, is Akiko Kimura, "A Study of John Keats—The Evolution of Keats's Idea of Beauty" (*Essays and Studies,* Tokyo Woman's Christian College, 1965). The most recent study of Keats's aesthetic theory is M. A. Goldberg, *The Poetics of Romanticism: Toward a Reading of John Keats* (1969), which, despite its comparative brevity, combines many things. In particular Goldberg re-examines such central concepts as, e.g., the "vale of soul-making" letter, the idea of the "sympathetic imagination," "truth and the intellect," as well as Keats's own poetic practice as it reflects or extends the implications of his poetic. He places Keats, as well as some of his English contemporaries, in the "tradition he inherited, the classicism of ancient Greece as it developed through the eighteenth century," and, in a final section, discusses the twentieth-century development. The book is also an eloquent personal credo: that, after a half century of alienation from the Romantic, modern art and criticism could profitably return to the most fertile Romantic insights as a guide and inspiration in the Neo-Romanticism that seems about to develop.

Two studies that had already presented unqualified statements about Keats as a poet of thought are Alexander W. Crawford's *The Genius of Keats* (1932; rpt. 1967) and Margaret Sherwood's "Keats' Approach to Myth," in *Undercurrents of Influence in English Romantic Poetry* (1934). To Crawford, Keats was an intellectual as well as an aesthetic poet whose genius lay in his ability to achieve "harmony out of the diverse elements of our humanity." Crawford sees Keats as winning his way to this harmony through the exercise of philosophic powers which, contrary to Garrod, formed an important part of his natural endowment. Miss Sherwood elaborates the idea that Keats utilized myth for the expression of "complex aspects of thought and feeling which he could hardly have expressed . . . in any other way." The thought and feelings are about life, the problems of man, his troubles and joys, his aspirations and conflicts. Thus *Endymion* is a poem about aspiration for fullness of knowledge and experience, fundamentally a poem of the development of a man from a lower to a higher state of knowledge. Answers to the problems of relationship raised are (1) that there is a fundamental "oneness of life in all things," (2) that development is an inherent part of the organic conception of life: "that which lives grows."

It was indeed through a profounder and more sophisticated conception of myth that the deeper consideration of Keats's actual poetry began to unite effectively with the interest in his intellectual promise and his ideas as revealed in the letters. Here again we must refer to the central discussion in Bush's *Mythology and the Romantic Tradition* (1937; rpt. 1969). Bush simultaneously does several things. He brings together Keats's use of sources (Elizabethan as well as classical) with full consideration of his imaginative use of them (from general theme down to image or phrase). In this light all the major poems and many of the minor ones are freshly illuminated. At the same time, since the subject is taken up chronologically, Keats's general intellectual growth is disclosed, as well as his growth in artistry, with full recognition of stylistic and thematic innovation as well as development. Finally, all this is seen in the contexts both of Keats's own period and the periods before and after. The result is so impressive a critique that later works concerned with the same subject have tended either to ramify, magnify, or minimize particular details or interests in order to find a point of issue or difference.

Published about the same time, C. L. Finney's *The Evolution of Keats's Poetry* (1936), discussed above, also applies the use of sources and influences to Keats's poetic theory and philosophical interests. In various articles Finney had previously dealt with some of the main phases of Keats's thought: particularly in his "Keats's Philosophy of Beauty: An Interpretation of the Allegory of *Endymion*" (*PQ*, 1926) and in *"The Fall of Hyperion"* (*JEGP*, 1927). In his 1926 article, he had made Miss Lowell's denial of allegorical intent in *Endymion* the occasion for a reinterpretation of the poem in terms of Spenserian Neoplatonism. In his study of *The Fall of Hyperion* Finney had argued for an interpretation and a date from his reading of evidence for Keats's alternate acceptance and rejection of "Wordsworth's humanitarianism" and of "the ideals of Elizabethan humanism." The Wordsworthian influence was dominant from early 1818 to October 1818. The opening of *The Fall* is in the Wordsworthian spirit (its lesson being that unless the poet leaves his palace of art and acquires a knowledge of humanity, he will perish); therefore it was written before the end of October 1818, hence before *Hyperion,* which was written under the influence of Milton, to whom Keats turned after deserting Wordsworth. These ideas are, with some modifications, carried into *The Evolution of Keats's Poetry,* constituting the most individual, and one may add most controversial, of Finney's theories about Keats's thought.[10]

The latest work to concentrate on myth is Walter H. Evert, *Aesthetic and Myth in the Poetry of Keats* (1965). Here Evert, taking for granted that previous discussions render comprehensiveness less urgent, focuses primarily, with close analysis, on Keats's attraction to and use of the Apollo myth, or rather "the late-Greek conception of the God Apollo." With this in mind as a key to general interpretation, he retraces Keats's thought and poetic treatment of myth. He inevitably concentrates more on the earlier poems, since, as he argues, Keats after the spring of 1818 begins to retreat from the myth of Apollo and his idealization of the imaginative realm into a more "willing acceptance of whatever response the experience of the moment may bring forth." One could argue in return, that this represents an important step forward (indeed this is a central theme of much critical reinterpretation of Keats). Particularly valuable, in Evert's book, is the detailed criticism of *Endymion.* One's only regret is that so

---

[10] When Amy Lowell, without evidence, committed herself to the view that the composition of *The Fall of Hyperion* preceded that of *Hyperion* she stirred up a bit of a hornet's nest in criticism. Both de Selincourt (*TLS,* 19 March 1925; 5th ed., 1926) and J. M. Murry (Appendix, *Keats and Shakespeare*) proceeded to demolish her position. Likewise, when Finney, supporting his case by reference to Keats's thought, followed Miss Lowell to the extent of dating part of *The Fall* first, he drew conclusive rebuttal, notably from Douglas Bush in "The Date of Keats's *Fall of Hyperion*" (*MLN,* 1934).

brief a portion of the book is able to concentrate on the principal poems after *Endymion*. Of related interest is Charles Patterson's perceptive study of *The Daemonic in the Poetry of Keats* (1970), which explores Keats's use of the non-Christian (classical and Celtic) concept of the "daemonic," and conceives the principal conflict in Keats's poetry to be that between the "real" and the "daemonic," resulting in an increasing rejection of the "daemonic" as a means of human fulfillment. Though his thesis especially applies to "La Belle Dame" and *Lamia*, Patterson provides suggestive explications of most of the other major poems with psychological acumen and imaginative knowledge of Keats generally.

The principal concern of Albert Gérard is with ideas Keats shares and exemplifies in common with other major English Romantics. In "Coleridge, Keats and the Modern Mind" (*EC*, 1951) he sees Keats as always striving to reconcile experience with philosophic thought. Though Coleridge is ordinarily regarded as more idealistic and Keats as more concrete, they were similar in their hope for synthesis. Gérard stresses the modernity of Keats, in whom we find "a desperate hankering after Truth, and a devastating honesty in recognizing that Truth—if there be such a thing—lies beyond human reach." This, says Gérard, is the "existential predicament" of our time. In "Keats and the Romantic *Sehnsucht*" (*UTQ*, 1959), *Endymion* is seen as showing Keats's growing awareness that "the dream of perfection," though unattainable, is formative, and even the suffering that the *Sehnsucht* entails is a challenge to the soul. "Romance and Reality: Continuity and Growth in Keats's View of Art" (*KSJ*, 1962) is concerned primarily with the "Grecian Urn" and its background in Keats's thinking. The movement of the ode is dialectical: "There is truth (in a somewhat Platonic sense) in the first scene; and there is beauty in the vision of ordinary life, suffering, and death described in the second." The theme is the relation of art to life. Art (whatever its limits) can "actualize the ideal" and make perceptible "the presence of the ideal in the actual." In this respect, it is a true "friend to man." Gérard's book, *English Romantic Poetry: Ethos, Structure, and Symbol in Coleridge, Wordsworth, Shelley, and Keats* (1968), drawing on his earlier articles, discusses particular Romantic poems as belonging to two groups: (1) "poems of perplexity," which exemplify "the poet's puzzlement and/or anguish as he becomes aware of the contradiction between his youthful idealism and the hard realities of life"; and (2) "poems of reconciliation," in which, through "enlarged experience and deepened meditation," the Romantic poet emerged from puzzlement and despair to "reconcile the antinomies of expectation and experience into a further synthesis." It is in and with this hope of reconciliation that the Romantic use of the "symbol" develops. The poems of Keats on which Gérard concentrates are *Endymion,* Book IV, exemplifying the first category mentioned above; the "Epistle to J. H. Reynolds," a transitional poem; and, as a poem of reconciliation, the "Grecian Urn." Aside from regret that Gérard did not extend his criticism to one or two more poems, the only reservation one might have about this excellent book is that the "symbol" is construed in such completely Coleridgean terms. For actual practice—as distinct from Coleridge's own transcendental theory—the symbol may be more profitably viewed in looser or more fluid terms as a significant image, tapping or expressing a variety of responses and emotions, from or through which synthesis (though not necessarily in Coleridgean terms) is often achieved but just as often achieved only partially (in which case the symbol remains "open" and even—especially in Keats—a subject for inner debate).

A book difficult to describe briefly, since it is disarmingly individualistic but provocative, is Bernard Blackstone's *The Consecrated Urn: An Interpretation of Keats in Terms of Growth and Form* (1959), an original and independent work that jostles our customary attitudes by approaching Keats through Blake, the Hermetic tradition, and what he calls a "botanico-physiologico-cosmogonical" concept of growth, fruition, metamorphosis, and rebirth, which is seen as Keats's central interest. In particular Blackstone tries to relate Keats to the scientific interests of the late eighteenth and early nineteenth centuries (Erasmus Darwin, whose scientific poetry is preoccupied with the growth and decay of life, especially that of plants, is "the best introduction to Keats"). Blackstone concentrates especially on *Endymion,* the "pilgrimage pattern" of which is "penetrated" with ideas of growth and rebirth. He is less successful, except at particular moments, with the later work, and is sometimes disarmingly capricious (Keats, instead of writing the odes, "marred by technical and emotional imperfections," might better have spent the time "sleeping his winter out undisturbed by love, ambition, or poetry"). Despite its gusto, and even though it makes many original and suggestive points, the book leaves one with a sense of enthusiastic but wasted ingenuity.

More difficult to classify—perhaps of only marginal interest as criticism—is Katharine Wilson, *The Nightingale and the Hawk: A Psychological Study of Keats's Ode* (1964). We mention it here rather than in the section on individual poems (IV, 4) since only a relatively short space (pp. 120–38) is devoted explicitly to the "Ode to a Nightingale" itself.

The book discusses parts or aspects of Keats's poetry generally as it reflects or fits into Jung's psychology of unconscious archetypes, claiming that "a fantastic correspondence exists between Keats and aspects of Jung's psychology. Jung can be elucidated in terms of Keats and Keats in terms of Jung." The "Nightingale" was written "to clarify a meeting with the Self not in imagination . . . but as an overwhelming experience." Even within its own terms—since Keats unquestionably had a strong imaginative sense of and reaction to what we now call the "archetypal"—this work does not seem to open up this rich subject to the extent one would hope. Also, as with most interpretations of a complex writer through a single-minded approach, psychoanalytic or otherwise, one finds the approach quickly becomes a filter excluding many of the most important factors that coalesce into what makes a work (especially a group of works) great as art.[11]

A paragraph should be added about the continued interest in the influence of Wordsworth on Keats. While it is amply discussed in general works (especially Thorpe, Murry, Finney, and Bush), we should also mention Hermann Anders, *Die Bedeutung Wordsworthscher Gedankengänge für das Denken und Dichten von John Keats* (1932). This was an ambitious study of the subject for its time. But its chief virtue is the summation within two covers of what had been noticed in one way or another by earlier critics. E. von Schaubert's "Zu Wordsworths Bedeutung für John Keats," in *Neueren Sprachen* (1932), does little more than run briefly over the same ground covered by Anders. A more recent review is Thora Balslev, *Keats and Wordsworth: A Comparative Study* (1962). Though the book does not attempt a general critical interpretation of this important subject, it provides a detailed catalogue of parallels (imagery,

---

[11] For Keats as for other major poets, psychiatric comment is volunteered usually by observers somewhat on the fringes of both psychiatry and literary study. Of tangential interest, however, are Arthur Wormhoudt's "Cold Pastoral," in *American Imago* (1951), and G. H. Pederson-Krag's two articles, "The Genesis of a Sonnet," in *Psychoanalysis and the Social Sciences* (1951), and "O Poesy! for thee I hold my pen," in *Psychoanalysis and Culture* (1951). A different approach is represented in W. R. Betts's "John Keats," in *The Infirmities of Genius* (1952). Approaching the view of Betts, who interprets Keats as haunted by the spectre of tuberculosis and preoccupied with images of death, is the idea of Tarquinio Vallese in "Il pessimismo di Keats," in *Saggi Di Letteratura Inglese* (Napoli, 1949). Vallese finds that "a black pessimism," "a Hamlet-like resignation and cynicism," characterizes the later Keats and that by the time he wrote "Ode to a Nightingale," he had come to look on life not so much with tragic vision as with "a superior indifference." Of almost hilarious interest is Robert Rogers, "Keats's Strenuous Tongue: A Study of 'Ode on Melancholy'" (*L&P*, 1967), which sees, in the "strenuous eroticism" of the poem, a manic-depressive approach to life and love (see the reply by A. Ward, in the same journal, 1967).

diction, versification, and occasionally in general theme and interest), and has a suggestive but thin chapter comparing their use of symbolism.

Keats's interest in and the relation of his poetry to the visual arts is discussed in the following shorter works, listed chronologically: Edmund Blunden, "Romantic Poetry and the Fine Arts" (*Proceedings of the British Academy*, 1942), in which Keats is presented as a special example of the Romantic interest in painting, sculpture, and architecture; the chapter on Keats in Stephen Larrabee, *English Bards and Grecian Marbles* (1943); D. S. Bland, "Painting and the Poetry of Keats: Some Further Identifications" (*MLR*, 1955); M. A. Goldberg, "John Keats and the Elgin Marbles" (*Apollo*, 1965), which argues that what inspired Keats in the Marbles was not the truly classical so much as a romanticized conception of it; and Dieter Riesner, "John Keats, Benjamin Robert Haydon und die Parthenon skulpturen," in *Versdichtung der englischen Romantik: Interpretationen* (1968), ed. Teut A. Riese and Dieter Riesner, which provides an informed and condensed analysis of an important episode in Keats's life. But by far the most comprehensive study of this general aspect of Keats— or of any other poet of the time—is Ian Jack, *Keats and the Mirror of Art* (1967). Here Jack explores, with numerous parallels and with unrivalled fullness of detail, Keats's debt to the visual arts, and the effect of this interest and knowledge in helping "to sharpen his perceptions, and so increase the range and power of his descriptions."

We should add discussion of two special problems in Keats's thought: his interest in politics and world affairs, and his relation to the art-for-art's-sake creed. Among critics of the last twenty-five years H. G. Wright and C. D. Thorpe have dealt specifically with the first question and Louise Rosenblatt and F. R. Leavis with the second. Wright ("Keats and Politics," *E&S*, 1933) assembles evidence to support his argument that Keats had "a keen sense of the traditional liberties of an Englishman" and that though he was no born reformer his writings reveal the sympathies and anger of one who had known and felt keenly the miseries of the world. In an earlier paper ("Keats's Interest in Politics and World Affairs," *PMLA*, 1931), Thorpe had covered much the same ground, replying in effect to previous denials of Keats's concern with public matters by such critics as S. J. Mary Suddard (*Studies and Essays*, 1912), W. J. Courthope (*The Liberal Movement in English Poetry*, 1885), and Sir Arthur Quiller-Couch (*Charles Dickens and Other Victorians*, 1925), and supporting with more detailed evidence the recognition of Keats's wider interests by such writers as Morris, Colvin, Garrod, de Selincourt, Shaw, and Saito. Keats was in fact keenly alive to the social and political movements of his day, Thorpe concludes. More recently, Carl Woodring's authoritative *Politics in English Romantic Poetry* (1970), though understandably concerned almost entirely with other poets (Wordsworth, Coleridge, Byron, Shelley), provides a distilled, balanced statement of the subject as it applies to Keats (pp. 77–83).

Though advocates of art-for-art's sake of the later nineteenth century were eager to claim Keats as forerunner, Louise Rosenblatt (*L'Idée de l'art pour l'art dans la littérature anglaise pendant la période Victorienne*, 1931) concludes that Keats reveals too much interest in the mystery and comprehension of life, is too much concerned with reflection and knowledge, to be classed with the true aesthetes. Admittedly, he put aesthetic intuition above all else; but he saw clearly that to be adequate for great poetry this intuition must be prepared for by such knowledge and thought as would give a harmonious vision of the real world. In *Revaluation* (1936; rpt. 1947) F. R. Leavis arrives at a similar denial of Keats's real affinity with the art-for-art's sake group. The basis of the denial is that, though Keats is related to the Victorian aesthetic movement, he presents this essential difference: he has a grasp of actualities, shows a refusal to mistake dreams for realities, has a "magnificent vital energy" in a strong "grasping at fullness of life," reveals a joy which is in life rather than in art (even in "The Grecian Urn") that one does not find in the later cultists.

Such is some of the evidence for belief in a Keats of no little profundity of thought, whose mind was peculiarly susceptible to growth, with humility to recognize past error, with insight to embrace the gains of experience. As D. G. James puts it, Keats died young, "Yet his mind in its quality and range, in its passionate desire for what is ideal, in its exquisite and balanced scepticism, in its acceptance, in serenity, of sorrow and suffering, is wonderful to contemplate. He set himself high standards, in a plenitude of critical power; and he knew what was failure and what was not."[12]

---

[12] Additional titles concerned with Keats's modes of thought and general temperament include: A. von Bentheim, *Symbol und Mythus bei Keats* (1932); V. Orend, *John Keats Schönheitsideal* . . . (1928); T. B. Haber, "The Unifying Influence of Love in Keats's Poetry" (*PQ*, 1937); Hildegard Schumann, *John Keats und das romantische Bewusstsein* (1938); B. S. Chowdhuri, "Keats, the Development of His Mind" (*Journal, Department of Letters, Calcutta*, 1939); H. N. Fairchild, "Keats and the Struggle-for-Existence Tradition" (*PMLA*, 1949); R. Lloyd, "Keats and the Limitations of Pantheism" (*QR*, 1952); Earl Wasserman, "Keats and Benjamin Bailey on the Imagination" (*MLN*, 1953); Dorothy Van Ghent, "Keats's Myth of the Hero" (*KSJ*, 1954); Paul de Man, "Keats and Hölderlin" (*CL*, 1956), which compares some of the principal themes in *Endymion* and

3. WORKS CONCERNED PRIMARILY WITH LITERARY ARTISTRY AND STYLE

Recognition of Keats's artistry was a Victorian commonplace; discovery of his intellect came later, and like most literary discoveries was for some time the center of attention, with studies of Keats's thought overshadowing, in volume at least, those of his art. But, in the last thirty years, Keats's craftsmanship (style, imagery, diction, his art in general) has increasingly excited the interest of critics, with the net result of a pendulum-swing to special studies of these topics. One who wished to examine the art of Keats should not, however, limit himself to these more specialized writings; for most of the main works that have been mentioned in this survey contain relevant material.

For example, Robert Bridges essay (see above) contains penetrative analyses of Keats's diction and rhythm, his use of the couplet, stylistic debts to Milton, even his pronunciation. De Selincourt's editions, in introduction, notes, and appendices, furnish illuminating comment on Keats's style and art: incidental remarks on diction and metrics, sources of vocabulary, revisions, and a systematic examination of Keats's poetic vocabulary, with special reference to Spenser and Milton. In this he draws on such earlier studies as W. T. Read's *Keats and Spenser* (1897), Johannes Hoops's introduction to his edition of *Hyperion* (1899)—where Keats's verbal debts to Milton are examined—and W. T. Arnold's study of Keats's diction in relation to his predecessors in the introduction to his *Poems of Keats* (1884). The editions of H. B. Forman include materials on Keats's style and poetic methods, with suggestions of parallels and sources. These, with additions, are carried over into M. B. Forman's Hampstead Edition. The best place to go for variant readings, for help in

---

Hyperion with Hölderlin's treatment of similar ones; John Rosenberg, "Keats and Milton: The Paradox of Rejection" (*KSJ*, 1957), which stresses Keats's closeness to the mind and thought of Milton despite attempts to free himself from Milton as a dominant model; Hanspeter Schelp, "Der Tod im Leben und Werk von John Keats" (*Neueren Sprachen*, 1958); R. T. Davies, "Some Ideas and Usages," in *John Keats: A Reassessment* (1958), ed. K. Muir, a discussion of Keats's use of six key words (speculation, truth, spirit, sublime, sensation, ethereal); D. G. James, "Keats and *King Lear*" (*Shakespeare Survey*, 1960); George Yost, "The Poetic Drive in the Early Keats" (*TSLL*, 1964); Edward Carben, "John Keats: Pioneer of Modern Existential Thought" (*Trace*, 1964); Martin Halpern, "Keats and the 'Spirit that Laughest'" (*KSJ*, 1966), which reviews the subject of Keats's humor and its place in his total sensibility; Stanley C. Russell, "'Self-Destroying' Love in Keats" (*KSJ*, 1967), also of biographical interest; Gerald Enscoe, *Eros and the Romantics: Sexual Love as a Theme in Coleridge, Shelley, and Keats* (1967).

understanding Keats's ways of composition, is now, of course, H. W. Garrod's *Poetical Works*. Brief discussions of Keats's artistry are to be found in the introductions to other editions. (See Editions, above.)

Of the biographers Colvin, Amy Lowell, and especially Wolff and Bate do most in exploring Keats's literary art. Wolff, in both the 1910 *La Vie* and the 1929 *Keats,* makes fine analyses of the important poems; and Bate devotes substantial chapters to each of the major poems, concentrating on artistry, including diction and metrics, as much as ideas. In his *Evolution of Keats's Poetry,* Claude Finney tracks down parallels and sources in a wide range of authors from Virgil and Ovid to Wordsworth and Hazlitt and points to stylistic influences by Keats's English predecessors. Some of his findings are convincing, others overdrawn, as when he says, in effect, that the *Hyperion* is a direct imitation of *Paradise Lost*—the reverse of R. D. Havens' conclusion that, instead of copying, "Keats . . . tried to write a poem as Milton would have written it" (*The Influence of Milton,* 1922).[13]

Among earlier studies was David Watson Rannie's "Keats's Epithets," in *Essays and Studies* for 1912, precursor of B. W. A. Massey's *The Compound Epithets of Shelley and Keats* (1923), a work, like Rannie's, aimed at better understanding of an important element in Keats's art. In the same general category are Josephine Miles's examination of Keats's adjectives in "From Good to Bright: A Note in Poetic History" (*PMLA,* 1945) and a section on Keats in *Major Adjectives in English Poetry from Wyatt to Auden* (1946), in which she concludes that Keats is "the great fourth poet of the adjective" in English—in the line of Spenser, Milton, and Collins. Herbert Read ("The True Voice of John Keats," *HudR,* 1953) finds three stages of development: (1) *Endymion,* in which Spenser is the dominant influence; (2) *Hyperion,* with Milton in control; (3) *The Fall of Hyperion,* where Keats has finally found his own mode of expression, his own true voice: "The style, the poetic diction and vocal accent, of *The Fall of Hyperion* is at last his own."

The most detailed discussion of Keats's metrics, diction, and use of rhetorical patterns is W. J. Bate's *Stylistic Development in John Keats*

---

[13] Finney repeats in this book his argument for Keats's debts to Drayton, previously developed in "Drayton's *Endimion and Phoebe* and Keats's *Endymion*" (*PMLA,* 1924)— accepted by Amy Lowell, rejected by Douglas Bush; and, along with more on the Shakespearean relationship, includes the substance of his earlier "Shakespeare and Keats's *Hyperion*: A Study in the Processes of Poetic Composition" (*PQ,* 1924), where he had contended that Shakespeare, not Spenser, was the dominant influence in Keats's poetry, particularly in imagery.

(1945; rpt. 1958).[14] Bate's direct concern is with prosodic and rhetorical matters related to a remarkable growth in restraint and artistic power, as Keats moves, after "Isabella," toward the poetic discipline which in *Hyperion,* "The Eve of St. Agnes," *Lamia,* and the odes manifests itself in a style with fewer adjectives and more verbs, a firmer line and more rigorous structure, a greater inevitability of word and form. Bate's book is full of prosodic lore, close and productive analyses, perceptive critical comment, as well as the first (and still most complete) study of Keats's use of assonance and vowel-interplay.[15] Qualifications appear to be in order on only two points: the comparative neglect of earlier poems, and the theory that *Lamia* and *The Fall of Hyperion* represent a sudden revision of Keats's conception of poetry—since the basic poetic ideals revealed in these poems are to be found in previous writings. This interpretation, it should be added, was considerably modified in Bate's critical biography, discussed above. Bate also presents a brief reconsideration of the development of Keats's artistry, including imagery and general tone, in "Keats's Style: Evolution Toward Qualities of Permanent Value," in *The Major English Romantic Poets.* Particularly stressed are the increasing intrusion of the dramatic in the odes, the creative rapidity with which Keats develops different styles in his final year of writing, and the relevance of his example to modern poetry. A companion essay on Keats's style in the same volume is Cleanth Brooks, "The Artistry of Keats: A Modern Tribute," which points out that, in the twentieth-century shift from Romantic and nineteenth-century poetic idiom to a more oblique and involved idiom ("metaphysical," ironic, ambiguous, intellectual), Keats not only survived better than any other Romantic but, especially in the odes, could serve as "one of the heroes of modernist criticism." The essay, though justified and well-intended, seems now a little condescending as well as out of date (Keats, by passing the test of the Donne revival, qualifies for "modern" approval).

[14] We should also mention three earlier discussions of versification: Lucien Wolff, *An Essay on Keats's Treatment of the Heroic Rhythm and Blank Verse* (1909); N. S. Bushnell, "Notes on Professor Garrod's Keats" (*MLN,* 1929), a discussion of Keats's development of the ode-stanza; and C. A. Langworthy, "Dryden's Influence on the Versification of *Lamia,*" in *Research Studies of the State Coll. of Washington* (1930).

[15] For later discussions of Keats's use of vowel and consonant patterning or interplay, see E. C. Pettet. *On the Poetry of Keats* (1957), pp. 90–122; David Masson, "The Keatsian Incantation," in *John Keats: A Reassessment* (1958), ed. K. Muir, pp. 159–80; and Ann Lozano, "Phonemic Patterning in Keats's 'Ode on Melancholy' " (*KSJ,* 1968). For further observations on the diction, though from a rather specialized conception of what Keats's famous phrase implies, see Nathan Starr, "Negative Capability in Keats's Diction" (*KSJ,* 1966).

Keats's imagery has been a subject of growing interest. In "Romanticism and Synaesthesia: A Comparative Study of Sense Transfer in Keats and Byron" (*PMLA*, 1945), Stephen de Ullmann shows that whereas Byron's synaesthetic imagery, less frequent than Keats's, is conventional and ornamental, Keats's sense transfers are "striking, personal, and original," the result of experience of psychological realities. In "Empathic Imagery in Keats and Shelley" (*PMLA*, 1946), Richard Fogle finds that Keats is "a poet typically empathic," in contrast with Shelley, who tends more to sympathy and personification. Beginning again with analysis of imagery Fogle concludes in "Keats's 'Ode to a Nightingale'" (*MLQ*, 1947) that some of the odes, the "Nightingale" in particular, reveal awareness of the inseparability of the elements of human experience. Less specialized, but invaluable for its brilliant, many-faceted treatment of Keats's imagery is G. Wilson Knight's "The Priest-Like Task: An Essay on Keats," in *The Starlit Dome* (1941). Psychological, perceptive, comparative—Shelley, Coleridge, Shakespeare are frequently brought in—this illuminating essay has such near-bewildering detail as to defy summary. But it certainly should be read. It is one of the score or so most fertile single discussions of Keats, in essay length, and, since it appeared, has provided suggestions for later critics of Keats and of poetry generally.

Richard Fogle's *The Imagery of Keats and Shelley: A Comparative Study* (1949; rpt. 1962) is the only full-length work on the subject yet published. Fogle's method is to classify and analyze Keats's characteristic imagery in comparison with that of Shelley, and to examine specific poems illustrative of the modes in which each poet works. Contrary to general belief, he finds that Shelley's poetry is scarcely less sensuous than that of Keats. The difference lies in the specific quality of their imagery. That of Keats is concentrated, definite, spontaneous, preoccupied with "human, natural, and artistic objects," holding itself to the context of reality even when, as in the later poems, it is symbolic of higher meanings; Shelley's imagery, though sensuous in origin and body, is likely to be expansive and highly symbolic and is generally conscious and intellectual, striving to reach beyond the material world into the realm of infinity, seeking "to grasp and express an unattainable truth." Hence the "concreteness" of Keats, the "abstractness" of Shelley. The importance of this study is enhanced by the fact that while sharply at variance with the "New Criticism" in its tendency toward absolutism and exclusiveness, Fogle subscribes to its general objectives and illustrates the value of its favorite procedure of close analysis of works.

Theodor Wolpers' "Zur Struktur der Bildlichkeit bei Keats" (*Anglia*, 1962) is a valuable discussion, at once condensed and comprehensive, in which Keats's imagery is seen as expressing the general habits of his imagination. The article is perceptive in detail and rich in thoughtful generalization. Moreover, every point is amply supported by indicated examples and references to secondary literature. Wolpers stresses the union of two qualities in Keats's imagery: (1) the richly concrete detail; (2) the sense of a whole form against which the detail is seen as a part. With respect to objects that exist primarily in space—urns, temples, etc.—the movement of the poem is the movement of the eye from one detail to another along or within the total form, the standpoint of the observer not usually changing. With objects in motion, the motion tends to be gradual, continual, and completed, so that the total curve of the action makes up the whole in which individual phases may be dwelt on. Similarly, time in Keats's imagery is likely to figure as process, that is, as natural and purposeful transition from phase to phase, leading to a culmination. In the representation of objects Keats gives a sense of their past and future as well as their present. Thus his imagery mediates between such qualities as change and permanence, the plastic and the kinetic. These same habits of imagination enter into the formation of whole poems as well as images, and Wolpers particularly remarks that this is true even in the narrative poems. Though some of these observations are not new, several others are; and they are put here with a compression, implication, and concatenation that makes this one of the best interpretative discussions, of this length, of Keats's poetic style.

David Perkins ("Keats's Odes and Letters: Recurrent Diction and Imagery in Keats," *KSJ*, 1953) traces likenesses between the odes and the letters in image and language. The interest in such parallels is in finding "common counters" of thought and expression, to throw some light on Keats's habitual imagery. At times it is the idea, not the exact wording, that is carried over from letter to poem. The idea of recurrent imagery, along with recurrent situation and idea, is considered in "The Feast and the Lady" in Gittings' *John Keats: The Living Year* (Section III, above), when the author relates the feast scenes in "The Eve of St. Agnes," "La Belle Dame," *Lamia*, and *Otho the Great* to Keats's supper with Mrs. Isabella Jones.[16]

---

[16] Miriam Allott, in " 'The Feast and the Lady': . . . " (*N&Q*, 1954), takes exception to Gittings' case. The elements of the situation occur earlier, and more inclusively, she avers, in *Endymion*. A reply from Gittings elicits further argument from Miss Allott, followed in turn by a second rejoinder (*N&Q*, 1954).

Studies in the craftsmanship of Keats have in general followed two natural lines, one related to pattern and structure, the other to internal workings—imagery, phrase, and verse. The essays on "The Grecian Urn" by Cleanth Brooks and Kenneth Burke mentioned in the next section (IV, 4) are examples of analysis to show both the thought and the organic structure, the essential unity, of the poem; each is interested in revealing how part fits into part, how step by step each detail moves toward the final inevitable statement. Garrod's examination of the odes in his *Keats* (1926), with the suggestion that Keats arrived at the forms he employed through experimentation with the sonnet, also belongs in this first category. Such, too, is the case with H. M. McLuhan's "Aesthetic Pattern in Keats's Odes" (*UTQ*, 1943); for, though the author is also dealing with central images (or symbols), his main quest is for inner organic pattern.

In a sense all studies of style and imagery belong in the second group, but more specifically we may place here M. R. Ridley's *Keats' Craftsmanship* (1933; rpt. 1962, 1963), in which the author sets himself to study what he calls the "verbal carpentry" of Keats's poems. In his book Ridley takes up all the major poems of which we possess Keats's manuscript revisions, and follows them through various stages of revision to their final form. Much of the book (especially the section on "The Eve of St. Agnes") has been of immense interest not only to scholars and critics of Keats but to students of poetry generally. The reason is that of few other major English poets do we have anything like this detail of manuscript revision, where (especially with "The Eve of St. Agnes") we can follow the poet, line by line, as he is writing. Of course, since Garrod's edition (1939)—stimulated partly by the knowledge of the book Ridley was writing—it can be said that we now have, in Garrod's textual notes, the basic material with which to work. Still, Ridley guides the student helpfully, often with imagination, through this maze. Scores of teachers have found that one of the surest ways to introduce students to what is meant by the craft of poetry is to follow—or to enlarge upon—what Ridley does with some of the great passages in Keats.[17]

A combination of the two modes is to be found in J. M. Murry's discussion of the Chapman sonnet—"one of the greatest sonnets in the English language; . . . the first great sonnet Keats wrote"—in "When Keats Discovered Homer" (*HJ*, 1928; *Essays and Studies in Keats*, 1930).

---

[17] A similar kind of study, though in a minor way, was Sidney Colvin's account of the writing of the "Ode to a Nightingale," in "A Morning's Work in a Hampstead Garden" (*Memorial Volume*, 1921).

Because of its influence as an example, we mention Murry's essay here, though in general citation of discussions of particular poems appears in the next section. "The poem is a perfect whole—one single and complex metaphor, as intricate as it is clear," says Murry. The emotion is one with the imagery, and "the rhythm of imagery and emotion of the whole sonnet is reduplicated in either part: in the octave the imagery and emotion of eager exploration; in the sestet the rhythm of eager discovery." The poem is, moreover, "a perfect crystallization" of the attitudes and thoughts and emotions that prevail in the 1817 volume: exploration in the realms of poetry and nature and self, exciting discovery of nature, of the fuller beauty of poetry, of his own creative powers.

Mario D'Avanzo, *Keats's Metaphors for the Poetic Imagination* (1967), in considering recurring metaphors and imagery in Keats, finds that the dominant subject of metaphor for Keats is the imaginative act of poetic conception itself. The pattern of development reveals the concreteness of his mind. The metaphors—like the creative procedure itself—begin with the experience of objective reality, and then follow an arc through imaginative arousal to fulfillment, decline, and a final return to reality. Of related though more specialized interest is Helen Haworth, "Keats and the Metaphor of Vision" (*JEGP*, 1968). The point is the non-mystical nature of Keats: his descriptions of or apparent attitudes toward imaginative and poetic "vision" are "merely" metaphoric; and we make a mistake if we try to "transform" his use of metaphor "into metaphysics."

Difficult to classify or summarize briefly, since it touches on many aspects of style (and theme), is Karl Kroeber, *The Artifice of Reality: Poetic Style in Wordsworth, Foscolo, Keats, and Leopardi* (1964). Taking issue with interpretations of Romanticism as an attempt to transcend the split between subject and object, self and nature, Kroeber stresses the effort of the Romantics (particularly those discussed here) to maintain this separation. As such they anticipate the later development of civilized values into something at once more unified (supranational, even worldwide) and yet personally more diverse. The book then focusses on the role of "artifice" in poetic style as a means of securing this complex end. Also difficult to classify briefly is Gerald Kauvar's suggestive *The Other Poetry of Keats* (1969), the aim of which is "analysis of the expressive functioning of Keats's figurative language." The principal limitation is frankly stated at the start. He is concerned less with the major poems than with those less frequently discussed in detail. This, of course, has its advantage. In any case, the approach is broad. To close analysis of figurative expression,

Kauvar joins both psychological and general thematic considerations, an informed knowledge of what Keats criticism has done, and an awake and generally thoughtful independence of mind.

Two studies of special forms are Lawrence Zillman's *John Keats and the Sonnet Tradition: A Critical and Comparative Study* (1939) and George Shuster's *The English Ode from Milton to Keats* (1940; rpt. 1964). Zillman's is a painstaking examination of Keats's use of the sonnet form, especially in his comparison of Keats with previous and contemporary English writers; Shuster's additions to our knowledge of Keats's odes are slight, but he does place Keats in the development of the ode in English. (Works more specifically concerned with Keats's odes—meaning the great odes of 1819—are mentioned in Section IV, 4.) On the use of narrative, Karl Kroeber's valuable *Romantic Narrative Art* (1960) contains passim many insights that apply to Keats (detailed discussion of Keats, as of Shelley, is deferred for a later work). Hermann Fischer, *Die romantische Verserzählung in England* (1964), discusses Keats briefly (pp. 202–28).

Examining the broader problems of Keats's artistic mode, R. W. Stallman, in "Keats the Apollonian: The Time and Space Logic of His Poems as Paintings" (*UTQ*, 1947), finds that whereas Shelley is Faustian, Keats is Apollonian. In "Keats and Crane: An Airy Citadel" (*Accent*, Autumn 1947) Frajam Taylor also concludes that Keats is Apollonian; Hart Crane, in contrast, is Dionysian. Another study related to artistic mode is Elmer Stoll's "The Validity of the Poetic Vision: Keats and Spenser" (*MLR*, 1945). This is an argument for placing the "internal consistency" of a poem and the "inner reality" from which it was created above any demand that it be "true to life." Using "Ode to a Nightingale" and "On a Grecian Urn" as illustrations, Stoll declares for the autonomy and independence of poetry.

Source-hunting—always a perilous scholarly pursuit—became increasingly popular among writers on Keats from the 1930's to the 1950's, and still continues. A potential evil is the tendency to trace everything in a poet back to someone else, so that in the end he may be left devoid of virtue beyond that of being an adept borrower. This comes close to being the net result of Gittings' pursuit of sources in *John Keats: The Living Year* (discussed in Section II, above). But there are values to investigations of sources when judiciously made, as Lowes's *Road to Xanadu* illustrates. Lowes himself had shown the direction a comparable study of Keats might take: first, in two minor studies, "Keats, Diodorus Siculus, and Rabelais"

(*MP*, 1937) and "*Hyperion* and the *Purgatorio*" (*TLS*, 11 Jan. 1936), then in a major one, "Moneta's Temple" (*PMLA*, 1936). In the last, dealing with only the few lines descriptive of the Temple of Saturn, Lowes does for Keats, on a small scale, the same kind of thing he had done for Coleridge. Lowes here shows how imagery from Plutarch's *Pericles* and John Potter's *Archaeologia Graeca* (*The Antiquities of Greece*), materials about Egyptian monuments in current periodicals, passages in the Bible from Exodus to Revelation, Dante's Mount of Purgatory, and Fingal's Cave—along with other sources—coalesced to enrich Keats's conception of Moneta's Temple, its priestess and appointments. Lowes is not talking of direct borrowing, but of probable materials of a storehouse of memories from which Keats's imagination drew in its new creation: "was there ever, indeed," he inquires, "a more amazing coalescence of five great architectonic conceptions into a sixth, which—compact of all of them, yet itself none of them—achieves its own majestic individuality?"

Some years before Lowes's study Helen Darbishire had prepared the way for the parts of it about Egyptian art in "Keats and Egypt" (*RES*, 1927), which traces a number of images in *Hyperion* and *The Fall of Hyperion* to accounts of Egyptian monuments and sculpture with which Keats was familiar. (For further discussion see Barbara Garlitz, "Egypt and *Hyperion*," in *PQ*, 1955.) Douglas Bush had likewise detected signs of Potter's *Antiquities* in *The Fall of Hyperion*, as well as in *Lamia* and elsewhere, in his "Notes on Keats's Reading" (*PMLA*, 1935). Other critics—de Selincourt, Colvin, Forman—had noted the influence of Dante in the *Fall*. There had been some references to the Bible and *Hyperion*—for example, by de Selincourt; and, among others, Martha Shackford ("*Hyperion*," *SP*, 1925) had called attention to evidence of memories of scenery encountered by Keats on his walking trip. But it remained for Lowes to indicate something of the multiplicity of sources from which Keats's imagination drew in the creation of one single great passage of his poem.

In addition to finding evidence for Keats's use of Potter's *Antiquities*, Douglas Bush (above) points out possible debts by Keats to a wide range of authors, including Gray, Thomson, Dryden, Jonson, Browne, Dante, Ovid, Apuleius, Virgil, Chapman, Shakespeare, Lyly, Milton, Robertson, Southey, Landor, Shelley—an impressive list. Employing the method of Lowes, B. Ifor Evans, in "Keats's Approach to the Chapman Sonnet" (*E&S*, 1931), makes one of the most elaborate attempts to account for the ideas and imagery of Keats's sonnet. The materials are the matter of Keats's reading from the time he received Bonnycastle's *Introduction to Astronomy* in 1811 to the night's "ramp" through Chapman's Homer, including imagery and ideas from Keats's own earlier and current poems. In "Keats's Realms of Gold" (*PMLA*, 1934), J. W. Beach builds a case for the influence of Robertson's *History of America* on the sonnet on Chapman. Others had mentioned a connection, but Beach makes a thorough examination. Robertson appears again in H. E. Briggs, "Keats, Robertson, and 'That Most Hateful Land'" (*PMLA*, 1944), which relates the *History* to parts of the second ode to Fanny. In "Keats and Coleridge: A Note" (*KSMB*, 1950), J. M. Murry sees Coleridge's "The Nightingale" as having some part in shaping Keats's own ode, especially in his suggestion of the quality of the bird's song—as being neither melancholy nor merry, but deeply, soberly happy. Keats's "While thou art pouring forth thy soul abroad" may also owe something to "And sent my soul abroad" of "Dejection: An Ode."[18]

In his *"Trompe-l'œil* in Shakespeare and Keats" (*SR*, 1953), Robert Adams examines Keats in comparison with Shakespeare in the use of the over-reached frame or broken context. Adams says that Shakespeare used the device to show the hardness and light of the real world while Keats uses it to show its darkness and dullness. In the "Ode to a Nightingale" and "Ode on a Grecian Urn," Adams asserts that Keats withdraws further from the world and then oversteps his context in order to contrast the dream with reality. Joan Grundy's "Keats and William Browne" (*RES*, 1955) furnishes a model of what studies of influence should be: knowledgeable, guarded, balanced, with suggestions of resemblance, not assertions of positive borrowings. She finds that Keats's treatment of the nature of poetry and of his own ambitions are conducted in much the same spirit as similar discussions in Browne's *Britannia's Pastorals*; also that the sensuous and decorative, the overripe quality in some of Keats's early poetry has its analogue in Browne's verse. The purpose of her article is to show, not deliberate borrowing, but the "unconscious selective and assimilative processes of Keats's memory." Her later essay, "Keats and the

---

[18] A further ascription of relationship between Coleridge and Keats occurs in Barbara Hardy's "Keats, Coleridge, and Negative Capability" (*N&Q*, July 1955). Miss Hardy believes Keats and Coleridge are less apart in thinking than is generally believed. An earlier comment on the similarity of the ideas of Coleridge and Keats on this concept occurs in "Coleridge as Aesthetician and Critic" (*JHI*, 1949). Robert Daniel's "Odes to Dejection" (*KR*, 1953) examines Keats's report of his conversation with Coleridge, pointing out that the nightingale heads the list; then, comparing Keats's ode with Coleridge's "Dejection," concludes that Keats borrowed imagery, form, and feeling from Coleridge.

Elizabethans," in *John Keats: A Reassessment* (1958), ed. K. Muir (pp. 1–19), discusses Keats's general affinities with the Elizabethans and the limitations of those affinities. At first his principal affinity was in range, energy, and looseness of style. Later it appears in direct uses of technique, vocabulary, and imagery. By *The Fall of Hyperion* he again, after successful assimilation, returns to a more general and spacious use of them as suggestive models or examples.

Chatterton has received attention as an influence in Robert Gittings' "Keats and Chatterton" (*KSJ*, 1955) and in Nai-tung Ting's "The Influence of Chatterton on Keats" (*KSJ*, 1956). Gittings traces by exact day and poem the non-appearance, the appearance, and the disappearance of Chatterton as a poetic influence in Keats's work. Gittings has read Chatterton and Keats closely, and in spite of his tendency to overwork evidence, presents a number of interesting parallels. Nai-tung Ting, following the lead of Gittings, turns up additional examples of likeness in diction and idea.

Other discussions of sources include: B. Ifor Evans, "Keats and the Golden Ass" (*Nineteenth Century*, 1926); G. W. Landrum, "More Concerning Chapman's Homer and Keats" (*PMLA*, 1927); E. V. Weller, "Keats and Mary Tighe" (*PMLA*, 1927), in which he evolves a case for Tighe's influence, later amplified in his *Keats and Mary Tighe* (1928; rpt. 1966)—a book of which Bush ("Notes on Keats's Reading") drily remarks, "Weller proves that Keats and Mrs. Tighe both wrote in English, and that they shared some current fashions in diction"; Floyd Dell, "Keats's Debt to Robert Burton" (*The Bookman*, 1928); T. Saito, "Collins and Keats" (*TLS*, 20 Nov. 1930); F. E. L. Priestley, "Keats and Chaucer" (*MLQ*, 1944); H. E. Briggs, "A Note on Keats and Addison" (*MLN*, 1944) and "Swift and Keats" (*PMLA*, 1946); R. K. Gordon, "Notes on Keats's 'Eve of St. Agnes' " (*MLR*, 1946); R. F. Rashbrook, "Keats and Others" (*N&Q*, 1947); D. T. Starnes, "Spenser and Keats's 'Ode to Psyche' " (*N&Q*, 1947); Aileen Ward, "Keats and Burton" (*PQ*, 1961); H. Felperin, "Keats and Shakespeare: Two New Sources" (*ELN*, 1964); Burton Pollin, "Keats, Charlotte Smith, and the Nightingale" (*N&Q*, 1966).

In "Keats's Odes: Further Notes" (*KSJ*, 1954), Edmund Blunden discusses the early training in literature that led Keats to accept the austerities of the ode in the classical tradition, and speculates upon the part writers like Cowley, Gray, and Coleridge may have played in Keats's decision to try his hand at a form as pindaric as the "Ode to Psyche": "As if

Keats was for once aiming at the theatre-suited effect of the Greek ode."
From Cowley Blunden moves to Anacreon, back to Keats's "Fancy," then
to Cowley's grasshopper in No. x of the "Anacreontiques," then to Keats's
charming sonnet; and from there to reflections on "Ode to Fanny," with a
possible glint of Horace in it, and to Congreve's Ode "On Mrs. Arabella
Hunt," from which the author quotes anticipatory Keatsian intonations.
Blunden does not overdo the matter of influence. Keats owed much to his
reading, but through his artistry what he borrowed became his own, "all to
one thing wrought."

Reference to classic writers brings us to Keats's relationship to things
and authors Greek and Latin. This has been a frequent theme in Keats
criticism from Milnes to the present. Critics have made much of apparent
debts to Homer, Virgil, and Ovid; and few have missed calling attention to
the poet's response to the Elgin Marbles and his use of them in his poetry
and letters. Studies on various phases of this subject have already been
mentioned, especially those on his interest in the visual arts generally (IV,
2). Approaching the classical from a more strictly literary point of view,
Herbert Warren, "Keats as a Classical Scholar" (*Nineteenth Century,*
1923), makes a vigorous case for Keats's acquaintance with and grasp—
intuitive rather than scholarly—of Greek and Latin literature. Also to be
noticed here are Martha Shackford, *"Hyperion"* (*SP,* 1925), Paul Shorey,
"Keats and Lucan" (*Classical Philology,* 1927), John A. Scott, "Keats and
the Epic Cycle" (*CJ,* 1922–23), Paul de Reul, *La Poésie anglaise de
Wordsworth à Keats* (1933), J. H. Wagenblass, "Keats and Lucretius"
(*MLR,* 1937), and de Reul's earlier "Keats et le néo-hellenisme dans la
poésie anglaise," in *Etudes de littérature européenne* (1898). But the most
important of such studies is that of Douglas Bush in *Mythology and the
Romantic Tradition in English Poetry* (discussed above in IV, 2). Bush
shows here how Keats, a natural myth-maker, brings mythology alive by
recreating classical myths and by giving them modern implications. Even in
his earlier verse, where mythological allusions are mainly symbols of
sensuous joys, there are intimations of the applications of myths to personal problems; in his more mature poems fresh, creative vision of myth
becomes increasingly a basis for a pattern of thought, so that in the
completed work myth and personal philosophy are integrated, mythmaking genius combining with earnest endeavor to know and explain
essentials. Abundant cases of parallels and apparent sources do not mislead
Bush into implying Keats is a mere borrower. Wisely he remarks, "But of
course no array of parallels is of much account. When Keats mixes three

sounds . . . they become, not a fourth sound, but a star." Illuminating interpretations of *Endymion, Hyperion,* and other poems add to the value of this indispensable study.

4. OTHER WORKS ON INDIVIDUAL POEMS

Most of the valuable discussion of particular poems is to be found in works already listed: general works on Keats, or criticism primarily concerned either with thought and theme or with special aspects of artistry. We mention other works here, occasionally titles already cited in other contexts.

Endymion quickly became a sort of touchstone in assessing Keats as a thinker, and in a sense continues to be. Of works after Colvin's *Life* (1917), a provocative early discussion was H. C. Notcutt, *An Interpretation of Keats's Endymion* (1919; rpt. 1964), which conceives the work as more allegorical than had previously been thought, and as having two meanings: the more specific has to do with the experience of the individual, stirred by poetic imagination, in seeking to realize the ideal; the wider meaning is the new birth of poetry just taking place in the Romantic movement. In his *Studies in Keats* (1930, 1939), J. M. Murry writes at length on the meaning of *Endymion,* presenting an interpretation which centers in Love as "a faculty of understanding" and as a transmuting power "through which fact is changed into truth." Endymion's quest has for its end a realization of the wholeness of reality through experience of the various kinds of love. Leonard Brown, in "The Genesis, Growth, and Meaning of *Endymion*" (*SP,* 1933), argues that the "genesis of the thought" of the poem is to be found in Hunt's social ideas and "the genesis of the structure" in Drayton, but that the source for "the growth of the idea" is to be traced to Wordsworth and the immediate stimulus of the poem to Shelley—specifically to his "Alastor," against which Keats is in revolt.

Studies of *Endymion* continued with Newell Ford in *"Endymion*—a Neo-Platonic Allegory" (*ELH,* 1947) and "The Meaning of 'Fellowship with Essence' in *Endymion*" (*PMLA,* 1947); Werner Beyer in *Keats and the Daemon King* (1947); Newell Ford again in *The Prefigurative Imagination of John Keats* (1951); and J. D. Wigod in "The Meaning of *Endymion*" (*PMLA,* 1953). Ford's thesis is briefly discussed above (IV, 2). It opposes critics like Finney who see Neoplatonic tendencies in *Endymion.* Beyer approaches *Endymion* by way of Wieland's *Oberon,* which he sees as the immediate source of the poem, both in story and idea. The interpretation educed is a confirmation with modifications rather than a rejection of the older readings, and therefore need not be reviewed here. The book is in part a record of source hunting, with some of the familiar limitations and exaggerations peculiar to that method (Beyer tends to overemphasize the Wieland influence); but it comes to more than that. Beyer is able not only to offer clarifying comment on *Endymion,* thus more specifically defining its import, but to suggest revised meanings for various other poems. Replying to Ford's arguments against allegory, J. D. Wigod maintains that, however concealed, the poem is nonetheless a personal Romantic allegory depicting three main factors of Keats's poetic growth culminating in *Endymion*: joy in nature and myth, a theory of poetic ascents, the importance of being a poet.

Later discussions include S. R. Swaminathan, "The Meaning of *Endymion*" (*Saugar Univ. Journal,* 1955), which reconsiders three central ideas or concepts in the poem—the imagination, immortality, and the ultimate union of concrete and ideal; Carroll Arnett, "Thematic Structure in Keats's *Endymion*" (*TexSE,* 1957), which argues that the poem has a "dialectical" pattern in which the movements toward the "earthly" and the "spiritual" alternate; Glen Allen, "The Fall of Endymion: A Study in Keats's Intellectual Growth" (*KSJ,* 1957), the theme of which is that, as Keats wrote *Endymion,* he began to surrender his association of poetry with visions and "etherealized pleasures" and to prize more the "unimpassioned analytical intellect"; Clarisse Godfrey, "*Endymion,*" in *John Keats: A Reassessment* (1958), ed. K. Muir (pp. 20–38), which takes issue with attempts to find systematic allegory, and states the poem should be read simply as an open narrative of human love although (reflecting Keats's own development) it becomes more deeply serious near the end; Robert Harrison, "Symbolism of the Cyclical Myth of *Endymion*" (*TSLL,* 1960); Stuart Sperry, "The Allegory of *Endymion*" (*SIR,* 1962), which discusses the poem generally as a reflection of Keats's "concern with visionary experience"; Bruce Miller, "On the Meaning of Keats's *Endymion*" (*KSJ,* 1965), which follows Thorpe in viewing the "fellowship with essence" passage (1.777–842) as central to the poem but stresses again the element of physical and passionate love; and Mario D'Avanzo, "Keats's and Vergil's Underworlds" (*KSJ,* 1967), on *Aeneid,* Book VI, as a major source of Book II of *Endymion.*

Hyperion has been carefully considered by all the major critics of Keats. It has been interpreted as a poem of conflict but also of progress or evolution. Further studies include Martha H. Shackford, who, in an early article, *"Hyperion" (SP,* 1925), states that Keats is facing squarely the old natural law of mutability, recognizing with sanity and courage that change in the universe is inevitable. Both *Endymion* and *Hyperion* figure in John H. Roberts, "Poetry of Sensation or of Thought?" (*PMLA,* 1930), where the author underlines conflict in Keats. Keats's career became "a matter of writing either what he wants to write or what he thinks he ought to write," with continued effort to reconcile the rival claims. *Endymion* represents an attempt to show that the ideal and the real are one. The conflict continues in *Hyperion,* in which the poet tries unsuccessfully to show that "the poetry of philosophic humanitarianism is better than the poetry of sensation"—tries and gives up. In "The Meaning of *Hyperion*" (*PMLA,* 1936), J. R. Caldwell, rejecting the arguments of Roberts that *Hyperion* reflects a conflict between sensation and intellect, the claims of imagination and those of humanity, maintains that Keats means simply that Apollo, the poet, the ideal, surpasses the "unpoetic" order of the Titans by his capacity for passionate experience. Kenneth Muir's important essay, "The Meaning of *Hyperion*" (*EC,* 1952; rpt. 1958, in *John Keats: A Reassessment*), because of its range of implication, has already been discussed above (IV, 2). Another significant discussion is Karl Kroeber, "The Commemorative Prophecy of *Hyperion*" (*Transactions, Wisconsin Academy,* 1963), in which the poem is seen as uniting "a commemorative, traditionalistic impulse . . . with a prophetic, progressive impulse"; the traditional is not to be obliterated but "absorbed into a more complicated and comprehensive unity." The revised version speaks even more than the first in "two voices, one commemorative, one prophetic."

For "The Eve of St. Agnes," an article of central importance, involving a general reconsideration of the whole poem, is Jack Stillinger's "The Hoodwinking of Madeline: Scepticism in *The Eve of St. Agnes*" (*SP,* 1961). Madeline, as "the self-hoodwinked dreamer," illustrates a dominant preoccupation of all Keats's major poems in 1819: that an individual cannot release his grasp of "the realities of this world" without disaster or grief. Stillinger arrives at this conclusion through a penetrating analysis of the poem itself; a balanced, judicious consideration of what other commentary has said about the poem; and a close knowledge of the context provided by Keats's other poems and his thought generally. H. G. Wright raised the question "Has Keats's *Eve of St. Agnes* a Tragic Ending?" (*MLR,* 1945), to which M. Whitely made a spirited reply, "The Tragic Ending of Keats's *Eve of St. Agnes*" (*MLR,* 1947). Miriam Allott, *"Isa-*

bella, The Eve of St. Agnes, and *Lamia,"* in *John Keats: A Reassessment* (pp. 39–62), discusses these three narrative poems as a symbolic expression of "the romantic dissatisfaction with the actual." R. A. Foakes, *The Romantic Assertion: A Study in the Language of Nineteenth Century Poetry* (1958), points out the loss to the Romantic poet of the Renaissance and neoclassic concept of order, and a new use of imagery and symbolic expression, evoking familiar natural impressions, as a means of "reasserting" an "ideal order." The three Romantic poems to which Foakes applies this theme, before turning to the Victorians, are "The Prelude," "The Eve of St. Agnes," and "Adonais." Roger Sharrock, "Keats and the Young Lovers" (*REL,* 1961), concludes that the "Eve," like "Isabella" and *Lamia,* proves that "Keats is supremely the adolescent poet." M. H. Cusac, "Keats as Enchanter: An Organizing Principle of *The Eve of St. Agnes*" (*KSJ,* 1968), comments on the stance and persona of the narrator as "enchanter" or "story-teller," inducing us to accept the witchery of the tale. Discussions of Keats's reading and possible or probable sources include: M. H. Shackford, *"The Eve of St. Agnes* and *The Mysteries of Udolpho"* (*PMLA,* 1921); J. C. Jordan, *"The Eve of St. Agnes* and *The Lay of the Last Minstrel"* (*MLN,* 1928); M. E. Wells, *"The Eve of St. Agnes* and 'The Legend of Britomartis' " (*MLN,* 1942); R. K. Gordon, "Notes on Keats's 'Eve of St. Agnes' " (*MLR,* 1946); E. C. Pettet, "Echoes of 'The Lay of the Last Minstrel' in 'The Eve of St. Agnes' " (*RES,* 1952); Arthur Carr, "John Keats' Other 'Urn' " (*UKCR,* 1954), where the "Eve" is presented as another "imagined work of art" analogous to the "Grecian Urn"; Stuart Sperry, "Madeline and Ophelia" (*N&Q,* 1957). For discussions of particular themes and/or stanzas in the *Explicator,* see R. Whidden (1943), R. P. Basler (1944), Elmo Howell (1956), E. A. Bloom (1961), E. H. Scholl (1961); and Cecil Seronsy on "The Concluding Stanzas" (*KSJ,* 1957).

Discussions of other poems written before the odes include: Jack Stillinger, "The Order of Poems in Keats's First Volume" (*PQ,* 1969); Stuart Sperry, "Keats's First Published Poem" (*HLQ,* 1966), on the sonnet "To Solitude"; Carl Woodring, "On Looking into Keats's Voyagers" (*KSJ,* 1965), which considers the theme of the "Chapman's Homer" sonnet as discovery in all its ramifications organically coalescing in the experience the poem expresses, and Bernice Slote, "Of Chapman's Homer and Other Books" (*CE,* 1962); Paul Baumgartner on the sonnet "After dark vapours" (*KSJ,* 1959); on "Shed no tear," J. B. Severs (*Explicator,* 1955, Item 3) and Jack Stillinger, "The Context of Keats's

'Fairy's Song' " (*KSJ*, 1961); on "When I have fears," T. E. Connolly (*Explicator*, 1954, Item 14) and M. A. Goldberg, "The 'Fears' of John Keats" (*MLQ*, 1957); on "To Homer," Thomas Cook (*KSJ*, 1962); Mary Visick, " 'Tease Us Out of Thought': Keats's *Epistle to Reynolds* and the Odes" (*KSJ*, 1966), and Stuart Sperry, "Keats's *Epistle to J. H. Reynolds*" (*ELH*, 1969), the latter of which especially illuminates the poem as the product of a crucial period in Keats's development; Jack Stillinger's discussion of *Isabella* in "Keats and Romance" (*SEL*, 1968); W. E. Houghton, "The Meaning of Keats's *Eve of St. Mark*" (*ELH*, 1946), and Jack Stillinger, "The Meaning of 'Poor Cheated Soul' in Keats's *Eve of St. Mark*" (*ELN*, 1968); John L. Mahoney, "Theme and Image in a Keats Sonnet on Fame" (*English Record*, 1961) and "Keats and the Metaphor of Fame" (*ES*, 1963); and, for "La Belle Dame," S. R. Swaminathan on Apuleius as a source (*Saugar Univ. Journal*, 1952–53), F. L. Utley on Lucretius as another (*ELH*, 1958), Grant Webster on Sackville's "Induction" as still another (*ELN*, 1965); Bernice Slote, "The Climate of Keats's 'La Belle Dame' " (*MLQ*, 1960) and "La Belle Dame as Naiad" (*JEGP*, 1961); and D. R. Mathur, "A Study of Keats's 'La Belle Dame' " (*Calcutta Review*, 1961). For "Bright star," the date of which continues to be argued, thoughtful explications have been provided by Martin Kallich (*Ball State College Forum*, 1964) and David Ormerod (*KSJ*, 1967).

In his *Twentieth Century Interpretations of Keats's Odes* (1968), Jack Stillinger provides selected discussions from sixteen critics: M. H. Abrams ("Grecian Urn"), Kenneth Allott ("Psyche"), W. J. Bate ("Grecian Urn"), F. W. Bateson ("Grecian Urn"), Harold Bloom ("Autumn"), Cleanth Brooks and R. P. Warren ("Nightingale"), Douglas Bush ("Grecian Urn"), R. H. Fogle ("Nightingale"), Albert Gérard ("Grecian Urn"), Anthony Hecht ("Nightingale"), Leonidas Jones ("Psyche"), C. I. Patterson ("Grecian Urn"), David Perkins ("Psyche," "Melancholy," "Autumn"), Leonard Unger ("Autumn"), Jacob Wigod ("Grecian Urn"); and a general essay by Cleanth Brooks ("The Artistry of Keats"). Most of these discussions have been already mentioned or are discussed below under individual odes. Professor Stillinger's "Introduction: Imagination and Reality in the Odes of Keats" itself provides the best condensed treatment of its length of the odes generally, analyzing succinctly their structure and theme, and placing them in their context in Keats's development generally. For other discussions of the odes generally, see B. Ifor Evans, "Keats and the Golden Ass" (*Nineteenth Century*,

1926); H. M. McLuhan, "Aesthetic Pattern in Keats's Odes" (*UTQ,* 1943); John Holloway, "The Odes of Keats" (*CJ,* 1952); Kenneth Muir, "The Meaning of the Odes," in *John Keats: A Reassessment;* D. G. James, *Three Odes of Keats* (Thomas Memorial Lecture, Wales Univ., 1959); and Karl Kroeber, "The New Humanism of Keats's Odes" (*Proceedings of the American Philosophical Society,* 1963). Some observations about the place of Keats in the history of the English ode are made in the relevant parts of George Shuster, *The English Ode from Milton to Keats,* cited above under IV, 3, and especially Kurt Schlüter, *Die englische Ode* (1964). A not too convincing argument that Keats's odes are more rooted in the English Pindaric tradition than is usually believed is made by Ian Gordon, "Keats and the English Pindaric" (*RES,* 1967).

To turn to discussions of individual odes: (1) Kenneth Allott, "Keats's 'Ode to Psyche'" (*EC,* 1956), reprinted in *John Keats: A Reassessment* (pp. 74–94), argues that this, which he calls the most neglected of the odes, is the most "architectural," the most judiciously contrived and detached. Leonidas Jones, "The 'Ode to Psyche': An Allegorical Introduction to Keats's Great Odes" (*KSMB,* 1958) is an important article, establishing "Psyche" as a major announcement by Keats of his intention to become a psychological poet—to turn increasingly to the human mind as his central theme: an intention he immediately began to fulfill in the later odes. Max Schulz, "Keats's Timeless Order of Things" (*Criticism,* 1960) provides a thoughtful explication of the poem; and Robert D. Wagner, "Keats: 'Ode to Psyche' and the Second *Hyperion*" (*KSJ,* 1964), argues that the two poems are "anti-Romantic"; in the case of "Psyche," because he is celebrating the imagination as a "limited" part of life shut off from other things. For discussions of the imagery as it might reflect Keats's medical interest, see H. Pettit and C. W. Hagelman (II, above). (2) Allen Tate, "A Reading of Keats" (*American Scholar,* 1946; rpt. in *On the Limits of Poetry,* 1948, and *Essays of Four Decades,* 1959, 1968), discussing the "Nightingale" and the "Grecian Urn," places Keats "among the few heroes of literature." Though the "Nightingale tries at least to say everything that poetry can say," and is by any standard "one of the great poems of the world," it fails to resolve the antithesis of common experience and ideality. Janet Spens, "A Study of Keats's 'Ode to a Nightingale'" (*RES,* 1952), defends the integrity and unity of the poem against strictures of Bridges (above) and Garrod (above); and Richard Fogle, "Keats's 'Ode to a Nightingale'" (*PMLA,* 1953), also arrives at a vindication of the ode as a poem whose purpose is not to answer the question of which is better, the ideal world or the actual, but to portray an inner experience, ending in realization that the ideal can be attained by man only tentatively. Other discussions include: Lowry Nelson, "The Rhetoric of Ineffability" (*CL,* 1956); T. B. Harrison, "Keats and a Nightingale" (*ES,* 1960); Ethelbert Flood, "Keats's Nightingale Ode" (*Culture* [Quebec], 1961); Irene Chayes, "Rhetoric as Drama" (*PMLA,* 1964), which applies some of Aristotle's dramatic and rhetorical criteria to three Romantic odes, Coleridge's "Dejection," Shelley's "West Wind," and Keats's "Nightingale"; Arno Esch on the "Nightingale" ode in *Versdichtung der englischen Romantik* (1968), ed. Teut A. Riese and Dieter Riesner; and F. Matthey, "Interplay of Structure and Meaning in the 'Ode to a Nightingale' " (*ES,* 1968). (3) The "Ode on Melancholy" has received little specialized discussion in article form. But we should mention B. H. Smith, "Sorrow's Mysteries" (*SEL,* 1966), and G. L. Little, "Keats's Ode on 'Melancholy' " (*Explicator,* 1967, Item 46). (4) Jack Stillinger perceptively discusses "The Text of Keats's 'Ode on Indolence' " (*SB,* 1969). (5) To jump ahead a few months to the ode "To Autumn," deferring for separate mention, because of its bulk, commentary on the "Grecian Urn": "The Genesis of Keats's Ode 'To Autumn' " is discussed by E. J. Lovell (*TexSE,* 1950). Leonard Unger, "Keats and the Music of Autumn" (*WR,* 1950; rpt. 1956 in *The Man in the Name,* pp. 18–29) provides an excellent explication, stressing the rich unity and decorum of the ode's structure while also seeing the poem in relation to the other odes, especially "Melancholy." Reuben Brower uses the poem in *Fields of Light* (1951) to show "how a succession of images . . . imperceptibly blends into metaphor" and "how groups of images are linked and how images work as design." Other helpful discussions include: B. L. Woodruff, "Keats's Wailful Choir" (*MLN,* 1953); Stewart C. Wilcox, "The Seasonal Motif of Keats's Ode 'To Autumn' " (*PQ,* 1956); Arnold Davenport, "A Note on 'To Autumn,' " in *John Keats: A Reassessment* (pp. 95–101); John Hollander, "The Metrical Emblem" (*KR,* 1959); B. C. Southam, "The Ode 'To Autumn' " (*KSJ,* 1960); Michael Quinn, "The Objectivity of Keats's Ode 'To Autumn' " (*Critical Survey,* 1965).

The "Ode on a Grecian Urn" remains by far the most frequently discussed of the odes or of any of Keats's poems. Keats's *Well-Read Urn* (1958), ed. Harvey Lyon, provides a convenient summary of critical remarks, frequently with selected passages, from eighty-eight works published from 1828 to 1957. Almost all of the more valuable discussions before 1950, and a large number of those between 1950 and 1965, are to be found in general books on Keats already discussed. Among other works, an essay of primary importance is Kenneth Burke's "Symbolic Action in a Poem by Keats" (*Accent,* Autumn 1943; *Transformations,* Two, 1944; *A Grammar of Motives,* 1945), which attempts "to analyze the poem as a viaticum that leads, by a series of transformations, into the 'Beauty is truth, truth, beauty.' " The transformations as adumbrated by Burke are too intricate to be traced here, but they lead to a transcendent scene, a "new internal sky" in which contradictions between the spiritual and the material are reconciled in a proclamation of the unity of science and art (truth and beauty). Allen Tate, who rates the "Nightingale" above the "Urn" ("A Reading of Keats," above), believes that the latter poem is defective because the final stanza tries to say too much, tries to say, indeed, what poetry should not say, and is, moreover, irrelevant. Cleanth Brooks ("Keats's Sylvan Historian: History without Footnotes," in *The Well Wrought Urn,* 1947) joins Kenneth Burke in defense of the integrity of the "Urn" and the logic of the last lines. The Urn tells a story which says in effect that in art in general "basic and fundamental perception of man and nature" is embodied in "formed experience," or "imaginative insight," and that its own particular beauty has its origin in "an imaginative perception of essentials." Hence the validity of equating beauty and truth. Brooks is here close to some of the older interpretations, though the approach, the finesse of his argument, and the detailed reasons are all his own. C. M. Bowra's chapter in *The Romantic Imagination* (1949; rpt. 1969) accepts the message at the close of the Ode, which he believes is spoken entirely by the Urn, as a statement of Keats's belief that for the poet, or for any other artist, truth is another name for ultimate reality and is discovered not by the reasoning mind but by the imagination; the reality thus discovered Keats calls "beauty." The Urn, then, is speaking of a special kind of experience, which Keats identifies with art. Keats knows that this art is not everything, but for him, at this moment, it is of first importance. Alvin Whitley, in "The Message of the Grecian Urn" (*KSMB,* 1952), argues convincingly against the theory that the Urn speaks the initial words, and Keats the part beginning "That is all": "It is artistically as well as philosophically unthinkable that Keats would suddenly intrude himself in this way," he declares. His strongest appeal, however, is to the authority of four known transcripts in none of which is "Beauty is truth, truth, beauty" set off by quotation marks; all read as one unit with the basic punctuation of

> *Beauty is truth,—Truth, Beauty,—that is all*
> *Ye know on Earth, and all ye need to know.*

The only inference to be drawn is that the Urn makes a single uninterrupted statement. But conflicting interpretations continue to chew at the two closing lines. The truth is that, as Jack Stillinger says, none of the readings in the transcripts, the *Annals,* or the *Lamia* volume can be used as conclusive proof of what Keats intended ("Keats's Grecian Urn and the Evidence of Transcripts," *PMLA,* 1958). Meanwhile, a valuable condensed statement of all the major possible interpretations, and a succinct weighing of the evidence *pro* and *con* in each case is also provided by Jack Stillinger in an Appendix ("Who Says What to Whom at the End of the *Ode on a Grecian Urn?"*) in his edition of selected essays, *Twentieth Century Interpretations of Keats's Odes,* cited above.

Charles Patterson, "Passion and Permanence in Keats's 'Ode on a Grecian Urn' " (*ELH,* 1954), effectively refutes Garrod's idea (*Keats,* above) that the theme is "the supremacy of ideal art over nature," that truth to his theme carries Keats further than he intended, and that nothing has prepared for the last stanza. Patterson argues that the poem is a unity, that there is in it as much eulogy of passion as of permanence. There is throughout a tension between something unchanging because it is dead, and something transient because it is alive; only to those who so read it will the poem yield its full value. "Beauty is truth," says Patterson, means that beauty is total reality properly understood; that is, beauty is the true significance of things not only in the ideal world, or the world of art as Bowra would have Keats say, but in the world of phenomenal reality. Martha H. Shackford ("The *Ode on a Grecian Urn,"* *KSJ,* 1955) argues for the complete artistic integrity of the Ode: it "is in structure, style, diction, imagery and music of stately verse completely a unit with its subject matter." It is "an assertion of faith, a triumphal hymn in praise of beauty in achieved form." Unlike Patterson, who in the course of his article finds occasion to discount the idea of Platonism in Keats, Miss Shackford also argues for its Platonic concept: Beauty at its best is truthfulness, in idea, in wisdom, in imaginative penetration. In "The 'Ode on a Grecian Urn,' or Content vs. Metagrammar" (*CL,* 1955), Leo Spitzer provides an occasionally penetrating but oversimplified attempt to argue against some of the main points in Wasserman's notable critique in *The Finer Tone.* J. D. Wigod, "Keats's Ideal in the 'Ode on a Grecian Urn' " (*PMLA,* 1957), argues that the ideal Keats has in mind can be found in neither art nor life separately but only in both together. D. R. Godfrey, "Keats and the Grecian Urn" (*Hermathena,* 1965), states that the final two lines (spoken as a unit by the urn) are meant to apply to its own world, that of classical Greece, "not our world or Keats's." James A. Notopoulos, " 'Truth-Beauty' in the 'Ode on a Grecian Urn' and the Elgin Marbles" (*MLR,* 1966), states that the aesthetic philosophy behind Keats's "Truth-Beauty" equation is that of Haydon defending and describing the Elgin Marbles. Rudolf Sühnel, "Ode on a Grecian Urn," in *Versdichtung der englischen Romantik,* provides a welcome distilled account of attitudes of the time toward classical sculpture, relates Keats to them, cites analogous responses in English and German poetry of the period, and takes into account previous scholarship and criticism of the poem. Suggestive explication or other discussion is found in the *Explicator* by R. C. Pettigrew (1946–47, Item 13), S. C. Wilcox (1947–48, Item 2, and 1948–49, Item 47), Robert Fox (1956, Item 58), Virgil Hutton (1961, Item 40), David Cornelius (1962, Item 57), C. F. Burgess (1964, Item 30), and Blair Kenney (1969, Item 69); in Helmut Viebrock, *"Die griechise Urne und die angelsächischen Kritiker"* (1957); and in articles by E. M. Schero (*Chicago Review,* 1951), K. M. Hamilton (*DR,* 1954), Martha H. Shackford (*KSJ,* 1955), Alwyn Berland (*Kansas Magazine,* 1956), Robert Berkelman (*SAQ,* 1958), Kurt Schlüter (*Neophilologus,* 1958), I. B. Cauthen (*KSJ,* 1959), C. R. B. Combellack (*KSJ,* 1962), R. A. Swanson (*CE,* 1962), Martin Halpern (*CE,* 1963), Allen Austin (*CE,* 1964), Philip Hobsbaum (*KSMB,* 1964), and R. J. Fusco (*Massachusetts Studies in English,* 1969).

Especially in comparison with the odes, *Lamia* and *The Fall of Hyperion,* though extensively discussed in some of the longer works on Keats, have not been the subject of many discussions of article length. This is understandable since both poems, coming as they do at the end of Keats's writing career and marking significant changes, involve reconsideration of Keats's writing and thought generally throughout 1818 and 1819. J. H. Roberts, "The Significance of *Lamia*" (*PMLA,* 1935), continues the theme developed in his earlier article, "Poetry of Sensation or of Thought" (above)—the conflict of intellect and sentiment—and expresses a now discredited interpretation: Keats is bitterly admitting that "once the intellectual ideal has made entry into his life the inevitable result is destruction." Lord Gorell, in *John Keats: The Principle of Beauty* (1948), takes issue with Murry's admittedly overpersonal interpretation of Lamia as Fanny Brawne and Apollonius as C. A. Brown, but is not able to offer a constructive interpretation of his own. O. B. Hardison, "The Decorum of *Lamia*" (*MLQ*, 1958), concentrates on form and style, and stresses the extent to which the parts fit, in classical decorum, into the whole. Georgia Dunbar, "The Significance of the Humor in *Lamia*" (*KSJ*, 1959), points out the use of mockery and humor in the poem to relieve the painful sense of what is "the central agony of Keats's life: the inevitable evanescence of love and beauty and illusion." James D. Boulger, "Keats's Symbolism" (*ELH*, 1961), concentrates on *Lamia* as well as "The Eve of St. Agnes" and the "Ode to a Nightingale." For *The Fall of Hyperion,* the best condensed treatment of Keats's use of sources is John Livingston Lowes, "Moneta's Temple" (*PMLA,* 1936), discussed in the general section on sources (III, above). Brian Wicker, "The Disputed Lines in *The Fall of Hyperion*" (*EC,* 1957), provides a searching discussion of the element of "sacrament" in Keats's struggle to attain poetic identity. Kenneth Muir's important "The Meaning of *Hyperion*" (1958), discussed above under *Hyperion* as well as in IV, 2, considers *The Fall* as well as the first version; W. R. Manierre, "Versification and Imagery in *The Fall of Hyperion*" (*TSLL,* 1961), finds the narrative inadequate as a vehicle for the ideas Keats had in mind. Stuart Sperry, "Keats, Milton, and *The Fall of Hyperion*" (*PMLA,* 1962), shows that the influence of Milton is more pervasive than is ordinarily thought, transcending similarities in structure and style, and apparent in the whole conception of the allegory. Dorothy Hewlett, "Some Thoughts on *The Fall of Hyperion*" (*Aryan Path,* 1964), stresses again Keats's personal application of the myth to himself ("It is the making of a poet, not of a god, which now occupied his mind"). John Saly, "Keats's Answer to Dante" (*KSJ,* 1965), cites further evidence of Dante as an influence on *The Fall*; and C. S. Hooker, "The Poet and the Dreamer" (*McNeese Review,* 1966), focuses on one of the crucial issues of the poem. Finally, we should especially notice Paul Sheats, "Keats's Second *Hyperion* and the *Purgatorio*: Further Notes" (*N&Q,* 1968), and his valuable general article, "Stylistic Discipline in *The Fall of Hyperion*" (*KSJ,* 1968). The latter is one of the best distilled discussions of the poem yet published. "Stylistic discipline" is interpreted not only in its more technical aspects (diction, imagery, versification), on all of which Sheats is closely informed, but in the broadest sense, involving the total imaginative conception of the poem and its place in the chronology of Keats's development.

INDEX

McClintock, W. D., 49
McDonald, Daniel, 177
McDowell, Frederick P. W., 164, 243
McElderry, Bruce R., Jr., 179, 189, 207, 326, 337, 357
McFarland, G. F., 257
McFarland, Thomas, 140, 149, 207, 236, 238, 241
McGann, Jerome J., 268, 319–20, 374
McGill, Mildred S., 367
McKeehan, Irene P., 41, 124
McKenzie, Gordon, 225
McKillop, Alan Dugald, 8, 11, 21
McLaughlin, Elizabeth T., 256
McLean, Kenneth, 118
Mclean, Norman, 19
McLuhan, H. Marshall, 164, 431, 443
McMahan, Anna B., 296
McNamee, Lawrence F., 330
McNiece, Gerald, 356, 361, 373
McNulty, John Bard, 129
Medwin, Thomas, 280, 282, 285, 286, 287, 340, 360
Meier, Hans Heinrich, 186
Meinecke, Frederich, 22
Mercer, Dorothy F., 187
Merchant, W. M., 78
Merkel, Gottfried F., 58
Mertens, Helmut, 375
Metzger, Lore, 149, 237
Meyer, George Wilbur, 81, 85, 89, 126, 130, 199
Meyer, Hans, 361
Meyerstein, E. H. W., 172, 183
Middleton, Charles S., 340
Miles, Hamish, 276
Miles, Josephine, 18, 40, 99, 120, 427
Mill, John Stuart, 109, 162, 216
Miller, Bruce, 439
Miller, Craig W., 246–47
Miller, J. Hillis, 55
Miller, Henry Knight, 8
Milley, H. J. W., 195
Millingen, Julius, 283
Milnes, Richard Monckton (Lord Houghton), 383, 385, 388
Miner, Earl, 19
Mirsky, D. S., 299
Miyoshi, Masao, 18
Monk, Samuel Holt, 21, 114, 125
Moore, C. A., 9, 10
Moore, Doris Langley, 286
Moore, J. M., 213
Moore, John R., 173
Moore, Thomas, 191, 265, 271, 277, 281
Moorman, Mary, 78, 80, 81, 84, 97, 125

Moraud, Marcel, 32
Mordell, Albert, 66
More, Paul Elmer, 59–60, 102, 267, 268, 325
Morgan, Bayard Quincey, 22, 204
Morgan, Roberta, 229
Morley, Edith J., 78, 150, 157
Morley, John, 110
Morpurgo, J. E., 282, 384, 386
Morrill, Dorothy J., 229
Morris, William, 424
Mortenson, Robert, 359
Moss, Howard, 384
Motter, T. H. V., 297
Mousel, M. E., 346
Mueschke, Paul, 98, 126, 364
Muir, Kenneth, 376, 408, 415, 417, 426n., 428n., 436, 439, 440, 443, 448
Muirhead, J. H., 209, 212, 217, 227
Müller, Curt Richard, 225
Müller, G., 218
Müller, Joachim, 30
Müller, Rotrand, 418
Munson, Gorham, 60
Murchie, Guy, 394
Murray, E. B., 365, 366
Murray, John, 269
Murray, Robert Henry, 219
Murray, Roger N., 119
Murry, John Middleton, 67, 221, 383, 384, 394, 395, 397, 400–02, 408, 410, 412, 416, 420n., 423, 431–32, 435, 438, 447
Muschg, Walter, 48

Nabholtz, John R., 124
Natthey, Pierre Louis, 385n.
Needham, Joseph, 220
Nelson, Lowry, Jr., 17, 149, 235, 444
Nelson, N. E., 61
Nelson, Sophia Phillips, 330
Nesbitt, George L., 109
Nethercot, Arthur H., 191, 193
Nettesheim, Josefine, 218
Neumann, Joshua H., 224
Newdeck, Robert S., 154
Newell, K. B., 267
Newman, John Henry, 325
Newton, Eric, 34
Nichols, Stephen G., 4
Nicoll, Allardyce, 43
Nicolson, Harold, 35, 272, 299, 300
Nicolson, Marjorie Hope, 11, 45, 125, 230
Nidecker, Henri, 149, 161, 212, 214, 220
Nitchie, Elizabeth, 42, 175, 340, 344, 365